WHEN PIGS FLY

WHEN PIGS FLY

THE IRREVERENT TALES OF A BEAR IN THE AIR

RICK CARNEVALI

authorHOUSE®

AuthorHouse™ LLC
1663 Liberty Drive
Bloomington, IN 47403
www.authorhouse.com
Phone: 1-800-839-8640

Published by AuthorHouse   01/21/2014

ISBN: 978-1-4918-4323-9 (sc)
ISBN: 978-1-4918-4324-6 (e)

Library of Congress Control Number: 2013922924

CONTENTS

DEDICATION

Four people have had a tremendous influence on my life and career. My Dad, Roy and Mother, Rose who taught me how to respect and be responsible with dangerous farm machinery at an early age which helped me tremendously during my aviation career. Jim Kieran, owner of the *Hangar Flying Club* at Felts Field, who showed me how to finesse an airplane for maximum passenger comfort and gave me my first flying job. Most of all my lovely bride Debbie who waited up for me on those late night shifts when I often came home at sunrise with a uniform smelling of blood, antifreeze, battery acid, and gas from some awful grinder I'd investigated the night before. Even though she was working full time while pursuing her BS and later Master's Degree she always was excited for me, offered loving support and encouraged me to keep climbing the aviation ladder. She never once over-reacted or complained when I told her how much the latest flying certificate or rating was going to cost. My love and thanks to all of you guys!

Ten WSP troopers were killed in the line of duty during my career and shortly after I retired. As a traffic pilot I had the unique opportunity to work with and get to know just about every line trooper in Eastern and Western Washington. We often had lunch together and many became my friends. Later as a transport pilot I flew most of them to annual In-Service training at the Academy and spent countless hours shooting the breeze with them while hanging around FBO's all over the state waiting for the weather to get above landing minimums in Olympia or Shelton. Of those ten troops who gave their lives for us, I knew or had worked with all of them except Glenda Thomas whose career was so brief before someone took her life on the Seattle Freeway. Frank Noble had once investigated a wreck I was in near Toppenish and was kind enough to not write me a ticket. I spent ten days at In-Service training at the Academy with Tom Hendrickson where we were both trained as EMTs back in 1974, and I used to ride with Jim Gain out on the Mountain Road in Tacoma when I was a cadet. I worked the airplane with Steve Frink up in Issaquah lots of times, went to In-Service training and got to know Cliff Hansell at the Academy one year, and spent many hours with Ray Hawn at a burger joint in Sunnyside sharing laughs at lunch after working with him near Grandview. Jim Saunders was the Tri-Cities designated governor's driver and just days before he was killed I was laughing and joking with the "Big Guy" at the Walla Walla Airport fire station during a governor's flight. I worked the airplane at Sedgwick or Trigger and had fish and chips with Tony Radulescu at the Bremerton airport café often and had lunch with Sean O'Connell near the Bayview Airport several times after working traffic with him at Conway, Bow Hill, or Freeborn.

I just can't express how much I miss every one of those troops or how deeply I appreciate the ultimate sacrifice they had to make while keeping us all safe . . . . This story is dedicated to those ten, to all the other WSP troopers and patrolmen who died before them while serving the citizens of Washington State, and to the nearly 20,000 other police officers across Washington and the United States who have sacrificed their lives for us in the line of duty over the years.

INTRODUCTION

There were many tragic, ugly, smelly, bloody, and occasionally violent episodes that I experienced in my career as a road trooper and later as a State Patrol pilot. I have included many of those stories in this book but have tried to focus more on the humorous, outrageous, and wild or gross out type experiences I survived or witnessed instead. As the saying goes if whatever had happened could "Gag a Maggot" then I almost always found it hilarious and just had to write about it! If you're expecting a big city type cop story brimming with gun battles, wild chases, and fighting off hordes of Columbian drug lords, or flying episodes that begin with the line: "There I was flat on my back with a raging fire in the cockpit and a Mig 21 on my tail" . . . . you'll be reading the wrong book. Similarly, I worked with a number of characters whose freak-show personal and professional lives would no doubt be of interest to all . . . . But after careful consideration and introspection I have chosen not to bring **all** of those episodes to light. I feel the people involved would most certainly be humiliated, even with the passage of time, and would probably sue me even if I changed their names. Just as they probably now regret what they did in the line of duty or elsewhere, I also committed a number of borderline unethical, and possibly illegal infractions (sorry Mom) and would just as soon not have to relive my missteps or see them in print again. As is the case with our elected officials, state troopers are drawn from that same old generic cross section of society that always includes the usual mix of egomaniacs, sex crazed-power hungry back stabbers, and brown-nosers . . . Oh so many freakin brown-nosers!! However, when I eventually transferred into the WSP Aviation Section I had no idea I was getting mixed up with the cream of the crop of that genre! Anal retentive narcissistic trooper pilots, with ego's the size of Cleveland, carrying badges and guns and all suffering from A.D.D. and O.C.D . . . . OMG!! As hard as it is for me to acknowledge, I've been told by my wife that I too fell into that category at one time . . . . However, I would like to think I was one of the more benign examples and have most certainly been "born again" having left that competitive atmosphere behind in retirement.

I've read many biographies of World War II pilots and most of them spoke of joining the service after Pearl Harbor out of a tremendous sense of patriotism, call to duty, defending the homeland, honor, country, etc. I have to admit that when I joined the Washington State Patrol back in October of 1971, I did not share any of those sentiments towards the State of Washington or any of its citizens. My sole purpose for joining the force was knowing that I would have a license to speed while driving one of those great Plymouth Fury Interceptors of the day with a Mopar 440 Magnum under the hood. I felt that writing a couple tickets a day and investigating a few fender benders now and again was a small price to pay while pursuing my passion for speed. Back then there were no polygraph tests, urine tests, and not much of a background check in order to get hired. As long as you were over six feet tall, didn't have a felony conviction on your record, and showed up at your interview sober with a pulse, you were in. The minimum six feet tall rule was removed a few years later to allow aspiring females to apply. That height rule had originated back in the late twenties when the Highway Patrol pretty much only hired big bruisers for their physical intimidation factor alone. In that era they were quite often forced to do battle with the aggressive violators of the Prohibition and Great Depression era and to those guys, size mattered!

Anyway, to all you fellow pilots, police officers, troopers, corrections officers, deputies, military police, park rangers, wildlife officers, firemen, EMT's, or anyone else that has to deal with "The Public" in an enforcement role, (retired or still grinding it out), enjoy the read. For everyone else and especially those with delicate sensitivities or certain religious proclivities, please excuse the language, irreverent attitudes, and colorful metaphors I've employed. Some of them are a bit crude/harsh from time to time, but applicable for the age group/time period/job description and situation. Please keep in mind that police officers and pilots are often placed in very stressful life threatening situations (usually self-induced in my case) where politically correct responses and perfect grammar are occasionally replaced with quite "colorful" adrenaline enhanced adjectives and metaphors, some of which occasionally escaped onto the police radio airwaves for all to hear and enjoy.

Please refer to the **Glossary of Terms** in the back if any abbreviations, airplane talk, or slang terms need further explanation or definition. If anyone wonders how I could recall so much detail and dialogue from violator contacts 40 years ago I should point out that all troopers were required to maintain a "Bluebook" (officer's notebook) of all our daily activities for court. I kept all of mine until just recently . . . . However, I really did not want to lift and carry all those boxes of bluebooks again so just prior to our most recent move, we had a large bon-fire/weenie roast with them instead. But before that fire, re-reading my arrest reports and daily activities from those years helped jog my memory quite a bit and consequently allowed me tell this story fairly accurately. I also kept a separate diary of some of the funnier incidents just in case I ever decided to become a stand-up comic and needed some good material. I should point out that I have omitted a few names from certain stories and changed a couple others here and there to protect the guilty . . . .

Again, to those who might nitpick or take offense to the contents of this story, my apologies. Since it has been almost 40 years now since many of these events occurred, please forgive any minor inaccuracies, names or dates slightly askew, or unintended personal slights. Finally, I should acknowledge that some of the actions during my career weren't exactly in keeping with WSP policy or the excellent training I had received . . . I tried as hard as I could to abide by them but sometimes, in the heat of the moment, I failed to live up to those lofty goals and standards. I take full responsibility for the results of those occasional deviations and solemnly pray that the statute of limitations has expired for some of the more egregious infractions I possibly committed against humanity in the line of duty . . . .

If it seems that I'm occasionally critical of WSP supervisors and managers, I have to admit from time to time, that I did experience some frustration with a few of them and often wondered how they ever got hired or made rank . . . . However, in almost every case, my dissatisfaction was with an individual not with over-all WSP policy which by and large was usually in keeping with my own personal goals and ideals throughout those 33 years. Nearly all of my supervisors and managers were good people but as can be found in any large organization a few of them were hubris laden, narcissistic jerks . . . . It's my failing but I have never been able to effectively deal with that type of individual and never will be! I can only pray that the clowns who made life miserable for so many of us back then, have since reviewed their life, taken some measure of personal inventory, and are now repentant for the sins of their youth (as I am for mine).

Lastly, in keeping with the spirit of full disclosure, I need to reveal that many of my family members have been diagnosed with a deadly communicative condition known as "Excessive Use of Hyperbole" . . . . I suppose I share that propensity as well but I assure you that I have tried my best to control those latent impulses while writing this.

I wish to acknowledge the following three gentlemen who were all official State Patrol photographers at one time; they are responsible for most of the WSP photos displayed in this book. Lee Fagan, Chuck Miller, and Weldon Wilson were all former troopers and excellent professional photographers. My thanks to all you guys and especially Weldon who never once barfed in the plane during the occasional unusual attitude!

CHAPTER 1

THE U.S. AIR FORCE SAVES THE DAY

While cruising to the Tyler area from Ephrata one morning, gazing down on the Moses Coulee (gouged out aftermath of the 15,000 year old Lake Missoula ice dam burst) I couldn't help but reflect on my career to date and appreciate just how lucky I was to be actually getting paid to fly airplanes for the State of Washington . . . . It was a dream come true and I can't begin to describe the relief I felt knowing I no longer had to grind it out as a road trooper any longer. I had a lot of close calls during those 13 years on the line in Olympia and Spokane and like so many other police officers, I had become rather fatalistic about my long term prospects for survival after so many guys I knew were getting killed doing the same job as I. I often had bad dreams about that final night shift where things would somehow go terribly awry and while walking up to the car I'd just stopped I'd see that flash of light and hear that loud report . . . . Thankfully, it turned out I was one of the lucky ones. Whether we wanted to admit it or not, we all knew deep in our hearts that no amount of officer safety or survival training can keep someone determined (or drunk enough) from taking you out . . . . And as we all know from recent events, a texting driver's car is no less a deadly weapon than any handgun or drunk driver could be!

On the other hand, trying to independently kill your own damn self in an airplane every day is a totally different matter! Although I unsuccessfully attempted to do just that many times over in the next twenty years, as events unfolded on this particular day, I thought for sure this was the occasion where I'd bought the farm once and for all!

1

My WSP (Washington State Patrol) flying career started after my transfer from Spokane to the lovely Basin metropolis of Ephrata where one of the five WSP traffic airplanes was based. Leaving the big city behind had been quite a shock for us since 1985 Ephrata could have been easily mistaken for a settlement that might have existed during the Pleistocene. However, life there as a traffic pilot was like one continuous vacation and I counted my blessings for every minute that I no longer had to speak face to face with a member of the vast motoring public!! It was just "so clean" dealing with them from altitude and as they say I was in 'hog' heaven! On the day in question however, my typical traffic pilot sort of day ended with some excitement harking back to my road trooper years . . . . As usual, I was up at 0645, and at the WSP office by 0800. After wolfing down several of secretary Sue Spencer's great cookies by 0830 I was soon outa there to go preflight our trusty Cessna 182 traffic plane (N95879) in the old WWII hangar at the Ephrata Airport. My flying partner in those years, Trooper Ben Hamilton 314, had the day off so I launched myself alone towards the designated target area of the day, I-90 at Fishtrap, west of Spokane at 0930.

First a little (well, several pages) primer on traffic pilot activities and a little overview of the whole WSP Aviation program. Most of the major state highways and interstates in Washington have areas (traffic courses) designated for airborne traffic enforcement. You can easily tell when you're in one by the painted white marks on the shoulder of the highway. The marks are about six feet long and a foot wide and are arranged in an alternating 'bar' and 'V' shaped format exactly one half mile apart. They are painted and maintained by the Wash State Dept. of Transportation whose technicians measure and certify the distance between the marks with extremely accurate laser equipment. They have to be exactly 2,640 feet apart since the airborne pilot's stopwatches, which measure the speed of vehicles traveling between them, are calibrated for that ½ mile distance. When speed enforcement action is taken both the marks and the stopwatches and all their certifying documents have to be in order in case a violator takes a ticket to court. The digital stopwatches are checked monthly, for a 24 hour period, against the time tone transmitter from the atomic clock in Boulder,

Colorado, as well as against each other before and after each shift. We even had a device that measured the vibration level of the quartz crystal in the stopwatches to ensure their continued accuracy. I never saw one of the digital stopwatches off more than one ten thousandth of a second after running it against the atomic clock for 24 hours.

The tried and true method the pilots used was to establish a race track traffic pattern over a three or four mile section of highway with local ground troopers waiting on a freeway on-ramp. Sometimes, they just staged in a wide spot in the road, over the crest of a hill, or around a corner where motorists couldn't see all the patrol cars waiting and get spooked. Although we often worked two lane sections of state highway the results were usually not as good as out on the interstate. The problem on two lane roads was the traffic going the other direction would flash their headlights, honk their horns, and wave their arms at the cars approaching that gaggle of troopers waiting for them over the next little hill. Consequently, the fast ones would usually slow down before I could get a decent speed check on them. Of course the truck drivers would also start hollering on their CB radios about the Bear in the Air and cause more slowdowns. Thankfully, most of the ground troops also had CB radios . . . . The wily veterans often countered the truck driver calls with realistic sounding reports on channel 19 that the Smokeys had all headed into town for coffee and everyone was now free to put the hammer down if so desired, or so I've heard.

We flew at around 1,500 to 2,000 feet AGL (above ground level) but often a bit lower in Western Washington where the weather didn't always cooperate. The airplane was flown with approach flaps, around 13 inches of manifold pressure, and trimmed to maintain around 90 knots. One beautiful characteristic of Cessna 182's is that once the trim is set for hands off flying, the pilot could easily watch traffic, spot the fast ones, operate two stopwatches, document the speeds and times, and radio down to the waiting ground troops as necessary. Cessna 182's are perhaps the most stable airplane ever designed and once properly trimmed they basically flew themselves with only the occasional nudge from the pilot on the controls. Sometimes it was necessary to horse the plane around quite violently to keep sight of a car when trees, terrain, and other obstacles blocked the pilot from seeing that next mark or keep the violator's car continuously in sight. This usually wasn't a problem working traffic courses in Eastern Washington which are usually painted on long straight-aways with only sagebrush for vegetation and great weather. Western Washington was quite a different story with the predominant rain and low clouds and tall timber along the highways.

Once a pilot spotted a "fast one" and believe me they are very easy to spot from our high perch, he waited for the car to get to the first mark and started a stopwatch when the car's front bumper was adjacent to the mark. When the car reached the next mark the pilot clicked the stopwatch and it immediately displayed that car's average speed for that last half mile. The stopwatch automatically starts a second check beginning when the pilot clicked it. On some traffic courses a pilot might get as many as six or seven half mile long checks on one car. Needless to say some of the folks we "hung a greenie on" or "gave some WSP green stamps to" . . . . (the violators copy of the citation was green in those years) would often set a court date to protest their innocence even though they knew their speed had been monitored and averaged for several miles. The usual claim in court was how unfair it was, or that we had the wrong car, that they never saw an airplane and doubted if there was one in the air at all, that there were no warning signs to indicate airborne speed enforcement was in progress, and that the whole WSP operation was a sham, and some kind of unfair-unconstitutional commie-pinko speed trap. The most common defense attorney tactic was to try to prove that there is no way any pilot on earth could fly the plane, maintain altitude and airspeed, monitor its systems, keep track of traffic on the road and in the sky, talk to ATC (air traffic control), talk on the WSP radio and direct the ground troops, check the speed on two different cars simultaneously with two stopwatches, write everything down, and manage the whole affair without making a mistake. However, this tactic often fell on deaf ears as nearly every district court judge in the state had come up with us to observe the operation and saw how effortless it really was. Although occasionally challenging, especially in turbulence, it's just like any other job requiring a little multi-tasking . . . once you establish a system, prioritize your activities in a timely manner, and develop that hand, tongue, and eyeball muscle memory through daily repetition, anyone with basic coordination skills could become adept at it.

Unfortunately for those making the accusation that our program was unconstitutional, there is a separate statute in the Revised Code of Washington allowing for airborne speed enforcement. However, this did not dissuade some violators to question the legality, morality, legitimacy, etc., etc., of the operation. In almost every case I was aware of, during my 33 year career, when there was a long drawn out court appeal, for a simple $17.00 airplane speeding ticket, it nearly always stemmed from a traffic stop where an arrogant perpetrator had unsuccessfully utilized a radar detector to avoid getting caught speeding. The really serious guys often had two detectors . . . one aimed forward and one aimed rearwards in case they were getting 'back shot' off an overpass or on-ramp . . . . The ultra-serious guys also utilized a CB radio and routinely asked the truck drivers on channel 19 for a "smoke report" (where are the smokeys/bears/troopers hiding). Sadly for them no company has ever produced a stopwatch detector yet. Unfortunately, this sort of individual cost all the citizens of the State of Washington thousands of dollars each year in court costs, time spent issuing subpoenas, writing affidavits, trooper overtime, public disclosure procedures, etc., etc . . . All that money and time wasted just to assuage the bruised ego of some hubris laden snob who could not or would not take responsibility for his/her actions . . . . Really quite sad . . . . The only saving grace from these episodes was knowing that those guys had just spent many thousands of their own dollars in attorney fees, took time off from work, and hopefully got an ulcer just so his ambulance chasing attorney might find a poorly copied document somewhere in the system where a date stamp or signature was not legible. The most common and successful defense attorney tactic of all was to keep getting a court date continuance until the ground trooper or pilot was eventually on vacation, sick leave, or otherwise occupied. Sadly, depending on the leanings of a particular judge, that was usually all it took to have the case dismissed . . .

The primary difference between getting a speeding ticket from an officer using a laser radar gun versus an airplane is as follows: the laser radar is extremely accurate but the actual speed measuring probably only lasts a second or two; the violator might have been passing, maneuvering, getting away from a tailgater, going around a truck, etc. With airplane speed enforcement, the pilot might have been checking your speed continuously for several minutes and would certainly take into account any passing, tailgating, or any other cause for necessary and temporary speed increases. It's just a much more fair, comprehensive, and timely method (when available). Additionally, with the bird's eye view afforded the pilot, so many other serious violations are easily spotted that a ground unit parked behind an abutment would never sees. My favorite violators were those who would follow too closely and tailgate six or seven different cars in a short distance, while violently changing lanes in heavy traffic and getting nowhere fast but really pissing off a lot of other motorists who occasionally responded in kind resulting in an ugly road rage incident of some sort. Often, when looking down on these serial tailgaters, I could not see any daylight between their front bumper and the rear bumper of the other motorist they were 'violating'. Getting this kind of Type A bonehead pulled over and cited brought me tremendous satisfaction! They would not have been stopped nor the extent of their reckless driving documented were the plane not up getting that 'bird's eye view of things. Speaking of boneheads, I once took one of our 'esteemed' and highly respected district commanders (a WSP Captain in charge of a huge area of Washington State) up for an airplane ride to show him our traffic operation. Just after takeoff he commented, "I've always wanted to see just how you guys manage to work the **radar** from an airplane . . . ." Jesus Christ . . . . I was flabbergasted by that remark and assumed he was kidding . . . . But when I realized by the look on his face that he wasn't, I showed him the stopwatches and explained the program . . . . He became very quiet for the rest of the flight and just stared out the side window at the scenery . . . . He did write me a nice comp letter which I assume was his attempt to guilt me into not telling everyone what a nincompoop he was . . . ?

Typical results of tail-gating…No injuries.

The most rewarding words a traffic pilot could hear from a ground troop who was contacting one of the above described serial tailgaters was; "He's got a bug (radar detector)". That made my day but more so when he added: . . . ."and . . . he's wearing . . . (oh be still my heart . . . . wait for it . . . . wait for it) . . . . DG'S" !! (driving gloves) . . . Oh Good Lord . . . this was the 'Trifecta' of satisfaction for all of us, for we all knew we had just bagged one of the poster children of the "Wannabee Formula One 'Nerd' Driving Community." Better yet was the gratification enjoyed by all of us when passing motorists would slow as they went past shaking their fists and honking their horns at the idiot we had just pulled over!! Ahhhh, the ultimate in job satisfaction!!! Later in my career they began labeling these tailgating lane changing jerks as aggressive drivers and the WSP launched several departmental and media campaigns to battle them . . . . But I can tell you from experience, this is a battle that will never be won, just perpetually sustained.

Anyway, I digress . . . . back to Traffic Pilot 101 School. When the pilot had a speeding motorist in his sights, and had documented several good speed checks on his kneeboard log sheet, and the selected violator had about a half mile to go to reach the waiting troopers, he would announce on the radio: "Half mile, red car, 86 at **1520**" (24 hour time for when the highest speed check occurred). As the red car was just about to go under the overpass or approach the waiting troopers the pilot would announce: "Red car, left lane, next car to you now" or some other similar identifying language such as: "It's the red car in the outside lane next to the motorcycle and behind the blue pickup." When the ground troop got behind the correct car, under the pilot's watchful eye, the pilot would verify that was the correct car, and turn back onto the traffic course to look for another. The ground troops would identify themselves with their badge number, and usually read back something to me such as: "Got it **305**, (my badge number) red car 86 at 1520, **378**" (his or her badge number). I usually had many other speed checks on the car but we normally didn't tie up the radio airwaves unless the ground troop wanted all of them documented on his case report. This process would be repeated around 50 or 60 times until the ground troops got tired and bored or I got low on gas and/or began to have bulging bladder issues whereupon I headed for the nearest regional airport, or in some cases the closest crop duster strip.

WSP Pilot verifying trooper has correct car stopped.

Since we now seem to be discussing urination issues I should point out that all of the WSP planes were equipped with Port-a-Johns (with a Port-a-Jill adaptor), mainly for the heavy coffee drinker crowd. Their usage, however, was not usually recommended and actually extremely frowned upon by all of the pilots! . . . . These containers would probably work just fine in the office cubicle environment but trying to use it while strapped in, sitting down, flying a plane in turbulence, with someone certain to call you on the radio just when you got all prepared and un-zipped, was always for me a real 'Three Stooges' moment . . . Watching someone else attempt it was just wrong . . . As for myself, after several unsuccessful attempts where I ended up returning to the airport with a flight suit in need of immediate laundering and the airplane seat and carpeting in need of an immediate shampooing, I gave up and familiarized myself with the location of every dirt strip in Washington State for possible future emergency usage. I have heard that there are some pilots endowed with freakazoid type 'personal units', who could successfully penetrate a Port a John, even in clear air turbulence, and not spill or leak a drop . . . . However, I never heard of one of those particular sized units in our group of aviators . . . . One of the more senior pilots I used to fly with, Dave Gardner, once told me that any dipshit could successfully piss in a Port-a-John in flight even in moderate turbulence but that it took a "real" man to take a dump in one under those conditions . . . . I'll give you that one Dave!! I also noted a direct correlation between increased urination urgency and increased headwind component towards your landing airport . . . you just never saw a tailwind when you needed it most! I was very happy I never had to witness, assist, or be asked to produce one of the Port a Jill adaptors on a flight. It was one nasty looking contraption and I just don't see how it could be successfully utilized, even on the ground let alone in a pitching airplane, without a hazmat spill of some sort resulting. I always felt that if I was in an airplane with a female passenger trying to use that thing, and the inevitable stinky mess ensued, there is no doubt in my mind that everything would have somehow been my fault, and a lawsuit would soon follow claiming pain, suffering, and PTSD.

Later in my career while flying WSP King Airs and Beechjets, we actually had factory installed bathrooms on board with doors no less. The Beechjet had a nice and secure unit in the back of the plane but the King Airs were a different story. N88SP, a real old King Air 90, had a sideways facing toilet right among the passenger seats. The metal toilet receptacle looked remarkably like an upside down trooper's campaign hat (drill instructor/smokey bear type) and it was our duty after a flight to pick this thing up and dump the contents. This chore was automatically assigned to the FNG co-pilot. Most of our passengers were reluctant to use it since the "secure" door was actually a folding curtain with a magnet to hold it closed. When you were on the throne your butt was about 12 inches from a passenger seat with that occupant's nose and ears in close proximity. We usually briefed our passengers that this was an emergency toilet only but there was always some clown who just had to try it out in flight. A nice feature on the King Air 90 and 200 aircraft was the location of the outflow valves in the tail section of the plane . . . . if anybody barfed or used the toilet, at least we didn't have to smell anything horrible since recirculating cabin air was vented to the rear. However, the Beechjet was a different story; the outflow valve was under a panel near the co-pilot's feet so if any nasty odors were created in the plane, we weren't the first to find out about it but those horrible odors lingered there the longest. As I recall, it was one of our gorilla sized SWAT team guys who thought it would be hilarious to take a massive dump in the tiny little toilet in the Beechjet, filling it to the brim with what can only be described as some sort of hideous alien material accompanied by an odor that immediately caused myself and my co-pilot to don our oxygen masks. Thank God they were the quick donning type as we immediately went to 100% to make sure we didn't lose control of the plane. Just prior to being assaulted by the odor we heard the screams and death threats, somewhat muffled by our Dave Clark headsets, from the other SWAT team members, being directed at the perpetrator. I don't know where or what those guys ate and drank before a mission but I assume it must have been something necessary to maintain their bravery and courage. More importantly for the pilots, we didn't have to empty the Beechjet's toilet receptacle as it was a complicated affair that only a trained jet technician could handle . . . My special thanks to Chris, Gary, and Brian for their courage!

One of my very small bladder capacity flying partners, during my latter tenure in Ephrata, used to get on his knees on the backseat of a 182 in flight and try to use the Port a John. But, unlike Colonel Bill Kilgore in *"Apocalypse Now"*, who loved the smell of napalm in the morning, I for one did **not** enjoy the pungent odor of cheap recycled WSP coffee in the morning especially when it was being slowly dripped and drizzled into a plastic pot inches behind my head . . . . After about the third episode I issued a stern directive to that FNG to never do that again or the next time I would roll the plane inverted, just as the Port a John got to the full line, and drench him with its contents . . . . He began drinking less coffee in the morning but was "pissed" at me for some time for being so insensitive about his small bladder issues . . . .

Working traffic, as described above, was only one of many roles filled by the WSP traffic pilots and aircraft. We did a lot of search and rescue, drug interdiction (following a car load of morons around with a trunk load of cocaine/marijuana/heroin for hours on end), plain old personnel transportation flights, emergency organ, tissue and blood flights, photo flights, and many types of surveillance flights. We were available to just about any city, county, state, or federal agency. My favorite non-traffic related activity was summertime marijuana field observation flights. This usually entailed looking for outdoor grows, usually on state or federal lands in mountainous terrain, but quite often on private property such as in the middle of an 80 acre corn circle . . . Quite fulfilling when a big grow (1,000+ plants) was discovered!) More on this later.

Sorry, I really got side-tracked there . . . . back to the day in question . . . . After launching myself in my favorite old Skylane, N95879, I relaxed on my way to Fishtrap as the DME (distance measuring equipment) in the King KNS 80 Area Navigation unit (this was 1985 by the way—no GPS yet) slowly counted down to zero to let me know it was time to go to work. As usual, there were four or five troopers waiting for me on the eastbound on-ramp to I-90, all expecting to get at least one triple digit stop today (a speeder over 100 mph). However, those were actually fairly uncommon except during a Friday afternoon or Sunday evening on a holiday weekend, when 100+ cars became blasé. Those holiday weekends were the days when we occasionally went home with 150+ violators called out during a single session . . . Very tiring and my biceps were usually aching after six hours (all our Skylanes had the long range 92 gal. tanks) of yanking and banking a 182 all over the sky . . . . the Port a John would also be looking very attractive to me by then.

After an hour or so of turning circles over Fishtrap I got a call from Spokane WSP radio to proceed to Felts Field, East of Spokane, and to call the office immediately upon landing. (Remember, no cell phones, no texting, and no pagers in those years). During the call I was connected to a local DEA agent who needed me airborne immediately to follow a guy in a Beech Bonanza to see where he was going. He was either transporting a load of cocaine or going to get it and they needed to know where that might be and who he might be meeting there. I immediately knew there might be a problem since a Bonanza is quite a bit faster than a Skylane and told the agent that . . . He said to do the best I could and gave me a discreet frequency to talk to him on as well as another discreet frequency to talk to ATC on and finally a pre-arranged transponder code so ATC could track me. Apparently the twin engine Beech Baron DEA had chartered for this mission had engine problems and I was the emergency back-up. Well, this sounded like fun and beat the hell out of turning circles out at Fishtrap all day!

I had the tail number on the Bonanza and actually watched him takeoff from Felts Field ahead of me. The DEA agent called me again on the Wulfsburg UHF radio and said if I lose him they now had credible intelligence that he was headed for the Yakima Valley, just didn't know exactly where. At least that was familiar territory to me as I was raised there and knew where some of the small airports and dirt strips were located. Initially, Spokane approach control was able to paint him easily on radar while he was in the relatively flat terrain North of Geiger Field and had some altitude. But he apparently soon dipped down into the Spokane River valley and they lost radar contact. I lost sight of him almost immediately due to the speed differential between our planes but kept on a southwesterly heading in anticipation of him turning for the Yakima Valley. When Spokane approach lost him I didn't think I had much of a chance to find this guy again. However, when the Spokane ATC Departure controller handed me off to Seattle Center, they had good news for me: a quick thinking controller there just had an F-111 (might have been an F4) Air Force fighter, out of Mountain Home AFB near Boise, handed over to him that was just exiting the Roosevelt MOA (military operating area) North of Moses Lake. He apprised the pilot of our situation and asked if he had the gas and time to help us track this guy. He said he had a few extra minutes of gas and would do his best while on his way back to Mountain Home. We assumed the Bonanza was flying at sagebrush level by now so the F111 was looking for him down in the weeds with his sophisticated downward looking radar. I kept up my southwesterly heading praying I could eventually intercept him somewhere near the Wapato, Sunnyside, Toppenish area where most of the drug activity was located in the Yakima Valley. Surprisingly, within a few minutes the Air Force pilot said he had a low flying target westbound in the Palisades which is a deep narrow valley just southeast of Wenatchee. I was about ten miles south of there so this was great news. His next transmission advised that the low flying target had now turned south low level over the Columbia River . . . even better for me. The F111 pilot then announced he was at bingo fuel (gas minimums to get home) and had to bug out. I had Center pass on my heartfelt thanks to him.

I felt pretty confident of this guy's intentions now and proceeded to a point near the Vernita Bridge over the Columbia, just northwest of the WWII Hanford atomic works. I knew the Bonanza would turn towards the lower Yakima Valley here after skirting the boundaries of the Yakima Firing Center, another military restricted area and usually 'hot' (active military operations in progress), just west of him. I knew he wouldn't take the shortcut across there as he would most certainly be picked up on their radar. I hadn't been in the Vernita area over 5 minutes when I spotted the Bonanza again right down on the water . . . As my old hero Hannibal used to say on the *A-Team* . . . ."I love it when a plan comes together!" I had climbed to about 8500 ft and had a pretty good altitude advantage on him and hoped I could keep up with him if I stayed wide open in a shallow dive, and thought I might be able to keep him in sight as far as the Sunnyside area. I even had the sun more or less in my favor so it would be hard for him to see me if he was even looking. As soon as he cleared the firing center he took up what looked like to me a direct heading to Sunnyside. I put the Sunnyside coordinates in my KNS80 navigation box and our courses matched perfectly. I notified the DEA agent that I felt he was going to Sunnyside and he said he would try to get one of his undercover agents there in time to monitor things. After saying that I immediately regretted it as there are several other small airports in the Sunnyside vicinity and I was just guessing that was his destination based on my previous experience with druggers in that area. To my great relief, as the Bonanza approached Sunnyside, he slowed down, circled the airport a couple times, and landed without talking on the local Unicom frequency. The local DEA agent did manage to get there in time to watch the proceedings so I stayed well away from the airport and set up a holding pattern 5 miles northeast, in case he decided to return to the Spokane area afterwards.

About 95% of my previous experience following drug traffickers could best be described as some crazy made up episode from The Three Stooges meet Abbot and Costello. These guys are the most erratic, illogical, disconnected morons I've ever watched. Most of the time I would have an agent with me who was in radio contact with other agents on the ground who kept us apprised of the whole ground situation. The supposed drug traffickers spent quite a bit of their time lost, distracted, eating, or dealing with broken down cars; this often happened when they had the drugs or a big bag of money with them. It was quite obvious to me from 2,500 ft above them that they had no contingency plans for security or a back-up plan when something went amiss. When things did go awry, they would often just get out and mill around the car for awhile . . . . Sooner or later one of them would be dispatched to the nearest 711 or Qwik-E-Mart to get a couple bags of jo-jo's, greasy fried chicken, or a similar box of gut bombs. The agents on the ground would be cracking up as they gave us a running commentary on the unfolding culinary circus. There was usually a confidential informant mixed in with the group of bad guys; I did attend a post mission de-briefing once and it was hilarious when all the additional stories of the druggies' ineptitude were revealed.

After holding for about 20 minutes, I saw the Bonanza pilot take off again and initially head southbound towards Grandview. I prayed this was just another diversionary tactic and stayed northeast. I was able to keep him in sight and he soon turned towards me and proceeded back towards Spokane. I now had a lot of altitude on him again and while keeping a shallow dive going I didn't lose him until we were in the Moses Lake area. His heading looked good for direct Spokane so I proceeded to the Felts Field airport hoping that was his destination. I was quite surprised that he wasn't down in the weeds flying the canyons, as he did on his trip down, and assumed he might be getting low on gas by now. In the meantime, the confidential informant involved in the drop at the Sunnyside airport advised the DEA agent that he thought the pilot was going to Mead, a small airport North of Spokane. When the agent gave me the news, I made a slight heading adjustment to the left, quickly determined the distance and radial from the GEG VOR to Mead off my enroute low IFR map, input the data into the KNS80, and proceeded there wide open. I hoped my direct flight would get me there first and offset his speed advantage since he would probably be involved with his low level zigzagging routine as he got closer . . . . However, drug traffickers aren't exactly the most reliable types even if some of them are pilots. I arrived over the Mead airport and entered the pattern pretending to practice touch and go landings. The Bonanza was nowhere in sight and none of the ground units had seen it yet . . . . After twenty minutes or so I thought he must have gone to Felts Field and started to head that way but I was barely out of the pattern when the DEA agent said he thought he saw a V-tail Bonanza overfly the airport behind me. I cranked it around hard and finally spotted it circling Mead at about 1000 ft AGL. I was at 2500 ft by then and when he turned away from me I dove on him and got within 100 yds of his tail. He got down to around 500 ft AGL over the airport, slowed to about 100 knots, started circling and appeared to be looking for his contact or any sign of trouble on the ground. There were no radio calls to Mead Unicom from him and I wasn't talking either. He increased his bank to about 45 degrees in a left turn and I eventually ended up just aft of his right wing at full power to stay with him. He went wings level and I was sure he must have spotted me. I was now within 100 ft of him when I saw him making furtive movements in the cockpit . . . I wasn't sure if he was getting ready to make a drop but in my excitement it sure as hell looked like he was hauling out a Mini Mac 10 or something with which to do me harm!! Although our WSP planes are unmarked I was in full trooper uniform in those years and thought he must have seen my big yellow WSP shoulder patches. The side windows on our Skylanes had the retaining arms removed so they could be opened 90 degrees to the fuselage in flight, mainly for taking photos over fatal accident scenes. I flipped open the window, horsed out my S&W 357 magnum, and prepared myself for any eventuality. While I was fiddling around getting my hogleg out he banked hard into me and I had to dive under him . . . . It sure seemed to me that this was turning into a dog-fight of sorts . . . . I maneuvered back to his right and behind him again just as he started a hard turn to the left. We ended up in a real tight 70 to 80 degree bank turning battle with me slightly lower than him . . . I was flying with my right hand and was trying to hold the window open with my hogleg stuck out about a foot with my left . . . (**Please Remember**, I was an Aviation Section FNG and have never purported to be very smart or quick on the uptake) . . . Anyway, I knew he couldn't out-turn me since maintaining 70 to 80 degree bank angles was what I did all day long working traffic . . . I could see his tail pretty well but couldn't quite tell what he had in his hands. I was convinced he was trying to ID me and after doing so would probably attempt some nut-job suicide by cop stunt and try to take me out . . . . Just after I glanced away from him for a split second to check my manifold pressure, there was a huge "Whuumpp" and all hell broke loose! I suddenly found myself inverted, nose low, and a bunch of God damn trees quickly filling my windscreen!! Son of a bi . . . .

CHAPTER 2

LIFE ON THE FARM

All four of my grandparents immigrated to America from Italy in the early 1900's. Arranged marriages in Italy were common in those years and both my grandmothers had to suffer through these forced unions with older husbands they despised. However, since these men had sponsors here in Philadelphia and Baltimore the skids were already greased for them to become American citizens. Curiously both of them ended up working in boarding houses on the east coast where they each met their future husbands who had just arrived from Italy as well. Like so many other immigrants of that era from Poland, Germany, and Ireland my future grandfathers had found work in the coal mines. Eventually, my paternal Grandmother Antonina Grilli ran off with the dashing Tomaso Carnevali, and my Maternal Grandmother Ersiglia Lombardozzi ran off with the equally handsome Francesco Sauverigno Logozzo. The Logozzo's settled in the Seattle area where my Mom was born and the Carnevali's in Cle Elum where my grandfather worked in the coal mines near Roslyn where my Dad was born. Eventually, they all moved to the Yakima area, bought some land, and began to farm it. My Dad Roy grew up on the Tieton ranch where my grandfather began the *Carnevali Dairy* and planted an apple orchard. My Mom Rose ended up West of Yakima where her folks also started a fruit ranch. Life was tough during the Great Depression but they all worked extremely hard. Many of the kids didn't get to go to high school but somehow they all prospered. Mom once told me the best job she had during the Depression was picking apricots for 10 cents an hour. My parents finally met at an Italian party at Joe Batali's in Harrah and were married in 1938. My sister Rita (Hanses) came along in 1940 and my brother Ray in 1943. I was the baby arriving in 1949. Soon after getting married, my folks moved off the Tieton ranch and started their own apple orchards first in the Selah area and later near Wide

Hollow West of Yakima. When my grandfather could no longer run the Tieton ranch due to failing health we all moved back to the home ranch when I was about four.

Mom and Dad in 1938.

Initially, life on the farm was quite idyllic. We had a huge ranch with a nice creek running through it loaded with trout, a winding road going up to the top of the property which was great for sledding in the winter, and all kinds of wildlife. One of my first memories of those years was counting the airplanes that went over our house every day. Although I didn't know it then I was witnessing the end of an era as I counted all the DC-3's, 4's, and 6's and the occasional Connie drone overhead on their way in or out of Seattle. As luck would have it, a Victor Airway (airplane freeway) went right over our house; we lived directly under TITON intersection on V4 (Victor 4). More importantly, fighters and bombers from McChord Air Force Base in Tacoma also came right over the house on their way to the Yakima

Firing Center Restricted Area, just a few miles away, to drop their bombs and shoot up ground targets. This was during and just after the Korean War and the training must have been quite intense. We heard a lot of window rattling BA-BOOMS in those years which I later deduced could have only been created by the supersonic F86 Sabre Jets of that era. My interest in aviation began in those years and has never waned and the F86 is still my favorite jet fighter of all time.

The idyllic farm life came to an end quite rapidly when I was around six. My brother Ray seemed to be having all the fun and I couldn't figure out why he was always complaining about it. So I told my Dad I wanted to do all the neat stuff Ray got to do like: (get ready to feel real sorry for me) changing the water, hoeing all the young apple trees, cutting water sprouts, thinning apples and pears, propping the fruit laden limbs up, pruning, spraying weed killer, ditching, grafting, cutting blight out of the pear trees, disking, spraying DDT, Parathion, etc., spreading empty boxes and bins out in the orchard for the harvest, picking apples and pears, picking the props back up, cutting mildew out of the apple trees, hauling the filled boxes and bins out to the truck, shredding grass, spring-toothing, disking, rotovating, getting up at O-dark thirty to light the smudge pots in the spring, wind-rowing brush, pushing brush, burning brush, shredding brush, fixing broken pipe lines, spreading manure, spreading hay-hauls, more spraying, getting back up again before sunrise to extinguish the smudge pots, then fill them up again with diesel oil for the next cold night, spraying more Paraquat and 2-4D weed killer, gopher baiting, more spraying, subsoiling, rototilling, dragging and climbing up and down these huge herkin wooden ladders, etc., etc., etc . . . . I think my Dad liked my 'can do' attitude and so for the next twenty years or so I got to do all those things as often as I liked . . . . What a moron I was!! Our sister Rita would occasionally make an appearance on the porch, see the hired help (us) sweating out in the orchard, become faint and retreat inside to be comforted by Mom. She then had to lie down and rest up for her next date.

Smudging was a dirty messy routine. Although we used diesel in our 'pots' some of our neighbors were still burning piles of tires to raise the temperature in their orchards a few degrees to ward off the frost in the Spring. Burning the old tires left a residue of sticky melted rubber strands floating in the air that got all over you, in your ears and nose, the house, the trees, you name it. As one can imagine the local atmosphere in the morning after a heavy night of smudging was thick and dense; the whole Yakima Valley would be obliterated by this gray-brown smog until the wind blew it away. In the forties Dad had constructed several portable wind generators which we would drag around the orchard on skids and place them in favorable areas to keep the air mass moving a bit in the normal 'frost pocket' low spots. These wind machines were crazy looking monsters with straight eight Buick engines attached to huge WWI era wooden propellers off God knows what kind of ancient flying machines. They were loud as hell and no one ever doubted it was smudging season when Dad cranked those babies up. Today, everyone mounts their wind machines on tall towers where the Chev 454 V8's are required to be muffled somewhat.

I was about seven when I inherited the gopher traps from my brother. He had started high school and didn't have the time anymore to take care of a trap line (for gophers anyway) . . . . Pocket Gophers were the bane of our existence then for a couple of reasons; they loved to gnaw on the roots of all the new varieties of small apple trees we had inter-planted the whole ranch with, often killing them. Secondly, all of our tree rows had three small ditches on either side which were used to irrigate them. Problem was, the irrigation water would sometimes find its way into a gopher tunnel and get diverted away from the trees. One of the everlasting, and oft repeated memories from my childhood, was when the old man would get the huge Bean speed sprayer and tractor stuck in one of these almost invisible wet spots created by the gophers in the wide area between the rows of trees. We would hear his shrieking whistle first, which I'm pretty sure could be heard in space, then the yelling and cussing to go get the other tractor and bring the big chain. Anyway, to prevent repetitions of these episodes, and keep his blood pressure from boiling over again, first my brother then myself were paid handsomely to trap the gophers . . . if you call 2 bits (25 cents) per gopher handsome . . . . But some days I made a buck or so and felt like I was really helping out.

First Grade photo, Tieton Elementary . . . I'm
the middle guy in the middle row

Dad spraying the pears with the Bean Speed Sprayer.

About this time I was presented with a single shot 22 and was directed to kill every cottontail rabbit and grey digger (a type of ground squirrel) that I saw. The rabbits would gnaw the bark all the way around the small trees at the top of the snow in the winter usually killing them. The squirrels would run up the props that supported the heavily fruit laden tree limbs in the fall, and take random bites out of many different apples ruining them for market. I believe I got 4 bits apiece for the bigger critters and if I hadn't massacred the cottontails too badly, my Mom would sometimes soak them overnight in a bucket of vinegar brine, reducing the sagebrush flavor, and then we'd have spaghetti with rabbit. At the time, I believed it was a perfect life and thought every kid should be slaughtering dozens of animals a week and getting paid for it. I became a pretty good shot and later when I had to qualify once a quarter with the WSP I didn't have too much trouble. However, as I got older, I began to abhor hunting and killing things and quit altogether about 30 years ago. I still carry a lot of guilt for the animal serial killing of my youth even though I knew it was necessary at the time. Most of the other farmers of the era poisoned those critters with strychnine but my Dad felt there was too much potential for collateral damage to the local cats and dogs so we just shot the offenders instead.

Our entertainment in those years after the farm work was done was initially limited to listening to shows like Jack Benny, Amos and Andy, and Gunsmoke on the **radio**. When the folks bought our first black and white TV around 1955 or so it was a tremendous leap into the 'modern' age for us. My favorite shows of that era were Rin Tin Tin, The Cisco Kid, Zorro, The Three Stooges, and my favorite of all, Sky King. Schuyler made flying look so easy as he flung his trusty old Cessna 310 'Songbird' around the Arizona skies chasing bad guys with his gorgeous niece Penny at his side . . . . Man, every red-blooded kid my age was in love with Penny! My cousin Jack Logozzo married Sky King's (Kirby Grant) real life niece Nancy and on our last visit to Montana she had many stories to tell from those years about her famous uncle Kirby. Regarding the Three Stooges, my best buddy from that era, Gil Martin and I had most of their eye poking, face slapping, spinning circles on the floor, nyuk, nyuk, nyuk routines down to a science . . . I'm sorry, but I will always think they are the funniest guys ever and we still have a large portrait of them hanging in our bedroom entitled; 'Golf With Your Friends.' The Sky King series sure held a lot of significance and similarities for me about 30 years later.

When I was about ten I started to get paid for the farm work, starting out at 50 cents an hour with a raise to $1.00 an hour when I was sixteen. Saving up to buy a jeep was the sole purpose of my life in those days as Dad, my Uncle Joe, and family friend Dino Paganelli all had them. Bouncing around in my own jeep up in the hills West of Yakima was all I thought about. Dad was friends with a guy named Ronnie Huff who specialized in installing Chev 283 V8's in jeeps. The stock four cylinder engine in CJ5 jeeps was pretty anemic so the who's who of the Yakima jeeping community all had 283's installed under the hood. My savings account began to grow and when I turned sixteen I was told I could buy a jeep and Dad said he might help me put a 283 in it if I didn't wreck up too much more of the farm equipment or bark up and kill too many trees between now and then.

Family photo at the Batali's in Harrah circa 1956 Standing from left: Rita, Rose, Roy, Ray, and Ricky (kneeling) The 5 R's!

In the meantime I was privileged to view, hear, ride in, and occasionally drive some of the greatest cars of the 50's and 60's. My sister Rita dated several guys with really cool sports cars'; one had a '58 Vette, another a really nice Austin Healey, Mark Hanses had a gorgeous maroon Pontiac Ventura with a 389 under the hood, and Ronnie Anderson had my favorite, a '57 Triumph TR3. I don't know if Rita or my parents ever found out about this but one day when Ronnie came over, he left the Triumph at our place, and took off with Rita and my parents for parts unknown. Of course being a farmboy, my brother Ray was quite adept at hot wiring a simple mid-50's engine and in seconds it was running and we jumped in and went for a great ride down to Naches and back. I got to drive it in the driveway and had no trouble with the stick shift since all our tractors were so equipped. Shortly thereafter Ray traded in his '53 Chevy (which he let me drive on the highway when I was nine) on a beautiful '56 T-Bird. Well, not beautiful at first, since it arrived with the factory 'salmon' color paint job. When he had it painted candy apple red, it was transformed! There was an unfortunate incident one afternoon while he was washing it on the lawn. He had parked it kind of close to the shrubs next to the house and as I rode my bike around that day I kept eye-balling that gap and felt I could squeeze it in there and display my superior bike riding skills. I got it up to full speed, thought I hit the gap clean but apparently my left handlebar, which didn't have a grip on its rusty-jagged end, caught his right front fender as I whizzed by. There was a screeching metal rendering noise and as I looked back I noticed an ugly 10 inch scratch that was deep and wide in that brand new candy apple red paint . . . . Well, I have never peddled faster in my life and headed straight for my grandmother's house about two hundred yards away. I laid the bike down hard in front of her steps and crashed through her front door as I heard footsteps pounding closely behind me. I crawled under her bed and just managed to grab hold of springs and boards before I felt my brother's hands grab my ankles. There was a lot of yanking and crying and unintelligible yelling and cursing going on, most of it in Italian, as my grandmother wasn't too keen on big surprises like this. She was hitting Ray with a broom when he finally let go but I stayed under the bed for some time. My Mom finally came in and said it was safe to come home.

Getting back to wrecked farm equipment. Our farm was hilly, rocky, had big cliffs, and was very spread out with little three and four acre patches of good dirt with trees planted in them scattered around between huge piles of volcanic rock. When my grandfather bought the land back in 1915, he got it cheap, but to turn it into orchard land took some doing. Now I know for a fact that my Dad, Ray, and other hired help, wrecked up a lot of machinery themselves . . . But as everyone knows when an adult pulls a bonehead maneuver it was just an unavoidable 'accident.' However, when a ten year old kid breaks a tooth off the rotovator, or barks up an apple or pear tree with the disk, then it's just pure stupidity to be expected from someone with no common sense.

Well, during the mid-fifties, Dad had started a land leveling business to supplement the farm income and was away a lot on jobs with the cat and can (D7 and later D8 with Cat 70 and 80 scrapers). The winter of '55-'56 had been very severe killing a lot of our trees and Dad needed to work two full time jobs to keep us afloat. Consequently, Ray and I were left un-supervised operating some very dangerous farm equipment on some pretty scary land with steep cliffs, drop offs into creeks, steep grades, rocks hidden just inches underground waiting to tear up rotovator and disk blades, let alone all the rows and rows of freaking trees just begging to be run into, cut, sliced, and gouged. The huge old variety winesap, standard delicious, and red rome trees had monster limbs to become trapped under when operating machinery near them; those limbs would get caught on the equipment and sometimes would release back and either slap you in the face, or knock you right off the tractor. Ray got in a nasty pickle one day on the old Ford 9N while shredding grass; a big springy limb pinned his arms onto the steering wheel so he couldn't shift gears or touch the hand throttle or disengage the PTO . . . . He managed to push the clutch in and stop but that was it. Keeping that stiff clutch lever pushed in took a lot of leg strength and if he let it up the limb would swipe him right off the tractor into the swirling blades of the shredder . . . . Luckily our hired hand Earl Buck heard his yells for help and came to the rescue.

On the rare day when the ranch work was caught up, Dad would take us with him to his job site and let us ride on the Cat with him while he was land leveling, making roads, building levees, water retention ponds, and my favorite, clearing the snow off SR-410 up at Chinook Pass. He had this job every spring for 25 years or so and it was always his favorite. The scenery was unmatched, it was easy on the equipment with no dust or rocks to beat up the Cat, but it was very dangerous. The last couple of miles of SR-410, east of the summit, are carved out of the side of a mountain with one helluva drop off on the low side. On some years, the road was completely snowed in so you couldn't even tell where the road was since the slope was so steep. Dad's contract with the Highway Dept. labeled him as the 'pioneer' cat. He had to find the general road path, cut and plow the snow down to within a couple feet of the pavement, then let the huge Highway Dept. rubber tired snowblowers take it down to the road surface. Riding with him on the Cat up there was another one of those situations where several of his 'unknown' personality traits were revealed. Unfortunately for me there were a few moments of stark terror until I looked over at Dad and saw him having the time of his life so I guess I was somewhat comforted. While normally a very conservative person and not a risk taker at all doing farm work and conventional land leveling work, on Chinook Pass he was transformed into Evel Knievel on a D8. The first Cat he used up there was an older model D7 that had a rather short track base, was underpowered at that elevation (5,500 ft), and tended to sink into the snow too much due to its short-narrow tracks. However, when Dad traded that D7 for a 14A D8, and added a turbo charger to it, it was the perfect machine for the job. The D8 had a longer track base, wider track pads, and even though heavier than the D7 it did not sink into the snow as much. Dad installed a huge U-blade up front (with late model hydraulics and tilt cylinder of course) and attached a vertical eight foot 'knife' to the right side of the blade to keep the cut nice and straight in the snow. With the added turbo, he could now maintain sea level horsepower on the engine and was able to literally push a mountain of snow. The D8 had a stick shift set up, three speed transmission with a hand clutch on the left and a forward reverse lever on the right. I still have the occasional flashback from my time up there and see myself sitting on the battery box of that D8 while Dad approached a two thousand foot drop off with a huge pile of snow up front completely obliterating where we were going . . . . As my pucker factor increased to the point where I swore my ass was sucking the bolt heads off the top of that battery box, Dad would calmly keep the Cat going forward into certain oblivion . . . . At the last goddamn second, just as the mounded up snow began to slide off the blade, he would smoothly and simultaneously shove the clutch forward with his left hand while bringing the shift lever into reverse with his right then deftly bring the clutch lever back to get the Cat back in gear and us the hell out of there. While this was going on he was also steering the Cat with the foot brakes, without benefit of the usually required steering clutches (they required free hands) and tapping the throttle de-celerator with whichever foot he had free for a second to reduce engine rpm's as we neared the drop off. He would then release it to go back to full power in reverse. Now this was multi-tasking at a very high level with a considerable price to pay for a second's lapse in judgment or coordination. I often thought about those moments when later in my career I had to shoot instrument approaches down to minimums in the Beechjet in a snowstorm, then couldn't land due to zero visibility, and ended up performing a very complicated missed approach procedure at night in the mountains of Colorado with lots of very steep climb gradients to maintain. Dad would have been a good jet pilot; he had excellent situational awareness and the best hand eye coordination I've ever seen . . . .

Back to the snow falling off the blade over the precipice . . . There were several instances when just as he got the transmission into reverse the whole front end of the Cat would drop sharply several feet just as we started getting traction to back the hell off the edge of that cliff. As he reefed the Cat back from the brink with perfect timing I clearly remember him glancing over at me occasionally with that look which clearly sent the message . . ."Now that's how it's done kid." . . . . Every year on Dad's birthday my wife Debbie and I make a pilgrimage to the summit of Chinook Pass where we scattered his ashes so many years ago . . . . It's a beautiful spot in the shadow of Mt. Rainier near Lake Tipsoo and I'm pretty sure he would have thought it to be the perfect spot to rest up a bit in the shade and have lunch.

Dad pushing snow on Chinook Pass on his D7.

Dad standing by D7 on Chinook Pass.

I had my own scary moment a few years later while rotovating the apple trees in the spring . . . I was coming downhill towards a fifty foot cliff with the old Massey Ferguson 65 running *a Northwest* 72 inch rotovator . . . It was set to till the top 10 inches of soil with its circular rows of self-sharpening blades. When I got to within 10 feet of the cliff I put the clutch in to stop, back up and turn around . . . . Unfortunately, the clutch had two levels . . . 3/4 of the way down disengaged the tractor transmission and all the way down stopped the PTO from driving the rotovator . . . . This time I only pushed it part way down which just put the tractor in neutral . . . . However, the rotovator was still churning away in thick sod getting excellent grip and immediately accelerated the tractor like crazy . . . . I hit both brakes as fast as I could but it was still pushing me towards the cliff with the brakes locked up . . . I finally got the clutch lever pushed all the way down just as the front wheels of the tractor dropped over the edge of the cliff and dumped the tractor onto its frame . . . . I just sat there stunned for a second afraid to touch anything as my left leg started to quiver holding down that very stiff clutch . . . . I finally got the damn thing in reverse and raised the rotovator out of the ground but when I let the clutch out only one rear wheel was turning and I was still hanging over the cliff. It finally dawned on me to use the locking differential pedal under my right heel . . . When I got that pushed down and let the clutch out, both rear wheels churned away and hauled my ass out of there . . . I thought of that episode many times later in my aviation career when I got myself in a bad spot and tried to remember the lesson learned that day . . . . Always know your equipment and systems and keep the **memory items** on the emergency checklists fresh in your mind!!!

The scariest piece of farm equipment we had was the brush shredder. We primarily used it to shred the wind-rowed brush left in between the rows of trees after the pruners were done in the spring. The Dept. of Agriculture actually paid farmers to shred it and disk it in to enhance the soil. The old man bought this huge shredder, must have been eight feet wide, put hydraulics on it to raise it up and down and also installed an off-setting hydraulic side-shift mechanism. He also fabricated a huge brush shield that he mounted from the front to the rear of the tractor, flared up in the rear to protect the driver from flying pieces of shredded tree limbs. The design also allowed us to drive over and straddle the fairly tall and rough rows of brush without getting it all hung up under the tractor. Altogether, a great design theory but operating this thing was extremely dangerous. Large pieces of shredded tree limbs would coming flying out of the front of the shredder at warp speed and hit the shield with resounding clangs. Other pieces would go over the top of the shield and slam into my back, elbows, and head. I started wearing my motorcycle helmet and several jackets to protect myself. However the biggest threat was when a piece of wood or a rock came flying out of the shredder low, went under or alongside the tractor, hit the front tire, and bounced back into your face. I used to come in for dinner after a day of shredding brush looking like somebody had just drug me down a dirt road behind their pickup for a couple miles.

Getting back to busting up the equipment . . . . Those events usually occurred while operating this shredder. With the hydraulic side shift mechanism Dad had installed it allowed us to get the low riding shredder shifted over about four feet to the right. While cutting grass in the summer, you could get it under the low hanging apple tree limbs, without damaging or knocking any fruit off the trees with the tall tractor tires. Unfortunately, this put a hell of a strain on the PTO drivelines and universals which were already stretched to their limits at crazy angles. You had to be really careful when turning around at the end of the tree rows to not exceed the limitations of this set-up. If you accidentally tried to turn in the same direction the shredder was off-set to, mechanical doom soon ensued. The little welded tower holding the drivelines would separate from the shredder hitch, and begin to spin at the same rpm as the drivelines. It would beat the bejeezus out of everything in its proximity including hydraulic hoses, hitch, side shift cylinder, etc., etc. with pieces flying in all directions. When this happened, the noise was unbelievably loud and like Dad's piercing whistle was surely audible in space. Since he was usually gone on a Cat job when these breakdowns happened, I would limp the whole sorry affair down the hill to the shop and first try to fix it myself. Sometimes I was able to heat and beat the tower back into place with the cutting torch and huge sledge hammer and weld it up myself. I never had any electric welder training but had watched Dad enough to get the general idea of things. If nothing else was amiss, I would throw water over everything to cool it down, smear grease all over the new weld, then finish it off with an appropriate amount of dirt thrown onto the grease until everything was symmetrically dirty again and nothing looked amiss . . . Then it was back to work. The grease and dirt trick worked well when I nicked, gouged, or sliced a tree with the disk or rotovator too. Surprisingly the old man never caught on to my tactics until I told him years later. He thought it was hilarious then but most certainly wouldn't have at the time. Sometimes the damage was so extensive I had to take the whole thing up to Jim's Garage in Tieton. I drove through the neighbor's orchard to get there otherwise Mom would have seen me drive by the house. It was usually a quick fix to replace a couple torn up hydraulic hoses, and perhaps some welding when it was a bit more complicated than I could handle. I was soon back in business after spreading grease and dirt all over the new hoses and welds. Thank God Dad had an account at Jim's and I guess he never looked at the billing too closely as I never got caught.

Speaking of hydraulics . . . Dad had a tremendous aversion to getting stuck, especially while towing the speed sprayer around which when loaded with spray was extremely heavy. He initially began looking for a WWII era White Motor Car military half-track to replace the two wheel drive tractors he was always getting stuck. I remember going with him to look at a couple of them at some army surplus yards near Everett and Seattle . . . I don't remember why he didn't go that route, but probably had something to do with getting parts for those funky looking cleat tracks. He finally decided on a four wheel drive tractor but since no one built one back in 1958 he did what any frustrated engineer would do . . . . he built one himself. He found an old army WWII six by six chassis with the 270 Jimmy engine to use as the basic tractor . . . With a lot of modifications and a little help from Carl Brand down at Brand's Truck Repair in Yakima, he developed it into a usable farm tractor geared down to handle orchard work. It was a rear engine design with a forklift at the front. The four wheel drive system worked well and Dad fitted it with high narrow tires for maximum traction and ground clearance. He let his fascination with hydraulics get the better of him in its first iteration however . . . He determined a conventional steering wheel was inefficient and installed a single hydraulic push pull lever to steer the tractor with . . . push to turn right and pull to turn left . . . It worked OK at slow speeds or low engine rpm but once you got moving or had that big ole 270 Jimmy wound up a bit with a lot of pressure built up in its hydraulic pump, the tractor turned into a real monster. It took a real fine touch on the hydraulic lever to not get it into a series of P.I.O.'s . . . . (aviation terminology for pilot induced oscillations) whereupon with each driver input the tractor began jerking left and right with ever increasing frequency and violence until you just had to stop the damn thing and start over. Dad named the tractor the **Beast** and it is still spoken of with great reverence in family circles some 50 years later. He finally retrofitted it with a normal power steering unit and steering wheel complete with suicide knob in the early sixties and it gave us many years of great service without any problems. It was nearly impossible to get it stuck and had an excellent fork-lift in front with the engine and all the weight in the rear. Dad also made attachments to the fork lift for a huge brush rake that would allow you to clear out a whole row of brush in one pass, as well as a snow plow which got a lot of use during those nasty winters of the late fifties and early sixties. Dad had a tremendous inherent mechanical engineering talent and had his folks allowed him to go to school he could have written his own ticket anywhere.

Dad pushing snow on his homemade tractor the "Beast".

The entertainment highlight of my youth was waterskiing at O'Sullivan Lake (Potholes Reservoir) each summer. We started out with a 14 foot Reinell with a Mark 58 Mercury motor; it proved to be way too small so Dad soon upgraded to an eighteen foot Glaspar with a 100 horse Merc. Man we had a lot of fun in those years up in the sand dunes from 1957 to 1962. I'll always remember the time we invited my Mom's aunt Perina from Italy to go water skiing with us; you might say she was a little 'old fashioned'. This was a 100+ degree day and she showed up in a full length black dress with black lace up shoes, black hat and black parasol . . . . We all wondered who had just died? She had a helluva time getting in and out of the boat and was not comfortable at all once we got to the sand dunes. We all got to bring friends along and since I was a bit young to be dating then I usually invited my best friend Gil Martin; we had many adventures in the water and sand dunes as well as finding many dead carp and sea gulls to poke with a stick.

A tremendous innovation for pruning all our huge old growth apple trees was invented in the early sixties; it was called a Girette. Earlier versions of the Girette were called squirrels, monkeys, or cherry pickers but were very limited and got stuck easy. When Dad saw the Girette demonstrated at the Fair one year, he just had to have one. Nothing was more tedious and hairy than dragging those huge old wooden ladders around in the dead of winter and climbing up and down ice covered steps loaded down with saws and pruning shears. The Girette was a five wheeled affair that you steered with your feet and had a rotating boom-lift-arm affair similar to the pole trucks lineman use working on power lines now days. The operator was encased in a cage at the end of the boom and it was perfect for getting up high into our huge old trees for pruning. It came with air and hydraulic powered clippers and buzz saws. It was absolutely an engineering marvel. When the boom-arm was fully extended and as high as it would go it became a little top heavy and was known to tip over . . . My Dad examined the problem carefully and determined two things: 1). The Girette was underpowered and 2). A bigger engine would not only solve 1). but should also stabilize and decrease the top heavy situation due to the increased weight of the bigger motor lowering its center of gravity. Dad consulted with his new Boeing engineer son in law Mark Hanses who concurred and told him it was a tremendous idea . . . Of course Mark might have just been sucking up to his new father in law too. Anyway, Dad removed the factory single cylinder engine and its air compressor which he also determined had too little capacity. He installed an air-cooled V4 Wisconsin engine, bigger air compressor, and larger wheels with tires filled with some kind of calcium solution. When topped off with tires-chains this new and improved Girette was a pruners dream and real hard to get stuck. With the increased air compressor capacity bigger faster loppers could be used which really sped up how many trees per hour could be pruned. Dad was pretty protective of his Girette and none of us got to operate it much except on level ground or just to relocate it from one field to another. I can still hear those air-loppers and the distinctive 'put-shooo' sound they made while making short order of a winter's pruning. The little circular air driven buzz saw sounded just like those Gatling guns on some of the newer jet fighters.

Brother Ray decided to test his D7 Cat operating skills one Sunday when the folks were gone and the Cat was at home in between jobs. It was hot and our little creek only had a few small pools where the water might be just two feet deep or so. He decided we needed a large swimming hole so together we tried to figure out how to start a D7 and dig one out. It had a separate but integrated starting engine, like all Cats of that era, and there was quite a routine to just get the little engine running. Next you had to flip some clutch levers and gear shifts to get it to begin turning over the big engine. Finally when you felt the time was right you introduced fuel to the big engine and it usually, except in very cold weather, sprung to life immediately. After getting all the levers and clutches back in order Ray drove down into the creek and started digging it out. I think he was about 13 at the time and his excavating skills were a bit undeveloped. He managed to build up a good sized dam and its newly made reservoir began to fill quite rapidly. I was only 7 or so but it seemed to me that while he was putting the finishing touches on the dam he had eliminated his only escape route as the banks were pretty steep in that spot. He was forced to come back through some pretty deep water that was already over the top of the tracks. The big engine fan started catching water and spraying him down while he sought an exit out of this trap. Luckily, just then his newly formed 'mud dam' breached and solved the whole problem for him. The flood related debris field downstream was quite a mess but we still ended up with a pretty good and fairly deep swimming hole after the water cleared up. My wife Deb, who spent her career as a wildlife biologist with the state, dealt with these same type of 'hydraulic violations,' usually involving big timber companies, on a daily basis and she just cringes when I tell this story. For some unknown reason when Dad came home and saw the mess he wasn't too upset and seemed somewhat impressed with Ray's Cat driving skills . . . . I think it had more to do with the fact that we had hosed all the mud off the Cat and cleaned it up though.

One last funny episode with the equipment. I was shredding brush one day, all hunkered down behind the shield with my helmet on trying to make myself as small a target as possible when I noticed the usual thrashing, crashing, and grinding noises from the shredder seemed to be getting more distant; this was something really different. I instinctively shoved the clutch in but waited to turn around and take a look as I didn't want to get hit in the face by any flying debris . . . When I did look it was a crazy scene . . . . The shredder was about 20 feet behind me and the four hydraulic hoses to it were stretched out like rubber bands . . . . the PTO driveshafts had disconnected but unbelievably were not crashing around at all . . . both of them were just winding down smoothly which really blew me away. I backed up carefully to release the tension on the hoses and then saw the problem; some brush had gotten under the hitch pin and pushed it out and I saw it lying on the ground about 15 feet back. Once I got everything hooked up and applied pressure to the hydraulics, nothing leaked, but the hoses appeared to be about a foot longer . . . What a freaky and lucky break. Another lesson learned about listening to your equipment and always making sure the important parts are either safety wired or cotter keyed. I'm glad I survived those farm years 'cause I think I established somewhat of an affinity for knowing when machinery was about to break. However, that affinity was not to be confused with me actually understanding how it all worked . . . . These experiences on the farm were of great benefit to me later in my flying career; I didn't always understand all the complex airplane systems but I usually could recognize when something wasn't quite right and dealt with it before it became an in-flight emergency.

Occasionally in the winter, when there wasn't too much to do on the farm, Dad would let brother Ray and I go to work with him on one of his land-leveling jobs usually down in the Zillah area. We were allowed to go jack rabbit hunting up in the Rattlesnake Hills North of Zillah with our .22s, while he clattered around some guys mint field on the D8 dragging that old 80 scraper back and forth. During the Korean War this area had been part of the Yakima Firing Center and there was still lots of ammo. debris scattered around, mainly empty .50 cal. and 20mm shell casings ejected from the machine guns and cannons of the aircraft of the day shooting at ground targets. We often found live rounds and I vividly remember watching brother Ray in the shop at home one day with one of those intact .50 cal. rounds we'd found in the vice; he got a center punch and was in the process of tapping the primer to see if he could get it to fire . . . . Man, I was only 9 or 10 but this seemed a little risky even to me . . . . Luckily the damn thing wouldn't detonate. We had a huge collection of those shell casings; we polished up some of them with the wire brush on the grinder and I still have a couple of the 20mm shells out in the garage. Anyway, on one of those rabbit hunting expeditions up in the hills, we came across the ass end of some kind of little rocket sticking out of the ground. It was made of cast iron and had four little fins on it. I think we later determined it was either a mortar round of some sort or a small aircraft practice rocket or bomb. Man, this was a helluva find for a couple morons like us so we proceeded to beat on it with a rock to try to dislodge it from the frozen ground. It finally came out so we cleaned it up to take home. We noticed it was kind of hollow but had some gunk and debris inside . . . Brother Ray determined that a well placed .22 round down the center of it might clean it up a bit more. He laid it out level on a flat rock then laid himself out prone with the end of his rifle barrel level with the mortar just a few feet away . . . . I was just standing there close by but turned my back just in case . . . I didn't even hear the .22 shot . . . . all I remember was suddenly being thrown forward and getting knocked down by the concussion blast when that thing blew up. I couldn't hear a thing for a few minutes and noticed that Ray was writhing around on the ground grabbing his ankle. The little bomb was gone and a piece of shrapnel from the thing was imbedded in Ray's leg . . . As I stood there deaf as a stone watching him flipping around on the ground I thought it was about the funniest thing I'd ever seen and began laughing my ass off . . . . I assume it was just some sort of adrenaline fed—survivor response or something but then again I've always had a strange sense of humor . . . . so I've been told . . . Anyway, after things quieted down a little, Ray seemed pretty much unscathed and got his pocketknife out to see if he could dig the shrapnel out of his leg since a bloody piece of it was protruding out a little. He dug it out and on examination we determined it to be a 12 gage shotgun shell brass casing that apparently was designed to detonate the explosives in whatever that was . . . We never told Dad about that episode until many years later and we often counted our blessing from that day!

My interest in aviation was peaked when I began reading the *True* Magazines Dad left in the bathroom. In the fifties there were great stories in *True* about famous test pilots like Chuck Yeager, Scott Crossfield, and Marion Carl flying those X-Planes and rockets down at Edwards. When I found out that some of those guys had also been World War II fighter pilot aces I really got interested. I begged my folks to buy me all the Revell plastic airplane models of the day and spent a lot of time in the basement gluing together P51's, F4U's, Bell X1's, etc. Not much has changed some 55 years later as I look around my office at newer versions of those same models except they are all metal units autographed by guys like Yeager, Bud Anderson, Bob Hoover, and Greg Boyington. However, the greatest day of my young life occurred in 1958 when my best buddy Gil Martin, got me my first airplane ride. His Dad Linn, had been a decorated P51 pilot in the war and somehow arranged for Gil's Cub Scout pack to go for a ride in a DC3 operated by (I think) West Coast Airlines out of Yakima. I was invited to go along as a guest and was thrilled beyond comprehension. I remember the day like it was yesterday. Just walking up that steep aisle to my seat was a thrill and when the pilot actually said hi and welcome aboard . . . . man I thought life just doesn't get any better than this! When he started cranking those big ole Wright Cyclones to life I was enthralled . . . . That crazy staccato uneven firing, as all the cylinders tried to come to life, smoking and belching, was unbelievable! You just gotta love round engines! Another huge thrill was when just after takeoff the pilot turned northwest and in a couple minutes we were flying right over our ranch . . . I couldn't believe it!

Well, the seed was planted and I was definitely hooked on flying but had to wait about 20 more years before I got serious about it. Lin was still in the Reserves in those years and I would see him all dressed up in his Air Force blues from time to time. After initially flying Spitfires in combat Lin was assigned a P51C to conduct bomb assessment photo flights. Returning to England from one of those missions he noticed a German staff car speeding down a French road so he came back around and strafed the car. He came back around again and while kicking rudder he fired into the ditches on either side of the road in case anybody had jumped out and was hiding there. He later found out that General Rommel, the Desert Fox, was injured during that strafing attack as he lay in the ditch. Many years later I tried to get Lin to write a book about his experiences during the war but he was reluctant and like so many members of the greatest generation, too quiet and humble to talk about himself. Lin survived the war in Europe intact but upon reassignment stateside was 'shot down' in Florida by one of his own countrymen. He was flying a Bell P63 King Cobra designated 'Pinball' during a training mission near Eglin AFB in Northern Florida. These planes were painted bright orange and fitted with heavy armor plating; gunners on B17s and B24s would fire plastic bullets at them for aerial gunnery practice . . . . Sounds kind of 'iffy' to me now and didn't turn out too well for Lin back in 1945. The oil radiator in the belly of the P63 was hit as he banked away from a bomber, even though the gunners were instructed not to shoot unless the P63 was straight and level. He was forced to bail out in a swampy area. Getting out of his stricken fighter didn't go well and he broke his leg on the horizontal stabilizer while jumping out of the Pinball machine . . . . Lin was one of the typical quiet heroes of the greatest generation and it was my privilege to have known him!

Another enjoyable aspect of my early years was going Steelhead fishing with Dad. We would get up around 0300 and drive to Goldendale for breakfast. From there it was a short 20 minutes to the upper Klickitat River where we would normally hit the water at sunrise. Summer Steelhead fishing is always a hit and miss proposition; experiencing the perfect combination of water color and water temperature was nearly impossible so we were often skunked after a day of flogging the water to death. But like most other outdoor activities it was the total package that mattered and if you landed a fish that was just gravy. Lunch was always the highlight for me and usually consisted of: a can of baby smoked oysters, a small can of pork and beans, some French bread and a fresh tomato. We always ate this gourmet repast while sitting in the back of the pickup on top of Dad's 'huge' homemade insulated fish box (always the optimist). While brother Ray was away in England with the USAF, Dad and I made many trips to the Klickitat. I'll always remember one memorable incident when I had hooked a nice steelhead on the far side of the river, fought him all the way across some rough water, and just as I had him near my feet he broke off and got away . . . Well, hooking a nice fish like that was quite rare on the Klickitat, but getting one that close only to lose him at my feet was more than I could handle . . . . I was shaking with rage and without thinking yelled out at the top of my voice "Son of a fu***ng bitch!!" My Dad was pretty close and heard me very clearly . . . . I don't think he expected a fourth year divinity student to be capable of such language let alone spew it out with such venom . . . He didn't say anything then or for most of the ride home but finally, somewhere near Toppenish, calmly responded "You know, I'm not going to tell your Mother about this because it would kill her and she wouldn't believe me anyway but if I ever hear that kind of language again I'll make you thin, prune, and hoe, every Goddamn tree on the place by yourself and you'll never get on a tractor again . . ." Well, the tractor part hit home hard as that was the only farm work I enjoyed, so I definitely cleaned up my act, at least around the folks, from then on . . . . However, I was amazed at the incongruity of it all since most of the invectives I heard from him when he got the speed sprayer stuck or mashed his fingers or knuckles while fixing something on the Cat, would have made a combat Marine blush . . . and those were just the English swear words . . . God knows what he was yelling in Italian!? I also remember seeing that same 'look' on his face that I saw up at Chinook while fishing the Klickitat . . . . When he had a steelhead on he handled the fish the same way he handled the Cat . . . so smooth, so careful, and so meticulous in every detail. When he ended up with the fish at his feet and it was done struggling, he would reach down effortlessly, slip a finger behind the gill flap, and hoist it up to show me a beautiful silvery steelhead accompanied by that 'look' that said; 'That's how it's done kid . . . . '

Each fall, when all the tree limbs were hanging low, heavily laden with fruit, we had to apply a spray called 'stop drop'. This spray attached itself to the stems of the apples, toughened them up and was supposed to prevent the stems from breaking when the fruit got heavy with sugar, as they ripened up in the Fall, especially when the wind kicked up. We couldn't get the speed sprayer through the low hanging limbs anymore without knocking a lot of apples down so Dad hired a crop dusting outfit out of Yakima to spray the whole place. In the early years all the crop dusters were WWII era Stearman trainers modified with large hoppers and spray bars behind their wings. The pilot would have a guy on the ground with a flag on a pole to indicate which row he needed to line up on for the next pass. I used to follow the flagger around and was in seventh heaven as the Stearmans came right over us only thirty feet up or so . . . Man did I look forward to those days! Unfortunately, in the late sixties, most of the crop duster outfits began switching over to helicopters. It was determined that the down-wash effect from the rotor-craft did a lot better job of getting the spray swirled around inside the tree branches for better coverage on the leaves, stems, and fruit. There was a tremendous upside to this change of equipment for me however. The pilot we used for a couple years wanted a rider with him to help identify all the little segmented areas of our ranch where we had scattered patches of pears interspersed with small grows of apples since the stop drop was only used on apple trees. Thus began my career as a Bell 47 co-pilot. The Bell 47 was the famous helicopter from the Korean War used to evacuate wounded troops off the battlefield to M.A.S.H. units as depicted in the TV series. We just called them whirlybirds at the time and it was my privilege to spend countless hours flying all over our ranch in one. The most exciting memory I have from those years was when the pilot would fly under a huge set of power lines, that bisected our upper ranch, pull up steeply and execute a beautiful hammerhead type course reversal, then swoop back down under the power lines for the next pass . . . What a thrilling ride and along with that DC3 flight was the highlight of my youth! Many years later, as my Dad sat in his pickup eating his lunch one day, while on a land leveling job near Zillah, he was watching a helicopter spray a nearby field. Apparently there were power lines at one end of the run. When the pilot was almost done and nearly on his last pass he got tangled up in the lines and crashed hard near some trees. There was no fire and Dad ran over to help. He saw a guy sitting at the base of a tree near the wreckage with no apparent injuries but when he got closer he saw that he had been killed. Just another one of those crazy accidents similar to the ones I investigated so many times in my career, where the thin line between surviving a crash or not was hard to define. I remember driving up on wrecks that we used to describe as 'rip-snorters' where the car had basically disintegrated and there was no chance anyone could have survived it. Often there would be some guy milling around the scene who I assumed was a witness. When I went up to him, to get a statement, I would discover this person to be the driver of the wrecked car. He had suffered no apparent injuries, and was often only 'dead' drunk. Conversely, I drove up on just as many minor accidents, where the damage was hardly noticeable and the car looked drivable, only to discover a deceased driver behind the wheel with no apparent injuries. Many of those folks were driving older cars that didn't have collapsible steering wheels; if they hit a power pole or something solid, the bottom of the steering wheel would often slip under their rib cage on impact and cause severe internal bleeding or a ruptured spleen. I heard the following statement more than once from witnesses at accident scenes . . . ."But I was just talking to him a minute ago and he seemed OK . . . ." Unfortunately, the pilot of the helicopter in the Zillah crash was the same gentleman I used to fly with on our ranch . . . .

Bell 47 spraying "stop drop" on the apples right before picking circa 1957 . . . This is the aircraft I spent many hours in later.

As the sixties rolled around, my sister got married to Mark Hanses, a Boeing Engineer, who had the cool Ventura, and my brother Ray joined the Air Force and was soon stationed in England. I transferred to St. Paul's Cathedral School in Yakima starting in the seventh grade which began my ten year association with the Catholic school system. The Dominican nuns who taught at St Pauls were very dedicated but strict disciplinarians. The escapades I used to get away with at the Tieton and Cowiche public schools just were not tolerated here and I was soon on the receiving end of many hacks and other disciplinary actions from the nuns. Occasionally they called in the big guns and that was when I met Father Wood (I know, I know, not the most appropriate name considering events involving priests and altar boys that have recently come to light). He was a kindly looking man but possessed a vicious looking custom made hack paddle with holes drilled in it, a long curved handle, with a leather strap attached. Hacks were delivered at the front of the class for all to see and crying was just not an option. Thankfully, I was quite used to getting wailed on at home and adept at not giving the hacker the satisfaction of crying. When we had committed an infraction on the farm, my brother and I would have to march out into the orchard and cut our own water sprout switches out of the crotch of an apple tree, peel the leaves off, and hand it to the old man for our punishment. When we bent over to get our lashes, he would make sure our jeans were nice and tight to maximize the effect. So, I took the hacks from Father Wood upon my calloused ass with dignity and self control. Soon, the frequency of the hack sessions diminished as I slowly adjusted to the system and settled down. I guess I had impressed Father Wood somewhat because over the next few years he began to tell me I might have what it takes to become a priest. So being an impressionable 13 year old I joined the "seminarian club" with about ten other guys where we learned what having a 'vocation' was all about. It sounded pretty good as I had by now realized that being a farmer was a helluva lot of round the clock work, all year long, where the vagaries of the weather dictated everything. So in September of 1963 I was sent off to St. Peter the Apostle Seminary in Cowiche, WA exactly 2 miles from our farm, to begin my priestly training.

CHAPTER 3

VOCATION INTERRUPTUS

Most of the other seminarians came from cities hundreds of miles from Cowiche. I was pretty lucky living so close to home and used to see my Mom and Dad driving by from time to time. We still only went home on the major holidays but I didn't get as homesick as some of the others. My Mom used to do my laundry for me twice a month and left it in a black mailer box outside the chapel vestibule. Although I wasn't allowed to talk to her she always left a letter in the mailer with some fresh chocolate chip cookies (flavored with rum) which I usually shared with the guys.

The strict seminarian life wasn't much different than dealing with the nuns at St Pauls except the seminary staff didn't beat us up anymore. After two years of having the Dominican nuns wail on my fingers with their triangular rulers as I grasped the front edge of my desk, my knuckles had finally started to heal a little. Looking back, the most terrible crime I ever committed at St Pauls was putting a note in an upside down eraser one day and sliding it down the chalk tray in the back of the classroom to my girlfriend Kathy Draper at the other end. She zipped her response back to me a few minutes later when the nun had her back turned. Unfortunately, the one time we were apprehended committing this heinous violation the note contained some unflattering comments about the nun who caught us. Even though Kathy had penned the derogatory comments I was apparently profiled and got blamed for the whole affair due to my previous history of violations. However, this time the punishment went a little overboard. The chalk tray incident had occurred during apple picking season and this was the busiest time of the year for us on the ranch. When I got home from school I had to work until dark hauling out filled fruit bins with one of the tractors so Dad could load them on the truck with the Beast. I hadn't had time to get a haircut for a couple months so a couple days after the eraser note incident the nuns accused me of having a shaggy and unkempt appearance, sat me down in front of the class and proceeded to give me the worst haircut I've ever had. I wasn't particularly embarrassed by this episode, after having endured their wrath so many other times, and kind of enjoyed the notoriety. But when I got home and my Mom saw how they had butchered me she went ballistic. The next morning, although busy as hell picking apples, she was in Father Wood's office unloading on him. He was unaware of the incident and a few minutes later he called me out of class. When he saw the haircut his jaw dropped and I'll never forget his quiet response under his breath: 'Son of a bitch!! . . . . ' I was sent back into the class and he called out the offending nun, and her helper from another classroom. He then proceeded to rip them each a new 'one' right out in the hallway where we could hear everything for about five minutes. As we all sat snickering, I for one knew this was probably not going to end well for me. When he got done chewing them out he called me out again and told me to get in his car. He took me to his barber in Yakima who was instructed to fix the mess on my head. He did but I ended up with a Marine boot camp buzz cut since that was the only way he could fix all the gouges and bare spots the nuns left. Crazy thing about it all was my hair was no more than an inch long anywhere before the nuns went nuts on me but I guess they had other issues. Father Wood then took me to Jeds, a sporting goods store in Yakima, and got me a NY Yankees baseball cap. He said I could wear the hat in class until my hair grew out. Although I very much appreciated this gesture, I hated the Yankees as they had just beaten the San Francisco Giants and my hero Willy Mays in the World Series that fall. I wore the hat for a couple days anyway. Surprisingly, the nuns didn't retaliate and the rest of the school year was fairly uneventful, except for one unrelated incident . . . .

Just prior to graduating from the eighth grade and moving on to St Peters I was involved in a semi-unprofessional attempt at "arresting" the behavior of a reckless driver one afternoon. This so called 'driver' operated our little school bus van that picked up all the Catholic kids from the remote areas around Tieton and Cowiche and took them to either St Pauls Cathedral School or Central Catholic High School in Yakima. The driver at that time was a local greaser whose girlfriend was one of the high school students who always sat up front with him as he ran his route. While driving that bus full of kids this dipshit would be kissing and groping her and weaving all over the road. A few years later I learned that this kind of activity (embracing while driving) was *prima facie* evidence of reckless driving! At the time however, I just thought the guy was a total moron and could have killed us all on several different occasions. So, one afternoon after school, when I was needed at home for picking apples, we all had to just sit in that bus at Central Catholic and watch the dipshit make out with his fifteen year old girlfriend on a bench near the bus stop . . . . Even at that age this sort of irresponsible behavior just galled the living shit out of me! . . . . After several minutes of watching those two enjoy a heavy petting session, I just lost it, jumped in the driver's seat, and stole the bus to teach that stupid mother a lesson! I drove it about a half mile and then circled round the gymnasium and football field parking lot for a few minutes while being cheered on by all the other students in the bus . . . . Eventually I drove back to the bus stop only to find that rat bastard standing there with Father McDermitt, the principal of Central Catholic. McDermitt read me the riot act and said he was going to call the police . . . . I was pretty hyped up by then and just blurted out what that shithead had been doing with his skanky girlfriend while driving the bus and was able to recount dates, times, and places with amazing accuracy . . . Father McDermitt seemed somewhat stunned, told me to go sit in the bus, and went over to have a little heart to heart with the driver. The greaser finally came back to the bus and we all got to enjoy an uneventful ride home without any hanky panky and wild swerving for a change. I was always the last student on the route but this time he drove me all the way up our long driveway and dropped me off at the front door for a change. He gave me one helluva shit stare (the first of many more to come) as he drove away. The cops never came to get me and I never heard another thing about the incident. A couple weeks later however, we had a brand new driver who just so happened **to not be** a total douche bag!

This was only the second year of existence for St Peters Seminary so there was only the sophomore class ahead of us. Unlike the media perception of priests, altar boys and seminary types in the Catholic Church now-a-days, all of the guys I knew then were heterosexual and actually believed they had a real **vocation** to the priesthood. We all felt it was a noble calling and that a life of abstinence, public service, and sacrifice would be very rewarding. Priests were highly respected in those years and I felt becoming one was a pretty lofty goal for a thirteen year old kid. In my eight years in the seminary I never saw, heard about, or even remotely suspected any of the priests or seminarians I knew to be pedophiles or sexually abusing anyone. Of course years later, to my horror, I discovered that several of the priests and fellow seminarians that I had known then were indeed pedophiles and were later found guilty of terrible acts with young boys. I never saw it when I was among these guys and I'm still amazed at the extent of the cover-up perpetrated by the Vatican, various bishops, and cardinals on their behalf. It's my opinion that when the allegations of abuse and/or a cover-up arose, the current pope (there were at least six popes who knew about the pedophile priests) should have **immediately** demanded that every single one of them, the priests as well as the bishops and cardinals, be investigated by the local police. If the allegations were proven then each and every one of those bastards should have been publicly excommunicated and criminally prosecuted . . . . Had the church taken the high road then it would be in such a better place than it is now!! Sadly, the Vatican treated those horrendous events as an internal administrative matter, labeled the accusers psychopathic liars, then quietly transferred those (now empowered) pedophile monsters around the country where they could terrorize more children in a new location! As a result of the cover-up the Vatican hierarchy demonstrated themselves to be no better than their Italian Mafia cousins . . . . worse really . . . At least the Mafia goons only whacked other bad guys . . . . But those Vatican bastards were responsible for destroying the lives of **thousands of innocent children** and their families as well!! It's hard for me to say but I am truly ashamed to have ever been associated with the Catholic Church . . . . The ultimate "bitch slap" for me is the current movement within the church to canonize (make a saint) out of Pope John Paul II. Along with his henchman Benedict, they knew the most about the pedophile priest problem early on. Unbelievably, they **still** chose to protect all those pedophiles, as well as all those dirty cardinals and bishops involved in the cover-up. The Holy Pontiff John Paul allowed all those poor falsely accused kids to suffer in agony and disgrace for years!! OhYeah, that's really **"saintly"** behavior!! If they succeed in canonizing him, to me he will just be known as the "Patron Saint" of pedophiles!

In spite of everything, I feel a tremendous amount of sympathy for the vast majority of innocent, dedicated, hardworking priests and lay people around the world whose past, present, and future activities involving young boys will probably always be under suspicion and scrutiny . . . . My heart goes out to them and especially to all the victims of clerical abuse. I have been impressed with brand new Pope Francis who seems to be showing some guts and appears to be trying to repair some of the damage done by his predecessors . . . . He's setting a fine example with his austere lifestyle but has a real tough row to hoe trying to convince all the remaining ultra conservative deadwood cardinals and bishops that "Change is Good!"

The fall of 1963 was really the last perceived innocent period of time that most of my generation lived through where the old values, simple pleasures, and widespread feelings of contentment and patriotism, were still common and unquestioned. As I sat in religion class the morning of Nov. 22, 1963, Father Chris Breen burst into the classroom and announced that President Kennedy had just been shot in Dallas. We were really laid low by his assassination since he was our first Catholic president and really a hero and role model for all of us young Catholic guys. Even though we have since learned that JFK wasn't as 'clean cut' as we were all led to believe back then, it still hurts today as I remember the overwhelming sadness we felt that morning.

Life in the seminary began at 0600 with the loud clanging of a hand rung bell, followed by a shower and shave (some of us) and into the chapel for morning prayers and Mass at 0630, breakfast at 0700, with the first class at 0800. Classes consisted of the usual high school curriculum except we all had to take Latin for four years. We started out in our freshman year translating Caesar's Gallic Wars, and then graduated to Cicero, Pliny, Virgil, et al. in subsequent school years. Although I can still conjugate a few Latin verbs the only lasting result that four years of Latin gave me is the ability to occasionally come up with the correct question on *Jeopardy* when the answer has something to do with word origins. For physics and chemistry lab we were bussed to Central Catholic High School in Yakima on Saturdays and used their equipment for our experiments. We were also bussed to all of the Marquette High School home football games in Yakima so we had some semblance of a normal life during our teenage years, minus the dating part . . . .

We shared the chapel for Sunday Mass at the Seminary with the local parishioners. At the 0900 Mass we would sing all the liturgical hymns of the day usually in Latin. My singing voice was so bad that our choir director told me to just move my lips and not make any sounds that would ruin everything. I was labeled a 'crow' and thankfully only had to be in the choir on Sundays. The parishioners ate all this up and thought it was marvelous to have a trained choral group performing for them every Sunday. However, the feelings were not mutual as most of us were only concerned with what the parishioner's young nubile teenage daughters were wearing as we strained to get a whiff of their perfume during Mass. We competed vigorously to be the altar boys for Sunday Mass since this meant we'd get to follow the priest around during communion with the little plate to catch any crumbs from the communion wafers. I realize this will come as a tremendous shock to those devout Catholics out there but the highlight of our week was viewing the aforementioned nubile teenagers up close and personal with their tongues stuck out waiting for communion while serving Mass . . . . The personal highlight of my four years in the seminary occurred one Sunday while I was serving as one of the altar boys. A communion host was fumbled by the priest, missed one of the young nubile teenage girls tongue, bounced off the catch plate I was holding under her chin, and landed down the front of her dress in her developing cleavage. I was horrified by this eventuality and had no idea what the proper protocol would be . . . . I assumed only a priest could touch the body of Jesus which was now located in a precarious physical and ethical position . . . . quite a dilemma. The young nubile princess solved it herself by deftly extricating the wafer from her cleavage and putting it in her mouth thus ending the drama. Although very exhilarating for me I assumed she had just committed a grievous mortal sin of some sort for illegally touching the body of Jesus . . . . I prayed for her soul, and other things.

Tenure as an altar boy both at the seminary and earlier at St. Pauls revealed some interesting facts about the various priests we served Mass for. They all had their individual chalices which they used during Mass to offer up the blood of Christ (red wine). Most of the priests had fairly small, common looking, low volume chalices; however, one guy had a chalice that resembled a small gilded bucket adorned with precious stones of some sort. I believe it was during the 'offertory' part of the Mass when we as altar boys offered the glass cruets of wine and water to the priest to mix in his chalice. Again, most priests utilized small little cruets holding just a couple tablespoons of wine and would only put a few drops into their chalice. However, this particular priest must have gotten his cruets at a 'Carafes Are Us' store because they were huge and probably held a whole fifth of wine. When he poured the wine into his chalice it was to the brim . . . At the time we just assumed that since the wine was transformed into the blood of Jesus that the alcohol was somehow divinely deactivated. We felt this particular guy must have been 'holier' than the other priests due to his seniority and was entitled to a much larger dose of Christ's blood. Obviously a life teeming with great spiritual deeds and self-sacrifice had elevated him to this privileged level. We did occasionally have this priest for a first period class an hour later and often noticed that his speech was slightly slurred and he seemed a bit clumsy sometimes . . . We assumed he was just sleepy . . . . How innocent we all were . . . .

Most of our instructors had been parish priests from the Yakima area but now resided at the seminary which was just a renovated old stone public school house built around 1912. Its distinguishing feature was a large enclosed metal fire-escape that ran steeply down the North side of the building from the third story to the ground. From our daily recreational usage of the fire escape the inside bottom became very polished and slick. Occasionally we would have an Open House at the seminary where the many benefactors from the Yakima Diocese could view the results of their donations. Since most of us were 13 or 14 we thought it was hilarious to run a rope down the fire escape to within 5 ft from the bottom and tie it to a five gallon bucket of water at the top of the escape. When some unsuspecting child would look up the escape and see that rope they assumed it was an aid to climb up. To our immense satisfaction, someone always got wet and we laughed our asses off when we saw some soaked kid come boiling out of there.

Back to the schedule: lunch at noon, classes again until 1530 followed by building maintenance and house cleaning then intramural sports until 1700. We played all the seasonal sports and usually very aggressively as many of us had a lot of excess energy/hostility to vent. During my four years at St Peters I recall a number of guys being taken to the hospital after some really hard hits during our flag football games. With no pads and a lack of training we still went at it very hard and worked off all our youthful energy and other 'repressed issues' during sports. Ruptured kidneys, concussions, broken arms and legs, were just a few of the injuries I recall. We had a couple tremendous athletes during those years who could have easily started for any AAA local high school team. Our basketball games were a farce; we all had to rotate as referees and many games would end up in the third quarter with only one person left on each team as the others had all fouled out. There were some real iffy calls by the 'in-house' refs. who might have a slight grudge or two to settle with a couple of the players. Consequently, I held the school record with 68 points for quite some time when during a game everyone fouled out except me (6'2") and my opponent (5'3"). Baseball season was always highly anticipated as we got to occasionally play against local high school teams, usually their junior varsity, and some semi-pro teams from the American Legion league who used us to get tuned up for the summer season. We practiced like hell for those games as we did not want to be perceived as a bunch of inept 'holy joe weenies'. Some of the games turned rather violent when we would 'accidentally' crash into opposing players long after it was even a close play. A lot of this aggression was driven by the antics of some of the local Highland High School kids. When we were out playing ball in the afternoon, these rednecks would drive by slowly in their beat up pickups and yell out various epitaphs such as: 'F***ing fairies' . . . ." Or usually just 'Hoooommmooossss' . . . . I recognized several of them from grade school and couldn't believe that my former buddies were doing this. On one occasion, when a pickup drove by slowly yelling "queers", myself and Steve LaFramboise ran after them with baseball bats while screaming "Why don't you stop you f***ing cowards . . . ." They didn't stop and I'm quite glad they didn't as I'm sure I would have most certainly been beaten half to death with my own bat.

Just a quick side-light about my buddy Steve LaFramboise . . . . He was my constant ping pong opponent in those years and I think after three years of battling we were about even in the win/loss stats. His hero was Micky Mantle whereas mine was Willy Mays but my memory of Steve will always be intertwined with Carl Sandburg's poem *"Chicago"*. We had a sadistic English teacher back then who made each class member memorize the whole damn thing and wouldn't pass us until we had recited it perfectly in front of the whole class. Anyway, there is a passage in *Chicago* that went: ". . . . The painted women were luring the farm boys". When most of us recited it we changed that one line to: "The painted women were luring LaFramboise" . . . Even our sadistic prof. enjoyed that one and always laughed heartily when we made that small change . . .

During the winter months we had access to a pond about a quarter mile away for ice skating. Sunday after Mass and lunch was the only time all week we had a whole afternoon off so the pond was very popular then. There is no doubt in my mind that the winters were a lot colder in those years as that pond stayed frozen from November until March. One Christmas vacation when brother Ray was home from college we decided to go play hockey there. Not having hockey sticks wasn't a problem. We went out into the orchard and cut a couple likely looking limbs down with the appropriate bend in one end to slap a puck with. We finished them off in Dad's shop until they looked like issued equipment in the NHL. We found an old puck sized Timken roller bearing and were soon off to the pond. Neither of us had ever played hockey before but we had a lot of ice skating experience between us. Mom & Dad used to take us out onto the big irrigation canals where there was always good skating after the water had been turned off. So we started whacking the puck-bearing around using rocks to outline the goals. Even though he had six years on me, I was holding my own since I had been ice skating a lot lately and my legs were in good shape. At some point I took a big ass round house swing at the Timken, missed it, but my follow through caught Ray right in the eye with the end of my stick. He went down like a sack of spuds but I kept my distance since his behavior often became somewhat erratic following similar past incidents. Eventually, after the appropriate profanity laced tirade, and graphic descriptions of the future bodily harm he was going to inflict on me, we drove home. When Mom saw that huge yellow, red, and orange black eye swollen up and shut tight, she was freaked out a bit but fairly used to these 'minor' farm type injuries. Problem was, Ray had an ROTC ball to attend the next night in Seattle and thought the 'eye' might detract from how sharp he looked in his uniform. I however, had no feelings of guilt or remorse, and felt it was a simple case of payback for an incident that occurred several years before. We had been clearing rocks off the lawn from a new sewer line ditch when I strayed behind Ray as he was throwing them out between his legs. One sharp edged one got me in the nose and did a neat job of peeling one side back so you could look inside and examine my nasal passages. Of course there was a lot of blood; Ray sensed big trouble and took off up into the rocks to hide as Mom and Dad took me to the hospital to get stitched up. I think he might have been up there all night. He still talks like he's traumatized by this episode almost 60 years later and still blames me for getting into his throwing zone . . . I think I was 4.

A seminary bathroom prank of that era was to cover the toilet bowl with Saran wrap, clear cellophane, put the lid down, and wait for an unsuspecting user to suffer the consequences. It actually worked better when the urinals were occupied and the toilet was being utilized from the standing position as the spray effect was much more pronounced. Another more disgusting game was what we called the 'turd races'. Several of us would gather around the pulled back septic tank lid for the whole school where the main sewer line entered it, and await the exciting competition. When all participants signaled they were ready, the designated controller would signal for the simultaneous double flush of the two contestants competing after they had just taken dumps in toilets in separate areas of the building. They would have marked their 'entries' with identifying colored paper or similar material of some sort prior to flushing. The scoring was a two part affair: first entry to arrive at the tank was the session winner. However, a larger prize was awarded to that lucky seminarian who, after a month of fierce competition, had the best elapsed time for his deposit to travel from toilet to tank. I don't believe our diocesan benefactors ever found out about this activity . . . .

So, dinner was at 1800 which was a silent meal. We always had a designated student reading a popular novel out loud for us during dinner. The only ones I remember were Von Ryan's Express and The Heart is a Lonely Hunter. After dinner, when those assigned to kitchen duty were done, and we had burned all the garbage, it was rosary time and evening prayers in the chapel. We alternated saying the rosary in Spanish, Latin, and English. With all the prayer time, Mass, and rosaries, we all suffered from nicely developed calluses on our knees from the hundreds of hours spent kneeling on the spartan wooden kneelers in the chapel that had no padding. Study hall followed and then we hit the rack around 2130 with lights out at 2200.

Without a doubt, the most interesting and "uplifting" sport during my 8 years as a seminarian was "flipping". For the intended victim, flipping was usually preceded by short sheeting. This procedure involved tearing a guy's bed apart and folding the sheets in such a way so when he got into bed he could only get about half way in, the rest of the way blocked by tightly folded sheets which prevented him from getting his feet to the bottom. Sounds childish but the victim would then have to remake his bed in the dark while the rest of us silently chuckled since we were still under the no talking ban. Now when the intended victim's crimes were so severe that a flipping was ordered, things got very serious. A severe enough crime that would warrant a flipping was: taking the last pork chop during our silent dinner, ratting a classmate off to the priests for some minor offense such as smoking at the burn barrel, not showering for several days, or silently farting in chapel during rosary or Mass, then blaming someone else. A flip usually involved one flipper but sometimes called for two if longer hang time was desired for the flipee or if that person had some over-eating issues. Usually around 0200, the two flippers would silently approach the victim's bed, which was a single mattress on a wooden frame. Each guy would grab hold of a mattress handle, and on the silent count of three would lift and shove with all their might, with the intention being to send the occupant airborne onto the next occupied bed about six feet away. Sometimes, there would be a slight technique error resulting in the flipee striking the side of the wooden bed frame next to him with a crashing head bonking thud. With all the noise and confusion, the flippers were long gone before anyone realized what had happened or recognized the perpetrators. Flipping was a semi-monthly occurrence that served as a constant reminder and deterrence to the brown-nosers, jerks, stinky people, and backstabbers that their behavior would not be tolerated.

We occasionally had to resort to the ultimate in house punishment when faced with an incorrigible prick who was unfazed by a flipping; we called it flushing. This involved grabbing the offender, and transporting him to the toilets. After properly and legally advising the offender why this was happening to him, we'd dangle him by his feet and dunk his head into the bowl. We always finished the dunking with a nice clean flush to tidy the offender up a bit prior to release. Most victims of the combined flipping/flushing protocol never offended again and order was soon returned to our little community. One might perceive these rituals as slightly brutal and cruel but we did not consider it hazing nor did we pick on the weak sisters among us . . . Those who suffered through those ordeals truly deserved it, had already been verbally warned and had chosen to not heed said warning. They just needed to be shown the true path to virtuosity. The faculty was usually unaware of their deeds so an in-house dose of "roadside justice" really was the only meaningful solution. More importantly, since knowledge of these episodes was kept among ourselves, and if the victim mended his ways, it was a win-win situation with no one having to face any official disciplinary action. A Marine pilot friend of mine at the WSP told me that at his boot camp training during Vietnam, they called these types of sessions "blanket parties". However, their methods were a tad more dramatic and usually involved wrapping up a dozen or so bars of soap in a blanket, grabbing the usually stinky & unshowered victim, and then beating the bejeezus out of him. Then the offender was escorted to the showers and cleaned up with an extremely rough brush coated with Ajax or something similar . . . . Hey, I can't argue with their methods . . . there was a war on for Crissakes.

Activities in this same vein seemed to be a recurring theme for me in later years as a road trooper . . . I occasionally ran across loud mouthed, venom spewing, smart ass pukes who began our violator contact with a pleasant "What did you stop me for pig?" Now, a casual observer might assume that this sort of initial rhetoric from a violator would immediately inflame the situation . . . . It did initially for me but over the years I eventually learned to remain calm, take a step back, and quietly ignore the asshole's protestations while systematically evaluating and assessing every single additional violation I could possibly cite this moron for such as: not signing his registration, no litter bag, cracked windshield, loose steering, bald tires, cracked taillight lens, etc., etc. Now if that same puke was a redneck bigot still fighting the Civil War and displaying a Confederate battle flag sticker on his rear window or had a pair of those huge plastic testicles dangling from his hitch, I somehow **always** found sufficient cause to call for a tow truck and impound his piece of shit pickup . . . . If the tow truck's arrival caused any further cursing, spitting, or threatening language then charges of resisting arrest and provoking an assault were always on the table followed by a lovely booking ceremony at the county jail . . . . There are many facets to roadside justice and just as many different ways to productively validate the old axiom of "what goes around comes around."

Anyway, I was too big to get hoisted for a flushing but did suffer through several attempted revenge flippings. The incompetent flippers only managed to slide me onto the floor off my mattress since I weighed about 200 lbs. in those years. On one occasion after I thought someone had recognized me during a flip I came up with a foolproof plan to avoid possible disciplinary action were the flippee to rat me out. Right before Mass each morning we were privileged to avail ourselves of the sacred sacrament of confession . . . So I went in to the confessional where Father Auve sat half asleep and confessed to the horrible mortal sin of flipping. I assumed my sacred confession would somehow grant me immunity from prosecution as he would not be able to break the seal of confession if the flipee reported me to him and there was an investigation. I determined he would probably feel somehow conflicted and obligated to not reveal any prior knowledge of my sins after the ensuing investigation and perhaps let me slide. After Mass he called me into his office and explained to me that my tactics, although fairly sound and not totally without some canon law merit, were probably unethical and not in keeping with the high moral standards expected of future priests . . . However, I did slide on this one.

Summer vacation during those years was punctuated by more responsibilities on the ranch as Dad was increasingly busy with Cat work all over the Yakima Valley, and Ray was still in England finishing his Air Force gig. I began to do a lot of the spraying which was a never ending task from April through October. In the spring it was oil and Seven, to kill the codling moth that wintered over just under the bark of the trees with other similar pests. Next, came a dose of sulfur on everything which stunk up the whole region for a few weeks. This was followed by a course of blossom thinner, then the initial spray of Parathion, Guthion, Moricide, Ethion, TEP, Moristan, Diaznone, or one of oh so many other similar sprays of that era to kill the aphids, mites, worms, maggots, and other bugs destroying our apple crop.

These sprayings were repeated one after the other all summer long. Additionally, the pears had to be sprayed separately with streptomycin and some other concoction with soap in it to kill the blight and control the pear psylla. Pear psylla was a horrible sticky honey like infestation that would get all over you when thinning or picking pears and was a terrible scourge. Problem was the bugs just adapted to each new spray variety and the resilient survivors of each spraying passed on their now resistant DNA to the next batch of insects and so on and so on. The spray companies kept coming out with new, improved, and horrendously expensive sprays each season, guaranteeing immediate results but it was always the same outcome . . . the insects adapted to it, the strongest mutations evolved and prospered, and the farmers got screwed. One of the major reasons Dad had to start his land leveling business had been the escalating cost of the various insecticides eating up all the profits each year. If anyone were ever to doubt Darwin's survival of the fittest theory, talk to an apple grower!

The Bean speed sprayer Dad bought back in 1947 was the marvel of its day for apple growers and he got one of the first ones in the Yakima Valley. Before the advent of the speed sprayer a large crew had to drag pressurized and very heavy hoses all around the orchard while spraying the trees with a hand held nozzle under terrific pressure. Everything was hooked up to a stationary pump and nurse tank on skids where someone was continually mixing the water and spray. Horses and later iron wheeled tractors were used to drag the pump and nurse tank to the next water valve which were spread out equidistant around the place. In the twenties and thirties the sprays of choice were arsenic and lead. When DDT became available in the early forties in conjunction with self-contained engine driven speed sprayers, and smaller more manageable orchard friendly tractors, pest control was revolutionized. However, we are all still suffering the consequences and long term effects of dumping thousands of tons of lead, arsenic, DDT, Paraquat, TEP, Parathion, 2-4-D, and many other poisons into the soils of the Yakima Valley. Much less harmful sprays are now being used but it's unknown what future issues we might all be facing. I know I would certainly think twice about planting a garden in an old orchard anywhere in the country!!

When the folks bought the Bean it was a huge gamble for the family and they really couldn't afford it. All the grand folks told them they were crazy to waste their money but I think Dad just had a gut feeling about it. It didn't take long for nearly all the other farmers in the area to begin hiring him to spray their orchards once they saw how fast and efficient it was. Mom and Dad soon paid the sprayer off and actually made more money from it than the apple crop for a few years. When I began spraying with the Bean, Dad (of course) by then had attached hydraulic lines to the various pumps and valves and sprayer jets so he could control the whole operation from the comfort of the tractor seat. Before that he had to use a complicated harness array of ropes and pulleys to turn things off and on and they were forever getting caught in tree limbs or run over by the tractor. The sprayer had its own engine, a six cylinder flat head Hercules that ran the massive pumps and circular spray bars that followed the round contours of the 600 gallon stainless steel tank. Dad also installed a locking engine throttle control for that big ole Hercules and mounted it on the tractor as well. At the back of the sprayer was a huge fan with a massive screen cover. That fan was the secret to the whole system. Its tornado like wind caught the spray coming out of the circular jet array just in front of it and swirled it beautifully up into the apple trees applying a never before seen consistent and even application of spray to all sides of the leaves and small fruit. The farmers all loved it and within a few years nearly every orchardist in the Yakima Valley had a new Bean.

The Bean originally came equipped with a long and low exhaust pipe down one side. With his engineering mind ever churning and sharp eye for innovation, Dad believed that re-installing a real short exhaust pipe with a slightly rearward dump angle, directly behind the engine and just in front of the spray nozzle array, might actually enhance the swirling spray pattern due to the vertical velocity of the exhaust gases. One has to remember that the old variety trees we had on the ranch in those days were 'old growth' monsters and in no way resemble the short, trim, manicured hedge-row apple orchards of today. You needed as much 'lifting' action as possible to get the spray into the upper branches of those trees. After seeing the sprayer in action both before and after the modification I think it truly worked better with the 'exhaust assist'. However, I still feel the best result of the exhaust mod. was the beautiful sound of that Hercules at full song with that short stack . . . it was horrendous! When the water ran out in the tank and the huge pump released its drag on the Hercules the tremendous rpm increase of the engine could be heard all over the upper valley . . . . there was never any doubt in my mind when that tank was empty! We usually sprayed in the early morning or late evening when the wind wasn't too much of a factor. If you tried spraying with too much of a cross-wind there would always be one side of the trees that didn't get coated very well. Sometimes we'd spray all day long when the wind was calm but it wasn't advised since we would lose so much to evaporation in the heat of the day. Spraying with a significant wind was OK as long as you only sprayed in one direction then made a dry run back so you were always spraying with the wind in your face. If you tried it with a tailwind you would get drenched. Even though we usually wore rubber spray suits you would inevitably get soaked anyway. Considering that all the bags of spray we emptied into the tank at filling time had big old red skull and cross bone labels all over them, getting soaked with this stuff wasn't a real good idea. However, when the sprayer operator is 15 or 16 and has so many other more interesting things he could be doing besides dragging a bellowing speed sprayer around the place, especially when the wind dictated a dry run, shortcuts were taken. The first thing to go was the rubber suit which really made me sweat like crazy. Secondly, I just didn't see the need for a wind driven dry run if I just went a little faster with the tractor to keep the blowing spray behind me. Well this worked sometimes but more often than not when I got back to the water-box to fill up I was usually drenched in everything from Parathion to Moricide. The water box was a large double concrete weir affair where the irrigation district could measure your water usage. We'd drop the filler hose into the water, reverse the pump direction on speed sprayer, and start filling the six hundred gallon tank. Meanwhile, I would jump into the water box, if I had been soaked with spray, to wash it all off while trying to avoid getting caught in the suction of that hose. This usually worked fine and I never had any ill effects for several years. The spray that finally got me was Guthion. I had been spraying on a hot day and did my usual water box clean up procedure, after getting soaked several times on a couple of runs, then went home for a late dinner. Afterwards I started to really feel sick and suffered just about every symptom you can imagine. I was afraid to tell the folks about my spraying tactics so I suffered alone all night long alternately sweating, vomiting, experiencing excruciating headaches, hallucinations, freezing, shaking, temporary blindness, you name it, I experienced it that night. I was still a wreck in the morning and just told Mom I thought I had food poisoning or something. She was skeptical and thought I was faking it, but I did get a day off from work. I was screwed up for a week but finally started feeling better. It goes without saying that the rubber suit became a fixture with me from that day forward. Dry runs were my new best friend when the wind wasn't right, and I began using Dad's respirator too. It's funny how so many tractor jobs on the farm made learning and understanding how to fly much easier later on; so many of the mechanical principles involved were the same. Whether it was dealing with crosswinds and tailwinds while spraying, keeping precise headings, speeds, and rpm settings while cultivating and spraying, steering tractors with your feet (differential braking) or utilizing the split brake pedals, dealing with the adverse effects of torque on so many machines, and through osmosis I was getting a pretty solid understanding of general mechanics and system integration. The flying time I got in that Bell 47 asking lots of crazy questions, also helped tremendously. I feel very lucky to have survived my life on the farm and still consider those years as having been much more hazardous to my health than my time as a road trooper or the 14,000+ hours spent as a full time pilot flying in some of the worst weather in the U.S. However, I still get the shivers when I hear someone mention Guthion.

Brother Ray finally came home in 1966 with his beautiful new English bride Chris. I had my jeep by then and finally had a full time fishing and hunting partner again, at least in the summer. Ray immediately got a job with Bell Telephone and Chris with Global Travel in Yakima. They both continued in those professions for nearly 45 years each. While I was in the sem, for those 8 years, Chris wrote to me regularly and kept me advised of what was happening out in the real world.

Seminary life remained relatively unchanged over the years except the size of my class shrunk from 25+ in 1963 to just the six of us that graduated in 1967. The bishop of the Yakima Diocese somehow arranged for our little group to spend our freshman year of college in Waukesha, Wisconsin at Mt. St. Paul College. It was affiliated with the Salvatorian order of the Society of the Divine Savior (whatever that all signified) and life there was quite a bit more laid back than St Peters. Getting there did afford me my first ride in a jet, a gorgeous Boeing 707. Maneuvering around the terminal and concourses at O'Hare was quite an eye opener for a farm-boy from Cowiche however. At Mt St Paul my classmates came from all over America. My new roommates were stereotypical to say the least. Al was a wisecracking fellow Italian from New Jersey and Eddie was a black kid from New Orleans whose Southern/Cajun accent I had one helluva time understanding. They were good guys and I learned a lot about various cultural/ethnic issues and life in the big city outside of rural Washington State. I know they considered me to be a real hick; when I started rambling on about farm related topics their eyes glazed over rapidly.

Mt St Paul had it all: a bar and restaurant (drinking age 18), indoor shooting range, movie theater, bookstore, nine hole golf course, huge gymnasium with every kind of athletic equipment imaginable, real sports teams with uniforms, etc., etc. What a shock! Within a month of arriving I noticed a lot of excitement in the air and was finally told it had to do with the upcoming October-Fest celebration. I still don't know if it was a German tradition or just a local Milwaukee area month long beer party but it was something else. We hosted a huge affair in our gymnasium for the whole town and must have had six different local beer companies set up exhibits and booths in there. There were huge banners proclaiming the wonders of all the great Milwaukee beers: Schiltz, Blatz, Pabst, Miller, Old Milwaukee, etc., etc. This will seem hard to comprehend but I had never drank a beer or consumed any alcohol for that matter by the time I got to Wisconsin. While at St Peters I got conned into joining a no drinking club and proudly wore a little lapel pin professing my abstinence to everyone. Well that pin did not go over well in Wisconsin where not sampling several of the locally brewed beers daily was akin to being a commie. Anyway, after the last day of the October-Fest, we had quite a bit of leftover beer lying around. Several of us ended up in the huge TV room watching Johnny Carson. I got stuck with the Blatz beer and began sipping a few. From the vantage point of 45 years later I have to say that Blatz was the worst beer I have ever tasted . . . bitter goat piss comes to mind as the best flavor descriptor. However, I had nothing to compare it to then so I persevered until there were nine or ten empties scattered around my seat. I think Jack Benny was Johnny's guest and that's the last thing I remember before the room started rotating . . . I held on to the armrests for all I was worth but man that TV room was really spinning . . . I tried to act nonchalant and began to work my way to the can. Between the TV room and the restrooms were several pool tables . . . Someone later told me I pitched forward onto one, hesitated just a second, and then barfed all ten of those Blatz beers right onto the table. Apparently there were some harsh words by the players as I crawled into the can. I have a brief recollection of my face in the bottom of a urinal pressed up against the little white hockey puck. My roommates were notified to come and get me and next thing I remember was being drug all the way to our room by my feet. Apparently, it was one ugly scene and I was informed of all the gruesome details in the morning. My roommate Al was particularly disgusted with me as he couldn't believe that a fellow Italian would dis-respect himself like that. Again, as with every other unpleasant episode in my own life, I was to revisit this type of behavior many times over when working the swing shift as a road trooper. My little initiation to drinking was very tame compared to some of the messes I saw with the hundreds of drunk drivers I arrested over the years; but more on those guys later.

Myself in cassock and collar, 1968, during Mt St Paul seminary years.

I didn't go home at Thanksgiving that year but was invited to a friend's for the holiday, way up North in Antigo, Wisconsin. Man, the drive up there was gorgeous and the names of the towns we went through were unbelievable: Wauwatosa, Fond du Lac, Menomonee Falls, Oconowomoc, etc., etc. Beautiful Native American names similar to the ones I was familiar with in Washington such as: Skokomish, Duckabush, Dosewallips, Bogachiel, Humptulips, etc., etc. Antigo had about five feet of snow on the ground and very few cars were on the roads; everyone got around on snowmobiles. This was the first time I had experienced bitterly cold weather in the minus 30 degree zone; what a shock when the snot froze in your nose! A big surprise was the arrival of my buddy's sister home from college as well. He hadn't mentioned that she could have been a clone of Sophia Loren as well as being a huge flirt. However, I kept reminding myself how sacred the vow of chastity was and tried not to be led astray by this foul and evil temptress. Anyway, we played a lot of Scrabble but unfortunately most of the time was spent discussing the Packer's season. Antigo was just a few miles from Green Bay and my buddy's dad was a crazy fan. He knew every detail about Starr, Nitschke, McGee, Kramer, et al.

Consequently, that Sunday we were all glued to the TV as the Packers barely beat the Bears. The Pack went on to win the Super Bowl that year and I have to admit it was pretty exciting living in Wisconsin in those months!

Traveling home for Christmas proved to be quite an ordeal. We were diverted to Portland and had to take a bus to Yakima since all the airports in Eastern Wash. were closed due to a massive snowfall. I was traveling with Wayne Perrault from Sunnyside and we were so fortunate to be seated right next to a drunk on a very crowded bus for nine hours. That was the first and last time I ever rode on a bus . . . I still can get a whiff of this guy's b.o. all these years later, when combined with the oh so lovely stale barf/cheap wine/urine/fecal matter mix I'm pretty sure there must be some military applications for that kind of stench. Of course I came across this horrible smell combo cocktail many times in my career but contact time was usually limited to the ride to the county jail and never lasted for nine agonizing hours.

Once back in Waukesha I was awoken one morning by a sweet sounding machine out in the parking lot. One of the upper-classmen had brought his motorcycle back with him, a brand new 1967 BSA 650 Lightning. Man it sounded good and was probably the most beautiful bike I had ever seen. My brother Ray came back from England with tales of riding a Triumph Trophy 500 around the countryside and had high praise for all British machines. The triple play occurred when my cousin Jack Logozzo showed up at our ranch in Tieton one summer on his 650 Triumph Bonneville. He took me for a ride down to Cowiche and back and I was really blown away! Thus far my only experience on bikes was when our barber Bud Phipps brought his Tote-Goat out to the ranch to ride around. When he let me have a shot at it I promptly drove it wide open straight into a big bush by the house and got thrown off. It got all tangled up in the bush with the throttle still stuck open and tried to tear itself apart in there. Anyway, I was told by the old man that I was too uncoordinated to ever ride a bike; if only I had heeded his warning . . . .

Life at Mt St Paul was going quite smoothly when one day after lunch one of the kitchen staff suddenly flopped onto the floor and began having some sort of seizure. It was a pretty bad one with foaming at the mouth and lots of jerking around. (I learned later during my EMT training that this was a grand mal). Well, I had earned a first aid merit badge while in Boy Scouts but all I could remember was something about putting a stick between the teeth of someone suffering a seizure to keep them from biting their tongue off. I have to tell you that is a task much easier said than done; I grabbed a rolled up linen napkin and tried getting that in there while holding this guy down . . . . Man what a cluster this was . . . Finally a couple other people laid on him too and we were able to control him somewhat until the ambulance arrived. One of the folks helping me was a very pretty blonde waitress that worked in the cafeteria. After they hauled this guy away we talked a little and next thing you know she invited me over to her folks for dinner. I was always ready for free chow and besides the fare offered at Mt St Paul was usually unpalatable since the cooking staff were all Germans who tended to boil everything; steak, fruit, sausage, veggies, you name it. So a couple days later I walked a couple miles to her place for Sunday dinner in the suburbs of Waukesha. Her folks were quite nice but the brother seemed a bit strange. Dinner was a nice roast beef affair. Her old man had always wanted to see Mt. Rainier so I was telling him of my adventures up there as a boy scout trying to get my 50 Mile Hike badge back in 1961. Although the Tote Goat episode was still fairly fresh in my mind, I apparently still had not recognized that I had a multi-tasking disorder of some sort. I was as surprised as anyone when I suddenly found myself with a full gravy ladle in my hand while trying to describe how magnificent the panorama was up on Rainier overlooking the Emmons Glacier. With a grandiose sweeping of my hand I attempted to portray the overwhelming scope of the vista up there . . . Unfortunately, the sweeping hand I chose was the one holding the gravy ladle. I have to admit that unlike my orchard spraying I got some good coverage in this time . . . The Mom, Dad, and the brother, were now all dripping with hot gravy. Thankfully none got on my new girlfriend who was sitting too close to me I guess. Well, there was a pregnant pause then a totally uncalled for eruption of maniac type laughter from the brother who I already surmised was somewhat demented anyway. I had never been quite this humiliated in my life and the folks just glared at me like I was human garbage. Many apologies followed but fell on deaf ears. Finally my new girlfriend suggested we go to a show and we got the hell out of there. We walked in silence for a few blocks when she suddenly started shaking and I thought, shit, she's gonna have a seizure too. Well the shaking soon developed into the same maniac laughter that her unhinged brother had displayed, so I just figured the whole family must be nuts. Choking and gasping while tears and snot flowed freely she had to recount the whole horrendous episode for me step by step again and again until she got it all out of her system. I eventually started laughing as well but still wake up at night from a dream after having thrown more hot gravy on some new and unsuspecting victims. We went to see Bonnie & Clyde that night and then went for a pizza as neither of us had eaten much at dinner.

My old Rector Chris Breen from St Peters came out for a visit in the spring and told all of us Washington boys that the next school year we would be enrolled at St Thomas Seminary in Kenmore, Wash. I was pretty disappointed as I really liked Wisconsin and all the jet travel it took to get there. While there he took us out to see the Lakers play in Milwaukee, when Elgin Baylor and Jerry West were still with the team. He also took us to see a play called 'Waiting for Godot' by Samuel Beckett. This was a production from the theater of the absurd I believe and that's about all I can say too . . . . it was absurd. By then my new 'girlfriend' had taken up with another seminarian friend of mine who I assume was a multi-tasker and not a gravy tosser. So I was really looking forward to getting home ASAP as my Dad had written and said he had found a real nice 327 Chev V8 at a wrecking yard in Yakima and thought it would be perfect to drop in my jeep. We had already installed a really neat Koenig PTO winch in it, and Dad had welded together a gorgeous 2 &1/2 inch roll bar too. The 327 would make this the ultimate jeep! After I retired from the WSP I briefly flew for a fractional jet outfit and once had a trip back to Wisconsin. We had two days to kill before heading back to Santa Rosa so I was able to re-visit Mt St Paul after nearly 40 years. It looked remarkably the same except that it was now some sort of half-way house for recovering addicts . . . .

Homecoming was great and brother Ray now had a jeep as well; a '65 CJ5 with the aluminum V6 under the hood. More importantly by far was when Ray showed up at the ranch with a bike stuffed in the back of his jeep! It was the coolest looking machine I had ever seen: a 250 Ducati Scrambler. Man, it was loud, fast, and Italian made . . . what more could you ask for? My grandmother who still lived on the ranch wasn't as impressed with the Ducati even though it was made in Bologna near her home town in Italy. I think the big loud sliding broadies Ray laid down right in front of her house might have put her off a bit. Anyway, I was a little hesitant to ride the monster at first, remembering the Tote Goat incident, but I found it very easy to operate and soon was looking around town for one of my own. Ray found one first, but it was the Diana Street model. The scrambler looked a lot meaner with the smaller gas tank and little banana seat. So, I bought the scrambler from him and he got the Diana and converted it into a dirt bike. Metzler knobbies were the tires of choice back then and both bikes were soon equipped with a new set. When ranch work would allow, usually on Sundays, we loaded the Ducatis into our jeeps and off we went into the wilderness West of Yakima.

The Ducatis were very trouble free bikes for the most part but they had a real aversion to water. The ignition points were located under a round plate on the lower right side of the engine. The gasket protecting them was quite thin and the ignition wire came out of an unsealed hole. Consequently, every time we crashed through a little stream all it took was just one water molecule anywhere near the points or condenser and the engine would quit dead. Sometimes, when lucky, it would just begin 'eight stroking' (get spark every eight strokes). Usually after several minutes with the engine in this mode the offending water molecule would evaporate and the engine would revert to its normal four stroke cycle. We always carried paper matches with us which were perfect for drying the points out but everywhere we rode was wet so this became quite a hassle. Finally, brother Ray 'expropriated' some really great black silicon sealer that came in small round rolls about a quarter inch thick from the phone company. Remember, this is 1968 and silicon was a very high tech material then. Man that stuff was made to order and once we sealed up those points covers and wire holes with this stuff we never had ignition issues again unless we completely submerged the whole bike when all bets were off. We had many enjoyable outings and some of the most memorable were up on top of Darlin Mountain West of Yakima. We were always able to get into the snow up there even in August. My favorite situation was trying to stay on top of wet hard packed snow while in fourth gear wide open, feet paddling away, traveling about ten mph with that big ole Metzler digging in and sending up a huge rooster tail of snow . . . Still better was getting in front of brother Ray and sending the rooster tail onto him. However, that took extreme multi-tasking talents and I found myself being the recipient of rooster tails more often than being the sender. We also rode in the sagebrush Northwest of Wapato and developed a game of motorcycle tag which was a blast. After a tagging all the other rider had to do was try to catch up and tag you back with a big slug in the back. During one episode I had just tagged him and during my escape maneuvers feigned a turn to the right, and then went left and for some crazy reason I went hard right again colliding into him pretty hard . . . I stayed up somehow but he hit the dirt with a mighty crash. When I circled back he was lying motionless on the ground and I figured I'd killed him for sure. However, when I got closer he suddenly sprang to his feet and was all assholes and elbows for a few seconds as he apparently was trying to get his pants off for some reason. I laid my bike down close by and ran to help. However, I pulled up short when I saw what the problem was . . . He had landed on a ground wasp nest with his pants partially pulled down from the crash and they seemed pretty upset by his sudden intrusion into their home! Ray was jumping around all over the place spewing forth invectives that even my Dad wouldn't have thought of after getting the speedsprayer stuck. After he ridded himself of all the offending pests it was determined that two and maybe three of them had actually stung him. Unfortunately, one got him on a testicle and that hairy thing eventually swelled up to the size of an orange. It goes without saying that the five mile ride back to the jeeps was a bit uncomfortable for him and he had to stand on the footpegs the whole way as sitting just wasn't an option. On the way home I was thankfully alone in my jeep because I did an exact rendition of my old girlfriend's delayed reaction to my gravy spraying act. Every Christmas, Easter, and Thanksgiving since that day he usually regales every one present with that story emphasizing what a lousy biker I was and that no self respecting rider would ever feign turning in one direction and then a split second later actually go in that direction . . . Just not proper motorcycle tag etiquette!

Mom on my 250 Ducati Dirt Bike, 1969

A life altering seminal moment occurred for me while we were riding our Ducatis up on the mud flats at Rimrock Lake one fall. There was a seasonal motocross track set up out there and a few guys were racing around it pretty quickly. After a couple laps I thought I was doing OK except there was this skinny little kid riding a tiny Yamaha 90 or something that kept passing me. I thought he must be cutting across the track or something but realized that he was legally passing everyone out there like we were all standing still . . . This kid was awesome. On the way back to shore I saw this kid again with his folks all huddled around a magnificent looking Maroon and White Triumph 650 that had no street equipment just two big freakin exhaust pipes tucked under the frame with what looked like the biggest Metzler knobbies I've ever seen mounted. While we ate lunch the kid's old man got on this monster and cranked it up. Man it was loud, almost up there with the Hercules in the speed sprayer. Anyway, the old man got out there in the mud and proceeded to lay down a beautiful series of slow lazy eights in top gear with that Triumph engine just bellowing away . . . . What a sight, the rooster tails of mud and sand must have been twenty feet high! After hearing that gorgeous BSA run back in Wisconsin, riding on Jack's Bonnie, and then to witness this Triumph in action, I began to seriously rethink my choice of future bikes.

After a couple years of riding the Ducatis around I convinced myself I could be competitive on it and actually entered a couple racing events. The first was a hill climb out near the Roza Dam North of Yakima. I had been practicing at home on the same hill I almost drove the tractor over with the rotovator and thought I had the 250cc class event in the bag. Only trouble was at the hill climb you had to start right at the bottom of an extremely steep slope . . . At home, I always took a hundred yard head start and more or less let momentum carry me up and over. As can be expected I didn't get too far up the hill and had a helluva time coming back down that cliff without going end over end. That little kid that had smoked us up at Rimrock was there and won the whole damn event riding a 250 Yamaha. He even beat all the old timers riding their nitro burning Harleys and Triumphs with the stretched rear ends with chains on their tires. He came over to my brother and I and made several disparaging remarks about the "Du-Pussys" we were riding. Later that year, not deterred by my humiliating outing at the hill climb, I entered a 100 mile cross country race north of Zillah. It was to be three laps around a sage brush and canyon filled course. I was by myself as no-one was interested in being my pit crew that day. It was a running to your parked bike start which was problematic for me since I had taken the kickstand off to save some weight. I propped it up with a stick but before I got to it at the start of the race someone had knocked it over. I hung back a little at first to let all the Triumphs and other desert sleds go past then started picking off all the weenies, old ladies, and little kids at the back of the pack. I made it to the first couple of check points OK where a guy stuck a colored piece of tape to your helmet and waved you on. Although brother Ray and I had ridden many miles on our little weekend outings we always stopped every 15 min. or so for a smoke break and quick rest. This racing gig was a bit different and I found myself getting a little tired about two thirds of the way through the first lap. I started falling off pretty hard and shed a few bike parts each time. I broke a footpeg off on a rock and had to rest my foot up on the engine case which was hotter than hell by now. Next I broke off the kick starter lever and had to resort to bump starting it after each fall. Finally, as I neared the pits, the exhaust pipe rattled off and I barely made it to my jeep before it quit running. I was totally exhausted and even if I had fixed everything there was no way I could go on. Thus ended my competitive bike racing career. By the time I had loaded up the bike the winner crossed the finish line having already completed all three laps just a few minutes after I only managed one . . . It was that same kid again . . . what an animal he was!

Starting my sophomore year at St Thomas was fun with lots of guys I knew from St Pauls and St Peters now enrolled. This seminary was run by yet another different order of the church, the Sulpicians. Again, I have no idea who these guys were or where their order came from. Many of my new classmates had graduated from St Edwards Seminary just down the road the previous year. I was most gratified to find that most of them shared my sense of righteousness regarding the handling of in-house issues as we had at St Peters. I also discovered that flipping, flushing, and toilet bowl wrapping had all been common practices at St Edwards too . . . this was going to be a fun group! Some of my new almost immediate best friends were Pat Noone (Gooner), John Haydu (Donger), Jim Bender (Ralph), Ron Hertz, Miles Kessler, Jim Borte (BA), Jim Hardiman (Gabby), and Mike O'Halloran who had been my classmate at St Pauls in grade school. We had a lot of fun together the next three years and never took any of the mandatory philosophical and theological curriculum, none of the uptight upper-classmen, or any of the profs. too seriously. I found myself to be almost immediately quite popular with this group but sadly I learned it had nothing to do with my sterling personality at all . . . . I was the only guy who brought wheels to school. We crammed almost all the above guys into that jeep many times while making mid-night runs down to Dicks in Lake City. Those were the best burgers around at the time and you could get a bag full for a buck as I remember.

Although my grades had been pretty good in high school and at Mt St Paul I started to notice a slow decline at St Thomas. The subject matters weren't too tough by any means, I just spent so much time goofin off with the guys that my available study time began to suffer as there were just too many distractions. All of us had to do volunteer work in the community. For a couple years I was a tutor for some low income kids in the central area of Seattle, just working on basic math, reading, and writing skills. It was rewarding work but occasionally the child's father would show up drunk and want to know what the hell this white guy was doing with his daughter. It was so sad to see just how many young black kids were being raised in these broken violent households.

Later I became a Sunday school teacher for 5th & 6th graders out at the Catholic Church in Duvall. I tried to tell the upper classman in charge of these duty assignments that I would not be very good with these kids since the lesson plan they wanted me to teach was so antiquated and boring. When he went into the "You will teach them as you are told" mode I acquiesced but already knew I was going to develop my own more relevant lesson plan for these youngsters to enjoy and try to make it fun for them. Instead of regurgitating the usual bible fantasies and requiring the forced memorization of totally irrelevant passages from scripture, as the nuns had been doing for centuries, I tried a new "radical" (this was 1969 remember) approach. Rather than focusing on all the horrible sins they shouldn't be committing, and the terrible punishment they could expect from the vengeful Almighty if they did, I would have one of them read a selected passage, usually about love or forgiveness, followed by a little round table discussion about the "true" message . . . . I know, crazy left wing crap. They all seemed to like it and we covered many appropriate topics, handpicked from actual bible passages that related to issues of tolerance, anger management, respect, ethnic and cultural issues, etc., etc. I always summed up the discussion with the moral for the day and tied it into the actual scripture passage translated into modern language the kids could relate to. Everything went well until the Spring of 1970 when one of the parents heard that some hippie was teaching blasphemous notions and heresy to their little Sally. The rector at St Thomas was informed that my methods were in total contradistinction to the precepts of the church, the Sunday catechism, Canon law and that I was inculcating their child with left wing hippie ideology. Well, I wasn't totally surprised by these allegations but I honestly felt it had been my duty to try to modernize the Sunday School format, at least with my own small little class, before they too became warped by an out of touch church. Anyway, I was immediately re-assigned as the medical assistant to the visiting doctor who came by St Thomas once a week to our closet sized clinic . . . No doubt knowledge of my Boy Scout First Aid merit badge had been discovered in my transcripts. Now this was a critical volunteer position if there ever was one: when a patient needed a band-aid, man I knew where to look . . . Pepto Bismol, I had it out on the counter in seconds . . . . and so on . . .

We attended Mass every day in our huge chapel and all upperclassman had to rotate on a weekly basis as the liturgical director of operations (I can't remember what it was really called then) . . . . Anyway, when so assigned we were responsible for choosing some appropriate music to play during Mass, which might include some subdued guitar playing, a recording of a current popular song of love or peace, or something similar. Usually, the chosen seminarian would read an appropriate passage or two from some approved holy source as well . . . These services had been conducted in a very conservative and appropriate manner for many years that is until a classmate of mine, Larry Trelevyn (Tree) decided to shake things up a bit . . . He had kept his musical liturgical intentions a secret from us until the day in question . . . . So there we were, having just received the sacred sacrament of holy communion, all kneeling with our heads bowed, contemplating all our sinful shortcomings, when our post communion

music started and began blaring out on the stereo chapel speakers . . . .
In contradistinction to the usual "mild" secular songs of peace
and love the staff allowed us to play such as: *"Get Together"* by the
Youngbloods or *"Peace Train"* by Cat Stevens today we were shocked
to hear Bob Dylan singing his famous ditty; *"Lay Lady Lay"* . . . . Man,
talk about pandemonium especially when those memorable lyrics "Lay
across my big brass bed . . . and stay with your man awhile" rang out!!
We all turned and looked towards the upstairs choir loft where Larry
was controlling the music from . . . . He was trying to act like nothing
out of the ordinary was occurring but we were all beside ourselves
laughing and snorting our approval!! One of our Sulpician profs, who
must have been at least 75 then and limped pretty badly, semi stormed
out of his pew and tried to run upstairs to put a stop to this horrific
sacrilege . . . . Of course by the time he got there the song was over and
the liturgical damage had been done . . . . I still laugh myself to sleep
at night remembering that episode!

As the years in the seminary crept by it was slowly starting to dawn
on me just how far the Catholic Church was out of touch with
reality . . . . Sadly, no-one in a position to do so, wanted to or had
the courage to take on the Vatican to change or modernize things
then. Just as they did in the handling of the pedophile priests, the
local bishop's and cardinal's attitudes were and probably always will
be to take whatever action necessary to ensure there are no major
scandals, or breaks from tradition, on my watch that you can blame
on me. However, the realization was growing in my mind just how
intransigent and unwilling to change the church really was I
started to doubt my resolve that I could spend my life associated with
such a stagnant and corrupt organization no matter the good work I
might have accomplished in spite of them.

So, I became a Pizza Haven delivery truck driver. Money was getting
short as a result of all the late night runs to Dick's and our new favorite
Italian restaurant, Venettis on Aurora. Besides, none of my buddy's
ever pitched in for gas money. I worked primarily in the evenings
after class, two or three nights a week out of the University restaurant

just a couple blocks from the UW campus. Being unfamiliar with the Seattle area initially proved to be quite an issue as I seemed to be spending most of my time lost or stuck on a one way street somewhere with pizzas getting dried out in the back. These trucks had neat little warming ovens with a huge sponge underneath to keep the pizza hot and moist. But if you didn't stop at a gas station every 15 min or so to re-wet the sponge, the pizzas would dry up pretty fast. Delivering pizzas was a lot like stopping cars as a trooper, you just never knew what weird situation you might find yourself in during each contact with the 'public'. On nearly every delivery I made around the U. District I would be met at the door by a semi-nude, intoxicated and/or high fraternity/sorority brother/sister followed by a wave of marijuana smoke from the party within. However, as a result, there was often an unexpected benefit when it came time for the tip; the door greeter was often confused and intoxicated and occasionally mixed up the currency denominations resulting in me getting a five dollar tip for a three dollar pizza . . . . I was torn about keeping the money at first but eventually just considered it "pay-off money" for not reporting the criminal activity going on inside, so my conscience was clear. I have to say that at most other locations tips of the paper variety were not usually offered; a couple quarters or a dime was my usual fare. I experienced one other more serious episode of criminal activity up in the central area one evening. As I was returning to my truck I noticed several inner city youths hanging around the back near the oven. While I put the big warming mitten away they moved in close with one of them asking; "Hey man, you got any free pizza in there?" I might not have been much of a multi-tasker but did have fairly good survival instincts and courteously responded; "As a matter of fact I do." I gave them one of our standard cheese pizzas that we always carried around as a spare. I threw in a box of chicken that had been in there all night too and they seemed satisfied. I drove around the block and radioed the boss what happened but he wasn't concerned and told me to just come back and reload the oven. Those spare pizzas were usually never sold and at the end of our shifts the boss said it was OK to take them home with us. After I tried one of those dried up pieces of cardboard and almost broke a tooth on it I usually found some left over fried chicken at the store and snacked on that on the drive back instead.

There was a guy at the seminary named Ron Hertz and when he found out I had access to 'free pizza' he literally became apoplectic and begged me to bring some back for him. I just knew he wouldn't like it but brought one back anyway one night. It was all cold, hard, and shriveled up, and it was one in the morning, but Ron tore into that thing like it was a sizzling filet mignon. I was just utterly amazed not only at how fast he ate it but that he did so without breaking any teeth or drinking anything . . . . What a guy! Almost every work night thereafter, whenever he heard my jeep coming up the hill to the seminary, he would meet me at my parking spot for his free pizza. There was another separate incident involving Ron and pizza eating. At 145th and Lake City Way, on our way to Dick's one night, we noticed a grand opening special at a new Pizza Hut restaurant, Pizza Haven's sworn enemy. The banner proclaimed 'All You Can Eat for $2.99'. Well, Ron was in the jeep that night and nearly went berserk at the prospect of an all you can eat offer. So, couple nights later about eight of us showed up there for dinner. Now we were all pretty good sized starving seminarians with very healthy appetites. The Sulpician Nuns who cooked for us at St Thomas were wonderful ladies but again, I think they might have been English or German as most of their entrees had been boiled into submission. Anyway, each of us easily put away the equivalent of three large pizzas apiece. However, Ron was really in his element that night; he would pound away three pieces to our one piece and reminded me exactly of those guys you see in those hot dog eating contests at the fair. He was rolling the pieces up like large cannolis, gobbling them down, and doing the best imitation of Homer Simpson I've ever seen. Well, not surprisingly, the store manager finally came over and asked us all to leave. Ron was outraged, stood up and while poking his finger in this guy's chest exclaimed "It says—all you can eat Bub!" The manager sort of backed down, as Ron was a pretty intimidating character. To his credit the manager held his ground and quietly advised us we were not in keeping with the 'spirit' of an all you can eat promotion. The rest of us were already stuffed to the gills so we carefully edged Ron outside.

My jeep had a rag top so when the rain Seattle is so famous for became so bad that no one wanted to venture out to Dick's in such a leaky rig and get soaked we came up with plan B. The priests had a private refectory near their sleeping quarters with a well stocked fridge. We would wait until the wee hours of the morning to be safe and launch ourselves on a 'raid'. We had convinced ourselves this was a legal and justifiable undertaking since the primary mission statement for the Sulpician order had words to the effect of share and share alike. Well, these guys weren't sharing and we felt they were in violation of their own sacred vows so we concluded we had a moral obligation to partially rectify their sinful behavior. Anyhow, we would crawl down the corridor on hands and knees with no shoes on to prevent inadvertent sneaker squeaks, quietly skulk into the carpeted refectory, and unplug the refrigerator so it's light wouldn't give us away upon opening. Initially we used to gobble down all the goodies we found on site . . . cheese, salami, olives, ham, etc. But after a couple of close calls due to our lingering, we expedited the operation and began taking the booty back to our rooms. We noticed there was beer and Cold Duck in there as well. We all felt that alcohol was off limits at first but after several months of successful raids the beer and Cold Duck was expropriated as well. Apparently, the staff never figured out that students were to blame for their occasionally semi empty fridge (we always left a few representative items) and hoped they would assume one of their own was raiding it . . . . We never got caught. However, the year after I graduated I got word that several 'raiders' had gotten very greedy, crossed the line, and while hitting the big freezers in the kitchen got caught and subsequently kicked out of the seminary. By then I had been transformed into an upstanding member of society, having just been hired by the WSP, and was just shocked and horrified at their reckless criminal behavior . . . .

The school year 1970-71 was a pivotal year in my life; so many career and life changing events took place that I just lost track after awhile. It had all started to unwind in the spring of 1970 after brother Ray and I had gone to Seattle Raceway Park to see our AMA motorcycle racing heroes fling their machines around the road racing course there. I was just overwhelmed by the howling Triumph Tridents and BSA Rocket Threes that dominated the event. Soon after the race I was on spring break back home where I was thinking a lot about those

Triumphs at the races, the memory of that ride on Jack's Triumph and watching that gorgeous BSA back in Waukesha . . . . Before I realized it I found myself walking into Don Pomeroy's Triumph shop in Yakima. I immediately noticed pictures on the wall of a very familiar looking skinny kid holding up a ton of trophies . . . Turned out it was Don's son Jimmy Pomeroy who at the time was fast becoming a world famous Motocross racer in Europe. He was also the same guy who had waxed my brother and me up at Rimrock a few years back, and at the Hill climb, and at the cross country race. Surprisingly, Jimmy became my sister Rita's baby-sitter around that time and my nephews and niece (Mark, Teri, & Mike) thought it was pretty cool that a world famous motocross champion was their nanny! Additionally, Ray's daughter Lisa later married a great guy by the name of Chris Dunn, who was also a championship Motocrosser in the Pacific Northwest! Lisa's brother Kevin (who like Lisa and her daughter Sam) was a fantastic all around athlete but had unfortunately inherited some Carnevali DNA that contained a mutated Motocross gene of some kind, as I had . . . I seem to remember an incident where Kevin tumbled off a thirty foot cliff up north of Ellensburg, while riding with his Dad, but was saved by a large sagebrush . . . As I'm writing this Lisa and Chris are on their annual trip to Sturgis on their Hog . . . . Anyway, Don had a new 750 Triumph Trident on the showroom floor . . . . Sadly, this was the most butt-ugly machine I had ever seen . . . Square gas tank, stupid looking triple mufflers on each side, putrid color . . . . This machine in no way, shape, or form resembled the racing versions we saw in Seattle. I was pretty bummed until Don said he had a new 1970 T120 650 Bonneville in the back still in the crate. Well, when I saw that Bonnie it was love at first sight . . . The classic looking engine, gorgeous maroon/silver paint job, perfectly sculpted gas tank, and I already knew about that beautiful Triumph rumble that would soon come roaring out those pipes . . . . WOW!! Mainly though, it was that image I recalled of Don riding his '67 Bonnie TT Special up at Rimrock, throwing up those rooster tails of mud and sand, that convinced me I just had to have this one. Needless to say, I immediately put the jeep for sale never having time to get that 327 installed. Brother Ray's best friend immediately bought it and within a couple days I was back to buy that Bonnie. When I came into the store with money in hand there was some guy sitting on my bike pumping the forks pretty aggressively. I was about to say something when Don came over and introduced me to his buddy Bob Knievel. I had seen this guy jump a bunch of Greyhound Buses at Seattle Raceway park and was pretty impressed with him but more so when he got off my bike and proclaimed it to be a nice Bonnie. Unfortunately for Evel, the next night he fell off his Laverda while jumping a bunch of Darigold milk trucks in Yakima and broke his arm.

As gorgeous as the new Triumph was on the outside it had quite a few internal demons and I suffered through several engine failures with it in short order and finally traded it in on a new Harley Sportster XLCH that summer . . . . (This wasn't my last Triumph or the end of my love affair with them however.) Before trading in my Bonnie I had one final moment on her that was a harbinger of things to come . . . I was riding into a very stiff headwind on I-90 near Thorp and was really getting buffeted when I had a brilliant idea . . . . I'll just tuck in behind this semi trailer ahead of me, get into his draft, and let him pull me along, hopefully getting a smoother ride as an added benefit! Well, it was a pretty smooth ride in there (about three feet off that trailer's bumper) and I was able to roll off a little throttle. I really had to keep an eagle eye on his brake lights though to keep from decapitating myself in case the driver suddenly stepped on his brake pedal hard. I got a couple miles in like this when I caught a quick glimpse of a patrolman sitting in the U-turn just west of the Thorp exit . . . . Shit! Shit! Shit! . . . . Maybe he didn't see me! I quickly took the Thorp exit and wheeled my bike behind the Chevron station that was there in those years . . . Nothing happened so I took my helmet off and lit up a smoke to celebrate my 'victory'. I was congratulating myself about my lightening like reflexes and quick thinking when a trooper suddenly walks around the corner of the station with a big smile on his face . . . . All he says is "Hey Slick, I saw your little Evel Knievel act out there . . . very impressive!" The grin then left his face as he asked for my license and registration . . . . Man, I knew this was going to be bad so I put on my best innocent looking seminarian face and plead stupidity & insanity (not too difficult) . . . . He could have easily written me a ticket for negligent driving or even reckless for that matter but he was kind to me and simply wrote me for following too closely . . . . I was really thankful for the break and thought of that trooper's leniency to me often over the ensuing years . . . .

Four years later when I transferred into the Spokane West Beat after having finally made it through my probationary period with the WSP, one of the first guys in my new detachment to greet me was Trooper Gene Osburn 483 . . . the same guy that let me off easy that day! As I shook hands with Gene I asked him if he recognized me. He didn't at first but after refreshing his memory about our first meeting he laughed and remembered everything . . . He said that was the worst tailgating episode he had ever witnessed and that he should have written me for reckless!! If he had, I wouldn't be writing this story now as a reckless conviction would have been disqualifying for a new cadet applicant. Thanks again Geno!

Before I traded that Bonneville in on the Sportster, I did an engine overhaul on it all by myself in my room at the sem. The motor had seized up near Cle Elum but I managed to get a ride to Bellevue in the back of some guys U-Haul. I picked up a couple of new pistons at the Triumph shop in Seattle and after considering my vast wrenching experience on the farm thought it would be a snap to install them . . . . I hadn't really thought things through much since pistons don't usually seize for no reason . . . I just thought they had just been badly forged or something . . . . !? I did the top end over-haul using a pair of vice-grips and the under seat tool kit that came with the bike. When I was finished it started on the first kick and I congratulated myself for being quite the intuitive mechanic! Sadly, it only ran for a couple days then seized again . . . . A 'real' Triumph mechanic found the timing to be way off and re-built the top end one more time.

When summer vacation started I just couldn't resist the allure of that new Sportster and finally bid my dream machine a sad farewell. The Sportster handled like a tractor towing a disk but did it ever sound good! I was riding it when I happened to meet a lovely sweet young thing named Debbie Carls down at Rest Haven Lake one afternoon.

Brother Ray and I had taken to water-skiing in irrigation canals near Cowiche in those years as Dad had sold the boat we had skied behind up at O'Sullivan a few years back. So I invited her and her girlfriend to give the canal experience a try. The tow vehicle was my brother's CJ5 Jeep, to which we attached an extra long tow rope hooked to the top of the roll bar. When Debbie first saw how narrow the canal was I think she had some second thoughts about our sanity but she didn't flinch, which impressed me a lot. Both girls made several valiant attempts to get up on one ski but neither made it having never skied before. Many years later, when we had our own boat, Deb became an excellent skier . . . and as long as we were out on Lake Pend Oreille or Coeur d'Alene she never had to worry about horses and cows in her path!! Of course, on the day in question, brother Ray and I had to put on a show of our daring-do, and wowed them with our slalom skiing prowess. Afterwards he told me in confidence that Debbie was indeed 'a keeper' after he too noticed that she didn't back down from such a daunting challenge. (The fact that she was drop dead gorgeous helped somewhat too) There were three interesting aspects involved with skiing on a canal not usually encountered on a lake; first it's the only water sport where you ended up covered in dusty mud at the end of a run since the jeep had to be driven on the narrow dusty canal frontage road with the skier eating all the dirt blown his way. Secondly, when skiing around some of the blind hairpin turns in the canal, which was a real feat in itself, you would often be surprised by a horse or cow having a drink in the very narrow confines of the ditch. Those hairpin turns added another water-skiing dimension not usually associated with lake skiing; the jeep would be around a sharp corner, long before the skier, with the tow rope cutting quickly across the apex of that curve. This required the skier to lay over onto his left shoulder to maneuver through it, often with the ski's skag slicing into the cat-tails and occasionally hitting rocks on the right bank. Lastly, there were a couple tall iron water gates with big wheels on top that we had to deal with. When you got close to them you'd have to pull some slack on the ski rope, try to time it just right, then fling the slack in the rope over the iron wheel so you didn't get sucked into it . . . . Just another activity on the list of what I needed to master on my path to multi-tasking competence. We were able to stretch out about a three mile run of drivable canal road before encountering a siphon where the canal went into a huge underground tube to cross a small valley. Normally we'd make every attempt to do a lot of cutting back and forth to get some water on the road to keep the dust down but it evaporated too quickly to do much good. We took brother-in-law Mark Hanses up once and he thought it was great fun too. Our only regret from those years is that we never took any pictures or got any video of ourselves during our redneck water skiing forays but it sure was a gas and one of my fondest memories from my youth!

During summer break that year, although it was never a vacation for me, Pete McCarthy, an upperclassman friend of mine from the seminary who lived in Yakima, called and invited me to the drive-in one night with Mike Ibach and another Seattle upperclassman. Although strictly forbidden by our seminarian code of conduct laws, I seem to recall some adult beverages becoming available in the car. Pete had also constructed a homemade "used beer" elimination device, basically a funnel and five foot hose, that could be conveniently slipped under a slightly open door so we didn't have to get out during the show. But more importantly for me was getting to meet Pete's Dad before we took off. He was a State Patrolman in Yakima and had been since WWII. He broke out his scrapbook and photo albums and told us all about his life as a State Trooper over the last 30 years. Man he had some terrific stories and photos of all those great patrol cars from his era. He also showed us some horrendous fatal pictures with mangled cars and bodies but I tried not to look at those too long. One photo really caught my eye; it showed a patrolman sitting in an old WWII era plane that carried the WSP logo on its side. Sergeant McCarthy told me the guy's name was Bill Gebinini and that he used to fly a "forties" version of traffic patrol (as I later discovered) in his own personal North American AT6 Texan out of the Olympia Airport. Seeing that great looking plane and all those cool patrol cars really got my juices flowing and I tried to imagine life as state patrolman and maybe someday a trooper-pilot. I wasn't even sure that the WSP had an aviation department at the time but as it turned out they did, but it was pretty small and underfunded. Anyway, when I started my senior year at St Thomas, I was slightly conflicted about my future life of public service; life as a parish priest versus life as a highway patrolman . . . I have to say the latter sounded a helluva lot more exciting! The only lasting benefit that my years in the seminary inculcated in me was an understanding of just how vital public service of some sort is during your life. Whether it's accomplished in the military, at church, through a service organization, or a life toiling away as a lowly state employee, I think we all need to give something back to society and fill that void in our lives we often don't understand as we get older . . . .

Before making any long term plans there was the small issue of the upcoming draft lottery for the Viet Nam War. They published all the numbers which I think went from 1 to 365 with the low numbers getting drafted first. Luckily, my number was 344, so it was pretty unlikely they would get to me but no-one knew then just how much longer the war might drag on. I decided to see if I met the minimum requirements to be an aircraft crewmember either with the Air Force or Navy. I was told ahead of time by the recruiters that you had to have 20/20 vision to be any kind of crewmember let alone be accepted for pilot training; my vision was around 20/80 then. However, they told me I would be a shoe-in for officer candidate school in either branch if I graduated from college in the spring. So I kept that plan in reserve if they started to get down near my lottery number after graduation. One of the Air Force recruiters told me flat out that I'd never get any kind of flying job, civilian or military, and probably couldn't even be a pilot without perfect vision. That startling declaration, from someone I assumed knew what he was talking about, really hit home hard and set my dreams back of becoming a pilot awhile.

My last year at St Thomas went by all too quickly although we had some fun at the expense of one of the newly assigned instructors, Father Bill DeVino. He wasn't much older than us and was a pretty good guy from the East coast. St Thomas was his first assignment so he was pretty green and straight laced. When alone with him we all asked him the same question: 'Why do you act like you have a stick up your ass all the time?' He became quite indignant after that revelation but soon warmed up to us as he sensed we had accepted him as one of the gang. From that point on we all started using the shortened phrase, 'What's up your butt', whenever any of us starting acting superior or pompous. At one point we felt DeVino might have been slipping back into his east coast uppity persona but we engineered the perfect fix. He fancied himself as quite the dramatic actor and even wiggled his way into a starring role in the 1971 St Thomas Seminary production of the play 'Martin Luther'. At one point in the play DeVino, playing an important church official, unrolled this large scroll and had to read all the charges the church was bringing against Martin Luther, being played by my good friend Jim (Ralph) Bender. Well, the first couple of nights the play went well and DeVino was on a roll . . . . His final performance, not so much . . . . All the big wigs from the Seattle Arch Diocese were there in our huge theater that night including the Archbishop and many other clergy and nuns. Additionally, all the big seminary benefactors and several celebrities from the area showed up including Lenny Wilkens from the Super Sonics and Marilee Rush and the Turnabouts. Well, unknown to DeVino, backstage Jim Bender was able to tape last month's Playboy Centerfold into the scroll that DeVino would later unfurl during the play to read the charges against Jim from. Of course our little group of malcontents sat in the audience barely able to control ourselves knowing what was about to happen. When the unfurling of the scroll finally occurred during the play, DeVino was uncharacteristically quiet for a couple seconds . . . Jim had a huge grin on his face but DeVino's just turned crimson, with rage I believe. We all just busted a gut from the hours of pent up anticipation but were somewhat disappointed when DeVino bounced back pretty well, put the centerfold aside, and got all the charges read against Martin without further ado. Later that evening, things got a bit ugly and I guess DeVino had to finally get serious and gave all the suspected perpetrators quite an ass chewing. We never felt the chewing had anything to do with our violations of the seminarian code of conduct but had everything to do with the fact that we almost made him look bad on stage. The next morning in our Civil War History class DeVino walked into the classroom only to be rudely greeted by a large chalk inscription on the board asking: "What's up your butt?"

By now my Harley had also given up the ghost several times as the rear piston kept seizing. I finally unloaded it on a poor sap in the Bothell area and to this day keep waiting for him to come after me for dumping that slug on him. The factory quality control at AMF Harley in those years was just horrendous and I was just one more lucky recipient of one of their fine machines—better suited as a boat anchor. Prior to selling it however, it did manage to stay running long enough one day to take my girlfriend Debbie on a nice ride up to Chinook Pass. On the way back down a couple of real losers riding piece of crap Triumphs passed us at a high rate of speed. Well I refused to be disrespected like that in front of my girlfriend so I dropped a gear and pushed my streamlined boat anchor to its limit . . . . I finally caught up to the Triumphs when they got stuck in traffic near Naches . . . I thought I had room so I didn't slow down, passed them both and the truck they were behind and just got back into my lane as a pickup had to swerve onto the shoulder and almost nailed us going the other way. Shortly thereafter I felt a slight pounding vibration and figured it was either my heart from all the excitement or that rear cylinder was packing up again. As I slowed I realized it was Debbie pounding on my back and yelling some unintelligible obscenities at me. I pulled over on the shoulder and as I was leaning the bike over onto its kick stand she attempted to get off the high side of the bike where both of those big herkin red hot mufflers were installed pretty high up. Before I could say or do anything I heard the sound of fresh meat being thrown on a hot grill with a sickening sizzle. Shortly thereafter I heard some more gratuitous profanity, then some screaming and crying. Apparently I only exacerbated the situation when I said rather matter of factly: "Aw for Crissakes, I told you not to wear cut-offs!" 42 years later this event still seems to be fresh in her mind; every time her calf starts to itch a little she just scratches that monster burn scar down there and looks over at me with that "you did this to me you moron" look . . . . Geez . . .

My other big Harley memory was starting that thing up at night. 1970 Sportsters were fitted with a humungous Tillotson Carburetor. That bike never started very well but when it caught it was preceded by a massive flaming backfire that came out the Tillotson's throat and lit up the neighborhood pretty well at 0230. After Deb's folks complained that I was scaring their Collie, I took to coasting down the street and starting it on the roll.

After the Sportster was gone I entered a brief muscle car period starting with a '65 GTO with the three deuces (tri-power) on top of that 389. But, by Spring I missed bike riding again. So I sold the GTO and actually made some money for a change and bought a new Triumph Trident 750. This was the same bike I had seen at Pomeroys but by then Triumph had added a 'beauty package' which really cleaned it up. It now looked the same as a Bonneville with the same gas tank and mufflers. This was by far the best bike I had ever owned and the fastest machine I have ever ridden.

When I finally graduated in June of '71 I bid a somewhat fond farewell to my seminary days and hit the road on my Trident with my freshly minted BA Degree in History crammed under the seat and headed home. Before re-visiting the Air Force recruiter I stopped by the Yakima WSP office to pick up an application to be a trooper. There was a heavy set sergeant sitting behind a desk with his shoes off who asked if he could help me . . . He didn't even stand up . . . . When I told him I was interested in joining the force and would like an application he grimaced a little and really gave me the hairy eyeball once over. Although my hair was down to my shoulders my beard was neatly trimmed and I had taken a shower that morning. He just matter of factly stated, "Tell you what slick, why don't you come back when you've had a haircut and shave." I guess I should have known better but he was probably right and I should have presented myself a little more professionally on this initial contact with a possible new employer. So a week later I was back all cleaned up and meeting society's standards of decency for the day. I filled in the application on the spot and turned it in. Before I got out the door somebody asked me if I really had a BA degree; when I said yes they seemed quite shocked as this apparently was quite rare in those days. Then he asked me how tall I was and when I told him 6'2" he said that's great because they would have been willing to knock 2 inches off the six foot minimum height requirement since I had a degree. I guess the WSP was trying to clean up its image back then and apparently they were under the **very** mistaken impression that obtaining a degree somehow transformed a person into a quality human being!? Man, the guys back at the sem. would have busted a gut laughing at that premise! Anyway, I was ordered to come back in a couple weeks to take a written test, physical, and an eye test.

The written test wasn't too bad as it was the Army entrance exam and contained pretty basic stuff. The physical was a snap as I was still in great shape from playing basketball and handball at the sem. However, during the eye test I noticed the examiner expressing some concern. He asked me how bad I thought my eyes were and I said about 20/60. He told me I was right at 20/100 and said I would need a notarized statement from my eye doctor indicating they were no worse than 20/80 or they couldn't take me. Man, this eye situation was going to cost me another dream job! Well, I went to see my ophthalmologist and pleaded my case to him . . . After I read the eye chart he concurred that my vision was hovering around the 20/100 mark. He then said he needed to leave the room for a few minutes so I figured he had another patient to attend to. After about five minutes all my college training the WSP was so envious of finally kicked in and I realized he was giving me time to memorize the eye chart. I didn't want to seem greedy so I just memorized the 20/80 line. When he came back in he said "why don't you try again . . . ." Miraculously, I was able to read the 20/80 line, even throwing in some hesitation for dramatic effect. He tried to act surprised at my improvement and I told him my eyes must have been tired or something earlier. So I was soon back at the WSP office where I dropped off my "doctored up" eye exam results. I did get a new set of contact lenses right away with which I did see 20/20 so I didn't feel too guilty about this whole affair. They told me I would be contacted from someone in Olympia after they did a thorough background investigation of me and checked my traffic record . . . . Ah shit, now I had all kinds of things to worry about! There were several priests at St Thomas who I just knew would unload on a WSP investigator about what an insufferable prick I was. One was my old philosophy prof. who really got miffed at me once when I jokingly posted a bunch of existential nonsense on the bulletin board with him as the butt of the joke. The other was an elderly history prof. we called Flick. He had a very annoying habit while lecturing us out of a book, where he never even bothered to look up for 20 min. at a time. During this period, he would unconsciously be picking his nose then indiscriminately, and I hope unconsciously, 'flick' his boogers at us. I might have accidentally mentioned his unsanitary habit to one of the other profs. who I'm sure brought the whole revelation to Flick's attention wherein my name figured prominently. Unfortunately, I had to present my senior thesis to Flick before I could graduate, and it took me about four tries before he finally accepted it. Additionally, I had accrued about six tickets in the last two years. None were too serious just the usual motorcycle type violations; no mufflers, no lights, no helmet, a couple for speeding, and one for following too closely that really should have been negligent driving. Anyway, I tried to think positively.

Deb standing by my '69 GTO Judge near Duvall, 1971

While riding my Triumph down Yakima Avenue one night I noticed a gorgeous Orange '69 GTO Judge stopped at a light with a for sale sign in the window. I called the guy right away and soon went for a test drive. Holy shit, this car was something else . . . it had it all . . . Best looking muscle car of the day, almost as fast as my Triumph, sounded great, price was right . . . Only thing was I didn't want to sell my Triumph this time to get it. I had no collateral to get a loan so I begged brother Ray for help. He graciously put up his furniture and a few other things and with the $500 I had in savings I was able to get that Goat. What a car! My wife Deb still carries a picture of it in her wallet!

For several weeks prior to getting the GTO I had been carefully watching the fish count over Bonneville Dam on the lower Columbia River in the paper; the Coho Salmon (silvers) had been running very strong and heavy so I felt it was about time to go hit the Klickitat River since it was just a few miles upstream from Bonneville. I picked up Deb about 0400, just two days after getting the Goat, and we were on the water at sunrise. I don't know if the moon was wrong or what happened that day but we got skunked and finally gave up flogging the water around 1500 and headed home. About 10 miles Southwest of Toppenish on SR 97, I was getting a little sleepy so I cranked the air conditioner all the way up hoping that would keep me awake. The next thing I remember was a very loud noise like someone was spraying gravel into a 50 gallon barrel . . . When I opened my eyes all I saw was dust and dirt flying and noticed I was in a real unusual attitude, about a 60 degree bank to the left. We seemed to be in a ditch and still doing about 50 mph . . . I got the car level but just then saw a culvert coming up fast and hit it doing about 35 mph. Deb, who had been asleep as well during this ride, smashed into the dash board pretty hard which knocked her kind of silly. When I got out I could see exactly what happened; I had been on a long straight-away and when I got to a curve to the right I just kept going straight into this ditch on the other side of the road. Well, I wish I had a nickel for all the one car accidents I covered later in my career identical to this one. But for now I was just so grateful I hadn't hit somebody head-on and that we both seemed to be OK. The car however looked totaled . . . I'd only had it for 3 days and now it was junk! About 30 minutes later a trooper showed up and he asked me what happened. The left front tire was flat so I just blurted out that I guess I had a blowout; well that was true but not necessarily the cause of the accident. He looked at me with the same look I was to give so many people under similar circumstances soon enough which basically said: "Kid, do I have stupid written all over my face or something?" Luckily for me I had this accident during a brief period of time where the police could not take enforcement on a one car accident if there weren't any witnesses. So all I had to do was fill out an accident report and that was it. The name of that courteous trooper was Frank Noble. Less than a year from that day he would be gunned down by an ex-con just outside Zillah. Sadly, Frank would be the first of **ten** troopers I knew during my 33 year career to be killed in the line of duty. As I write this in Feb 2012, another friend of mine, Trooper Tony Radulescu 557, was just shot and killed by a deranged ex-con near Bremerton last night . . . . God dammit, it just never ends . . . . !

The tow truck took the car to a body shop in Yakima then dropped us off at Deb's place. Deb's Mom was a little upset but also said that my Mom had called and told her someone from the WSP wanted to talk to me right away. I thought I was screwed for sure and assumed a witness to my accident had surfaced and I was going to get a ticket for reckless driving and for lying to a state trooper. So when I called Mom it was with a heavy feeling of dread as this had already been a pretty bad day. Unbelievably, she said some WSP lieutenant from the personnel office in Olympia Headquarters had called and wanted me to schedule an interview in Olympia right away. I didn't quite know how to take this news; I was excited but felt that somehow they were going to find out I'd been in a wreck, lied to a trooper about having a blowout, and rescind the interview offer since I was obviously a sociopath. I hadn't told Trooper Noble I was applying to be a trooper since I knew he'd probably just laugh in my face. Man, this day was all over the place!

I called the lieutenant about the interview the next morning and he seemed friendly and polite so I thought that maybe he didn't know about the wreck yet. The folks wouldn't let me take their car (a gorgeous '62 Riviera) over to Olympia as they seemed to have recently lost faith in my driving skills. So about a week after the accident I put on my leather jacket, grabbed my Bell Star helmet and headed to Olympia on my 750 Triumph. The weather had been perfect all summer but the day I headed over for the interview it was raining hard on White Pass and I got soaked. As I sat in the WSP waiting room wet, cold, and miserable I hoped what that Air Force recruiter promised me was true 'cause I felt my chances of getting hired by the WSP were pretty remote right now. Additionally, I had been chatting with two other guys waiting for their interviews and they were both impeccably groomed and had freshly pressed suits on. I caught a reflection of my head in the door glass and saw some moron doing his best impression of a wet dog with helmet hair wearing muddy jeans, stained leather jacket, and a soggy turtle neck sweater . . . . Looked like more spraying, rotovating and picking apples for me . . . .

CHAPTER 4

WELCOME TO THE REAL WORLD

I was finally summoned into Lieutenant Maltby's office to face the music. When he saw how I was dressed I thought for a moment he was going to tell me to leave like the sergeant in Yakima did. However, he handled things very diplomatically but did ask why I was not dressed more appropriately. Not wanting to get into the wrecked GTO saga I just said the motorcycle was the only ride available to me today and apologized for being wet and underdressed. He told me that if I were to be hired I would have to commute to work in a car since I would be in uniform; I assured him that would not be a problem . . . (as long as the Goat was out of the body shop by then I thought to myself). He ran down a list of people his team had talked to during my background check. He said that my mother spoke highly of me and said I was a good boy!!! Jesus Christ, I would hope to shout my own mother would have something nice to say about me!! However, I was grateful she hadn't shot me down in order to keep me working on the ranch! The next guy they talked to was Father Gerald Stanley, my old philosophy prof from St Thomas . . . . He must have been the only guy at the Sem. the day they went up to Kenmore, and my pucker factor level immediately approached that of being on Dad's Cat up on Chinook pass! Father Stanley had spent several years trying to force feed us the existential ideologies of Nietzche, Kierkegaard, and Sartre where we studied such useful topics such as the essence of existence and consciousness . . . . When he occasionally gazed out upon us after proposing some crazy notion he thought we might be able to comment on intelligently he was usually met with a classroom of blank faces. So quite often he had to revise his terminology (dumb it down) to fit the crowd. His next sentence might begin like this: "OK, a big Maple Tree down by St Edwards fell over last night, but everyone was asleep and no one heard the crash . . . So, did it really make a sound if no one heard it?" As usual, most of us missed the point altogether and started asking questions like; "Was it that big one by the fountain?" or "Which way was the wind blowing 'cause that would really affect how far the sound would travel . . . ?" He was a kindly man and kept his cool even in the face of overwhelming stupidity. I always felt that he was looking right at me when he seemed to be most overwhelmed at our lack of comprehension. When the WSP personnel folks told him I was applying to be a trooper I could just see him cringe while choking back a laugh and then asking; "Are you seriously thinking about giving Rick a gun and a fast car too . . . . ? Well I hope you're self insured 'cause no one will ever write you guys a policy if he's on the force!!" Well that's what I thought anyway . . . . Luckily for me, Father Stanley lied like a senator facing an ethics probe and apparently had a couple complimentary things to say about me. I just thank God that none of the other profs. who knew me better were there that day. Then Maltby asked me the $64 question: "Why do you want to be a state trooper?" I knew I couldn't admit to my true aspiration which was only to get to drive one of those Plymouth Interceptor's with a 440 Magnum under the hood as fast as I wanted anytime and anywhere, as that probably wouldn't be received well. So on the spot I made up some comparison that my seminary training had been preparing me for a life full of altruistic service to the souls of my parishioners and a state patrolman's job was to likewise selflessly administer to and ensure the safety of the fine upstanding motorists of Washington State . . . . After almost gagging on my own words I thought to myself that I hadn't heard of too many parish priests who routinely had to pull out a hogleg, mace, or cuffs to protect themselves from a wayward parishioner. Anyway, apparently that was a satisfactory response and after he grilled me about all the tickets on my record he said he would be in touch in a couple weeks. I left not knowing which way this was going to go but had a feeling that my ridiculous "degree" would probably trump all the red flags regarding my personality and driving record.

Back at home my Mom seemed somewhat bewildered at my possible new career path and asked why I hadn't sought out her advice before taking this big step. I diplomatically tried to tell her that several months earlier Dad had quietly advised me that he would support me if I wanted to be an apple rancher or join him in his land leveling business . . . . I did enjoy operating the D8 from time to time but Jesus that thing was rough riding, hot as hell with that big old torque converter right under your feet, and the noise from those clattering track pads was horrendous! I told her that Dad had strongly urged me to find a profession with a retirement system and paid medical . . . . I believe brother Ray got the same speech when he came home from the Air Force. He really did not have to convince me how unstable and tenuous the life of a farmer was after I saw firsthand, year after year, how every new weather system brought potential ruin to this year's crop. Anyway, I spent a couple more weeks doing ranch work before the inevitable phone call from Lieutenant Maltby. All he said was they had an opening for a communications officer cadet in Tacoma radio and could I report to Olympia Fleet and Supply on October 1st? Little did I realize that I was about to embark on a surreal trip into the real world where so many of the people I met and events I witnessed would be indelibly burned into my consciousness never to be forgotten.

The body shop had bad news. They had to take my Goat to another facility that had a frame straightener and it would be another couple weeks. Debbie offered me her car to use in the interim and I arrived at Olympia Fleet and Supply bright and early on Oct. 1st, 1971 driving her '64 Nova SS. Of all the people to meet in the waiting room was a fellow classmate from St Pauls in Yakima, John Broome. We had a nice reunion and discussed nun atrocities before being ushered in to receive our indoctrination speech and new uniforms and equipment. One of the other new cadets and his family was from Tacoma and he was being assigned to Yakima and couldn't believe that a single guy from Yakima was being assigned to his hometown. A third cadet was just back from Viet Nam, noticed our consternation over the assignments and advised us not to say anything about this obvious screw up. He had learned his lesson the hard way in the Army about the perils of pointing out obvious oversights to the brass . . . . We deferred to his sound advice . . . So I was sent home with a box of coats, hats, badges, buttons, shoes, and uniforms. They said I was on the payroll but didn't have to report to Tacoma Radio until Oct. 15th. Back on the ranch it was pear picking time and those two weeks flew by with all the work.

I had already found a studio apartment just off 38th St in Tacoma for
$50.00 a month. I was only there for a couple of months before one of
the other radio cadets, Nick Brewer, was selected for the 48th Trooper
Basic Academy Class. His former roommate and fellow cadet, Rick
Nelson, asked me to be his new roommate in the same apartment
complex I was in. It was a two bedroom two bath unit and I finally
had a real bed to sleep in instead of that crummy hide-a-bed couch in
my studio unit. Rick and I hit it off immediately and spent most of our
free time together. Rick liked Rainier Beer and I was still trying to get
over my Blatz complex. Within a few weeks however I was matching
him beer for beer as we tossed the empties behind the couch not to be
removed until they started spilling out the ends and got in the way too
much. We dined on some of the finest boxes of dried out food of the
day including: Hamburger Helper, Tuna Helper, Mac & Cheese mixed
with leftover Hamburger or Tuna Helper, Top Ramen mixed with all
three, etc., etc. More often than not we just went out for pizza then
brought enough back to have for breakfast and lunch the next day . . .
it was a simple yet elegant life.

My first day at work was somewhat comical since I wasn't at the office
for three minutes before I was sent home. No one had instructed me
on the finer points of putting a uniform together and I had left off
several of the brass buttons on my sleeves and epaulets which I had
deemed redundant to hold my shirt together. My new supervisor
wasn't impressed and just told me to go back home and don't return
until I was in uniform. After studying the uniform a bit more I soon
got all the buttons attached in the proper manner. Back at work I was
introduced to the wild and crazy life of a communications officer. I
was shown how to key a mike, by foot or by hand, what to say on
the radio, how to answer, and where to log it. This was before the era
of automatic recorders and we had to type every single transmission
from a trooper and to a trooper verbatim as it was being said into a
radio log. I was a fair typist but this was high test and you never had
the time or luxury of looking at the keyboard while logging some of
the long winded proclamations from some of the troops. The craziest
piece of "modern" equipment was the huge teletype machines. I
really enjoyed learning how to use them to run driver's checks and

looking for wants and warrants on various violators the troopers were inquiring about. You just typed in the driver's name and D.O.B. onto the keyboard and the machine kicked out a yellow tape full of appropriately spaced holes about ten inches long. Then you just peeled that off, placed it in another receptacle, clamped it down, typed in what type of checks you wanted on this guy, pushed a button then sat back and waited as the machine sucked that tape into its guts. When the response came back there was a tremendous thrashing noise from the teletype: keys and rollers were jumping and clattering all over the place, as it ground out a response to your inquiry on a piece of paper. This was pretty high test back then and I was always thrilled to get on the air to advise some lucky trooper that his violator had a warrant in Arizona for trespassing or some similar non-extraditable offense. We also had a public counter to help the walk-in traffic where we handed out accident reports, sold permits, tried to answer general questions, etc. Apparently this office had also been the site of the DMV for many years where the public came to renew their driver's licenses. The DMV had recently moved to another site and the WSP had erected large signs out on the street and on the front door advising the public that they could no longer renew their licenses here and gave directions to the new DMV location. Regardless, there were always a few folks who did not read the signs or just could not comprehend how the DMV, which had been there since 1938, could just up and move away like that. As a result, several times a day citizens would come to the counter and hand me their old license and ask to renew it. Well the motto of the WSP is "Service with Humility" but after several months of this I just wanted to take those licenses they handed me, rip them up, slap them in the face ala Moe on the Three Stooges, and sternly inform them they shouldn't be allowed to drive anyway if this attempted license renewal was an indicator of their driving skills . . . . But my priestly seminary training kicked in and I never did. Thus began my personal 33 year battle of dealing with the motoring public of Washington State. I always provided the "Service" when called to do so but there were moments when the "Humility" aspect suffered somewhat. The other type of walk in traffic were those who wanted to complain about a ticket or wanted to know how the radar worked. When they realized I was merely a cadet and not a real policeman I would be forced to summon one of the Detachment Sergeants from the back to come and help them. One of the Sergeants was a bit volatile and after sending back a complainer to him we often would soon hear a very animated and loud one-way conversation occurring in his office. This was always followed be a brief period of silence and soon we would view the two of them walking out together all friendly. This same sergeant had quite a colorful history including one famous episode I still laugh about. There had been a freezing rain downpour in the Fife area and the ole Sarge drug himself out of the office to go help with all the accidents in the vicinity of the Puyallup River Bridge. In those years the fusees (road flares) still had a spike in one end originally designed to be stuck in road sign posts, trees, guard rail posts, etc., near an accident scene after being lit. Well ole Sarge was standing in the road near a multi-car pileup on the bridge with one of those lit flares in hand waving it around and warning traffic to slow down and stop since the road was completely blocked ahead. The roadway was so slick no one could get over 10 mph or so. However, one intrepid motorist managed to get up to 15 mph and was fast approaching the flare wielding sarge. When the driver finally noticed the arm waving patrolman who was by now yelling quite specific profanities at him, he locked up his brakes but continued sliding towards him. Due to the slope of the bridge decking his car started to rotate and just as he went spinning slowly past the flare wielding and still screaming patrolman, the driver should have heard a muffled thump on the rear of his big old Cadillac. As his Fleetwood, still slowly rotating, slid on down the slope of the bridge, it must have been quite a sight with a burning flare professionally impaled in its trunk lid. By the time ole Sarge had slid his way down to this moron, whose Caddy was now resting quietly facing the wrong direction against the guardrail on the low side of the bridge, he deftly pulled the fusee out of the bodywork, chucked it into the river, and hoped the driver hadn't noticed his temporary trunk ornament. I never knew what really went on back in his office but whatever happened was a good lesson for me nonetheless. I learned to always end a shouting match with a citizen by being the first to offer the olive branch even though you knew the other guy was a flaming idiot . . . This tactic seemed to lessen the severity of the inevitable "bitch letter" that was soon to follow . . . . And man, did I get a lot of bitch letters!

One of the finest men I have ever known was also one of those detachment sergeants in Tacoma back then; his name was Lorne Hughes 137. Lorne had been a sailor during WWII and had been badly burned during combat in the Pacific. Lorne was in the hospital for quite some time but finally recovered enough to join the WSP back in 1946. In early 1972, Lorne was issued a brand new Dodge Polara with the 440 Magnum. They came equipped with two huge exhaust pipes that year which made it the best sounding and loudest patrol car in the history of the WSP. When Lorne drove into the 38th St. office he really knew how to make an entrance! First we would hear him key his mike followed by the background roar of his 440 being floorboarded and the secondary jets on the huge Carter carburetor dumping large amounts of fuel into the engine causing it to sound something like . . . wah—WAHH—WAAAHHH!!! While this was happening he would simultaneously scream into his mike, **"137 TACOMA!!!!!"** Of course we would initially think he had just been shot or was chasing a bank robber or something equally disastrous and would excitedly answer . . ."**TACOMA 137 GO AHEAD!!**" . . . Then after a slight pause for effect he would calmly and quietly announce on the radio . . . ."At the office, 137." Even after I got used to this routine it never failed to get my blood pumping for a second or two the next time. Another trooper, Dick Bush 711, had a rather unique way to call radio. Rather than saying 711 Tacoma his call in was: "O Thank Heavens Tacoma." (For those of you not getting this one that was the early catch phrase for *7-Eleven Stores* many years ago). Lastly, and I won't mention any names with this character, but we had a trooper who didn't use his badge number or any other snappy phrase while calling in . . . I shudder to think of this even today, since I used to go on training rides with this guy and had put my lips near or on his patrol car microphone from time to time when I ran a driver's check for him . . . . Anyway, he would occasionally rip a huge wet fart into his mike while it was pressed somewhere near his "nether" regions and then just say "Tacoma" . . . . I know, very disgusting and juvenile, but when we heard this in radio we knew who it was and as trained professional dispatchers we would calmly respond with his badge number as if nothing unusual had just happened, do whatever task he asked for, then laugh so hard for several minutes that nothing got done. More on some serial farting later . . .

In those years the WSP required cadets to ride with troopers for a whole shift as often as possible . . . We weren't paid for those shifts and they were in addition to your 40+ hour work week in radio. We were led to believe that if we ever wanted to go to the Academy that as 'often as possible' meant around 32 to 40 more hours a month . . . . At the time I had no problem with this requirement and probably went way over the extra 40 hours a month many times. I thought riding with troopers was pretty exciting since they used to let me talk on the radio and light flares at accident scenes . . . . woo hoo!! Several years later a group of new cadets going through the Academy filed a class action lawsuit about not getting paid for all the extra hours they had to put in while there. They won, and as a result all future Academy classes lasted a couple months longer. Additionally, when pre-academy cadets rode with troopers it was considered a regular shift and they got reimbursed for it . . . . Some 42 years later I'm still waiting for my check for the 1,280 hours of work I never got paid for . . . .

Some of the troopers we had to ride with were a real pain in the ass; they would make you stand at attention before a ride while they inspected your brass, buttons, shoeshine, uniform, badge, haircut, hat, etc., etc. The ride itself with these kind of guys was pure hell; it was a nonstop quiz fest on all the obscure RCW's for the whole eight hour shift while having to address them as Sir or trooper so and so every time you spoke . . . . Thankfully after our six month probation was up we could ride with whomever would take us. One of the troopers I rode with the most was Bruce Hume 387. He was a wily seasoned veteran driving my dream car, a 1970 Plymouth Fury III with the 440 Magnum under the hood and man could Bruce drive it! He worked the peninsula beat, Narrows Bridge, Gig Harbor, Purdy area but we always seemed to end up on some narrow power line road around the Tacoma Industrial Airport. Late at night while negotiating one of these narrow twisty dirt roads at warp speed, Bruce would suddenly turn his lights off . . . . Now you'd think he might slow down somewhat but Bruce had owl-like night vision and it was full speed ahead . . . I honestly could not see a thing and really began to doubt if I had what it takes to be a trooper if these were the skills necessary to do the job. Eventually, the lights would come on, including the spotlight, as we came to a sliding stop usually in front of some hapless teenagers drinking beer in the back of a pickup or engaging in various forms of "carnal knowledge" with each other. Bruce would always end up writing several tickets for minor in possession while giving stern lectures to the others on the various forms of VD they had probably just contracted. Although these crazy late night driving escapades were very exciting what I really enjoyed the most was visiting the Span Café. This was a tiny little restaurant just West of the Narrows Bridge and normally was closed around 9pm. Bruce was very good friends with Larry the owner and had a key to the place. We would "open" it up, sometimes at 3am, and have a late dinner. Bruce knew how to heat up the deep fat fryer and soon had shrimp, chicken, or fish and chips boiling away in the oil. I thought that life couldn't get much better than this . . . but wait, there's more! About an hour later Bruce would usually get a craving for fresh donuts and coffee. He had more friends at a bakery on the other side of the bridge where they started cooking the donuts around 4am. At least this place was open and we'd head right into the kitchen and help ourselves to donuts just coming out of the deep fat fryer . . . . We weren't total slobs though . . . we'd let them cool for a minute and then sprinkled powdered sugar on them . . . Gawd they were good . . . and they always had the best fresh coffee brewing . . . . my mouth is watering right now. I always wondered if the age old stereotype of the cop and donut shop routine didn't originate with Bruce at that bakery? . . . It was after nights like this that I decided I could not have made any better decision in my life than to join the WSP!

One day we were at the shooting range for the trooper's quarterly qualifications when I was privileged to witness the superb shooting skills Bruce possessed as well. After he had completely shot out about a two inch round portion of paper in the middle of his target, all in the 10 ring, and had secured his Master's pin once again, he aimed his 357 at his neighbors target to get rid of his last few rounds. This fellow trooper was a decorated Korean War soldier and was extremely proud of his perfect shooting skills; like Bruce he always got all his rounds in a two inch circle in the center of the target eventually leaving a neat blown out hole. Anyway, Bruce purposefully placed a few of his rounds in his neighbor's target 7 or 8 ring ruining his perfect score. When we walked up to score the targets I heard language so foul and vile from that poor guy that even my Dad would have winced a little. There was some payback for Bruce though shortly after this episode when the old "what goes around comes around" rule finally caught up to him. I was riding with him on one of his powerline road sorties when he again turned his lights off . . . By this time I had come to realize that he normally only did this on night's with a really bright moon which gave him a slight advantage. However, it was overcast on this particular evening and he had no sooner doused the lights when there was a big thump and we were suddenly spun sideways. When we got out to investigate we immediately saw the offending stump root sticking out into the road behind us. There was quite a bit of damage to the right front fender and the bumper was pushed in a bit. Bruce was quite cool and collected and we immediately drove to Paul's Chevron in Purdy where Bruce was good friends with the owner Paul who just happened to be an excellent body and fender man. We spent the next several hours watching Paul hammer, beat, pound, sand, grind, and bondo that fender back into shape. He finished it with a coat of WSP white paint but told Bruce to come back the next night when he would sand it and give it another coat. I was beginning to realize that there was a helluva lot of unknown aspects to being a state trooper that no one had told me about . . . Bruce had a heck of a time pronouncing my last name so he just shortened it to Carnal Knowledge and eventually just Carnal; I was **so** pleased when my new nickname caught on with everyone thanks to Bruce. He also thought my Italian heritage was hilarious and I would frequently find official looking documents in my mailbox, apparently from him, including such items as: "Application For 2 Joina Mafia" that included a long list of stereotypical bullshit questions and a newspaper ad describing the benefits of Italian snow tires: "Dago thru Mud, Dago thru Snow and when Dago Flat Dago Wop, Wop, Wop." I just figured it was some kind of rookie cadet hazing and tried not to get too upset about it even though I was really pissed! Another senior trooper who had been around since the thirties told me that I would never have been hired back then since I was a Catholic, my name ended in a vowel, and I wasn't a Mason . . . I guess things had changed. Bruce passed away just last year and I sure miss the big guy!

One of Bruce's best friends was a great guy named Mario Parisio 325, il mio paisan, (my countryman) and I rode with him a lot out on the Gig Harbor Peninsula. I'll always remember one incident where we had just pulled a guy over out on SR-16 near Purdy for speeding . . . . As we were walking up to the car some dipshit riding a chopper goes by with a real loud exhaust . . . Mario tosses me his 4W book and as he's running back to his patrol car yells at me to give the speeder a warning ticket then took off after the chopper. Well, I had never contacted a violator before so there I was with no gun, all by myself, hoping this guy wasn't a psycho . . . Luckily he was just a nice family man so I took my time printing out a real nice warning ticket and sent him on his way. I couldn't even see where Mario had gone to so I just sat down on the freeway embankment and watched as passing motorists stared at me as I sat there wearing my stupid looking bus driver's hat . . . . He finally came back after about twenty minutes and was laughing like a madman as he drove up. His first words as I climbed in were "You looked like a real "buffone" (moron) out there!

I had my own "incident" on the Puyallup River Bridge while riding with Trooper Jim Gallagher during a winter storm. We had stopped Northbound on the right shoulder (high-side) of the bridge to investigate a couple minor accidents. Our issued shoes in those years were slick leather soled affairs that worked great on dry pavement but not so well on compact snow, covered with a fresh dose of freezing rain. I had been instructed to grab a handful of fusees out of the trooper's trunk and place them on the road to warn oncoming traffic of the mess ahead. Well, I got to the trunk OK but as soon as I didn't have anything to hold onto I was off for a nice evening slide to the bottom of the freeway across all three lanes of traffic . . . Thankfully, no traffic was moving since it was a virtual skating rink or I would have been creamed. The slope was quite steep and try as I might with those slick shoes I couldn't get back up to his patrol car or anywhere for that matter. So I tried to look professional as I laid out a nice flare path on the bottom of the freeway where there weren't any accidents while never letting go of the guard-rail. Eventually, the Highway Dept. came through the area with a sand truck and I was finally able to crawl my way back up to the patrol car. The trooper hadn't even noticed I was missing for the last twenty minutes but commented on all the fresh fusee burn-holes on my jacket, shoes, and pants and assumed I had been doing something useful.

Another character I spent a lot of time riding with during my cadet years was Don Lee 788. Had he not chosen to be a trooper Don could have easily been a stand-up comic in Vegas, hosted the Tonight Show, or starred in his own comedy sit-com . . . He was probably the funniest guy I've ever known and could get away with saying the most outlandish things to violators without getting a bitch letter. I guess it was his delivery style because later on when I tried those same lines on violators I stopped I was always met with icy stares and promises they would have my badge. Don worked out in the Puyallup Valley where the big trooper hang out was The Daffodil Bowl. We seemed to spend an inordinate amount of time at this bowling alley where Don would regale the other troopers with perfect renditions of his latest outrageous violator contacts, usually the slobbering drunk variety. He remembered and recounted every single statement, mannerism, voice inflection, burp, fart, slurred word, etc., etc., until all of us were just laughing and crying and making a scene for all the bowlers.

In that era violators were occasionally issued a written warning called a 4W. If the moving violation wasn't too severe or the car just had a headlight out or a cracked windshield or something they would be issued the 4W instead of a citation. The violator didn't have to do anything with it and we just told them it served as a reminder to slow down or get whatever was broken fixed. Don however viewed issuing 4Ws as an opportunity to try out his latest comedy sketch. Most troopers would explain what the 4W was for and what to do with it as the violator was signing. Don however, would just hand the violator his 4W ticket book and tell them to sign it . . . . Usually they just signed it with no questions asked and went on their way since right at the top of their copy it clearly stated it was a warning ticket. About one out of twenty violators didn't read that part and after getting their copy from Don would turn and ask him: "What am I supposed to do with this thing?" This was the response Don was waiting for; he would immediately launch into his best Don Rickles imitation and loudly state: "I don't care what you do with it mister, you can line your shoes with it or wall-paper your ceiling . . . . It's just a **warning ticket!**" I thought this gag was just hilarious and each time he used it I'd have to turn back towards the patrol car so the violator wouldn't see me laughing . . . . This was one of Don's lines that I tried out a number of times later in my career but was usually rewarded with a bitch letter for my efforts. The hats cadets had to wear in those years resembled a bus driver's cap and Don would not be seen in public with one of us wearing it. He always gave me his winter "fur" arctic hat to wear when I rode with him (even in the summer) and banned me from ever wearing the other in his presence.

One early day shift I was riding with Don after I had just worked the graveyard shift in radio. I did OK for a couple hours but after breakfast at the Daffodil Bowl I started to fade a bit . . . . I was rudely awakened by screeching brakes and tires during a violent U-turn and Don was screaming that some son of a bitch had just fired several shots at us . . . He was driving like crazy after someone I couldn't quite see, that he said was just around the next corner . . . Man, I was frantic and was trying to remember how to get Don's shotgun out of its boot under the front seat in case I had to use it. Cadets were not armed and had no firearms training whatsoever but I was familiar with shotguns from years of hunting pheasants. After a couple of minutes Don saw how nervous I was getting, slowed down and started to laugh uncontrollably . . . Shortly thereafter he launched into a reenactment skit of all my supposed frightened reactions using all the colorful adjectives and metaphors of a New York comic . . . . During his little monologue he was able to masterfully capture the look of fear on my face, the tremble in my voice, the shaking of my hands, the smell of fear about my person, etc., etc . . . then finished with an admonition and stern warning about the pitfalls of trying to work 16 hours straight! Of course none of his descriptions were true other than the one about how bad I smelled . . . . Later at coffee, which usually included some of the regulars like: Jim Gleason, Byron Rake, Pat Halliday, Bob Lucas, or Mark Pitttenger, I had to sit through another retelling of the episode . . . Of course Don ramped it up a couple notches for effect and had me screaming like a school girl while I simultaneously wet and soiled my uniform pants . . . What a guy!

There was another trooper in the valley detachment who was a lot like Don except for one small distinction . . . . He saw a Sasquatch run across the road one night out near Eatonville and then **"Talked publicly about it!"** He also managed to get a plaster cast of its footprint . . . . Later, a photo of his son holding that plaster cast up, along with a big feature story about the sighting, was soon published in the *Tacoma News Tribune*. Needless to say coffee time at the *Daffodil Bowl* was never the same after this incident and Don was in rare form for several years recounting all the hilarious details of this event over and over. On a more disgusting note, the trooper who saw the Sasquatch once related to me a horrible incident when I was riding with him. He had arrested a stewardess from a major airline for DWI and had placed her in the backseat of his patrol car un-handcuffed. While waiting for the tow truck she became enraged and began screaming and shouting obscenities at the trooper. Eventually she really went off the deep end . . . . She defecated on his back seat, then smeared her shit all over the plexi-glass shield in his patrol car . . . . The coup de grace was when she took her finger and scrolled in her own excrement "Fuck You Pig" backwards so the trooper could read it from the front seat . . . . I guess that was her way of proving that she wasn't "that" drunk but I think her delivery method was a bit over the top . . . . Just another story about dealing with the wonderful motoring public we all had to serve . . . . Later in Don's career he ran into a burning building to save some folks inside and was awarded the WSP's highest award for bravery . . . He was quite a guy! Like Bruce, Don also passed away way too soon just a couple years back . . . . Everyone who knew him, and especially me, misses him dearly.

On a quiet November morning in 1971 I was suddenly indoctrinated into the violent world of what really being a state trooper is all about. I was riding with Trooper Sam Shimko 740 and we had just taken the Tillicum exit Northbound on I-5. We stopped just short of the stop sign at the end of the exit so we could watch the railroad crossing on the other side of the freeway. Sam told me this was a good place to catch people blowing through the train crossing when the red lights were flashing and warning bells were ringing as a train approached. Sure enough in a couple minutes we heard the loud horn from an approaching Northbound train, saw the crossing lights start flashing and heard the ding, ding, ding, of the crossing bell. When the train was about 50 yards from the crossing a guy in a '69 Chev Nova, who had been stopped on the freeway exit ramp on the Southbound side, suddenly pulled out of line, turned right, and stopped right on the tracks in the middle of the crossing . . . . Sam and I both simultaneously shouted **SHIIITTTT** as the engine plowed into the Nova around 45 mph! I remember seeing all the glass on the passenger side of the car exploding out like spray . . . . At first the train just pushed the car down the tracks for 100 ft or so; then the rear end of the car hit a switching box which pirouetted it into the air spinning it around several times to the right landing on its wheels in a blackberry bramble. Sam was on the radio in a heartbeat advising everyone we had just witnessed a car-train at Tillicum and needed assistance. When we got over to the car the train was still moving since it takes them awhile to get stopped. I'll never forget the scene inside that car; the driver's legs were trapped under the dashboard under the steering wheel but he was all stretched out with his head resting in the right corner of the rear seat. There was some involuntary body movement but it was pretty obvious he was gone. It looked as if the forces of the impact had somehow stretched his body out and dislocated all his joints since he looked like he was now 7 feet tall. By the time the fire trucks got there he had no pulse and his pupils were dilated. This was the first dead guy I had ever seen and to witness his death was something else . . . . We were so busy initially that I didn't really have time to mentally process the whole scene right away. Later at the hospital, with him lying on a table, it started to bother me a little although I tried mightily not to show it. It had shaken Sam up a little too but he put on the brave face for me and even asked if I wanted to go get a greasy cheeseburger covered in Ketchup when we were done. The driver was a young Infantry soldier from Ft Lewis and had just gotten his orders to Viet Nam; apparently he became overwhelmed that morning about his survival prospects over there.

When word got out in the "radio cadet" world that I had witnessed a fatal I became somewhat of a temporary celebrity. Usually just going to a fatal scene, even after all the bodies had been removed, carried significant bragging rights about what a seasoned veteran one had become. Witnessing one was just unprecedented and I even had senior troopers ask me about what it was like.

Not long after the car-train I finally got the call from the body shop in Yakima that my GTO was finally ready. Although I sincerely appreciated Debbie letting me drive her '64 Nova I was anxious to get back in my Goat. The first day I drove it to work I was accosted in the parking lot by a couple senior troopers. Although I didn't expect them to immediately lavish praise on my choice of wheels I thought they might at least offer up some sort of veiled compliment . . . . Unfortunately, that was not the case. The exact quote was: "Jesus H. f***ing Christ, this orange piece of shit looks like some kind of French whorehouse pimp-mobile . . . !" Of course that remark was followed by loud guffaws of uncontrollable laughter from the other trooper . . . I was slightly stunned but even though my tenure with the outfit had been brief I was already starting to catch on to WSP humor. Eventually I countered with: "Yeah I know, but my girlfriend bought it for me and I hated to complain too much about the color." By their subdued grunted acknowledgement and sideways looks at each other I could tell that my improvised response was satisfactory and I was allowed to pass. Shortly thereafter I was confronted by Sam Shimko out in the lobby one evening. He was in his civvies and told me to come out into the parking lot with him. Parked right next to my goat was his brand new green 1971 Dodge Charger. Man, it was gorgeous but I immediately noticed that it was one of the new "plain jane" Chargers with an automatic and the 383 V8 instead of the HEMI under the hood. Back in the office Sam took me aside and advised me in no uncertain terms that I would be the world's biggest pussy if I didn't run him title for title in my goat. Of course this immediately scared the shit out of me as I was sure he must be wearing a wire and was setting me up for some kind of undercover cadet ethics probe. I initially told him I couldn't do it but he started with the chicken clucking noises and various pussy remarks so I told him I'd think about it. I knew his Charger was an old ladies car and there was absolutely no doubt in my mind I could wipe his ass with my 370 hp Ram Air IV Goat . . . . He had put me in quite a *Catch 22* situation but after much consideration I told him I just couldn't do it; I lied and said I knew my car was almost as fast as his but that he was no doubt the better driver with all his years of high speed patrol car driving and would ultimately win . . . . He seemed placated but later told everyone I was a chicken-shit pussy anyway . . . . What a guy . . . .

My assigned "coach" during my cadet time was Trooper Bob Orth 752. He was a terrific guy and I learned all the daily nuts and bolts of what really being a trooper was all about from him. He politely tried to steer me away from emulating some of the more extreme habits and tactics of some of the more "zany" troopers I had ridden with. He also warned me about the "up-tight" ladder climber crowd; these were the guys who applied Glo Coat floor wax to their patrol car tires and dashboards, regularly re-baked their gun leather in the oven after coating it with Flecto Verathane or Plasolux, washed their patrol cars twice a day, and went home and changed their uniforms, in the middle of their shift, if they sweated in them a little . . . Bob told me he really did not want me to develop into an anal retentive, brown-noser like those guys . . . . I felt like telling him that he was preaching to the choir and that he really did not have to pursue this message too far with me. I was already well aware of these kinds of individuals from my seminary days and already knew how to steer clear of them. Bob liked to give me lots of hands on training when I rode with him; he always let me do all the talking on the patrol car radio, write the tickets, and fill out the accident reports. Soon he was even letting me contact violators which was a big no-no but much appreciated by me. Unfortunately, while I was getting a violator's signature on a warning ticket one night, Bob's supervisor drove by and saw me out there. I didn't get in trouble but Bob got his ass chewed pretty good. Undaunted, he still let me contact violators but was just smarter about it and we didn't get caught again. Later, Bob let me drive his patrol car and pull violators over but he always did the initial contact. All this "extra" on the job training was a huge advantage for me when I eventually went to the Academy; some of the other guys in my class were really green blank slate types who struggled with the basics because no-one had ever taken the time to prepare them for the real world.

I learned a huge lesson one night about always setting your parking brake while riding with Trooper Dave Drakeford 252. Dave had stopped a car Southbound on I-5 near Ft Lewis. He had positioned his patrol car correctly with the front end angled out towards the lanes of travel in case it got rear ended by a drunk it wouldn't strike us or the violator's car. As we were walking up to his car I thought I noticed some unusual movement behind me; when I looked I was horrified to see Dave's patrol car just about going into the ditch backwards behind us . . . I yelled to Dave and we both started running after it . . . It had a mind of its own though and with the steering wheel still cranked to the left it just missed going off the shoulder and began a very slow arc back out onto the freeway in reverse; it crossed all three lanes and just missed scraping the new jersey barrier with its right side. More miraculously, it wasn't hit by any other cars as it came right back across all three lanes again headed straight for the violator's car that Dave had just stopped. God was with old 252 that night 'cause his brand new '71 Dodge just missed that guy's car, backed on down over the shoulder and continued down a little incline coming to rest up against the freeway fence with the engine still idling away. Dave told his violator to just leave then we ran down to his Dodge. Once back up on the shoulder he started playing with the shifter and saw that the indicator would indicate it was in park but the transmission would occasionally drop back into reverse if you hadn't shoved the selector all the way to the end of its travel and into a little detent. Good lesson for both of us but Dave immediately manned up and admitted he hadn't set his park brake which would have precluded this episode from ever happening. To this day I set my park brake in whatever I'm driving no matter where I am even in the garage; this drives my wife crazy as she often drives off and can't figure out why the car is so sluggish and then later smells something getting hot . . . .

Working radio was where you really learned how to politely deal with the public, usually on the phone. During inclement weather on the mountain passes, the phone rang constantly. We would rotate phone duties and working radio every couple hours with the other communication officers so we didn't go nuts dealing with the morons on the phones. Most of the calls were in the same vein: how far is the snow coming down . . . . is it slick . . . . when will it not be slick . . . . can I make it without snow tires . . . . how long will it take to get to Yakima . . . what pass do you recommend . . . should I put my chains on now or wait till I get up there, etc., etc. Right in the middle of the weather question barrage someone would inevitably call and want to complain about a rude trooper who just gave them a ticket for driving too fast in the snow . . . When I told them to contact the district court to contest the ticket they would immediately want to talk to my supervisor since I was now being rude too; then they would inform me that I was a public servant and they paid my salary . . . . blah, blah, blah . . . It just never ended. When it was quieter some of the calls were more of a learning experience for me; people would have questions about how far a load could extend past the end of a trailer, how many tons a particular sized truck could haul, when did you have to display gross weight signs on a pickup, how bald did a tire have to be before it had to be replaced, etc., etc. I usually didn't know the answer but told them I'd call them right back after I looked it up. All of us got real familiar with the RCW Codebook which contained all the traffic laws for the State of Washington. For you pilots the RCW was the FAR/AIM for an aspiring trooper cadet.

Our radio communications crew was evenly split between trooper cadets and permanent civilian communication officers. Some of these guys were WWII veterans and a bit on the crusty side. Since they did not have to worry about qualifying for the next academy class I noticed that their telephone courtesy procedures were considerably more brief, curt, and to the point. They really didn't care if they got a bitch call back or letter so just hanging up on some of the more irritating callers was just accepted procedure. Of course when that person called right back these guys would turn to me and say, 'Rick, can you take this, I gotta hit the head . . . ' One of the coolest was Charles Duffy. He was a no-nonsense veteran who I had the privilege of working graveyard with several times. Usually around 3am he would leave me alone in radio and head downstairs into the furnace room. He was an excellent cook and when he came back up he'd announce on the local frequency for all the graveyard troopers that the 'soup was on'. Very soon we'd have two or three troops in radio enjoying some of Duffy's fantastic Mulligan Stew. A couple of the other permanents spent most of their time worrying about the rumor that the WSP would soon be hiring 'female' radio operators. Man, they really got worked up about that prospect and carried on for hours about all the bad things that would soon occur and how the women would ruin the WSP forever, and the world was coming to an end, etc., etc. Well, they not only soon hired civilian women in radio but when I went to the Academy my replacement was the first female trooper cadet ever hired . . . As the song went in those days: 'The times they are a changin'.'

One of the most memorable days of my cadet time was when I finally got to go for a ride in one of the patrol's airplanes. The Aviation Section had just moved their operation from a small hangar at the Boeing Field Airport to the original Olympia Airport hangar that was built back in 1937 by the Works Progress Administration (WPA) during the Great Depression. It was and still is a great historical monument saluting all the hard work carried out in those years not only by the WPA but also the CCC (Civilian Conservation Corps). If you look at all the old bridges in Washington State you will usually see a year stamped in it and the date is always around the mid to late thirties. Anyway, Lieutenant Dick Swier was the Aviation Commander then and he was polite enough to give me a quick tour of the hangar and its airplanes. At that time they were operating a Piper PA23-250 Aztec, a Beech King Air 90, and an almost new Cessna 182. Then as now the Patrol was responsible for transporting the governor, other state officials, and WSP personnel as needed. The Cessna 182 was used primarily to conduct traffic operations as previously described. My pilot for the day was Trooper Bob Boos and he gave me quite the introduction to "traffic flying". We were to be working South of Chehalis on I-5 and the commute time was a brief fifteen minutes. However, on the way down we veered a little east of course as Bob decided to demonstrate to me an age old principle of thermodynamics which stated that hot air rises. Near Bucoda was a massive open pit coal mine which fired a huge power plant for the local electric company. Its main distinctive feature was a huge smoke stack which continuously sent a massive plume of steam thousands of feet into the air and could be seen a hundred miles away on a clear day (not many of those days ever occurred). So Bob is chatting away smoking a cigarette and seems to be headed straight for the middle of the plume but acts like he doesn't see it. I'd seen this act before while riding with troopers as they drove a 100 mph with one arm resting on the top of the passenger seat, while maneuvering down some twisty county road, trying to get a rise out of the green cadet. When we hit the hot plume we of course got the familiar big bump and temporary zoom climb and pulled a couple positive g's. Having taken Physics in high school and college I knew what to expect and had quietly braced myself for the impact. Bob casually glanced over at me and I think was disappointed at my lack of a reaction. Once more, my previous "training" with Don Lee had saved me from embarrassment. We soon settled in to calling out speeders Northbound on I-5 at the SR-12 junction. Round and round and round we went in the left hand traffic pattern while Bob would occasionally glance at one of his "manual" Minerva stopwatches then calmly call out a speeder to one of the waiting troops on the onramp. Bob had it good in those days; he didn't have to document all the details of every speeder on a kneeboard sheet, as we did a few years later, so he had it pretty easy. He didn't have a built in WSP radio with a push to talk switch on the yoke as we did later and it was inconvenient having to grab the hand mike off the portable bag radio all the time. I guess as pilot workload went we were about even. Bob still tried to get a rise out of me with some wild wingovers and 3 and 4 g turns but I kept it together. However, when he lit up a cigarette, and then executed a few of those maneuvers, I was right on the verge of barfing. Thank God he turned for home about then and finally uttered those words I had been waiting for; "You want to take it?" I tried to remain calm as I politely responded, yes please. Wow, this was awesome . . . I got a little overly concerned about what to do with my feet, as I'd seen Bob jamming those pedals down there quite a bit while working traffic, but he said to ignore them and just keep the wings level. He let me think I landed it although I knew he had control the whole time but I was elated over my first real flying experience. I submitted a flowery thank you IOC (inter office communiqué) to Lieutenant Swier the next day in a not too subtle attempt to "feather" my bed for some future eventuality.

I'll never forget working radio late one evening with fellow cadet Rick Nelson when one of the more "gregarious" troopers, shall we say, pulls up out front with a drunk in his back seat. As he brought her through the lobby, enroute the breathalyzer machine in the squad room, Rick and I couldn't help but notice that she was really hammered and was pretty much being dragged along and didn't seem capable of walking unsupported. If there was ever to be a poster girl for a slobbering— drunk—skank . . . . man, she was it!! Anyway, an hour or so later they came strolling out together and it sure as hell looked like they were having a good time with all the laughing and what appeared to be excessive assistance being proffered by this trooper . . . Rick and I just looked at each other with a silent WTF?? It wasn't even a week later when this same trooper pulls up out front again but this time he was off duty and driving a pretty fancy luxury car. He strolled on in to use the restroom and Rick and I both noticed a faint odor of stale beer following in his wake. I was at the counter and glanced through the large glass entry doors at his big ole ride outside. There was someone in the front seat and when she turned her head towards the front door I half screamed to Rick to come look at this . . . . We were utterly flabbergasted when we recognized her as that same skank this trooper had arrested for DWI last week . . . . And now there're out on a date!! Holy shit . . . was this even legal? He came strolling out of the can, not in the least embarrassed by his actions, and jumped in his car . . . She cuddled up next to him as he roared out of the parking lot!! By this time, Rick and I had seen quite a few strange occurrences but this one was near the top of the list for quite awhile. A year or so later, when I was a rookie trooper working the road in Olympia, radio put out a Tacoma trooper (same guy) chasing a drunk southbound in the northbound lanes of I-5 near Dupont. I didn't know quite what to do, but I knew I wasn't going to go the wrong way on the freeway for any reason . . . . (That mindset changed a few years later) . . . . Anyway, I saw them coming at me at Nisqually, got on southbound and came up alongside the drunk (separated by a ten foot median area) who was still in the northbound inside lane. This trooper was yelling something at me on the radio but all I could think of doing was to pull slightly ahead and shine my spotlight backwards into the drunk's eyes . . . . In those years it was a common practice to replace the patrol car stock spotlight with an airplane landing light and this is what I was using that night. This super bright light in the face caused the drunk to start swerving all over the place and he finally came to a stop in the Median north of Marvin Road. Before I could even get over to them the Tacoma trooper had drug the drunk out of his car, had him cuffed and in his backseat already . . . . This guy was a man of action when he was working but I sure couldn't say much about his choices on the dating scene!

After 18 months of working radio and riding with troopers as often as I could we started to hear rumors that the legislature might be appropriating funds for an academy class in the Spring of 1973. By this time there were six cadets in Tacoma radio and we all started getting real competitive for one of those academy slots. Normal staffing for a day or swing shift in radio was two communication officers who alternated answering radio calls in between phone traffic, counter traffic and teletype work. Suddenly we all became hyper active multi-taskers, especially when the brass was in the office or listening on the radio; we would all try to do the other guy's job if he hesitated for a microsecond on some task to make him look bad. It was pretty impressive just how much work an individual could accomplish when the competitive juices started flowing. If we were paired with one of the civilian radio operators they just sat back, had a smoke and coffee, and watched us put on our act.

I had also been a smoker during those years and had worked up to around a pack and a half a day, and occasionally two during busy shifts in radio. We had been told by our trooper coaches that we had better be in shape before the academy since they would be running our asses off there. I thought I could handle the running if I cut back to a pack a day. Anyway, I went out running with a couple other cadets one night in early January 1973 and immediately saw the error of my ways. I could only jog about two blocks before I had to stop to hock up a couple huge green lugies the size of a small potatoes followed by several minutes of gagging, choking, and coughing. Of course the other cadets viewed this as great news for them, sensed weakness in my camp, and never suggested to me that I might quit smoking. However, I got the message loud and clear on my own and took my last drag on a *Marlboro* shortly thereafter. In those days a **carton** of smokes ran about $3.25 (at least on the Puyallup Indian Reservation) somewhat cheaper than the $8.00 a **pack** now. My running endurance picked up almost immediately and I was soon keeping up with everyone during those painful four and five mile runs. We started playing a lot of basketball after work as well and by late March I felt I was in the best shape of my life . . . . I couldn't have been more wrong!

CHAPTER 5

One evening while working the swing shift in radio the teletype machine suddenly burst into action and cranked out a message regarding an upcoming cadet class. It began: the following patrol cadets have been selected for the 49th Trooper Cadet class . . . Unbelievably, my name was right near the top in alphabetical order and I was just stunned beyond belief. As another cadet and I read and re-read the message we began to question its validity since several "senior cadets" who had more time on than us weren't even on the list. Disturbingly, one cadet, who didn't even meet the minimum cadet time criteria previously laid out by the training section to even be considered for this Academy class, was. The other cadet I was working with that night was just livid about not making the list especially since he was beat out by a new hire that was still very green. The chosen cadet was a big gangly dude who didn't even know how to drive when he first reported to work a few months ago, and was a total blank slate. Shortly after his arrival I was given a direct order by Captain Jack Todd 21, to take him out one day, while on duty, and help him select his first car. I took him around to several used car lots on South Tacoma Way and tried to steer him towards a nice Chevy Chevelle and a real cherry '70 Challenger that we found in his price range. Regardless, about a week later he showed up at work in this gawd-awful Dodge Dart with a huge three foot tall home-made wing-spoiler glued on the trunk lid and of all things a grotesque looking after market water bumper on the front end . . . . Worst of all it had a six cylinder engine with a slush box! . . . Jesus, you couldn't have written a worse prescription for the most dicked up car of all time for a twenty-one year old to be driving! When Captain Todd saw it, he was horrified and called me into his office and chewed **me** out royally for allowing this to happen!! However, the FNG cadet was quite proud of his find and loved it to death. One day we noticed the water bumper seemed to be sagging a bit; upon investigation we discovered its plugs had popped and it had drained out. He finally admitted that he got mixed up with the gas and brake pedals while maneuvering into his parking place and had run into his apartment building.

We finally got orders to report to the University of Washington Hospital for our pre-boot camp physicals where I finally got to meet the 35 other guys I'd be spending the next five months with. It was quite a diverse group of guys that included several combat helicopter pilots from Viet Nam, jocks, school teachers, bartenders, nerds, and even a former divinity student. We were all a bit suspicious of the so called 'doctors' that performed our physical exams that evening; a couple of them looked to be about 19 or 20 and they seemed to spend an inordinate amount of time probing our rectal areas while apparently trying to locate our prostates with their bony index fingers.

Arriving at the Academy in Shelton we were greeted by several instructors who acted out their part as the stereotypical Marine boot camp drill sergeants who soon had us doing push-ups out in the parking lot for not positioning our cars perfectly between the parking stall lines or for displaying hair too long. However, I thought they were quite tame compared to the Nazi SS nuns at St Pauls. I immediately found out I had two other issues to deal with and had to resolve quickly; although I thought I was in good shape I soon realized my six weeks of daily jogging was not near enough conditioning to prepare me for what they were asking of us. Secondly, our primary drill sergeant had in fact been a real drill sergeant in the Marine Corps. He expected us all to already know about marching, counting cadence, making oblique marching turns and reversals, the dress right dress routine, keeping in perfect step, etc., etc. Since I seemed to be the only cadet who had no aptitude or natural 'rhythm' for this sort of thing I was immediately singled out as some kind of spastic farmboy-holy-joe who had no business being in the company of real men. Worse yet, when we had to sing those crazy Marine Corps marching songs while counting cadence such as: "I don't know but I've been told, Eskimo

119

pussy is mighty cold," I just couldn't keep from laughing out loud as I thought they were hilarious. Apparently everyone else was much more mature than I was since I seemed to be the only guy often down in a mud puddle doing twenty push-ups during these exercises after failing to maintain proper decorum. The other huge test of manhood and self control that I failed was the flag formation every morning. I think it was right before breakfast and after our morning run when we had to assemble in the courtyard for the raising of the colors. I thought this was very patriotic and we all rotated being the flag raisers. My downfall was my inability to not react when someone standing close by me in our tight formation ripped a huge fart when all was very quiet during the solemn flag ceremony. Although I never laughed out loud the drill sergeant always seemed to notice my shaking shoulders and smothered-choked laughing. When he suddenly appeared right in my face asking "What seems to be so fu***ng funny cadet Carnevali?" I just said "nothing sergeant" while thinking his need to even ask was even funnier than the farting since there was no doubt he had heard it too. I was finally called before my designated personal training officer-advisor, Sergeant Ed Crawford, to explain my inappropriate behavior. I knew Ed pretty well as he had been a trooper I rode with while I was a radio cadet in Tacoma. I was at a loss for words but finally blurted out that I guess I spent too much time riding with Don Lee . . . . I saw a quick but instantly covered up smile flash on Ed's face where upon he laid into me about my irresponsible-adolescent behavior and how I better get my shit together or else! Then I was suddenly dismissed . . . . No one could ever argue that Don Lee was not an irresistible force of nature.

My roommate was a guy named Joe Cortez. He was already a partially commissioned trooper, although he was limited to stopping trucks for size, weight, and load violations only. He was probably in his mid-thirties and really helped keeping me focused and out of trouble during those hectic days. When we started our firearms training we were all issued temporary gun belts, holsters, cuff cases, ammo pouches, and brass buckles the night before our first shoot. These gun belts were not new and were labeled as field leather as they were pretty beat up and worn out. Apparently our homework was light that night since Joe came up with the brilliant idea that we should polish up our dull looking brass buckles and various buttons with Brasso and should shine up our leather with KIWI shoe polish. During brother Ray's stint in the USAF he had shown me how to "light up" a large can of KIWI then dab the melted liquid polish onto your shoes . . . We tried this method on the field leather and it worked great! By lights out our leather and brass looked brand new! Bright and early on the range the next morning it didn't take long for our drill sergeant to notice how sharp we looked compared to everyone else wearing their dull looking scratched up leather and brass. He immediately had us front and center facing our classmates; instead of praising us he accused us of not being team players and for trying to make everyone else look bad!! He said nothing about our initiative or attention to our uniform appearance which we had been told was the most important aspect of being a trooper. To make matters worse he then chewed out everyone else for not polishing up their leather and made all of them do twenty push-ups in the gravel while we looked on in horror! Man, did we ever get the evil stink eye from the rest of the cadets that day! Needless to say Joe and I didn't do anything out of the ordinary from then on. It was during this first firearms exercise that the cadet with the goofy Dodge Dart dropped his 357 in the gravel while it was cocked which caused our firearms instructor to go apoplectic. He dressed the guy down pretty severely in front of all of us and came very close to assaulting him after the cadet had acted rather indifferently about the whole incident. We later found out that he had to personally apologize to this cadet for losing his temper that day which must have been very painful for him.

Our days at the Academy were normally divided equally between classroom time and outside field exercises. Classroom topics covered the expected police curriculum such as laws of arrest, RCW statutes, various court decisions, gruesome videos of police officers getting assaulted and/or killed, first aid, etc., etc. Outside activities included firearms, self-defense, pursuit driving, violator contact, accident investigation, etc., etc. The first classroom session when we arrived began with a spelling test, which was done in pencil; when we were done we were told to leave them face down on our desks and to go take a break. When we came back we were told to grade our own tests and hand them in. We were not aware that while we were on break the instructor had made copies of all the tests then placed them back on our desks. Of course after class they compared the 'graded' tests to the originals to see if anyone had 'adjusted' their spelling during the self grading process. Although no one in my class cheated on this spelling test, over the years I heard of quite a few cadets who got fired on their first day at the academy after succumbing to such an obvious ploy. While I'm on the subject of test grading I guess I need to relate a disturbing series of events regarding the cadet with the crazy looking Dodge Dart. We took tests sometimes before and after every class; we always exchanged our tests with the guy sitting behind us for grading. He sat behind me and I graded every single one of his tests during our time at the Academy. He failed nearly every single one of his tests and occasionally scored a zero. I was utterly amazed that he was allowed to continue when there were so many other qualified cadets out there who could have replaced him in those first few weeks. But politics trumps common sense sometimes and the WSP sure paid for enabling this guy's ineptitude several years later.

That summer of 1973 was a hot one for Western Washington and as luck would have it the air conditioning system went out in our classroom building. When we occasionally had classes right after lunch it was almost impossible to not fall asleep during riveting lectures on such spellbinding topics such as recent appellate court decisions affecting police work. On one occasion our normal instructor, Trooper Russ Lybecker, was sitting in a chair propped up against a wall in the back of the classroom while an FBI agent presented his class on inter-agency cooperation. At one point the FBI agent was hammering home a significant point and said; "Isn't that right Russ? Russ . . . . Isn't that right? Of course Russ was only human and as we turned to see what was wrong we saw that he had succumbed to the warm room while his lunch was slowly digesting away releasing all those calming endorphins. Another not so funny incident occurred when we had another guest lecturer presenting a class on Mexican American-migrant worker issues. She was a young pregnant Mexican American woman who we all thought had done an excellent job. When done she asked if there were any questions; Rick Phillips asked her a very pertinent innocuous question that seemed relevant . . . . For some unknown reason she burst into tears and ran out of the classroom. We all glared at Phillips for asking a question in the first place, since we wanted to get out of that hot classroom ASAP. We called him a few unprintable names for causing the big ugly yellow shit-storm that we knew was soon going to descend upon us . . . . A few minutes later Sergeant George Wehnes rolls into the classroom livid with rage and didn't even bother to listen to our side of the story. George was a very devout and religious man so there were no screaming expletives; he just told us all that we made him sick, he was disgusted with us, and ordered us out into the parking lot. We all just kept wondering what the hell had she told him?? Anyway, no time to change into our sweats as we were only given two minutes to get out there by our enraged instructor. He soon had us doing every combination of sit-ups, push-ups, eight count burpees, and then had to run several miles in formation. He also stopped us in an area of sharp gravel for more push-ups, all while in uniform during a 90 degree day. After an hour of this torture we were finally allowed to drag ourselves into the showers. It goes without saying that no matter how excellent or ridiculous future guest speakers were we never again asked any questions.

The seating arrangement in the classrooms left a lot to be desired and it never changed in the five months we were there. There were four cadets on the left side of the aisle, and another four cadets on the right in the first row. My seat was the first on the right next to the aisle which means I sat almost directly in front of the podium with the quickest access to it. Whenever an instructor needed a live body to humiliate, demonstrate, or experiment on, I was almost always selected. The first aid instructor once presented a rambling ten minute oration on how to do CPR then called me up cold to perform it on a 'resusci-annie' doll lying on the floor. Of course under pressure I did everything wrong, was chastised severely, and had to do my usual 20 push-ups with one for the governor right next to Annie. Next time I had to dismantle a shotgun after the instructor had given a fast one minute demo showing how it was done. I was familiar with the

Winchester pump but he handed me a Remington and I stumbled around for a few minutes to the delight of all the other cadets who were just thanking God it wasn't them up there making a fool out of themselves . . . Needless to say, I was down doing twenty shortly thereafter. Next time it was our self-defense class indoctrination. We were given instruction in about twenty different holds, takedowns, reach-arounds, arm twisting, grabs, etc., and were somehow expected to remember all those crazy complicated moves in about five minutes. I was called upon to demonstrate some come up from behind takedown maneuver demonstrating the "Koga" method and I had no idea what I was doing. So as soon as I touched the instructor he wheeled around and slam dunked me onto the floor while twisting my wrist until I was forced to cry out in pain. Then I had to do my twenty with what felt like a broken wrist. We all felt the Koga self-defense system was just too complicated and only worked well if you practiced all the time and if the person you were doing it to sat perfectly still and didn't struggle . . . Not too practical in the real world but it was better than the previous WSP self-defense training methods. The old timers had been taught that when they got into a fight to just get their nightstick out and then commence wailing away on their target until it quit moving so much . . . . When their nightstick broke, their back-up weapon was the butt end of their shotgun. I have to say I did use Koga a couple times when I was working the road. It only worked for me when I had to get an unconscious drunk out of their car so the wrecker driver could hook up to it and tow it in. As soon as I put that twisting wrist lock on those drunks, and found that right nerve to press on, man they often just popped right up and I was able to maneuver them into my backseat without too much trouble. We also used to carry ammonia inhalants in our first aid kits and those worked equally well except on the full blown alcoholics.

The food at the Academy was really good and the highlight of the day for me but I wasn't allowed to partake of most of it for almost a month when I first got there. We all had to meet very exacting height and weight standards or we had to suffer the indignity of eating at the "fat table". I was 6'-2' and weighed 205 when I arrived and by today's body mass index criteria I was just right; however back then the WSP said I needed to weigh 195 to be considered fit. Anyway, about five of us had to eat at the 'fat table' for all three meal. It was just fruit for breakfast, soup and crackers for lunch, and a salad with a small piece of lean meat for dinner. Man that just wasn't enough to eat considering all the running and extra push-ups we were doing and I was starving all the time. We got to go home every couple weeks and after picking Debbie up in Yakima we headed straight for the IHOP'S at the Valley Mall where I would wolf down a huge ice cream sundae with the works on it. Later, I would catch up on my sleep on the couch at Deb's place while she typed up all my classroom notes I had accumulated during the last several weeks. Her folks were not very impressed with me as all they ever saw me do was eat and sleep. We had to organize all our notes from each different class into a separate binder which had to be handed in and graded before we could graduate. It was a tremendous help having a full time legal secretary take care of this chore for me and I was looked at quite suspiciously by my advisor when I handed my immaculate notebooks in.

My seminary training in some of the more absurd philosophical disciplines kicked in one afternoon to give me quite a boost (in my mind at least). We were taking a class in public speaking to prepare us for testifying in court, I think. Each of us was assigned a crazy topic, then given a couple minutes to prepare a ten minute speech with no notes. My topic was 'the inside of a light bulb'. In the seminary we used to play at this sort of game all the time, especially right after having endured a thoroughly confusing philosophy session with Father Stanley, so making up ridiculous esoteric or metaphysical non-sense, that sounded impressive, was my strong suit. I presented a speech on the theory of the existential proportionalities of the vacuum that existed in the light bulb, whether time and other various vicissitudes existed in that vacuum, and how that reality was altered when the filament was excited by an electric current. Needless to say, no one was impressed with my babble and from that day forward I was looked upon as some sort of freakazoid by my classmates and instructors. I toned down my rhetoric a bit later in my career when I would be testifying in court during a DWI jury trial. I liked to scan the jury beforehand looking for that one easily 'excitable' or innocent looking juror. When I had some really disgusting and/or gross testimony concerning the behavior of the defendant I would try to look that particular juror right in the eye while describing in morbid detail, using every ultra-graphic adjective I could think of, how the defendant not only criminally defecated and vomited in my back seat but also negligently urinated in his pants in the elevator on the way up to the booking desk . . . This almost always resulted in a good gasp or burst of laughter from the selected juror and stink-eye looks from both the defense attorney and prosecutor.

I thoroughly enjoyed my time at the Academy once I was allowed to eat with everyone else and really looked forward to the day when we got to go out on the local highways and practice pulling people over in patrol cars. Prior to these outings we were always briefed on all the horrible and unexpected things that could occur during a violator stop; but more importantly, when we wrote a ticket, it had to be perfectly printed and extremely neat. In those years appearance and perfect paper work was stressed way too much by the Academy staff and it took many more years before they started concentrating more on officer survival skills instead of that bullshit. Anyway, one day I was pulling over another car load of cadets, who had an instructor driving, for some imaginary violation. It was pouring rain and when I contacted the driver he deflected all knowledge of any violation that might have occurred and started rambling on about his upcoming trip to Reno and wanted me to give him directions there. When I finally got back to my patrol car I was soaked to the bone. I tried to write out the fake ticket as neatly as possible but kept getting it all wet; while I fretted with the paperwork I finally glanced up after a minute or so to discover my violator had disappeared. Shit, now I'm going to get canned for sure . . . I took off down that narrow county road looking down every driveway and into every barn trying to find them. I finally came around a blind corner and there they were. The instructor got out and told me to assume the position and to give him twenty. I tried to maneuver around a huge mud puddle but he directed me right into the middle of it for the push-ups. While I was thus occupied a citizen drove by and must have really wondered how his tax dollars were being spent as he witnessed a bunch of state patrolmen standing around watching while one of them apparently was drowning in a mud puddle. As usual, I never forgot that lesson and never let a violator get away from me . . . . drunk drivers backing-up and hitting my patrol car did occur . . . . but none of them ever drove away without me noticing. That particular instructor, Wayne Small, came back to save my ass several years later when I was trying to get into the Aviation Section; for some unknown reason he gave me a good recommendation and helped me secure a pilot position. Wayne had his own issues one afternoon while investigating a combine rollover in a wheat field near Colfax. The catalytic converter on his '75 Ford Patrol Car caught the wheat stubble on fire under his car and burned it up along with all his WSP notebooks and records he had stored in his trunk . . . Before the computer age dawned this was a huge loss of information.

One afternoon we were being given instruction on how to remove some bad guys embedded in a building after they had committed some heinous act against society. Myself and another cadet were going through the old structure, room by room, trying to ferret out the perpetrators. We were armed with Smith & Wesson 357 revolvers with blank ammunition and were instructed to shoot if we felt threatened. As we worked our way through the building, which was some old WWII Navy barracks and part of the original WSP Academy, we could hear the evil perpetrators mocking us in the distance with snorting pig noises. Their names were Bubba and Billy Bob, twin brothers from a lovely southern coastal state. I had no idea what I was doing as we had not been given any tactical training whatsoever on how to clear a building . . . . We were going to be traffic cops for Chrissakes, why the hell would we ever be inside a building doing real police work? Anyway, as luck would have it, as I crawled around a corner on my hands and knees I spotted Billy Bob, (Academy Instructor Jerry Baxter), peering around another corner with his back to me: the bastard was trying to get a bead on my fellow cadet in order to waste him . . . . Just then he yells out to brother Bubba that "He smells himself some pork!" . . . . In my adrenaline induced state I immediately shot him in the back three times **then** remembered to shout out "State Police, halt or I'll shoot!" Sergeant Baxter turned and calmly addressed me with his nickname for me; "Look Spaghetti, you stupid shit, you're supposed to warn the bad guys first then shoot them . . . . !" Anyway, later during the classroom de-brief I was labeled a back shooting coward and not given credit for apprehending the dangerous felon Billy Bob . . . .

On another afternoon we were practicing investigating injury accidents in the streets around these same old Navy buildings. Some of them were now occupied by a group of highly functioning State Mental Health patients known as "Exceptional Foresters". The Academy staff had sought out their participation to volunteer as accident victims and witnesses while we practiced our mock accident investigations. As we drove up on these staged accident scenes we would be met with these guys and all kinds of conflicting 'first hand eye witness' information as to what happened. It was a real chore sorting out the facts especially when some of the so called 'eye witnesses' actually turned out to be the drivers of the cars involved. The ones wearing baseball caps were often hiding head injuries highlighted by a nice dollop of Ketchup smeared on top of their heads. As comical and outrageous as these scenarios seemed at the time, some of the incidents I was involved with in the real world a few years later made them seem quite realistic in comparison . . . . In fact, some of the real world eye witness testimony from 'normal average' citizens wasn't half as accurate or informative as that from the Exceptional Foresters.

All of our pursuit driving training was conducted on the runways and old taxiways of the Shelton Airport. Prior to each session we had to place the large yellow X's on the approach ends of each runway, to notify pilots they were temporarily closed. Then another group of cadets would lay out all the traffic cones marking off our various training areas where we practiced backing up, high speed evasive lane changes, dodging cardboards boxes (pedestrians) thrown out in front of us, etc. The Academy staff placed a tremendous amount of importance on us becoming 'expert' drivers, as they should have, and there was very little margin for error. When a cadet screwed up on any driving segment his punishment was to wear a sign around his neck, for a 24 hour period, which indicated what his personal driving deficiency was. These signs were professional looking cardboard cutouts held by the claspers of a braided set of jumper cables. Some of them read: I'M A LEFT FOOT BRAKER . . . I DON'T KNOW HOW TO BACK UP . . . I GOT LOST ON THE PURSUIT COURSE . . . I KILLED SEVERAL PEDESTRIANS, etc., etc. I got caught left foot braking while an instructor was riding with me one day and suffered the ignominy of wearing the jumper cable sign for a day. In my defense, nearly every trooper I had ridden with drove that way during a pursuit and so did I when I worked the road later on . . . It's just so much more efficient when you're in a hurry! We also had to wear smaller versions of the jumper cable signs when our rooms failed an inspection. The violations which necessitated wearing a sign usually involved an instructor finding a dead insect, a bedspread with a wrinkle in it, a toiletry item cap not secured in your locker, etc., etc. My second roommate, John Broome, had to carry around his offending dead insect in a small box for a day and was required to introduce it to all of us; he named it 'John 'd Bug'.

As the summer of '73 rolled by and our Academy training peaked, we all got closer to our much anticipated "coaching trip". This was a two week period of intensified training with a 'real' trooper out in a real detachment where we would be driving the patrol car, contacting violators, and investigating the accidents under the intense scrutiny of our 'coach'. How we performed on our coaching trip really decided whether or not we would be commissioned as troopers or sent packing. Just prior to being assigned coaches we were finally issued some 'real' trooper equipment which included our Smith & Wesson 357 Magnums, newer used leather gun belts, handcuffs, and a for real trooper's "Smokey Bear" campaign hat. Now we knew we had arrived and the only item left was our badges. With the badge came the assignment of a personnel number (badge number) that would stay with us the rest of our careers (lives). When that moment came one day in the classroom, Sergeant Baxter called our names then just threw the badges to us from the podium as if getting them meant nothing. Some of them landed on the floor . . . . This really upset a lot of us but I guess it was just his way to put things in perspective . . . . ? My badge and new personnel number was 305 and even though I've been retired for 9 years I still associate myself with that number and include it in my email address and other secret stuff.

Initially, I was to be assigned to Trooper Ron Snyder in Newport for my coaching trip. I was really excited about going to Newport as I loved that corner of the state. At the last moment I was notified that Ron was sick and my new coach would be Trooper Tom Adams 307 out of the Hoquiam Detachment. I was fine with that too as I had worked radio in Hoquiam several times as a cadet, filling in for their operators when they had Christmas parties and such. When I first met my coach he seemed a bit upset about something and finally told me that he was 'pissed' because I had a lower personnel number than him. In spite of that, we got along fine right away. I couldn't have been assigned a more picturesque location for the next two weeks . . . right on the ocean with Westport and Ocean Shores part of our beat with gorgeous views of the towering Olympic Mountains and daily drives by beautiful Lake Quinault. After I retired from the WSP I spent hundreds of hours flying over this same country while locating and tracking radio collared elk for the Quinault Indian Nation. It's still one of my favorite spots in the State of Washington.

Coaching trips were all about racking up drunk drivers and getting some big numbers (lots of violators) and we got quite a few. Sadly, that first day was marred by another grisly train accident. This one involved a kid on a bicycle trying to race a train to a crossing down by Porter; unfortunately the kid lost. He was ground to a pulp and like so many other images in my mind from those years that one just won't go away. A couple nights later we were advised by dispatch of an orange Porsche 914 driving erratically on SR 109 between Hoquiam and Humptulips; we were in the vicinity but never saw him. Right after that we got called to a pick-up with camper blocking the roadway just outside Bay City on SR 105. Sure enough, we found the pickup blocking the eastbound lane with the lights on and engine running. We knocked on the door of the camper but when it opened I immediately wished I was back at the scene of the bicycle train wreck. A gentleman in his eighties greeted us in his birthday suit and seemed to be quite intoxicated. Another 'toothless' senior citizen somewhat younger but still in her late seventies or so, also in her birthday suit, was seen in the background trying to find her underwear or something. Man, that camper just reeked of booze, sweat, and various other 'old people' odors. Those horrendous visual images were burned into my brain forever and I started to gag uncontrollably. She was drunk too so we had to call a tow for the rig and put the old man under arrest for being in physical control of a motor vehicle while intoxicated . . . I didn't quite 'get' the physical control aspect since he wasn't in the driver's seat but the law's the law I guess? He was fairly cooperative, and blew in the breathalyzer down at Westport PD for us, but kept telling us to hurry up as he wanted to get back and finish his activities with his newfound paramour. This would not be the last time I had to deal with seniors in compromising situations and after living the semi-cloistered life of a seminarian for so many years these kinds of incidents were quite the wake up call for me. The next night we got another call about a recklessly driven orange Porsche 914 Westbound from Hoquiam on SR 109. It was about the same time as the night before so this guy had a little pattern going on. We were way out of position but vowed to be in that area the next night to see if we could get lucky and nail the stupid shit.

It was about this time that everyone started talking about a movie that John Wayne was filming down near Moclips and Pacific Beach. It was called *Mc Q* and the Duke was supposed to be a Seattle PD detective chasing bad guys in our area. We were working the radar down near Ocean City on SR 109 when we got a motor home in the beam at ten over the speed limit. I pulled it over and while we were talking to the driver at the bottom of its steps I see this quite elderly gentleman peering out from inside but who quickly went out of sight when I noticed him. It was the Duke but man he looked pretty rough; I sure wished he had come out so we could have met him though . . . I gave the driver a warning. Soon it was time to head back towards Hoquiam to see if perhaps we could catch the Porsche driver doing something crazy. As we were crossing the Humtulips River bridge radio put out a one car injury accident in the Grays Harbor City curves just outside

Hoquiam with someone trapped in the car . . . . Tom and I just looked at each other and we each knew without saying what our thoughts were . . . . We were there in less than five minutes. This was just one of those what goes around comes around moments as we worked our way down the embankment to an upside down Orange Porsche 914. The car had left the road at a high rate of speed in a curve to the left, hit a tree fairly high up, and then slid on down the tree trunk landing upside down in a heap at its base. The driver didn't appear to be injured too badly, just couldn't get his door open and he was too fat to get out the windows. When we finally got a door open for him and got him out it was pretty obvious he was bombed. He was your stereotypical loudmouth moron wearing the big gold watch with several layers of gold chains around his neck . . . The kind of drunk I eventually learned to just feel sorry for since we ran across his type so often. Booking this guy for DWI was very rewarding in light of his activities the last few nights and for me was the highlight of my coaching trip.

After about a week on my coaching trip I was allowed to go home for the weekend. I had been issued a worn out '70 Plymouth Fury III Patrol Car to commute in but that old 440 was still in decent shape! It was pretty late when 307 finally turned me loose so when I headed out to Yakima over White Pass there was absolutely no traffic on the road. In an area called the Randle Flats on SR-12, I opened the old girl up and found she would still do 130 mph without even breathing hard. Right before one of the Cowlitz River bridges I thought I caught a glimpse of a car parked down a dirt road a little bit and a red light came on for a second then went out . . . Just then an inquiring voice comes on the State Common Radio Frequency and asks; "Who dat?" . . . . Well I was quite familiar with how most old timers would answer that query which was; "Who dat who say who dat?" but I was only a cadet and one in jeopardy right then so I just identified myself as cadet 305 going home from my coaching trip . . . . I knew the next few moments might have a severe impact on my career and was overjoyed when Trooper Harry Minton 868 just came back with a laugh and told me to watch out for Elk on the road at this hour . . . . What a guy! I worked with Harry for many years afterwards both on the road in

Spokane and with the airplane down in the Tri-Cities . . . Harry was a good friend of mine and especially of Cisco Cortez 306 (my Academy roomate's brother). Harry died so very young and so long ago already.

One of the most enjoyable aspects of 'coaching' in the harbor was patrolling the sandy ocean beaches near Copalis and Ocean City. At low tide several hundred yards of beach with hard packed sand was available to drive on and the WSP investigated all accidents and incidents in those areas. My coach wasn't particularly thrilled with driving on the beach as it always required an immediate car wash afterwards to get rid of all the corrosive salty sand. Secondly, it was very easy to get stuck in the approaches to the beach area where the sand was dry, soft, and deep. I think we covered a dune-buggy rollover down there and got a DWI out of it. I did manage to get a bitch letter on one of my last days there stemming from a bootleg-u-turn I conducted after radio put out an accident behind us. After I was completely turned around and was proceeding in the other direction with my red light on for a couple hundred yards or so a guy going the other way suddenly jerks his car onto the shoulder as we passed by. We didn't think anything about it until a couple days later when Tom's Sergeant, Lynden Woodmansee, called us into his office. Apparently the motorist who jerked his car onto the shoulder was claiming that we had forced him off the road, after we had made an illegal u-turn right in front of him, nearly colliding with him and his whole family. He went on to say that had it not been for his cat-like reflexes all of us would have been killed. Tom and I were both flabbergasted at this claim since nothing remotely like that had happened. Thankfully, Sergeant Woodmansee said he didn't believe the guy either. However this served as the "unfounded complaint" opening salvo for me and was just one of so many more to come. Manufactured and totally untrue complaints became a quite common occurrence that myself and most of my colleagues had to suffer through in our careers. There are just so many disgruntled drivers who just can't pass up an opportunity to exact a little vengeance for their last speeding ticket or DWI arrest. The time spent on investigating erroneous and frivolous complaints like these was and still is a tremendous waste of taxpayer dollars.

To cap off my coaching trip I stopped a red-neck driving a fully loaded log truck for speeding on my last day. When we checked out his truck we discovered so many equipment violations (broken off lug nuts, cracked wheels, broken tie-down chains, no brake lights, no turn signals, missing mud flaps, and probably over-weight) that I wanted to immediately write him for everything and call for one of the big Kenworth tow trucks for this piece of shit!! But my coach stressed that this was a logging community and if he impounded every illegal log truck he saw the local industry would collapse and his wife and kids would probably be retaliated against. So we took the politically correct action and decided to just give him a warning on all the equipment violations, as long as he promised to fix them, and to just write him the $17 speeding ticket. When I walked back up to this guy and let him know we were just giving him a warning on those items but that we could have easily impounded his rig costing him thousands of dollars he just glared at me and said; "I bet you think you're some kind of fu***ng hero don't you?" Man, I immediately saw red and really wanted to go 'old school' on this guy's ugly tobacco juice stained semi-toothless face with my flashlight . . . . My coach saw that I was about to lose it and urged me to just walk away . . . . Later on I always sort of expected rude and stupid behavior from kids who didn't know any better and usually let it slide but when a guy in his fifties talks to you like that, then as far as I was concerned, he is a lost cause and deserves no consideration whatsoever. After my coaching trip I made it a point to hammer those kinds of assholes for every RCW violation I found and could articulate on a case report . . . . At the Academy we had been instructed to never make an "attitude" arrest no matter how severely you had been provoked . . . . Well, in the real world I always felt that if some stupid bastard could speak to a trooper like that then what was he doing to his wife and kids? I never once regretted the comprehensive enforcement action I occasionally dealt out. Even worse in my mind were the people you'd stop to help change a flat tire for in the pouring rain, or put their tire chains on for them in the wintertime . . . . Some of those shitheads, even before their tires had hardly touched the ground after I let the jack down, would take off without even the slightest acknowledgement or muffled utterance of a thank you . . . Man that was hard to take . . . . Dealing with the never ending supply of those kind of individuals was one of the main reasons

I eventually got into flying . . . . Sooner or later I was going to lose it with one of those pukes and then I'd be the one on the evening news as the focus of one more story about police brutality . . . . I obviously don't condone kicking the shit out of some asshole on the ground but I can understand how the guys working the metropolitan areas occasionally just get over whelmed by the constant flow of maggots and eventually experience a momentary break . . . . Usually a career ender though . . . .

When we all re-convened back at the Academy in early August things were a lot more laid back. We had to write up a summary of our coaching trip and do a presentation in front of the class. Awards were given for most DWI arrests and although I thought I had quite a few one of the cadets had something like 17 in that two week period . . . hard to beat those numbers. The most anticipated and important announcements to be made were our duty assignments after graduation. We each had filled out a form indicating where we would like to be assigned, listing three in order of preference. I had selected Spokane, Okanogan, and Yakima on my wish list. Had I known that our personnel department usually assigned you to the direct opposite of the type of community you wanted to live and work in I most certainly would have indicated Seattle, Tacoma, and Everett as my choices. The last thing I expected was to be assigned a non-line position at the Capitol Campus, but there it was in black and white . . . Capitol Security. What a let down for the nine or ten of us who got thusly hosed. However, I was fortunate not to be included in that half of my group that was assigned to the governor's mansion detachment of Capitol Security. They didn't even get a patrol car to drive and basically were baby sitters for Governor Dan Evan's kids, his mother in law, and their huge dog. There was a light at the end of the tunnel though; apparently this was only a temporary assignment for three or four months, then all of us would be transferred into one of the Olympia Freeway detachments and those guys would fill our positions. There had been some sort of 'uprising' against their sergeant and the punishment was for most of the offenders to be re-assigned to Capitol Security. I found out later that the whole thing was more or less planned as most of these guys had 20+ years on and were looking for a 'cushy' job to finish out their careers . . . or so I heard . . . .

Anyway, back at the Academy we knew we had it made so we felt we could relax a little and felt brave enough to pull a couple pranks on some of the instructors. Lieutenant Lloyd Danielson had been one of the better instructors and was the assistant Academy Commander so obviously we selected him one evening for a 'special' flag ceremony. We tackled him right after dinner, cuffed him, drug him over to the flag pole and tied his feet to the lanyard. We hoisted him up until he head was about three feet off the ground then waited for him to beg for mercy. He was struggling quite a bit but not saying anything and after a minute or so it looked like he was gagging or choking on something so we started to let him down but the lanyard took off and he dropped pretty hard on his head. His false teeth had become dislodged and he was not a happy camper as he stormed into the admin building. We all thought we were screwed for sure so we just retired to the TV room waiting for the ensuing PA announcement to gather in the parking lot for several hours of running and push-ups. However, the PA stayed quiet and eventually we all went to our rooms. Around 0200 the fire alarm went off and we all ran outside according to protocol. Nothing happened, there was no fire, and no-one came out to shut off the alarm. It finally dawned on us that Lloyd was getting his revenge for being roughed up so we all tried to go back to sleep with that clanging alarm still ringing. When he didn't shut it down after an hour we decided to make him suffer a little more. We went to his room to get him but he had locked himself in. One of the cadets had access to the main patrol car key lock box where we got the duplicate for his patrol car parked out front. While a couple of us kept him occupied pounding on his door another cadet who happened to be an electronic whiz, re-wired his patrol car siren to come on and stay on when he started his car to go home in the morning. Lloyd finally shut the damn alarm off around 0330 and we finally got some sleep. Around 0700 when the day shift admin people started to show up for work we were finally rewarded with the beautiful music of a '72 Dodge Polara siren wound up to the max where it stayed for quite awhile waking up everyone in a five mile radius of the Academy. I'm sure some of the local residents thought it was a tsunami warning and started heading for high ground. Lloyd never said a word about any of these shenanigans and we respected him all the more for it.

Graduation day finally arrived but instead of being commissioned in the state capitol building like all previous and subsequent trooper cadet classes, our ceremony was held at the Tyee Motor Inn in Tumwater in a banquet room which still pisses me off! I think they were refurbishing the capitol rotunda or something that week. Governor Dan Evans gave us our commission cards, Chief Will Bachofner presided over the affair and congratulated each of us, and a Supreme Court justice administered our oath of office. It was all pretty exciting and I was now a graduate of the 49th trooper cadet class and a full fledged trooper with a license to speed . . . life was good! Since my life finally seemed headed in the right direction shortly thereafter I worked up the nerve and proposed to Debbie. Like an idiot she said yes but I told her we had to wait until I got off my one year probation to get married and she seemed OK with that. I went home for a few days to help out on the farm one last time then reported to Sergeant John Kelley at the Capitol Campus Detachment in Olympia.

CHAPTER 6

My new boss, Sergeant John Kelley 177, had just been re-assigned to Capitol Security after leaving the TAC Squad (General Support Division). These guys were the ones that responded to all the student anti-war protests of the day, the blocking of the I-5 freeway up by the UW, riots, rock festivals, and other 'hippie' gatherings. You would expect such a guy to be a rip snortin no holds barred SWAT team type, but John was just the opposite. He was a quiet unassuming man, soft spoken, extremely sociable, and didn't mind dealing with a whole new detachment of FNGs . . . Along with Lorne Hughes, John was one of the finest guys I knew in my career with the WSP. His previous group of troopers were all seasoned veterans looking for a fight and a chance to beat up some hippies. John's main pre-occupation in life was fishing for tuna then canning them in his basement; it's all he ever talked about. We all sampled his tuna and it was fantastic and there was just no resemblance to the Starkist or Chicken of the Sea tuna you get at Safeway. We hadn't been there a month when he decided to throw a Halloween costume party. He came as Bozo the Clown complete with a flashing red light in his big bulbous nose. When Deb and I got to the party, he had already set up camp in a big easy chair and from all appearances was feeling no pain as he relaxed there with his blinking red nose. At work he calmly came on the radio from time to time to give us a parking violation to tend to in one of the many underground parking lots under the capitol campus. Writing parking tickets was a real drag during day shift but swing and graveyard turned out to be the worst job ever. Each patrol car had a jockey box full of keys to every state office building on the capitol campus and our job was to check every door on every office building to see if they were locked . . . . Man, this was not what I had signed up for. To make matters worse, our patrol cars were old Dodges with 383 V8's with two barrel carbs which couldn't get out of their own way. When we occasionally got out onto the freeway to blow the carbon out of them and a "real" local road trooper saw us we had to endure snide little comments like; "Get that portable roadblock off my freeway" or "Hey man, you're stinking up my beat with that piece of crap" . . . . What a bunch of sweethearts . . . During one of my freeway runs out to get gas at Fleet and Supply late one night I had finished filling up and then parked my car next to a row of other parked patrol cars, killed my lights, and was writing in my 'Bluebook' (officer's notebook). I saw an older Suburban approaching the gas pumps and killed my dome light to see what was going on. This was during the period when the speed limit on the freeway was 50 mph, there were severe gas shortages, rationing was in effect and you could only get gas every other day and usually had to wait in long lines. Anyway, the driver of the Suburban gets out at the pumps and I recognize him as a colonel in the WSP. He's acting real hinky, looking around and making sure nobody sees him . . . . I was about 75 feet away but I guess I fit in with all the other empty new patrol cars and he didn't notice a body in one of them. Anyway, he pulls out three five gallon gas cans and proceeds to fill them all with WSP gas! He then tops off his Suburban and leaves in a hurry. I got his license number and ran a registration check with radio and sure enough it comes back registered to the colonel. I really couldn't quite believe what I was seeing and figured he must be doing some undercover work or was going to put the gas in his patrol car later . . . . Yes, I was very naïve back then . . . . Anyway, I told Sgt Kelley about it and he didn't react very much just squinted a little and said he'd handle it. I don't know what he did or who he talked to (I was never contacted by anyone) but about a month later we were reading the daily teletype in our squad room one morning and saw that this particular colonel had announced his retirement. Apparently he had a stellar career with the WSP dating back to WWII and I can only assume that he was experiencing early onset Alzheimer's, or something, to attempt such a stunt.

Several days later Chief Will Bachofner comes on the radio and says; "1 to any local patrol, contact me at Fleet and Supply". No one answered so when he repeated his request and still no one answered I finally said; "305-1 I'll be enroute, eta 5." I guess he initially thought I was a real road trooper but when he saw the campus patrol car pull up alongside him I could see the slight look of disappointment in his eyes as he knew he would be talking to an FNG and a lowly door shaker FNG at that. He was cordial at first but when he realized I was also a blank slate and had no opinions or suggestions to offer about anything, he made a quick exit. At that time he was also putting out feelers to see if any of us would be willing to work an extra hour a day without getting paid for it. He was trying to forestall a big pay cut a couple state senators were considering for us by offering this plan up to the legislature beforehand. Those were the days before we had a Troopers Association and we were basically helpless. Before you could spit, each of us was giving the state an extra hour of 'love' time each day. This situation wasn't fixed until many years later when our association got stronger. At the time, I didn't care, but there sure was a lot of grumbling from the old timers (guys in their 30's) about that extra hour a day they had to work. Right before this new policy was enacted the Chief went around the state and gave every gathering of troopers the same motivational speech about how important this extra hour was and how we needed to support him. Chief Bachofner was one hell of a charismatic speaker; he reminded me a lot of the famous faith healer Oral Roberts. Anyway, the Olympia troopers all gathered at the Armory in Chehalis to hear his pitch and as usual he worked the crowd up to a fever frenzy and ended his speech with a very patriotic "Well boys, are you with me?" One of the guys in the Olympia detachment, who unbeknownst to any of us was apparently very susceptible to this sort of rhetoric, jumps up and screams out: "We're all with you 100% Chief!!" Well, even the chief was a bit taken aback with this sudden outburst and the rest of us just looked around at each other with that WTF look in our eyes . . . .

The most memorable incident from those four months at Capitol Security occurred one snowy-icy morning between the governor's mansion and the legislative building. I had just come around the corner in my patrol car when I saw Governor Evans descending a long set of concrete steps towards the back door of the Leg Building. I stopped so he could walk in front of me but apparently those last couple steps were icy and the next thing I see is the bottoms of his shoes up in the air and his brief case sailing towards me . . . He then went bumpity bumpity down the last couple steps on his ass and ended up in a disheveled heap at the base of the steps right in front of me . . . . Geez, I was a little stunned but hopped out to help him right away . . . . He noticed that I was really working hard at fighting back a laugh so to hide my shame I turned around and picked up his briefcase for him and then for some reason thought I should say something appropriate . . . . All that came out was "Nice weather huh?" But my voice broke at the end and revealed an obvious choked back snicker . . . . He grabbed his briefcase out of my hand and stormed into the building . . . . Yes sir, working Capitol Security was going to be a thrill a minute . . . .

One of the buildings we had to secure was the WSP Hangar at the airport and I seemed to migrate down there quite often to ogle the airplanes. I was really drawn to the King Air 90, N88SP, and just thought it was the most gorgeous plane I'd ever seen. I finally got to fly the old girl about 16 years later when all the older FAA controllers still called her 88 Sugar Pop. While assigned to Capitol Security I ended up working with one of my Academy classmates Trooper Loren Ottenbriet 378. That was the beginning of a 40 year friendship and our families still see each other all the time. Loren's wife Chris brought their little baby Kim down to the campus one evening back in '73 and I can still remember a huge head of red hair attached to a beautiful little girl.

Our time on the campus finally came to an end in December and most of us were assigned to one of the Olympia Freeway detachments. I think there were only two veteran troops in our newly formed unit and they were not too happy to be surrounded by a bunch of rookies always asking stupid questions and needing help with routine duties. I finally was issued an almost brand new '73 Dodge Polara which had belonged to Trooper Swede Leland who was now taking my place as a campus trooper. It only had a couple thousand miles on it but more importantly it had a 440 under the hood and those big freakin dual exhaust pipes that sounded so good! I was in hog heaven (ha ha) and took a bunch of photos of my new ride especially of that long coveted license plate displaying WSP305 . . . . I still have one of those original plates hanging on the garage wall. None of us had too much time to revel in our new found glory as the winter of '73-'74 roared in right after our new assignment with an uncustomary heavy snow for the Olympia area. It was one accident after another and I soon discovered that Westside drivers do not know how to drive in the snow. The nice thing was we could now take enforcement at one car accidents when there were no witnesses so I wrote a lot of tickets for Failure to Exercise Due Care and Caution . . . sort of a catch all charge for winter-time screw-ups. Later some genius in the legislature had the nomenclature changed to Driving Too Fast For Conditions . . . . Apparently too many voters were confused by the original terminology?? I only got to keep me '73 Dodge for a few months when they told me they needed it for the next cadet class. So off I went to Fleet and Supply again where I was finally issued a brand new patrol car, a '74 Dodge Monaco. It wasn't quite as good looking as the '73 but still had the 440 and those great sounding pipes. I hadn't been driving it for even a week when one night on graveyard they gave me a one car accident out on SR-8 near the Grays Harbor County line. There was a deputy at the scene and he informed me the driver was very drunk. I tried to get the guy to do the field sobriety tests but he couldn't even stand up unassisted let alone close his eyes and touch his nose so I arrested him for DWI and called for a tow. At three in the morning tow truck drivers aren't exactly waiting in their trucks for a call so it took almost an hour before the wrecker showed up. After finally clearing the scene I headed for the county jail in Olympia. I thought my drunk was being pretty quiet and that's when I noticed the unmistakable odor of fresh urine. I slammed on my brakes got out and jerked him out of my brand new car before he soaked my new seats . . . too late. The dip shit had quietly pissed a couple quarts onto my back seat, soaking it, and even managed to get some on the carpeting as well . . . . So much for my new car smell. I got a blanket out of my trunk and wrapped him up in that just in case he had any more left. Geez I was mad and I knew it was going to take a lot of work to get that smell out of there. I spent almost all of the next day scrubbing, deodorizing, shampooing, etc. to get the piss smell out and finally thought I had got it all. However, on my next shift as soon as I turned the heater on that piss odor came back strong as ever. The only good aspect was that my new sergeant didn't ride with me much to evaluate my progress while on probation since my car stunk so bad it made him sick. Finally, some Seattle area troop totaled his '74 Dodge and while its carcass sat at Fleet and Supply I was able to swap his back seat for mine before they took his car away to the crusher. I kept shampooing the carpet and after a few more months my car was pretty much odor free. Later patrol cars came standard with a thick plastic rear seat cover and rubberized footwells that were a helluva lot more user friendly and easier to clean out when drunks did their thing back there.

I was driving through the downtown Olympia area on Capitol Blvd. one afternoon and accidentally came up behind a 'student driver' car from one of the local high schools at a red light. I could tell that the instructor in the right seat had noticed me and no doubt had briefed the student driver of my presence and warned him to not do anything stupid. Everything was fine until they got to the next red light when the kid's panic level apparently rose to a fever pitch and he suddenly gunned the accelerator and drove through the light without stopping. I really hated to stop the poor sap but I turned on the lights and pulled him over. I had no intention of writing him a ticket but thought a little humor might diffuse the situation and leave the young driver with a favorable impression of the police. There was a very funny *Midas Muffler* TV commercial in those years where an old couple were seen driving a car with a very loud worn out muffler. When they pulled up and stopped at a red light a Hells Angel biker puke pulled alongside on his chopper and seemed very aggravated with them because of all the noise. The Hells Angel looks over at the timid car driver and says, "Man, you are a menace to society!" He then roars away on his chopper. Well, as I was walking up to the car I thought that line might be appropriate for this kid so when I greeted him I said; "Junior, you are a menace to Olympia society!" The other two kids in the backseat burst out laughing, the instructor just glared at me, but the poor kid driving burst into tears and started sobbing like a three year old. Geez, I felt pretty bad and just told him to be more careful and got out of there before anybody got my badge number. I didn't try that one again.

A real confusing incident occurred in early 1974 involving one of our radio operators. I was given an injury accident out North of Olympia and was going through town with my lights and siren on. As I approached a left hand turn I had to travel over a series of railroad tracks while turning which caused my tires to squeal somewhat and then I accelerated away. I covered the accident and thought everything was routine. Unfortunately, the next morning I get called into my sergeant's office and he solemnly informs me that there has been a 'major' complaint filed against me for reckless driving and to make matters worse he tells me that since I'm still on probation I could be terminated for this heinous offense. He asked me if I was on such and such street at such and such time and I said yes, that I was responding to an injury accident out on South Bay Road. He seemed stunned by this announcement and asked me to leave his office for a few minutes. When I came back in he wanted to know if I had 'lost control' of my patrol car while going to this accident. I told him no way! Then he specifically asked about the area near the railroad tracks. I replied that my tires might have squealed a little while crossing them but said I never skidded or slid sideways; I admitted that I wasn't wasting any time since **I was responding to an injury accident** where I did end up performing first aid to an injured bicyclist. I asked who the complainant was and he informs me it was one of the radio operators. I had known this guy for several years, and had mistakenly thought he was my friend. Additionally, I had never had a cross word with the guy! I just couldn't believe that he would fabricate some crazy reckless driving scenario after I apparently passed him near those railroad tracks enroute to the accident. Now I'm not saying that I occasionally didn't mash the accelerator down late at night out on the freeway when there was no traffic around me but I never drove as he described in town or anywhere else there was witnesses (I mean heavy traffic) . . . . I knew if I contacted him to ask what's up his butt he'd probably fabricate some other bullshit story and then report that I was harassing him or something so I had to let it go. Years later, when I was in Spokane, I found out this guy had tried to become a trooper around this time but had failed some aspect of the process and was turned down. I guess he was just mad at the world right then and decided to take out his frustrations on a vulnerable rookie troop on probation. That dipstick sergeant who over-reacted to this whole situation just wouldn't let my complaint drop even after he got all the facts. He still wrote me a written reprimand for unspecific "driving deficiencies" mainly because I got a little surly with him during his so-called professional interrogation where he didn't even have his facts straight . . . What I learned from this incident and similar ones to follow is that there are very few people you can trust in your life but when you do find a good friend that has your back no matter what, it is a very rare occurrence and you should nourish that relationship!

There were a couple interesting diversions in early winter 1974 that were definitely a lot more interesting than going out and working the radar all day. Chief Bachofner decided that we should all be EMT's for some reason so all troopers had to attend a ten day course of instruction at the academy to get the necessary training. Before we could get certified we also had to spend at least four hours in an emergency room and four hours observing surgery; I did mine at St Peters in Olympia . . . . The emergency room session went fairly well except for a little girl who showed up with her foot mutilated by a lawn mower which was a little grisly. The surgery session the next day "was" going pretty well until they brought in a little boy who had a dislocated elbow they had to repair under anesthesia for some reason. I had just witnessed a hernia repair, which only took a few minutes, and a total hip replacement and was amazed at how much pulling, jerking, twisting, and grunting went on, let alone the amount of blood thrown everywhere, so I didn't think a dislocated elbow was going to be very interesting . . . . However, after they put the kid under and the doctor started manipulating that kid's upper and lower arm bones, I apparently spent too much time watching those bones moving around under the skin near his elbow because the next thing I knew I woke up on my back staring at the ceiling in the operating room . . . . The first face I saw was one of the O.R. nurses who had a huge smile on her face I could see around the edges of her mask. She bent over and quietly whispered to me; "Oh, did the big bad state trooper fall down go boom?" Man, I was really humiliated and to this day still can't figure out what the hell happened!

The other exciting event that winter was when I was selected to be part of the security team for the National Governor's Conference being held up in Seattle that year. Some of the guys got to be drivers for the various governors but most of us FNG's ended up doing hotel room security grunt work. We spent four hour shifts standing outside our assigned governor's door trying to stay awake at 3am. I was privileged to be assigned to Governor Ron Reagan and got to meet him a couple times. Just as I finished my shift around 6am on the last day, one of the Calif. State Troopers, serving as his executive protection, said there would be a photo shoot with the governor in a few minutes if I cared to hang around for it . . . . Man, I thought that would be great and was pretty excited. Well, after about an hour, that trooper came out and said it was going to be awhile and if I wanted to go back to my room to wait it might be a good idea. I told the on duty WSP troop to come and get me when the governor was ready and went to lie down. When I woke up it was around 9am so I anxiously ran down to Reagan's room to see if he'd come out yet. The on duty troop had a real sheepish look on his face, said he was really sorry, but told me that right after I left the governor sprang out of the room, took a hasty photo with everyone there, and left in a rush . . . . Well, that was certainly a missed opportunity but 34 years later, while flying a Citation Jet for a private company, I was privileged to take a tour of Reagan's "Rancho del Cielo" up in the hills north of Santa Barbara. It was known as the Western White House during his presidential years and it was a beautiful place. The house was quite small but the setting up in the mountains was magnificent! I guess that made up for not getting that photo with him . . . . ?

At the end of a graveyard shift one morning I came across a car parked mostly on the shoulder but partially blocking a lane of travel on the freeway. The driver was passed out behind the wheel with the car in gear and his foot on the brake. I reached in and put the shifter in park and tried to wake him up. He was really out of it and I wanted to get home and go to bed and not spend the next two hours with a messy drunk . . . . So, I called for a day shift trooper to see if any of them wanted a DWI (physical control). An old crusty veteran showed up a few minutes later and said; "Whadaya got here kid?" I said it looked like a physical control and he quickly agreed. Most of the guys his age had either retired or were "colonels" so I was eager to observe how a trooper from the mid-1940s handled a drunk . . . I have to say that he was a man of action. He immediately began shaking the shit out of that poor sap while yelling "Wake up Bub!" When the guy finally came around a little the crusty old trooper drug him out of his car and began advising him of his constitutional rights; however his version of the Miranda Warnings were a somewhat abbreviated version to the rights that I was just taught at the Academy. As he drug him to his patrol car he informed his drunk thusly; "You got rights to a lawyer and you got rights to a phone." That was it, brief and concise. In retrospect I think he only 'Mirandized' that guy for my benefit as he knew all too well that most drunks never remember a thing about their arrest anyway. I had another run in with this same old codger about a week later. Again, with only an hour to go till the end of my graveyard shift radio pumps out a one car injury accident in Rainier at the narrow railroad underpass. When I got there the driver was still sitting in his car which had struck part of the wooden supports for the overpass. There wasn't a lot of damage and he was only complaining that his side hurt a little and thought he had cracked a rib or something. The ambulance took him away to St Peters and I was about to call for a tow truck when "Krusty the Trooper" shows up unannounced and asks his now trademark inquiry; "Whadaya got here kid?" I told him it seemed to be a pretty straight forward one car minor injury accident and that the driver might have a cracked rib or something, and that I was off in twenty minutes. He must have been feeling magnanimous after I gave him the 'free drunk' the other day and told me to go on home and he'd take the accident for me. That was fine with me so I headed for the barn. Early the next morning he calls me on the radio and tells me to contact him at the pumps (Fleet and Supply). When I get there he seemed to be pretty miffed and then he lays into me for lying to him about the accident. He said when he got to the hospital that the guy was already dead and that I must have known his injuries were life threatening and what kind of asshole was

I to be dumping fatals and messy drunks on other troopers. He went on to say that he had to do a 'shitload' of paperwork and it ruined his whole day. Man I was really surprised and tried to tell him that I was just talking to the guy and he seemed fine. The old codger finally lightened up and told me he'd covered a lot of accidents just like that one where the drivers got a ruptured spleen from the steering wheel hitting them under the rib cage causing internal bleeding. He ended our contact with; "I really had you goin there for a minute didn't I boy". He then said he was late for coffee and took off. Needless to say that wasn't the end of it and from that day forward I kept hearing rumors (started by him I'm sure) that I was afraid of messy drunks and had a habit of dumping fatals on other troopers . . . what a guy . . . .

There were a series of incidents during my first year on the road that are still stuck in my mind all these years later probably since they occurred during my 'formative' years' as a young trooper and taught me life lessons I never forgot and served as my ongoing initiation into the real world. The first one began when radio put out an apparent naked female driving erratically Northbound through town in a yellow VW Bug. Well, the response was just the opposite of what happened when the Chief called for a contact . . . everybody and his mother's uncle was on the radio all at once saying that they were in the best position to make the contact. It must have been dumb rookie luck but she drove by me as I waited on the shoulder about thirty seconds later. Man when I announced I had her in sight no-one said a word but I knew what they were thinking; "Lucky dumb-shit rookie . . ." Well, she was naked alright, and her driving was pretty erratic so I pulled her over near Martin Way. When I walked up she made no attempt to cover up and I started to wonder how the hell I was going to handle this without getting a major complaint of some sort levied against me. She was a real space cadet and obviously high and feeling really "groovy" on some feel good substance; I asked her politely if she would mind putting her flower child mumu back on. This took some time as backwards and inside out all looked the same to her. While this was going on several patrol cars stopped by 'to help' . . . . but when they saw the show was pretty much over, off they went without even asking if I needed any assistance. I eventually arrested her for driving under the influence of 'something' and took her to the hospital for a blood and urine test. Turned out to be LSD and she wouldn't be the last person I stopped to be high on that; I filed away those symptoms and reactions for the next time.

During another day shift I pulled a young kid over for improper lane travel; he was polite enough, and told me his Dad was a cop too. I didn't smell intoxicants on his person but he just seemed out of it. All of us had just completed EMT training at the Academy and I recalled learning that dilated pupils might indicate someone is on barbiturates. Well this kid's pupils were as big as saucers which I thought was a bit unusual in broad daylight. He was acting just like a drunk just no odor but he also failed all the field sobriety tests. The DWI charging verbiage included the use of drugs so we just had to go to the hospital for the urine test instead of the county jail for a breathalyzer. I patted him down but didn't cuff him as it was optional in those days. While I was waiting for the tow truck I noticed him squirming around in the back seat and thought I saw him put something in his mouth. I got him out immediately and did a much more thorough search; to my chagrin I found some red pills wrapped flat in tinfoil that I had missed the first time. I immediately assumed that he had probably been trying to get rid of all the evidence and had swallowed a bunch of them. I knew this could turn ugly real fast so I took off for the hospital at a high rate! It only took me a few minutes but he was unconscious by the time I got there. The ER staff was pretty familiar with overdose cases and immediately began pumping his stomach. I checked in on him a couple times during the day but he hadn't regained consciousness yet. The next morning my sergeant calls me and lets me know my suspect had woken up in the middle of the night at the hospital and escaped. We notified his Dad who was the Chief of Police down in Chula Vista but he didn't seem too surprised and said he'd call us if he heard from his kid. Eventually, the kid did go home and his Dad convinced him to come back to Olympia and face the music which he did. Altogether, another lesson learned about conducting a thorough search and always cuffing anybody you put in the back seat no matter how friendly they seem. The final installment of this particular story occurred several weeks later at Fleet and Supply when I was trading my '73 Dodge for that new '74 Dodge. Whenever a car was brought to Fleet either for a trade or when it was turned in at the end of its life, a thorough inspection was conducted. The WSP really didn't like taking those old patrol cars to auction with a gun or knife still in it that some drunk had ditched under the back seat. In my case with the '73 they didn't find any weapons under the back seat but did discover several more tinfoil packets with the little red barbiturate pills . . . I guess I really did a lousy job searching that guy!

Speaking of Chiefs of Police my next incident involved one. I had been called to a one car accident Northeast of Olympia around 2am. At the scene I found an unmarked patrol car slammed into a large Maple tree with the highly intoxicated driver partially pinned in the now reclined driver's seat; it had collapsed during the accident and was now resting against the back seat. He had straightened out a left curve and hit the tree pretty hard. A large limb from near the top of the tree was snapped off by the impact and landed on top of the car smashing the roof in and trapping him. He had a pretty serious bleeding laceration to his neck so I was able to put some of my recent EMT training to good use. After applying direct pressure for a while I taped a 24x72 all purpose gauze bandage onto his injury. After the ambulance hauled him off I noticed a pool of liquid of some sort in the recessed rear footwell of this old Chevy behind the driver's seat. I thought it was rainwater but when I shined my flashlight on it I discovered it was blood and man there was a lot of it! I had radio call the hospital to advise the ER personnel that this guy had lost several pints of blood at the scene. He was a really big guy but this was still a lot to lose. When I finally got to the hospital they had already completed a non-legal medical blood alcohol test which was near the .40 mark which usually is the level for alcohol poisoning. We drew another "legal" blood test which ended up pretty close to the medical blood test. I felt pretty sorry for this guy as he had been a good chief for his small department over the years. Unfortunately, this incident finished his career.

There were two seasoned veterans in my detachment and neither guy suffered rookies kindly or wanted to be seen with any of us. So

I was quite surprised one evening when the really elderly (he had 8 years on at the time) of the two calls me for a contact down at Nisqually . . . . Man, this was unprecedented and could only mean one thing . . . he was inviting me to have coffee at the VIPS Restaurant there . . . . !! Wow, I started to feel like one of the gang as I rushed down the hill to meet him but when I got there I didn't see him in the parking lot . . . . However, I did see a patrol car stopped in the middle of Old Hwy 99 just up the road a bit with its wig-wags flashing so I went on over. He had his spotlight aimed at a lump of rags in the middle of the road and when I walked up all he says is: "It's all yours . . . ." Before I could ask "What's all mine" he took off! I walked up to that pile of rags and when I gently probed it with my foot it moaned . . . So began the history of "ah shit" moments in my career. The "lump" turned out to be a highly intoxicated female who hadn't quite made it crawling home after staggering out of a local bar. I tried the KOGA wake-up technique and broke some ammonia inhalants in her nose but nothing would rouse her. I finally just drug her into the rear seat of my patrol car and headed off for the local Detoxification Facility downtown while I plotted how I was going to get my revenge on that old timer. Again to my chagrin I made another rookie mistake; since she was unconscious I hadn't cuffed her nor did I close the little sliding window that was installed at the top of the floor to ceiling shield between the front and rear seats in all our patrol cars. So, while travelling 70 mph down the freeway I suddenly felt two slimy hands grab me around the throat and start choking me! Worse yet this gesture was accompanied by a shrieking-screaming chant of some sort that scared the living shit out of me! I have to say, that got my undivided attention and I slammed on the brakes as hard as I could to get her to let go of my neck before I got to experience a knife slicing into my carotid . . . . Well, that improvised slam dunk maneuver worked pretty well and when I stopped to cuff her she was thankfully unconscious again and stayed that way until we unloaded her at the detox facility. I am ashamed to admit that I used this technique several more times in my career in order to "quiet down" various malicious prisoners but I reserved its usage for only the violent psychopaths. If they had assaulted me or threatened to track me or my family members down and then kill or rape everyone when they got out of jail then the were rewarded with the slam dunk routine. I re-named and perfected my "slam **drunk**" maneuver as follows: Once the maggot had punched all the necessary threatening and inflammatory buttons I would let off the gas abruptly to allow the prisoner to come forward a few inches off the seat back . . . . I would then floorboard the accelerator for a split second to suck them back into the seatback in order to obtain maximum seatback foam compression. The coup'd grace was then applied a second later by jamming on the brakes as hard as I could to get the perfect rebound off the seat for the maximum energy slamming effect of the puke's face into the steel shield while simultaneously exclaiming as loud as I could: "Jesus Christ, did you see that fu**ing deer jump out in front of us?!!" Of course the timing had to be perfect, in order to obtain maximum effectiveness. The subsequent concussion they often sustained usually erased all the evil intentions they harbored against me, or any memory of the incident, so I was often able to score a twofer! I know, I know, horrible police brutality; but be honest, who wouldn't do something similar if their children, wife, or family members were threatened by a psychopath?

The lesson I learned about conducting thorough prisoner searches was re-enforced soon after the kid with the downers in the tinfoil episode. I had arrested a DWI near Trosper Road and was performing my enhanced pat down search when I felt something lumpy in his front pocket. Of course when I asked him what it was he just said it was his keys and I almost fell for it. However, when I fished his "keys" out they looked surprisingly like a little derringer that someone had even made shorter by sawing the barrel off to a nub. It also carried a nice little .32 cal. bullet in the chamber I might add. He acted surprised and said he "didn't know" how that got in there . . . . Yeah, sure! After putting the cuffs and leg restraints on this clown, the dumb shit actually gave me permission to search his car. I found quite an array of knives, beat down sticks, throwing stars and other rough looking homemade weapons . . . . I had to have a deputy contact me at the scene as I really didn't know what was legal or not. He didn't have a concealed weapons permit so that was the only other charge I filed on him but who knows what could have happened had I not learned my lesson a few weeks before? The last time I saw that little derringer it was sitting in a display case in the WSP Academy lobby with an assortment of other crazy looking weapons taken off prisoners over the years. Looking back, I really have to thank that old timer (and I mean "really" ancient now) for dumping that DIP (drunk in public) on me . . . . The lesson I learned about properly securing prisoners that night probably helped keep me alive for the rest of my career. I did get my revenge on him a little later . . . He invited everyone over to his place for poker one night and probably assumed that an ex-divinity student pussy like me would be an easy mark. Unfortunately for him, we played poker almost every night at the sem . . . . I got some good cards that night and was lucky enough to extract my "pound of flesh" from his hide for dumping that DIP on me.

One afternoon I was working radar out on SR 8 near Summit Lake and stopped a guy for the usual ten or twelve mph over the posted limit. In those years we were still wearing our 357 Magnums in a cross draw holster which hung on the left side of our gun belts with the pistol butt facing forward. On the other side of the buckle we wore our cartridge case, which carried around 20 loose bullets in its two pouches, and then our handcuff case. Anyway, as I was getting out and trying to keep an eye on the violator, as I was trained to do, six distinct yet separate events occurred almost simultaneously . . . . Apparently, due to the speed of my exiting, the seat belt shoulder harness caught and hooked itself onto my holster strap, unsnapping it . . . I noticed my gun starting to fall out of the cavernous holster they issued us back then while I was leaning to the left so my stupid campaign hat would clear the door frame . . . I twisted to catch my gun with my right hand since I had my 'blue mousetrap ticket book' in my left hand and jammed that into the gravel shoulder to help stabilize myself since I now seemed to be on the verge of falling out of the car . . . . While all twisted up my right foot got caught under the emergency brake pedal somehow which resulted in me 'definitely' falling out of the car . . . . Just then the edge of the door frame caught both snaps on my cartridge cases and snap-sprayed all my bullets out onto the highway . . . . As I was going down I tried to grab the door with my right hand and of course my beautiful Smith & Wesson 357 hit the dirt and I was fortunate the damn thing didn't fire and blow my nuts off or something . . . . What I thought was the last indignity was when my blue mousetrap ticket holder exploded open, after I had jammed it into the ground, scattering a variety of new blank tickets and my copies of several tickets I had just written all over the freeway as well . . . . I had also knocked my campaign hat off which I last caught a glimpse of rolling across the freeway and picking up speed with a little tailwind . . . . The last and final indignity, as I lay there defenseless all twisted-up, half in and half out of my patrol car, was when that God damned violator walks up to me, hands me several of my bullets and asks if I needed any help . . . . I was a bit flustered to say the least and was slightly unkind to him when I told him to just 'Get the f**k out of here' . . . I felt bad for saying that but he definitely left in a hurry . . . It took me quite awhile to find everything and regain my composure . . . My gun barrel was full of dirt and I'd lost several bullets . . . I couldn't find all my tickets and my hat looked like something had driven over it . . . . Jesus, I was a mess that day!!

In spite of the above incident by the summer of 1974 I felt like I was finally getting the hang of this trooper job and found I didn't have to keep asking for help all the time while investigating and trying to sort out some of the crazy accident scenes. Conflicting driver and witness statements or skid marks and vehicle damage that didn't make sense seemed to be quite common. I also quickly learned to not talk to the press at accident scenes; whatever you told them would end up all screwed up in the paper the next morning with names reversed, and the wrong driver being blamed for the wreck. When that happened, the phones started ringing in radio as the 'wronged' drivers called the office wanting everything straightened out immediately or they were going to sue. I really got in the grease after I made the front page of *The Olympian* one morning when a story about a fatal I had covered the day before showed up there. Apparently the chief saw the paper that morning and immediately called my sergeant to complain about me. It all started when a passing motorist had reported a car in a blackberry bramble south of town on a remote county road. When I got there I could barely see the car from the roadway as it was way down an embankment and really buried. As I was fighting my way down to it I knew this thing was going to get ugly real fast; there was a real bad odor coming from somewhere and I was praying it wasn't near the car. Well, it wasn't near the car but more or less coming from inside of it. The car had no damage to speak of but it was on its left side in the blackberries with an obviously deceased driver hanging part way out. When I got closer I could finally see what happened. As the car had gone down the embankment the driver's door had somehow come partially open and the driver fell out a little and got all tangled up in the thorny blackberry vines. They were wrapped tightly around his neck and arms and it looked like he had suffocated or choked to death since he didn't really have any other apparent injuries. It really kind of spooked me to think of that poor guy struggling with those vines and not being able to free himself; from the look of things he'd been there awhile too. I finally crawled back up the cliff and called for the duty sergeant, the coroner, and a photographer as was the protocol then. After a couple hours we finally got the poor guy onto a stretcher and myself and another 'strong' trooper attempted to carry him up the steep gravelly slope to the coroner's van. As we got close to the road my shoes were filling with gravel, as this guy was heavy, and I was really sinking in. I told the other troop about the gravel in my shoes and he made some comment about not dumping him as that would look real bad to all the bystanders that had gathered. Unfortunately, I inadvertently grinned for a split second and that just happened to be the same split second some idiot cub reporter from *The Olympian* snaps a picture of us. The other troop had his head down and his campaign hat covered his smile but my face was fully exposed. Anyway, the next morning my sergeant calls me into his office and slams that day's edition of *The Daily 'O'* on his desk for me to review. Of course I was terribly embarrassed to see that photo of me callously laughing away as I carried some family's deceased loved one out of the brush. At least my sergeant handled things a little better than the last time and turned this episode into a training session for me about never trusting reporters. I felt the blame was with the editor of the paper who allowed this photo to be published in the first place since they no doubt had several others they could have chosen to print. As usual, I didn't make that mistake again and never trusted anyone with a camera at an accident scene in the future. I would certainly hate working the road now considering every moron on earth has a digital camera device of some sort permanently attached to their person somewhere.

About this time I got the Jeep and motorcycle bug again. I had sold my 750 Triumph the year before, and bought a gorgeous 450 Ducati Desmo Scrambler. I also traded in my '69 Goat on a brand new CJ5 Jeep that came from the factory with a V8 already in it that year . . . . Several people have asked me if I have ever regretted selling those two (now priceless) GTO's . . . . **YES!!** Every God damned second of every day thank you very much!!! The Ducati was the ultimate "Thumper" of its day and I rode it along the powerline trails around Thurston County as much as I could. One evening myself and fellow trooper Chad Johnson 878 went for a ride up at Rock Candy Mountain. We got separated somehow and at one point I apparently was momentarily distracted and flew off a twenty foot cliff landing in a brush pile at the bottom. The bike wasn't damaged but I couldn't budge it out of the blackberry brambles. I took off walking hoping that Chad would find me but never saw him. It got dark as I followed the powerlines down to a road and finally got picked up by a local. Well, he was drunk but beggars can't be choosers so I had him take me to Rick Taylor's place, another one of our radio operators who lived nearby, so I could have him take me back to my Jeep. When I got to Rick's place there was a lot of activity in front of his house. When I stepped out of the drunk's car I found out that Chad had assumed I was lost and injured, rode his bike to Rick's and arranged a search and rescue mission to find me from there . . . Jesus, I was humiliated and sooooo embarrassed . . . I wanted to crawl under a rock and die. I got stink eye shit stares from everyone there and I think they all would have been much happier had one of them just found my stinking dismembered carcass lying in a ditch somewhere. To make matters worse when I went up to retrieve the bike the next day, I couldn't find it. I drove around for hours investigating every drop off along the power line road and started to think someone else had located it and claimed it as their own. Again, it was almost dark when I finally found the damn thing; I had to drag it out of that brush pile with a long rope and chain before I finally got it loaded on the bike trailer . . . . My sergeant wanted a total debriefing on the whole episode and not too subtly indicated that I was becoming a real problem child for him. I really started to worry that I wasn't going to make it off probation. Debbie and I had already set a wedding date for September but that was before this last series of incidents. Now I began to feel I would be quite fortunate not to get fired by then and could only pray that I might get lucky and they would only extend my probation for six months. With documented driving deficiencies on my record, pissing the Chief off for laughing at fatal scenes, and now getting lost while bike riding . . . there was no doubt in my mind that Deb was about to dump my sorry ass and I'd soon be back on the farm picking apples or running Dad's D8 for him in a few weeks . . . I guess I just wasn't trooper material after all.

I had a four day-off shift change roll about then so Deb and I decided to drive to Eastern Wash and check out a remote area we both loved. If I did manage to get off probation we were both very interested in transferring there after we got married. Deb and I had taken a Harley ride through the area several years before and thought it would be a terrific part of the state to live in. It was gorgeous apple country, good fishing, and perfect for dirt bike riding. By this time Deb had bought a brand new Hodaka Dirt Squirt and was becoming an accomplished dirt bike enthusiast. Her first ride on it didn't go exactly by the book though. We had just unloaded it off my brand new three rail bike trailer when she started it up. I was still getting my Ducati unloaded when I hear the ring, ding, ding, of the Dirt Squirt's mighty 100cc engine revving up. I looked up just in time to see her coming right at me full bore . . . . !! Jesus Christ, I barely had time to jump out of the way as she crashed right into my new trailer folding her front fender in half and putting a big ole dent in the gas tank of her brand new Hodaka! I didn't know whether to laugh, scream, or cry but since my first bike riding attempt on Bud Phipp's Tote Goat wasn't much better I tried to be supportive. However, I was later criticized for checking out the damage to my new bike trailer before seeing if she was OK . . . . She was a cautious rider and when we finally sold it I was honestly able to tell the new owner that 3rd and 4th gears were brand new as Deb had never engaged them. Anyway, I had called the sergeant in that remote area to see if I could meet with him and discuss my possible transfer to his beautiful city. He asked me a lot of detailed questions before finally agreeing to meet with me and seemed a little unfriendly on the phone. When Deb and I finally sat down in his office it was apparent he had made some calls as he immediately lays into me about my so called driving deficiencies, lack of respect for my superiors, bad judgment, laughing at fatals, getting lost, etc., etc. and how he certainly didn't want **someone like me** in his detachment . . . . I wasn't allowed to speak, defend myself, or give my side of the story and was just flabbergasted that someone could be so mean spirited and disrespectful to myself and Debbie during a casual **off duty** meet and greet . . . . I was really mad but my first thoughts were to feel sympathy for the poor bastards that had to actually work for this cretin . . . . More importantly, after his bombastic display, was the sense of relief I felt that I'd never have to!! Deb started kicking my leg and was giving me the sideways hairy eyeball look so we got the hell out of there before I said or did something inappropriate. Apparently my wonderful sergeant in Olympia had briefed him on all my recent activity . . . . Jesus, you'd think he would have been glad to get rid of me and given me all kinds of glowing reviews!! Several years later I was regularly flying up in that cretin's old detachment area and worked traffic with some of his former troopers. Thankfully, they now had a terrific new boss but they told me that it had been the shits working for that clown and they always referred to those years as the "dark ages" . . . . Man did they have a lot of horror stories to piss and moan about . . . . I was quickly learning that there were a lot of good men in the WSP but an almost equal number of pure boneheads. This outfit just wasn't like the seminary had been at all . . . . There, we could "tune up" the idiots with a little in house re-training. In the WSP the wheels of justice often turned very slowly for some of the more prominent misbehaving assholes . . . . Thankfully, nearly 100% of them eventually stepped on their dick in some way, shape, or form and ultimately paid the price for being a shithead . . . . Their inevitable downfalls and slides into disgrace almost always involved one of the three B's that the academy staff had warned all us cadets about: booze, broads, or bills . . . . As they say, Karma's a bitch!! . . . .

We continued driving east and began to investigate the Spokane area instead. My brother Ray had just moved there after being recently promoted by the phone company. Deb and I loved Spokane almost immediately and I'm embarrassed to admit that it was primarily because of two terrific Italian restaurants that brother Ray introduced us to; Pupos, and Luigis. Pupos was a family owned place downtown and was very similar to my Aunt Minnie and Uncle Mario's restaurant in Yakima, Gasperettis. The veal saltimbocca at Pupos was out of this world and my Mom and Dad came over to visit us many times in those years, mainly to eat there I think. Luigis, just up the street from Gonzaga Univ. on Division, was just a once in a lifetime pizza place; although they only stayed open for a year or so after we moved to Spokane; it was absolutely the best pizza we will ever have.

But before all that could happen, Deb and I got married in Sept. of 1974 after finally getting my letter from Chief Bachofner indicating that my probationary period was over . . . . I was tremendously relieved! After a really neat honeymoon trip fishing in British Columbia, where we flew into a remote lake by float plane, we began our life together in a small apartment overlooking Budd Inlet on Puget Sound. I can still hear that fog horn blaring away all night long . . . But at the time we didn't care! Our meals for the next few months consisted primarily of the Kamloops Trout we caught on our honeymoon. We had baked fish, barbecued fish, fried fish, poached fish, smoked fish, deep fried fish, you name it . . . We finally had to give the rest away as we were finally just "fished out". Almost immediately after I got off probation a few of the local Olympia cadets heard that I might be fun to ride with and started calling. The one I remember the most was Ethan Reavis; he was a cool guy but slightly naïve back then. We had him over for dinner one night during a ride and Deb made a nice casserole with cheese on top. Apparently he couldn't identify the meat inside and asked what it was; without missing a beat Deb calmly replied that it was a Possum that Rick had shot in the woods from off the balcony this morning. To his credit he didn't even flinch and said it was delicious. I didn't tell him it was chicken until many years later after he made sergeant. In December my transfer to Spokane finally came through so off we went cross state on the first big adventure of our lives together.

I thought the winter of '73-'74 had been rough in Olympia but when we got to Spokane that December we were introduced to the never ending winter of '74-'75. Man, it was brutal . . . we were just not prepared for a real Eastern Washington winter! I have never chained up my patrol car so many times as I did that year. Unlike the Westsiders, Spokane drivers figured out fairly quickly and seemed to understand that ice covered roadways mean you must slow down if you want to get somewhere. There weren't as many accidents to cover as you might think although I was pretty damn busy. It was during that winter when I patented my innovative "chaining up" procedure. Most people lay their chains out in the snow, drive over them, and try to get them tight but never can and have to stop several more times to get them just right. Having learned my lesson on the farm, I just jacked my car up with that big old herkin freeway jack they issued to Westside troopers then, whipped the chains on in no time, got them nice and tight, and off I went . . . took about ten minutes, tops. Out on the beat, I used to carry that jack on the floor in front of the back seat to speed up my chaining time. I really enjoyed the look on most people's faces when I got their chains on for them in less than ten minutes . . . they were astonished. Of course if I could make it to Duke's Chevron, they just put my patrol car up on the rack, and it took even less time to mount them and I didn't get wet. Duke's was the West Beat trooper's hangout and we all spent hundreds of hours there drinking their coffee and bullshitting with Duke and his brother Pat. They were great guys and took really good care of us. One day I got a call from Trooper Gene Osburn 483 to contact him at Dukes for a ride while he got an oil change. When I got there Gene was standing near the rack and his patrol car was up in the air. Duke let his car down and just as the tires touched the floor Pat springs out of Gene's trunk and grabs him by the throat . . . . Man, I about split a gut but Gene damn near pulled out his hog leg and drilled Pat . . . He didn't think it was too funny at first but finally thought it was a pretty good one. Gene was able to get his revenge a few weeks later when he snuck up behind Pat one evening, after parking his patrol car unnoticed in back of the station, and stuck a cold piece of pipe onto Pat's neck while grabbing him and demanding all his money. Apparently, Pat had a slight heart condition and damn near croaked. He later said that the cold piece of pipe sure as hell felt like a revolver barrel and really freaked him out.

In those years we had a pink handout with holes in it that we attached to the radio antennas of abandoned cars to let the other troops know it had been checked. If the car was still there after a couple days we towed it. Anyway, the "cool" Westside troopers in those days were cutting those handouts into a circular shape and putting them inside their dome lights in order to diffuse the white light somewhat. The theory was when you didn't 'light up' the inside of your car so much at night you made yourself less of a target. I also used to hang a green scented tree in my car to help with the still lingering stale urine odor. While I was sitting at an accident scene waiting for a tow truck one night one of the senior troops in my new detachment stops by and hops in my car to introduce himself. Trooper Mike Barr 653 was not impressed with the subdued pink glow inside my patrol car. It turned out that most of the Eastside troopers were not up to speed yet on all the current and more advanced procedures that us Westside troops were privy to so his first words to me were; "Jesus Christ, it looks and smells like a fu***ng French Whorehouse in here!" Like the guys who complained about my GTO Judge, I guess this French Whorehouse comment was pretty much the standard remark a senior trooper made while addressing a rookie. About a month later another one of the other senior detachment mates, Pete Powell 641, got in my car one night and said it really does smell like a French Whorehouse in here but he had more to complain about. Apparently he had rummaged through the sergeant's in basket and saw my activity report for the last month. Those reports were called 68s and they documented how many and what kind of violators we had contacted in the last month. In Olympia we had all averaged about 200 to 220 violators a month and that's about what I turned in for my first full month on the Spokane West Beat. Pete politely informed me that those kinds of numbers were totally unrealistic and unsustainable for a West Beat trooper and if I wanted to fit in I had better get my activity down in the 120-130 range like everyone else. Well, that worked out to around six cars a night . . . what the hell was I supposed to do with the other five or six hours of my shift? I tried to be polite and said I'd attempt to conform to the new standard . . . . I have to say that it was always quite difficult to take anything Pete said too seriously . . . . After his own wedding reception at the Longhorn Barbecue, while out in the parking lot, he dropped his pants and "Mooned" fellow Trooper Loren Ottenbreit and his wife Chris for no apparent reason . . . . What a special night that was! As of this writing in 2012, after consulting with a current road trooper, I was advised that the average monthly activity standard now is in the 300+ range . . . . Good Lord, it's a good thing I'm retired 'cause there's no way in hell I could have ever produced those kind of numbers back then!

My new sergeant was a peach of a guy named Dale McLeod 182. We hit it off right away and enjoyed a really good working relationship. Everyone called him Rocky and it turns out he had been quite a scamp during his trooper days. One evening he and his best buddy Don Graybill decided to prank their good friend who owned a local restaurant. They were having coffee at the counter as usual one night when they began to argue about something. It got louder and louder and pretty soon Rocky pulls out his hogleg and shoots Don in the chest several times with his S&W 357 Magnum! Don falls to the floor grasping his chest while Dale is still shouting expletives at him . . . Dale then turns to the owner and calmly announced "He said my boat was a piece of shit!!" Of course the owner is backing up crying Omigod, Omigod, and tries to run away. About this time, Don pops up and yells out "Oh for Chrissakes Bill they were just blanks . . . !" Well, I have to say I didn't think this escapade was too funny when I first heard about it and still don't but that was Rocky.

Our favorite restaurant hangout in those days was *The Longhorn Barbecue* at Spotted and SR 2. It was owned and run by a group of brothers from Texas and was and still is the best barbecue I have ever had. We had our own table there and a special hat rack for our smokey bear lids. Rocky loved the place and his favorite sandwich was the barbecue beef which was served just oozing with the Longhorn's special sauce. He really got into it while eating those mothers and when it was over he gave new meaning to the term "wearing your lunch" . . . . The waitresses there all looked like Playboy Bunnies and all wore little skimpy cowgirl outfits that appeared to be several sizes too small. Old 641 just happened to be dating one of them and was kind enough to introduce me to her one morning. As I got up to shake hands Pete loudly announces; "Jesus Rick, is that a flashlight in your pocket or are you just happy to meet Sally??" By this time I had nearly become immune to tasteless remarks and trooper banter so I just said; "I don't think the folks over in that corner heard you Pete" while I shook hands with Sally. Pete turned out to be the Spokane version of Don Lee and there was never a dull moment when Pete was around. Pete's Dad had been a Captain in the WSP and his brother Chris, 448, was also a trooper in Cle Elum soon to transfer to the West Beat as well . . . . What a crew!

As if my high activity standards (which would be considered being lazy now days) hadn't alienated me enough from my new detachment mates another incident soon followed which really left me isolated for awhile. As I was driving up Sunset Hill on I-90 late one night I noticed a dark shape approaching me, going the wrong way on the freeway; it had no lights on and was in my freakin lane!! As usual with me there was a brief moment of dis-belief but I finally flipped on all my lights and just barely swerved in time and missed hitting him head on by a couple feet . . . . It must have woke him up too as he slowed down and stopped right in the middle of the freeway. I backed up to him and as you might have guessed the driver was very intoxicated. He was a nice old guy and kept apologizing to me over and over. After the breathalyzer test, and writing him a ticket for DWI, as was our prerogative then, I just took him home and didn't book him. When we got to his house he invited me in for coffee and cookies but I declined. Well, being the rookie in town, I didn't recognize the name or who this guy was but soon found out when several of my detachment mates quit talking to me and treated me like I had suddenly developed leprosy. Turned out my drunk was one of the owner/brothers from the Longhorn and a long time friend of all the troopers, except me. They all felt I shouldn't have arrested him and should have just taken him home . . . How the hell was I supposed to know?? I've thought about this arrest a lot over the years and still think I did the right thing. Hell, even if I had known who he was I would have still arrested him. I talked to one of his brothers several years later who told me this episode shook his brother up pretty badly and he really cleaned up his act thereafter and quit drinking . . . . Who knows what might have befallen him, or some other innocent party, if I had let him go that night further enabling his drinking and driving in the future?

Deb and I settled into a little apartment out in the Spokane Valley off Argonne Road which is now the site of a Holiday Inn Express. I don't know what we were thinking when we rented that place but it was the last time we ever lived in a congested residential area in our lives. People would see my patrol car out front and feel free to knock on our door at all hours of night and day to report all matters of criminal activity ranging from the neighbor's dog pooping in their flower bed, loud fornication activity, bitching about some bum ticket another trooper wrote them, various domestic violence issues, etc., etc . . . . Man, we had absolutely no privacy and could not wait for our six month lease to be up so we could get the hell out of there! One afternoon on my day off there was a loud banging on our front door where I was greeted by an excited young lady who was screaming that her boyfriend had just tried to kill her by running her down with his car; then she yelled; "And there he is right there!" Sure enough, the dumb shit had followed her to our place and then got stuck in the snow when he tried to turn around after seeing my patrol car out front. I told Deb to call the office and send a trooper over as I just wanted to enjoy my day off a little and not have to mess with this. I walked on over to this idiot who was rocking his car back and forth trying to get unstuck. I immediately noticed a strong odor of intoxicants and the usual bloodshot and watery eyes. I told him I was the trooper who lived here and that he was under arrest for DWI and that an on duty trooper would soon be here to take him to jail. He didn't like hearing that news so he resumed rocking his car back and forth further burying it in the snow bank he had backed into. At one point he killed it so I reached in and grabbed his keys to get him to stop. That set him off pretty good so he got out and came at me; he was pretty drunk so it wasn't too hard to keep shoving him aside. Debbie was watching from the front porch and didn't like the looks of this scene at all. Finally, Trooper Jim Swartz showed up, slammed dunked the idiot into the snow and cuffed him. He gave me that "why didn't you take care of this guy yourself you lazy asshole" look. However, I think he was secretly happy to get a day time drunk to boost his 68 a bit since he was trying to get promoted then and needed all the extra activity he could get to make himself look good on his evaluations! A couple nights later there was a knock on the door and when I opened it there stands the same drunk that had created that ruckus. I was just about ready to slam the door and go get my gun when he starts apologizing profusely, crying, and began describing how his life was in the toilet, his girlfriend left him, etc., etc. I heard this act nearly every night when I was working and certainly didn't need to hear it when I was off duty but I listened for a few minutes anyway. We finally shook hands and he seemed to feel a little better about himself. Later when he came to court, he pled guilty, and apologized again to me in front of the judge . . . . I hope he got his life turned around.

I finally got to meet the West beat legend Trooper Dick Alm 506. He was probably the coolest trooper I'd ever met and was quite a smooth talker; the Longhorn girls loved him as he was very handsome. Dick already had about twenty years on by then and nothing ever got him very excited. When we were out at the "Horn" together and would get a phone call from radio about an accident I would jump up and bolt for the door. Dick would just tell me to calm down, and finish my coffee and butterhorn . . . He said the accident will still be there when we're done . . . We hit it off pretty good after he found out about my Italian heritage and especially when he discovered I knew how to cook a little. I used to write out all of my Mom's recipes for him as he was quite a gourmet chef himself. He especially liked my Mom's gnocchi recipe but like me had a lot of trouble with it since there were a hundred ways to make a mess out of those little potato dumplings. I think he got the sauce down pretty well and finally caught on that you can't make decent sauce in less than four hours.

1976 West Beat Detachment. Back row from left: Dale McLeod 182, Bob Watkins 849, Self 305, Chief Will Bachofner 1, Pete Powell 641, Jack Humphrey 668, Jim McKillip 24. Front row from left: Jack Obenland 357, Mike Barr 653, Larry Lane 495, Gene Osburn 483, Dick Alm 506.

Another local trooper-hero legend was Jack Brazington 761. He was in the freeway detachment at the time and we shared the same office out at the airport. One day Jack and I were reading an IOC on the bulletin board from Olympia Headquarters that sought input from line troopers about what we thought of allowing bicycles on the freeway. Jack didn't seem to care one way or the other but this request really pissed me off. I thought it would just cause more messy accidents since cars traveling 70 mph just don't mingle well with bikes doing 15 mph. Anyway, since I was now off probation I wrote a scathing IOC addressed to my new lieutenant, John Colwill, wherein I said in no uncertain terms that I thought it was a misconceived idea. I went on to say that I felt that to even broach the subject in the first place revealed just how uninformed and out of touch with the real world the current headquarters personnel must be to not recognize how inappropriate it was to even seek input on such a ridiculous matter. I had Jack read it and he liked it a lot; he encouraged me to send it up the flag pole chain of command to see if anybody saluted. Well when a documented hero gives a rookie such a solid endorsement I had no choice and dropped the IOC in Sergeant McLeod's in-box. I was off for a couple days but when I eventually signed into service radio advised me to contact Lieutenant Colwill in his office. Geez, I haven't even been in Spokane for six months and I have to go see the lieutenant already. I had a hunch it was about the IOC but felt that the brass were the one's asking for input and that's what I gave them so how could I get in trouble? I hadn't used any profanity and it was written professionally. Lieutenant Colwill was cordial enough and understood and semi agreed with my central premise but didn't like the semi derogatory and accusatory tone of the epistle. When I glanced at the IOC on his desk I noticed that my sergeant had given it a strong endorsement, agreed with me 100%, but said it might have been worded a little strongly. Just what I needed, a sergeant who was a rebel who also got all worked up when headquarters weenies churned out drivel like that IOC. He was supposed to be my filter and should have sat me down so we could have cleaned the thing up a little before he submitted it, but he hadn't. Anyway, the lieutenant went on to say that I was going to have a long and difficult career if I didn't tone down the rhetoric in my paperwork a little and that I needed to start showing my superiors a little more respect. He finished with a line I was to hear many more times in my career: "Just because you think you are educated doesn't give you the right to be so critical of everyone else." I suppose he was right and I thanked him for the good advice and vowed to be more diplomatic. I had a feeling he was more upset at Dale for endorsing that IOC so quickly instead of talking to me first about it. Unfortunately, the damage had been done and that IOC brought both of us some grief over the years after it went through the chain of command, was flagged, and became a permanent part of my personnel file. However, one guy was singing my praises to everyone he talked to; Jack Brazington thought I was a brave and gifted writer/trooper who told it like it was even though I was probably committing professional suicide in front of everyone. Just as my visit to the lieutenant's office wouldn't be my last I would also have a few more encounters with Jack before he retired and a couple more after that as well.

The West office out at the airport was an old WWII building that we shared with an FBO (fixed base operator) called *Flight Craft*. Most general aviation flights originated and arrived at this FBO so there was always a lot of activity out on the ramp in front of our office. Sports teams, military personnel, celebrities, even Hugh Hefner's personal black DC9 with a pink bunny painted on the tail graced our ramp from time to time. We got to tour a lot of the planes and I remember that Hefner's DC9 had pink carpeting and a hot tub in it. This period in the mid-seventies was also when they were filming the Black Sheep TV series. One of the Corsair owner/pilots from that series was a local gentleman named John Scaufhausen and he came into Flight Craft or Spokane Airways from time to time with his beautiful F4U-7 Corsair. Man, when I got to sit in that bird all my old dreams of becoming a pilot were re-born and I started checking around on where I could take lessons.

A somewhat funny incident, for the rest of us anyway, occurred in the restroom of our office one night involving one of the "older" West Beat troops. I wasn't there but apparently he was in the toilet stall practicing his quick draw, which in itself was quite a feat since we were still using those big old cross draw holsters in those days which were useless. (Sorry—being critical of WSP procedures again). Anyway, he was getting pretty fast but during his last quick draw he accidentally touched the trigger and fired off a 357 Magnum round into the wall right towards Flight Craft. Of course he was temporarily deaf from the blast but immediately ran over to the Flight Craft lobby to see how many people he had killed. Luckily, it was a quiet evening and I don't think anybody was even there that late. Every time I used that toilet stall I always looked at that bullet hole patch job and reminded myself to try not to pull a similar stunt.

Getting back to the legendary Jack Brazington . . . One evening I was working the West Beat graveyard shift which really covered nearly all of District Four and I just happened to be out in the Spokane Valley near Harvard Road Eastbound around 1am finishing up writing a ticket. When my violator took off, I noticed a car on the shoulder about a quarter mile ahead with its four way flashers on. I drove up to see if I could help when the car suddenly took off. I guess everything was alright except that the car seemed to be accelerating pretty damn hard. I had a hell of a time keeping up and soon realized it was pulling away from me at 100 mph. We were fast approaching the Idaho State line so I advised radio to notify the ISP that I was chasing a fast one into Idaho and needed assistance. Approaching the big metropolis of Post Falls, which was several miles into Idaho, I yelled into my mike that I was now chasing this car at 130+ mph and asked where the ISP was! Just then I hear a familiar voice on the radio announce; "I don't know what's wrong with your speedometer 305 but I'm only showing 125 . . . ." Of course it was Jack and he had just suckered me in to chasing him into another state and getting another police agency involved in the whole damn thing . . . He had me contact him back at the scale house at state line where he laughed so hard I thought he had ruptured himself . . . . I remember some of the adjectives he used to describe me and my pursuit technique . . . : 'Moron, dip-stick, shit-for-brains, idiot FNG, etc., etc' . . . . He finally got it all out of his system. Again, my lesson to learn was: 'if it seems too good to be true . . . . it probably is.' As with all the other 'lessons learned' I filed this one away as well for future reference.

When we first got to Spokane Debbie was able to get hired almost immediately by a law firm since she had several years of legal secretary experience in Yakima. Luckily, one of the senior partners at that firm was the brother of the Assistant Attorney General in Spokane. Our goal had always been for both of us to get jobs with the state and it wasn't long before he wrote Deb a nice recommendation letter to his brother, AAG John Lamp. Shortly thereafter, when she passed all the necessary tests, Deb was hired at the Attorney General's office as a legal secretary. We finally had achieved the goal we had set for ourselves long before we got married; to both be state employees each with our own retirement plan. There was a young law clerk there at the time named Christine Gregoire who Deb eventually worked for when Chris became the AG in Spokane. Chris has just finished her second term as our governor and I had the distinct privilege to fly her around our lovely state on many occasions when she was the head of the Dept. of Ecology and as the Attorney General.

Deb and I finally got out of that shit-hole apartment and rented a nice house on five acres off Bigelow Gulch Road. We could ride our bikes on our own place but found out the neighbors weren't quite as thrilled with the noise from my open piped 450 Ducati Desmo. There was an ORV park near Seven Mile, NW of town, so we started riding up there. One day radio operator Bill Silvernail and I were riding in the park and I might have been in a little over my head while racing him to a narrow crossing over a deep gulch. He made it OK but it didn't look too good for me. I missed the crossing but gassed it hard and tried to jump the mother at the last second but didn't quite make it. The Ducati dropped into the gulch and I almost cleared the far bank but my left shoulder hit just below the top and got crunched. Man did that ever hurt but nothing like the ride to the hospital in my jeep where every bump felt like someone cramming a piece of red hot re-bar into my shoulder. After lifting a bunch of sandbags while they watched my clavicle excruciatingly move around under my skin a doctor finally announced it was an A/C separation. Shortly thereafter during surgery, a crazy looking orthopedic surgeon crammed a 5 inch long stainless pin into that A/C joint and told me to come back each week for two months so he could rotate it. I really hated those visits and nervously waited for him to make his grand appearance. He would invariably burst into the room with a pair of vice-grips in his hand and just say "brace yourself", grab the end of that pin (which was sticking out of my shoulder an inch with a 90 degree bend in it) with his vice grips and twist it around a few times to keep gunk from building up on it. I finally asked him why he always burst into the room like that and he said there was less chance of the muscles tightening up if the procedure was done quickly rather than talking about it for too long . . . . What hurt the most though was when I was sleeping and would roll over onto that pin at night and drive it a couple more millimeters into my

A/C joint . . . I don't think Deb has ever gotten over the sheer volume of my screaming ability nor the variety of never before heard expletives she heard me verbalize on those occasions.

In the mid-seventies we were still not allowed to even have an AM radio in our patrol cars since the brass thought we would be totally distracted listening to music and miss that all important official radio call about some dumb bastard out of gas near Fishtrap. A few of the 'rebels' were known to bring portable radios into their cars, secure them under a headrest with a bungee cord, and entertain themselves while working those lonely night shifts out West where all you saw for hours on end was the occasional jackrabbit. The craziest of the rebels would sometimes go so far as to key their patrol radio mike next to the AM speaker to share some golden oldie with all of us . . . Unfortunately, most of the Westside troopers were country western fans and when they keyed that mike I'd have to endure some twangy song about some dip-shit wrecking his pickup after his girlfriend caught him drunk with her sister . . . . I would like to think that I was personally responsible for raising the bar somewhat when it came to late night listening pleasure. Having always been a huge fan of that big ole Mopar 440 under my hood I was able to enhance the carburetor intake roar even more by flipping the air cleaner lid over and exposing a lot more air filter to the outside world. Now, when you mashed the accelerator down, the wah-WAH-WAAAAHHHH roar when the secondary's kicked in was really wild! So after being forced to listen to another Country Western tale of woe I liked to bring my car to a stop, put my WSP mike right down on top of the transmission drive-line tunnel between the seats, mash the accelerator down with the mike keyed and run through the gears until I was doing around a hundred or so. I never knew how good that sounded on the air until another trooper buddy of mine, Mike Wunsch 636, did the same thing with his car . . . Man, that did sound good! But eventually even this new and exciting form of entertainment became blasé and late night entertainment once again deteriorated into farting and belching into the mike followed by the age old game of attempting to guess who the perpetrator was by his unique audio fart signature. A couple times when I was driving someone else's car that had one of those illegal radios under the headrest I would key the mike during a *Peter, Paul, & Mary* or *Mamas & Papas* song. Apparently my choice of music was a dead giveaway to who the disc jockey was and I would be verbally assaulted with cat calls and insults about playing hippie-commie trash on area frequency. This was all great fun and made the late night shifts pass a little quicker but reality was once more about to raise its ugly head and end my age of innocence as an FNG.

CHAPTER 7

REALITY BITES, BLOWS, AND SUCKS

My quiet summer evening sipping iced tea at the Horn was rudely interrupted by a phone call from radio advising of a one car injury accident on SR 902 out near Medical Lake. The scene was the usual mess of car parts, tree limbs, beer cans, and barbed wire scattered everywhere. Biting mosquitoes added a nice touch along with that ever present fatal accident smell-mix of anti-freeze, battery acid, gas, beer, and blood. A badly injured guy was crammed behind the steering wheel and another trooper helped me get him out; he wasn't breathing so I started CPR on him. Unfortunately, each of my chest compressions caused his avulsed eye to bulge in and out accompanied by bone crunching noises from within his chest. He had bad head injuries, a flailed chest, and we both felt he wasn't going to make it. He had a strong odor of intoxicants about him as did the other occupant of the car who was staggering around the scene. I got the severely injured guy's wallet when they put him into the ambulance and the car turned out to be registered to him. Before they loaded the other guy I asked him who had been driving and he indicated his unconscious buddy had been. Radio notified me shortly thereafter that the driver was DOA at Fairchild AFB Hospital. When I finally cleared the scene several hours later I went to the hospital to get a formal statement from the passenger in the car. He reiterated that his buddy was driving and that they both had been partying at the lake all day. As was customary in those days we had to call radio and give them a brief synopsis of the accident, who was involved, what happened, and whether or not the next of kin had been notified. I had talked to the deceased's family at the hospital so felt it was alright to give radio the memo they needed for the press release.

The next morning while still asleep I got a call from my sergeant who advised me that I had really screwed that fatal up last night and to come to the office immediately to fix things! I was advised that several witnesses had now come forward after reading the morning newspaper article on the accident, saying that we had the wrong person driving at the time of the crash . . . . My first thought was where the hell were these so called witnesses last night when I needed them and secondly we had found the registered owner pinned behind the steering wheel of his own car for Crissakes!!?? I already knew the answer to the first one; they were all drunk and probably thought it wouldn't be too prudent to hang out around a police officer in such a state. Anyway, they all claimed that several minutes before the crash had occurred the injured passenger got behind the wheel since the car owner was too drunk to drive when they left the lake. Obviously, he wasn't in much better shape himself as he only made it about a mile before missing a curve and hitting a tree. Well we now had a real mess on our hands and the simple one car fatal with the deceased driver causing had now turned into a possible negligent homicide. To make matters worse, we didn't have a breathalyzer or a blood draw on the other guy. We immediately went back to the hospital, advised this guy of his rights, and got another statement; he stuck to his guns and still said his dead buddy was the driver. Well I was now officially in over my head with this one so my sergeant called in ole 653, who was a trained accident specialist, to sort this thing out. The first thing we did was get a warrant for this guy's clothes and shoes then proceeded to the wrecking yard and began going over the car with a fine toothed comb. 653 quickly noticed there was a fresh blood smear on the pooched out windshield glass on the passenger side with some hair and flesh attached. Next he removed the brake pedal rubber, took hundreds of detailed photos, and measured the steering wheel height, its distance from the seat, and seat position very carefully. It only took a week or so but 653 was able to prove that the injured dude at the hospital was more than likely the driver based on his lack of a head laceration and driver seat position. Additionally, the blood type, hair, and tissue match (this was long before DNA was in vogue) on the windshield passenger side matched the deceased. Lastly, there was an impression of a brake pedal rubber on the bottom of the injured guys right shoe that our WSP crime lab in Spokane said matched perfectly with the one we had in evidence.

This guy also had a corresponding impression/bruise under his ribs that matched up nicely with the location of the steering wheel, seat position in the car, and the driver's body size. The only thing 653 was really concerned about was figuring out the physics involved during the crash that resulted in the passenger ending up behind the wheel. We spent a lot of time out at the accident scene going over the skid marks, determining the road surface coefficient of friction with a drag sled to determine the car's speed. Mike figured out what angle the car rotated to after impact with the tree, and how the crash forces would act upon the occupants. We finally could see (and prove) how the driver had been ejected out into an open field after hitting the tree, and that the passenger was forcefully pushed across the seat and was jammed against the steering wheel as the car spun violently . . . .

Well, I certainly had my eyes opened with this one and couldn't believe that rat bastard would try to blame the wreck on his dead best friend!! Needless to say, I **never** jumped to conclusions again at an accident scene! We finally wrote it all up and presented it to the prosecutor to see if there was enough viable evidence to charge this guy with negligent homicide. He was very reluctant to proceed since we didn't have a blood alcohol on him . . . However, I reminded him we had about twenty people who witnessed him drinking all afternoon at the lake, saw him get behind the wheel when they left, and that he admitted to heavy drinking himself after we advised him of his rights . . . . But even that didn't persuade him. After a couple days he finally thought of a way to make the results of the hospital blood alcohol test admissible in court through some sort of 'backdoor' legal procedure. (that was the first time I witnessed a prosecutor using questionable tactics usually reserved for defense attorneys, but certainly wouldn't be the last.) After the prosecutor presented the case to a judge he signed the warrant for negligent homicide without much hesitation. I went down to the tow truck company on Sprague where the guy worked and arrested him without any trouble. He seemed very subdued by this time and I'm sure that his conscience was starting to weigh heavily on him. Of course it went to court about a year later and the defense attorney spent a lot of time flashing that newspaper article in front of the jurors quoting me as saying someone other than his client had been driving that night. Thankfully, the jury focused on the real facts of the case and eventually convicted the guy. I still have that article in my WSP scrapbook . . . . From embarrassment I've tried to throw it away many times over the years but always end up keeping it as a reminder to think things through before making an important decision! Every time I read one of those terrible internet blogs where some moron jumps to conclusions and crucifies some other poor sap based on some sketchy and unverified information, I think back on my own stupidity and vow once more to try to get **all** the facts and look at both sides of a story before forming a conclusion about anything!

Everybody who worked with old 761 has their own Brazington stories. Similar accounts of these next two incidents that I witnessed were often retold by others since he seemed to repeat this sort of activity on a regular basis. I was driving Eastbound on I-90 near Thor Freya when I saw Jack standing in the 'V' of his open car door on the shoulder holding an old TR6 radar head in his hands apparently aiming it at traffic. I slowed a little as I went by and then noticed that he was "possibly" taking a leak and using the radar as a distraction of some sort. I thought he must have had to go pretty badly since the office was only two minutes away. I thought that for Jack to even bother to carry around a real radar unit was only for show anyway to appease his sergeant. Usually when violators would ask him how he measured their speed Jack was known to pull his tiny little yellow Civil Defense Dosimeter out of his shirt pocket and display it as 'the radar unit'. Those dosimeters were always a joke with us as we had absolutely no training in their usage nor in the big old Geiger Counters we carried around in our trunks in wooden boxes to be used after a nuclear attack. The dosimeters registered how many roentgens of radioactivity you have been exposed to and if any of those violators had looked into it they would have seen that Jack was bullshitting them. Jack had a good eye for speed though and really didn't need a stinking radar unit to tell him someone was over the limit . . . In the Aviation Section we referred to Jack's natural ability as 'having calibrated eyeballs' and it was a highly desirable trait for a traffic pilot.

One morning during my second winter in Spokane I was given several one car accidents out near Tyler. Man, the roads were super slick in that area after a localized freezing rain event had occurred on top of compact snow and I called for a Highway Dept. sand truck to get out here ASAP. The safe speed in that area was around 20 to 25 mph even if you had studded tires or chains on. I investigated the accidents and was driving back to Spokane when I noticed a car coming up behind me at around 55mph which was the posted speed limit then. The car went right past me and the driver seemed oblivious to the world and the still un-sanded greasy road surface. I actually had a lot of trouble catching up to her so I could get her stopped. When I turned on my blue lights there was hardly any response from her. After several minutes she finally seemed to notice me and locked up her brakes as I could see that all four tires had quit rotating; to make matters worse her tires were slicks, no studs or even a snow tread to be seen. With her brakes locked up she was still blissfully sliding along hardly slowing down at all. Her car finally began to slowly rotate and when she finally slid to a stop she was sideways to the roadway with her rear end almost in the ditch. Man, to say I was hot would have been the understatement of the year; I just couldn't believe that anyone could be such a bonehead! I told myself to remain calm but when I got up to her she screamed; "Look what you've made me do . . . why are you stopping me I was doing the speed limit?" Well, that did it and I yelled back; "You stupid Nerd, the safe speed is 20 mph, and you were doing 55 on glare ice! Did you notice it took you a mile of sliding just to get stopped?" Well she took umbrage with my remarks and retorted with a "How dare you talk to me in that manner . . ." I wrote her a ticket for speed too fast for conditions (even though reckless driving would have been a more appropriate charge) and got out of there before I said or did anything else. Needless to say a four page bitch letter quickly arrived at the District office and I was soon sitting in front of Lieutenant Colwill again to explain myself. I could tell by the look on his face that he was suppressing the verbalization of his true feelings towards me which no doubt would have included some statement of disbelief that I was even allowed to wear the same uniform as him. However, he did seem somewhat sympathetic towards me but was hung up on the word "nerd". Apparently he wasn't a fan of the then hit TV show "Happy Days" wherein 'The Fonz' originated and used that term quite liberally. Lt Colwill said he had looked it up in the dictionary, couldn't find it, and assumed it was some sort of vulgar 'hippie' profanity. I assured him it was merely an inoffensive word to describe a bookworm type person with no common sense. I don't think he believed me and was convinced it was some sort of horrible derogatory insult and that I should be severely reprimanded for uttering it. He said he was going to do more investigating and finished the meeting with an admonition that I still chuckle about it. His parting shot was: "It would have been OK to tell her that you are driving 'like' a stupid Nerd but not OK to say that you are one . . . . ?" I left the office somewhat confused and wondered how my old philosophy prof. would have interpreted that one. Apparently the lieutenant must have finally watched an episode of 'Happy Days' as the written reprimand I was eventually issued merely stated that I had made inappropriate remarks to a violator. I'm ashamed to admit that uttering inappropriate remarks to violators did not end there. Eventually my inability to stem the flow was the primary reason I started taking flying lessons since I knew I couldn't hack 25 years of dealing with the 'stupid nerds' of the world and needed an out before they fired me due to the sheer weight of my disciplinary file.

Another memorable winter-time complaint was generated while I was off duty and trying to be a good Samaritan. While driving to Yakima for Christmas one year Deb and I drove up on a one car accident just east of Ellensburg on I-90. An oriental gentleman had lost control of his brand new Cadillac on very icy roads, and rolled it over a couple times pretty much totaling it. Against my better judgment I stopped to help . . . . No one was hurt too badly and since it was bitterly cold out I had the old couple get in our car to warm up while waiting for a trooper to hopefully show. (before cell phone era) While waiting I cringed when Deb told them I was a trooper . . . . Upon hearing that news the first words out of this guy's mouth were; "Why no warning sign say road slick?" When I politely reminded him that the roads were icy for a hundred miles in either direction today and that it should have been pretty evident they were slick, he just said; "Why no sand on road . . . Where highway department truck?" While trying to control myself Trooper Dave Standish finally showed up to investigate the accident. After escorting the couple to Dave's patrol car I took him aside and warned him that the old man was an asshole.

Well, we had a nice Christmas but a couple days later I got called into my sergeant's office where he was holding a bitch letter from the Cadillac owner . . . . Of course the letter contained no thank yous or any mention of the fact that I was off duty when I stopped to help or that we kept him and his wife from freezing to death. He just went right to the point and accused either me or Dave of stealing the hood ornament off of his wrecked Cadillac since it wasn't there when he went to the tow truck facility the next day to get some stuff . . . . WTF!! Even off duty I couldn't escape from the stupid shits of the world! Apparently it hadn't occurred to this genius that perhaps while he was violently rolling his car through the median of the freeway at 60 mph that **just maybe** his sacred Cadillac hood ornament got torn off and embedded in the mud and snow during the crash . . . Anyway, my sergeant just laughed it off but since Dave was on duty there was an investigation at his end. I had to write an affidavit stating that at no time did I see Trooper Standish remove the hood ornament from this dipshit's Cadillac which by the way was upside down with its hood buried in deep snow when I last saw it! Dave and I shared many a laugh over that one for years afterwards!

That same winter I was sitting on the shoulder near Granite Lake one afternoon writing in my bluebook after covering an accident there; it was snowing and the temperature was around zero. I noticed a guy come up and stop behind me driving a VW dune-buggy of some sort. It had no top and when the driver got out I noticed he was dressed like Nanuk of the North. He came up and knocked on my window and that's when I realized it was Rocky! Holy shit, he was frozen solid! I had him get in and turned my heater up to max to get him defrosted. He was blue, had icicles all over his face, and was shivering uncontrollably. I asked him if he wanted to go to the clinic in Cheney to treat his hypothermia but he declined and asked me if I had some cocoa. I always carried some in the winter and he finished it off. I don't know why he picked that particular day to bring his dune buggy over from Everett but that was Rocky . . . . my boss!

Deb and I sold our bikes after I recovered from my last crash and we started looking for a house to buy. We had no money saved so our plan was to sell my '72 Jeep Renegade as a down payment on one. However, within a couple weeks I really missed having a bike to ride. I saw a gorgeous '65 Triumph TR6 in a display window at a Yamaha bike shop out on East Trent. The owner was the chief mechanic there and he had maintained the bike in factory new condition. Having always been somewhat blinded when it came to nice looking British bikes I was somehow able to convince Deb that riding on the street was much safer than riding dirt bikes. Surprisingly she agreed and we became the proud owners of that beautiful machine, the sweetest and most trouble-free bike I've ever ridden . . . . Deb and I enjoyed many day trips up to Mt. Spokane, Steptoe Butte, and Grand Coulee Dam with our little black tank bag containing our picnic lunch strapped to the parcel grid on the tank. All was going well and we even managed to buy a brand new house down in Hangman Valley for $27,500. Work was fun and we had just finished putting in our new lawn when my new sergeant, Rick Jensen 125 called, and told me to take my now worn out '74 Dodge Monaco Patrol Car to Olympia in the morning and pick up my new '76 Chevy with a 454 under the hood. I was excited about getting a new patrol car, as we all were then, since that car was a large part of your identity as a trooper especially since your own personnel/badge number was on your license plate (WSP305). I rode my 650 Triumph down to the district office to pick up all my vehicle maintenance files which they would need in Olympia when they sent my old patrol car to auction. I ran into Dan Davis 360 while there and it turned out he was also going over to Olympia the next day to get his new Chevy too and was also picking up his vehicle files. Dan and I had been classmates so we agreed to leave together for Olympia in the morning. We lived in the same general area south of town so I followed him out of the parking lot on our way home. On a short little straight section of roadway I decided to pass Dan and give him a little friendly one finger salute before we split to go our separate ways home. I got around him OK and then had to lay the bike over pretty hard while maneuvering through a series of sharp curves. I slowed down after that and then caught a glimpse of Dan overtaking me in his old '75 Ford Patrol Car with his blue lights on. He had his siren all wound up too and I thought he was really making our little rat race seem pretty realistic. When he got right up on me I pulled over onto the right shoulder and then was going to turn around and park next to his driver window so we could talk about all the fun we were having. As I was turning all I heard was the intake roar of his big four barrel carburetor accompanied by the wah, WAH, WAAHHH noise as the secondary jets kicked in . . . . I suddenly found myself flying through the air in slow motion and looking down to see my beautiful Triumph now crammed under the push bars of his patrol car . . . . Son of a bitch!!! If ever there was a WTF moment, this was it! I crashed down on the sidewalk and immediately noticed my left leg was bent back under my knee at a crazy angle. The next thing I see is Dan glowering over me and saying something about how I was going to be the last guy to ever run from him . . . . Man, this just did not make sense . . . we had just been at the office bullshitting 5 minutes ago! When I took my helmet off Dan was really shaken to discover that it was me . . . Apparently his mind was in the ozone layer when we pulled out of the parking lot together and he didn't notice that it was me on the bike behind him. Additionally, I guess he didn't see me dragging that same bright orange Bell Star helmet around the office while wearing a leather motorcycle jacket a few moments before either . . . . Regardless of why it happened or whose fault it was we were both in a pickle at this stage. My first comment to him was "You didn't have to break my fu***ng leg you moron!" I don't think he was listening as he had gone into EMT mode. He straightened my leg out, wrapped it in a cardboard splint, and loaded me into the back seat of his car. He drug my wrecked bike into some guy's garage and off we went to Sacred Heart. By now the pain was horrendous and I could only wish it was as mild as when I rolled over in bed on that pin sticking out of my shoulder. We also needed to report this incident and spent most of the ride to the hospital devising a plan that would have minimal impact on our careers. When the ER doctor asked how it happened the best we could come up with was that I had fallen off my deck and Dan was the closest guy to call to come get me . . . . He looked at both of us rather skeptically and said that my broken tibia and fibula were not consistent with a fall off a deck. That was sort of a wakeup call so Dan called the office and told his sergeant what had happened. I called Deb and for the second time in less than a year she had to drive to the hospital after I had crashed another motorcycle. They had to rush me into surgery as the blood flow to my lower leg was being cut off. Right before I went under I looked up to see that same crazy looking doctor that had fixed my shoulder staring down at me again . . . . As I went to sleep I wondered how many stainless rods he was going to cram up my leg bones . . . When I woke up he was there to tell me that he was able to do a closed reduction on the two leg bones and didn't have to use any pins, plates, or screws. Shortly thereafter my sergeant, Rick Jensen 125 came for a visit and being the great guy he was said not to worry about anything, just get better, and we'd sort it all out later.

All was OK for awhile until the pain kicked in again and it was excruciating! They had me on Demerol and it would work for an hour or so then all hell would break loose when it wore off. The on-call doctor finally determined that my leg was swelling inside the cast so he split it open to relieve the pressure. The nurse later added another dose of Demerol to my IV but it had absolutely no effect and I was really hurting even with the reduced pressure. She gave it another hit and I started to feel the pain subside a bit. Just about then there was a shift change and a new nurse came into the room, read my chart and told me that it looked like I needed more Demerol as the chart showed it had been four or five hours since my last injection. I was kind of groggy and didn't quite understand what she said . . . When Deb came back after grabbing a bite to eat I was asleep and wasn't aware of those extra injections. Shortly thereafter Deb noticed that my breathing had become quite labored and raspy so she called the nurse to check me out. The nurse said I was just sleeping soundly and that everything was OK. Apparently a few minutes later Deb said I got very quiet . . . She screamed down to the nursing station that I had quit breathing which finally got their attention that something might be wrong. I guess they had to intubate me and put me on a respirator since I had lapsed into a drug overdose coma. Deb was beside herself but I owe her my life since if she hadn't been there those nurses would have never known what was going on! In the meantime I was moved into the intensive care unit and a priest showed up; he thought I might be a goner, and gave me the last rights. This shook Deb up a lot so the priest had to call my folks in Yakima at 3am and told them they might want to drive to Spokane to say goodbye to their son. I hadn't even told them I'd been in a wreck yet so they were a bit surprised to say the least.

When I finally woke up about 24 hours later I was overcome by a choking sensation because of that respirator tube crammed down my windpipe. The doctor told me to try not to breathe and just get in sync with the machine and let it do the work . . . Man, that was easier said than done! Mom and Dad were there and looked pretty rough but everyone seemed pretty happy that they didn't have to plan a funeral right away . . . most of all me! I was finally briefed on everything that happened and eventually had that damn tube pulled out of my throat. Boy it felt good to breathe on my own again but I couldn't talk as those nurses had really dinged up my vocal cords when they had intubated me. Then they hit me with the really bad news; while jostling me around with that cast split open they had re-broken my leg and I would have to have another surgery to put the bones back together again. Shit-O-Dear, this was turning into a real nightmare!! The doctor wanted to wait a few days for me to get stronger so I had to endure many more painful hours with no medication whatsoever since the staff was now really freaked out about over-dosing me again. While I was in the coma my good friend and fellow trooper Don Campbell (Cambie) 273 stayed at the hospital with Deb until my folks arrived; he was a tremendous help during that time and I have never forgotten his thoughtfulness. He also notified all the District 4 brass that it didn't look like I would make it. They, along with their wives, came down to stay with Deb that night!

We never received an apology or even an acknowledgement from the hospital that they had screwed up but I'm sure the hospital attorneys told the staff to handle it that way anticipating a lawsuit. 360 came for a brief visit before my second surgery and seemed pretty upset . . . I was pretty mad at him for a long time afterwards, mainly because he had trashed my beautiful Triumph. I finally accepted the fact that had I been in his position and some "unknown" moron flipped me off, I might have done the same thing . . . . I eventually let the anger go. The second surgery went well but they still wouldn't let me go home until I had extensive physical therapy; apparently I had aspirated into my lungs at some point in the fracas and now needed to clean the gunk out of them. I finally got to go home after about two weeks and it was a tremendous relief to get out of that god-damned torture chamber loosely called a hospital. My sergeant Rick Jenson and 360's sergeant showed up at the house one day to report on the findings of their investigation into our 'incident'. It was officially determined, and I quote Sergeant Ed Crawford verbatim, that "Boys will be boys" and we were each given a written reprimand: mine was for speeding and Dan's was for using excessive force during a violator stop. They now call ramming motorcycles a use of deadly force and lethal intervention. The guy you use it on had better have just killed several people or blown up a church full of parishioners otherwise you could expect to be fired, criminally charged, and probably end up making a trip to the 'big house'. Trying to kill someone for a misdemeanor traffic violation was largely frowned upon then and still is now. After his retirement, Dan became a defense attorney in Spokane . . . .

After about a month I was allowed to go back to work in radio while I recuperated. They gave me an old unmarked patrol car to commute in and it was a real hassle getting in and out of that thing, let alone driving it with a full length cast on up to my crotch. It was fun to be working radio again but those stupid phone calls from the public were the same as before. However, I tried to be a little more sympathetic with them since I hadn't exactly been on top of my game lately. Trooper Phil Giles 851 came in one day to autograph my cast; he was a tremendous artist but the final result of his creation was somewhat on the pornographic side and definitely needed an XXX rating. I had to wear longer pants to cover it up until I went back to the hospital to have it cut off and have a fiberglass (waterproof) cast installed. The doctor sawing the old cast off laughed like crazy when he saw Phil's artwork and I had him preserve that section for posterity. The new cast was a huge improvement since I could now take a shower with it without having to put my leg in a garbage bag tied off with rubber bands.

As the spring of 1977 rolled around 273 came over to the house to help me finish off our basement. He was a tremendous all around handyman and was an expert framer, plumber, electrician, sheet rocker, tiler, you name it. While I hobbled around fetching tools for him he did most of the work and in no time Deb and I had a finished basement. All Cambie required was a supply of Olympia beer to keep him motivated. I learned just about everything about home construction from him and it was a joy to watch him work. After a couple of beers he was able to drive home a 16 penny nail with one swing of the hammer. His construction skills were just the tip of the iceberg though; Cambie had a photographic memory and could remember every detail of every violator contact he ever had. When he heard someone else running a drivers check on a particular guy he would come on the air and ask that trooper if so and so was still driving his green '66 Ford PU and then give a synopsis of his violator contact with the guy that might have occurred seven or eight years ago. He later became a total accident scene reconstructionist detective and just blew people away in court with his accuracy, technical knowledge, and detail. Cambie was taken from us way too soon while still a young man and every time Deb and I pass through Cheney we stop by his grave up on the hill West of town to say hi.

By late Spring I was finally given the OK to go back to work and boy was I ready. I had put on quite a bit of weight while working radio and had ballooned up to 245 from my regular 205. I couldn't handle running yet so we bought an exercise bike which I worked out on religiously. When Captain McKillip 24 saw me in my bulged out uniform he said I looked like Buddha . . . . That remark was my motivation to lose the weight! Someone else had gone over to Olympia to fetch my new Chev patrol car but I wished they had left it there. Even though it had a 454 in it, it was a gutless wonder and couldn't get out of its own way; we just called them tuna boats. At that same time there was an older trooper named Dick Schroeder who primarily worked as a Safety Education Officer but was driving a very low mileage '74 Dodge Monaco like the one I had just turned in. I asked him if he'd like to trade cars and he said sure. I was ecstatic to be back in a real patrol car again and out of that lumbering Tuna Boat.

I slowly had fixed up my old Triumph while recuperating and by the summer of '77 decided it was time to go for a ride again. There is a lovely county road south of the Hangman area called Valley Chapel. Deb and I were cruising down it one evening and coming up to a long sweeping corner when for some unknown reason the hackles stood up on the back of my neck and I unconsciously eased the bike towards the right shoulder a bit. Just then two Corvettes came around the sweeper side by side going the other way wide open . . . The one in our lane came so close that I felt its mirror graze my pant leg . . . I pulled over and was shaking worse than Deb this time. Well, we drove home and parked that TR6. That was 35 years ago and I haven't ridden a bike on the street since. I spent a lot of time while working the next few months driving around that same area looking for those two Vettes but never saw them again. It was probably for the best since my contacting them would have no doubt generated the bitch letter to end all bitch letters . . .

In the next few years I covered quite a few motorcycle injury accidents and a couple fatals; the horrible carnage from those wrecks always reinforced my decision to stay off bikes forever. One non fatal motorcycle accident really sticks in my mind. An Airman from Fairchild AFB lost his bike on Hayford Road one evening and rolled himself down the pavement and gravel shoulder for a hundred yards or so; we called this doing an eggbeater. He had a helmet on but that was about it; cutoff jeans, a tank top, and thongs finished off his wardrobe. Needless to say he was a mass of abrasions, cuts, bruises, and there must have been several pounds of gravel imbedded in all his wounds. He absolutely did not want to get in an ambulance, go to the hospital, or be treated anywhere 'officially'. Apparently he was on some kind of 'probation' at the base and if his boss found out he had been in a bike accident, serious grief would rain down upon him. I could relate to this guy's dilemma. He asked me if I could clean him up a little and make him presentable. This was going to take awhile but I opened up my first aid kit and broke open several viles of Merthiolate. This was a heavy duty iodine type disinfectant and stung like hell on just a tiny little scrape let alone open wounds and gashes. I had to soak a huge bandage in the stuff and then basically drenched the poor guy in it to clean him up while trying to brush all the gravel out of his wounds. I could see I was really hurting him but he kept telling me to keep going. I finally used up all the Merthiolate I had and bandaged him up the best I could. I helped him drag his bike out of the ditch, straightened out his forks and handlebars, and sent him on his way. I called it a non-reportable accident and just prayed I didn't get a call from the AFB that he had died of sepsis or some other horrible infection in the next few weeks.

Motorcycle fatal South of Cheney.

The next bike accident I covered that summer didn't turn out quite so well for a young couple South of Cheney. They were riding their motorcycle Southbound on the Cheney Plaza Road and drifted over the center-line into the path of an oncoming pickup. When I got there the carnage really took my breath away. The driver of the pickup was just devastated. The image of those two torn up bodies is still vivid in my mind so I can't imagine how he's dealt with it all these years. I vowed once more that I would never ride a bike again on the street; you can make a mistake in a car and probably survive but riding bikes is just so unforgiving of even a momentary lapse in judgment.

It didn't take long before I got back into the usual routine of grabbing a radar unit every day and heading out to my favorite fishing hole near Four Lakes on I-90 Westbound. There was a great overpass there to hide behind and drivers never saw you until it was too late. So many troopers used the spot that we had to have the Highway Dept. come out occasionally to grade and smooth out the washboards we created when accelerating hard out of our hiding spot to chase the fast ones down. I was always amazed at how many people thought it was 'unfair' for us to hide behind bridge abutments . . . When they made that statement I always queried them right back if they thought it was fair to only go the speed limit when they saw a patrolman on the shoulder instead of maintaining a constant speed all the time as the law requires . . . I guess such simple logic was too overwhelming for a lot of folks since their next statement was usually; "I don't like the tone of your voice followed by "What's your badge number and how do I get a hold of your supervisor?"

When I was a rookie troop the excuses I would hear for speeding seemed somewhat interesting for a few months. Eventually, I was just amazed at the total lack of imagination most drivers had when it came time to explain why they were speeding. The excuses always seemed to come down to the same lame examples that troopers have heard on a daily basis for the last 90 years or so, such as: 'It must be my snow tires', 'My cruise control doesn't work right', 'The wife was yakking in my ear and I couldn't concentrate', 'The kids were acting up in the back and I had to swat them', 'My car has a real bad vibration right at the speed limit', 'I have diarrhea and I'm trying to get to the rest area,' 'I'm taking my wife to the hospital', 'I just sped up for a second to get around that truck,' etc., etc. The other class of violators were the control freaks who immediately liked to take over the contact by making accusations, such as: 'Let me see that radar reading' . . . When you showed them their flashing speed locked on the screen . . . their response was; 'How do I know that's **my** speed there?' or 'Car and Driver says these radars are extremely inaccurate because of the inherent cosine error', or 'You got the wrong car', or 'My car won't go that fast', or 'My wife was watching the speedometer and she said I never went over the speed limit . . . and 'Are you calling my wife a liar'? 'You look like a rookie, why should I believe you?' 'Motor Trend' says radars are illegal', 'You're nothing but a speed cop . . . . Why aren't you stopping all the rapists and murderers instead of picking on innocent people?' That one always made me laugh as if every other car had a rapist or a murderer in it and like we were supposed to know who the hell they were . . . 'You're just making this shit up to get your quota, that radar isn't even turned on is it?' etc., etc . . . .

A sub-class of the control freak violators was the serial impeders. These were the clowns usually travelling 5-10 mph under the speed limit on a two lane highway with seven or eight very aggravated motorists stacked up behind them. Trying to catch up to and stop one of those morons was often just as aggravating for the troopers. You had to move a number of upset people out of the way, with lights and siren, and never knew which one might decide to execute a frustrated "pissed off pass" without looking in their mirror just as you went by them. When I finally caught up to the perpetrator they often refused to pull over for quite a distance since the self righteous driver just knew he wasn't doing anything wrong. Usually, it was just an elderly driver whose first words were always: "Why are you stopping me officer, I was travelling **under** the speed limit?" I tried to be diplomatic with that crowd while writing them a ticket for impeding traffic. Sadly, some of them were just first class assholes who impeded traffic on purpose just to fulfill some deep seated need for control. There was always a confrontation with these types and the "Why aren't you stopping all the rapists and murderers" comment was the most common remark spat out by them.

Another class of control freaks were the 'briber/deflectors' and their methods were evenly split along gender lines. The method that most men used was fairly uninspired but direct: they would casually hand me their driver's license and registration with a neatly tucked $10 or occasionally a $20 bill folded in with their paperwork. I was always amused at how cheap those dipsticks were . . . . I mean Jesus, only a $20 bribe to get out of a $20.00 ticket . . . . Come-on, let's be reasonable . . . . should have been at least $40 . . . $20 was just an insult!! When I "**ALWAYS**" handed them back their $10 or $20 along with a polite but caustic remark, most of them came back with the same ridiculous line; 'Oh I don't know how that got stuck in there . . . !?' The controlling women were a little more crafty and innovative. On the initial contact their skirts would be at a normal knee length and their blouses buttoned up to normal and acceptable standards. When they were told they would be receiving a ticket and that I would be a couple minutes there was quite often a very radical change in their appearance by the time I came back to their car to have them sign it. The skirt had somehow been hiked up to within a cats whisker of their panties, a strong odor of cologne now filled the air, their blouses had somehow become unbuttoned or unzipped to the extent that copius cleavage and/or bra material was now being exposed and their demeanor and speech had suddenly devolved into the sultry—dripping with concern variety . . . The most often heard remark was: "Oh, it must be sooo dangerous and exciting being a state trooper" with corresponding eye, upper body movement, and facial expressions matching their newfound concern for my well being . . . . Of course, I heard of other less professional (usually single) troopers who would drag out this type of contact for several minutes . . . . But I was all business and just gave them the ticket and left . . . . ?! (Hey, Debbie might read this sometime . . .) It got to the point that when I walked up to a car and the driver admitted exactly what his speed was that I would just be beside myself with disbelief! I almost always gave those types a warning, praised them if their kids were present, and always thanked them for their honesty. If the other 95% of the motoring public would just try that simple method when they get stopped, everyone could sure save themselves a butt load of money! Contacting violators and expecting them to tell the truth reminds me of a recurring line from the great TV series *House:* 'Everybody Lies!' Nothing could be more true!!

Another common response we got from a large number of violators after they were presented with a ticket, told how much the bail was (back then $15.00 was a lot of money) and were asked to sign it was: "I pay your salary and this is just highway robbery . . . ." Now usually when I heard this one I just let it go and patiently waited for them as they scribbled some infantile remarks on the face of the ticket such as: "This is illegal and I am signing under protest!!" However, on one memorable occasion I guess I sort of lost it since this particular violator had been a real "Dick of the Woods" type throughout the whole contact. After his stupid "You work for me and I pay your salary remark" without thinking I said: "You know sir, stopping you today makes it 400 violators I've caught this month alone . . . . Since you pay my salary, how 'bout a small color TV or a microwave as a bonus for all my hard work??" Holy shit, that didn't go over well at all and I have to admit I was a little ashamed of myself . . . . Of course, a week later I was called into Lt. Colwill's office yet again . . . . As usual, I could clearly see his carotid pulse pounding away on the side of his neck as he tried to maintain his composure with me . . . . But he was cool and just said: "I have a letter here from a Mr. Snodgrass who claims that you told him you would not write him a ticket if he bought you a TV or a microwave . . . . !!" Well, I had to admit that Mr. Snodgrass could certainly "turn a phrase" pretty well but it still took me quite awhile to convince the lieutenant that I wasn't out there taking bribes . . . .

Rick Meyers 24 eventually took over as our district commander but I was a little concerned about his winter-time driving decisions after a funny incident out on Trails Rd. one morning. We had experienced another localized freezing rain episode in a small area of the West Beat near Fort George Wright and there were numerous cars in the ditch. There was a fairly steep grade on this portion of Trails Rd. and nearly every car coming down the hill ended up in the ditch. When I arrived, I had already chained up my patrol car at Dukes, and didn't have too much trouble going from one accident to the other. I asked Trooper Fred Swan 843 to close the road at the top of the hill until we got it salted and sanded. Captain Meyers had been monitoring events in radio, where I'm sure the weather was just fine. When he heard that I had closed a road he felt he had to come out and investigate the conditions himself. I was at a school bus in the ditch facing downhill when I noticed his unmarked blue Pontiac patrol car coming towards me. He nonchalantly pulled along side me, driver door to driver door, as if this was just a normal roadside contact between two troopers. He started to say "Rick, what are you doing closing a main arterial without my permis . . ." Just then I noticed his voice starting to fade away as he found himself sliding backwards towards the school bus . . . . In so doing I believe he just answered his own question. I have to admit he pulled off a pretty slick course reversal maneuver without hitting anything and had that blue Pontiac pointed downhill in no time. There was no further contact between the captain and myself and the county sand trucks showed up shortly thereafter and fixed the whole problem in short order.

Trails Rd turns into Government Way a little further down the hill from where those accidents were and near a cemetery in that area we used to conduct 'Spot Checks'. I'm pretty sure they are illegal now but they were a commonly used tool back then to jack up your monthly activity. You just had to find a safe wide area, have several troopers on hand, turn on all your red & blue lights and start 'randomly' flagging cars in to supposedly 'inspect' their equipment. We were primarily looking for bald tires, cracked windshields, broken light lenses, loud mufflers, inoperative horns, weak brakes, loose steering, etc. We weren't supposed to ask for a driver's license unless we found an equipment violation . . . Well, you can always find 'something' even on a brand new car; no litter bag, misplaced license plate tags, failure to signal when being flagged in, too many bugs on the windshield, etc. Although we were not supposed to flag in obvious 'junkers' the spot checks usually devolved to that level quite rapidly. The problem was that if you didn't find anything wrong with a car you didn't get credit for a stop on your monthly 68 Activity Report so it was counterproductive to flag in Ma & Pa in their new Cadillac just because they were the next car coming. Each trooper had his own spot check style; some only flagged in convertibles loaded with pretty co-eds from the nearby community college even timing the spot check for known break times there. Others went after specific 'pet peeve' vehicles; one troop hated taxis for some reason and really raked those guys over the coals. Other guys singled out trucks, some older Volkswagons, (which were always good for something), or even wreckers. One guy even held 'one man' spot checks which were really forbidden; those usually occurred near the end of the month when a quick review of your monthly totals revealed that your 68 was going to be a little on the 'light' side. The randomness aspect of spot checks sort of lost meaning after awhile and probably had something to do with them being discontinued. You always had to keep your head on a swivel during a spot check; when you saw some guy doing a u-turn on either side of the designated area, you had to immediately drop everything and chase him down. 99% of the time he either had a suspended license or warrants; nice thing was you just saw him make an illegal u-turn so if he was clean you at least got a pinch for that. I once got a DWI once out of this scenario as did several other guys. After one spot check I was dropping off my tickets and written warnings in the sergeant's inbox and noticed a warning that 641 had issued to some poor sap sitting on top of the pile; the first charge was for 'unsafe tires' but the second one was a charge I was unfamiliar with; 'Masturbating in public without a permit . . . .' I only hoped that Pete had 'added' that second charge after the fact, to see if the sergeant was even checking his work, and didn't actually witness that sort of activity at a spot check . . . .

This story really reinforces '*House's*' 'Everybody Lies' prediction . . . . I stopped a brand new Cadillac one evening out near the Sprague overpass Westbound. It was doing about 25 over the limit and the driver took a long time stopping, driving down the shoulder for almost a mile. When I contacted the driver and got his license I recognized the family name immediately before he even opened his mouth. I knew I was about to be treated to a real cock and bull story as this family was notorious for their criminal activity in the Spokane area. Before he could speak an elderly lady sitting in the front seat lashed out at me saying; 'Can't you see we have a family emergency here?' I played along and asked what that might be . . . She screamed at me and said her husband was having a heart attack in the back seat! I took a look at him and recognized the patriarch of the local crime family himself. His name and photo had been in the paper several times lately usually associated with some sort of used car or fortune telling scam . . . . He was just staring straight ahead and not talking but seemed intoxicated; apparently he was letting junior be the designated driver for the evening. He was not in distress and refused to answer my questions about his medical condition. Against my better judgement I told junior I would follow them to the hospital and he'd better keep it at the speed limit. So off we went and then I realized they never said which hospital they were going to; I thought this might turn out to be fairly entertaining since I was sure they had no idea where the hospitals were and now they had a cop following them to one. Well, junior indeed did not know where he was going, and I could see a lot of violent gesturing going on in the car as the old lady yelled directions at him. I watched the old man turn around several times to see if I was still there. I was really enjoying the show and while following them ran a driver's check on junior and a registration/check stolen on the car. Everything came back OK on the car but junior's license was suspended for continuing offenses. After taking 30 minutes to make the ten minute drive to Deaconess Hospital they arrived at the emergency room sally port. I parked back a ways just out of their sight and turned my lights off. I could just barely see them but no one got out for about five minutes . . . . However, there was a lot of twisting and turning activity in the car as they tried to determine if I was still there or not. Finally, junior went in and came out with an ER attendant. They loaded the old man in a wheel chair and took him in. At this point it wasn't fun anymore so I finally took off to go have coffee and brag about my encounter with these dip shits. Several hours later I stopped by the ER room to inquire how the old man was doing. They all laughed out loud after I filled them in on all the details and said as soon as they saw me leave the old man sprung out of his wheelchair, got in the car and left. Thankfully, I had written down everything I needed to arrest junior for and sent him a ticket, via the prosecutor, for speeding and driving while suspended. About a year later I saw in the paper where junior had been busted in an FBI sting for dealing in stolen car parts and rolling back odometers; couldn't have happened to a nicer family!

Another day as I rolled into my 'radar hole' out at Four Lakes I thought I saw some movement up under the concrete bridge girders in a dirty dark corner right under the freeway decking. I got on my PA (public address speaker) and asked whoever was up there to come down so I could talk to them; it was a pretty steep slope and two guys basically slid and rolled on down to me. They pretty much met the textbook definition of unkempt and disheveled and didn't smell too good either! However they both had ID's and their names were immediately seared into my memory forever; I didn't even have to refer to my old bluebooks while writing this since I have never forgotten them. They were both proud Native Americans currently living in Alberta and just hitchhiking around the country. I don't recall which tribe they were from but their names were; Johnny Drag Guts Through the Fence and Peter Pretty Weasel Walks Along. They were nice guys and we chatted for awhile but I had no intention of writing them tickets for anything. I thought their names were very special and meaningful and quite symbolic of a different era in U.S. history. I gave them a couple of the Hostess Fruit Pies I always carried around in the car, for the sad and hungry folks I always seemed to run into, and took them off the freeway. After I set the radar up again I thought I better run driver's checks on them just in case. In those years a driver's check was run last name first, then first name, middle initial, and DOB. So my call to radio was; '305 Spokane two drivers checks, check WACIC-NCIC.' (wacic was the Washington Crime Information Computer and ncic was the National Crime Information Computer) 'Spokane 305 go ahead' . . . . 'Number 1 . . . Drag Guts Through The Fence, Johnny, no middle initial 9-9-99—**common spelling** and number two' . . . long pause from radio then . . . 'go ahead number two 305' . . . 'Pretty Weasel Walks Along, Peter, no middle initial, 8-8-88—**common spelling** . . . . There was another long pause then Radio Supervisor Bill Reilly himself finally came on the air and asked me if there were any other aliases they should run as well . . . . I responded with 'That's an unknown Spokane' . . . . But good old Bill just wouldn't leave it alone now since I had made that smart ass 'common spelling' comment which was normally reserved for guys named Jones or Smith . . . He then asked me to phonetically spell their names out letter by letter. So I played along and began: 'Number 1, david, george, tom, tom, frank, etc., etc. until I got through them all; he then just routinely signed me off. A few minutes later Bill came back with the no wants or warrants call on both of them and calmly asked me to contact radio at my convenience . . . . I wonder why? On a Salmon fishing trip to Smithers B.C. one year my Dad and I had the pleasure of meeting several of the local Native Canadians in that area and several of them had similar names to Peter and Johnny; I hope their trip went well!

The PA system on our patrol cars was a tremendous tool for working the road but like any other electronic tool the operators often abused or misused it. The misuse of the PA was demonstrated to quite a few of us early on one day shift. Everything was quiet and peaceful, you could hear the birds singing, not a cloud in the sky, not a whisper of wind when out of no-where this idyllic setting was blasted into oblivion by the following scream on the radio: "If you don't pull that fu***ng motorcycle over right now I'm going to shove my push bars up your fu***ng ass!!!" Jesus Christ . . . . I about creamed my jeans when I heard that transmission on Spokane area frequency! I immediately looked down at my PA-Radio-Microphone switching panel to make sure I had my own PA switch in the right position unlike the one of this particular trooper . . . This was an easy mistake to make and I have done it myself several times . . . . just not quite as memorable as this episode. I've also heard airline pilots make the same switch mistake while cruising along in the Beechjet at FL410; suddenly the FAA radio would come alive and for our listening pleasure we'd be treated to some nearby Delta Captain announcing to everyone on the Salt Lake Center frequency that it was now OK to get up and move about the cabin since I have turned off the seat belt sign and the beverage cart would soon be coming down the aisle . . . or the other stuff I described earlier in the Preface . . . . Anyway, poor old 1643 had to endure several minutes of abusive comments from his work-mates that sounded something like this: "You're gonna do what with what there 1643?" 'Did that Moped driver stop for you 1643?" "Don't forget to hose off your push bars when you're done with that guy 1643!" etc., etc . . . Well, we were pretty hard on him but everyone knew in his heart that "there but by the grace of God go I".

Myself and '78 Plymouth patrol car at District IV Office in Spokane, 1980

My '78 Plymouth . . . . Last of the good patrol cars with a Mopar 440

In 1978 I finally traded in my second '74 Dodge on the last good patrol car I would ever be issued, a '78 Plymouth Fury, last patrol car with the 440 in it. This car had it all; it was very fast, a lot lighter than that old '74, great brakes, super suspension, radial tires, and was the best handling car I had driven yet. I wanted to keep it forever because word was that the department was looking to purchase more fuel efficient fleet cars in the future. (the age of those stinking Dodge Diplomats was soon to be upon us)

On a trip to Seattle Deb and I were browsing around at Pier 54 when I came across a battery operated 'Laughing Box.' I immediately saw the PA abuse potential with this sweet little box and bought two of them since I knew it was going to get a lot of use in my brand new patrol car. I practiced with it at home to get the proper volume settings and to see how close I needed to get it to the mike to achieve the perfect crazy-demented laugh volume I was looking for. Man, when amplified by the PA in my new Plymouth it was just awesome . . . . you could hear it for a mile or more! I still have that box, doesn't work anymore but sure brings back a lot of memories. Anyway, my first day back to work I was trolling around looking for an innocent victim to attack when I saw it; right at Thor Freya Eastbound Phil Giles 851 had a violator pulled over. I stopped on the shoulder several hundred yards behind him since my timing would have to be perfect to get the full blast effect on both him and his violator. When I saw him walking back up to the violator's car to have the driver sign the ticket I went into action; I wanted to keep my speed fairly slow but needed another car between myself and Phil so Phil's violator wouldn't suspect the laughter was coming from me. Things worked out pretty well but when I keyed the mike I scared the shit out of the guy I was driving next to and he almost crashed into me. I saw Phil look up in astonishment and his violator did not seem pleased at all to hear this maniacal laughter exacerbating his predicament for all to see. Jesus, I never laughed so hard in my whole life and was pretty pleased with myself. Phil saw me hiding next to that car as I went past and called for a contact a few minutes later. Our favorite coffee joint was at the Spokane House near the top of Old Sunset where we normally met on Sunday mornings to relive the latest episode of Saturday Night Live. Man, we both thought that John Belushi, Dan Akroyd, and that whole crew were the craziest mothers on the planet. Anyway, far from being mad Phil was beside himself with envy and wanted to know all the details about my box. I didn't tell him I had two of them because this was 'my' new gig and I didn't want any competition for the laughs. I asked him to keep quiet about it for awhile so I could get as many attacks in as possible before the brass found out and confiscated it. Most of the other troopers I nailed with it told me it was childish and stupid . . . . But I could see the envy in their eyes . . . . at least I thought it was envy back then. Anyway, in the real world new technology doesn't last long and parity shall always reign. While I was out contacting a very disagreeable violator on Geiger Hill and was just about ready to drag the shithead out of the car to cuff him we were suddenly blasted by a terrific crazy maniacal demented laughter of biblical proportions!! Of course I looked up to see Phil driving by, but he had no car running interference for him. I could see him laughing hysterically in his car but I thought he had pulled a major boner by not hiding himself in traffic better. I had to let my shithead go since there was no doubt he would bring up the laughing box usage in court and rat us out. When we debriefed Phil admitted he had 'blown it' but said he just couldn't get the timing down right for a perfect pass. We both had a lot of fun with those boxes and it sure helped ease the pain sometimes during or after a bad day.

I had my own 'different' sort of radio related fiasco several months later. Thankfully it occurred late at night unlike poor 1643's day shift episode; however there was still three or four troops on the air and two radio operators who heard me. I'm jumping ahead in time a bit but I had just been issued a brand new '81 Dodge Diplomat, which I will trash talk later. That was the first year they switched over to these rather large but all plastic lightweight microphones. The old solid iron Motorola mikes had worked well over the years and were so heavy that some guys had ripped them out and used them as a weapon. Anyway, these new mikes had a lot of rough plastic edges on the outside and apparently on the inside as well. I had just run a driver's check and hung the mike up on its dashboard clip. Unbeknownst to me a piece of jagged plastic had jammed up the mike push to talk button in the transmit position and I had just hung up a 'hot mike'. Normally we only used it as a hot mike when we had a drunk in the back yelling and screaming profanities and wanted to share their tirade with everyone that was working. By 1981 the brass had finally conceded that AM Radios in patrol cars would not cause Armageddon so I just happened to be listening to KJRB that night on my factory installed radio. Just as I hung the mike up Neil Diamond came on singing "He Ain't Heavy He's My Brother". Man, I loved that song and turned the volume up and began singing along . . . . As you might recall from an earlier chapter I had been officially classified as a 'crow' and was not allowed to sing in public. Anyway I'm loudly groaning away for all to hear; 'The road is long, with many a winding turn that leads us to who knows where . . . .' When suddenly my CB radio comes alive; (this was another piece of equipment that the brass had fought against for years to install in our patrol cars believing they would also cause patrol car accidents and distracted troopers). "Rick, Rick, you're transmitting on area frequency!!" Shit Shit Shit!! Then I prayed I had only thought those profanities to myself and hadn't actually transmitted them too! Anyway, I grabbed that mike and unstuck the button. Thankfully, there weren't too many unsavory comments just Buzz Binsfield in radio who professionally advised me to skip whatever audition I was practicing for . . . There were a couple 'nice one 305' and lastly a 'Sounds like you've got laryngitis there Neil'.

We all had made up our own CB handles by then and had devised an automatic system whereby we rotated which channel we would use for bullshitting each day; I think it was the number of the month plus the day of the week or something stupid like that. Channel 19 was reserved for the truckers and channel 9 was the emergency channel. Anyway, my call sign or CB handle was Dogsbody. Nobody knew what that meant but I had just read WWII British Spitfire Pilot Douglas Bader's autobiography and that was his call sign during the Battle of Britain and I thought it was cool. I wish I could remember all the other guys handles but I can only recall a couple: Loren Ottenbriet 378 was "The Silver Bullit", Fred Swan 843 was "Moondoggie" and my personal favorite was Chris Powell's 448 who had chosen a very classy yet strangely appropriate handle "Dorkbreath". We would chat for hours on the CB which really were the late seventies early eighties version of cell phones and texting. They really made the shift go faster but we never had anything to talk about at coffee since we had already exhausted all our conversation topics by then. So as predicted it didn't take long until many of those low life troopers began to abuse those CB's just as the brass had predicted . . .

National Guard UH1 fatal crash on a frozen Medical
Lake with Loren Ottenbreit 378 having a look.

I had just left the west office one foggy morning when radio put out an
airplane crash into Medical Lake. I was there in a couple minutes and
my initial reaction was really gut-wrenching . . . . Medical Lake was
frozen solid and there was red liquid scattered all around the remains
of an Army Guard UH1 helicopter on top of the ice. Thankfully,
the crewmen had already been taken to the hospital at Fairchild
AFB where I think two of them didn't make it. As myself and Loren
Ottenbreit 378 walked around the grisly scene we discovered that the
red liquid wasn't blood after all but hydraulic fluid from the UH1.
Later when the fog lifted to about 200 ft we could see what happened.
The UH1 had departed Geiger Field and continued westbound into
an area of lowering ceiling and visibility conditions. We saw that the
tops of a couple pine trees on the east shore of Medical Lake had been
sheared off and were scattered on the ice in a line with the crash site.
During the crash one of the rotor blades flew all the way across the
lake and imbedded itself into a frozen dirt bank on the far side . . . .

The very next morning, I was asked to help out one of the Ritzville detachment troops with a semi-snow plow fatal out between Davenport and Reardan. It was still foggy out with lots of black ice everywhere. The snow plow had been scattering sand on the roadway when the semi driver apparently fell asleep, crossed the center line, and hit him nearly head-on. After I'd spent several hours out there helping the other troop his sergeant finally showed up to supervise the investigation. This clown comes over to me and doesn't offer a word of thanks for helping his troop investigate and clean up a messy fatal out of my detachment area. He just takes a long sneering sideways look at some one inch long hair sticking out from under my campaign hat strap and says; "Why don't you just head on back to Spokane boy and get yourself a haircut . . ." Man, there were so many great guys in the WSP but sadly just as many jerks to match . . . .

Semi-Snow Plow fatal near Reardan.

One of our (mine at least) favorite pastimes on a quiet night was to get on channel 19 and do a little 'Redneck Baiting.' Sometimes it took awhile but we would monitor the trucker's conversations until we heard a distinct southern drawl, usually belonging to some citizen of the great states of Mississippi or Alabama, bragging about the Cat engine in his Pete and how he could out-pull any Cummins powered Kenworth down on the grapevine with 90K in back. One of my "fellow" detachment mates was an extremely talented mimic and was just praying for those moments. He would get on the air and insult the living shit out of the Pete driver that was bragging about his Cat power. The remarks were usually along the same derogatory lines and were always intended to enrage the Redneck types. Some of the remarks were: 'Only pussies drive Peterbilts', 'My girlfriend's VW could out pull that piece of shit', 'Maybe your Momma will buy you a Kenworth when you grow a couple', etc., etc. On one occasion a real serious Alabama redneck, who sounded like a Klansman and said his handle was the Mobile Marauder or something just as stupid, got on the air but included several racial epithets while bragging about his Peterbilt. Well this was way too much for my fellow trooper to take without a response and he quickly got on channel 19 with a vengeance to set things straight. He did a perfect impression of a very agitated black truck driver operating a Kenworth; the derogatory and insulting comments were not only aimed at that moron's Peterbilt but at the driver as well. His sexuality was called into question, the size of his Johnson was ridiculed, and lastly he announced that it was common knowledge that all Alabama truck drivers kept a sheep in their sleeper as a girlfriend and 'in your case it was probably a dead one!!' Man that last crack really put the redneck into orbit!! He went totally tits up and was screaming into his mike and every other word was MF 'N' word this and MF 'N' word that and I'm gonna kick your MF black ass from here to breakfast, etc., etc. My buddy calmly advised the redneck that he would gladly meet him at the Broadway Truck Stop in twenty minutes to settle the matter and that he was driving a Blue KW with Michigan plates towing a flatbed loaded with re-bar. The Redneck screamed a few more profanities and racial slurs and said he'd be there!! When my fellow trooper got back on our regularly scheduled CB channel of the day we all congratulated him on his command performance . . . man he had been brilliant . . . ! We all talked about the image of that dip shit redneck searching all over that huge truck-stop trying to find that blue KW with a load of rebar and often wondered how long it took him to realize he'd been scammed.

While on the subject of the Broadway Truck Stop I should add that there were quite a few hookers working the facility ready to service the rednecks whose sheep had died. The only one whose handle I can remember went by Red Rider on the CB. She would get on channel 19 from time to time and ask if anybody wanted to party and sometimes give a brief description of what she was going to do to you. I'm sure she had bills to pay like everyone else and I always felt kind of sorry for those lost souls. On one occasion when I was working graveyard and covering the East beat, radio put out an injured female lying on the ground at the Broadway Truck Stop. When I arrived there was no question who she was since she had a large Red Rider tattoo across her chest. Some john had shoved her out of his sleeper and she got banged up a little. A deputy showed up but nothing much happened as she was not about to name names, file any charges, or get in an ambulance. She was a real mess; dozens of raunchy tattoos, drunk, smelly, fat, only a couple teeth left, just the stereotypical worn out hooker. I never knew when my seminarian training was going to kick in but I felt I could at least spend a little time with her since her life seemed to be at quite a low ebb right then. I told her not to worry, I wasn't about to arrest her for anything, and asked if she just wanted to 'rap' a little. We talked for twenty minutes or so in my patrol car and she calmed down a little but it was obvious that no amount of talking was ever going to heal her wounds so I gave her one of my Hostess Fruit Pies. I honestly felt sorry for old Red Rider and all the others like her trapped in that miserable profession.

Trooper Loren Ottenbreit 378 had transferred to Spokane by now and joined the West beat. We spent a lot of time together in those years, as we still do, and we all get along very well together. Their second baby, Jon, was born in 1976 and went on to play football for WSU during their Rose Bowl year of 1998. We bought a ski boat in 1979 and the Ottenbreits were our automatic guests for skiing every summer at Lake Coeur d' Alene and Lake Pend Orielle for many years thereafter.

I hadn't skied since the canal days with brother Ray so it was fun to get back on a lake with lots of room with no cows or horses to run into. Loren was already an accomplished slalom skier having grown up in Kalispell where his family skied on Flathead Lake. We just had to get the wives up to speed and Deb and Chris learned very quickly. The boat ramp at Rockford Bay on Coeur d' Alene, where we normally put in, was always a challenge. It was quite steep and narrow and had a bend in the middle which made unloading a real event. The most fun was in the evening when we got to watch all the drunks try to back down that wet ramp and then pull a large boat out with a small two wheel drive pickup. The number of jack-knife events was always impressive but when they started spinning their tires trying to climb up that steep wet ramp until they were smoking and burning, it was a sight to behold.

Three times a year the West Beat troopers had to sweat out the most horrible assignments known to man . . . . performing manual traffic control duties at either the Fairchild AFB Air Show on SR-2, the Cheney Rodeo on SR-904, or the Summer National Drag Races at Hayford and SR-2. I hated those assignments with a passion and as I recall might have called in sick a couple times to avoid them . . . . My most memorable (or forgettable) episode occurred while assigned to the drag races one afternoon after the Sunday final eliminations were over. I was parked on the south side of SR-2 near the old Longhorn Burger Stop, watching southbound traffic on Hayford Rd coming out of the drags. By then, DOT had installed a hand held stop light controller, with a long extension cord, so we could control which way we wanted traffic to flow according to which highway was getting backed up the most. For the most part I was giving the southbound traffic on Hayford Rd the green light the longest due to the heavy traffic coming out of the drags but at some point I had to let the SR-2 traffic flow as well. Just after I had given the east-west SR-2 traffic the green light for a couple minutes I switched it back to let the drag race crowd out . . . . I was sitting at a picnic table near the intersection with the controller in my hand when I noticed a British Columbia licensed pickup turning left right in front of me . . . . Now to say that there was a lot of drinking going on at the drags would be quite the understatement . . . . In reality there was a huge SHITLOAD of drinking going on and about 95% of the cars coming out were full of drunks. Every year we waited for them with lots of extra troopers and always racked up several dozen DWIs!! Anyway as the Blue Plate Special (Our term for British Columbia cars) went by I noticed three guys in the back standing up with their backs to me . . . Just as they passed they all bent over and dropped their pants and gave me the first and only triple 'Moon Job' I had ever seen or heard of . . . Apparently I had really pissed them off by holding them up at the light for a couple minutes . . . . I have to admit that it was a very well done BA job and choreographed perfectly . . . My first reaction was to just laugh out loud but I soon recaptured my composure and radioed the license plate and description of the vehicle to some waiting troops down the road a bit . . . They got the pickup stopped but unbelievably the driver was sober . . . Man, that was just unheard of for a Blue Plate Special . . . . !! The troop asked me what I wanted done with the three in the back who had hung the BA's . . . . Having been involved in similar incidents myself in college I just said, "Ahh, nothing, let's focus on the DWI's . . . ." I used to regularly encounter "blue plate specials" during my road trooper years. Whenever I asked the driver what he was doing down in "the states" today their response was invariably: "Oh, we're just down and "aboot" on holiday ehh!" Don't know why, but that always cracked me up!

Speaking of sights to behold, it was around this time that I felt I needed to 'educate' some of the teenagers I was stopping about the real perils and hazards of drinking and driving and/or general reckless driving that all of us succumb to when we're in that 16 to 21 'invulnerable' age bracket. I carried copies of some very gruesome and graphic fatal photos in the jockey box of my patrol car in those days which depicted some decapitated bodies and mutilated corpses from a few of the fatals I'd covered. Whenever I'd stop some kids who didn't seem or want to understand how serious the repercussions of bad driving was I'd show them those horrible photos to jar their senses a little. Those photos would normally make adults want to vomit immediately and I knew I was making an impression on those kids. But like so many other of my 'brainstorms' I eventually was ordered to cease and desist this activity by my sergeant after the parents of one kid filed a lengthy complaint against me. They claimed I had done irreparable harm to their son's gentle psyche by exposing him to the graphic images of mutilated bodies from a high speed crash . . . I remembered that little puke had laughed his ass off when I first showed him those photos, putting on quite the macho show for his little buddies in the car with him . . . . So, back into my evidence locker went my personal 'safety education' curriculum.

A sort of funny incident occurred one afternoon as I was taking an 'assist' on Sunset Hill, which is how we classified changing a tire on our 68 reports. I had my freeway jack out and in hardly no time had that flat tire off and the spare going on for the 'helpless' motorist. While so engaged another motorist from out of state saw me at work and slowed to take a photo of the scene. They were from New York where they indicated in a later comp letter (one of the few) that the Highway Patrol there didn't stoop to such mundane tasks where they might soil their uniforms so they wanted to record this event for posterity. Just before the New Yorkers drove by Trooper Chris Powell 448 stopped behind me to shoot the breeze when I got done. I guess he was afflicted with the same small bladder syndrome as old 761 however. While waiting for me to finish, he walked up into a nearby small stand of pine trees to relieve himself. About a week later my sergeant gets this nice letter from the New York couple praising the wonderful troopers of the WSP who actually serve the public. When I took a look at that photo I could clearly see 448's backside up in the trees as he was casually pissing away just behind me and thought it was hilarious. I still have that photo in my album and have a good chuckle every time I see it!

Speaking of the Powell brothers, Chris's brother Pete, 641, told me a funny story about an accident he investigated out near the Fairchild AFB main gate one afternoon during a dust storm. Apparently a couple of airmen from some lovely southern state had rear ended a semi trailer they didn't see and one of them sustained a bad laceration to one of his biceps. His uninjured buddy sprang into action when he saw all the blood flowing freely and deftly applied a tourniquet to save his friend's life. When Pete arrived at the scene and scrutinized the quality of the first aid that had been administered to the injured driver he said he had a lot of difficulty not laughing out loud . . . . Apparently, this guy's lower arm was turning quite pale from a too tight tourniquet but more importantly was its placement; the budding EMT had attached it just **below** the guys elbow and well below the laceration! The laceration wasn't that severe in the first place and a compress took care of the bleeding. The things you see as a trooper . . . . and yet, there are still folks out there who are against birth control!!

Since we seem to be talking about funny stories I will never forget a one car accident I covered out near Cheney where the car was crammed full of HUGE football players. These dudes were all members of the Seattle Seahawks, where in those years they completed their summer training camp at EWU in Cheney prior to the regular season. Anyway, these guys were all defensive linemen and the smallest was probably 6' 6" and 245 and there was **five** of them jammed into a BMW 320i 2dr . . . . Somehow the driver had lost control on gravel in a curve just north of the stadium, where the road was being re-surfaced, and rolled that poor old Beemer out into a wheat field landing on its wheels. I had to respond from quite a distance so it took me almost 30 minutes to get to the scene. When I drove up I saw this dust covered BMW 2dr sitting out in the wheat stubble with all of those massive guys still sitting in the car all hunched over as the roof was partially collapsed and the glass was all busted out. I immediately thought they must all be hurt pretty badly but there was no ambulance or fire trucks around . . . Man, this was really odd! It was hotter than hell that day and as I walked up I could see the sweat glistening off all of them. Those guys were like statues in there, all looking straight ahead and nobody was talking. The driver was a player I recognized immediately, as I was a huge Seahawks fan, and he cordially handed me his license and registration. I finally couldn't take it any longer and asked him why the hell everyone was still inside that sweatbox out in the middle of a wheat field? One of the big guys in back blurted out that Coach Knox had instructed the whole team, in no uncertain terms, that if anyone ever got in a wreck to **stay at the scene** and cooperate with the police . . . . I thought that was sound advice but holy shit, I think Coach Knox sort of meant for them to stay in the **vicinity** of the accident scene not to sit all jammed up inside a sweltering wrecked car that might catch on fire . . . . I had them all get out immediately, which was quite a show in itself, and reminded me of those circus scenes where a bunch of clowns started climbing out of a Volkswagen Bug . . . . Now, most of these guys had multi-million dollar contracts and one went on to become a Hall of Famer so it seemed like quite the non sequitur when one of the millionaires told me they were just coming back from seeing *Friday the 13*ᵗʰ*" Part 7* . . . . ?! I don't know why but I expected gentlemen in that income range to be a little more discriminating regarding their entertainment choices . . . Anyway, if you are wondering, I admit I showed the driver a little preferential treatment and didn't write him a ticket . . . . Far be it from me to besmirch the record of a potential NFL Hall of Famer!! Every summer some of us always took our afternoon coffee breaks out in Cheney watching these guys on the practice field at EWU and we always enjoyed the show! I clearly remember back in 1977 or '78 when Jim Zorn and Steve Largent (minus their milk moustaches) came over to the fence and said hi to us. We all had a special affinity with Dave Kreig, whose dad was a Wisconsin State Trooper, and he came over to say hi to us every year after he took over from Jim Zorn as quarterback.

I don't think that many people would classify me as a 'violent' man, quite to the contrary. I always tried to reign in my anger impulses that could result in injuring someone. I 'usually' reacted to extremely rude or provocative violators in a verbal manner and tried to match them insult for insult at the same level of intensity. I almost always abstained from using profanity and never was responsible for escalating the threatening language. On one occasion however I really lost my cool and could have easily broken every bone in the stupid mother fu**er's body had there not been witnesses present . . . . I received a call for assistance (again) from the Ritzville detachment troops to help out with several accidents down on SR 261 between Ritzville and Washtucna. It had been a dry winter and the wind was just howling down there causing 'brown outs' of blowing dirt coming off the cultivated wheat fields. The visibility would be fine for miles and miles then all of a sudden you'd come upon a solid wall of blowing dirt and dust, usually in a little valley or gully, where the visibility was about three feet at best. The first accident I arrived at was totally invisible to me but there was an Adams County deputy there who said he would 'direct me' to the scene. He sat on the hood of my patrol car as we penetrated one of those brown outs and gave me hand signals to keep me going straight. I hadn't started my instrument flying syllabus yet but as I soon found out this was exactly the same as penetrating a very dark cloud, I got vertigo almost immediately and I had difficulty even seeing the deputy sitting on my hood from time to time. He finally gave me the all stop signal. I still couldn't see anything until I got near the front of my car where I discovered the rear end of another car. It had rear ended yet another car that had stopped in the middle of the road due to the total lack of visibility. There were no injuries since the guy doing the rear-ending had at least slowed down somewhat. While I was getting their information I thought I saw a car on the other side of the road stop right next to me in the northbound lane; it was hard to see him even though he was only several feet away. The wind was just howling and I couldn't hear a thing. I started to walk over to him when suddenly there was a flash of light coinciding with a very loud metal to metal crunching sound that I heard quite clearly over the howling wind!! I was also pelted with a shower of what I later discovered was window glass since I was no more than three feet away from that car when it got rear ended by a stupid shit in a pickup doing around 50 mph! Of course the impact took both of them out of sight in the brown out and up the road about 75 feet or so. I was really stunned by this and my initial reaction was how could anyone on the face of the earth be so fu**ing stupid to keep driving into a total brown out at those kinds of speeds . . . ?? As I groped my way up to the wreck I started to get very angry as I realized just how close I had come to getting creamed . . . . When I found the two cars the driver of the first one was thankfully OK but really shaken up. The offending driver was sort of pinned in his car and was complaining that he couldn't open his door. I'm very ashamed to admit what I did next or that every other phrase that came out of my mouth while addressing this miscreant began with 'You stupid mother fu**ing SOB' . . . I screamed at him to get out but he kept saying his door was jammed shut . . . The door glass was broken out of his side window (some of which I was already wearing) and the next thing I knew I had pulled that cretin out the window with such force that I actually got some 'air' with him and then threw him down onto the roadway as hard as I could! He probably weighed around 180 lbs. and I assume

I must have had some adrenaline assistance during that ugly little episode . . . . While I stood over that miserable piece of crap I heard a wind muffled 'Jesus Christ!!' coming from somewhere. Apparently the Adams County deputy had been right behind me the whole time but I hadn't seen him with all the excitement and blowing dust. I'm afraid I was a little terse with him too and told him in no uncertain terms to go and flare off both ends of this dust storm before someone gets killed out here! . . . . He went out of sight immediately. It took awhile but we finally got everything all cleaned up and I wrote both of the offending drivers in those two wrecks tickets for reckless driving . . . . On the way back to Spokane I just couldn't calm down and kept thinking about how close I had just come to making Deb a widow. Of the ten troops killed in the line of duty that I mentioned in the Dedication, seven of them had been killed in car accidents similar to this one . . . . Anyway, I knew that a terrible complaint was going to be filed by the stupid ass I'd slam dunked on the road but I really didn't give a shit right then. This incident was just another in a series of bad scenes that together acted as the final impetus for me to start taking flying lessons. It was just too damn dangerous being a road trooper and I knew I had to find a safer line of work. Additionally, I knew if I kept encountering morons like this one sooner or later there would be a video of me on the six o'clock news beating the living crap out of some puke with my Kel-Lite! A few days later we were having a District 4 (Spokane Area) training session downtown when one of the Ritzville troopers, Brian Holliday 907, came up to me. He was friends with the deputy that had witnessed my little 'indiscretion' and told me that I was the 'talk' of the town. It sounded like the deputy had embellished the events a little since Brian asked me if I had really pulled that guy out through the wing window of his car . . . . I told him I didn't but if he'd had one I think I could have. Well, thankfully the complaint letter never materialized but unbelievably I ended up getting a comp letter from the Ritzville sergeant for helping his troops out that day . . . . What the fu** next??

This story is about a 'drive by' complaint I once received . . . . One snowy day radio gave me a one car 'abandoned' accident out near Reardan. I wasn't too far away as I had just finished up with another accident near Deep Creek and was at the scene in a few minutes. There was no-one around the scene so I called for a tow truck. I walked out to the upside down pickup, which was about a hundred feet off the road in deep snow, to inventory it for the impound. I didn't notice the driver was still in there until I got pretty close and heard him moaning and groaning. Jesus, so much for the abandoned aspect of this accident! He was all hung up in debris and to make matters worse, the gas tank, which was right behind the big bench seat, was ruptured and dripping fuel on him. His radio was on so I knew there was still power being supplied. The fact that he was soaked in gas worried me a bit and I wanted to get him out of there before trudging all the way back to my patrol car to call for an ambulance and get my back board out of the trunk. Anytime a car is upside down I was always nervous about electrical issues and spurious sparks starting a fire so I got him untangled and very carefully drug him out of the pickup by his shirt collar and slid him flat on his back about fifty feet away on top of the snow. I ran to my car to call for the ambulance, got my blankets, and ran back to cover him up and keep him warm. Later when I contacted him at the hospital he was OK in stable condition and I thought that was the end of it . . . . Wrong!! About a week later my sergeant calls me into his office and advises me that some passing motorist had filed a bitch letter about my actions at this accident scene. Apparently the complainant said he was a trained EMT and saw me unprofessionally dragging a guy out of a car without use of a backboard or any head and neck restraints. He went on to say that I could have inflicted all kinds of permanent spinal injuries on that poor victim and that I must be a real untrained idiot. Well I agreed with the idiot description but told my boss that I found it incomprehensible that a trained EMT would just drive by an accident scene without stopping to help a trooper who was obviously struggling with an injured person. My boss agreed and called the moron back and advised him of 'the rest of the story' then chastised him for not stopping to help me. My Boss then was Steve Robertson and he was one of the finest guys I had ever worked for. Unfortunately there was a real ugly incident involving myself and Steve that I will describe in the next chapter.

There was something about that stretch of SR-2 between Fairchild AFB and Reardan; it seemed like every time radio gave me an accident out there it was usually a doozy. The next event was a car pedestrian accident just west of Deep Creek. I arrived to find a very dead hitchhiker lying on the shoulder in front of a Cadillac Fleetwood. He had been walking across a bridge with a narrow shoulder just as the Cadillac approached and drifted over onto that same narrow piece of shoulder he was occupying with disastrous results. The driver of the Cadillac was an elderly man and had not been drinking; he was devastated and inconsolable. I called for my sergeant, the coroner, a photographer, and good ole 653 to help me establish exactly where the hitchhiker was standing when he was struck. Mike was there first and pointed out some interesting Levi Jeans impressions on the hood of the car as well as a belt buckle impression left there. It looked like the hitchhiker had been facing the car when it hit him and it must have been a very scary last moment for the poor guy. The coroner's representative that showed up was a crusty old soul; when she arrived at the scene the first thing she picked up on was what appeared to be a bullet hole in the forehead of the deceased. She looked over the front of the car very carefully and finally had one of those 'Aha!' moments. She focused in on the broken off radio antenna that was located near the rear of the Cadillac's right front fender and noticed it had blood on it. She asked the driver if that antenna had been broken off before the accident and he said yes. She went back to the deceased and performed a medical 'procedure' on his head wound which still makes me gag some 35 years later. She pulled a pencil out of her pocket, and stuck the pencil, eraser end first, into the 'bullet hole' in the poor guy's head until she apparently met some resistance. She marked the length of penetration with her fingertips on the pencil, then pulled it out making a horrible sucking sound. She walked back to the car and measured that length against the height of the radio antenna stub . . . . They were exactly the same. She then announced to us that the broken off antenna stub penetration into his left cerebral hemisphere was the cause of death. Mike and I thought this was a great deduction and all but we both felt that the two broken femurs, two broken arms, crushed pelvis, flailed chest, and extensive internal injuries he had also sustained **might** have had some impact on his death as well. She then performed another semi-medical procedure which also still makes me gag thinking back on it . . . . Before she put her pencil back in her pocket she wiped the guy's gray matter and blood off on her sock then put it back in her pocket. Man, that was a lot to take in, and I thought that maybe she was the only coroner who acted like that . . . . Wrong! Unfortunately, I was privileged to witness two more different representatives from the coroner's office in action within the next year or so acting in a similar manner.

Only two or three miles from the car pedestrian fatal I was called to a vehicle fire early one morning with a confirmed fatality inside. It took me awhile to get there as I had to come all the way from state line. It looked like the driver had fallen asleep, drifted across the centerline on a small bridge, hit a short guard rail and catapulted his van over it down into a gully landing on its wheels. The van had been loaded with paper pull tabs from all the taverns in the area, caught fire as a result of the impact with the bridge, and had burned ferociously. The Deep Creek Volunteer Fire Dept. had already put out the fire and left right after I got there. All that remained was the smoking metal framework of a Ford Van. With all the paper inside it had been a very hot fire that had quickly consumed everything, including the driver. I made the usual call for the sergeant, coroner, and a photographer. The van was still smoldering and too hot to get close to so I just sat on the shoulder all by myself waiting for everyone to show up. I shined my spotlight on the front of the van which was facing me and kept getting a bright reflection off something that I couldn't make out. Against my better judgement I went down in that gully to see what it was. Well, right off, I filled my shoes with mud since the fire dept. had sprayed several thousand gallons in the area fighting the fire. I was able to get a license number off the burned up front plate and then saw what I had been looking at; it was the top of the driver's skull. His skeletal remains were hunched over the top of the steering wheel and his bones were really seared. I had only been to one other fatal where someone had burned up and I can tell you that once you smell the odor of burnt human flesh it sticks with you forever. I beat a hasty retreat back to my patrol car and turned my spotlight off. After getting the registration information I still had to wait a long time before anybody showed up and it really was a little spooky with just me and that poor guy down there . . . Anyway, the coroner's rep. finally showed up and did his investigation. He handed me a partially burned up wallet with quite a bit of 'residue' on it. I grabbed it without thinking and was immediately sorry I had. I went back up to my car and tried to clean the 'gunk' off the wallet and my hands and was finally able to retrieve the guy's half melted driver's license. The coroner had gone back to his van for a body bag and then asked me to 'help' him! Jesus, I didn't know if I was up for this or not but what the hell—I was already covered in mud and other gunk so it couldn't get much worse. The sun was coming up by then and now we could see all the gory details of what was left of the poor guy's body. There was just a little solid material left in the center of his lower abdomen but the rest of him looked just like the skeletons hanging in a biology lab. The coroner tried to pull him out of the van but the deceased's hands were still grasping the steering wheel and were kind of melted and stuck to it. Then he started reefing on the poor guy; the sounds of cracking cartilage and god-awful smells coming out of there really made me weak in the knees and that was the closest I ever came to hurling at an accident scene. He finally pried everything loose and told me to open the body bag. He brought the skeleton over grasping it by the spine. It was all curled up and looked like a bony suitcase as he dropped it into the body bag . . . . Man, I now knew for sure that I wasn't going to sleep well when I got home!! When I got back to my patrol car the early day shift trooper had showed up; it was Jack Obenland 357. He was an old timer ready to retire and not much phased him anymore; all he said was "Crispy critter huh?" He said to call him when I was done and he would buy me a cup of panther piss down at the *Shack*.

The last incident in this stretch of SR2 occurred while I was stopped with a violator near Deep Creek right around dusk. It was really windy that day and there was quite a thunderstorm going on nearby. Just as I was walking back up to the violator's car with a ticket to get signed there was a tremendous flash of light followed by a huge explosion right above us. I ducked down the best I could next to his car just as what looked like molten lava started spraying down on us. I yelled at him to get going and I ran back to my car. I backed up a couple hundred feet and saw what had happened. Lightening had struck a huge transformer right above us and blew the thing up! It was really on fire now and dripping some kind of hot flaming oily goop. I called for help and pretty soon there were all kinds of fire trucks and utility trucks out there. However, I wasn't so shaken that I forgot the WSP prime directive; "Get Your Numbers!" I mailed that violator his ticket via the prosecutor's office and got my scratch!

Car-semi head-on fatal near Spangle.

My last grisly encounter with the coroner's office occurred down on SR195 just south of Spangle one snowy morning. A well known local gentleman was heading south towards Pullman when he apparently fell asleep. The roadways were covered in about three inches of slush as he drifted over the centerline in his small car. A northbound Freightliner driver saw the small car coming across the centerline at him on an apparent collision course and swerved right onto the shoulder until there was no more room. The horrific head-on collision did not end well for the occupant of the small car as it ended up well underneath the front of the big semi truck . . . . At least it was quick and painless for him with no awareness whatsoever. When I arrived at the scene I had already called for all the normal fatal responders since radio had already announced there was a confirmed fatality at the scene. There were perfectly preserved tracks and skid marks in the slush on the shoulder from both vehicles when I first arrived. However, while I was out of the car checking on the deceased a Highway Dept. snow plow came blasting through my scene and before I could wave him off, he plowed away all my skid mark evidence before we could photograph them, while simultaneously sanding and salting the living shit out of the highway! Eventually Trooper Bob Watkins 849 arrived to help me investigate. The coroner soon arrived as well and quickly had the driver in a body bag. The gruesome part was when the coroner asked Bob to retrieve the driver's brain which was lying perfectly intact in the back seat of his car. The impact had severed the driver's head right above his lower jaw and somehow his brain remained intact during that awful decapitation. I don't know why Bob agreed to pick that brain up as I would have told that coroner to do it himself. Anyway, Bob got a shop rag out of his car then fetched that brain for the coroner. I can still see that squeamish look on Bob's face as he picked it up, brought it over, and deposited it into the body bag . . . .

849 and I were at another fatal scene one evening just after dusk north of Medical Lake. Again we were just waiting for the sergeant and coroner to arrive when it was Bob's turn to answer the call of nature this time. We were in a fairly remote farming area, there was hardly any traffic, and the closest house was several hundred yards away. 849 walked out into a wheat field a little ways and was busy irrigating the farmer's winter wheat when I thought I heard something over there. I looked up to see five or six people, apparently from the farm house, standing no more than 50 feet away from Bob who was facing them! They were laughing, snickering, and pointing and I couldn't believe he didn't hear or see them! Of course I hadn't seen them either in

the semi darkness . . . . I yelled out 'BOB' and pointed to the mob of onlookers. He about ruptured himself spinning around and pissed all over his shoes. Man, we laughed about that one for a long time!

OK, I'm done talking about dead people for awhile . . . . I really hated taking my uniforms to the dry cleaners every other day so I usually tried to stretch out their usage to four or five days which Debbie thought was a bit unsanitary but I thought was just being thrifty . . . . In the winter I could get away with it but in the summer I really got those mothers pitted out pretty quickly . . . . I had always relied on the tried and true "tree ring" method to determine when they needed to be changed out . . . . I felt that if a disinterested observer could count three salty "distinct" sweat rings in your armpit area then it was time to swap out all the buttons, pins, badges, and shit onto a fresh shirt. But as it turned out we had a much better method to determine change out time right in our own little household . . . . During those years we had two Burmese kitties at home named Nikki and Teenie . . . . They were wonderful cats and lived to be 21 and 23 respectively. Anyway, Nikki had a somewhat weird fetish that had begun to manifest itself with Debbie's Dad Jerry. She would jump up into his lap and would start rubbing her face in his armpits while purring loudly . . . . Jerry would always respond with a kind "Boy your cat is sure friendly . . ." Soon after that episode I caught her doing the same thing to my uniform shirt laying on the bed but she seemed to be really getting into it . . . . She started by just rolling her face in the armpit of my shirt and purring for awhile but I soon noticed that if the shirt had three or more dried sweat rings that seemed to really set her off . . . . She would bite down on the collar and then began to viciously kick the shit out of my armpits with her hind feet while growling loudly . . . . I thought this was great and it became my new method to absolutely determine the expiration date on a pitted out uniform shirt!

I never had to discharge my issued duty weapon at a suspect or violator in my 33 year career; however I did dispatch quite a few severely injured animals with it during that period and most of those didn't go well. I remember being sent to a car horse accident south of town late one evening. When I arrived I was greeted by a mob of folks around a young horse with two broken front legs. It kept trying to stand up and was making horrible screaming cries as his broken and exposed lower leg bones contacted the pavement with each effort. Several people said I needed to dispatch it immediately and several others said I needed to wait for the owner to arrive to make that determination. I wasn't about to let it suffer any longer and asked if anyone knew where the best place was to shoot a horse in order to drop it immediately. I got several different opinions so just decided to place a round right in its ear. I had someone hold my flashlight on the spot and took careful aim . . . No one bothered to tell me that the horse's owner had just showed up as everyone was concentrating on me making a clean shot . . . Apparently just as I fired my 357 Magnum the owner was just about to tap me on the shoulder and didn't realize that I was in the process of shooting her horse. Well the horrific blast and tremendous elongated fireball that erupted out of the barrel of my 357 that night caused the owner to faint straight away and fall in a heap beside me. I saw her go down and immediately thought the bullet had somehow ricocheted of the horse's skull and nailed her . . . . I checked her all over for injuries but couldn't find any and she soon woke up. Amazingly, the shot in the ear dropped the horse and dispatched it immediately but I was still worried that the owner was going to sue me. However she was fine with everything just very sad to lose such a beautiful young philly. The next incident involved a car and a large Angus bull. It was similar to the story about the horse with the bull suffering two broken front legs and the owner no where to be found. I took careful aim again with a bystander holding my flashlight beam on the poor suffering critter's head and fired . . . . All hell broke loose with the now screaming bull trying to run away from me on those two broken front legs . . . I hadn't missed but I guess the bullet just glanced off that thick skull of his . . . . I got in front of him and with his head weaving all over the place fired again . . . . The bullet bounced off that thick skull again and now he was really suffering and crying! Jesus, everyone was yelling at me and giving me conflicting advice of where to shoot next . . . I tried another shot in the side of the head with the same result . . . . Shit, I was going to have to reload pretty soon if I didn't get a good shot in. Now the bull was bleeding all over the place and really suffering badly . . . He finally fell down on his belly and I panicked and went in real close and placed a shot in the back of his head in that little depression there . . . . Well that finally did it and he quit moving immediately. Jesus, I was worn out and the spectators looked at me like I was just a total dick of the woods! I hoped I would never have to dispatch another animal . . . Wrong! Not even a week later just as I was about to turn off SR 195 onto Hatch Rd to go home for '60' (dinner) I saw a jogger trying to flag me in. I stopped and saw that there was a whitetail deer lying on the shoulder with severe abdominal injuries after being hit by a car. I thought this couldn't be happening again but knew I wasn't going to let it suffer. At least it was lying on the ground. I told the jogger to stand back and walked up to the poor deer and fired into the back of its skull hoping to get a quick kill shot like I did on that bull. The son of a bitch leapt to its feet and with its intestines dragging on the ground and two broken legs tried to run away!! God damn it, what do I have to do to finish these poor bastards off? Is there something wrong with this shitty ammo they issue us? The jogger went tits up and started yelling profanities at me because I was torturing the poor thing and that I should have called for a vet! The damn deer started dragging itself across the freeway . . . I checked around to make sure of my line of fire and pumped two more rounds into its head. Thank god it finally quit moving and I hauled the poor thing off the highway by its hind legs before I got run over too. In those days we had a list of people who came out to pick up road kills for their exotic animals. I called radio and within ten minutes a young lady showed up and was ecstatic to have a fresh deer kill for her two cheetahs. I really started to question why the department was issuing us these 357 Magnums; I could have done a better job with my old single shot 22!

Early one morning, I drug myself out of my patrol car at home after having had a really rough night on a late swing shift. I had just investigated a one car fatal out near Tyler where a young mother had been killed after she fell asleep and ran off the road hitting a rock embankment . . . However, her young four year old son had survived with hardly a scratch . . . . When I got to the scene, the young child was sitting in a passing motorist's car . . . His Mom was lying across the front seat of her wrecked car, had obviously suffered fatal injuries in the crash, and had been killed instantly. When I got the toddler in my patrol car he kept asking me where his Mom was and if she was OK? The ambulance had showed up by then so I told him I didn't know and moved my patrol car so he couldn't see what was happening outside. Since she was obviously dead the ambulance crew just left her there for the coroner to examine and took off . . . . I tried to keep distracting him with other things and told him that the ambulance had taken her to the hospital to get checked out . . . . I hated lying to him but didn't know what else to do. After an eternity the on-call coroner finally showed up to do his thing and I was finally able to take the child to his Aunt's place out in Greenacres after radio made a few phone calls for me. I broke the news privately to them and asked if they could somehow let the little guy know what had happened . . . .

After I finished most of my paperwork and got home it was almost daylight. I was pretty keyed up and not sleepy but was kind of hungry . . . . In those years our local Rosauers grocery store had weekly specials on day old glazed blueberry cake donuts for like 50 cents a dozen (I know-big time cop cliché) . . . . But they were unbelievable!! So I found a dozen of them in the freezer and not wanting to wake up Deb by cranking up our old first generation and very noisy microwave to defrost them I just started eating them frozen . . . . They were kind of dry that way so I had to wash them down with something . . . . I had recently given a fellow troopers wife, Mrs. Rick Frizzell, a battery jumpstart out in the Spokane Airport parking lot one really cold night . . . . Rick later sent me a half gallon of *Crown Royal* to thank me for saving her from freezing that evening, which I thought was extremely generous of him!! So I figured this was a good time to pop its top and sat down in front of the TV for a fantastic breakfast . . . . As I recall, I went through the donuts in just a couple minutes so I was forced to break out another dozen . . . . I got through about half of those before I noticed I was getting a little sleepy and finally rolled into the old fartsack around 0700. When I woke up around 1100 or so, Deb was at work and I had the worst gut-ache I'd ever experienced in my life and felt like there was a bowling ball in my stomach! The other issue I became aware of was that I seemed to be kinda hammered and couldn't quite remember how this all had come to pass . . . I tried to give myself the standard field sobriety tests but failed all of them . . .

I noticed that the Crown Royal was out on my TV table and that it was over half gone . . . I thought that either Deb was going to work drunk or that it all might have been somehow my doing . . . . I took a handful of Tums and tried to go back to sleep. When I finally woke up again about 3pm my stomach was better but now I had a splitting headache. I had to work the 7p to 3a shift but said screw it and called in sick. When Deb came home she wanted to know what the hell had happened last night so I filled her in on all the grisly details . . . . We still laugh about that night but unfortunately in my mind's eye all I can remember is that poor little guy sitting in the front seat of my patrol car asking for his Mom . . . .

It was in the late seventies that the WSP Aviation Division traded in their old Piper Aztec on a brand new Super King Air 200 turbine airplane. Each winter every trooper in the state had to attend what was called 'In-Service Training' at the WSP Academy in Shelton. Those training sessions lasted anywhere from 3 days to a week depending on how many issues had surfaced in the last year. We all had to requalify for our EMT certificates and breathalyzer operating permits every other year. There was always extra shooting and driving classes mixed in with lots of interesting classes and gory videos of police officers getting killed all over the United States. All the troops from Western Washington had to drive to the academy but the brass had determined that it was more cost effective to fly the Eastern Wash. troopers there. Well I was all for that 'cause it took forever to drive to Shelton from Spokane after stopping for disabled motorists and helping out at accidents along the way. My first ride in that King Air was fantastic! Troopers Ray Riepe and Conrad Pederson were the two pilots that day and was I ever thrilled to ride in old N222KA! We made several stops along the way in Wenatchee, Pasco, and Yakima to pick up other troopers before landing near the Academy. It was real foggy in Shelton that day (as usual) and when I felt the plane slowing down and still couldn't see anything I started getting pretty nervous. But they pulled off that NDB approach and got us all there uninjured. While waiting for the academy van to come and pick us up I grilled Ray Riepe about what it took to get into the aviation section and he filled me in on all the details. An applicant needed to have a commercial license with an instrument rating and at least 500 to 600 hours of flying time. He went on to say that most 'successful' applicants have additional ratings such as multi engine and flight instructor. Well that all sounded pretty expensive to me so I thought I'd better check out their program carefully when I got back to Spokane. At that time the WSP had a Cessna 182 traffic plane based in Moses Lake that provided service to all the Eastern Washington detachments. I called their office and arranged a ride with Trooper Jack Mulder. Jack had been in my West Beat detachment for awhile where he was the outpost trooper in Sprague. He was an ex-Navy Jet pilot and former A4 instructor. He picked me up out at Geiger Field one day and we proceeded out to the Salnave overpass to work traffic. I picked his brain as thoroughly as I could in between traffic stops and concentrated my questions on the 'real' costs of the flying lessons. It didn't sound good and worse yet looked like it would take several years to get it all done while working full time. Later I went up with Troopers Godber and Harshman to get their take on the program and real world costs. Everybody was singing the same song so the only person I had to convince was my wife.

There was one other incident that pretty much cemented the whole deal though. Late one afternoon radio called me and asked if I could contact the pilots of the WSP King Air (Air 1) who were staying out at the Airport Ramada Inn. They apparently weren't answering their room phone (no pagers or cell phones yet) and someone needed to get a hold of them about some changes to their governor flight itinerary the next morning. I went to their rooms but no one answered; they weren't at the bar either so I checked out by the pool. Sure enough, there they were sunning themselves on a couple chaise lounges in their swim suits and each had a fresh gin and tonic by their side . . . . I laughed out loud at this scene but they just acted like 'hey, what else are we supposed to be doing?' I passed on the schedule change info but that image of them lounging by the pool never left my mind and served as my continual stimulus to become a pilot and to hopefully enjoy those kinds of benefits one day myself. However, during some of the rougher training days ahead when I couldn't find my ass with either hand I felt like bagging the whole idea!

Convincing Deb about dropping thousands of dollars on my flying lessons turned out to be fairly uneventful. She had spent a lot of sleepless nights over the years worrying about me when I was working a late night shift and didn't come home on time. She would lie awake until she finally heard my patrol car pull up. Then when I came in I often smelled like anti-freeze, battery acid, gas, blood, beer, piss, shit, barf, or smoke and she wasn't often impressed. So it wasn't a real hard sell and Deb quickly gave me the OK to start taking lessons. She actually believed me when I told her that a career path change would bring some semblance of normalcy into our lives . . . . At that time there was a weekly aviation column in the Spokesman Review newspaper authored by a highly experienced pilot and FAA Designated Examiner named Jim Kieran. I loved his column and thought I'd start my flying career by getting his advice. He and his beautiful wife Karen were the proprietors of 'The Hangar Flying Club' out at Felts Field (SFF). As soon as I walked in to the lobby and spoke briefly with him and Karen I knew I needed to look no further! I signed up for flying lessons on the spot and never looked back! Karen had also been a nun for quite awhile so we had some interesting stories to share about seminary and convent life!

Jim assigned me a crusty old WWII aviator named George Thiele to be my primary flight instructor. He was in his sixties and had flown B24's in the China, India, Burma Theater during the war. He liked to talk about his ability to back up a B24 on the tarmac by applying power to an outboard engine until the plane was almost 90 degrees to its initial heading then going to the other outboard while holding the opposite brake until the plane again reached the 90 degree point and it started to back up . . . I would sure like to see that in real time. He flew the 'Hump' during the war mainly flying gasoline to a forward airbase in China where the B29's initially were based to hit Japan from. He was a hero in my eyes and I'll never forget him. As a flight instructor he was usually quite calm but his most oft repeated remark that I recall from my early student pilot days while flying with him was; "Jesus Christ Rick, I've got it!!" Followed by a very stern glare in my direction! What can I say I was a slow learner . . . . One day he worked up his courage somewhat and finally let me go solo after about

9 hours of dual instruction. It was one of the greatest days of my life and as most pilots will agree, trainer planes sure felt lighter without all that excess instructor weight in the right seat. I was flying a Beechcraft B19 Sport and would spend many thousands of happy hours flying Beechcraft products later in my career as well.

Most new student pilots have never talked on a radio before and quite often are a bit hesitant when they call up ground or tower for the first few times and often get a bit tongue tied. At any airport in the world it's not uncommon to hear a student pilot key his mike, followed by a long "Uhhhhhhh . . . . Felts Ground this is N1234 . . . . uhhhhhh . . . . *What do I say now Mr. Phillips?*" Then in the background you could hear his instructor shouting: "*GA ramp, taxi for takeoff . . . .*" Well, I wasn't afraid to talk on the radio since I'd been making dozens of WSP radio calls every day for the last ten years . . . My problem was the god damned letter phonetics . . . . The police letter phonetics went: A=adam, B=boy, C=charles, D=david, E=edward, F=frank, etc, etc . . . . However the FAA and airplane phonetics were based on what the military used: A=alpha, B=bravo, C=charlie, D=delta, E=echo, F=foxtrot, etc, etc . . . . Needless to say for the first few years of my flying career I fell back on what I knew best so when I needed to spell something out to a controller, such as the name of some intersection I was cleared to, it often came out like this: "OK Seattle, N6594E is cleared to Whiskey, Hotel, Young, Tango, Edward (WHYTE) then as filed . . . ." Where upon the ATC controllers would come back with some sort of smart ass reply like; "You're going where and doing what now 94E??" Conversely, when I was in my patrol car and calling in a drivers check or check stolen, and was spelling out some name or license plate, I would inevitably give them a mix of police and FAA phonetics, causing all kinds of trouble with the radio operators who were only used to hearing a prescribed set of letter designators . . . Not funny, I know, but I was sure confused for awhile . . . .

George ended up having some health issues about this time so Rick Morris became my new flight instructor. He was quite young but very enthusiastic and finally got me to the point where I passed my Private Pilot check ride with the local designated examiner at 47 hours. I immediately took Deb for a ride and discovered that she was not a comfortable passenger and freaked out quite often during normal maneuvers. I immediately started work on my instrument rating as Deb and I watched our savings account quite rapidly become diminished. I was assigned an instrument instructor named Norm Hjelm who had flown F100s and F111s in Viet Nam. He was a no nonsense sort of guy and you had better get it right the first time or be prepared to have your asshole ripped out and handed to you. On one of our first flights he directed me to an NDB out near Coeur d' Alene and told me to hold as published. I didn't know jack shit about holding let alone NDB holding which is the toughest of all. When I turned to the wrong outbound heading after crossing the beacon he grabs the controls away from me and screams "You don't know what the hell you're doing or where the hell you're at do you?" I immediately got a little testy myself and said "No I don't, that's why I'm paying you to show me how to do this shit for Crissakes . . . !" He glared at me for a second or two but slowly I saw a big grin creep across his ugly puss . . . . We soon established a pretty good working relationship. Man, he never did cut me any slack but looking back, his no nonsense training probably saved my life a number of times later flying Skylanes solo in really hairy instrument conditions. I always felt that any dipstick pilot can fly a King Air or Beechjet equipped with flight directors, autopilots, full anti-ice and de-icing capabilities in heavy IFR weather; but plodding along in those same conditions, at a third the speed, in an old Skylane was where you really learned the instrument flying trade. Later on I made many solo flights in the winter flying a 182 across the Cascades, just downwind from Mt. Rainier, iced up to the point where I couldn't hold altitude any longer with a 50 knot headwind in moderate turbulence . . . . Those flights were real character builders!!

Unfortunately, before I could look forward to a full time flying career I had to endure several more years of dealing with the motoring public while patrolling the highways and byways of Spokane County . . . . And there was never a dull moment!

CHAPTER 8

VIOLATORS... YOU GOTTA LOVE 'UM

A lot of people say you can judge a person's character by how they react during an emergency; I think most police officers will agree with that dictum. I personally feel that a more valid evaluation of a person's character is how they react after being placed under arrest for DWI when they suddenly realize their life is probably getting flushed down the toilet . . . . Problem is, when you're falling down drunk, you're just not in any kind of cognitive state to appreciate just how bad the whole scene really is . . . Now the next morning . . . that's when reality hits the fan and the totality of last night's "life emergency" suddenly presents itself!! The majority of the folks I contacted just took it in stride when I handed them a speeding ticket and most refrained from making too many caustic remarks. It's the guys and gals who were the exception to the norm that made life interesting for us and obviously the ones we remember most vividly. The following are some of the more memorable violators I contacted along with some of the crazy accident scenes I rolled up on during my 13 years spent working the road . . . . Some of these stories aren't so funny but I just can't get some of those crazy and occasionally horrible images out of my head even 40 years after the fact.

One evening I pulled a guy over that was weaving all over the freeway out near Altamont eastbound. Of course he was drunk and was soon sitting in my backseat under arrest. While waiting for the tow truck I got to listen to the inevitable sad story of how he got to this point in his life and who was at fault for all his troubles. It was remarkable how similar those stories were from one drunk driver to another . . . . and the fact that nearly all drunks performed exactly the same on the field sobriety tests . . . . They couldn't walk a straight line, their eyes were always watery and bloodshot, their speech was always slurred, they couldn't touch the tip of their nose with their index finger, they couldn't stand on one leg, couldn't say the ABC's, etc., etc. I once had a young defense attorney ask me why all of our drunk driver affidavits all sounded the same; he even asked if we could spice them up a little . . . . When I suggested to him that alcohol usually affects all humans in the same manner he seemed unimpressed . . . . Anyway, my drunk was rambling on about how he got injured at work, took too much time off from his job and when he did start showing up again was often late, through no fault of his own of course, and then got fired by his asshole boss. He got depressed, started drinking and gambling too much, got pulled over by the state bulls for speeding several times, didn't pay those tickets, had his license suspended and then they cancelled his insurance. Not having any extra cash he got stopped for an expired license tab, and was of course subsequently arrested for driving while suspended and then booked on the warrants for the unpaid tickets he'd accumulated . . . . When he couldn't make bail, his good for nothing wife left, eventually divorced him and then demanded child support for their four kids under eighteen . . . . I arrested over 1,000 drunks in my 13 years working the road full time and nearly every one of their stories was just a slight variation of the above series of events. No matter how sorry I felt for these guys each of them was just a heartbeat away from killing my wife, my folks, or any other innocent driver in some horrendous crash. There is no doubt they would feel just terrible about causing such a catastrophe, after they sobered up, but that's not the point. So, I never cut those guys any slack whatsoever. The other similarity I noticed among drunks was what the fairly cooperative examples said and did in the backseat while waiting for the tow truck to arrive to impound their car (pickup 90% of the time). First words out of their mouth were "Can I have one of my smokes now?" (I always confiscated their smokes and lighters after arresting them so they wouldn't stink up or burn up my patrol car). This was followed by "Whadaya gonna do with my pickup?" Next was "Can I have a smoke now?" Then, "What's that guy doin with my pickup?" 30 sec. later, "Can I have a smoke now?" Finally, "Where's that guy takin my pickup??" Those questions were only topped in frequency by their common response to my question of "How much did you have to drink tonight?" . . . . Invariably it was always, "Jus a couple beers, I dunno . . ."

I was also able to document a common similarity about the vehicles driven by most of the drunks I stopped: without fail their wheels and tires (which were usually 5 times too big for that model of pickup) were by themselves often worth three times as much as the whole pickup was. Additionally, I discovered a direct correlation between the height of the lift kit (how far the pickup's body was jacked up off the frame) and the driver's apparent IQ . . . . Allowing for a median IQ of 100 (pretty generous I believe) that most of the drunks I encountered seemed to possess, I was eventually able to extrapolate enough statistical data to prove that for each additional inch of lift above the standard 6 inches most of them built into their rigs, there was a corresponding 10% reduction in that individual's IQ . . . . The next statistic I was able to document related to how much mud and dirt some of these idiots purposefully accumulated on their rigs in order to give it that really authentic "Bold Redneck" appearance . . . . I'm convinced that those cretins who spend an hour or so driving back and forth in a huge mud puddle, trying to cover every square inch of their pickup's body with mud and dirt, should be labeled the poster children of this whole genre . . . . Consequently, when a police officer stops a vehicle decorated as described above, I firmly believe they should immediately assume a 25% reduction in that driver's IQ even **without** any of the other supporting characteristics described in this section. Finally, as I stated earlier in the book, displaying a Confederate battle flag or hanging a pair of those plastic testicles off your hitch was **always** a dead giveaway to the level of intelligence of that vehicle's operator. I believe those two vehicle conditions were each good for an additional 15% reduction. Therefore, due to my extensive and well documented observations over the years, I eventually felt I could prove to a jury that a drunk driver operating a pickup jacked up 12 inches, equipped with huge wheels and tires, covered in mud, adorned with a Confederate flag and dangling testicles, more likely than not had the IQ equivalent of a small cantelope and should be found guilty of all charges, regardless of the BA reading . . . . I really should have published my data but was never quite sure who might have been interested in it? I suppose a sharp defense attorney could have used these conditions to support an insanity defense for their client but I would sure hate to see them denigrate the reputation of a cantelope like that . . . .

Anyway, I finally got to the WSP District Office at First and Park and hauled my drunk into the squad room to administer the breathalyzer. There were two other troopers already sitting around the large squad room table with their drunks. Sgt. Steve Robertson was sitting to my right with a very quiet and well mannered drunk. My guy was pretty disheveled and stinky and Steve looked over at me with that 'couldn't you find a little higher class drunk to bring in here' look. Things were going well and my guy was cooperating when he suddenly started displaying certain characteristics that during my flying career I would recognize instantly as the precursors to airsickness. He got quiet, seemed to be searching for something, and started sweating. Next it was the loud burping, a little dry heave action, and then the serious ralphing started . . . . Somehow I saw the finale coming, since he was looking right at me just then, and at the very last second I just shoved his face away from me . . . Man, he just blew chunks all over that huge squad room table in a huge graceful 'arc of barf' . . . . Unfortunately, my little slap to his face resulted in most of the projectus being propelled right onto Steve and his quiet drunk . . . Now when I say 'blew chunks' I mean that quite literally . . . . This guy had been at some raunchy bar somewhere and apparently had eaten about two pounds of pepperoni but had failed to spend much time chewing it. Most of the chunks, now bouncing all over the squad room table, were nice little bite sized pieces about an inch in diameter. Well, Steve jumps up and bellows at me "God Dammit Rick, get that fu**er out of here!!" . . . . I did and later made him clean up his own mess . . . . I remember talking to janitor Lou Tyacke several weeks later who said he was still finding pieces of pepperoni in various nooks and crannies and that he had a helluva time getting the stale beer barf odor out of that room. Steve never really forgave me for that incident and I'm sure still thinks I did it on purpose.

The next one involved a very lovely female drunk driver out near State Line. It started out as the all too familiar case of a driver weaving from lane to lane then over the fog line and back . . . . Today you would think it was just some dufus texting or getting real involved on their cell phone but back then it could only be a drunk driver. She failed the field sobriety tests miserably, her speech was almost incoherent, and she reeked of alcohol. I placed her under arrest for DWI, advised her of her rights, and started to put the handcuffs on . . . . As soon as she felt that cold steel on her wrist all hell broke loose! Her fight or flight defense mechanism kicked in and she took off running; luckily I still had hold of the other end of the cuffs. I didn't want to just jerk her to the ground so I gave her a little rope and tried to just keep her close until she wore herself out a little . . . . She got as far as the freeway fence, tried to climb that, but I pulled her down. Then she tried to get back in her car but I pulled her away from it. At this point she started screaming profanities at me, accused me of trying to rape her, and said she was going to sue me and the WSP for millions . . . . Well, that was the end of playing nice with this little bitch . . . I slammed her onto the trunk of my patrol car, got the other cuff on, threw her in the backseat and in lieu of searching her I hog-tied her with our issued "ski-rope" leg restraints, wrapped it through the cuffs and cinched it up tight so she couldn't move. Man she was screaming and yelling like a total psycho so I called radio so they could document the time of arrest and informed them that she had made rape accusations against me. I left my mike keyed for a minute or so to record all her ranting and raving. Another trooper showed up while I waited for the tow truck to further document her insanity. At the county jail I requested a matron to meet me in the sally port to assist me getting her in the elevator for the ride upstairs to the booking desk. She was still yelling and making accusations so when the matron finally did a pat down search on her she became the new object of the sexual assault accusations. She refused the breathalyzer, which was fine with me, as I just wanted to get away from this maniac! I documented everything the best I could, and wrote her tickets for driving under the influence and resisting arrest. In today's politically correct society the resisting arrest nomenclature has been changed to 'Not being law enforcement friendly'. I just knew there was going to be a long drawn out court case, no doubt with media attention, followed by a big internal investigation by the WSP on me for sexual assault. I was quite surprised when after a few days had passed there were no calls to contact the lieutenant ASAP. When a few weeks had gone by I was really stunned. At some point she pled guilty to the resisting arrest charge and even to the DWI which was amazing since there was no breathalyzer . . . I was somewhat surprised but thought that was the end of the story . . . But wait, there's more!

About 25 years later I was attending a cultural diversity, ethnic sensitivity seminar, mandatory for all state employees, at the huge L & I facility in Olympia. After each lecture we were broken up into smaller groups to discuss and rehash everything we had just been lectured on to further enhance the learning experience. We were all in our civilian clothes and had to wear little name tags indicating which agency we worked for. During one of these sessions I noticed a middle aged woman staring at me so I assumed my zipper was down or I was wearing part of my lunch again. At the break she came up to me, introduced herself, and asked if I used to be a trooper in Spokane around 1980. Still not recognizing her I said yes whereupon she went off on a five minute re-cap about the time I had arrested her for DWI out by state line Idaho, how she had made a total fool out of herself struggling and fighting me. When she sobered up she just felt terrible about her actions, and later pled guilty to all the charges. She went on to say that she quit drinking immediately, turned her life around, and was now working for another state agency thanks to my intervention that night. She was crying and sobbing and then gave me a huge bear hug which I will always remember . . . It was **so very nice** to get a little positive feedback from my days working the road after so many years . . . . Usually after a "questionable" incident like that one, a visit to the lieutenant's office soon followed where you were assumed to be guilty of something and even when exonerated still felt dirty after having been made to feel totally worthless by said office weenie.

While on the topic of women caught in bad situations I will always remember two elderly German sisters involved in a very serious one car accident out near Tyler. It was a nice summer day but for some reason the older of the two sisters lost control of her car on a straight section of freeway, ran off the roadway down an embankment and hit a tree. It was a pretty severe impact and both of them suffered double compound fractures of their lower legs . . . Now this is serious stuff, excruciatingly painful (as I can attest to) and both were in jeopardy of losing their legs if not their lives. I got there before the ambulance and as I walked up to their car I thought it might not be too bad since both ladies were just quietly sitting there not saying a word. When I glanced in and saw those tibias protruding out of their lower legs I thought 'holy shit' these two are really being pretty cool customers about this! Surprisingly, there was very little blood so I ran back to my patrol car to get my cardboard leg splints. They still didn't react or say a word as I lifted and moved their legs around while getting them splinted up. Even jostling them onto the stretchers when the ambulance showed up didn't seem to faze them . . . I was just amazed at how resilient, strong willed, and seemingly impervious to pain these two ladies were. It turned out they were descendants from a pioneer family that had settled in the Sprague area back in the 1850's . . . Tough old birds from tough stock . . . . They just don't crank out people like that anymore!

Early one morning as I was just about to go home following a boring graveyard shift radio gave me an abandoned car at SR2 and the Airport exit to the Old Sunset Hwy. I almost told them to give it to the day shift guy when he signed in service but decided to go on out there anyway. It was a bitterly cold morning about—20 degrees and when I drove up to the scene it was still dark. I saw a van just off the road parked up near a rocky outcropping just where the exit splits off SR2 for the airport and splits again to Old Sunset. I took my time, ran a registration on the car, filled out a pink tag (abandoned vehicle slip), wrote everything in my bluebook, pulled on my arctic hat and gloves and finally walked up to the van to hang the pink tag on its radio antenna. When I got closer to the driver's side door I noticed with my flashlight what appeared to be a hand barely sticking out of the window . . . . I once again experienced that all too familiar 'ah shit' sensation and when I got closer saw that there was a guy all crunched up behind the wheel. I checked for a pulse but not only was there not one but this gentleman was ashen gray and nearly frozen solid.

It was such a surreal scene. There were no skid marks, his vehicle was quite a ways back from the rocky outcropping, and how had he gone unnoticed in that van for so long? I initially thought the van was the older style flat nose type but soon discovered it was a newer van with a protruding nose. Its nose and engine had been evenly pushed back into the driver's compartment after impact with the rock wall and to somebody driving by you would not suspect this van had been in an accident. Absolutely no doubt the driver was killed instantly. We later determined he was doing about 70 mph when he left the road, hit that rock wall airborne, then bounced straight back about ten feet. When I advised radio that this abandoned car had just turned into a one car, one confirmed fatality accident, they were beside themselves, as I was! We soon found out what the 'rest of the story' was. The gentleman had terminal cancer and not long to live. Although we could not absolutely prove it, it was pretty obvious he had committed suicide by 'car accident' so his widow could collect on the insurance money. I'm sure there are those who might think otherwise but I thought that was a pretty noble and courageous act on his part. I had to be pretty careful how I worded things on my fatal report so it didn't smell like a suicide to the insurance investigators. There used to be a box on our accident reports you could check which stated; 'Apparently Asleep.' I checked that box and submitted everything to my boss. I really didn't get along with the sergeant I had at that time but he surprisingly agreed with me and left my accident report alone. He had contacted the man's wife to do the next of kin notification and had heard the guy's life story from her; he had been a WWII hero and a great family man . . . . He was obviously looking out for them up until his last moments . . . .

The next guy I ran into should have been a cast member on *Saturday Night Live* . . . I was eastbound near Division when I noticed an older Cadillac Eldorado ahead of me driving fairly slowly and weaving within its lane, nothing too egregious, but still a pretty obvious indicator of a drunk driver. As I was walking up to the car I saw that the driver was wearing a lovely evening gown and made a quick assumption that this wasn't a DWI but possibly a lady trying to adjust her makeup while driving. When I got to the window and saw the driver up close I was a little stunned by who was wearing that nice dress . . . . It was a very large black guy, about 6'5" probably weighing in around 280. Man, I was at a loss for words for a second or two . . . . However, he was very polite and formal and asked if he had done anything wrong . . . I asked him to get out and try the usual field sobriety tests, which he performed miserably. I then tried out our 'then' new tool, the gaze nystagmus test . . . . This sobriety test involved having the suspect follow a moving pencil with their eyes only, while not moving their head . . . . getting these guys to not move their head during this test was always a huge challenge! Anyway, when their eyeballs got to the end of their travel if they started flicking back and forth at a certain frequency, they were drunk . . . . as if we didn't already know that! So . . . his eyes were bouncing all over the place and I placed 'him' under arrest for DWI. During the pat down search I noticed that his dress was not cheap, he had on a matching shoes and bag ensemble, expensive hosiery, simple but elegant earrings, and understated makeup. The only incongruous aspect to his feminine get-up and finery was his voice . . . Man he sounded just like the character played by Michael Duncan in the *"Green Mile"* . . . . (the big guy on death row with the pet mouse in his cage) . . . . I just knew that when I got to the booking desk the jailors were going to have a field day with this cat. He started crying while we waited for the tow truck and began to fill me in on his life and how things had gotten to this point. Apparently he was at the stage where trans-sexuals have to try living as a woman for awhile before they actually committed to it and have the surgery and hormone injections. As usual with these kinds of cases my seminary training kicked in and we had a nice talk as I listened to him vent. When we got to the jail I temporarily put him in a holding cell myself and then asked the jailors to please be respectful to him as a favor to me . . . They acted shocked and hurt that I would even insinuate they might do otherwise. He was a nice guy and I hope he got his life going in the right direction . . . .

Late one evening radio gave me a one car accident out near Long Lake Dam. There were no injuries but the driver was highly intoxicated and passed out behind the wheel of her car in the ditch. She was probably in her late fifties and was wearing her favorite tavern jacket from the big city of Wellpinit. Now it was a standing joke among most of us in those years that the sign of a "classy drunk" was the one who was wearing a tavern jacket with the words spelled correctly on the back . . . . Regardless of the spelling on the jacket—underneath it they would almost always be wearing the ubiquitous *Budweiser* T-Shirt. Well, on this night the words on her jacket were spelled correctly but she turned out to be a little less than a class act!! She was missing quite a few teeth, was considerably overweight, and just reeked of beer and smoke. I woke her up with the old standby ammonia inhalants. She could not even get out of her car unassisted so I didn't even ask her to try the field sobriety tests since I knew she would probably injure herself attempting them. I just placed her under arrest for DWI and basically carried her to my patrol car where I assumed she would pass out again . . . but that wasn't the case. While waiting for the tow truck things started to get a little dicey. She started asking me what it would take to get out of this ticket since it was her sixth or seventh DWI in five years and she didn't want to go to jail again. I immediately experienced one of those 'ah shit' feelings and had a hunch where she was going with this but prayed that nothing 'unsightly' was about to occur. However, my prayers were not answered and she soon began to describe several 'acts' that she could perform on me if I would just show her some leniency . . . Jesus, I didn't know if I was going to laugh or vomit; I just wanted that God Damn tow truck to get here fast! I got out to inventory her car to get away from her. The inside of her car was a mass of beer and wine bottles and other detritus from several years back. I stayed outside and hoped she would just pass out again. Finally the tow arrived and we got the hell out of there. We were in Lincoln County so it was a fairly short ride to Davenport to book her. We didn't even make it to Reardan before she decided to escalate things further. I knew I had made a big mistake in not cuffing her and now I was gonna pay the price. When I looked in my mirror I saw that she had removed her tavern jacket and Budweiser T-shirt but seemed to be struggling with her bra . . . . I was just horrified at what I was going to see next and seriously considered using my patented 'slam drunk' maneuver on her . . . but I just couldn't do it as I normally reserved that for the psychopaths. She started asking me if I knew of any gravel pits in the area that we might pull into for a few minutes . . . . I had already advised radio that I was enroute the Davenport jail with a drunk female, and had given them my mileage which was a standard practice. I now had to make the additional call that my prisoner was disrobing in my backseat. We always kept radio advised of unusual circumstances but this call would also let everyone know that I probably hadn't cuffed her and as a result would no doubt cause me untold grief later. After I got on the other side of Reardan, I killed my dash lights so she couldn't see my speedometer, and floor boarded my old '78 Plymouth! She was still talking but at those speeds I couldn't hear what she was saying which was fine with me. The last time I glanced in the mirror she had everything off but her socks and was giving me a 'detailed' preview 'look' of what I could expect in return for leniency if I would just stop at the nearest gravel pit . . . . Jesus Christ, I thought I would be blind forever after seeing her display her thing like that! I had radio call the Lincoln Co. jail to have someone meet me outside to help me with this gal but they only had one person on duty and he couldn't leave the booking desk. I had been fairly polite with her so far but when we got into the parking lot and she was still naked I decided to proceed with the 'bad cop' routine. I told her to get her fu**ing clothes on immediately or I was going to charge her with bribery, prostitution, and obstructing an officer and I would make sure she spent at least ten years in prison! I wasn't sure if this threat would work but I was starting to panic and that was the best I could think of. She didn't react at first and seemed a little stunned and hurt that I wasn't going to be her boyfriend any longer . . . She finally pulled her pants and tavern jacket on which was good enough for me and I immediately drug her inside the jail. I asked her quickly if I should even bother with the breathalyzer test . . . . When she said 'I don't know', I took that as a BA test refusal, dropped off her ticket, and got the hell out of there.

One other drunk female sticks in my mind to this day since I have to look at the aftermath of trying to arrest her every day on my right hand. I was driving down East Sprague about to pull into the WSP office at First and Park to get gas when a car blows through the red light right in front of me, almost completely over the center line, and nearly takes me out. I chased it North on Park a couple blocks until she of course stops right in the middle of the road . . . . Next thing I see is her white back-up lights come on as her car starts rolling back towards me . . . . I get on my PA, while backing up myself, and yelled at her to put the brakes on and put the car in park. It took a couple seconds but she finally got it stopped . . . . However, her brake lights and white back up lights were still on so I yelled at her again on the PA to put her car in park but there was no response. I then pulled ahead until my push bars gently made contact with her rear bumper, hoping that would hold her car if she took her foot off the brake while I was walking up to her. As soon as I got to the driver side window I could see she was hammered so I just reached in, put the gear shift lever in park for her, and took her keys out of the ignition . . . . I think that little "safety gesture" on my part was the first straw that eventually set her off a few minutes later. When I asked her to step out of the car she basically fell out and to use the trooper parlance of the day, she appeared to be one of those "piece of shit sloppy drunks." She couldn't even attempt to do the field sobriety tests since once she took a hand off her car to try them she just started sliding down the fender and couldn't catch herself. So I just told her she was under arrest for DWI, patted her down, and walked her back to my patrol car. As she was climbing in she whacked her head pretty hard against the door frame . . . . I think that was the second straw as I'm pretty sure she thought I was the one who had just bonked her. On her second attempt I gently pushed her head down so it would clear the door frame . . . . Apparently my touching her hair was the final straw . . . . She turned her head and before I could react bit down sideways on my right thumb just above the knuckle!! Just one more of those WTF— Ahh Shit moments in my road trooper career! Man, she really had a good hold on it and I was afraid she'd bite it off if I struggled too much . . . . I had my heavy duty six cell Kel-Lite flashlight in my left hand and really wanted to bash her in the face as hard as I could . . . . But sadly, my training kicked in and all I could think about at that moment was the WSP use of force review board, that would have most certainly been convened, after her battered picture appeared on the front page of the Spokesman Review newspaper the next morning where she would be claiming horrible police brutality at the very least! So, I dropped my Kel-Lite, fished my Mace can out of its little holder on my gun belt, and sprayed that stupid bitch down in every one of her bodily orifices I could see, concentrating on her mouth and nose!! She finally released pressure on my thumb a little but I pulled my hand away a little too soon causing quite a long laceration from the residual tooth pressure she had on it. Man, my hand was bleeding like crazy as she had laid my thumb open to the bone! After slamming the door on her feet a couple times until she reeled them in, I popped my trunk and got my first aid kit out, sprayed a bunch of Merthiolate in the cut, and wrapped a 24X72 compress on my hand secured with a bunch of gauztex. It stung like shit since most of the Mace I had sprayed on her apparently went into that laceration! I called for another troop to come and take her to the office for the BA test and the booking ceremony. I then drove myself down to Sacred Heart to get my thumb fixed. My sergeant finally showed up at the hospital just as I was being released, expressed his displeasure with me that I had taken matters into my own hands and hadn't waited for an ambulance. He didn't say a word about my hand! Man that guy was a piece of work! Anyway, I ended up getting ten or eleven stitches, a tetanus shot, and advice to have my "biter" tested for HIV and Hepatitis. Luckily, she came back negative on those tests after I had to sweat out the results for several weeks! I had charged her with DWI, resisting arrest, and second degree assault but our limp dick junior prosecutor, against my wishes and those of WSP management, let her slide on the resisting and assault and just accepted her guilty plea to the DWI charge in exchange . . . . Ahhhh, sweet justice . . . . ?

There was another funny incident with a drunk and a car full of empty beer and wine bottles I happened upon one day shift. Radio gave me a one car non-injury accident just south of the airport. When I arrived I saw this poor sap stuck backwards over a ditch, high-centered on the shoulder, with the rear wheels of his car not touching the ground. The car was almost level but it was perpendicular to the road and the driver could probably only see pine trees straight ahead. When I got out to talk to him I noticed his engine was running and the rear wheels were spinning merrily away at what looked like a moderate cruising speed. I noticed the driver had his hands on the wheel at ten and two and seemed to be concentrating very hard on his 'supposed' driving. I was immediately hit with a wave of déjà vu as I had just read a story in *Readers Digest* in the *'All in a Day's Work'* section about a police officer back East driving up on the same exact scenario. In his story he snuck up on the driver and then acted like he was running along side the car, knocked on his window, and breathlessly asked him to slow down so he could talk to him. I thought what the hell and decided to give it a try. When I got up next to his window and was just starting my running along side routine—he saw me . . . He jammed on his brakes as hard as he could which stopped the rear wheels from spinning but I doubt he felt any deceleration forces. His eyes were as big as saucers and I imagined him thinking how in the hell this state bull managed to catch him on foot. I have never seen so many empty wine bottles in my life. They were piled up several feet deep in the back seat. It turns out he made his own wine and just kept all the empties with him. I just couldn't keep a straight face with this guy and probably was a little insensitive during the booking process . . . I've told this story many times but hardly anyone believes me . . . . I guess most of them had already read the 'other' story in Readers Digest . . . . What can I say, it really happened!! I remember a TV show back in the fifties with Art Linkletter in which he had a segment called "Kids Say the Darndest Things" . . . If you ever got a few State Troopers together from anywhere in the U.S. and started talking about their DWI arrests you would soon have plenty of material for several seasons of a new TV show called "Drunks Do the Damndest Things".

I was out near Harvard Rd. late one night on the graveyard shift monitoring my CB for lack of anything better to do when I saw something big and shiny on the shoulder of the road and stopped to see what it was. Turned out to be a brand new 30 gal. galvanized garbage can . . . . And as luck would have it, with a little bit of 'compression,' I was able to squeeze it in my backseat. This was a good score and I always seemed to be finding great stuff scattered along the freeway; golf clubs, tools, chains, you name it! Anyway, back to listening to all the morons on the CB . . . . All of a sudden a guy comes on channel 19 calling himself the "Rusty Bucket" and starts asking for a "smoke report" (CB lingo for has anyone seen any troopers (Smokeys) around) . . . No one answers him, although I was sorely tempted to bait him a little. Then the dumb shit announces he's leaving a certain tavern out on SR-290 and is going to try to make it home to Rathdrum. Man, he really sounded drunk so I took the

Harvard exit and headed north at Mach 1 to try and intercept him before he crossed into Idaho. When I got to SR 290 good old 'Rusty' makes another progress report and says he's at a certain intersection and again asks for a 'smoke report.' This time a buddy of his answered him but said he was at home and didn't know where the Smokeys were. However, when Rusty called out the road he was crossing I knew I was only about a half mile from him but still didn't know what he was driving. There was hardly any traffic and I soon caught up to the only car on the road ahead of me which just happened to be a beat up old pickup with a taillight out. I really didn't need too much more CB help from Rusty at this point. That old pickup was weaving all over the road and apparently the driver had his high beams on since a car going the other way flashed their lights at him. When I turned on my blue lights to stop him I was privileged to hear another one of those world class drunk phrases that only cops and abused family members are privy to. But like so many other useless bits of trivia stuck in my brain I can never get this one to go away . . . . Just after I turned on my lights he comes on the CB talking to his buddy again and announces; "God dammit Billy, the Rusty Bucket's fu***d . . . I got a Smokey up my ass here" . . . . then . . . . "If I find out you've been boning my wife while I'm in the can I'll fu***ng kill you!!"

By this time I'm nearly into Idaho so I had to get him stopped pretty quickly. Thankfully he pulled over for me right away and when I walked up I finally got to meet good old Rusty. His CB mike was sitting on the front seat along with a six pack of Bud (what else) with an open one still emptying out onto the floorboards between his legs. The first thing that hit me was a foul stench and I prayed the odor was coming from something under his seat . . . . When I had him get out to attempt the field sobriety tests I discovered to my chagrin that the stench was emanating from Rusty himself . . . . I asked him what stunk so bad and he nonchalantly informed me that he was trying to fart a couple miles back but shit his pants accidentally . . . . I honestly thought about just taking him straight home at this point rather than having to endure what I knew was going to be several horrible hours with him . . . but it would be just my luck he would go back and get his pickup and then go out and kill somebody with it . . . . While talking to him I was reminded of a phrase my Dad used to use on occasion to describe some of the folks who came to pick apples for us; "This guy was dumber than a sled load of bricks!" And Drunk?? . . . . While he was doing the head back eyes closed test, trying to touch the tip of his nose with his index finger, he actually fell over backwards and didn't even realize he was falling . . . As he went down, he made no attempt to catch himself, and smacked the pavement flat still valiantly trying to touch his nose . . . . He was very determined but kind of knocked himself out a little with the fall . . . . So, into the backseat I drug him, arrested for DWI. A driver's check indicated his license was revoked for several DWI's and that he was classified as an 'Habitual Offender' . . . . So now I had to write another separate ticket for that while waiting for the tow truck. After several minutes ole Rusty regained his senses somewhat and noticed he was sharing the back seat with my new 30 gal. garbage can. I guess every guy has his limits and apparently his proximity to that garbage can really 'violated his personal space' and set him off . . . The next words he yelled at me were; 'You just think I'm human garbage don't you?' He went on for several minutes yelling, cursing, and threatening me and my wife with all kinds of mayhem . . . . I just turned up my AM radio to drown out most of his tirade while documenting the highlights in my blue book. I also had to roll down my windows and turn the A/C to max. to get rid of his stench as it was getting a lot worse the more he got worked up. The tow truck took forever and I was out of there like a bullet the second it arrived. As we were approaching the Spokane River on Harvard Rd he screamed out some horrible vulgar threat about my mother and what he was going to do to her when he got out of jail . . . . He was also lying on my backseat pounding on the side window with his feet trying to knock it out . . . . Well, I could give a shit about that side window but the threat against my Mom was just a little over the top for me . . . . I performed the slam drunk maneuver harder than I ever had and then stopped on the bridge . . . . I had every intention of just dragging that sack of shit out and throwing the stupid fu**er over the rail into the river . . . . However, just before I acted on that impulse I realized that some wimpy WSP review board weenie might consider that an excessive use of force since there was about a 50 foot drop to the river . . . . So instead, I opened the rear door and maced the living shit out of him for trying to escape and for breaking out my side window . . . . Mouth, eyes, nose, ears, crotch, you name it I soaked it with CN gas! I slammed the door and then listened to him choking and gasping in there for quite awhile. I got back in but started choking myself as I had emptied a whole can of mace on the stupid bastard. I had to leave all the windows down and run the A/C at max all the way to the jail to blow the fumes out . . . . At least the mace masked his horrible shit stench for the rest of the ride into town. The jailors were none too pleased when I drug this piece of crap out of the elevator over to the booking desk . . . . I seemed to recall that at some point he had refused to take the breathalyzer so I dropped off my tickets and headed off for home with my brand new garbage can . . . . About a month later his case went to court and in the meantime I had written about a ten page case report documenting every single word and threat he had made and filed it with the prosecutor's office . . . . I had to include the macing incident since it was pretty hard to overlook that part. With a public defender at his side he agreed to plead guilty to the DWI and the driving while revoked as long as the prosecutor dropped the obstructing and destruction of state property charges. I was stunned at this outcome as I had thought for sure this one was going to the Supreme Court mainly because his public defender was one of the biggest pricks on the face of the earth . . . . His sentencing was postponed for a week. While I was out in the hallway bullshitting with another trooper good old Rusty walks up to me and actually tried to apologize for his actions that night . . . . Man, all I wanted to do was drop kick this sack of shit in the nuts as hard as I could . . . . But, being the good "ex-seminarian" I acknowledged his apology . . . But when he stuck his hand out towards me I just said "don't push it man!" He seemed OK with that and walked away.

His jerk-off of a public defender achieved some notoriety a little while after this case when he was in private practice. His drunk client in that case had been travelling the wrong way on the freeway with his lights off out near Altamont late one night and struck a legally driven car head-on in the left lane. I believe this guy's passenger was killed so they charged the wrong way drunk with negligent homicide. I think the drunk was found guilty in Superior Court but it was what happened next that blew us all away. That dip shit attorney filed a civil lawsuit against the innocent party who was driving perfectly legally . . . He stated that the other driver's "Failure to take evasive action" resulted in disfiguring injuries to his drunk client's face . . . . Man, that was just the ultimate in horrendous defense attorney tactics and revealed to the world that ethics and morality were just not part of this cat's lexicon . . . . I would love to see just how fast that moron could react to a car coming at him the wrong way on the freeway at night with no lights on with a combined closing speed of around 140 mph . . . However, Karma came to the rescue a few years later when that little puke just happened to be found with large amounts of cocaine on his person one night and was eventually disbarred . . . . How sweet it was!!

The violator in my next encounter was a vast improvement over old Rusty. I pulled a brand new Porsche 911 over westbound at SR 902. The driver had been driving on the shoulder while traveling about 25 mph over the speed limit. When I contacted the driver I was stunned to see a gorgeous blonde behind the wheel wearing the thinnest, loose fitting, tiniest white silk dress open to her navel, I have ever seen! She looked like she belonged on the cover of Vogue or Cosmo. After dealing with ole Rusty this was indeed a paradigm shift in the quality of violators I had recently contacted! She got out and walked back to me barefooted. There was the usual strong odor of alcohol, poor performance on the field sobriety tests, and typical slurred and mush mouthed speech. When I placed her under arrest for DWI she didn't argue or disagree. There was hardly any need to pat her down or search her as there was absolutely nowhere she could have hidden a weapon that wouldn't be totally visible!! She was obviously educated and a real chatty Cathy; she immediately began spewing out all kinds of unsolicited tidbits about her lifestyle, who her rich boyfriend was, including all the gifts and money he bestowed on her (including the 911). He was the owner of a nearby Boat Manufacturing company on Hayford Rd and according to her was a millionaire. I was really enjoying her blabbing and when the tow truck arrived way too soon, I hated to get out and destroy the quality repertoire we were sharing. It was also a shame to see the tow truck operator roughly handle the Porsche like it was the typical '62 Ford F150 that most drunks drove.

On the way to the county jail she 'opened up' a little more about her true relationship with the millionaire boyfriend . . . Turns out she wasn't his real girlfriend but was in truth a highly paid 'call girl' from a local escort service . . . She was drunk enough to even brag that she made between $500 to $750 per night for various 'services' . . . That might not sound like a lot of cash now but for 1981 she was definitely a "player!" I thought I had gained her confidence somewhat so I facetiously asked her if she reported that income to the IRS . . . Man, talk about a mood killer . . . It was obvious from that point on that I was no longer her 'girlfriend!' In the sally port at the county jail they had recently installed cameras so the jailors upstairs could watch to see if we were having any trouble with our prisoners while we maneuvered them out of the car into the elevator. I secured my 357 in the gun locker and helped my prisoner out of the backseat. Normally, when the elevator door opened there was no one there . . . This time however, two 'very helpful' jailors suddenly appeared to offer their assistance . . . I guess they had watched my prisoner get out of the car and somehow had noticed that she wasn't wearing any underwear . . . . Very high quality video equipment indeed! Upstairs in the breathalyzer room it was like a peep show or something. Every two or three minutes a jailor would pop in to ask if I needed any coffee, more carbons for my reports, if they could adjust the room temperature for me, etc., etc . . . . Never before or since had I been treated so well by those guys . . . . Her case never came to court and I never saw her again. Her boyfriend however made the news 'big time' about a year later. Apparently his 'millionaire' status was somewhat ill-begotten . . . . His company had been importing raw fiberglass boat hulls from Mexico which were then assembled into complete boats at his plant on Hayford. It appeared that the reason he could lavish new Porsche 911's on his hookers had something to do with the marijuana, cocaine, and black tar heroin 'encased' in the deep 'V' of those boat hulls . . . It was a shame to see the family name dragged through the mud since his father had started the company and had built it into a well respected legitimate enterprise before junior took over.

One drunk I arrested set a record that as far as I know has never been broken in Spokane County. I was heading up Sunset Hill late one evening going from car to car looking for any of a multitude of somewhat subtle indicators of a drunk driver such as: weaving within a lane, driving over the skip lines (lane divider buttons), driving over the fog line, driving with the brake light on, travelling very slow, etc. Now the really obvious signs of a very bad drunk driver were: wrong way on the freeway, no headlights on, excessive speed, reckless driving, etc. These types are pretty hard to miss and a trained monkey could catch those guys. So on the night in question my driver was going the speed limit, not weaving, or doing any of the other above mentioned indicators; what caught my attention was the fact that he had his dome light on. So I quartered him (got in his blind spot) and watched his driving for a few seconds . . . Everything was good except I noted that he was sitting bolt upright in his seat and had his hands at ten and two . . . . Very admirable but man, I just had a real funny feeling about this guy . . . He just seemed to be trying too hard . . . . I know that's a pretty flimsy (non-existent) excuse to stop someone for and I was really searching for any small violation that I could later articulate in court to some smart ass defense attorney, on what my probable cause was to stop this guy. So I pulled along side of him and just stayed there . . . . Eventually he glanced over at me and when he finally noticed it was a big ole ugly State Bull, he bobbled a little and went over the fog line a foot or so. Ahh, finally some probable cause! When I hit the blue lights he pulled right over, even signaled (which was a rare sight) and I started to think I was mistaken about him. Once he got out of the car I did notice a very strong odor of intoxicants about his person but he actually performed pretty well on the field sobriety tests . . . His speech was OK, he didn't seem confused at all, eyes were a little bloodshot, and he was very polite. Eventually I just couldn't get past that heavy odor on his breath and went ahead and arrested him for DWI. When we got to the county he consented to the breathalyzer and gave me a really good sample when he blew. On the old machines you had to wait awhile to get the results and when I finally pushed the button the little needle on the null meter just zipped to the right and almost bent itself in two when it hit the peg . . . I knew right then that this was going to be a high reading . . . . As I thumbed the little wheel to center the needle again it seemed to take forever but finally came on back . . . . The resulting reading was .46% blood alcohol!! I was really shocked since a reading of .40% is considered to be alcohol poisoning and at that point we are supposed to take them to the hospital immediately. Considering the legal limit for intoxication now days is only .08% I think it's fair to say that this guy was an alcoholic!! I ran another test to confirm that reading and sure enough it was even a bit higher at .47%. Meanwhile, my guy was just acting as normal as can be and if I didn't know better would swear he was sober. So, I told the jailors what was going on and off to the hospital we went. I dropped him off at emergency, stuffed his ticket in his pocket, and went home. Next morning around 9am I get a phone call from an officer from Spokane PD. He told me he had just responded to a call from an upset home-owner near Deaconness Hospital about a guy passed out on their chaise lounge on their porch. The officer found my ticket in the guys back pocket and wanted to know what was going on. I kind of had to laugh about this one and gave him all the details. Turns out my drunk had escaped from the hospital during the night and just managed to stagger a block or so before passing out on that porch. The SPD officer kindly took him back to the hospital for me. As any police officer will tell you, always follow your gut, it's rarely wrong!

One sunny morning near the end of June I realized that my monthly 'activity totals' were a little shy of the norm and I needed to get some stops in, no matter how 'skinny,' to prevent my boss from accusing me of being lazy again. I was basically looking to stop anything that moved and was getting close to desperation when I finally saw my prey . . . . While sitting in the u-turn just west of Geiger there it was . . . . A misplaced license plate month tab partially obscuring one of the letters on the license plate . . . . I had to choke back a little bile coming up in my throat, as this was about the most "CS (chicken shit) stop" a trooper could make, but a contact was a contact . . . . I pulled in behind my target and turned on my blue lights . . . . Nothing happened . . . . I noticed that I could not see the driver's head above the seat and assumed I was dealing with a person of reduced stature who possibly couldn't see me in the mirror. I got very close and engaged my siren . . . . Still no response . . . . I pulled along side, looked over, and saw a quite elderly female driver with a very determined look on her face; she had her hands at ten and two on the wheel which again was very admirable. I laid on the siren again right next to her but still could not get her attention . . . . Man, this old gal was proving to be a very tough nut to crack. I pulled back until the front end of my car was abeam her window and with my PA set to maximum volume advised her that I was a state trooper and would like her to pull over . . . . I didn't even get a glance in my direction. Jesus, what do I have to do short of the PIT maneuver to get her stopped? I knew that the PA was my best weapon as most people could hear it a mile away. I put on my Smokey Bear hat, rolled down my passenger side window, and got on the PA again . . . I kept repeating; "Maam, Maam, this is the WSP . . . . Please pull over I want to talk to you . . ." Finally, just as I was about to give up and take the Medical Lake exit and bag this whole ridiculous scene she sort of glanced in my direction for a second . . . . I gave her my best state trooper smile under my Smokey Bear hat and pointed for her to pull over . . . . Her eyes got huge for a second and she slammed on her brakes for all she was worth . . . . I was sort of expecting this response and stayed right along side her during the deceleration . . . Unfortunately she stopped right in a lane of travel but I wasn't about to get back on the PA and spend ten minutes trying to rectify that minor issue . . . . The most memorable part of the stop was not talking to her later but what occurred in that split second after she slammed on her brakes . . . I was looking right at her as she was being flung forward and saw her chest hit the steering wheel setting off her horn . . . . Then, as if in slow motion, while her chest compressed against the steering wheel, I witnessed her teeth sail out of her mouth, accompanied by a considerable amount of saliva, and land on the dashboard . . . Man, this episode was like seeing a Sasquatch . . . . You could just never do the story justice when retelling it . . . . You just had to be there . . . . When I finally walked up to the car to see if she was OK, after her self induced Heimlich maneuver, I saw her fumbling with her false teeth and attempting to put them back in . . . . Problem was they had landed on some dead bugs on her dash, several of which were now stuck to her slimy teeth . . . . She apparently wasn't aware of this minor inconvenience and put them back in her mouth, bugs and all . . . . Well, that was bad enough, but after I gave her time to get squared away and finally greeted her I saw that she had also put her teeth back in upside down . . . . Jesus, my seminary training just wasn't there to bail me out this time and I just broke down laughing until I almost puked. I tried to make sure she didn't see me convulsing and choking and finally just told her to please leave . . . She seemed confused but at least she finally complied with my instructions in a timely manner.

While sitting in another u-turn out near Granite Lake one afternoon working the 'bug' (radar) I glanced up to see a sedan approaching me . . . . Its speed was OK but something just didn't seem right . . . . Holy Shit, this fu**er was coming at me the wrong way on the freeway and **why had it taken me a second or two to realize that??** . . . . I thought I was losing it but managed to turn on all my lights and siren to get this guy's attention . . . He pulled over very quickly onto the shoulder and when I walked up I certainly expected to find a slobbering drunk behind the wheel . . . . but that was not to be the case. The driver was a quite sober elderly oriental gentleman who politely asked why I was stopping him . . . When I pointed out that he was traveling Eastbound in the Westbound lanes of I-90 he honestly didn't believe me . . . . He looked at his car nose to nose with my patrol car on the shoulder, looked at westbound traffic going by, then looked over at the eastbound traffic before he finally realized he was 180 degrees out of position for the lanes of travel he was in and had really screwed up . . . . Man, this cat was slow on the up-take! I really hate to reveal what he did next, as it was so stereotypical, but let's just say that there was a lot of bowing and short three word apologies repeated over and over . . . My main concern was where he had gotten on the freeway as I thought there could be a "Wrong Way or Do Not Enter" sign knocked down somewhere and we might have to call the Highway Dept. out. It sounded like he got on at Salnave Rd which was just two miles west of our location. I wrote him a ticket for wrong way on the freeway, got him pointed in the right direction, and let him go. I went up to the Salnave on-ramp but all the Do Not Enter signs were in place so I had no idea how he got so screwed up. After a trip out to the Adams Co. line to check for disabled motorists I was soon back at the original u-turn location . . . and he was still there. When I recontacted him he was rocking back and forth in his seat . . . . When I asked what was wrong he said he had 'lost too much face' and just couldn't continue driving. We talked for awhile and I tried to give him an out by saying that perhaps the sun was in his eyes and that he should wear dark glasses from now on and perhaps he just might need to have his prescription checked as well . . . This seemed to help a little and he finally was able to drive away with some dignity restored.

Mid-way through a another graveyard shift I was cruising down Sunset Hill when I thought I saw something weird happen about a quarter mile ahead of me; it looked like the rear end of a semi trailer had exploded and for a second there was a trail of sparks then nothing. I caught up to it quickly since the truck driver had slowed and nearly stopped by the time I got to him. I soon saw the reason for all the sparks . . . . There was a small car crammed under the semi trailer right up to its back seat . . . . I immediately called radio and told them I was rolling up on the scene of an injury accident that was probably going to be a fatal and to roll an ambulance. The car was actually stuck under the rear of the trailer and as the truck driver pulled to the shoulder he was just dragging the car along with him. I just knew I was about to view another gory decapitation and mutilated body as I got out to confirm the fatality . . . . I saw the truck driver walking back to me and just then a person flew out of the left 'rear' door of the car and began running wildly out onto the freeway screaming and yelling like a crazy man!! This was yet another of those WTF moments in my career and I ran after the guy before he got hit by traffic . . . . I grabbed him and drug him over to the front of my patrol car to evaluate his injuries . . . He kept yelling that he was blind and I sure as hell could see why . . . His whole face was gone and all I saw was the top of his skull and the inside of his bloody red scalp hanging down to his mouth!! Somehow, during the high speed impact into the back of the semi trailer he had been surgically 'scalped' by the safety bar on the rear of the trailer. That bar apparently caught him on the 'impact rebound' near the top of his ears and ripped his scalp down to just above the eye balls as his head scraped underneath it . . . I don't know how he survived that impact but drunks are sometimes the luckiest people on earth. Apparently, during the impact, the front seat had collapsed and left him lying on the back seat "relatively" OK. Only problem was he now had about seven inches of excised scalp that had flopped down over his eyes and nose and was just about into his mouth . . . . Man, this was just about the freakiest thing I had ever seen and to make matters worse that dip-shit truck driver screams out for all to hear that this guy has his face ripped off!! Those comments didn't help the situation much and the injured guy went further beserk and was squirming all over the place and fighting me. I had to identify myself as a state trooper and tried to explain what had just happened to him . . . . I told him I thought his eyes and face were OK and that he just had part of his scalp hanging down blocking his vision . . . That seemed to calm him down a bit. I got out my first aid kit and did my best to control the fierce bleeding with some 24 x72's gauze packs . . . . Jesus, I got blood everywhere but I wasn't about to put this guy in my car since I just knew I would never get rid of that dried blood stink in there . . . I was covered in it and the hood and left front fender of my car were just dripping with blood! The ambulance finally showed up and hauled the poor f**ker away to Deaconess Hospital. However, my sympathy for his situation only went so far and since I had detected alcohol on his breath I placed him under arrest for DWI before they took him away. Later at the hospital I was able to obtain a legal blood draw since he wasn't able to blow into the breathalyzer with his FUBAR face.

This had occurred early Thanksgiving Day 1975 and Debbie's folks from Yakima had driven over the day before to celebrate Turkey Day with us. It was still dark when I got home around 7am and I parked my patrol car behind the house in front of the dining room window. I was beat and hung up my coat and gunbelt by the door and just flopped into bed without waking Deb up. Around 2pm I awoke to the wonderful smell of turkey simmering away in the oven . . . Shortly thereafter Deb came into the bedroom with a real grim look on her face . . . She asked me what the hell had happened last night?? I was a little puzzled how she would know that I had experienced a real weird episode during my shift but filled her in on all the details anyway. She just laughed and told me to come out into the dining room when I was ready. When I arrived I saw her folks sitting around the table drinking tea with somewhat reserved looks on their faces. I soon figured out what the problem was. In the darkness I hadn't really noticed what a mess my car was but in the bright sunshine it looked like someone had slaughtered a cow on it. When Deb's folks had gotten up they first saw my WSP jacket and gun belt smeared with blood and then were horrified to see my blood soaked patrol car parked just outside the window . . . I imagine they had several hours to ponder just what kind of violent brutal son of a bitch their sweet little girl had got mixed up with . . . For a moment I thought I might play them a bit and casually report that I had stopped a guy for a defective taillight and got a little carried away when he didn't think that was very important . . . . But I couldn't do it and recounted the real episode one more time. We all had a good laugh and I heard that story repeated by them many times in the years to come . . . . I hosed my car off and threw my jacket in the washer . . . . The guy with no face contested the DWI charge and in court said he wasn't drunk but had just fallen asleep . . . . His blood alcohol was nearly three times over the legal limit so the judge and jury weren't too impressed . . . The defendant did have a real Frankenstein like scar though which I'm sure served as a lifelong reminder of that crazy night . . . . What a wakeup that must have been for him to be violently jarred out of a nice nap only to discover you're blind!!

The first few nights of a graveyard shift were always the toughest for me and I always ran out of steam around 0400 and got really sleepy. Until I got adjusted to those crazy hours I often found myself sitting on the eastbound onramp to I-90 at Geiger facing east around that time. To disguise what I was actually doing I used to put my campaign hat on, tucked the adjustable head strap under my chin, rolled down my window until I could just get part of its wide brim outside, then rolled the window back up securing the whole affair (and my head) tightly. I would then turn the volume up on my WSP radio so I didn't miss any calls, locked my doors, and finished off this arrangement by putting on my RayBan sunglasses to preclude some snoopy motorist from detecting what I was really doing in there. In this configuration I was dead center in the middle of my beat ready for action. I was usually able to get a pretty good nap in especially when the rising sun started to warm me up. I felt that stretching out on the couch at the office was just wrong and to keep driving while sleepy was an accident waiting to happen. However, I occasionally over-slept a bit and once woke up an hour after my shift was over. However, being "a Model Trooper" I never put in for overtime when that occurred! On one memorable occasion a concerned citizen stopped just ahead of me after determining that I seemed to be fairly motionless inside my patrol car, and walked back to check on me. That dipstick started rapping loudly on the side window I had my hat jammed into and scared the living shit out of me! After that, I started parking out on the gravel on the left side of the on-ramp, real close to the edge, making it really hard for someone to sneak up on my left side anymore.

On a quiet day shift one afternoon radio gave me a disabled motorist out near Tyler westbound. When I got there I discovered it wasn't really a disabled but some sort of weird hitchhiker attempted hijacking scene. The bonehead driver had picked up a really goofy looking hitchhiker in the Granite Lake Rest Area a few miles back then after a few miles is surprised when he discovers the guy is nuts! The hitchhiker had grabbed the steering wheel and tried to commandeer the guy's car while they were doing 70 mph down the freeway. The dipshit driver finally managed to get pulled over, jumps out taking the keys, and leaves the crazy hitchhiker inside. When I got there the nut-job was still sitting behind the wheel looking straight ahead . . . . He wouldn't look or talk to me and really had a death grip on the wheel. I tried prying his fingers off to attempt a Koga extraction on his wrist but those fingers were glued on there. I asked the driver to help me but he said 'No way Man!' I managed to cuff him with his hands in front, which was a no no, but I really couldn't think of anything else at the moment. I called radio and told them to send me some help. About then the nut-job starts yelling and screaming gibberish and began to bang his head on the dash and steering wheel. I hated to use it, as it was rarely effective, but I pulled out my Mace canister and hosed him down pretty good . . . . He responded a little bit to that dousing but just glared at me with an 'Is that all you got?' look . . . . Now I was getting a little perturbed with this moron so I grabbed his left arm and one handcuff and jerked and pulled for all I was worth trying to break his grip . . . He did his best impersonation of an octopus and crammed his legs up under the dash . . . . I was still pulling and jerking on him when a big guy shows up and asks if I need some help . . . . I think I was a bit surly and said something like "What the f**k does it look like . . . ?" Turned out he was a Cheney Fireman and with him on the other side of the car kicking and pushing this puke, we finally got him out on the ground . . . The fireman sat on him while I got my leg restraints and ski-rope lasso out of my trunk. We finally got his arms around to his backside and re-cuffed him. We pulled his legs up behind his back and secured them to the cuffs with the lasso and pulled them up real tight . . . . This guy was still kicking, spitting, struggling, yelling gibberish, and was doing a helluva impression of a mad dog with Rabies! After searching him we drug that piece of shit back to my patrol car and threw him in. I put him in face down on the floor in front of the seat to try to immobilize him. About then my backup shows up and after a few minutes announces matter of factly that this guy is on Angel Dust or PCP . . . . Not being a drug recognition expert I assumed he knew what he was talking about. I told the driver to never pick up a hitchhiker again but he was pissed at me because his car smelled like tear gas . . . When I got to the county a couple jailors came down the elevator to help me drag this guy out of my car in the sally port. Once upstairs their shift supervisor came over, saw my prisoner all hog-tied (and momentarily quiet) and said something sarcastic like 'Is this really necessary?' I resisted saying something really vulgar and just said; 'He's all yours now.' I went over to the BA room to start typing up my case report when all hell broke loose again . . . The dipstick shift supervisor had undone his leg restraints and had just got one cuff off when Mr. Nutjob went berserk again . . . Mr. Supervisor did this out in the open and hadn't even put him in a holding cell!! Jesus, this just wouldn't end!! They tackled him by the elevator and were trying desperately to get that loose cuff back on his free arm . . . . This looked just like an episode of the "Keystone Cops" from the thirties! I jumped into the fray again and finally got his arm twisted back around. He kept struggling and yelling and pulled it free . . . Man, this guy just seemed to have super-human strength when he got agitated! I grabbed that arm again and pulled and twisted with all my strength until we all heard a loud pop! That slowed him down a little as I had just completely dislocated his elbow . . . It looked real ugly and the supervisor just says something like "Great, now we gotta get him a fu**ing ambulance!!" The other jailors just drug the puke into a holding cell and slammed the door on him. I went over to look at the asshole and he casually glances up at me and clear as day says: "Happy now?" I didn't know quite how to respond to that so just said "No, are you?" I finished my case report and got the hell outa there . . .

Somewhat easier violators to deal with were the old folks; now I have to go easy with this subject since I'm rapidly approaching the geezer category myself. Quite often what I thought for sure was a drunk driver turned out to be an elderly person who had simply got a little confused. The telltale signs that the geezer crowd laid down were usually fairly obvious to spot such as: driving 20mph under the speed limit (usually in the left lane of the freeway), leaving the trunk lid open, leaving a door open, seat belt and/or coat slammed in the door and dragging on the freeway, forgetting to turn their lights on at night, leaving the hi-beams on, leaving the turn signal on, driving 5 to 10 mph under the speed limit on a two lane impeding a bunch of cars behind them, and my personal biggest pet peeve of all time (for anyone) . . . . sitting at a red light with their right turn signal blinking with no traffic coming and then not making that **free right turn** until the light changes!! Don't get me started on my second biggest pet peeve . . . . The idiots who will not maintain a steady speed either on the freeway or a two lane; 70 one minute, 58 the next then 74, then back down to 63 . . . Those guys drive me crazy!! Anyway, back to geezers; most of the above indicators could also be attributed to a DWI so it was hard to tell . . . . Sometimes it was just an elderly drunk driver . . . Never knew what to expect! Several times in my career I came up to contact one of these folks only to discover someone born in the 1800's who was way past their prime time of being a safe driver any longer . . . . I don't know how many times I heard the phrase "Why I was driving for 30 years before you were born son . . ." This right after I had stopped them for driving the wrong way on a one way street without their lights on at night. I always sent the bad ones in for what was called a DOL License Re-Exam test, the result of which was almost always a loss of their driving privileges. It broke my heart sometimes to have to break the news to these folks that their driving days were over since that was usually the only real "freedom" they had left . . . But, almost every week we read about an elderly driver getting the brake pedal and accelerator mixed up and subsequently crashing into a crowd of people or into a Seven Eleven store somewhere . . . .

I had to turn those folks in . . . . I only hope that the officer that eventually has to say those words to me is gentle about it . . . .

Late one graveyard shift radio gave me a one car non-injury accident westbound on SR-2 just west of the Old Sunset on ramp. It was really slick out but I had studded F-32s all the way around on my brand new 1981 Dodge Diplomat and it handled pretty well on the ice. When I contacted the driver he was drunk and soon took up residence in my backseat. While waiting for the tow truck my drunk suddenly announces he has to piss real bad; I told him to hold it since we'd be at the county jail pretty quick. A couple minutes later he says he just can't hold it any longer and says he's gonna piss in the car! God Damn it, I **had** to let him out (which is really considered a big no-no) as I did not want another new patrol car that smelled like urine for three years! Without thinking I left the rear door open and escorted him to the ditch for his piss. This fucker must have pissed for three minutes straight and just as I started to walk him back to my patrol car I look up to see another bonehead lose control in that same curve that caught my drunk. He wasn't going all that fast but started rotating out of control coming right at us . . . . I dragged my drunk back into that piss filled ditch just as the rear end of this stupid shit's car spins around and just catches my open left rear door tearing it cleanly off its hinges tossing it about 75 feet out into the brush! Son of a bitch . . . I didn't have 1,500 miles on that car yet! My current drunk must have been a John Denver fan as he yelled out "Far out Man" when he saw that door go sailing away. The second drunk just missed hitting the first drunk's car and went into the ditch backwards just ahead of it. When I contacted him he looked up at me with those ubiquitous bloodshot watery eyes that all drunks possess and just said "Man, I must have hit a slick spot or somethun . . ." I wish I had a nickel for every time I heard that stupid ass excuse! My sergeant **finally** showed up to investigate my patrol car accident while my two drunks froze their asses off in the back of my now door-less patrol car waiting for him. He eventually traded patrol cars with me, after the wreckers towed the two drunks' cars off, and I finally headed to the county jail. Taking two drunks in at once was a fairly common occurrence but what happened next wasn't . . . . I hadn't gone two miles and had just merged onto I-90 Eastbound going down Sunset Hill when I glanced into my rear view mirror and honest to God saw some dumbass coming up behind me without his lights on!! Holy Shit!!! I would sometimes go two to three weeks without getting a drunk driver on graveyard but tonight I just can't get out of their way fast enough! I'm the only troop working at 0400 and I knew for sure that my sarge didn't want a drunk in my door-less freezing patrol car so I have to pull this guy over myself. Sure enough, bloodshot eyes, strong odor of alcohol, failed field sobriety tests . . . . When I stuffed him in the back seat with my other two drunks it took him a few minutes to soak up the totality of the situation . . . . But he finally blurted out one of the funniest things I ever heard working the road: "Well shit, since we're all here, we might as well have an AA meeting!" This guy was a real conversation catalyst and while waiting for the third tow truck of the night he got the other two drunks talking about their activities that evening and I soon found myself writing down priceless unsolicited self incriminating tidbits as fast as I could . . . . Keeping who said or did what straight was a chore but I managed to get quite a bit of good evidence written down about where and how much they drank, how they lost control of their vehicles, and what bad luck it was to hit a "fuc**ng" State Patrol car! Thankfully, all of these guys were pretty well behaved, which was a miracle, and after spending the rest of the morning at the jail processing these clowns I finally was able to go home almost on time. I spent the first three hours of my next shift trying to get my three case reports straight before submitting everything to the prosecutor . . . . Never had another DWI night quite like that one. There was some fallout however; thanks to my good ole sarge, who forgot to check the appropriate box on my patrol car accident report that stated my wreck had occurred while I was an on-duty State Trooper. This accident mistakenly went on my personal driving record. It took me about a year to get that straightened out then another year to get a refund for the jacked up premiums I had to pay as a result of my accident even though I wasn't at fault in the first place regardless of what the f**k I was driving!! Needless to say, we changed insurance companies shortly thereafter!

I'll finish this section with a couple of car-train accidents that are still vivid in my mind. Although the car drivers were mostly at fault in both of them there were other circumstances that make these accidents hard to forget. The first one occurred south of Cheney at a fairly remote train crossing on a lightly traveled county road. The crossing was marked by a railroad track warning painted on the roadway and a railroad track sign right at the crossing. Visibility was very good in both directions but there were no lights or cross arms that came down when a train was approaching. The car driver approached the crossing pulling a boat; he slowed to a crawl going over the tracks as they were elevated and bumpy. Just as he was centered over the tracks he heard the train's horn blaring and finally saw it coming at him from his left; it was close and traveling very fast. I found out later why he reacted the way he did at this moment. Instead of just floor boarding the accelerator which would have easily got him safely out of harm's way he stopped, tried to get his car into reverse, panicked, killed the engine and was struck by the train . . . . He was trying to back up because he didn't think he could make it across the tracks in time without the train hitting his new boat and trailer and thought backing up would save them . . . . Man, the crazy shit that goes through people's minds! When I got to the scene it was the usual car-train mess but thankfully there was a doctor there who just happened to be driving by. The driver's son had been killed instantly. When I walked up to the dad he was sitting on a rock rubbing his thigh. He was rocking back and forth complaining about how much his foot hurt . . . It took me a few seconds to take in his injury but when I did it was a real shocker. His leg had been amputated about half way between his knee and ankle and all his calf muscles had retracted up into a ball just below his knee. His tibia was protruding out of this mess like a stick but was covered in dirt and I didn't recognize what it was at first. I didn't see his foot anywhere but when the ambulance got there I started looking for it in earnest just in case it could be re-attached. I found it crammed under the dashboard of the car still in a sneaker. I brought it over to the ambulance crew but realized it was probably a fruitless endeavor . . . . Several years later I was subpoenaed by the train company to testify on their behalf in a civil case brought by the driver alleging the crossing was dangerous and wasn't marked adequately . . . . I was really torn since the poor guy had lost his son and a leg but unfortunately, the crossing was legally marked, there were no obstructions, and the train had been blowing its whistle . . . What can you say??

Car-train fatal near Tyler.

The other car-train occurred just northwest of Airway Heights on a really foggy very cold morning. The driver approached the train tracks cautiously and slowed almost to a stop. There were no crossing arms or red lights at this crossing either. She swore later that she did not hear the train's horn nor did it blow its whistle. After a very thorough investigation, where I contacted every household in the area, I was also convinced that the crew did not blow their horn or whistle too. Anyway, as she was slowly crossing the tracks the train came out of the thick fog and hit her broadside. She was drug down the tracks for about 200 feet when her car finally separated from the train. When I arrived at the scene and walked up to the fog shrouded car I expected to find at least one very deceased person inside. What I found was an ejected driver in the deep snow with her legs trapped under the left rear tire and her upper body wrapped up in a phone pole guy wire. She was blue, getting very hypothermic, and in my opinion near death. As I ran back to my car to get all my blankets, I could just make out two train crewmen, in the fog, just standing there by the train with their hands in their pockets . . . I sort of lost it and yelled at them "Why aren't you fu**ers helping her?' All the older dumb shit, who I later determined to be the brakeman, said was: "We put the emergency brakes on when we hit her!!" Jesus, I just couldn't believe that two supposed professionals could be so apathetic and uncaring to just stand there and watch a fellow human being die in front of them without helping her . . . . When I got back I laid down in the snow next to her and wrapped my blankets all around both of us to warm her up. Man, I don't know what kind of brain-washing the train company did to those two assholes but after I yelled at them they just walked away and climbed back into their nice warm cab like a couple of sociopaths . . . After the ambulance, fire truck, and a tow truck showed up we were finally able to cut those guy wires and get her untangled. I visited her in the hospital and she eventually recovered but had some lingering mobility issues. I got the names of those two railroad employees and contacted the prosecutor's office about filing charges against them for failing to render assistance to an injured person . . . . They did not want to pursue the issue!? All I could do was write a bitch letter to the CEO of the train company complaining about those two miscreants . . . The CEO apparently was also a sociopathic pussy and never responded to my letter.

It was after frustrating episodes like this when I could calmly sit back and review my "knee jerk reactions" to unpleasant people and situations that I really became convinced that my career as a successful road trooper was in serious jeopardy . . . . I know of troopers that have worked the road for over forty years (Gus Nilsson) that still seemed sane . . . I applaud them but I'm afraid I could never have lasted that long without getting into some serious trouble . . . The straw that sort of broke the camel's back and made me realize that I might be getting a little burnt out was when I caught myself 'chewing out' the so called 'innocent' parties in two car accidents. It always aggravated me when an accident could have easily been avoided if the non-causing driver would have just taken some simple evasive action instead of just locking up their brakes like a trained monkey. Had they just employed a tiny bit of defensive driving, such as looking both ways 'after' the light turned green just in case some other moron was blasting through the red light, or "God Forbid" looking in your rear view mirror before making a left turn to see if anybody was trying to pass you right then . . . . Unfortunately, the vast majority of our motoring public doesn't look down the road any further than their hood ornament (after they are done texting) and when they do sense trouble they just lock up the brakes, get rear-ended by the asshole tailgating them, and then plow right into what they could have easily driven around. Anyway, I might have made a few caustic/sarcastic remarks to a couple of those 'innocent victims' about their lack of defensive driving skills . . . . As usual, I was soon rewarded with a none too complimentary bitch letter several days later . . . . So, as a result of this 'burn-out' revelation I totally immersed myself in aviation and went after each new rating and certificate with renewed purpose and a vengeance!

CHAPTER 9

THE PHONE CALL

Late one evening, while I was eastbound on I-90 near the Harvard Rd. exit, I observed what I initially thought was part of an airplane slowly spinning down out of the sky over the freeway . . . When it hit the ground I also noticed a large cloud of dust and other debris settling back to earth in the same general area . . . As usual, being a little slow on the uptake, it took me a second or two to process what I was seeing . . . . I finally recognized what had happened . . . I had just witnessed the final seconds of an horrendous accident! The object spinning down out of the night sky was the hood of a car that had just failed to negotiate a curve on the freeway and had rolled several times ripping the hood off and launching it skyward in the process . . . . I advised radio I had just witnessed an injury accident at Harvard Westbound and needed assistance. I slammed my patrol car through the median and stopped at the scene. There were three females occupants, two of which had been ejected during the rollover, and one still in the car. I tried to remember my EMT triage training as I attempted to prioritize which victim to assist first. The one that was screaming inside the car was obviously going to be my number three priority. The other two were unconscious so I needed to quickly evaluate them for the ABC's (airway, breathing, circulation) . . . One had respirations and a pulse but I couldn't detect anything on the other . . . . I started CPR on the girl that wasn't breathing but after just a few seconds I felt someone pounding on my back and yelling "That's my girlfriend you fu**ing pig!" I told one of the other 'looky lous' to get this asshole off of me . . . I kept up the CPR for quite awhile before Trooper Les Wilson 648 and finally an ambulance showed up. I told Les to restrain that crazy S.O.B. beating on my back as I just knew he had something to do with this wreck. We eventually got all three of them off to Valley General Hospital. This accident turned out to be one of the most frustrating of my career. The two seriously injured young girls were sisters and both died; the other had very serious injuries but later recovered. We discovered several days later (no one was telling the truth at the scene) that the driver was racing her boyfriend at high speed and he was that same S.O.B. pounding on my back. She couldn't keep up with him and lost it in the sweeping curve at Harvard Rd. travelling close to 100 mph. They were all under the legal drinking age for Washington and were just coming home from Idaho where the legal age was 18. This had been a serious on-going problem for years and this accident brought renewed media attention to that issue.

I was soon contacted by a reporter from the Spokesman Review who wanted to do an in-depth story on this accident. However, I was much more focused on trying to get enough evidence together to arrest the asshole 'boyfriend' for aiding and abetting negligent homicide and/or at least reckless driving and put the reporter off for awhile. I had several witnesses who put him behind the wheel at the time the racing was occurring, including one inside his vehicle. I finally presented my case report to a prosecutor who immediately told me we probably should just reduce the charge to negligent driving since there had not been any contact between the two cars and there wasn't a blood alcohol on the guy. I was pissed and angry but went with his judgment. When the case came to court, two of the three 'eye-witnesses' didn't show up after apparently being intimidated with threats of violence from the 'puke' boyfriend. The other gave a somewhat altered and subdued version of the events that night making it sound like they were just out on a scenic drive . . . Of course the judge found the asshole not guilty in spite of my lengthy detailed case report. I was so mad I went to see the judge in his chambers afterwards and probably pushed the limits of professionalism somewhat. I none too subtly reminded him that the puke he just found not guilty was directly responsible for the deaths of two young girls, that he'd just made a huge mistake, and that I hoped he was proud of himself . . . Luckily, I had known this particular judge for quite awhile as he used to play cards with one of the other senior troopers in my detachment . . . . He sympathized but was really pissed at me for my outburst! Thankfully, he didn't tell my boss what happened in chambers that day.

That reporter from the local paper eventually came out and rode with me several times on the late night shift, gained my confidence, and finally got me to speak my mind during a weak moment. I had a few unsavory things to say about the criminal justice system, various judges, particular bars in Idaho that catered to our young people, and drunk drivers in general. When his 'exclusive' story came out in the paper the headlines read "Weekend Slaughter" . . . . An inside look at the fatal consequences of underage drinking according to Trooper Rick Carnevali. He even published a photo of me, without my hat on, where I looked like an angry deranged greaser . . . . He purposely selected that photo instead of several others where I had my campaign hat on and looked fairly normal, just for the shock effect I guess. Man was I ever mad at that jerk! Not because of the photo but because of his insensitivity towards the family involved by using such shocking language to describe the deaths of their daughters! I should have listened to my old Olympia sergeant who had warned me about **never** trusting reporters. I felt terribly ashamed and so sorry for the parents of the deceased who had to read about their loved ones deaths in such a horribly graphic article . . . The only saving grace from this story occurred about a month later when I went to visit the one survivor from the accident who was still convalescing at home. While there her brother took me aside and gave me some great news . . . . Several friends of the young deceased driver had confronted that asshole puke boyfriend one evening and beat the living shit out of him after he was acquitted by that spineless judge in court . . . Although I sort of had to remain impartial to that news, inwardly I felt gratified that once again some 'roadside justice' had evened the score a little with another sociopath.

The aftermath of this fatal was the final impetus for me to dedicate my life to aviation once and for all . . . . I needed to finish my career doing what I felt was a somewhat 'clean' law enforcement activity with minimum contact with the public. I was really sick and tired of the up close and personal battles with the courts, the media, and most of all the never-ending supply of assholes and pukes pervading our highways. I freely admit that I had grown very intolerant but felt I still had a lot to offer the WSP in a different career path. However, when I really got involved in some serious instrument flying, I began to doubt my resolve and/or ability to become a professional pilot and even started thinking about quitting the WSP altogether and joining my Dad in his land leveling business as a Cat Skinner (D8 driver).

Myself on D8H push-loading my Dad on Euclid scraper near Sunnyside.

When I told Norm about my new resolve and asked him to show me no mercy during my training flights he seemed to "perk" up a bit. His renewed interest in my instrument flying took on a "Tomas Torquemada" theme and I soon found myself being exposed to severe icing and moderate to severe turbulence on nearly every flight that winter. Needless to say, he did not consider either of those naturally occurring phenomenon an excuse for deviating more than 3 degrees off heading or 20 feet off altitude . . . Man, when I got home after some of those flights I needed a couple belts of CC and 7 to settle my nerves a bit . . . Unfortunately, I usually had to go to work so a glass of milk and a couple of Rosauer's blueberry donuts had to suffice. I was also logging countless hours in a Gat 1 flight simulator with Jim Kieran at the Community College which was very similar to the old Link Trainers from WWII. All I thought, dreamed, and fantasized about were non standard holding pattern entries, back course localizer approaches, ADF approaches, ILS approaches, NDB Holding with a direct crosswinds, VOR DME arcs, missed approaches, partial panel, etc., etc . . . . I never quite knew where I stood with Norm and even after a perfect ILS the only reaction I might get out of him was a slight shoulder shrug and a muffled 'meh'. Finally, after one more horrendous flight where we landed with almost an inch of ice, he said that I might not kill too many people on a check ride and signed me off. Man I was so relieved to be done with that meat grinder training but almost instantly started stressing out about a ride with an FAA examiner. He turned out to be a real laid back guy from the SFF FISDO named Del Randall. I was so used to flying in actual IFR with Norm that I was almost disappointed when the sun was shining the day of my check ride and I had to don that stupid hood for the whole flight. He worked me over pretty good after I told him during the oral what my ultimate goals were. I thought that I had made several small errors during the ride but didn't think any of them amounted to a failure by any means. When we finally landed back at SFF he was pretty quiet and just told me to park in front of the restaurant. We went in for coffee and he started detailing every single one of the small mistakes I'd made as if they were catastrophic career ending events!! Man, he really had me going and I just knew I'd be getting a pink slip (failed ride notice) . . . But, he finally said that I just barely met the practical test guideline standards and against his better judgment asked for my log book. He quickly wrote something in it, gave me a sly grin and said good luck with my career. I still wasn't sure if I had passed or not until I saw the satisfactory he had scribbled in there. Man, was I ever relieved to get that ride out of the way!

Looking back I still consider getting my instrument rating the toughest assignment I have ever undertaken in my life . . . . Later on, acquiring my CFII, ME-ATP, and type ratings in the BE40 and CE-525 were a breeze after the Norm Hjelm experience . . . He certainly made me a confident instrument pilot and I will forever be in his debt and probably owe him my life. I immediately started work on my Commercial License and Jim Kieran introduced me to another great ex-fighter pilot named John Koch at Spokane Airways. He had flown Skyraiders and A4s in the Navy during Viet Nam and shared a lot of great stories with me about his career. He was also quite the local celebrity in aviation circles after having flown his Varieze homebuilt airplane around the world. He also owned a Super Cub that he kept in his barn down near Rockford and used to brag about how much gear he could pack in that mother and still get it airborne to go hunting in Alaska. He was a fabulous instructor and with his expert help I knocked off my Commercial in a week.

I started right in on my Flight Instructor Certificate before the ink was even dry on my Commercial . . . I was on a mission from God and nothing was going to deter me from racking up every rating and certificate I could manage. Jim assigned another great guy to be my instructor for this phase named Howard Miller. He was a local veterinarian and a real cool cucumber . . . nothing ever excited him. Flying from the right seat wasn't as tough as I thought and soon became second nature. There was a Cessna 150 aerobatic plane in the club and we flew it for the spin sequence. I didn't tell Howard that Norm had already introduced me to spins while flying the Beech Sport during my instrument training since that was somewhat frowned upon in non-approved aircraft . . . Norm also had introduced me to several other aerobatic maneuvers in that poor old Sport as he just couldn't keep his fighter pilot instincts from surfacing. I loved the spin training with Howard and we probably did many more than required by the syllabus. I was finally able to roll out 'pretty close' to a designated heading without busting my hard altitude during recoveries. The most trouble I had during this phase was writing up lesson plans that met Howard's approval . . . . Everything seemed so redundant and simplistic but I finally managed to buckle down and get them all approved. The check ride with a different FAA examiner this time was a real ball-buster and we spent several hours on the oral before even getting near an airplane. I was real shaky on the principles of aerodynamics and the examiner recognized that immediately. Man, I was sweating like a whore in church before he finally said those magic words: 'Let's go out to the plane' . . . The flying portion was pretty anticlimactic and he eventually uttered the magic words I was so used to hearing: "That was a pretty marginal ride but you somehow just barely managed to meet the practical test guideline minimum standards . . ." Plenty good enough for me!! I ran to Jim to tell him the good news and he unbelievably offered me a job as a flight instructor with the Hangar Flying Club right on the spot! Man, I just couldn't believe that and was just beside myself with feelings of satisfaction and accomplishment! On the way home I began to wonder just how I was going to pull off having two high stress jobs at the same time. I was working for a great sergeant at the time, Pat Thomson 196, and he said it would be OK if I worked straight graveyard which would allow me to fly in the afternoons. That work schedule was a real bitch but when you're thirty years old anything is manageable. Jim didn't hesitate dumping about five student pilots on me immediately and Jesus was I ever busy!! One guy had previous training and just needed a little tune-up before his first solo. I had never been so anxious in my life when I uttered those fateful words to him "I think you're ready, go ahead and do two touch and go's and a full stop" . . . . And then I got out . . . ! Watching him in the pattern all alone was so nerve wracking I thought I was going to explode . . . Thank God he was a natural pilot and didn't kill himself and crash into a church somewhere! Looking back on my flight instructor days I think I learned more about flying watching others work through their mistakes than in any other flight scenario . . . You just get so focused on what your student is doing that the fundamentals of flight seem to get permanently hardwired into your core . . . . I will always remember and be grateful to Jim Kieran for giving me the opportunity to grow and mature as a pilot while working for The Hangar Flying Club!

I was on another roll so I immediately started work on my multi-engine rating. I really lucked out on this training segment when Jim told me that a Hangar Flying Club member, who owned a pristine Piper PA23-250 Aztec, was willing to let me use it for my rating just for the gas it took! Man, this was huge! He owned a local vacuum cleaner dealership and was one of the most generous and gracious guys I've ever met. That Aztec seemed like a lot of airplane for a neophyte like me but it turned out to be a dream to fly and was a super stable instrument platform. Jim handed me over to Ken Seay for this training and he was another excellent instructor that Jim had recommended. He was the guy who finally taught me a very simple method to determine holding pattern entries that took all the guess work out of it. I still use it today and will always be thankful to him for simplifying what can be a little confusing when you don't have an MFD or moving map display to guide you. Ken was also an FAA designated examiner so he was pretty much all business. We spent a lot of time losing an engine right after takeoff and performing countless single engine approaches and single engine go-arounds. I was just amazed at how sluggish an Aztec was on one engine and just couldn't imagine how some guys got their multi in an Apache (an underpowered version of the Aztec) . . . . I thought that Norm was fond of ice until Ken came along . . . Jesus, we loaded that poor old Aztec down with ice on nearly every flight and were forced to make several nearly full power landings to keep the thing in the air without stalling it on short final. Ken had just come off a job flying freight in Montana in Beech 18's so loading up with ice just didn't faze him in the least. Finally, Ken said I might be ready for my multi-instrument check ride and signed me off. It was Del Randall again and this time he really raked me over the coals . . . I was just a total wreck when we finally recovered at the SFF café where I honestly didn't care if I had passed or failed . . . I just wanted to go home, call in sick, grab a bottle of CC and not think about airplanes anymore! When he finally told me I had passed I just couldn't process the news at first . . . I thought I had made so many huge mistakes that he was going to just slap me in the face, demand I produce my other certificates, and then rip them up in front of me!! I drove home in stunned silence and went to bed to try to get a little sleep before my graveyard shift started at 2300.

During those years, 1980 to 1985, Jim Kieran had a contract with a local radio station to provide on the air 'Eye in the Sky' traffic reports during the evening rush hour in Spokane. One afternoon while we were lounging around the hangar bullshitting he asked if I would like to fly with him during those spots and occasionally provide professional 'traffic tips' for the listening audience in good old N59AM, a pristine C172. I had to ask permission from my district commander at the time, Roger Bruett, to see if there was any sort of conflict of interest. He thought it was a great idea and believed it would be tremendous publicity for the WSP . . . . So began my third career as a part time radio personality. Jim let me do all the flying from the right seat so I could log the time, while he made the radio calls to the station and did all the 'on air' spots every fifteen minutes. He would occasionally advise the listening audience that 'Trooper Rick' was onboard whereupon he would ask me to provide brief 'on the air' safety tips such as: when you could put on your studded tires, the dangers of following too closely, or what to carry in your trunk for emergency situations, etc., etc . . . . I loved this program and racked up hundreds of 'free' flying hours with Jim. There was a slight downside though; occasionally when I was talking on the air Jim would slide his seat back and grab a hidden old fashioned *Ooga Horn* (like the old Model T's had) and give it a blast while I was trying to sound like a seasoned broadcaster . . . Man, it was tough to recover after one of those blasts and still sound professional on the air . . . . The first time he did it I almost blurted out; "God dammit Jim, knock that shit off!" . . . Thankfully, that kind of language never slipped out on the air!!

Captain Bruett thought I was the cat's meow and as a result of all the positive free publicity the WSP got, he told me he would support me in my quest to get into the Aviation Section in spite of my history of insubordination and pile of bitch letters . . . . We remained good friends for many years thereafter. Roger eventually became chief of the WSP and I will always remember a flight with him to Whidbey Island Naval Air Station. We had dropped him off at the civilian terminal in the Beechjet and he told us he would be gone for three or four hours. Since this had been an O-Dark Thirty get up, my co-pilot and I reclined a couple of the seats, pulled out the blankets, and stretched out for a nice nap. We were sleeping quite soundly when all of a sudden the hatch drops down and the Chief pounds up the airstairs . . . . He glares at us and exclaims out loud . . ."What the hell kind of airline are you guys running here???!!!" Man we were all assholes and elbows, pulling our blankets off and looking at our watches trying to figure out how three hours had gone by so quickly . . . . After witnessing our reaction he started laughing so hard I thought he was going to blow chunks right on the spot!! . . . Turned out his secretary had the wrong day penciled in on his schedule and he wasn't expected at Whidbey until the following week! When Roger was a young trooper he jumped into a freezing cold/flooding river and saved a family from drowning and received the WSP's highest award for bravery. After retiring he went on to become Chief of security for Bill Gates at Microsoft. Roger was another of those wonderful guys I knew in my career that sadly passed away so young . . . I really miss him . . .

My students at the Hangar Flying Club ran the spectrum from 15 year old kids to elderly folks finally fulfilling their lifelong dream of learning to fly. I will always remember a young lady who said she wanted to learn to fly solely to get over her lifelong fear of flying . . . She was a very exuberant girl and prone to sudden physical outbursts of both joy and fear that occasionally caught me off guard. She did pretty well on the first couple flights where we just practiced the four basics: turns, climbs, descents, and level flight. However, when we proceeded into the stall series, it got very painful (for me). The Beech Sport has a very benign straight ahead power off stall characterized by a gentle wings level break. During the first couple attempts she just took her hands off the controls at the break, grabbed the arm rest, and let out a blood curdling scream . . . . I let her rest a bit then demonstrated several more for her and showed her that nothing bad was going to happen after the break. She tried another stall but the very first one turned out real ugly . . . . She apparently got frightened again just as it broke, jerked the yoke back real hard and held it there while cramming one of her legs to the firewall taking a rudder pedal with her!! . . . . Jesus, that little Sport did a perfect snap roll and scared the living shit out of me! At the time I didn't know what a snap roll was but 15 years later, when learning how to do them in a T6, I immediately recognized what my student had demonstrated to me that long ago day. After I over-powered her control inputs I was pretty confused but sort of recognized that we were now in a spin . . . . While I was shoving the yoke forward and cramming some opposite rudder in she let loose with another ear piercing scream and simultaneously buried her long sharp fingernails into the top of my left thigh!! Holy crap . . . . she really got in there deep and drew blood . . . I thought I had seen it all while working the road but this was a new one for me! We headed back to the airport and after landing sat down and had a long talk about the sensations of flight. I flew with her several more times but just couldn't in all good conscience solo her. By this time Ken Seay, my former instructor, was working at the club part time too. I asked him if he could evaluate her to see if there was any chance we could get her over her fears to the point where we could release her for solo. He gave me that "You stupid rookie, I'll take care of this" look and started flying with her. I went on vacation about this time and when I got back three weeks later discovered that she had now accumulated around 30 hours of dual instruction and still hadn't soloed. When I sat down with Ken all he said was "Man, she's a real piece of work!" I have to give her credit though for not giving up . . . . Finally, one very calm morning, Ken let her go solo. She pulled it off without creating a smoking hole in the ground somewhere but as I remember, she never flew again. I guess she had proved some kind of point to herself or whoever . . . . Only thing was she spent more money just to go solo than most students spent finishing their complete private pilot course.

My most memorable student was a character named Gene Stuckle. He already had logged thousands of hours, primarily flying his own crop-dusters on his own farm, but had never got around to getting his Commercial Certificate. Since we were both farmers Jim thought we'd be a good match so I got the nod to help him get his ticket. He had a beautifully maintained all polished aluminum 1956 Cessna 172 which we did most of the flying in. On one of our first flights together we landed at his own private strip just west of Davenport for lunch and he gave me the tour. Wow, what a place!! It was actually a vintage truck, tractor, and airplane museum . . . He had literally millions of dollars worth of restored antiques that he kept in several large hangars at his airport. The equipment he restored just ran the gamut of motorized

American history: iron wheel tractors, early crawlers, all the early Poppin Johnnies, a huge collection of Model T and Model A Fords, a Fairchild, a Stearman duster and several other old planes that I had no idea what they were. His truck collection included a gorgeous old Diamond Reo and some very early Kenworth trucks. His masterpiece was a 1932 Duesenberg convertible that he kept in his living room! It should have been in the Smithsonian . . . it was perfect in every way and had to be worth a million all by itself! He had flexible piping hooked up to the exhaust and vented outside so he could start it up and run it in the house . . . . It just purred like a kitten . . . Man, this guy just blew me away! He also maintained an "Autograph Wall" in his den . . . . It was adorned with a Who's Who of Washington State pilots and celebrity signatures from all over the country and I was very honored to be asked to add mine. He did just fine on all his Commercial maneuvers but just wasn't comfortable talking on the radio. He soon met all the minimum hours of dual instruction the FAA required and passed his check ride with no problems. I learned more about flying from Gene than he ever did from me! I didn't see him for about five years until one day Jeff Harshman 311 and I drove out to his place when we had a day to kill in Spokane during a King Air flight. We got the grand tour and Jeff was just as super-impressed as I had been with him and his museum. About a week later Jeff and I had a drop off in Spokane and were empty going home. We gave Gene a call from Flight Craft and told him to be outside in about 20 minutes. When we got to his place we had the King Air wide open and buzzed his strip at about 50 ft! We saw Gene waving his cowboy hat at us as we went past . . . I don't remember who was flying that day but I'm pretty sure it was Harshman . . . .

About this time in early 1983 I started hearing rumblings from some of the WSP Aviation Section pilots, who I had been riding with on my days off, that there might be a pilot position opening up pretty soon. Man, I was all over that news and began my final all-out blitz to make myself known to the Aviation Section managers. Every time I got a new rating I sent them an IOC (inter office communiqué) keeping them advised of my progress. I did the same each time I added another hundred hours and also detailed all the 'actual' instrument time and instructor time I was accumulating. During the summer of 1983 I even volunteered to drag the WSP's "Seat Belt Convincer" trailer around to all the county fairs in Eastern Washington. This was a device that demonstrated to its riders how important wearing a seatbelt was even in a simulated 20 mph crash. A driver's seat slid down a pretty steep ramp and smacked into a rubber stop cushion . . . I had ridden it myself and it was a fairly violent impact. Only problem was the only takers I got at most of the fairs were little kids who thought it was just another carnival ride and kept coming back for multiple "convincings". I really enjoyed my time that summer and at least I didn't have to work the road during those weekend outings with the "Convincer". After one session at Ritzville I was invited to go for a ride in Maynard Lund's AT 6 Texan. He was an on-call ambulance driver in the area but also owned a crop duster business. When we got to his little strip along the freeway he had me stow my campaign hat and gunbelt in the little baggage compartment in the back of his T6. For the next 20 minutes he did everything in his power to make me puke . . . . Snap rolls, immelmanns, split esses, loops, you name it, and I don't think we ever got over 1,000 feet AGL the whole time!! I admit I was damn close to barfing but I knew I couldn't let him see how screwed up I really was . . . . When we finally landed and opened up that little baggage door to get my gear, it was scattered everywhere . . . My hat was totally destroyed, all my bullets had come out of their little pouches, and the leather on my gunbelt was all tore up . . . My 357 had come out of its holster and was crammed in a corner! We were lucky we hadn't shot ourselves down!!

I also volunteered to work on a live TV telethon of some sort, answering the phone and taking pledges. Of course I shipped off more IOC's to Aviation Commander Dick Swier to let him know how involved in the community I was and what a sterling model trooper I had morphed into . . . . I'm sure he saw through my obvious cheap attempts at self aggrandizement but at least I was getting my name out there. I began riding with the two WSP pilots based in Ephrata as often as I could. Troopers Rheaume 685 and Hinchliffe 328 no doubt thought I was a pest. As I found out later myself it was always nice to have another body along to do all the writing for you on a busy day with lots of speeders to document. They let me fly sometimes and I eventually started to feel fairly comfortable in a Skylane and learned how to operate its KNS 80 Area Navigation system. After months of anticipation there was finally an announcement that the Aviation Section had two pilot openings and would all interested applicants please submit their names and resumes for consideration. Man this was really huge and I honestly felt I had a decent chance at getting one of those spots. There were about five of us that applied but first we had to submit to a grueling psychological written test and oral with the departmental psychologist in Bellevue. After that we drove down to the Olympia hangar for an interview with Captain Swier, his Lieutenant Jack Mulder, and the head of the personnel division. When it was finally my turn I sat down in front of these guys and was fairly nervous. I knew they would have my complete personnel file in front of them which by now was pretty thick considering all the complaints I had accumulated. However, to my dread, they focused in on an incident that had occurred between myself and one of my former supervisors several years before. The two of us had quite dissimilar personalities and life views and a slight shouting match had erupted one afternoon between us which had to be broken up by another trooper in my detachment . . . . Of course this sort of behavior was just not condoned by the quasi-militaristic WSP management types and although they were very polite to me I knew as soon as I left the room that I didn't have a chance. It was a long drive home back to Spokane and the news that I didn't get either of the positions wasn't too surprising. I immediately re-focused myself to becoming an even better candidate the next time around and just hoped it wouldn't be too long before that vacancy occurred.

There was an old tradition in the WSP that when you were trying to get promoted just stop a huge number of cars and write a shit-load of tickets and all sins would be forgiven. I had seen it happen before in my career and was always disgusted by those guys' cheap and obvious behavior . . . . So, being the reformed whore I had become, I started stopping everything that moved and wrote so many tickets I had calluses on the fingers of my right hand. I was stopping over 300+ cars a month which would be considered being lazy now but put me in the very "high roller" category back then. Working straight graveyard allowed me to really hammer the drunks and I lead the district in DWI activity for quite awhile. As the summer of 1984 rolled around I was contacted by the Stevens County Sheriff's office to see if I would be interested in flying marijuana spotting missions for them. One of the other Hangar Flying Club members, to whom I had earlier given a biennial flight review, owned a brand new Cessna 172 and he was gracious enough to let me fly it on those missions since the Sheriff's office was buying the gas. Luckily the spotter that rode with me was a real pro and could spot marijuana better than anyone I have ever seen. Captain Ken Myers had eagle eyes and could pick out individual marijuana plants from a thousand feet . . . he was just awesome! I only had a few flights with him as the prime marijuana spotting season is actually fairly short. Even so, we took down quite a few grows that fall and this indoctrination with a real pro sure helped me later in my career. Ken was kind enough to write me up a commendation since I was flying on my days off as a volunteer. Later that year the DEA had an awards banquet and I got a plaque from them as well for my volunteer flying. Of course, copies of everything got forwarded to Captain Swier and I hoped I was re-building my reputation a little, at least in his eyes. I even went so far as to placard the dashboard in my patrol car with the solution for what usually got me in trouble with people; it read: "Sta zitto e contare fino a dieci!!" Translated: "Shut up and count to ten" . . . . When my old sergeant saw it he thought it was some kind of Italian curse aimed at him . . . .

West Beat troops, 1984 Standing from left: Bob Watkins
849, Bob McCluskey 466, Gene Osburn 124, Pete Powell
641, Loren Ottenbreit 378 Kneeling from left: Fred Swan
843, Lee Boling 281, Gary Scott 330, Myself 305

Shortly after this episode another vacancy opened up in the
Aviation Section. Captain Bruett wrote me another very flattering
recommendation as did my brand new West beat sergeant, and
former trooper buddy, Gene Osburn . . . . I thought this one was in
the bag. I felt the interview went very well and Captain Swier also
showed me a letter of recommendation from Sergeant Wayne Small
that I wasn't even aware of. I was really surprised with that letter as my
only contact with him had been during a two week Stay Alive at "55"
emphasis patrol where a gang of about six of us roamed around Eastern
Washington writing speeding tickets until we were exhausted. I tried
to write twenty tickets a day and I guess Wayne was impressed with
my performance. Anyway, on the way home I felt pretty confident and
when I walked in the front door Deb said some captain from Olympia

had called and wanted to talk to me. When I called Captain Swier back he told me I had not been selected again. I was really shattered this time but didn't let him hear that in my voice . . . I just gave him some stupid line about how much harder I would try the next time and thanks for the privilege of letting me interview . . . . I guess he bought it but I knew in my heart that I would probably never get that transfer. I made up my mind right there to quit trying to impress everyone, resolved to just be myself from then on, and to quit stopping so many freaking cars . . . It was wearing me out!!

55 Emphasis Patrol Team 1983: Standing from left: Dave Karnitz 750, Becky Bryson 313, Self 305, Joe Kimball 672, Brian Holliday 907, kneeling: Kris Boness 345. (672's Mustang in background)

I went back to working a regular schedule and finally got off that permanent graveyard shift. I flew when I could but kept it reasonable so I could finally get some sleep at night. The Ephrata traffic pilots said it didn't look like there were going to be any vacancies for several years as all the pilots seemed to be settled in for the long haul and no one was talking about retiring. I finally relaxed a little, settled back into basic trooper mode and was actually a lot calmer than I had been in years. I was working for a great sergeant, with a good group of guys, and really found myself at peace after I quit trying to be someone I wasn't . . . . However, the life of a road trooper is always full of surprises as I was soon reminded.

I was working the "bug" in the turn-around west of Four Lakes when a beat up old pickup came into the beam at 75. I turned on my lights and looked right at the driver as he went past me . . . He was looking straight ahead and appeared to be a real grungy—maggot—puke . . . (we referred to these types as un-desirables on the radio). I fell in behind him as he slowed on the shoulder . . . Just before stopping he suddenly gunned it and took off . . . I immediately advised radio I was in pursuit and gave them the license and description of the pickup . . . He took the Cheney exit but instead of turning right he turns left and starts down the Westbound Exit ramp going the wrong way . . . . Ahhh shit, I just knew I was soon going to witness a head-on accident on I-90 which I would be blamed for. I had a split second to either chase him the wrong way on the freeway or get back on I-90 Eastbound and get a little ahead of him to try to warn oncoming traffic. I chose to chase him the wrong way. This was before the days of the PIT maneuver but I still wanted to get up along side him and just force him into the ditch any way I could before there was a real rip-snorter. Traffic was fairly light but I still watched in horror as several cars swerved to miss hitting him at the last second then almost hit me! I was keeping radio advised and told the other guys to stop westbound traffic at Geiger if they could. This was also before the days of spike strips and about all we could do was try to shoot out their tires with our shotguns as they went by . . . I know, real Stone Age stuff . . . After a couple more close calls I lost my nerve and crashed on down through the median and got going in the Eastbound Lanes. Just as I caught up to him he took the SR 902 exit. I took it on the other side but lost a lot of time with a car that stopped and blocked me and I still had to get over the overpass . . . I lost sight of him for a few seconds due to the overpass and when I came over the top I couldn't see his pickup anywhere . . . . I backed up thinking I would have a better view of where he went from on top of the overpass. Just then I saw the guy walking across the grassy area between the overpass and the Westbound on-ramp . . . . What I really focused on was what he had in his right hand . . . . It looked like an old WWII M1 carbine of some sort . . . . Well the sight of that thing gave me quite the adrenaline surge . . . . I jumped out, pulled my shotgun out of its boot, punched the safety off and yelled at him to "Drop the rifle or I will blow your fu**ing head off!!" I don't believe I identified myself again since he had already identified me a few minutes ago when he decided to run from me . . . . He didn't even look my way and was carrying that carbine low with his right hand with the barrel pointed straight ahead . . . . All I really was focused on was the tip of that rifle barrel . . . If it moved even an inch in my direction I was going to fire. I yelled more police type profanities at him and really wanted to shoot him in the legs to just stop him . . . . Unfortunately, all I could think of was some recent training at the Academy where the instructor told us if you feel threatened to the point that you've pulled your gun out, then it's time for deadly force not time for warning shots or wounding someone . . . You'll just get the department sued if you do that . . . Even though this guy had a gun I honestly didn't feel 'threatened' by him at that 'very' second . . . . I imagined his defense attorney later in court exclaiming: "Your honor, my client was innocently out hunting rabbits near the freeway when this cop showed up and blew his legs off for no reason . . . ." Unbelievably, the other thing that popped into my mind just then was that Godamned Carol King song *Flatwater Jack* and those lyrics; "You can't talk to a man with a shotgun in his hand . . . ." While all this craziness was going on in my head, he walked into some Pine trees and I lost sight of him. I also finally noticed why he was walking; his pickup was stuck in the ditch at the curve in the beginning of the on-ramp. I told radio what was going on, backed up onto the top of the overpass, and peered over the edge to see what was going on down below. He didn't come out the other side and I was praying that a car had run over him. I was just starting to climb down the steep slope having assumed he had lodged himself up under the bridge girders near the freeway decking like the two Native American guys had done. I was filling my shoes with gravel again, when a car stopped back on top the overpass. A guy jumped out yelling at me saying that some crazy mother fu**er had just jumped out in front of traffic, under the overpass, pointed his rifle at a car until they stopped! He then pulled the driver out and hi-jacked his yellow Volvo. Shit Oh dear, what the hell next?? I knew I should have shot that mother in the legs!! I scrambled back up the slope, told the guy to call the WSP with his name and number, and took off after the yellow Volvo . . . I was so thankful the guy gave me a pretty good description and gave radio all the new details. Ladonna Zavala was working and immediately put everyone on emergency traffic so someone didn't try to run a driver's check while I was involved in this mess . . . He probably had a good 90 second head start on me and my first decision was whether or not to take the Cheney exit or keep going Westbound on I-90. I didn't see anything yellow ahead of me on the freeway so I took the exit and hoped for the best. I had radio advise the Ritzville troops and Cheney PD that the Volvo might be coming their way. While I was racing down SR904 towards Cheney, Don Campbell 273, who had just arrived at the guy's pickup, comes on the air to tell me that the guy's pickup was full of guns and other items probably just taken in a burglary somewhere . . . . Gee, no wonder he didn't want to stop for me! As I neared Cheney I saw one of their officers and stopped to check with him; he said he'd been there the whole time and no yellow Volvos had come by. I still couldn't assume he had stayed on the freeway but was kicking myself that I hadn't! There were several county roads he could have turned off on between Four Lakes and Cheney so I headed East on Fish Lake Road for lack of a better plan . . . . After putzing around the Marshall area for a few minutes radio comes back on the air to report another car hi-jacking had just occurred on SR195 near the Cheney Spokane Road . . . . God Dammit, that was only about 5 miles from me. Several other troops were already on SR195 and said they had to be really close to him so I backed off rather than kill myself trying to catch up. A few minutes later someone in the small town of Spangle called radio to report a reckless driver going through town at Mach 1 headed toward Waverly . . . . Man, this guy was really honking . . . Just one troop was fairly close and thought he was only a mile or so behind him but wasn't sure. I already had radio call for an airplane and hoped that either Rheaume or Hinchliffe weren't too far away. I started working my way East since 273 was taking care of the guy's pickup and inventorying all the stolen articles. Another troop was contacting the 'original' driver of the yellow Volvo who wasn't too happy when he learned that it had just been wrecked. Spokane PD had the driver of the second hi-jacked car and so far no-one had been injured by this maniac. Captain Bruett and Lieutenant Peterson were on the air and were doing their mobile command post routine. It was only a few minutes later when the troop that was following the second hi-jacked car found it in the ditch near Fairfield . . . . Man that guy could not drive for shit and I assumed he was either drunk or messed up on some other substance. When I got to the farmhouse where everyone was congregating the farmer's wife said she saw a guy with no shirt on walking across their wheat field up towards a stand of Pine trees with a rifle. This was early March, it was about 32 degrees out with a howling wind. The field was very muddy and I'm sure this guy was freezing to death about now . . . Why he took his shirt off didn't really matter since crazy people do crazy things! At that time the Spokane Co. Sheriff's office had a small helicopter and it arrived over the scene. They spotted the guy hunkered down in the trees near the top of a small hill. After only circling a few minutes the pilot announced he was low on fuel and left. Thankfully, good old 685 showed up to save the day . . . He told me later he had one helluva tailwind coming from Moses Lake and it had only taken him twenty minutes to get here. He radioed to us that the guy was aiming and tracking him with a rifle whereupon Captain Bruett immediately told him to back off a ways. I think we were waiting for a county canine unit to show up when 685 came on the air again and said the guy was working his way back down a little gully towards a smaller county road. 685 skillfully maneuvered everybody into a position behind another little hill so when the suspect came around a little bend they should be able to capture him. When they did confront him he hesitated but finally dropped the rifle; they arrested him without any further problem . . . . Man this guy should have been dead about 5 times in the last hour and must have had somebody looking out for him. From my perspective 685 had saved the day and once again proved the value of having a plane overhead during these crazy fast moving types of incidents. Apparently the suspect was hypothermic and extremely muddy and I'm glad I didn't have to put him in my nice clean car. I went over to the deputy's patrol car to make sure this was the same guy and sure enough it was. Man, what a goat rope this turned out to be!

Captain Bruett came over and I gave him a blow by blow of how it all started. As usual he was the ultimate professional and told me I had exercised extremely good judgment in not shooting him initially in spite of everything that happened afterwards. I was a little worried about the outcome until he re-assured me right away . . . . Looking back I think he was just grateful that I hadn't created a ton of paperwork for him by offing that crazy bastard . . . He was the best district commander I ever worked for! Turned out the suspect had once been a highly decorated soldier and later became a military bomb technician. Apparently he had been severely injured while diffusing an explosive device during a training session and had to take a medical retirement from the Army. He became hooked on painkillers and was forced to take up a life of crime to buy his pain pills that the VA couldn't provide. The ironic part of the story was that the old WWII carbine he initially grabbed out of his pickup was the only gun he had taken in that burglary that had its firing pin removed . . . If I had killed him the headline would have no doubt read "Trooper Shoots Viet Nam Hero Carrying Historical Artifact". In spite of the fairly good outcome, which included a district commendation for me, one of the guys in my detachment started bad mouthing me . . . . He was telling the other guys at coffee that I was a chicken-shit pussy for not killing that guy right off the bat . . . Of course, he never approached me to get a blow by blow first-hand account of what had really happened. He told everyone that had it been him he would have blown the guy's head off right away . . . . It's like the old saying goes: "You can choose your friends but you're stuck with your family (and fellow detachment troopers)!"

I wrote 685 a nice comp. letter after this incident since he really deserved it. He called me at home one night and thanked me and we had a nice chat. I got back into the old routine of heading to the office, picking up a radar, and trudging on out to several of my favorite fishing holes to fill my 'quota'. Actually, we didn't have a quota but like any other job we were expected to generate a certain amount of 'activity' each shift like any other worker on an assembly line or warehouse fork lift driver to earn our paycheck. During a normal work day, if we didn't have too many accidents to cover or any other emergency situations to deal with we were expected to generally stop a minimum of around ten cars. Of those ten, 3 stops were expected to be citations (later called infraction notices), 3 were expected to be written warnings (4W's), and the other 4 verbal warnings for minor violations. Of course as the computer age gained momentum our sergeants started evaluating our 'spread'. At the end of the month they did not want to see just a shitload of speeding tickets; they were looking for a balanced enforcement effort with a nice even spread of tickets for all the major moving violations such as: stop sign violations, fail to yield, improper passing, impeding traffic, DWI's, negligent driving, improper lane travel, following too closely, failure to obey a restrictive sign, improper turn, driving over the centerline, etc., etc. The guys who had a lot of DWI's were always given a lot of 'latitude' regarding their spread and the sergeant would usually look the other way at the end of the month or quarter.

I was involved in several other pursuits during my road trooper years but none got quite as involved as that last one. I remember trying to stop a motorcycle in downtown Spokane one afternoon for some minor violation; when I flipped my lights on we were immediately off to the races! He wasn't going extremely fast just 45 to 50 on crowded city streets but the damn pursuit went on for about fifteen minutes . . . . I finally got him in an area where there was a high curb on the right . . . I got my right front fender right along side his bike and then made several feints towards him with ever increasing closeness until I had him slowed down right up against that curb. He was only doing about 15 mph when I saw a telephone pole coming up. I squeezed him right against that high curb so that when he got to it, his handlebars hit it and jammed them and him right up against my car's front fender and the pole. He didn't fight me and I arrested him for reckless driving (the felony eluding law had not been enacted yet) . . . The only reason he had taken off was because he didn't have a motorcycle endorsement on his license . . . . BFD! I would have just written him a $15 ticket and he would have been on his way!

The next chase was a little more fun and we got up to some pretty high speeds in the middle of it. This guy came through the radar at 10 over near the top of Sunset Hill E/B on I-90. Same as before he took off when I flipped the switch for the blue lights . . . . Down Sunset Hill at 95 to 100 mph and then he barely made the exit to SR-195 S/B without rolling it. Of course I was on the radio requesting assistance and keeping everyone advised of my location. We eventually circled around in some residential areas until he turned into the Arboretum between I-90 and Old Sunset Hill. This was pretty much a dead end and I slowed down to see what his next move was going to be . . . He ended up stopping against another one of those dreaded high curbs . . . . Before he could back up I parked my patrol car right against his rear bumper so he couldn't move . . . . I got on the PA system and started shouting the usual commands such as: "Throw your keys out, hands on the dash board, don't move, etc . . ." I finally got all three of the occupants (teenagers) out of the car and soon had them lying face down in the parking lot . . . . I might have accidentally thrown in a few colorful police metaphors during this process so they knew I meant business . . . . Everyone was cooperating and I was just about to take the driver into custody when my back-up suddenly arrives and screeches to a stop a few inches from one of the kids on the ground . . . He jumps out and I could see he was really worked up about this whole pursuit deal . . . Even though the kids were cooperating he jammed his shoe against one of the kid's neck, with his gun drawn and yells out something like "I'm gonna off you mother fu**er if you so much as blink!!" So much for my nice calm arrest scene . . . . The other two teenagers took umbrage to those remarks and tried to get up to help their little buddy . . . Now I had to get mean as well and laid into them with a few invectives of my own . . . . A Spokane PD car showed up about then and we soon had all of them cuffed and in patrol cars . . . . As usual, the reason for running was really stupid . . . they had a half-case of beer in the car and didn't want to get arrested for MIP (minor in possession) . . . . **Again** . . . BFD!!

The only other chase, or chases in this case, involved another teenager on a dirt bike this time. The first time I saw the little puke he was riding down the Old Palouse Highway near 57th on the South Hill on his red dirt bike . . . . No lights or license, just a basic off road dirt bike. When I hit the lights he accelerated away from me pretty quickly but his top speed was only about 80 mph so I quickly caught up and stayed right on his ass . . . . He kept turning and looking at me for a couple miles but once he realized he couldn't outrun me he just dropped down into the ditch and went cross country out into a field. He stopped out there about two hundred yards away and just sat there glaring at me . . . . apparently waiting for me to try and get him out in the pasture . . . Being a dirt bike rider myself I wasn't about to bite on this one so I just drove on home and forgot about it for the moment. This area was on my way home each night so I kept looking for him every evening thereafter. I finally saw the little turd again a couple weeks later. This time he was on a side street with no pastures nearby to retreat into. Again, soon as I hit the lights he took off . . . . He obviously knew this neighborhood pretty well and he lost me in a couple minutes. I suddenly realized that I would probably never get this kid trying to chase him down on his home turf so I went with plan B instead. I came back into this neighborhood the next day, before school let out, and started going door to door asking people if they knew where the kid riding the noisy red dirt bike wearing a white helmet lived . . . . I got no help that day or the day after. When I finally moved over into another development I finally hit pay dirt . . . While I was talking with one homeowner another guy comes over and says something like "Is this about that Harris punk riding his 125 Honda?" Finally, someone who knew this little prick! He gave me his address and when I knocked on the door his Mommy answered . . . . After I filled her in on all the details she was just livid with rage . . . She blamed her ex-husband for everything and said he was the one that got him the bike against her wishes. She showed it to me in the garage and there was his nice little white helmet on the shelf too. Trying to be family friendly I asked her how she would like me to handle his arrest as I had no intention of just letting this slide even though he came from a broken home . . . . She finally said she would arrange to have him at the house the next afternoon where I could arrest him and take him down to the juvenile detention facility near the courthouse. Sure enough, he was there, and no struggle ensued. I tried to have a polite man to man discussion with him on the way downtown but he was obviously damaged goods and wasn't listening to a word I said . . .

Naturally, he was immediately released and was home that night so this whole affair had been pretty much for nothing . . . . The only other chases I was involved in occurred while I was trying to get a couple routine drunk drivers to stop . . . . Both of them drove into the ditch after a brief "pursuit" and I was never quite sure if they even knew they were being chased by the police or if they just happened to drive into the ditch while I was behind them . . . ?

Every trooper I knew had his or her favorite violations to write people tickets for; just about everyone had a real passion to nail drunk drivers but they were pretty scarce on a day shift. Other less serious but just as aggravating violations had to fill the gap. I had two violations that I never gave anyone a warning ticket for; asshole tailgaters, and those stupid jerks that chucked their car garbage out the window. When I was a Boy Scout I wrote a letter to then Governor Rosselini complaining about the amount of litter along the Cowiche Tieton Road. He actually wrote me a nice letter back saying he was about to make littering a serious offense carrying a heavy fine. He did and I enforced that statute as often as I could! I saw a lot of great tailgating activity later as a pilot but working the road it was often hard to be in a good position to observe it. When I did it was instant citation time. In my mind, the egotistical morons who followed too closely were some of the biggest jerks on the road and nearly every one of them argued, pissed, bitched and moaned when you wrote them up. They were universally very aggressive type A people who thought every other peon on the road was personally preventing them from achieving their true potential in life. They let the "lesser" mortals know it by flashing their high beams and parking their rides three feet off some poor sap's trunk lid at 70 mph until they moved over. These types almost always flipped the poor guy off as they sped past. Catching the really good litterers was pretty tough. It was fairly easy finding idiots flipping their cigarettes out the window, especially at night, but getting a high quality littering violation was fairly rare. The most memorable occurred as I was crossing the Hangman Bridge Westbound one night. I was just about to move around a car when I saw what looked like a bird fly out of the right rear passenger window; the 'bird' flew right into the center of my windshield and splattered what looked like the remnants of a milkshake all over the place. I recognized a *McDonalds* logo on the bird as well as several of their tasty fries sliding up and over my roof. When I stopped the car I didn't even go to the driver door but walked right up to the little maggot sitting in the right rear; I asked him if he'd lost anything recently and of course he said "why no officer". When I observed several other bags of McDonalds goodies in the car I asked how he had enjoyed his dinner; he said he hadn't eaten any and was doing a real good impression of a 16 year old sociopath. He had no ID and I knew the name he gave me was a bunch of crap. I hauled him out of the car and as I was walking back I noticed his empty McDonalds bag wrapped around my light bar; I peeled it off and said "Does this look familiar?" I got no response so I put him in my backseat. I had been working on a new technique to get low IQ violators with no ID's or fake or altered ID's to tell me the truth. I asked them very seriously if they knew that the legislature had just passed a bill last January making it a Class C felony to lie to a police officer . . . The more savvy sociopaths recognized this as bullshit and would just smile at me. However, this kid fell into the other group of less than savvy individuals. When I saw him hesitate a second I went for the jugular and told him that he could expect to spend at least six months in jail and that a "young good looking kid like yourself could expect to get a lot of attention from some of the older inmates in your cell late at night" . . . . He soon gave me his real name and confessed to having an extensive juvenile record of MIP (minor in possession), a couple of burglaries and several other arrests that he might not have taken care of properly. However, when I ran a check wanted on him there were no current warrants so I just wrote him a ticket for the littering and let him go . . . . There was no doubt in my mind that three weeks later, after he forgot about this ticket, that there would be a fresh warrant for failure to appear on the littering citation that I just hung on him . . . . Just a side note but if I were still working the road today every idiot I saw texting or using a cell phone while driving would automatically be my **brand new favorite** violator to pinch . . . There would be no warning tickets!!

I had one other interesting littering violator when I was a rookie in Olympia. I was driving home on Cooper Point road late one night when I saw a shower of sparks come flying out of the driver side window of a Cadillac just ahead of me and land in the ditch. It was mid-summer and everything was very dry. I stopped the car immediately. When I contacted the driver I smelled a strong odor of cigar smoke still in the car and assumed he had just flipped his stogey overboard. He hands me a driver's license encased in some kind of fancy holder that said 'Supreme Court Justice' around the edges. I recognized his name but he was acting real pompous and I detected a slight odor of alcohol on his breath. He admitted flipping the cigar out so I had him walk back to find it and told him to put it out before it started a fire . . . Man he 'did not' like taking orders from a rookie trooper . . . but he begrudgingly complied. I got to watch his walking and balance control while he did that and he seemed OK. When he got back I put him through the field sobriety tests anyway just to piss him off. Geez, he was getting madder by the moment so I really took my time writing that ticket, making sure it was perfect. I kept my cool and was very professional and when I handed him the citation he scribbled a couple initials on it and just glared at me like a typical sociopath instead of an esteemed Supreme Court Justice. As I was handing him his copy he tore it out of my hand while I was still talking, got in his Caddie, took off fishtailing his car and sprayed gravel all over the front end of my patrol car . . . Now I was mad, as this was my new '73 Dodge Polara!! I took a few deep breaths and stopped him again . . . I walked up and advised him that what he had just done could be easily classified as negligent driving, possibly reckless driving, and reminded him that he was HBD (had been drinking) . . . Jesus, he was so mad I could see his pulse pounding in his carotid . . . . But I guess you don't get to be a supreme court judge by routinely 'blowing up' during a routine traffic stop. He somehow kept it together, gave me a real insincere and snotty apology, and then made some ridiculous excuse how his foot had slipped off the brake onto the gas pedal . . . What a flaming jerk! I felt nothing but pity for his poor staff that had to put up with this asshole every day at work!

By far the worst and most disgusting littering scenario I was aware of involved long haul truck drivers. Now I don't have a problem with them pissing into a jar or plastic milk jug while driving as long as they dispose of the contents properly at the next truck stop. But a certain few just can't be bothered with a jug of piss at the truck stop and would just fling the full ones out their window while they motored along the interstate. I never witnessed or got to write one of those SOB's a ticket for that but I sure saw a lot of those piss containers along the freeway in the ditch. I really felt sorry for the Highway Dept. and Ecology Dept. crews that had to pick them up later . . . . If I could have only seen just one guy chucking a jug of piss . . . but, I probably wouldn't be in a position to be writing this story right now if I had . . . .

Although this isn't a littering or following too closely story it does involve another big time Olympia celebrity. Right before we transferred to Spokane I was southbound on I-5 near Pacific Ave. late one evening when I came up on (what else) another Cadillac scraping along the New Jersey barrier sending out a shower of sparks as the driver attempted to grind off the left side of his car. Before I even turned on my lights the Cadillac slowly came to a stop against the barrier. When I got closer the driver appeared to be slumped over in the seat unconscious. Luckily, the passenger door was unlocked and I checked to see if he'd had a heart attack or something. But it wasn't anything that dramatic. The car reeked of booze and the driver had a bottle of Crown Royal between his legs. He was passed out but breathing OK so I got his registration out of the case on his visor and saw that it was registered to a famous eastside legislator whose drunk driving reputation was well known to all of us. Before I called my sergeant I had to make sure it was him so I shook him until he finally came around. He was able to locate his license after several minutes of struggling to find it and handed it to me. There was that pretty little license decoration again which announced in big green letters around the edges that the holder was a 'State Senator'. (BFD) It was him so I made the call to my sergeant. The legislature was in session and as hard as it was to swallow, these morons were immune from arrest during that period except for high treason, murder, and a couple other crimes. My boss was there in no time and we gently drug his limp carcass into his patrol car. I was ordered to lock up and leave my patrol car on the shoulder and drive that drunk bastard's Cadillac to the Governor House Hotel in downtown Olympia where a lot of the legislators stayed when they were in session. Man, I really hated this . . . . That moron could have easily killed somebody and here we were treating him like he was visiting royalty . . . I really felt dirty during this episode and have to say it was one of the low points of my career!! On top of everything else, his car handled like a real piece of shit. I don't know what he had hit or run over recently (other than the Jersey barrier) but it was almost uncontrollable. We took him upstairs in the service elevator at the hotel and my boss was acting like an old pro at this . . . . I kept my mouth shut but wondered how many other times this had happened. He took me back out to my patrol car, told me not to say a word to anyone about this, and dumped me out on the shoulder like I was the problem . . . . Man, I couldn't wait to get to Spokane and away from that guy!

Several years later this same senator wrecked his car in Eastern Washington once again . . . . Fortunately, this time the legislature wasn't in session. It happened within the city limits of a small town and he didn't have a State Patrol sergeant there to enable his drunkenness again. He received a lot of unflattering publicity when the media discovered this last incident was just one of many DWI accidents in his career but was the only one he ever got arrested for . . . . Thankfully, he didn't get re-elected next time around.

Life was good during the spring of 1985 and Deb had just finished her AA degree at Spokane Falls Community College while still working full time at the AG's office as an administrative assistant. Her emphasis was in the sciences as she really wanted to become a biologist for the state. She had just enrolled at Eastern Wash Univ. and was taking more math and science courses towards her BS Degree. I had accumulated almost a thousand hours by then and was seriously considering quitting the WSP and becoming a freight pilot for *Salair*. Jim Kieran had introduced me to Bruce Salerno, whose family ran the outfit. Bruce indicated that if I would get my DC3 type rating on my own he would hire me as a co-pilot for their growing freight company based out at Geiger Field. Man, I loved those old planes, going all the way back to my first ride in one back in 1958. Problem was the starting co-pilot salary would cut my pay by about 75% and there were no medical or retirement benefits. But I just knew in my heart that the WSP aviation section just wasn't interested in me so I got a copy of the POH (pilot's operating handbook) for the DC3 and began to prep for the type rating in the old *Gooney Bird*. I was hoping I could moonlight as a freight pilot and somehow make it all work . . . .

On the morning of May 15, just before I was leaving for the airport for another afternoon of crash and goes with my newest student, the phone rang. It was Captain Swier from the Aviation Section and he wanted to know how I felt about living in the Basin . . . I honestly didn't know what he was talking about since there had been no announcements or even a rumor of a pilot vacancy so I figured someone had killed themselves . . . He told me that I had really impressed him with my determination during the last few interviews and didn't really see any point in making me go through the whole competitive selection process again . . . . So he offered me a traffic pilot position in Ephrata starting July 1ˢᵗ . . . . Later on I found out that one of the Olympia King Air 200 pilots had 'stepped on his dick' in some fashion or another and was being allowed to leave the section. Dave Rheaume was going to take his place there and I was to take Dave's place in Ephrata as a traffic pilot. Well, needless to say this was a total shock and unexpected surprise!! I told Captain Swier that he had just made me the happiest guy on the planet which seemed to please him a lot . . . .

I was on cloud nine that day when I showed up at The Hangar Flying Club . . . Jim was there and asked me what was up? He was as excited as I was when I gave him the news and said he couldn't have been prouder of me than if I was his own son!! Man, I owed that guy so much for being my mentor and for assigning me to a wonderful series of no nonsense combat veteran instructors . . . Other than my wedding day this was the happiest day of my life!! A couple days later Jim called me into his office and presented me with a fitting trophy to proclaim my huge achievement with . . . . It was a red T-Shirt emblazoned with large white letters that spelled out: **FIGMO** . . . . (F**k It, Got My Orders) . . . . I still have it and occasionally wear it with pride . . . .

It was a little hard to stay focused working the road for the next six weeks and it was a great relief when Gene the Machine (my sergeant) said I could relax a little and didn't have to write so God-damn many tickets anymore . . . . I was more worried about all my students that I wasn't going to be able to finish up with . . . . As with most student-instructor relationships the students get a little attached sometimes and don't want any major changes to occur that might upset their delicate trust relationship during those early critical phases of flight training . . . Ken Seay took over most of my students and I'm sure they all were much better off with him than me . . . One student I would really miss was my old detachment mate Trooper Larry Lane 495 (LL). I hadn't quite got him to solo yet when I had to leave. Larry was one of the best snow and ice drivers I had ever seen! I tried following him to accidents several times on glare ice and scared the living shit out of myself trying to keep up with him . . . He was something else! Helluva good stick too!

I was winding down my last few days working the road one evening and coming back northbound on SR 195 after doing a Whitman County line check. Just as I came into the Spokane city limits and went under a railroad overpass near Cheney Spokane Road there was a God Awful explosion of glass and my whole shittin windshield came in on top of me . . . . I was doing about 80 mph at the time and I couldn't see a thing . . . . This was one occasion where I felt it would be OK to hammer the brakes regardless of the circumstances . . . I damn near broke my leg shoving that pedal to the floor and got stopped real fast! When I finally got my wits about me I immediately saw what had caused this explosion . . . There was a plastic jug full of small rocks resting on top of the windshield sitting on my chest and it was apparent that some rat f**k pukes had thrown it off the overpass with perfect timing just before I went underneath . . . . I backed up to the other side of the overpass and got on my PA immediately . . . . I'm afraid that once again I was unable to control my emotions for a few minutes and let loose a profane broadcast for everyone within a one mile radius to hear about what I was going to do to the limp dick, mother fu**in, SOB's that just tried to kill me . . . I wasn't proud of myself and I'm sure I scared the living shit out of the people that lived nearby but I was really pissed!! Thankfully I was wearing my glasses instead of my contact lenses, as I usually did on night shift, and if it hadn't been for them I know I would have gotten two eyefuls of glass shards and probably ruined my flying career . . . I called radio to have Spokane PD meet me at the scene then put my gloves on to see if I could get that 'so called' safety glass (shattered) windshield out of my front seat. The SPD guys were very helpful and knew almost immediately who was probably responsible. Apparently a couple of little local pukes had been doing this for several nights and SPD was real close to nailing them. They felt that they wouldn't be able to keep quiet about taking out a State Patrol car and would eventually start bragging to their little asshole buddies about it. They hoped that one of them would hand up the evil perpetrators in due time. I drove myself to the hospital to have a few cuts on my forehead looked at and had my eyes irrigated; it was a 'drafty' trip home. I had a new windshield installed the next day and they even vacuumed out all the glass which had gone everywhere inside my car which I hadn't noticed the night before. That evening was one hell of a 'farewell to Spokane' send off but for some reason my poor patrol car was to be victimized still again before I left town . . .

I got a tip from another troop in Spokane, Joe Pass 530, that an old lady in Ephrata had half of her house for rent and that it was very nice and reasonable. He had lived there for awhile during his cadet days and said it was very quiet and that the old gal was a super landlady. Deb and I drove down on my days off to check it out. For some reason the landlady had assumed I was single like Joe so when I showed up with Deb she went into sort of a tizzy and let us know that she would not stand for any 'hanky panky' in her house and that she did not approve of the consumption of spirits on her property either!! We finally were able to convince her that we were married but I think she kept her ear to the wall after I was living there to make sure I wasn't consorting with any painted women or (God Forbid) partaking of any illegal libations . . . .

I will always remember the last violator I stopped while I was still a full time road trooper . . . . I did stop quite a few more cars while driving to and from the hangar as a pilot over the next 20 years but for the most part it had to be either a good reckless or an obvious DWI before I flipped the switch on those blue lights. This last one was just a routine speeder I caught while sitting in my usual radar fishing hole out at Four Lakes. It just happened to be an 18 wheeler and when I walked up to the driver side the "occupant" didn't even roll down the window so we could talk. I was hanging there by the grab bar on that high step yelling to be heard over that noisy Cat engine growling away. The driver just sat inside, looking straight ahead, not saying a word. I had encountered this type before and they were usually members of the "Posse Commitatus" an organization of rednecks who only recognized the authority of the local county sheriff and no other police. They made up their own driver's licenses and the average member was extremely fortunate to attain even plant life I.Q. I finally yelled through the window that I was going back to my patrol car to call for a big rig wrecker and said I hope you have several thousand dollars with you to cover the tow bill . . . . That remark caused a bit of a stir and the window finally rolled down a couple inches. The first thing that struck me and I mean really physically assaulted my senses was a stench so foul that I immediately assumed the driver had his dead goat and/or sheep girlfriend stashed in the sleeper . . . When I looked inside I saw that was not the case however . . . . The odor seemed to be emanating solely from the driver . . . . God damn it, why did this have to happen to me on my last day?! It took me a couple seconds to realize but I finally noticed that the driver was a female and she wasn't exactly your typical *Cosmo* cover girl variety . . . . This is an absolutely true description of what she looked like: she was dressed exactly like *Larry The Cable Guy* now dresses for his act with the *Mack Truck* baseball cap, denim shirt with the sleeves cut off, and carpenter jeans with suspenders . . . . Her teeth were reddish brown and she had permanent chewing tobacco juice stains on both sides of her mouth extending down several inches. She was braless and her chest was adorned with a number of "apparently" self inscribed tattoos that I couldn't make out at all . . . . I saw some tobacco juice stains in her cleavage and I knew if I looked any lower than that I would surely go blind . . . . She had hairy armpits and as best as I could smell she apparently had just been shitting and pissing in her pants for the last several days . . . . Her breath would have stopped a charging Cape Buffalo in its tracks at two hundred yards . . . . Man, this had to be some kind of sign from heaven, maybe a reward, I don't know, that flying was now my occupation and having to deal with creatures like this was **over** once and for all!! I couldn't believe it when she actually produced a valid driver's license (Arkansas—filled out in pencil of course) but I needed to get the hell out of there and away from her immediately as I was right on the verge of puking my guts out . . . I wrote down her name and DOB on my hand, told her to slow down, and leaped off that high step and made my getaway. When I got inside my patrol car, I turned my AC on max, since all I could smell was her horrible stench . . . I felt like burning my uniform on the spot and going to have myself steam cleaned somewhere. To best describe her I must steal a line from old 685's extensive repertoire of descriptive metaphors; "She was **SOOO** ugly she'd make a train take a dirt road . . . !" Even writing about her 28 years later still somehow conjures up that odor from deep in the recesses of my olfactory storage area . . . . I went to the office, dropped off the radar, filled out my last 68 and went home . . . . When Deb saw me come in with that familiar crazy look in my eye she grabbed the *Tanqueray* and made me a nice gin and tonic . . . I had survived 13 years working the road and hadn't been killed!!

My detachment had a nice going away party for us down at Fish Lake Resort one evening and it was sad to leave the guys and gals I had spent the last dozen years with. A couple mornings later around 3am I left home to drive to Olympia to begin my indoctrination training in the Cessna 182 with Trooper Dave Gardner 476 who was the Aviation Section's training officer then. It was pitch dark out and I was Northbound on Hangman Valley Road just South of Hatch Rd when I thought I saw an owl flare up near my left front fender . . . . A split second later there was one hell of a crash, my god-damned windshield shattered and landed in my lap again, and something big hit the top of my car ripping off my light bar . . . . Judas Priest, this Dodge Diplomat of mine was like a magnet for windshield smashing UFO's!! I slammed on my brakes again as hard as I could, since I couldn't see a thing, but this time slid into the ditch as this was a narrow county road and I might have been exceeding the posted speed limit by a couple mph . . . Well, it wasn't a jug of rocks this time but a big God Damned Mule Deer the size of an elk! He was struggling and gurgling up blood in the ditch so I quickly put him out of his misery (only took one shot this time). My whole car was covered in blood and guts and I was just amazed that these two glass spraying crashes had happened so close together . . . . I prayed that at some point in time I could get the hell out of Spokane County before I was struck by a meteor or ran over a Sasquatch!!

Well, my car wasn't drivable this time and my sergeant had it towed to the district office for some reason. He let me use his unmarked car to commute to Olympia for my training which was just fine with me! Before I left town I **was** able to generate one final complaint however . . . . In my haste to get to Olympia to start my training that morning I had apparently committed a major 'faux pas' when I forgot to hose all the blood and guts off my car after it was towed to the district office. A previous sergeant, who I'd had the little shouting session with several years earlier, complained to the lieutenant that he was just 'incensed' that I'd left a stinking bloody patrol car, with deer guts hanging off the push bars, out in the parking lot like that . . . . What a sweet parting gesture from such a special guy . . . . I also felt like writing a letter to Chrysler to let them know how shitty their windshield securing hardware was but I was soon fairly busy trying to keep a Skylane right-side up and forgot about it. Spokane PD finally did arrest the two little pukes who took out my windshield but they were 12 years old and after an afternoon in Juvenile Hall they were home with Mommy and Daddy the same evening . . . . However, I didn't really give a shit about any of the above . . . I was **FIGMO!!!!**

CHAPTER 10

I ARE A TRAFFIC PILOT NOW

My indoctrination training with 476 was supposed to last for two weeks but luckily I was able to get pretty comfortable with the 182 right away due to my previous checkouts with the guys. Being instrument current, from instructing at the Hangar Flying Club, helped a lot too, but I could always use more dual. Dave concentrated most of his time showing me how to use the Minerva stopwatches to check speed. He had a favorite restaurant called the Oaktree down near the Woodland airport and we spent quite a few mornings down there pigging out on their huge two pound cinnamon rolls before training could begin . . . I was to spend many more hours there a few years later and I still start drooling just thinking about those big hummers! Learning to work traffic was really a handful at first but I quickly learned that each individual had to establish his own personal rhythm and style to get comfortable with it. You had a stopwatch in either hand, along with a pencil, a kneeboard sheet on your lap, and ended up flying with your knees a lot . . . As I look back on it now, working traffic was really an art form of sorts and every pilot had his own unique interpretation of how to do it most efficiently. For me, smooth flight was nearly impossible; un-coordinated rudder turns were the norm when your hands, elbows, or knees were unavailable on the controls . . . . It was quite common to drop a stopwatch from time to time while trying to activate the push to talk button or messing with the throttle or switching watches and pencil from one hand to the other especially during turbulence which was pretty much all the time . . . The watch usually slid under the seats and ended up in the baggage compartment sometimes for the duration of the flight. To retrieve it required a pretty good dive with a sharp pull up accompanied by a little left or right rudder to help navigate it around the seat supports as it slid forward . . . If all went as planned the watch would suddenly appear on the carpet near the gas shut-off valve in a second or two. While thusly occupied it was imperative you never lost sight of the car or cars you were clocking since that would really be considered bad form by the eager troops waiting on the on-ramp for a hot one . . . . If you looked away for a second, the gray car you were watching suddenly was right along side another gray car when you looked back down, and now you were confused . . . On holiday weekends with good weather it really turned into a goat rope . . . There was always good speed and lots of troopers to keep busy and my flight sheet was often a total mess after an hour or so. I would just wait until I got back to the hangar to straighten it up . . . . I really envied the old timers like Bob Boos and Ray Riepe who didn't have to write anything down . . . . man they had it easy! As I said before the trouble with working traffic in Western Wash. was the horrible weather and low ceilings which quite often put you in the treetops while you were turning circles over the freeway. You really had to keep your head on a swivel to miss the trees, not lose the car you had going, while trying to avoid other aircraft scud running along the freeway right at your altitude just under the overcast . . . At the end of some of those sessions I just ached all over!

Dave showed me how to "scud run" and how to get a "pop up" IFR clearance when the scud running got a little too hairy to stay with it any longer . . . . I wasn't familiar with either of those techniques but when I was later assigned to Olympia for 15 years they became second nature and pretty much became necessary to get our traffic patrol job done. Anyway, 476 said I was good to go after a week and my first official flight was to transport Capt. Mel Mooers 26 back to Wenatchee. After that I was also allowed to take the plane home to Spokane for the weekend which was a pretty big deal for me! On the flight back to Olympia to get my patrol car, I stopped in at Ephrata and was given the tour of the place by 328 who was on military leave at the time. Our blue T hangar was at the Grant County Airport in Moses Lake so there was a nice little commute each day that had to be figured in to our flight schedule. On my first day at work I was all by myself at the office when the Okanogan County Sheriff calls up and said he needed a plane right away to check out a huge marijuana grow up near Wauconda . . . Man, I had no idea where Wauconda was but quickly located it on my Sectional . . . . When I picked up the sheriff I just told him flat out that this was my first day on the job and he would have to help me out a little with the navigating in that remote part of the state. The KNS 80 Area Navigation unit installed in our Skylanes then required a VOR signal in order to go direct to a remote fix. I had measured the distance from the closest VOR which was EPH (Ephrata) and had measured a radial off of it that went through that area. Unfortunately, Wauconda was so far away I would have to climb to twelve thousand feet to get a good signal for the KNS 80 to use off EPH . . . . So, we did it the old fashion way and flew IFR (I Follow Roads) . . . We picked up SR20 out of Tonasket and 15 minutes later we were over a couple houses out in the sticks which the sheriff said was Wauconda . . . I thought shit, what else would there be to do except grow marijuana out here! We went a few miles south of town and the grow was right where his CI (confidential informant) said it would be. We took photos, looked for any signs of trouble, and got out of there fairly quickly before anyone on the ground got suspicious of a circling airplane. The sheriff went back the next day with some of his deputies and 'harvested' several hundred plants. They were not very big yet as this was early July . . . Later in September each year we would often see some ten to twelve foot high fully mature plants . . . . those size plants had some serious 'bud' going on. The really tall ones were usually surreptitiously planted in some farmer's corn field early in the year after which he would unknowingly water and fertilize them all summer long with his huge wheeled sprinkler systems. In early September the 'grower' would sneak in there at night, cut them down, and no one was ever the wiser . . . Pretty slick operation and hard to catch the growers unless someone ratted them out . . . More on this later.

The next day I begged one of the local Ephrata troops to work traffic with me for my first solo attempt. Trooper George Stanton 855 was very obliging and we headed out to the Winchester Wasteway area of I-90 where I had my solo baptism of fire working traffic. It turned out to be pretty anti-climatic since I only had one trooper. I could only call out a speeder about every ten minutes or so since that was about how long it took him with each violator. I gave him about 20 cars and we broke for lunch . . . . Being a 'basin' trooper he wasn't used to such huge amounts of activity and didn't want to go back out in the afternoon since his hands were all cramped up from writing tickets. I decided to familiarize myself with several of the more popular traffic courses I had been briefed on. I cruised around Eastern Wash. for the rest of the afternoon checking them all out. Yeah, this job was going to be a real bitch!

The Grant County airport was where JAL (Japan Airlines) conducted their B-747 transition training . . . . There were always two of them in the pattern, one doing touch and goes after an ILS approach, flying at normal turbojet pattern altitudes and the other flying what they called a minimum circling pattern which was at around 800 ft. I have to hand it to the controllers for being able to understand the JAL pilots heavily accented radio calls but after a few months I started to understand them as well. One of the standard requests they made after takeoff on Rwy 32 to Grant County Tower was a left 90 right 270 direct to Pelly to hold as published . . . . What we actually heard on tower frequency sounded slightly different: "Ahh, Grah Cowie Towahh, we reques . . . ahh, reft ninety, lite two selety, dilect Prelly, ahh hoad as pubish . . . ." Those crew persons had no contact with anyone except their own folks and were transported to and from the airport in a private bus . . . When we did see them getting in and out of the planes they were all business and very serious all the time . . . Man, they just did not look like they were having any fun . . . . Those 747's laid down so much rubber on the runways after all those touch and goes that about twice a year a crew went out with high pressure equipment to blast it off the concrete . . . When there was a big rubber accumulation it was rougher than hell to land a Skylane on. Needless to say you had to be very cautious around the heavies and always looking for their wake turbulence especially when they were doing their minimum circling pattern . . . . In that configuration the 747 would be dirty (gear and flaps down) with a huge angle of attack going on and we would often see monster dusty tornado like vortices following about a half mile behind them on the ground that had developed off their wingtips. The Grant County Airport was perfect for their operation with its 13,500 ft runway and lightly populated locale. The main runway was so wide that you could easily land or take off in a Skylane crossways on it if you got the urge. This airport used to be known as Larsen Air Force Base back in the 50's and 60's and was home for B36s and later B52s back then. With that long runway it was also designated as an alternate landing spot for the Space Shuttle. Every day was like an airshow there since the Boeing Company did a lot of their test flights at Grant County; the Air Force and Navy made appearances there almost every day as well. It was not uncommon at all to see brand new 757's, 767's, B52's, Navy P3 Orions, KC 135 Tankers, Navy EA6B Prowlers, and various other fighters and tankers in the pattern all in the same afternoon. To really confound the issue were dozens of Big Bend Community College student pilots fighting for traffic pattern space in their Beech Musketeers with everyone else . . . It could get a little hectic and I learned how to fly a very quick and tight pattern, holding off with flaps until the last second then getting out of the way ASAP.

Before we sold our house in Spokane there was quite a bit of "high speed" commuting going on for several months on my days off. We finally got it sold in October of '85 to of all people a B52 pilot from Fairchild AFB. I had a lot of WWII prints hanging on the walls autographed by famous fighter pilots like Yeager, Gabreski, Anderson, McCambell, Boyington, Carl, etc., etc. He told me later those pictures sold the house. There was a retired WSP Captain named Bob Grimstead living in Ephrata who just happened to have a rental house available at the time. We moved into it but didn't realize he lived right next door. He was a great guy but would occasionally get mixed up on which house he was currently living in and would sometimes barge right into our place at all hours of night and day. This was also the perfect time for Deb to finish up her BS degree so she immediately enrolled at CWU in Ellensburg and began that horrendous commute every day. I frankly don't know how she did it . . . . She would record all of her classes instead of taking notes then play them back for review while commuting. She eventually wore out two cars and got really good at driving long distances in the ice and snow. That first winter was a real nasty one with a prolonged cold spell of—20 degree temps for several days. One evening as the wind was howling outside we heard a loud 'clank' from underneath the house and didn't know what had happened until we heard the sound of rushing water filling up the crawl space. I called Bob and he came right over only wearing a T-shirt. He said the water shutoff valve was in the crawlspace and he would need to get down there right away. The access panel was under our bed so after flipping that against the wall he crawled down into that hole full of freezing water, accompanied by the howling wind blowing through the crawlspace vents that weren't blocked off. He finally got it shut off but then we didn't hear anything. I looked in the hole and saw that he was having a lot of difficulty getting back. I got down there and helped him out but he was already severely hypothermic and his lips were starting to turn blue. We had a fire going so we sat him down in front of it for quite awhile and wrapped him in blankets. I have never seen anyone shiver like that before! He was finally able to walk home about an hour later . . . . Man, he was a tough old bird!

After I had been in Ephrata for **over two months** my new sergeant finally showed up one day to fly with me for the first time . . . !? On the way back from working traffic out at Fishtrap, he said he was going to demonstrate his "long landing" technique to me on RWY 22 back at Grant County which was a 10,000 ft long runway. He said he would touch down beyond the main crossing runway, 32R, which would still leave us 6,000 ft of RWY 22 to land on . . ."no use wearing out the tires taxiing that far" he said. Well this was something I had already been doing for the last two months but I never was one to turn down additional dual instruction and kept my mouth shut. We crossed 32R at about 100 ft and still only had approach flaps out . . . We continued cruising along nicely with no power reduction when I saw the end of the runway coming up fairly quickly . . . . I finally had to ask him what his intentions were . . . Man, you talk about a flurry of activity all of a sudden . . . . full flaps, power off, and (gasp) a dive for the runway . . . . Jesus Christ, it sure looked like he was going to wreck the plane rather than do a go around . . . . Well, he smashed it in nosewheel first and we bounced about twenty feet high since we were still doing over 100 when we touched and I couldn't believe he didn't ding the prop . . . . Shortly thereafter we hit the asphalt several more times until we finally screeched to a halt with the brakes locked up right at the end of the runway . . . . I looked out at a severely flat spotted tire on my side and assumed the other one looked the same . . . . Having learned my lesson the hard way about being insubordinate to my supervisor I didn't say a word . . . . I only knew this guy by reputation but I thought right then and there that it was extremely fortunate for me that he was based in Yakima with another pilot, Ron McClinton 600 and I was in Ephrata with 328. I certainly don't want to imply that I didn't have some embarrassing flying moments myself in the years to come but this incident, played out by my very experienced supervisor, really surprised me . . . . I had Stan at Grant County Aviation do a firewall inspection, after my boss had left, as that was a weak spot on Skylanes especially after hard nosewheel landings . . . He said it looked OK. I knew I was going to be blamed for those flat spotted tires at the next 100 hr. inspection so I called old 476 in Olympia to get his advice. He just laughed and said it was no big deal so I tried not to worry about it.

Working traffic in Eastern Washington involved a lot of long distance commuting since we covered all the distant detachments in such places as Goldendale, Walla Walla, Tonasket, Chewelah, Colfax, Easton, and all points in between. I loved those commutes and after I got the bird trimmed to fly hands off I just sat back and reflected on how lucky I was to not have to be dragging some stinking drunk out of his wrecked pickup anymore or not having to put some ungrateful asshole's chains on for them in the middle of a blizzard . . . . Man, this was the best job in the WSP! Deb was already greasing the skids to get hired by the Dept. of Fish and Wildlife after graduation by volunteering at their Ephrata office in what little spare time she had. She was on her own 'mission from God' now and had dedicated herself to becoming a state biologist. There wasn't exactly a lot to do in Ephrata but they did have the best Mexican restaurant that we had ever eaten at, El Charro. We probably ate there way too much but Hector had the best refried beans and banditos that we've ever had! His Dad ran another El Charro in Moses Lake so we alternated there for variety . . . We both started to put on weight so we bought a couple of mountain bikes and started riding the canal banks up to Soap Lake and down to Winchester. I really had the urge to go skiing in those huge canals, which were ten times wider than the ones near Cowiche, but we had a boat now so it wasn't necessary to tie a couple tow ropes to the roll bar on our old '72 Blazer to ski any longer.

During my training when I asked about doing weight and balance calculations before a flight one of the 'senior' pilots told me very matter of factly that: "If you can close the doors on whatever you put in a Skylane, it will fly just fine . . ." I still did rough calculations from time to time but got away from it pretty soon when I observed for myself the tremendous load carrying capacity that a Skylane has to offer . . . . I just figured the engineers were being real conservative when they published all those figures in the back of the POH. One hot afternoon radio told me to proceed to the Colfax airport to pick up the Whitman Co. Sheriff and a couple of his deputies for a surveillance flight over some Posse Commitatus/Constitutionalist's farm where he was refusing to vacate the premises after a long drawn out court battle of some sort. When I landed, the Sheriff walks over to the plane with two of the biggest deputies I'd ever seen . . . The three of them must have totaled at least 800 lbs and with my bulk thrown into the mix we were way over the limits set forth in the POH. It was a hot day, a short strip, and the density altitude was around 6,500 ft. Any reasonable and prudent pilot would politely tell the Sheriff that he could only take one of the deputies along . . . A really sharp pilot would tell the sheriff that 'he' was going to be the only passenger. A really stupid FNG pilot, trying his best to please his boss and everyone else, told the sheriff and his boys to all hop on in . . . . I was able to close the doors so I felt like this flight was going to be a piece of cake. I was somewhat concerned when I gave her the gun on the takeoff roll when my first thought was that I had left the emergency brake on . . . . Since that wasn't the case I still didn't comprehend what I was getting myself into even after we very slowly started to roll down the runway . . . Near the departure end, after about a 2500 ft. ground roll, my airspeed was only about 50 . . . . I remembered another tip from one of those senior pilots who told me that you could always drop another notch of flaps to pop you up if needed . . . Well, I dropped another notch but the result certainly didn't resemble a pop up in any way . . . Just as I got to the weeds I gently pulled the yoke back until the stall horn came on . . . We were airborne but just barely clearing the wheat stalks, stuck in ground effect. It just would not accelerate at all with all those flaps hanging out. For the next minute or so all I could think of doing was bringing the flaps up in tiny increments to keep the plane from settling into the wheat. I was flying in a slight right turn up a little valley towards SR 26 and the Whitman County Fairgrounds when I suddenly realized there was no way I could get over the power lines . . . By then, I had just barely managed to get the flaps back to the approach detent; the stall horn was still buzzing every few seconds but at least it wasn't continuous any longer. When I got close to those power lines I just knew in my heart that if I tried to pop up over them I would stall out and kill everybody in the plane. So, just as I had learned while flying in that Bell 47 sprayer when I was a little kid I went right on under those lines then had to veer a little East to miss all the Fairground buildings. I expected the sheriff and his men to immediately say something about it but I came to realize later that they honestly understood and sensed we were all in a world of shit right then and none of them wanted to upset me at such a crucial juncture . . . Man, did I ever appreciate that!! I finally got over a light colored field with no crops in it and felt the thermal lift rising off of it. I was able to climb to about 50 feet and finally got rid of all the flaps. We were soon able to climb, albeit very slowly, but at least we were all alive . . . The sheriff was one of the coolest guys I'd ever met . . . never said a word about anything and just pointed a finger in the direction I needed to fly to get to numb nut's farm. They took their photos and got the lay of the land for a future raid if it became necessary. Any one of those guys could have burned me so easily and I no doubt would have been kicked out of the aviation section and probably had my license jerked by the FAA. I will always be thankful to that sheriff and his tight lipped deputies!! Thanks again guys!!

The weather around central Washington was almost always VFR and except for a few high pressure inversion situations during the winter months, when it would be 200 to 300 overcast for several weeks, (more on those inversions later) we didn't get much instrument flying in. The challenging flying occurred about once a month when we had to take our Skylane to Olympia for its 100 hour inspection. Since the Aviation Section had five Skylanes at that time we would drop ours off and bring a 'fresh' one back. Problem was getting into Olympia nearly any time of the year almost always necessitated filing IFR and shooting an approach, sometimes down to minimums, just to drop the thing off for its 100 hour. Now I had quite a lot of experience in actual IFR conditions by then but almost none shooting approaches down to minimums. The first time I had to shoot the ILS at OLM by myself I have to admit I was a nervous wreck. I was not only exchanging planes that day but also was there to attend a Section troopers meeting. I got off late from Moses Lake then was hit with a 60+ mph headwind while enroute. I remember looking down at traffic while I was abeam I-90, through the occasional breaks in the clouds, and seeing semi trucks parallel to me going faster than I was. Anyway, when Olympia Tower gave me the weather as 100 overcast and ¼ mi. visibility in mist I immediately thought I'd better just head for my alternate which was Tacoma Narrows (TIW) where the weather was above minimums. But, I had been advised by several of the pilots that if I ever wanted to fly the WSP King Airs then I sure as hell better demonstrate that I was a real confident instrument pilot . . . As I intercepted that Olympia localizer and captured the glide slope out at Habor intersection, tower was still reporting 100 overcast and ¼ mile. That was probably the most horrific 2 & ½ minutes of my life . . . . When I got to DH, I didn't have a thing . . . . I was just starting to power up to go missed when I saw a slight glow in the mist off to my right and it seemed to be pulsating . . . I reduced power and slid on over a bit . . . At 100 feet, as advertised, I clearly saw all the lead-in lights flashing away very nicely . . . I went to full flaps and the REIL (runway end lights) magically appeared out of the mist . . . . Man, that was the closest to death I had ever been and what a great feeling it was to come out alive!! My hands and legs were shaking quite severely and I knew I needed a few minutes to let the adrenaline settle before I walked into the hangar. I went on over to Pearsons to gas up during which time my nerves quieted down a bit and my knees quit shaking. When I finally walked into the pilots meeting I put on my macho mask and tried to act like I shot approaches like that all the time . . . . I think the guys thought I had passed the 'test' but Capt. Swier was no fool;

he asked me what they were reporting the weather at when I got to the outer marker . . . I told him the truth but said I thought it would be OK to just 'take a look' before flying to my alternate . . . Then I lied a little and told him I had the runway in sight at DH . . . He just glanced out the window, where he couldn't even see the runway which was just 150 feet away, then glanced back at me with that "Do you think I've got stupid written all over my face" look . . . . Anyway, I thought I had quietly joined 'the country club' and later at lunch endured several semi-insulting yet veiled congratulatory remarks from the other pilots about what a "stupid mother fu**ing macho duck" I was . . . Problem was, I got lucky that day; in the long haul I had to repeat that performance many more times before I was any good at it and was finally 'truly' accepted into 'the country club'. Even though hand flying those below minimums approaches was dangerous and ill advised it sure as hell ramped up my situational awareness a notch or two and really prepared me well for the transition into the turbine aircraft a few years later where the approach speeds were a helluva lot faster.

The other huge lesson learned during those Cascade crossings in a 182 was how to deal with icing . . . . There is a reason that Boeing has done all of its new model icing research in the Cascades for decades as well as Aerospatiale who brought the Concorde to the Cascades back in 1970 for icing certification purposes . . . . The Cascades just have consistent icing conditions nearly year round. The turbine class aircraft can usually punch right through the icing zones in a few seconds on their way up to the flight levels. Pooping around in a normally aspirated 182 between 8 and 11 thousand puts you right in the worst of it. After my first couple of experiences loading up with ice to the point I couldn't hold altitude any longer and having to ask ATC to vector me into a canyon, I finally got smart and started flying several thousand feet higher than the MEA's . . . Only problem was I found out that my personal altitude limitations, without supplemental oxygen, was fairly low so when I ended up at 13 or 14 thousand for very long I really got sleepy and lightheaded . . . It was comforting during extreme icing, when you couldn't hold altitude, to have an extra 2 or 3 thousand foot buffer for a nice controlled descent, without busting the MEA's for your route. Usually by the time you lost that altitude you were over flatter terrain and could ask for lower anyway. ATC was occasionally miffed at me but at least we got the job done even though it got a little ugly at times. The most amazing aspect of a Cessna 182 is its tremendous ability to carry ice. When I anticipated an icing flight I never fueled it up all the way which really helped when the stall horn came on abeam Mt. Rainier while in level flight! I have seen an inch and a half of rime ice on the struts of a 182 many times and it was still flying merrily along . . . albeit at a much reduced airspeed with a significant nose up attitude and the stall warning chirping away from time to time . . . but still flying and not losing altitude! I'm not proud of those flights but I wasn't totally crazy either . . . I turned around several times when the icing was really severe at low altitudes and the old girl just couldn't make it up to the MEA. When this happened the standby routine to get home was to fly the gorge . . . This entailed flying South to the Troutdale, OR area then flying right down the Columbia River Gorge until you got to The Dalles area where you could usually climb again in a non-icing environment and proceed direct to Ephrata . . . Problem was if there was bad icing in the Cascades there was usually severe turbulence in the gorge and man did you ever take a beating on that route. Even with the usual great tailwind pushing you along, the pounding was horrific . . . After a couple of those beat ups I quit that route and just took my chances with the icing on the traditional routes. On the Victor Airways you usually had a little altitude buffer, and could just turn around, put your nose down, and usually get out of it. In the gorge when you turned around you were suddenly facing a horrendous headwind, were already down on the water, and the pounding lasted twice as long. Long story short, when I got home after one of those rip snorters I was really beat . . . literally! It's just so hard to describe to a non-aviator the physical and emotional toll and just how fatiguing hand flying a very slow airplane in those kinds of conditions is . . . Those gorgeous, calm, VFR days were such a Godsend after one of those really ugly Cascade crossings!! A local freight pilot out of Olympia gave me some great advice one day to help me get over 'the hill' on bad icing days. He recommended asking for a West climb out of Olympia, get up to altitude in a non icing environment, then turn around and hit the Cascades and its ubiquitous icing, already above the icing layer . . . It worked for me many times and I tried to pass it on to my successors but unfortunately usually had no takers. So, life as an Ephrata traffic pilot was pretty routine for the most part but those trips over 'the hill' in the winter sure livened things up a bit! I still thank God every night for not letting me 'buy the farm' up there near Raddy or Whyte intersection while hovering along all iced up in one those old 182's!! I hope I'm never that stupid again!

There was absolutely nothing to do in either Ephrata or Moses Lake on our days off so Deb and I found ourselves driving back to Spokane a lot to eat lunch, go to a show, and do our shopping. Our two favorite restaurants then were The Asian, where Sammy served tremendous Thai cuisine, the best Kao Pod in the world, and The Casa Blanca down in River Front Park for great Mexican. We also kept all of our old doctors and dentists in Spokane so we got quite used to the commute. On the way home we usually picked up an order of ribs at the Longhorn and made a big mess in the car while driving and dipping ribs into their great sauce. While enroute I always brought Deb up to speed on the various familiar old fatal scenes we drove past and filled her in on all the gory details again and again while gorging ourselves on those delicious ribs. Years later while traveling all over the Southern states transporting prisoners I had many opportunities to sample the 'supposed' best ribs in the U.S. in Texas, Arkansas, Florida, Georgia, etc. However, none of them compared to the Longhorn's . . . They smoked those ribs with Cottonwood and absolutely nothing could touch them!

One afternoon in the Fall of 1986 I was coming back from working traffic in Ritzville and made the call to Grant County Tower about ten miles East for landing. They gave me the usual warning regarding the JAL 747's in the pattern then cleared me for a straight in to runway 22. On about a three mile final I saw the JAL 747 on a left downwind for 14L crossing from my left to right flying one of their minimum circling patterns at about 800 feet AGL. As usual, I held a good 500 feet above his altitude until the 747 had passed my nose and was a good two miles off to my right on his downwind leg before I started my descent to 22. Going through about 500 feet AGL I suddenly felt a tremendous impact and was jarred upwards; my head hit one of the 182's plexi-glass skylights so hard it knocked it clear out of the airplane. I was really stunned and it took me a couple seconds to realize I was still flying . . . . I thought that I had just had a mid-air with one of the Big Bend trainers and started looking around to see if I could spot one of their Beech Sports spinning into the ground . . . I had to refocus my attention on landing since I was now only about a hundred feet in the air. My depth perception was all screwed up and I made a landing similar to the one my boss had demonstrated to me the year before. As I was rolling out I noted that the wind was calm and that it had been a smooth flight all the way from Ritzville . . . . I couldn't figure out what had just happened. I rolled on in to Grant County Aviation to have Stan take a look at the plane since it was now missing a skylight. When I had a chance to calm down a bit I finally realized that there really wasn't a big mystery involved here . . . . It was simply an encounter with the wake turbulence off that JAL 747 while it was in the dirty configuration and causing those horrendous vortices that were just waiting to smuck a tiny little 182. What I couldn't understand was why those vortices hadn't sunk to the ground yet when I passed through that zone . . . I had given them plenty of time to sink and break up and yet there they were still right at my altitude . . . . I could only assume that a thermal or some other crazy phenomenon had kept those vortices merrily spinning away without sinking just waiting for some dumb shit like me to plow right into them! Well, I called Olympia and told our mechanics to order a new skylight and to overnight it to Grant County Aviation since the plane was now unflyable. I gave my boss a rundown on what had happened, gassed the bird up and put it away. At home that night I had a stiff neck, experienced some pain in my right bicep, and noticed that the tips of three of my fingers on my right hand were tingling. The next morning things were a whole lot worse and my shoulder, neck, and whole right arm were sore and aching and those fingers were now burning and alternately going numb. I knew this wasn't good and called my boss to let him know about my new symptoms. I started taking handfuls of Advil to kill the pain and began putting icepacks on my neck and shoulder. After three days off with no improvement we drove to Spokane to have a neurologist examine me. He injected some dye into my spinal cord with a needle he stuck in my skull behind my ear . . . . Jesus Christ, that hurt like a mother fu**er . . . . It was called a Myelogram and was state of the art before the MRI's became popular. Anyway, it was a very conclusive test and showed herniated disks at the C4 and C5 positions in my cervical spine. My options were surgery with a bone graft repair or physical therapy after wearing a cervical collar for a couple months to see if the swelling would go down and cause my symptoms to subside. Since the memory of my last surgery was still pretty fresh in my mind I elected to wear the collar for a couple months then try the physical therapy routine. I couldn't fly so I had to take sick leave and just stay at home. Deb was still commuting to CWU every day so it was a very lonely frustrating period for me. Luckily a local road trooper, Steve Smith 913, came by quite often to visit and we played chess and video games to pass the time . . . . His visits were a great help and I will always remember his kindness.

After the two months were up and after some physical therapy I felt a little better and thought I could go back to flying. I worked for a couple weeks but after a session of moderate turbulence coming home one day all the pain, burning, numbness, and tingling came back with a vengeance and I had to go back on sick leave again. On the next visit to my neurosurgeon he repeated the Myelogram and said the disks were now protruding out further than before and surgery would now be my only option. Man, I really didn't want those quacks trying to kill me again but the pain in my arm, shoulder, and fingers was just killing me so I had no choice. Before the surgery the doctor described how he was going to harvest some cartilage off my pelvis to insert between my vertebrae after he drilled out all the crushed disk material between C4 and C5. Sounded good but I sure wasn't prepared for what happened after the surgery was over. I guess everything went well and after the anesthesia wore off I felt pretty good with no pain in my shoulder, arm, or fingers. I couldn't talk since he had gone into my spine from the front and messed up my voice box in so doing. The next morning the nurse said I needed to get out of bed and try walking. That was when reality kicked in . . . I couldn't walk! Every step I took felt like someone was cramming a knife into my pelvis where he had taken the graft from . . . . Shit O Dear that hurt! My neck incision was virtually painless but my pelvis felt like a truck had backed into me and pinned me against my patrol car. I was in the hospital for three days mainly to recuperate from the hack job on my pelvis . . . . I had a limp for a long time thereafter.

I was finally pain free but still couldn't go back to work for three months to allow the graft to take hold. Luckily, Deb had a summer project with the Dept. of Fish and Wildlife that year counting ducklings and mosquito larvae at a whole series of small lakes in the Winchester Wasteway area. I was her chauffeur and it sure as hell beat staying at home and watching TV all day!

By late summer I was finally able to get rid of that bothersome cervical collar and get back to flying. I immediately noticed that my range of motion turning my head from side to side was really reduced due to the two fusions in my cervical spine. Since working traffic required a lot of head twisting to the left I had to readjust how I sat in the seat and kept myself cocked to the left as far as possible to offset my lack of neck turning capability. I also made several other adjustments to my flying style to increase my safety margin somewhat: I flew with the seat as low as I could adjust it to increase the distance between the top of my head and the Cessna's cabin ceiling, I kept my seat belt and shoulder harness as tight as possible at all times, and lastly I started flying hunched over a bit to offset the angle of an anticipated direct hit with my head and ceiling to possibly lesson the severity of the impact if I hit severe turbulence again. Later in my career I successfully lobbied our new section commander to install five point acrobatic type harnesses in all of our Skylanes which I felt greatly decreased the likelihood of injury in severe turbulence. Nobody liked them but me, and I was looked upon as a big pussy again for creating such a huge inconvenience for them all . . . . Anyway, I had no pain, even after some jarring episodes of turbulence, and felt like my old self again. I had been away from flying for over six months and had a lot of catching up to do. I knew Captain Swier felt I was now 'damaged goods' so I needed to prove to him that I was still a 'high roller' and that the minor inconvenience of a couple of cervical fusions certainly wasn't going to slow me down!

In those years the WSP was getting federal money to enforce the 55 mph speed limit so the aviation section became the prime facilitator to burn up those funds. The brass set up more roving 'gangs' of troopers whose sole purpose in life was to write as many speeding tickets as possible and in so doing work the living shit out of the pilots! Working those holiday weekends at hot spots like Thorp and Kittitas over I-90 with ten or more troopers was where the aviation term 'turning and burning' originated. As a pilot you didn't have a moment's rest and on every pass it wasn't uncommon to bring one or more fast cars for the waiting troopers to chase down. These guys and gals were all highly motivated and knew how to work with the airplane. There was a minimum of air to ground transmissions and no wasted time questioning the calls . . . It was a beautiful thing to witness. One of the West side pilots, Bob Cory 268, set the all time record for traffic pilots when he called out 404 violators at Fife in one day working with a 55 team . . . . His feat will always be remembered as the Thanksgiving Day Massacre.

A re-occurring weather phenomenon descends upon Eastern Washington almost every year like clockwork usually towards the end of December till the middle of January. It's a high pressure inversion situation where the surface temps are often in the low twenties but at around four or five thousand feet it could be as warm as 50 to 60 degrees. Those inversions usually last about two weeks and are characterized by very dense freezing fog conditions at the surface with very low ceilings and visibility. The fog always has a very finite top and you nearly always broke out into brilliant sunshine at around 3500 feet during the climb out where it started to warm up very quickly. Problem was, usually all of Eastern Washington was affected so we often had to fly over to the Westside of the state to work traffic where the weather was often clear. The closest traffic course for us was North Bend but we often found ourselves working Fife, Marysville, Chehalis, or any other spot we could find eager ground troops to help us out. The commute over the Cascades during those high pressure inversions was just spectacular. Mt Baker, Glacier Peak, Mt Rainier, Mt Adams, Mt St Helens, Mt Hood, and all of the peaks on the Olympic Peninsula stood out in all their splendor on those crystal clear days . . . . Opening the side window to let in some of that 60 degree air was always a treat in the middle of the winter!

Coming back to land at Moses Lake was a totally different story . . . . The ceiling and visibility was usually down to minimums (200 foot ceiling and ½ mile visibility) but often somewhat lower than that. Unlike FAR Part 135 operators we flew under Part 91 and could go ahead and attempt an IFR approach even if they were calling the weather a 100 foot ceiling with ¼ mile or less visibility . . . . Not always smart but we did have an ace in the hole at Moses Lake (MWH). The runway for the ILS to 32R was almost 14,000 feet long and well over 200 feet wide having been built to accommodate B-36 and B-52 bombers during the Cold War era. when it was Larsen Air Force Base. The area around the airport was totally flat with no obstructions and if a pilot was ever going to "cheat" a little on an ILS this was definitely the place to do it. You could follow the glide slope all the way to the ground, be off the localizer by almost a dot, but still have 11,000 feet of runway left. You would always be over **some kind** of pavement when you flared! However, if a pilot got a little nervous about flying below minimums, executing the published missed approach procedure really was not an option due to another characteristic of that dense freezing fog. Once you were cleared for the approach, and descended into that gloom and doom for the ILS, for the next three and ½ minutes you were guaranteed to accumulate at least ½ to ¾ of an inch of very sticky ice. It was not unusual at all to land with an inch of very rough looking rime and I was always amazed at how quickly it built! Since so much lift and smooth air flow was lost due to the ice accruel it would sometimes require nearly full power and zero flaps just to keep the old Skylane flying even while going down hill. Naturally, we accumulated that same amount of ice on the initial climb-outs but it usually sublimated off in the sunshine very quickly once we broke out on top. Attempting a missed approach with that much ice just would not have been possible as the plane would have collected another ½ inch but probably wouldn't have been able to climb at all . . . . So, there would be no go-arounds!! The landing itself was almost always made looking out the (open) side window since the wind screen and side window were **always** covered in thick ice that the defroster just couldn't keep up with . . . . I'll always remember one approach when I was wearing my glasses for some reason and had to stick my face outside slightly to get lined up on the runway at the last second. Unfortunately, even though I wasn't getting the full effect of the wind blast in my face, my glasses did "ice up" which forced me to make a truly "blind landing" (if you want to call my semi-controlled crash a landing) for the first time in my career! Those two weeks each year sure took a toll on my once dark brown hair!

Taxiing over to the old blue T-hangar, after gassing up, was when the real fun began. Since the temps were usually in the high teens to low twenties, the accumulated ice was not going to melt anytime soon but had to be removed before the next flight. Thankfully, we had a propane powered Red Dragon engine pre-heater on hand to solve the problem. It had a long flexible metal hose attachment but the procedure always took awhile since you had to be a careful not to burn the paint off the plane with it. It did a nice job melting the ice off as long as you took your time and wore heavy gloves! I was always a bit nervous heating the leading edges of an airplane with a flame thrower having just topped off those wing tanks with 92 gallons of very flammable 100 low lead gas!! It's a good thing an OSHA rep. never saw us performing this task as I think we all might have gotten in the grease a little over our de-icing procedures! One of my Ephrata flying partners thought that using a ball peen-hammer would be safer to clear that pesky ice off with. In his defense it was dark when he tried that method and he did a helluva good job breaking that nasty ice off. However, the next morning it was quite apparent those soft aluminum leading edges had taken the brunt of his pounding. There were dozens of golf ball size circular dents all over both leading edges and on the horizontal stabilizers as well . . . . The boss was not a happy camper when he saw all the damage! The other lasting memory I have of those days was when I would come home from a day of flying with a freshly sun-tanned face to be confronted by an exasperated (and quite jealous) spouse who had been living in that dense fog for several weeks by now and was starting to get a bit cranky from her lack of Vitamin D.

Sometimes, during normal traffic days we often worked with troopers in some of the outlying areas who weren't real familiar with aircraft operations . . . . When the pilot made the 'under now' call for a car doing 75 or 80 mph you would expect the waiting trooper to be accelerating like hell to match its speed asap so as not to end up ten miles down the freeway with the stop. Unfortunately there was always one or two troops who just couldn't get the hang of it and would come down the on-ramp at 45 or 50 mph and then come on the radio to ask 'Where is it 305?' Of course the violator doing 80 was now long gone over the next hill and I would have to 'politely' hold this guy's hand for several miles and lead him to the violator . . . . It wasted a lot of time and made me long for the '55 Teams' where this old lady kind of driving would be considered a crime against humanity. When I encountered these type individuals I would try to anticipate their 'snail like pursuit style' when I knew they were next up on the ramp . . . When the violator was a good **mile** from the overpass I would announce it was going under now . . . The troop would meander down the ramp and would eventually find himself right along side the violator . . . . Glory be! They would be just beside themselves with their great sense of timing and pursuit driving abilities . . . . As hard as it was to not say something since all the pilots felt that it was anathema to ever criticize a ground trooper about his or her driving abilities, we never said anything on the air when we encountered a 'slow mover trooper'. There were a number of ground troops who really didn't care to work with the airplane at all, even though it was very easy activity for them. Others just felt that the pilots were just a bunch of lazy over-paid pussies who couldn't make it as real troopers . . . These guys were always easy to spot when you started working with them . . . . If you called out a car as beige they would pull along side it and announce it was really light gold then refuse to stop it since we had obviously made a huge mistake . . . . These type individuals were really hard to deal with and I'm afraid I might have violated the cardinal pilot rule a couple times when encountering this type of attitude. After enduring the antics of one insufferable prick, after he passed on several violators

I'd called out, I finally lost it and told him: 'Hey Slick, why don't you head on back to the office and grab a radar . . . you'll be a lot more productive someplace else' . . . . Of course as soon as those words left my lips I regretted it and knew I was going to pay for my insolence. When we stopped for lunch a couple of his younger workmates were beside themselves with glee that someone had finally stood up to this bully. They told me some horror stories about working with him and his Attila the Hun attitude. I felt somewhat better but was still worried about the inevitable bitch call to my sergeant . . . . Luckily, Attila never called.

Besides working traffic we also were on call 24 hours a day for other missions such as: search and rescue, drug interdiction (following a car load of morons around with dope in their trunk), emergency blood and tissue transports, and plain old passenger transportation flights. I will always remember one flight from Bowers Field to Boeing Field transporting the remains from a possible homicide scene to the WSP crime lab near the old Rainier Brewery in Seattle. It was around 3am when I picked up the evidence in Ellensburg . . . It was in a little icebox and I assumed it contained some small remnant of evidence that needed to be analyzed. I asked the sergeant what was in there and he said it was some guys head they had found out in the sage brush . . . . Geez, that kind of freaked me out a little but I soldiered on and tried not to think about it too much. It was a clear night and for once I didn't even have to file IFR which was really rare . . . I did have a strong little headwind and had plenty of time to consider what was sitting on the seat next to me. I thought back about some of the crazy stories my old commercial instructor John Koch had told me about during his days flying corpses around in an unpressurized Cessna 206. He said that sometimes the deceased would just be thrown in the back in a body bag which creeped him out somewhat to begin with. He recounted several episodes while cruising along in calm air when he would hear a thump or thought he heard something move in the back! On one occasion he just happened to be looking to the rear when he saw a corpse try to sit up for a second . . . Being a steely eyed Marine Combat pilot he convinced himself it was just muscle contractions brought on by the pressure and temperature changes at altitude but

319

was nevertheless totally spooked by that episode! He said the worst was when the pressure changes caused horribly foul 'gas' emissions to erupt from the corpses . . . He said he actually heard one of those nasty fart/belches one time even though he was wearing a set of Dave Clark's finest headsets . . . . Apparently, that was the closest he ever came in his flying career to breaking out a barf bag. Sitting next to a head on ice didn't seem quite so bad in comparison!

I had an interesting marijuana flight in the late summer of '87 up North of Republic in an area known as Rose Valley. Even though this wasn't on an Indian Reservation I had an observer from the Bureau of Indian Affairs (BIA) flying with me that day. I had flown with him before in the Tonasket area and he was an excellent spotter. He was pretty cautious and always wore a flack vest and sat on another one to protect his family jewels from 'pot' shots (ha ha) taken at us from overly aggressive marijuana grow security personnel below. He was a cool guy and had eyes as good as Capt. Myers for spotting hidden grows. On this particular day we were looking for plastic pipe lines going from various water sources to the remotely located plants. We finally spotted an old camouflaged bathtub and after many low passes finally started to pick up the black plastic pipe leading to the grow areas. Once we pin-pointed the center of the grow we started to see more and more pipe leading to other plants and pretty soon realized that this was a huge operation and pretty sophisticated in a Homer Simpson sort of way. We went back to the Republic Airport and organized a team of deputies and volunteers to get in there to cut those plants down ASAP before the growers started harvesting their crop early since we had no doubt spooked the security guys and growers by all of our low passes while getting our photo evidence. I had to get back to Ephrata but was called later at home and filled in on all the details. Apparently, once the 'harvest' team got in there they found even more plants and ended up hacking down nearly 600 mature 10 to 12 feet high "BC Bud" plants. At the time those were the gold standard in marijuana circles with a very high THC content and each plant might bring upwards of $1,000. Pretty lucrative business! Later that evening the deputies heaped all the plants up in a gravel pit, threw diesel on them, and lit the pile off. Apparently the oily THC laden smoke cloud drifted over town . . . . I would imagine that most of the residents of Republic were feeling pretty 'mellow' later that night . . . . You might think this is the end of the story, but wait, there's more! About two weeks later I got a letter from my BIA observer in which he included a local newspaper article about our activities that day. It was published by the "Rose Valley Marijuana Growers Association" but was actually just a single sheet bi-monthly newsletter for their members . . . Anyway, the headlines read: 'Nazi Baby Killer' . . . . The article went on to describe how a State Patrol pilot was flying dangerously low and that the horrible engine noise he created had caused several hysterical abortions in their goat herd. The writer then stated that the illegal harvest of their crop would now cause several of their human babies to probably starve to death since those plants were their only source of income . . . . I have to say that looking back on my career and all the complaints I received from the public that being labeled a Nazi baby killer was absolutely the most unique of them all!

I had a couple other rather scary marijuana flights up north of Colville when I was still new at it. On one occasion I scared the be-jeezus out of myself after getting talked into flying up a semi-box canyon by my observer from the sheriff's office. It was really choppy that day with a lot of mountain wave activity with severe downdrafts but he assured me there was a "big grow" up at the other end. When I finally realized I was running out of altitude, canyon wall clearance, and ideas all at the same time, I was forced to make a really ugly course reversal that included the stall warning horn blaring, sagebrush going by the windscreen way too close for comfort, and some unsolicited screaming from my rider which I certainly did not appreciate! It really took awhile to regain my composure after that episode and I knew I needed to get some advice on how to handle those kinds of situations.

In those years Bob Heale was flying a Cessna 208 Caravan for *Empire Airlines* under contract with *Fed Ex* and I used to run into him up at the Omak airport about once a month or so where he was forced to sit most of the day waiting for packages. Bob was a gifted aerobatic pilot and Deb and I watched him race the famous T-6 *Lickity Split* at the

Reno Air Races many times. Bob's lovely wife Marion was also a WSP communications officer in Spokane at that time. Anyway, after my latest debacle in the box canyon I sought out Bob's advice on how to more professionally get out of those kinds of situations in the future. After he got through laughing his ass off at my lack of flying skills he described a semi split-ess/wing-over maneuver that with my lack of experience thought I might be able to pull off the next time . . . . He stressed that once I had decided to attempt this mother I had to be 100% committed to it and realize that there would be some significant G's pulled as a result. I wrote everything down and the next chance I was alone I practiced it at a safe altitude over some flat country. This was about 15 years before I had a formal 10 hour aerobatic course so I wasn't exactly a skilled acrobatic pilot at this time. The wing-over part went OK since I was already doing those all day long while working traffic . . . . Committing to a nearly full split-ess took me awhile but I finally worked up the courage to pitch up and sharply roll that old Skylane almost inverted and then to pull like hell until it felt like about 3 or 4 G's and I had reversed course without losing too much altitude. Eventually, I could pull one off with only losing about 300 ft. and felt a little more confident about my chances in a narrow canyon. Of course doing this successfully was all predicated on my not getting so low to the canyon floor in the first place so that I still had some room to pull off this last ditch maneuver without making a smoking hole in the ground. After all that effort and practice I only got to employ the split-ess once. I had matured a little by then and had avoided getting into those situations in the first place. It wasn't even on a marijuana flight when I had to use it . . . . I had a WSP photographer with me flying over a fatal scene in a pretty narrow gorge in the mountains when once again I got talked into doing something I wasn't comfortable with. We ended up flying over the scene at an angle that I knew would be troublesome for a safe egress considering the approaching terrain. Anyway, we got some good shots of that fatal scene but unfortunately my camera guy was rendered unconscious by the severe G's we encountered on that modified split-ess pull out I had to initiate to keep from smuckin my 182 into that canyon wall.

Later, after my aerobatic course in Florida, I determined that a half Cuban 8 was actually a much better (and safer) maneuver for the box canyon scenario. **If** you had the airspeed, just pull into a 3g loop and as you started downhill over the top roll the plane level and you'd soon be heading in the reverse direction out of the canyon, usually with no altitude loss at all! Of course practicing those maneuvers in a Skylane was strictly forbidden by WSP Aviation Section policy. I had to always practice them alone and keep my mouth shut or risk getting fired. I never had an opportunity to use one while working but felt absolutely certain that the half Cuban 8 would have been the best choice to get out of that situation safely. I had some trouble trying one a few years later in a T6 but that's another story for a later chapter.

Bob ended up flying the P51 *Miss America* at Reno and also performed his aerobatic routine at airshows all over the West Coast in his own plane. I last saw Bob and Marion at Reno in September of 1996. A couple days later Bob was killed at the Fairchild AFB Airshow in Spokane when during a low altitude maneuver, something broke on his plane and he went in . . . . I believe he experienced the same sort of issue that took the life of Art Scholl during the filming of *Top Gun* . . . . I was privileged to see those two guys fly for many years at Reno and they were both at the top of their game when a mechanical issue got them both.

While working traffic we normally flew around 1,500 to 2,000 feet above the ground and no longer had to deal with the face to face realities that a road trooper sees all day long, i.e . . . . really ugly violators. In my road trooper days I recall weaving my way through freeway traffic looking for that elusive expired plate, loud muffler, or the guy who left his studded tires on too long . . . However, what I often found, and was always surprised to see, was just how many people were serial nose-pickers . . . . When I caught a glimpse of some slob with his index finger buried deep in his sinus cavity I couldn't help but maneuver my patrol car into his blind spot and then observe just how long this mining episode might last . . . . It was amazing how absorbed and industrious some of these folks were during that

endeavor . . . I mean they would keep digging for five miles or so . . . .
But unlike 'Flick' my history prof. at the seminary, some of these idiots
didn't discard their 'nugget' after it was dug out of the recesses of their
skulls . . . . A few of them rolled that little booger around between
their fingertips, savoring its fine texture I guess, then popped that jewel
into their mouths!! Holy shit, I just about gagged every time I saw
that . . . . Although not technically illegal, even though it pushed the
outside of the 'due care and caution' envelope, I was unable to just sit
back without bringing that atrocious behavior to their attention. As
soon as possible after it was popped into the mouth I would pull along
side from out of their blind spot and wait for the offender to glance
my way . . . . As soon as we made eye contact I would simulate a nose
picking gesture then give them a horrible gagging look as I pointed at
them disgustingly . . . . I used to get some crazy looks back and the
occasional single finger salute which I tried not to react to since I had
just sort of infringed on their privacy somewhat . . . .

Anyway, back to working traffic . . . Some of the courses we worked
were not exactly commonly referred to as 'hotbeds of activity'. When
we saw Tonasket, Walla Walla, Chewelah, or Goldendale on the
schedule, especially on a weekday in the winter, we knew it was going
to be a long grind and that we'd be extremely lucky to come back
with even 15 or 20 violators and most of those would be warnings.
While we were circling these courses looking for 'anything moving' to
call out there would sometimes be gaps of ten or fifteen minutes with
no radio calls whatsoever . . . . It never failed that one of the ground
troops would eventually call me and ask; "Are you still up there 305?"
My patented response (courtesy of Ron McClinton 600) was to wait
a few seconds then come back to him sounding out of breath and say:
"Yeah, (gasp, gasp) I thought I heard something rattling around in
the trunk, so I had to **get out** and see what it was . . . ." Some of the
troops were a little slow on the uptake and just said "Yeah, I figured
you were busy doing something . . ." When those sort of unthinking
remarks were proffered, usually by an FNG troop, they were often
countered with some unflattering comments from one of the veteran
troops regarding the offenders IQ level and/or birthing location.

Another fun distraction to occupy our time when things got slow was to fly backwards. If the wind aloft was blowing hard enough, (usually needed at least 45 knots), full flaps were selected and the airplane was slowed down to its minimum controllable airspeed. With the nose pitched up to about 20 degrees, you could just hover there like a helicopter with no forward movement whatsoever. Once in awhile at Thorp and I-90, where the wind always howled, there would often be enough wind to actually fly backwards which always impressed the shit out of the ground troops! There would always be one guy who would shout out on the radio: "Hey, look what 305's doing!" My only claim to fame . . . .

Anyway, up in the air we had more serious matters to deal with . . . namely F15 Eagles and EA6B Intruders . . . . Several of our traffic courses were bisected by low level MTRs (military training routes) and we often hunted for marijuana grows in MOAs and other remote areas where military planes prowled at will. At the CRO Orchards traffic course south of Wenatchee on SR-2 near Rock Island Dam a low level MTR went right through the course. Navy Whidbey Prowlers and Intruders would come whistling down the Palisades Canyon usually around 500 feet above ground level and I often wouldn't see them until they went right underneath me . . . . I never got used to seeing a military jet going that fast right under me that close to the ground and it scared the bejezzus out of me every time! I knew what the cockpit conversation between the pilot and navigator must have been each time; 'I bet that moron in the Cessna has to go change his shorts now . . . ' A few years later a Prowler collided with a crop-duster down near Trinidad. Knowing that most cropduster pilots get nose bleeds above 100 feet I guess it must have been quite a 'challenge' for the Prowler crew to try to get under him . . . Once, while looking for marijuana in the Roosevelt MOA near Curlew with my BIA partner, I had just rolled out of a turn after finding some plants in an old granary with no top on it when two silvery F15 Eagles went by at about 450 knots, one on each side of me at my altitude, clearing my plane by about 150 feet on each side . . . . Man the noise was God Awful and I was really impressed . . . . The usual adrenaline rush was amplified even more when the F15 on the left made a hard 90 degree banked turn to his left and his wingman a similar turn to the right and they just disappeared . . . . I guess they just had to let me know they were in the vicinity and had just 'shot me down'.

Most of the time our biggest threat while working traffic was just plain old Cessna 150s and 172s pooping along the freeways right at the altitude where we were working traffic. It never ceased to amaze me how many pilots don't know how to navigate so instead just follow the Interstates like they are driving their cars . . . . How boring! Anyway, before we got TCAD and later TCAS units installed in our Cessnas we all had our fair share of close calls with student and private pilots flying IFR (I follow roads). I always tried to work traffic at 'in between' altitudes like 2250 ft or 2750 ft since most so called IFR pilots flew religiously at 2500 or 3500feet . . . . Nonetheless I can't even begin to count how many times I rolled out of a steep bank after concentrating hard on a violator's car for a few moments and came face to face with some guy in a 150 with his face buried in a sectional and not looking outside at all . . . . However, the really scary ones occurred when you rolled level and actually **heard** the engine noise of a plane going overhead and looked up just in time to catch a glimpse of a bunch of oil stained rivets whistling by on the belly of some Cessna . . . . Quite unnerving! Luckily, sometimes we were flying with somebody else and those second set of eyeballs sure came in handy! After several years of close calls all the pilots finally got together and identified several traffic courses where we felt it was mandatory to have two pilots in the planes if we were assigned to work them . . . The dangerous courses were near military airports and in those areas near the arrival and departure corridors out of SEATAC, Paine Field, and Boeing Field . . . . We stated our case at an Aviation Division meeting one day when Capt. Swier's boss, an assistant chief of some sort, was there to listen to our story . . . . Up until this day I had respected this guy but not after his accusatory statements towards us at that meeting . . . . A non-pilot he basically said we were a bunch of prima donnas and not doing real trooper work anyway since we just flitted around the sky all day in expensive toys not accomplishing much . . . . He went on to say that if we didn't want to work in certain areas that he could easily find someone who would and replace us with those troopers . . . . Man, what a piece of work that guy was . . . . He certainly never turned down an opportunity for us to fly him around the country in our King Airs or Beechjet but according to him a 'trained monkey' could work traffic in congested airspace all by himself . . . . I guess he felt that a mid-air accompanied by multiple fatalities was just the price of 'real troopers' doing business . . . .

A similar two or three star type once made a sneering remark to me that we were ten minutes past our ETA as he got out of the King Air after landing in Wenatchee . . . . Man, I wanted to kick him in the nuts so badly at that moment but those stars on his epaulets convinced me to take a more cautious approach . . . . The weather that morning was right at minimums and we had just flown a complicated DME Arc approach with multiple stepdowns and heading changes . . . Seattle Center had told us to slow down several times for traffic ahead of us, and we encountered severe icing throughout the approach . . . . Then, to make it more interesting, after we had 'sort of' broken out Seattle Center gave us our holding instructions since the Horizon flight ahead of us hadn't cancelled their IFR yet . . . . Through heavy snow I caught a glimpse of Horizon at the gate and told Seattle they were on the ground and de-planing passengers already . . . They said they needed to get that cancellation from the Horizon crew themselves before we could finish the approach no matter what we saw . . . . They let us shoot the approach but now wanted us to climb back into severe icing and hold . . . . Jesus Christ!! I cancelled IFR immediately even though I wasn't really sure we could stay VFR or maintain circling minimums prior to landing . . . . The pilot flying looked at me with one of those WTF expressions but didn't say anything. During that brief conversation with Seattle we had gone past the airport and it was now getting really tough to keep the runway in sight with the heavy snow and low ceiling . . . . My memory is a little hazy but I seem to recall a rather steep bank angle at some point followed by a downwind landing on an icy runway . . . . Putting the props in beta (and possibly reverse) while still airborne is an unapproved procedure and I don't have an independent recollection of that ever occurring . . . . Luckily the guy I was flying with was a magician with a King Air 200 and we didn't even run off the end of the runway . . . . So when the Assistant

Chief made his nasty little remark to me as he climbed down the air-stairs I wasn't in the best of moods . . . . I really wanted to go over and have a conversation with that bonehead Horizon crew but chose to have a butterhorn in the terminal instead . . . . I had several other "interesting" landing incidents at Wenatchee over the years but will save those stories for later. These days, Wenatchee has an ILS and I'm sure even a "trained monkey" could get in there now at minimums!

Self next to Cessna 182 traffic plane.

Shortly after arriving in Ephrata I began my ancillary career as a self proclaimed vomit specialist. The high incidence of airborne (and once while taxiing) regurgitating began when the WSP started its Explorer Scout aviation program. The scouts from the local Troops all had to ride with us at some point to get that coveted aviation merit badge. I always enjoyed meeting the young Explorers and they were really enthusiastic. I had been a senior patrol leader in Troop 23 in Yakima as a kid and always supported the BSA. The problem was almost all of the teenagers that showed up for their assigned ride had never flown before or if they had it was in an airliner . . . . There is very little commonality between riding in a big ole aluminum tube at FL350, with bathrooms, rows of seats, and beverage service, and stuffing oneself into a little ole Cessna 182 for a day of tight left turns for 5 or 6 hours at 1500 feet when it was hot and bumpy . . . . Most of the Explorers made it out to the traffic course without too much trouble but as soon as those dreaded left turns started it was usually just a matter of a few minutes before the telltale indicators of impending trouble began to surface . . . . To keep them occupied, I usually handed them my flight sheet kneeboard and showed them how to record each violator stop before we took off. The first indication of a possible problem was when the Explorer was having difficulty writing . . . . When I saw this I would quietly take the kneeboard sheet back for myself . . . . Next, they would usually quit talking and began to just stare out the window . . . This was shortly followed by some excess fidgiting and the onset of light sweating. By this time I had already located and opened a barf bag for them but made sure they did not see my preparations as that sight would surely initiate a premature eruption. I usually never briefed them on the ground of the possibility of airsickness as I felt that would definitely predispose them to the act . . . The last two signs of an impending explosion were usually simultaneous; there was the digging into the Cessna side pockets looking for something to puke in followed by a couple dry heave type burps and sometimes a muffled ' I think I'm gonna be sick' declaration . . . . Usually I was able to give them the prepared barf bag, with the edges already folded back for ease of usage. This act was followed by a terse and stern tutorial on barfing etiquette which consisted of: 'Hold onto the bag tightly, stick your face way inside and leave it there until you're done'. Unfortunately, most of those kids were in no condition to listen to last minute shouted instructions during their moment of personal agony and they usually barfed all over the outside of the bag instead of into it . . . . When I saw that they weren't listening to my instructions and that vomiting was imminent I would kindly reach over and shove their heads down so they at least barfed on the floor mat instead of all over the instrument panel or seat . . . . It is really hard picking pieces of an Explorers lunch out of all those little tiny plastic crevices in a Cessna panel . . . . Moreover, it seems like I was never able to find all the little pieces during the clean-up and sometimes several days later when the plane was nice and warm I would start to detect a stale and acidy bean with bacon soup odor emanating from somewhere in the cockpit and knew I had missed some lunch bits . . . . Anyway, unless they did a perfect job of puking, and had sealed the bag of barf up tightly, and still wanted to fly, it was usually back to the airport for the clean-up . . . . I have a pretty strong stomach but I just couldn't keep turning circles with that stench and visible mess all around me . . . . Usually by then the Explorer had seen enough WSP flying to last a life time and was pretty eager to get back on the ground. On one occasion I picked up a very cute 16 year old female Explorer at the Grant County Airport for her required flight . . . She filled out her little uniform quite nicely and was accompanied by a very serious looking gentleman who turned out to be her Dad. Man, he really gave me the hairy eyeball and demanded to know all the details of the flight, where we were going, ETA'S, FAA registration number, call signs, etc., etc. I could see why he was being so overly protective but he was acting like a real nut-job. We finally got airborne and headed to Sprague to work traffic. She was a very nice young lady and asked all the pertinent questions necessary to fill out her little merit badge checklist form. More importantly, she did not get sick while working traffic so I even let her call out a couple violators on the radio . . . . The guys on the ground really liked this turn of events and when we landed at the Sprague Airport (a gravel crop duster strip) for lunch several of my old workmates suddenly showed up to give us a ride to town . . . . Now on a normal traffic day when I was alone I usually had to walk into town . . . . However, on occasion, when they were all sitting down to eat someone would eventually ask "Where's 305?" . . . So, once in awhile someone might come and pick me up as I was trudging down the hill into town. Anyway, things got a little tense at lunch when one of the newly single troops started hitting on the little 16 year old Explorer . . . . His pick up line was pretty sad and started off with; "Hey, you're pretty cute, how old are you?" When she said 16 he was momentarily set back but then asked; "You got any older sisters?" When she said no he moved smartly along to "Is your

Mom single?" This was followed by comments about her freckles, her uniform, and invitations to come and ride with a real trooper instead of this doofus pilot here . . . . Man, all I could think about was her blabbing to her Dad about all those lecherous troopers leering at her and making suggestive remarks about how she looked in her tight fitting shirt . . . . I could just see a lawsuit coming with my name in bold print on the cover sheet . . . . When we got airborne I told her that those guys were just kidding and goofing around and to not take them seriously . . . . She laughed and seemed to take it all in stride . . . . When we got back to Moses Lake her Dad was waiting for us on the ramp . . . . Before the prop stopped he was at the door looking inside the plane for some kind of evidence of wrong doing I guess . . . . Man, this guy was really paranoid . . . I suppose he expected to find several used condoms, empty beer cans, and visible DNA residue . . . . When I got out, he actually came up very close and tried to smell me . . . . Now, I'm normally a patient man but I've never responded well to rude behavior . . . I gave him a little shove and told him to back off . . . This seemed to bring him to his senses and he calmed down a little. I gave him a brief rundown about the flight, praised his daughter about being a very good scout, and got the hell out of there. There were no lawsuits filed but she was one of the last Explorers I ever took up. The inevitable barfing and the awful clean-up work just got to be too much of a hassle. In the future whenever an Explorer showed up for a flight I did my best to discourage them from going out and actually working traffic. Instead, I usually just took them on a brief local flight, all straight and level, showed them the stopwatches and landed before anything happened. If they really wanted to observe traffic operations I told them in no uncertain terms that unless they had an iron stomach they were definitely going to puke and feel sick and weak for several days afterwards . . . I never had any takers after that disclaimer. All the other traffic pilots had similar experiences and we soon began referring to those scouts as "Exploders". All five of our Cessnas eventually smelled like stale puke. We sort of got used to it but when we cycled the planes through Olympia for their 100 hour inspections and annuals our mechanics always complained about the foul odors and the occasional discovery of chunks of petrified ham and other assorted lunch tidbits found lodged behind the instrument panel.

The quickest onset of airsickness I ever saw occurred at Felts Field one afternoon on a media flight. I had met a reporter from the Opportunity newspaper at the Felts Field Café for lunch who wanted to do an in depth story on WSP airborne traffic operations. I think her slant was going to be that our whole operation was nothing but a speed trap and she was going to get the 'scoop' on our whole illegal program. She was pleasant but was a rather 'large person' and had what I felt was way too much lunch when she knew she was going flying afterwards . . . . With my previous history of reporters fresh in mind I didn't say a word about anything and kept all my comments professional and to the point. As we taxied out she said she had never flown before . . . . That raised my anxiety level somewhat but it was a super calm day with nice smooth air . . . The traffic course was just over at Barker Rd so I felt I could get her back to the airport in a few minutes if she started to get sick . . . I thought I had it all covered . . . When the tower cleared me for takeoff on 21R I pushed the throttle to the stop and listened as all 230 horses of that mighty Continental O-470 roared to full song . . . . I noticed that she grabbed onto the armrest with both hands but didn't think too much of it . . . . Just as I rotated she suddenly sat bolt upright in her seat and the next thing I saw was a firehose like stream of projectile barf shooting out of her, exactly like Linda Blair in 'The Exorcist', striking the instrument panel and dash . . . When it hit the plastic panel it splashed all over her, me, and the entire cockpit . . . . All those cups of coffee, a large bowl of clam chowder, and a club sandwich with fries now decorated the whole inside of the plane . . . . I couldn't even see the airspeed indicator as a piece of bacon was laying across its face . . . She even managed to get some on the inside of the windshield and I damn near declared a Mayday until the puke dripped on down a little and I could see out again. Shit O Dear this was a real catastrophe! I came really close to barfing myself and if I didn't have to fly I'm sure I would have . . . I told tower I needed to come right back! I guess the tone of my voice must have alarmed them a little as they immediately cleared me to land in the opposite direction on 3R. I taxied up to the restaurant so she could get into the restroom to clean up . . . . I just shut it down, opened her door for her from the inside, and she got out . . . . I never said a word and neither did she. I taxied over to The Hangar Flying Club and proceeded to clean myself up as well as the plane. Jim came out and just laughed his ass off at my predicament but pitched right in to help me clean the plane up. I then called the Olympia hangar and told them how extensive the mess was; I was advised to bring the plane over the next day as it would need some sort of professional bio-hazard clean-up . . . Of course it was determined that I was to blame for the whole incident and was later presented with the bill for the 'haz-mat' clean up at our next Division meeting . . . . That reporter never called to apologize and as far as I know never did the story on our program . . . I'm sure she felt I had made her sick on purpose and that she was just another victim of the cruel police state she was forced to live in.

One thing I always warned passengers about was the danger of spending too much time either looking through a telephoto lens or binoculars while airborne. Most cautious and prudent passengers heeded the advice but it was sometimes more difficult to persuade the self described "seasoned" flyers from the media or other police agencies about the inevitable results of prolonged usage of those devices. I was called in to assist the DEA with an airborne drug surveillance operation in Kennewick one afternoon when their Cessna 206 had a mechanical issue. Time was of the essence so when I picked their agent up at Vista Field he briefed me about the operation while we were taxiing and climbing out . . . Apparently the bad guys receiving the drugs were making stops all over town trying to get enough money together to make the buy. Where they stopped to get the money was very important to the investigation so things got a little hectic as we tried to keep track of the whole operation and the different cars the ground agents were driving as they followed the bad guys around documenting the addresses of their stops. Everything was going fairly well until my passenger spent a little too long on the binoculars trying to identify some bad guy on the ground . . . . Suddenly, the Exploder scenario reared its ugly symptoms . . . . My agent started sweating, became disoriented, quit talking, and started the searching routine . . . . I wasn't expecting this so I had to scramble to dig out a barf bag and handed it to him with the usual instructions . . . . He took off his head set about the time his ground agents were calling him on his handheld radio . . . I just took it from him and tried to pass on

333

the info they needed . . . I could hear them in my headset but had to talk to them on his handheld . . . The ground guys immediately knew something was up when they heard me on their channel . . . . Right in the middle of this complicated and fairly serious operation they started making hilarious derogatory comments about 'Jim' losing it at such a critical time . . . . And, right on cue, Jim lost it shortly thereafter . . . . but being the consummate government trained professional, he got all the 'ejectus' in the bag and then sealed it up tight . . . . Good man! He wasn't able to get back to work right away so I tried the best I could to keep the good guys and bad guys separated but close to each other, handled and monitored two different WSP channels, and the DEA radio, all while talking to Pasco Tower and avoiding landing and departing aircraft there since I was just inside the traffic pattern . . . . What a goat rope! Jim finally regained his senses somewhat and was able to get things coordinated again on his DEA radio in spite of further insulting remarks from his ground compatriots about his weak stomach. We ended up flying for another two hours but after awhile that bag of barf was starting to make both of us sick . . . . I flew out over the Columbia, when I had a moment, and had Jim jettison the bag . . . . I felt bad about littering but didn't think I could take that smell on a hot day much longer . . . Jim's jettison job didn't go well either and I felt a thump after he chucked it . . . it hit the right horizontal stabilizer . . . When we finally landed, that barf bag was still glued to its leading edge . . .

During my tenure as a WSP pilot there was only one road trooper who we eventually had to ban from flying in any of our aircraft . . . . In the eighties and nineties the WSP budget was in pretty good shape and we used to fly troopers, radio operators, commercial vehicle personnel, secretaries, etc. from all over Eastern Washington to Shelton and Olympia for various training sessions, meetings, promotions, etc. on a weekly basis year round. The first leg was usually from Olympia to Spokane in either the King Air 200 or Beechjet 400A to pick up our first group of people. The next stop was usually in Pasco, followed by Wenatchee, Yakima, then on to either Shelton or Olympia. We occasionally made stops in Okanogan, Walla Walla, Ellensburg, Lewiston, or Pullman as well. The personnel we picked up in Spokane got to suffer through a lot of takeoffs and landings as well as having to deal with the turbulence at low cruise altitudes due to all the short legs. Most everyone was used to the routine and never gave us any trouble . . . . However, we had one problematic Spokane trooper who loved to fly but flying didn't love him too much. On nearly every flight he was on he got sick and sadly, he never learned how to use a sick sack properly . . . We would have to clean up after him each time since once he had blown chunks he became incapacitated and was unable to function for quite some time. The other passengers would become distressed as well since he usually lost it shortly after takeoff from Spokane when we still had several stops to make and more people to load up. The final straw leading to his banishment occurred when we picked him up at the Shelton airport one afternoon after his yearly re-current (In-Service) training at the academy. Apparently, the last class had run long and we were already waiting at the airport for everyone when they grabbed a quick lunch and jumped into the academy van which brought them to the airport. The lunch menu had included some sort of miniature cheeseburgers and as we later found out our boy had hastily consumed at least three of them while running out to the van for the short trip to the airport. We had already warned him quite sternly several times before to only eat dry toast or crackers before a flight . . . . Unfortunately, he had a voracious appetite and this always seemed to override his better judgment. When he got on the plane I was loading the bags and asked him straight out what he had for lunch as he climbed up the King Air stairs . . . . Before he could answer, Sergeant Kris Boness, who was right behind him on the air stairs, ratted him out and said he saw him eat four or five cheeseburgers on the ride to the airport . . . . Kris was familiar with his problem and told our boy flat-out that if he puked on this flight he was going to pull out his hogleg and gut-shoot him in his seat . . . . I was fine with that as I had cleaned up his mess several times before! Anyway, it was a severe clear high pressure day with very smooth air and I prayed that the calm-air gods would be with us on this one hour leg to Spokane. I begged the pilot flying to make smooth gentle turns and to keep a shallow climb going up to our normal cruise altitude of FL270. Everything was going so nicely until I glanced out my right-side window and saw a small round cloud just northeast of Mt Rainier . . . . I asked the pilot flying if he saw that 'rotor' cloud over there and he said he had . . . . We looked at each other and knew exactly what was going to happen next . . . . A rotor cloud in that area on a clear day near Mt. Rainier almost always signified some pretty severe high velocity winds usually accompanied by severe downdrafts as the air-mass rolled over the mountain then spun up on the other side condensing the moisture there. A rotor cloud isn't as dramatic as the stacks of lenticulars that would build up over the mountain during low pressure days but the turbulence associated was just as bad. We looked at our newly installed moving map display which indicated wind speeds aloft and their velocity. The wind had been very light until we went through about 14,000 where it picked up dramatically coming out of the Southwest, as usual . . . We could usually predict within a couple miles when the mountain wave would hit us; sometimes it was pretty short lived but occasionally it would beat the crap out of us for five minutes or longer . . . . We silently prayed for the former . . . . When we got closer I flicked the seat belt sign which was always a waste of time and cinched my belts down tight. Right on cue we got hit by a big sinker followed shortly thereafter by its ugly twin sister the big riser which immediately overwhelmed the servos in our overly sensitive autopilot causing it to disengage . . . For a change I got to watch someone else try to hand-fly a King Air through this mountain wave activity and did my best calling out vertical speed trends to assist him a little. We experienced the usual moderate to almost severe turbulence for a few minutes then as usual everything smoothed out. We had just finished the cruise checklist when I turned around to see how our 'special' passenger was doing . . . . I really didn't need to look since I had already picked up the faint odor of fresh barf a few seconds before . . . . However, what I saw on the cabin floor was a shocker . . . . I guess in the mad dash to the airport in the WSP van our special trooper had inhaled his cheeseburgers without chewing them . . . . I could see the remnants of at least three of them scattered around but none of the pieces were smaller than two or three inches in diameter . . . . Thankfully, there wasn't much liquid in the mess just those nearly intact-large chunks of cheeseburger . . . . This was the strangest barf pile I'd ever seen and I've seen a lot of them! Kris Boness was really glaring at the offender . . . . He seemed very conflicted right then and I'm quite sure he was wrestling with all his internal demons who were no doubt screaming at him to draw his service pistol and put that SOB out of his misery once and for all!! When we finally landed at Geiger Field I had everyone get out and coaxed one of the Flight Craft lineboys into cleaning up the mess . . . . That was the last time that guy ever rode in a WSP aircraft, at least while I was still around.

During a marijuana flight, up north of Republic again, my observer was the outpost trooper who lived in town. He was a great guy but sadly was not used to mountain flying on hot summer afternoons. We were flying just south of Grand Forks, British Columbia, still in the USA (I think), looking for evidence of a grow near the border. Our intel was that some fine upstanding B.C. residents had a marijuana garden in Wash. State but they retreated back into B.C. whenever there were any signs of trouble. We hoped to find the grow, flush them out and solve the case. Unfortunately, after a few tight turns near the Kettle River that was all she wrote for my observer. He was able to keep it all in the bag OK but his vomiting was accompanied by the most God-Awful ralphing and retching noises I will ever hear on this planet . . . . I still have trouble searching for adjectives to describe the sounds he made . . . . My best analogy would be the screams of a gut-shot bull elephant charging a Land Rover in Africa with his trunk up and ears back . . . . The racket inside a 182 is already deafening even with Dave Clarks on but man, when he cut loose it scared the shit out of me . . . . After that kind of show, I expected to see his liver and large intestine in that barf bag . . . Then, to aggravate the situation further, he kept up the hacking and yelling during several minutes of dry heaving . . . . Needless to say we were back at the Republic Airport in minutes . . . I taxied up to his patrol car and then tried to assist him out of the plane . . . He was completely 'done in' by now and it took him several minutes to work up the strength just to get out . . . He finally slithered onto the ground and just lay there in a heap by the wheel fairing moaning and groaning. I asked him if he wanted an ambulance; I think that keyed some sort of personal dignity response somewhere in his psyche and he declined . . . Republic is a very small town and if word of something like that got around his name and reputation would be permanently besmirched. After about twenty minutes he was finally able to get onto his hands and knees and I was able to assist him into his patrol car. It took me another twenty minutes to clean the plane up, make a call at the tiny Gen. Aviation Shack, go potty, and when I was done he was still sitting in his car with his seat reclined all the way back with his air-conditioner on max. Several years later we landed the King Air in Spokane one morning to pick up a bunch of troopers to take them to Shelton for In-Service training . . . He was in the group and when he saw me sitting up front I could see the blood drain from his face . . . . He seemed to be having a major PTSD flash-back of sorts so I reassured him immediately that there would be no tight turns and nothing but straight and level the rest of the morning . . . . I don't think he believed me . . . .

I'll finish this vomit section on a somewhat different note as I'm sure most readers have had enough really gross barf stories for awhile. During my stint in Olympia from 1990 to 2004 I was the Aviation Section training officer/check pilot and tested, evaluated, and trained all new pilot recruits prior to their assignment into the section. In 1995 Trooper Debby Jacobsen became our first female reserve pilot. She was already an experienced flight instructor and an excellent instrument pilot and showed up current and ready to fly for her indoc. training. She breezed through the instrument flying syllabus in record time so we began the traffic pilot training phase out near the county line on SR 8 one morning working with some of the Olympia troops. She caught on extremely quickly and made it look really easy . . . . We were working right on the downwind side of Rock Candy Mountain and it was a little breezy that morning. She had just finished calling out a car and documenting everything on her kneeboard flight log when she casually asked me if I could take it for a second. I thought she was just going to get a drink of water . . . . She calmly reached down into the Skylane's side pocket, fished out a sick sack, opened it up very deliberately then barfed her God damned guts out . . . . When she was done she secured the sack very tightly and put it in her flightbag and zipped it up in there . . . . She cleaned herself up with her own towelette, then calmly looked over at me and said "OK, I'm fine now, I've got it". She went right back to working traffic as if nothing had happened . . . Man, I was beyond impressed . . . I had never seen anyone handle themselves in such a cool and calm manner while blowing chunks in an airplane . . . .

When we were all done with the training I gave her glowing review as our newest "reserve" traffic pilot and the best evaluation I had ever given a new recruit . . . . Additionally, she had great recommendations from her district and a spotless record as a road trooper. Soon after, a vacancy for a traffic pilot in Yakima occurred. Unbelievably, our section commander at the time advised me that they weren't going to give her the assignment . . . . When I asked not too politely "Why the hell not?" He said it was the Assistant Chief's call and that he wanted someone else for the position!! WTF!! I had already flown with and evaluated "everyone else" for this position and there **were no other qualified applicants** . . . . I was told in no uncertain terms not to pursue the matter nor to tell anyone about this situation . . . . Man, talk about feeling useless!! A couple days later, after I had calmed down a little, I asked how she took the news . . . . He said he hadn't even told her!!! Then, he tells **me** to call her and give her the bad news myself!! The coup de grace was when he ordered me as the so called "training officer" to officially recommend the pilot the assistant chief wanted for that position . . . . Things got a little heated at that point and I flat refused to recommend a guy, who was certainly an **excellent road trooper** and who I personally liked and respected, but had demonstrated to me that he was an unqualified instrument pilot at that time. I told him I would resign as training/safety officer if he forced me to falsify my records and fabricate some fantasy about this guy being ready . . . He said that if I wouldn't recommend him then he would do it himself, even though he had never flown with him!! . . . . Sadly, that's exactly what happened. Looking back, I know my boss was in a tough spot too, just trying to keep that assistant chief off his ass . . . but Good Lord, at some juncture a manager has to stand up for what is right and show some guts . . . . People's lives were at stake for Chrissakes! This was just one more example of the age old WSP Aviation Division adage that non-aviators like that assistant chief will never fully comprehend the huge differences between being a successful road trooper and having the talent necessary to be a pilot involved in daily hard instrument flying . . . . They are two totally different skill sets and there are dead pilots scattered all over the world who never realized that the abilities required to be a success in a non-flying endeavor don't always translate into those that are necessary to be a safe instrument pilot. That was 20 years ago and I'm still pissed about that whole episode . . . Debby would have been a tremendous asset to the Aviation Section and probably would be its commander right now had they not treated her so unprofessionally. What a waste of a super talented pilot . . . . I did not blame her in the least for disassociating herself from us and never re-applying for any future pilot jobs. She has since promoted up through the ranks and has had a tremendously successful career and I am so happy for her!

As I mentioned earlier one of the greatest rewards for me was nailing one of those idiot serial tailgaters that seem to crop up in our rear view mirrors so often these days . . . . They are the aggressive drivers that we all hate so much and never want to see again except a few miles down the road with a trooper talking to them or with their car wrapped around a tree. They are very hard to catch unless there is a plane up so I was always looking for them and often didn't spend quite as much time messing with the dime a dozen "ten-over" speeders as I should have. I guess what pissed me off the most about those boneheads was the total absurdity of their actions . . . . They never got anywhere! . . . . Traffic was always heavy and after they had finally forced some poor slob they had been terrorizing to change lanes they were almost always faced with a never ending line of cars ahead of them all of which were blocking their path to the open road . . . . so what had they accomplished? These guys are the major cause of road rage in others and I thought I'd seen some of the worst . . . . But wait, I did get to see even worse driving that in fact made those home-grown morons look like student drivers with brand new learners' permits in comparison!!

After my Dad passed away back in '94, Deb and I decided to make a pilgrimage back to Italy to see my ancestral homeland. We toured all the tourist spots in Rome, Florence, and Pompeii and then headed for the Italian "Outback" to see where my grandparents came from. My Dad's family was from Grello in the Umbria region and my Mom's side of the family came from Roccacinquemiglia in Abruzzi. I have to say that those two regions were pretty remote and it didn't look like too much had changed there in the last 1500 years or so . . . . A number of the farmers were still using horses to drag their plows around and goat herding seemed to be the predominant endeavor! I could certainly see why my grandparents (and probably 5 million other Italians) got the hell out of there and immigrated to the USA!! . . . . Anyway, driving to and from these regions was quite the adventure! The main North South freeway in Italy is the A1 Autostrada and it was in beautiful shape. There was usually 4 to 5 lanes in each direction and as I recall the posted speed limit was just a "recommended" top speed of sorts . . . . We had a pretty snappy little rental car and since I was fairly used to driving quickly I thought the A1 would be a no sweat exercise . . . Man, was I ever wrong! Things weren't too bad as long as you stayed in the far right lane but if you even thought about venturing into the middle lanes or God Forbid the far left lane things got real dicey almost instantaneously! Before I worked up the courage to venture out into that far left mother I always checked my mirror really well and usually accelerated up to the max speed our little sports car would go which was around 200kmh (125mph) . . . There was always a lot of buffeting at those speeds especially if you were passing a truck which was often travelling around 100 mph itself . . . Anyway, out of nowhere would suddenly appear a top of the line Audi or BMW that three seconds before wasn't even in my mirror . . . . These guys would courteously start flashing their high beams at you a couple hundred yards back and you had better be clear of their lane when they caught up to you . . . I usually was but a few times I just couldn't get out of the way any quicker and they were on me in a heartbeat . . . Now when I say "on me" I mean within a millimeter of our rear bumper at 125 mph . . . . I guess if you're a NASCAR driver that's no big deal but it pretty much made me want to kill the stupid mother f**ker on the spot!! Additionally, I could clearly see the driver making obscene gestures at me as he weaved back and forth, laying on his horn, and flashing those high beams . . . When I finally was able to get out of the way, off he'd go at warp speed flipping me a couple parting gestures as he searched for his next victim. Another sure fire way to get flipped off and create bad feelings was to pass anyone on the right even though there was 4 or 5 lanes of travel and another lane between you . . . . It made no difference if traffic was light and speeds were slow as this was apparently a huge no-no to Italian drivers and judging by their over the top reactions, ten times more serious than whizzing by in the left lane at 300 kmh . . . . go figure!? However, the most impressive of all were the MV Augusta and Ducati motorcycles that ripped by us, smoothly weaving in and out of traffic, at those same speeds . . . . The fastest I had ever gone on my 750 Trident was around 130mph, so I was duly impressed with these cats!! I have to admit it was pretty awesome but we almost always saw those same guys filling up at the next gas station in the median. Ultimately, just like our own home-grown morons, they got nowhere fast! We saw a couple of the fast car drivers actually bump the car ahead of them at those speeds in an attempt to force them to move over . . . . !! Really made our I-5 aggressive drivers look like a bunch of pussies in comparison! Unbelievably, we didn't see one accident on our whole trip . . . still can't figure that one out!

This next little ditty is slightly off topic but I thought it was kind of unusual at the time . . . The rest areas on the Autostrada were also in the median which wasn't too bad of an idea but the restroom facilities themselves were a bit stark to say the least. Inside there were no toilets or urinals just holes in the floor, sometimes with a little short partition on each side for privacy but usually there was just a row of holes. The Italian DOT did provide omni-directional indents in the concrete on either side of the hole that looked like footprints and that is where you had to position yourself to hit that hole in the floor which was only about 4 inches in diameter . . . . Some of the fancier restrooms had little short 3 inch handles on either side of the hole to help stabilize you a bit during the aiming process while squatting . . . Trying to hit those holes while standing took some pretty accurate aiming and lots of practice if you didn't want to splatter your shoes . . . Debbie had similar complaints about the ladies' room! Using them reminded me of what Dave Gardner had told me about the plastic Port a Johns in our Cessnas: "Anyone can piss in one but it takes a real man to take a dump in it!" Even more amazing was the fact that almost every restroom in Italy had an "attendant" inside! I don't know what crime you had to commit to get that assignment but it had to have been the "shittiest job" in the world!! Most of the attendants I saw just sat in a corner, looking very forlorn, with hose in hand ready for the next clean-up . . . . Another surprise occurred in the restroom on the train between Florence and Bologna . . . . Not only was it extremely small and stinky but when I shoved the little pedal down on the floor to flush the toilet the little trap door in the bottom of the bowl opened up right onto the tracks "whizzing" by under the train . . . . And people complain about our environmental laws . . . .

One nasty winter's morning I woke up to view about 16 inches of fresh snow outside but it was an otherwise nice day and severe clear. I drove on down to the old blue T-hangar, and fired up our propane *Red Dragon* airplane pre-heater to warm the place up a bit. I assumed there would be no flying today, got on our creeper and commenced to clean the oily belly of the plane with some 100 low lead. I had the outside speaker on my patrol car cranked up in case radio called for any reason . . . . This was before the era of cell phones and pagers so communications were always by state radio or a land line. Sadly, just as I had fallen asleep on the creeper radio called and wanted to know if I was available for an emergency flight. This wasn't unusual after a snow storm as we were called out quite regularly to look for stranded motorists in drifting snow areas. However this time was a little different. They wanted me to pick up Sgt. Sackman in Wenatchee and go look for a sniper up on Blewett Pass . . . . A sniper?? WTF . . . I assumed a deranged skier or snowmobiler had lost his marbles up on the mountain . . . . I popped over to Grant County Aviation and found out that the Wenatchee Airport was still closed for snow removal and in fact the only open airport in the area was right here at Moses Lake. I called Sgt. Sackman and he told me to just go look for the guy by myself which was fine with me since I knew it was going to be pretty bumpy up in the mountains and I really didn't feel like cleaning up a pile of frozen barf today. I stuck the red dragon hose into the engine intakes for awhile and got the old Continental nice and toasty before I tried to crank it. Good old 9624E started right off and I soon found myself the only plane in the sky that morning. It was a long ride to Blewett as I was facing a real stiff headwind even at low altitude and got the snot beat out of me near the south end of Mission Ridge. I cruised around near the summit for about 30 minutes but never saw anything resembling a sniper . . . . I was really getting pounded so I finally told radio I couldn't find anything and headed back to Moses Lake. The first sign of trouble was when I noticed a really strong odor of raw gas in the cockpit . . . . I immediately turned off all the master switches . . . While I was doing that I heard a muffled clank followed by a loud metallic rattle . . . . the engine suddenly started running on what sounded like three cylinders and the whole plane started shaking like crazy . . . . At this point I could really give a shit about the moderate turbulence outside and my mind was racing to figure out what this was. I tried switching tanks, pumped the primer a couple times, switched mags, ran it lean, ran it rich, rocked the wings, nothing worked . . . . I finally had to reduce power to around fifteen inches of MP as I was really worried the engine was going to shake itself out of its motor mounts . . . . I was getting a severe headache from the raw gas and severe shaking and opened the side window to breath. I was descending at around 500 fpm but was going downslope over the Colockum with a great tailwind so altitude wasn't a big concern yet. I tried to retrieve the fire-extinguisher from under the co-pilot seat and found that someone had mounted it in such a way that the seat had to be all the way forward to get to its release strap . . . . Well, those seats will not go forward unless someone is sitting in them so this really pissed me off on top of everything else happening . . . . Right in the middle of this whole affair I got into the co-pilot seat, crammed it all the way forward, squeezed back into the left seat and finally got that god-damned extinguisher out . . . I gotta tell you, it is not easy for a guy my size to pull that maneuver off in that tiny cramped space . . . . The term "You look like a monkey fu**ing a football" pretty much describes that scene . . . . To top it off, I hit the flap lever with my leg so right in the middle of everything I ballooned up and nearly stalled the damn thing trying to get back in my seat. By now I was over the Quincy airport but could see it hadn't been plowed either . . . . I wanted to set this damn thing down before it caught on fire but even with all the shaking I was able to just hold altitude at about 1,000 feet indicating around 65 knots. I felt that if the fire broke out I could set it down immediately on a county road and hoped that the extinguisher would work . . . . I finally got close to the pattern at Moses Lake, turned on one radio, asked for a straight in to RWY 04 and never told them I had a problem . . . Capt. Swier was forever pounding it into our heads to always keep a low profile and to **never EVER** draw attention to any of our flying activities . . . I was just approaching Airman's Beach, on about a three mile final for RWY 04 when I pulled the power back slightly for the first time since just after the shaking started . . . . That God-damned Continental quit cold immediately!! . . . . I crammed the throttle all the way in but was rewarded with only a very quiet wind-milling prop . . . It was really nice to get rid of that God Awful shaking but making the runway was going to be a close one. I just barely managed to get it in the deep snow over the threshold gravel in a full stall, bounced it a couple times and just barely got up onto the plowed compact snow of the runway . . . I had tried to put some flaps down but nothing happened . . . . I forgot I had turned the Masters off again after calling tower . . . . Regardless, I was sure glad to get that bitch back on terra firma and onto a plowed runway nonetheless! I tried to restart it on the ground but it just wouldn't light off. I finally had to tell the tower that I needed a tow into Grant County Aviation . . . I expected them to have all kinds of questions since I was blocking an active runway but they just calmly said they would send Stan from Grant Co. Aviation over to tow me in . . . There wasn't exactly a lot of traffic around that day . . . . Once in Stan's nice heated hangar he pulled the top cowl off and immediately saw the problem . . . . The left cross-over (balance) tube had become detached from the intake manifold and was just hanging there . . . Stan said I was real lucky it was the left side since the other side would have dumped all that raw gas right onto the exhaust pipe. It was determined that one of our WSP mechanics forgot to tighten the balance tube clamp during the last 100 hour inspection and it eventually worked itself free . . . No wonder I only had three cylinders firing! I called Capt. Swier and filled him in on everything . . . Lieutenant Gary Smith came over the next morning to inspect the airplane. He was not a happy camper but did thank me for not getting on the radio and calling a Mayday and creating a lot of bad publicity.

As a result of the investigation they fired the mechanic responsible for the mistake and at my insistence, re-mounted that fu**ing fire extinguisher between the seats on the floor! They also set into place a system for the maintenance personnel where the mechanics always checked each other's work and then each marked the job with some colored wax or something. We never had another serious maintenance issue once that program was initiated. At our next troopers meeting Trooper Jeff Harshman 311 presented me with a real ugly branch off of a local Maple tree which was inscribed with the date of my dead stick landing and the tail number of good old N9624E . . . . As usual, nothing was ever put in my personnel file about "possibly" having done a good job that day . . . . When they eventually sold that plane some guy from Seattle bought it and I used to see it from time to time tied down outside in the weeds, at the North end of Boeing field. Her paint is all faded now and she's looking rather neglected and forlorn . . . . She was a good bird in spite of everything!

Speaking of good birds, while convalescing from my broken leg back in '76 I revived my long time love affair with WWII warbirds which started anew when I read *BAA BAA Black Sheep* by Greg Boyington. During that time I read many other classics from that era including *Serenade to the Big Bird, Honest John, A Yank in the RAF, Duel of Eagles*, etc., etc. I was really taken with those guys and saw early on why Tom Brokaw labeled them the greatest generation. So, in '79 Deb and I began our annual trek south every September for the next twenty years to Stead Field for the Reno Air Races and warbird heaven. That first trip was very memorable for Deb's Mom Toni who accompanied us that first time. During WWII she had been a member of the RAF in London and personally witnessed the carnage and devastation brought on by the Germans during the Blitz. Later in the war, while walking home from work one evening, a German V1 buzz bomb exploded near the end of the street she was walking down and the concussion from the blast knocked her down and rolled her into a ball. Anyway, at the '79 Air Races there was a guy there with a pristine Mark IX Spitfire demonstrating a Battle of Britain scramble. When the claxon sounded, he ran out to his bird, got it started while being strapped in, took off straight from his parking spot and flew a real tight 360 around the home pilon in less than two minutes from when the claxon went off . . . Man, that was an impressive sight and the roar of that Merlin was just awesome! I saw the tears in Toni's eyes and will never forget that moment. During the Gold Cup race on Sunday that year we were seated in the east end of the grandstands just as Steve Hinton came across the finish line on the last lap in his famous P51 *The Red Baron*, racing John Crocker for the win . . . . He pulled up rather dramatically just as he crossed and it was apparent he was having some serious trouble . . . He made a big sweeping right 90 left 270 turn to come back and land to the West but went out of sight below a steep hill just east of the airport . . . . The next thing we saw was a huge billowing black and orange cloud of flames and smoke boiling up from just below the approach end to the runway followed by a muffled 'ka-wuummpp' . . . . Jesus, this was just unbelievable . . . . I know it brought back a lot of bad memories for Toni and the whole crowd of 100,000+ spectators was just deathly quiet. Bob Hoover flew over the crash site in his familiar P51 chase plane, *Old Yeller*, performed a flawless aileron role to salute a fallen aviator, and just said 'So long Steve' on the radio . . . Man, that was one somber drive back to the hotel. It was with tremendous relief when we heard later on the news that Steve had survived the crash somehow but had sustained a broken back.

Anyway, I was hooked on P51's, the air races, and the warbird movement in general from that day forward. Not long afterwards while visiting The Planes of Fame museum in Chino I made reservations to go for a flight in their P51D *Spam Can* N5441V. Steve Hinton was supposed to take me up but on the day of the flight Mike DeMarino was assigned instead. I asked him to give me the full meal deal and did he ever!! We did loops, rolls, emmelmans, split esses, Cuban eights, and a high speed low level pass down a canyon in the San Gabriel Mountains that I will never forget . . . I have to say that was the high point of my aviation career until 6 years later when I actually got an hour of stick time in a P51 named *Crazy Horse* down in Florida. Lee Lauderback at Stallion 51 was the pilot that day and just after takeoff he gave me the stick which I had for the whole flight including the landing, (although I certainly felt him on the controls from time to time)! Rolls and loops were effortless but when we went into the stall series I learned a lot about flying airplanes with high-wing loading . . . . I was a bit too aggressive on the first couple stall recoveries and immediately found myself in a secondary stall which Lee was not too complimentary about . . . . My biggest memory of flying the Mustang was how much trimming you had to do to keep the stick forces reasonable . . . . It just accelerated so quickly and the aerodynamic control pressures build so rapidly . . . In my first P51 ride at Chino all I remembered was how hot and cramped it was in the back seat sitting all hunched over right on top of that huge oil radiator. In Crazy Horse I was so busy I didn't notice the heat and with its blown bubble canopy I had lots of head room. My lasting impression of flying in Mustangs is the total lack of that beautiful trademark Rolls Royce Merlin engine sound you normally hear from the ground. Inside a P51 at full power all you hear is the sound of twelve jackhammers trying to tear the plane apart . . . It was somewhat quieter with the prop pulled back in cruise though. We made a high speed low level run across a lake south of Orlando that I still have dreams about . . . . There is good reason they call the Mustang 'The Cadillac of the Sky'. When the guys back at work found out I had flown a Mustang some just came up to me and reverently touched my sleeve just to vicariously share in that rare aviation experience.

Myself in Lee Lauderback's P51D Mustang "Crazy Horse" just after the flight in 1990

Not long after my first P51 ride in Chino I got to witness a real WWII air show, minus the spectators, while I was at work. We had a real bad fire season one summer up north of Omak and myself and 328 were dispatched to the Omak airport for several days to handle various transportation duties. We were kept pretty busy hauling various elected officials, media, local law enforcement, Natural Resource personnel, making supply runs, etc., to and around the fire zone. In between flights was the highlight for me since several fire fighting companies had brought their WWII era planes, converted for use as water bombers, to the fire. There were several PBY Catalinas, TBM Avengers, A26 Invaders, converted single tail B24 bombers, and best of all, the greatest twin engine piston fighter ever manufactured, Grumman F7F Tigercats, two of them!! All of the planes appeared to be severely overloaded on every takeoff. . . . After gear retraction, they would always drop out of sight down in the valley after departing to the south from Omak. You could hear them growling away down there in the valley and just when I expected to see that big ball of orange and black smoke again you'd catch sight of them barely climbing and gingerly turning back north towards the fire. When those Tigercats came back over the airport, with their two huge Pratt and Whitney R2800's roaring away, I was just transported to a different time and era . . . Those were the best three days of my WSP career!

A few years later Steven Spielberg decided to film a large portion of his fantastic movie *"Always"* at the Ephrata airport. We had moved our operation from Moses Lake by that time into an old WWII hangar at Ephrata and Spielberg loved its nostalgic 'forties' look. So for the duration of the shoot, we had to move back to Moses Lake while the film crew "re-conditioned" our hangar to make it look more like a training firebase in "Flatrock, Colorado". We spent a lot of time with the film crew and asked a lot of stupid questions. I climbed into one of the A26 Invaders used in the movie and I was just itching to go fly it. My new flying partner, Trooper Curt Hattell 513, got a part time job at the local FBO, flying the daily movie film to Spokane each night after the day's shooting. From there it was jetted to Los Angeles for Spielberg to review when he wasn't in town. The only scene from the movie I got to watch was when John Goodman was sitting on top of an old WWII ammo. bunker at the Ephrata (Flatrock) airport sipping iced tea under his umbrella when he supposedly got a load of red fire retardant dumped on him by the new guy in an A26. In reality, they made about a dozen runs on that bunker (no-one was actually on the hill) until they got the right shot. That whole area was stained red for several years thereafter and when I was on a ten mile final for RWY 20, I could see that red hill quite clearly. A mechanic at the Ephrata FBO was an extra in the movie and can be seen in the background kibitzing after a runaway airplane tug crashed into Holly Hunter's house. Before Curt was assigned as my new partner, Trooper Ben Hamilton 314 was briefly assigned to Ephrata after 328 left the section and went back to working the road. Ben had a really cool early model jet ski that was faster than stink but was nearly impossible to mount (at least for me) in the water. Every time I tried to get on the damn thing the jet water blast blew my swim trunks off before I could get on the seat . . . Not a pretty sight! Ben soon transferred to Yakima to be "closer" to our sergeant . . . . I know, go figure . . . . ?

Deb finally graduated from CWU and got her BS Degree in Biology in 1987. That commute from Ephrata to Ellensburg every day wore her out as well as two of our cars.

She was soon hired by the Wash State Dept. of Fish and Wildlife and finally got her dream job as a wildlife biologist working right out of their Ephrata office. The next three years were very serene for us and we were quite happy and content with our lives and jobs. In our time off we went water-skiing at Billy Clapp Lake and O'Sullivan, fishing for Silvers and Rainbows in Lake Roosevelt behind Grand Coulee Dam, took our German Shorthair Tippi out for long runs and swims, and rode our mountain bikes around the countryside. The rest of the time was spent eating Mexican food at Hectors or his Dads place in Moses Lake . . . . Boy do I miss those guys!

One of the traffic courses we worked a lot was abeam the Yakima Firing Center Restricted Area 6714 at Milepost 22 on I-82. I loved this course since there was no general aviation planes to bother us due to its proximity to the Firing Center. We simply checked in with the Army's Vagabond Airport Tower and all they requested was we update them every 15 minutes on what we were doing. They would keep us informed if any 'fast movers' or bombers were coming our way and I always enjoyed the 'air show' when those guys did their thing close enough for me to see the results on the range. There just happened to be another 'distraction' in this stretch of I-82 . . . . Between the two rest areas there is one of the biggest structures on the West Coast of the U.S . . . . the Fred Redmond Memorial Bridges. They span a huge chasm with enough room underneath to fly a 747 with a space shuttle attached to it . . . . Getting a 182 under there just didn't seem like much of a problem. The first time I ventured down that canyon I was down in the sagebrush and when I looked up at the underside of the bridge it must have been 500 feet above me . . . . not a big deal. Over the years I worked my altitude clearance up to around 50 feet under but on my last pass I saw something that ended my bridge underflying career forever . . . . Just as I was directly under the southbound span I caught a glimpse of a really thick steel cable dangling down that I had never noticed before . . . It was just off my left wing tip . . . . Man, that set my little heart a pitter pattering and I vowed to never be so stupid ever again!! Several years later while on a flight with an old Westside pilot I shall refer to only as the "Destroyer," I was dared to fly under a bridge up near Hadlock in Puget Sound after I had been bragging to him about my Redmond Bridge escapades . . . . When we got closer to it I saw that this was an entirely different ballgame than the I-82 spans . . . . Jesus, this bridge was only about 100 feet long and even at low tide the clearance under it just might barely allow a small rowboat to go under as long as no-one stood up . . . I deferred but asked the "Destroyer" if he would demonstrate his technique for me . . . . He took the controls from the right seat and set up for what looked like to me was going to be a very low pass under that mother . . . . Just as I was about to pull some elevator myself he did the same and we sailed over the top unscathed . . . . He was cool and only said that the tide wasn't quite low enough yet and that we would try again later . . . . Sure we would!!

On another afternoon while working traffic again down on I-82, this time near Wapato at Milepost 44, I got an urgent call from radio to assist Toppenish PD looking for a homicide suspect just east of town. I was there in a couple minutes and was told by Toppenish PD on LERN frequency that the suspect had just shot his girlfriend and they thought he was hiding in a drainage ditch on the outskirts of town. I made passes from the East and from the West along the ditch, trying to get a good angle on the sun and to reduce shadow issues . . . . techniques that I had learned the hard way while looking for marijuana grows up in the mountains. Man, I wasn't seeing anything . . . The water was murky and I guessed he was underneath breathing through a straw or something . . . After about a half hour with no results I advised the ground guys I was going to try a couple of really low passes in hopes of flushing that bastard out of the ditch with all the noise . . . . I got that poor old Skylane all cross controlled and came down the canal about twenty feet off the water at max power, half flaps, with full rudder and full opposite aileron cranked in to keep my left wing right down in the ditch at about a 60 degree bank angle . . . . I popped up at the other end, did a course reversal then came back the other way . . . . Now I don't know if these maneuvers scared the bad guy or not but I had certainly scared myself shitless . . . . I was below the powerlines on one side of the canal and level with a fence on the other . . . . This might be 'all in a day's work' for a crop-duster pilot but I needed to head for the hangar after that last pass to change my shorts. I only got a few miles north when TPD came on the radio and said the suspect had just come boiling up out of the cat-tails with his hands up screaming "No Mas! No Mas!" . . . . Well, that felt really good but I was already thinking ahead to the case report that I would have to file about the incident. Even though we were given quite a bit of latitude by the FAA while conducting police flying operations, I decided to not be too specific about my "flushing out" altitude during that mission.

When the World's Fair 'EXPO 86' rolled around up in Vancouver, British Columbia, the brass determined there would be a lot of traffic coming northbound up I-5 from Oregon and California the first week or so of the event. Consequently, they wanted all five traffic airplanes in the air simultaneously, between Portland and Bellingham, evenly spaced to nail as many speeding out-of-staters as possible. Myself and 328 were sent to Bellingham for several nights and assigned to work the hell out of a stretch of I-5 in the vicinity of Government Way and the Birch Bay Lynden exits. The other four Cessnas were covering all the best traffic courses south of us. I have to say that it was a free-for-all and all of us racked up some huge numbers and worked some really long hours. It was a lot of fun and our efforts made all the papers although some of the more 'liberal' media sources condemned us for harassing all those innocent motorists using illegal and unfair 'Orwellian' big brother eye in the sky tactics . . . . Tough shit we all thought! There were several cars that got stopped multiple times on the same day during the trip between Portland and Bellingham with a lot of 'three-peaters'. The guy that took the grand Booby Prize was a moron out of California who got called out and stopped by every single Cessna traffic plane that day . . . Five speeding tickets from five different WSP airplanes in the span of three hours. I remember the ground trooper who stopped him after we called him out said the dipstick was bragging about it and showed that trooper all four of his previous tickets . . . . Man, this idiot really deserved the Darwin Award for failing to evolve!! It has always been my contention that when state troopers encounter morons of this caliber that if they were given the discretion to perform a "free" painless roadside sterilization procedure on them, with of course a well hidden government approved laser, I firmly believe the world would be a much safer and enjoyable place in the relatively near future!! These kind of days and people like that clown always made me think of the delightful *Alan Parsons Project* song *'Eye in the Sky'*. . . . I think the lyrics went: *'I am the eye in the sky, looking at you . . . I am the maker of rules dealing with fools'* Man, you just couldn't say it any better!!

One quiet afternoon while slowly circling over SR 2 out near Cashmere, working traffic with some of the Wenatchee regulars which usually included guys like Davis Richmond, Don Whitman, George Lang, or Bill McCunn, I caught a glimpse of a motorcycle weaving in and out of traffic at an horrendous rate of speed . . . I had never seen anything going this fast before . . . even in Italy! I almost missed the mark but just caught him with a watch . . . . At the ten second point he was almost to the next 1/2 mile mark . . . . Jesus, this guy was way over 150 mph . . . . I was fumbling with the watch and trying to keep an eye on him when I saw him just dynamite the brakes only a hundred yards from the next mark . . . . When he did cross the mark he looked like he was only doing 45 mph or so . . . . Son of a bitch!!! I immediately saw the problem . . . there was a Chelan County deputy going the other way in his green patrol car that had spooked him . . . . He still averaged 147 mph which was the highest speed I'd ever seen while a traffic pilot. I later did some calculations and estimated that he would have averaged around 170 mph if it weren't for the untimely passing of that deputy . . . Damn it!! Anyway, I called him out at 147 to my three waiting troopers and they were ecstatic to get some clown at nearly three times the speed limit . . . Bill advised me that it was a juvenile with no motorcycle endorsement and the bike was one of the latest Ninja, Assassin, Monster crotch rocket something or other probably capable of 200 mph. After a couple minutes I looked down and saw a pickup stopped in front of all the troopers . . . I assumed it was just another pissed off motorist who wanted to describe to those troopers how that asshole had recklessly passed him back a few miles doing better than Mach 1. As I circled above I thought I saw some kind of skirmish going on and thought I saw someone on the ground getting the shit kicked out of them. Turns out the owner of the bike had driven by the scene, saw his little brother getting arrested by the cops and his bike being impounded. When he walked up and found out what had happened he freaked and started to beat the crap out of his sibling before all those big strong troopers intervened . . . . I imagine that holiday get togethers for that family were a bit strained that year.

In 1989 I felt it was about time to get back into multi-engine flying since my last flight in that old Aztec was back in 1985 at the Hangar Flying Club. I ran into a great guy at the airport named Skip Gregoire who just happened to own a beautiful Beech Baron. Skip had been a King Air test pilot at the Beechcraft factory in Wichita, after his flying tours in Viet Nam were over, and luckily he was also a CFIIME. I asked him what he would charge me to get my ATP in that Baron and he just casually replied, 'Oh, just put some gas in it once an awhile . . . !!' Well, I couldn't pass that deal up so we started flying that beautiful bird a couple times a week. I was a bit rusty flying multi-engine birds at first but immediately became aware of the biggest difference between a Baron and an Aztec . . . It was most apparent when Skip would simulate a failed engine on takeoff or during a go-around . . . . In the Aztec, if it was a warm day, it simply wouldn't climb and certain death was imminent . . . . In the Baron on one engine, it climbed as good as a Skylane on a cool day . . . . It just wasn't an emergency at all . . . . Skip would have to reduce power on the "operating" engine just to make it feel like a real single engine emergency . . . What a great plane! He finally thought I was ready for the ATP check ride so I scheduled an FAA examiner from Renton for the test. Man, the practice flight plan he made me write up was brutal and I took way too long checking and re-checking my calculations . . . The damn thing was about 2500 miles long with multiple stops and constantly varying passenger and luggage loads . . . To make matters worse, he kept coming into my little cubicle, looking over my shoulder at my work and asking me if I was done yet . . . . When I finally finished and gave it to him he just put it in his briefcase without looking at it and said "It's getting dark, let's get this show on the road . . ." Geez, I did not have a good feeling about this ride at all!! I was under the hood the whole time and he was vectoring me all over the place . . . . We did a couple non precision approaches at Wenatchee and then he tells me to go direct to some obscure intersection out near Quincy and to hold West with left turns . . . Well, up until that moment I always felt I was pretty good at determining holding entries but he really threw a curve ball at me with this made up scenario . . . . Even after I made my first turn upon arriving at the fix I really didn't know if I had gone the right way or not . . . . I figured he'd say something immediately if I went the wrong way and was expecting the worse . . . . it stayed quiet and when my time was up I made the next turn and I guess it was right because then he said "Alright, let's do some stalls under the hood" . . . . Shit! Skip and I had never practiced that before but what the hell . . . . I was sweating like a whore in church but they seemed to be going pretty well right up until we started getting a bunch of smoke in the cockpit . . . . I had just cycled the landing gear several times for the various stalls he requested and thought that maybe we got that gear motor a little hot . . . . Before I could say anything he calmly replied that he saw this all the time in Barons and that it was indeed the landing gear motor burning the grease off itself . . . . The last thing we had to do was a single engine ILS down at Moses Lake so I was cleared direct to the Pelly outer marker for the full procedure. He failed the engine in the procedure turn as expected and after cleaning everything up and finishing the single engine approach checklist off we went down the glideslope . . . . Man, Skip and I had done this a bunch of times and I was feeling pretty confident . . . I never got more than half a dot off until about a one mile final . . . Just then, for some unknown reason, I touched the throttle and made some minute totally unnecessary power reduction . . . . Just a few seconds later when I looked back at the glide slope it was just going past two dots low . . . Shit! Shit! Shit! . . . . I immediately added power and got the glideslope back . . . . I was OK at DH . . . . He told me to take the hood off, gave me back the other engine and we did a touch and go. Then all he said was "Take us back to Ephrata". Half way there he says "You do realize that three dots low, even for a second, is a busted check ride . . . . ?" He didn't say another word until we were inside the FBO . . . . Then all he said was "That had to have been the weakest and most borderline ME ATP checkride I have ever witnessed in my career . . . . But . . . . since you never got to three dots deflection on the glide slope during that single engine approach, and caught your deviation in the nick of time, I'm going to pass you . . . ." He never even looked at my long distance cross country flight plan I had sweated blood over . . . . I guess he was in a hurry to get home . . . . Other than my instrument ride, that was the roughest checkride I'd ever been through!

I ran into Skip several years later while on a King Air flight hanging around the FBO at Wenatchee waiting for passengers. He said something very peculiar had happened to him while flying his Baron a few months ago. Apparently he was in cruise, smooth air, autopilot engaged, when his seat suddenly dropped a couple inches and became slightly canted to the inside . . . . At the time he thought it was just something wrong with the seat mechanism. When he landed he discovered the door was slightly jammed up as well. Unfortunately, when the mechanics took everything apart it turned out to be a little more than a broken seat . . . . The main wing spar had broken! Unbeknownst to Skip at purchase time, it had not been disclosed to him that his Baron had once been ditched in Tampa Bay (saltwater) for some reason . . . Apparently the mechanics there didn't do a real good job cleaning it up afterwards other than plastering on a gorgeous paint job followed by the owner immediately putting it for sale. Turned out the main spar was severely corroded and Skip was extremely lucky that the wings hadn't folded up on him the rest of the way as he sat in his collapsed seat that day . . . . He told me that he got the plane 'really cheap' . . . . and I think we all know why now! I also think that the glideslope deviation on my checkride was also somehow affected by that metal fatigue and corrosion . . . . Couldn't have been pilot error!?

Skip was also responsible for me getting appointed as a Grant County Port Commissioner in 1990 . . . A position whose job description I knew absolutely nothing about . . . . I went to one meeting and the highlight was when someone asked me if our hangar was OK . . . . It was . . . . Later I suggested it wouldn't hurt to spray some Paraquat on all the weeds growing up through the cracks out on all the taxiways at Ephrata since nearly every time after I shut down at the pumps I noticed my prop was now green. "We" took care of that awful problem right away!! That was the extent of my career as a port commissioner since we transferred to Olympia shortly thereafter . . . . Looked good on my resume a few years later though . . . .

Well, I guess you just can't read a cop or aviation story that doesn't include a little gratuitous sex, violence and nudity or no-one would ever read these books. All I can say about this episode is that I was very young (40) and since I don't remember at this time who my partner was when this episode occurred, I blame him for everything. After we had moved the plane to Ephrata we finally had a full service FBO to take care of us, pump our gas, and even had someone to wash our windshield for free. At Moses Lake, we had to do everything ourselves and there was nothing I hated more than standing up on that slippery ladder, in the blowing snow, filling those long range (92 Gal.) Skylane

tanks with a pump that barely put out a trickle . . . What a treat! The
new FBO owner at Ephrata was a little unconventional, by Ephrata
standards, and never wore shoes . . . even in the winter. He was a
very nice young man and hadn't been there for very long when one
day he showed up at work in a cast from his chest down to his toes.
Apparently, he had tried to cross the Cascades in the winter in a VFR
only plane, got boxed in while down in the treetops in a canyon during
a whiteout, and attempted to land in a clear cut . . . . Everything was
going pretty well until he suddenly hit a stump that some careless
logger had left in his pathway . . . . He suffered a compound femur
and was lucky that some media people just happened to be in the area
doing a story on low reservoir levels and saw him crash. He was a
long time recuperating from that incident . . . . Then one day, after
he was all better, we came back from flying to find him moaning and
groaning behind the counter on the floor inside the FBO . . . . Man,
he was a mess . . . two black eyes, cuts all over his face, a broken nose,
bent teeth, blood all over the place . . . We thought he must have been
in another rip-snorter with his plane and somehow just managed to
crawl into the office afterwards . . . . Turns out he just got beat up
this time . . . . He admitted it was all his fault and that it involved
a female employee who just happened to have a husband who did
not take too kindly at his inappropriate 'activity' with his wife . . . .
Anyway, shortly thereafter he hired another young lady to be his line
girl at the FBO. Luckily, for everyone concerned, this young lady was
single . . . . Additionally, she was drop dead gorgeous, and although
of little importance to myself, since I was happily married, she had a
chest that Dolly Parton would be envious of . . . .

Normally, when I returned to Ephrata, I would taxi up to the gas
pumps, note my ending Hobbs time, jump out of that Skylane
sweatbox and head for the potty ASAP while the line personnel
serviced the plane. However, when my current partner and I flew
together lately, I noted that our routine became slightly altered,
especially on those hot muggy days when the windshield would just
be covered in green and yellow bugs. I thought that he might be
having trouble with the heat as he seemed to go into "slow motion"
on those days. After I got out to go potty, he seemed to spend an

inordinate amount of time sitting in that hot airplane slowly totaling up our flight sheets, checking Hobbs times, messing with the fuel log, etc etc . . . While he was thusly occupied, one of the line guys would start pumping gas and then the new line girl trainee brought out her little three step ladder to clean our windshield. On some of those really hot days she was often forced to wear some kind of flimsy halter top or the occasional tube top . . . I'm sure her attire was under doctor's orders to prevent herself from suffering a heat stroke or some other hot weather related medical condition. Being of rather short stature, even with the three step ladder, she couldn't quite reach all the way across the windshield to wipe all the bugs off the other side . . . . She obviously had no choice but to lay herself prone across the windshield in order to get those stubborn bugs way over there. While she was so engaged I happened to notice one day that my partner, still sitting in the right seat, seemed to be having trouble breathing. The line girl's enormous and by now very 'wet' chest was smashed up against and rubbing back and forth across the windshield, polishing that portion right in front of him . . . . On those days I always felt that she was just exhibiting her excellent multi-tasking talents . . . . I never quite knew where my partner's thoughts were . . . . Later on, we discovered she was an excellent artist and she eventually did a portrait of my partner and I apparently "at work" somewhere in the Skylane. I felt the portrait was somewhat biased towards "younger" people since she painted me with grey hair, reclined in the right seat sleeping, coffee mug on my chest, with a box of donuts resting in my lap. My young partner was shown working his ass off all by himself, feverishly running two stopwatches while dealing with an outlaw motorcycle gang down below . . . . Life just isn't fair sometimes . . . . (My old partner still has that portrait by the way . . . .)

One cold winter's day I was returning from working traffic in Spokane and took a little bit of a circuitous route which brought me over Banks Lake just west of Grand Coulee Dam. It had been below zero for a week or so and the lake was frozen over. It hadn't snowed in that period and the ice was clear and smooth. I never did get my float plane rating so I felt that this was as good an opportunity as ever to start my own training. I let on down near the middle of the lake, just using approach flaps, and did a pretty smooth power on touch and go which in my mind qualified as a water landing. Just as I was powering up to climb out I noticed a herd of deer out on the ice just ahead of me. What they were doing out in the middle of a frozen lake I will never know . . . Anyway, they tried to scatter in all directions but none of them could get any traction on that glare ice and most of them fell onto their bellies as their legs splayed out from under them . . . . I felt pretty bad about scaring them like that but went ahead and recorded one 'non float' water landing in my log book.

During the summer months, after a long hot day of bug smashing, our Skylanes were often covered in a green and yellow sticky ooze from the thousands of insects we had murdered during the flight. We always washed the planes after gassing up but it really was a lot of work scrubbing that petrified bug juice off the wings, struts, windshield, tail, wheelpants, and nose of the plane when it was 100 degrees out. After awhile I got lazy and stupid and tried a different washing method a few times. There was almost always an afternoon buildup of cumulus clouds in the basin about the time I was returning from working traffic each afternoon. One day I penetrated a fairly innocuous looking specimen and found it to be very wet inside. Travelling at 150 mph gave me a pretty good wash job in only a few seconds. It was a little bumpy in there but no worse than all the hours I'd spent flying IFR over the mountains . . . . At least there was no ice in these mamas! When I landed I only had to do a light touch up on the remaining bugs and was back at the air conditioned Ephrata office sipping an iced tea with George Nutter in no time. On the days when there were some build-ups, and I was flying alone, this became my routine . . . . Not a particularly smart or safe routine but mine nonetheless. I got away with my cloud washing program for almost an entire summer until late one August afternoon when my luck caught up with me. While returning from Spokane I noticed some pretty good buildups near Central Grant County. By the time I was over Odessa I saw a nicely developed cumulus dead ahead and thought that it must be just chuck full of moisture. I had to climb a little to get a good angle on the thickest part of it and just as I went in I noticed that it suddenly got really dark. The next thing I knew I was being squashed down in the seat so hard that I grunted out like a cow giving birth . . . . It felt like about a four or five G updraft and within seconds I found myself about a thousand feet higher than when I entered this beast. It wasn't really too rough yet but getting darker and colder by the second . . . Then out of nowhere the whole plane was just splattered with clear ice like a fire truck was hosing me down . . . . Jesus it was loud, and with those nearly empty gas tanks that noise really reverberated inside the aluminum can I was flying. Then I found myself in a washing machine and for the first time in my life experienced what I knew could only be severe turbulence . . . . Man, I had no control of that plane whatsoever . . . I could not judge, react, think, or even imagine what control inputs I needed to do to save myself . . . . I truly felt helpless at that moment and expected the wings to come off at any second. While this was all going on I was still getting splattered with a combination of hail and very sticky clear ice and the whole plane was just covered in it. I kept thinking that when I first looked at this cloud it seemed to only be about a half mile thick . . . . What in the hell happened in just a couple minutes? Then out of nowhere there was a brilliant flash of white light that blinded the living shit out of me . . . I actually thought the plane had blown up for a second until I heard the ice splattering still going on. The next moment I found myself smashed into the cabin ceiling and I stayed there . . . . I had forgotten to cinch my belts down tight enough so the downdraft and negative G's were floating all 230 pounds of me quite easily. That poor old Continental O-470 started sputtering during the negative G's since these weren't the fuel injected models. I was going downhill like a freight train in a full blown microburst when I blew out the bottom of that bitch back into the sunshine . . . Although it seemed like I'd been in there for half an hour it had only been about 45 seconds or so before it spit me out like a popcorn kernel. It was really rough underneath that thing and I still couldn't see since my windshield was covered in ice. I kept the nose pointed down and was soon back in some 90 degree heat which took care of all the ice in short order. Jesus, I was really a mess and my whole body was shaking like a leaf . . . . That was absolutely the scariest thing I'd ever encountered in my life . . . If some macho pilot ever tries to say that severe turbulence is no big deal, I guarantee you he is a lying sack of shit! That was my last cloud washing flight but I have to say that my Skylane looked immaculate when I landed . . . . A heavy steam cleaning could not have done a better job on those bugs! In later years while flying radar equipped jets and turbo props I always gave any size build up a very wide berth usually to the consternation of my flying partners.

About this time I found out my old flight surgeon from Spokane had been killed in the crash of his Bonanza along with several of his buddies just after takeoff from Felts Field on their way to a fishing trip in British Columbia after his engine quit. They crashed right on Trent Ave. which is a busy four lane highway in the Spokane Valley. He had been an F6F Hellcat pilot in WWII and myself and Jim Kieran used to spend time in Jim's office with him, sipping adult beverages, listening to his tales of the war while the swing music of Tommy Dorsey and Glenn Miller played softly in the background. He was a great guy and his death really affected me for some reason. I started having nightmares about taking off from Felts Field and then getting caught flying low down Trent Ave. under all the power lines and phone wires unable to climb out. Every time I would try to pitch up some power lines appeared and I had to duck back down and was never able to get out of that predicament. I was in and out of Felts Field several times a week during this time and I thought about that dream on every takeoff. I continued to have that dream routinely throughout my flying career and its recurrence has only recently started to diminish since I retired.

Not all of our marijuana missions took place in the mountains or on forest service lands. Some of the 'smarter' growers took advantage of the flat land corn farmers who irrigated their big round circles with motorized wheeled sprinkler lines. The farmers only went out into their fields for planting the corn and harvesting it in the fall . . . They even fertilized the corn through the overhead sprinklers. The marijuana growers would fly over all of these corn fields looking for "planter skips" areas where the big wide corn planters would sometimes get clogged or run dry for a few seconds during the seeding process in the Spring and leave a fairly long 'arc' of unplanted soil. These arcs of unplanted ground were sometimes 50 to 75 feet long and around twenty feet wide. The bad guys would sneak on in to those spots at night, plant their small marijuana plants, and then let the farmer do all the watering and fertilizing all Summer long. The corn always grew faster than the cannabis so it was never visible from the edges of the field. Then right before the corn harvest the bad guys would sneak on in again and harvest all their huge plants that had been so lovingly cared for all summer long by the un-knowing corn farmers. We flew primarily with a deputy from the Grant County Sheriff's office who never got sick and knew where most of the illegal corn field marijuana grows were located. The marijuana plants have a very distinctive 'wet' emerald color when they are mature and stood out fairly well against the flatter corn leaf colors. Unfortunately, even though I had attended three airborne marijuana spotting schools, one at the OSP (Oregon State Police) Academy, one put on by the DEA in Spokane, and one at the WSP Academy, I still got fooled several times . . . There were at least three episodes when I got excited about some likely looking vegetation in the planter skips and started hollering on the radio to have someone hike in there to check them out . . . . Each time they turned out to be Canadian Thistles . . . . Dammit, they really looked like marijuana plants from 500 feet! Anyway, the trick was to try to fly between 10:30am and 1:30pm when the sun was high and there were no shadows to mess up your viewing. The flat country marijuana flying was so much more relaxing than some of those God-Awful flights up in the mountains with the horrible updrafts, downdrafts, and mountain wave activity (rolling winds following the terrain like water would). As I described earlier, getting caught in a narrow canyon and being unable to out climb the rising terrain at its end was really the pits!! Anyway, down in the corn fields none of that nonsense occurred and locating marijuana grows was a real gentleman's game . . . No canyon walls to run into, no huge fir trees, and no mountain wave . . . it was a piece of cake! I never did all that well finding it in the flat lands but a couple of the other guys found some monster grows out near Davenport a couple years after I left Ephrata. They were even able to make some arrests, which was actually pretty rare for those big grow operations, since the bad guys usually lived out of state and had some local help doing the dangerous stuff. Usually, after locating some plants, local deputies would march on in, cut all the plants down (some were 14 feet tall), and then have a big bon-fire in the closest gravel pit . . . . I heard rumors (unverified) that some guys were known to position themselves downwind during those burns . . . .

I was involved in quite an embarrassing incident one blustery winter day while working traffic near George on I-90. Radio advised us that a Ritzville trooper was chasing a stolen car Westbound from the Adams County line and coming our way at 100+. I headed back towards Moses Lake and picked them up near the Dodson Rd interchange. They looked like they were still moving pretty good but when I turned into the wind, which was out of the West that day, I suddenly realized just how fast they were going . . . which turned out to be a helluva lot faster than I could go in level flight! I had about a 40 knot headwind and since a Skylane is only good for about 135 knots on a good day I had a little problem. I was only at about 1,500 ft. AGL so I was able to stay with them for a little while in a slight dive but sooner or later I was going to have some terrain to deal with. I told the pursuing trooper that I probably wouldn't be able to stay with him for long . . . he didn't respond but I'm sure he was thinking something along the lines of what the f**k use is an airplane if it can't even keep up with a car?! However, the headwind wasn't quite as bad down at 100 ft and I was able to stay with them until George. When I made the slight turn to the southwest there I got the full brunt of the wind and started falling behind again. There were now about five patrol cars following this idiot so I knew that it was just a matter of time before he ran out of gas, blew his engine, or just ran off the road. The Ellensburg troops were set up near the Ryegrass Rest Area ready to deploy a spike strip . . . When they saw him coming they pulled it across the road and got him. Having to climb 2,000 ft. to get to the Ryegrass Summit, I missed the best part of the show by a minute. Since I was based in Moses Lake I saw and had coffee with the local troops all the time . . . They flipped me a lot of shit for several months about how slow I flew and what pieces of crap the WSP airplanes were since they couldn't even keep up with a Chevy Cavalier . . . . When I tried to explain headwinds and how they affect groundspeed they just laughed harder at my pathetic attempt with such a lame excuse . . . . It was pretty humiliating . . . .

So . . . . there I was flat on my back over the Mead airport with the ground rushing up at me, having just flown through the wake turbulence of that God damned Bonanza I was dog fighting with . . . . I was already in nearly a 90 degree bank when I hit his wake which tossed me inverted before I could even blink . . . . (Again . . . . I have never purported to be very quick on the up-take . . .) I was still ten years away from taking a 10 hour aerobatic course in an AT-6 but had always been told by the "old salts" that if you accidentally get inverted don't waste energy fighting it back the way you came, just go with the flow and finish the roll in the same direction . . . so that's what I did . . . However, I damned near dropped my 357 outside when the window came slamming down on my arm during my uncoordinated 5+ G roll recovery just above the Godamned trees . . . . I put my hogleg in the airplane side pocket and forgot about trading shots with this asshole for now and started climbing back up into the pattern . . . . It would have been just my luck to hit him and have his plane crash into a church and I no doubt would have gotten a couple complaint letters after an episode like that. Luckily, none of the DEA guys saw or at least said anything about my maneuver on the radio and I soon re-established a visual on the Bonanza. It looked like he was still doing a "heat check" (circling and looking for cops on the ground) and probably had never even seen me in the first place or if he had, just assumed I was some local moron doing touch and goes (which was actually a fairly accurate accounting of my activities). I tried to stay at his six and out of sight until he made up his mind what to do. I was also looking for any obvious signs of police activity on the ground myself but everything looked normal to me as the DEA guys were all driving non-descript vehicles most of which had been seized in previous drug raids. Well, Mr. Dipshit Bonanza driver finally sets her down and taxies over to a corner of the airport. The DEA guys waited until someone approached the plane before they moved in. It didn't take long and I suddenly saw four or five different cars come out of the woods and from behind houses and buildings and surround his plane and the other assholes. When everything looked under control I landed and taxied over to the arrest site. I walked over to the Bonanza driver who was cuffed and leaning against a car. The DEA agent told him that I was the guy that had been following him all over the state. He glanced over at my Skylane and casually says; "In that piece of shit?" I wasn't too offended but I'm sure he often wondered, while lying in his prison bunk cuddled up with his cellmate years later, how the hell I had kept up with him . . . . I certainly couldn't have without a 'little help from my friends' as the song goes . . . . Besides, I wasn't the one in cuffs about to lose my shorts forever. I wrote a really long affidavit about the day and was even interviewed by a federal prosecutor about the case since this dipshit had crossed state lines several times earlier in this drug deal. He eventually was found guilty of a myriad of drug trafficking charges, had his Bonanza seized, as well as his logging company and most of its assets which included his business property, trucks, pickups, several newer suburbans, and other neat stuff that the DEA got to confiscate. A trooper friend of mine, Jerry Devenpeck 419 owned a similar year and model Bonanza and eventually flew the plane out of Mead to its holding hangar during the trial. I don't recall now but I think Wash. State ended up with the bird afterwards. Before I took off from Mead that day one of the DEA agents walked over and asked me about that "wifferdoodle" thing I had pulled off while chasing that idiot. He said it looked pretty cool but thought for sure I was going into the trees.

Well, that was a fairly exciting day and it wasn't long afterwards that I started hearing rumors that there might be a vacancy opening up in Olympia for a King Air driver . . . . Now **that** was really exciting news!! It wasn't that I was getting tired of working traffic and turning circles every day, far from it . . . I really got a lot of satisfaction nailing tailgaters, the high speed junkies and those asshole aggressive drivers . . . . But like any other aviator climbing the ladder you always aspire to flying the turbine planes and taking the pressurized equipment up into the flight levels . . . More importantly, there were even better rumors afloat that the WSP was looking into buying a jet, courtesy of Governor Booth Gardner and Chief George Tellevik, to replace its old King Air 90 N88SP . . . . Now that kind of news went way beyond exciting!! . . . . This job was turning into a dream come true and I just hoped that I didn't 'screw the pooch' along the way and blow my shot. There were also many more opportunities for Deb in Olympia with Fish and Wildlife so dreaming about this possible transfer occupied a lot of our time.

I had one last exciting traffic pilot episode, while still based in Ephrata, back on my old turf in Spokane one afternoon. I was working with the West Beat troops (my old detachment) down near Spangle on SR-195 northbound. The guys were all lined up on the shoulder near Smythe Rd just over the crest of a hill. It was pretty slow and boring that day and I was having trouble keeping them busy. I finally noticed that a northbound car accelerated after he had gone by all the troops on the shoulder. The driver must have assumed there couldn't possibly be any more Staters ahead and thought it would be safe to gun it. I turned and stayed with him and my first check was 90 mph. I advised the troops what was going on and my buddy Loren Ottenbreit 378 took off to chase him down. My next check on this dipstick was 93 mph and I advised Loren he was really gonna have to put the hammer down to catch this idiot. I was half way through a third check, which I could already tell was going to be near 100 mph, when all of a sudden the car crashes down through the median, which had a pretty good high spot in that area, and from my vantage point I saw that he got quite a bit of air during this maneuver . . . . He landed hard right in the southbound lanes and took off like nothing had happened . . . Jesus, this was turning out to be a fun day after all!! I had Loren cross over the median ahead of him which he accomplished without getting quite as much air . . . Loren saw him go by and said it was an older Oldsmobile Toronado . . . . I thought man, those Toronados are really built tough to take that kind of abuse. Even after seeing a trooper crossing the median in front of him I still got a check of 88 mph on this clown southbound . . . . All the other troops had taken off northbound as well so the Smythe Rd intersection was now all clear of Staters and that's where the idiot turns in a huge sliding broadie and heads East. Smythe is a dirt road so it was pretty easy to follow the dust cloud he was laying down . . . . Obviously there were no marks for me to use but I could tell he was still doing about 80 or so. Loren was doing one helluva job overtaking him on a dirt road but had to eventually back off a little when all the dust began obstructing his vision . . . Finally the dipshit turns onto what I could see was a dead end spur road and I advised 378 that he probably had him now. I think the guy turned around but when he saw 378 blocking the road ahead of him he finally gave up. The driver was sober and had a clean record and said that he was just showing off to his little 8 year old brother what a great stunt driver he was . . . ??!! Another candidate for the trooper assisted "painless laser sterilization program" . . . .

I was changing the oil in the Skylane one afternoon and just finished safety wiring the oil filter when my newly issued pager went off in my shirt pocket. Radio told me to call Capt Swier in Olympia ASAP. Capt. Swier said that one of the King Air pilots, Trooper Brian Holliday 907, was being promoted to sergeant and would be transferring out of the section. He asked if I would be interested in taking his place in Olympia . . . . For the second time in five years, Dick had made me the happiest guy in the world!! When word got out that I was being promoted to multi-engine pilot, every single member of the aviation section called to congratulate me . . . It was one of those very memorable days!

CHAPTER 11

THE COUNTRY CLUB

Once again we had to put our home for sale and get ready to move across the state. We had just built a really neat house on 5 acres near Quincy the year before when it didn't look like there would be any openings in Olympia for a long time . . . . We loved that place and had the best garden we'll ever have there. I had to report for training with 476 the first of August 1990 so Deb got stuck listing the house and dealing with potential buyers. We decided to try the 'for sale by owner' route and initially just listed it in the local grocery store Nickel Nick newspaper to see if we got any bites. Surprisingly, we had an interested party call that first week and as luck would have it they made a great offer right away. They wanted to move right in so we had to put all our stuff in storage in Moses Lake and Deb went to live with her folks in Yakima with all our pets while I found a place for us in Olympia. I ran into a local builder who was just finishing a brand new house in a quiet area; he intended to rent it out for a few years before selling it. We really liked it and signed a lease right away. Since it wasn't done we got to pick colors and carpets and liked the idea of moving into a brand new rental. We wanted to build a house on secluded acreage eventually so this would be perfect for us in the interim. Before my training began I was given a stack of manuals for the King Air 90 and was told they weren't going to send me to Flight Safety for a KA90 initial since they would soon be selling the plane; so my co-pilot training was to be handled 'in house' by 476. N88SP was an A model King Air 90 and had seen some hard use; we couldn't fly it over 18,000 ft. since the cabin leak rate was pretty excessive, the autopilot didn't work, it had no flight director, and the radar was broken. Its saving grace was those big fat single main gear tires which made for a lot smoother landings than you normally got out of the KA200 with its tiny little dual donuts that were hard as a rock.

During training Dave and I flew all around the state and even landed it on the sod at Jeffco near Pt. Townsend. I was a little overwhelmed dealing with all the new turbine terminology and features such as: N1, N2, Condition Levers, Beta, Autofeather, Prop Synchrophaser, Yaw Damp, Compressor Stalls, Rudder Boost, Bleed Air, Auto ignition, Reversing Propellers, etc., etc . . . . Dave was a firm believer in the total immersion theory of ground school training so after a couple days of reading the POH and emergency procedures checklist we climbed in old 88 Sugar Pop (that's what all the Seattle Approach and Center controllers called her instead of the official 88Sierra Papa) and proceeded to bore some holes in the sky around Puget Sound . . . . I found it really easy to fly but all those crazy systems had me baffled and I could have really benefited from some sim. time and a structured initial at Flight Safety. Jumping from a C182 to a King Air was a quantum leap for me especially since I only had about 50 hours of multi-engine time in a PA23-250 Aztec and B55 Baron. I think Dave mistakenly felt I was doing fine overall, since my stick and rudder flying was OK, but before I could be considered a King Air co-pilot I had to pass an in depth oral with Capt. Swier. Man, I was not ready for him and knew my inadequate knowledge of systems was going to be quickly revealed. Sure enough, after we got through all the various Vspeeds and memory items he stumped me on the very first question on the fuel system . . . . He was not pleased at all . . . . Of all the guys in the world I did not want to disappoint it was him. Anyway, Dave and I spent a couple more days on systems until he felt I had them down cold. The next session with the captain went much better and I soon found myself added to the roster as a newly minted King Air 90 Co-Pilot. My first official turbine flight with paying passengers was to Ellensburg, Spokane, Lewiston, and back to Olympia on Aug. 17, 1990 with Dave as the PIC. What a thrill!

Myself climbing out of King Air 90 circa 1990

The new rental house was soon completed and Deb and I moved in right away. Due to her previous experience in Ephrata, she was soon offered a position as an Area Habitat Biologist with WSDFW and was able to continue with her dream job as well. They issued her a nice PU as her work vehicle and she parked it at home right along side my patrol car every night. She quickly found out that dealing with laid back, easy going, Eastern Washington folks was a thing of the past . . . . Nearly everyone she dealt with in Western Washington were up-tight, hyper-critical, Type A snobs . . . . My response to her complaints of "welcome to the club" was not well received . . . . More importantly for her, they classified our house as her "home office" since she was primarily responsible for Thurston Co. issues so she didn't have to drive to Montesano every day which was actually her base of operations. This home office situation became a huge issue later on but thankfully she was grandfathered (mothered) in due to her seniority and was able to keep that status until she retired while many other biologists lost that privilege.

Those first few years back in Olympia were the happiest of our lives and both of us were once again quite content especially since we knew that there would hopefully not be any more moves until we retired. In December of 1990 I was finally scheduled to attend *Simu Flite* down in Dallas for my King Air 200 Initial. This was pretty heady stuff and I really dug into the 200 manuals to hopefully avert repeating my debacle of an oral on the KA90 systems. Capt. Swier was kind enough to schedule me on a couple of 200 flights before I went and man what a difference between the two King Airs! . . . This machine climbed like a fighter, cruised easily at FL290 and with the *Raisbeck* Mod. (four bladed props), stopped on a dime when you went into full reverse, and it was a lot quieter in the cabin at cruise . . . . What a terrific bird she was . . . N222KA . . . BB49 . . . . I'm looking at a big custom model of her sitting on my desk as I write this . . . The WSP pilots normally attended *Flight Safety* in Wichita for Initials and recurrent training but I think *Simu Flite* was a little cheaper that year or they threw in the hotel or something for free and that's why I went to Dallas. My hotel was close to the facility and they had a free shuttle to *Simu Flite* every morning. Part of the ground school routine was to find an empty cubicle where you were supposed to study the various King Air Systems. At that time they had some sort of Sony computer that used a huge disc about a foot in diameter. About ten minutes after logging into the system the machine got hotter than hell and it was just impossible to not fall asleep in those cubicles . . . . There were always three or four guys walking around in that area trying to stay awake. More often than not I would glance into a cubicle and see some poor slob dead asleep in his chair while the "Sony Sauna" did its number on him. This study method worked fairly well and prepared you for the classroom work the next day. We had a ground instructor named Buck Weber . . . He was a terrific instructor but became a bit flustered with my first Sim partner Roxanne. She was extremely attractive and was already a very experienced freight pilot having flown Beech 99's for several years out of Raleigh Durham, So. Carolina. The transition to a 200 was a snap for her but Buck, who definitely qualified as a member of the "old school," treated her like she had a learning disability or something and always ended up right in front of her desk during his presentations. We all found it hilarious and Buck was always flabbergasted when Roxanne would ask a very detailed technical question to which he sometimes did not know the answer . . . . My second Sim partner was a southern gentleman from Alabama who was a pilot for NASA based in Huntsville I think . . . . After my earlier experiences with Alabama truck drivers he was certainly a breath of fresh from that region!! He was only there for a re-current and was as smooth as silk in the SIM; he was very patient with me and my ham-fisted Sim flying. He taught me several useful tips about flying 200's that I still use today. He also shared some very interesting astronaut stories with me that put some of those guys in a slightly different light than the "All American Wholesome" image Life Magazine portrayed them in back in the early sixties. Roxanne and I were staying in the same hotel and took the shuttle together every day, ate breakfast, lunch, and dinner together, and spent a lot of time in the King Air mock-ups (procedure trainers) going over checklists and emergency procedures. I know this all sounds slightly suspicious but it was all **very professional** . . . . Honest!!

Anyway, one afternoon Capt. Swier calls the *Simu Flite* business office and wants to talk to me . . . . Apparently the receptionist transferred him to the Sim instructor's offices. The guy there said something to Dick like "Oh, I think I saw Rick and his girlfriend going upstairs to the cafeteria to have lunch . . . ."Great, just what I needed . . . . Now Dick thinks I'm down here chasing skirts. When he finally got a hold of me he just asked if I was having fun and I said something like "No way, I'm busting my ass and sweating blood down here!" He just chuckled then told me he would be arriving in two days to do his own annual re-current training . . . . That was the first I'd heard about that . . . Later that night a couple of the other King Air students who had a car said they wanted to go out for Mexican. We all jumped in and headed for downtown Dallas. These guys were both Southerners and unlike my Sim Partner from Alabama, these clowns were not gentlemen. When we got downtown, we went past some black guys on the sidewalk and these two morons shouted out some vulgar racial obscenities at them then sped away . . . . Stupid ass redneck pricks! They didn't know I was a State Patrolman so I told them what my occupation was and promised to make their lives miserable if they ever tried that shit again . . . . When we got to the Mexican place,

Roxanne and I ate alone, and left those two racist pukes to themselves. They apologized later, saying they had too much to drink but I knew they were insincere and were just worried I might report them to their bosses (who were probably redneck pukes too) . . . .

Anyway, when Dick showed up I was in the break room having a bear claw with Roxanne. When I introduced them, Dick's eyes lit up and he suddenly was transformed into a clone of that debonair guy who does those *Dos Equis* beer commercials on TV, "the most interesting man on earth" . . . I felt myself being politely shuffled aside . . . About a half hour later he came over and told me we'd be flying in the Sim together during his recurrent . . . . I was surprised since I thought he was going to tell me that he and Roxanne would be flying in the Sim together and I was on my own . . . . That night he invites me into his room and pulls out a twenty or thirty year old bottle of *Glenlivet* Single Malt Scotch . . . I thought, man, this guy really knows how to travel! I don't really like Scotch but certainly wasn't about to turn down a drink from my boss . . . After several of those he finally starts asking me all kinds of political questions on environmental issues . . . . Geez, I didn't know where he was going with this . . . . I thought it might have something to do with Deb's line of work but wasn't sure . . . I guess he wanted to see if I was some sort of bleeding heart pinko commie due to my own liberal private school background. I pretty much stood my ground on the environmental issues and I think he liked that even though he disagreed with me on saving the Spotted Owl. After he lubricated himself a little more he revealed that after his recurrent he was flying up to Wichita to check on the status of the brand new Beechjet 400A he had ordered . . . . I tried to not act surprised but up until that moment I thought the Beechjet upgrade was just a rumor . . . Man, this was exciting news!! . . . . The 400A had the latest Collins Pro Line III FMS glass cockpit and was just the coolest jet out there . . . . I think I sort of violated some basic employee/employer decorum procedures when I asked if I could go along with him if I paid my own way and took annual leave . . . Dick then realized that he'd said too much and just said no and changed the subject . . . . Anyway, I went to bed excited and slightly hammered and soon woke up with a splitting headache . . . I do not like Scotch!

The next night Dick suddenly tells me we're going to *Billy Bobs* in Fort Worth! I had no idea what the hell that was but soon found out . . . . It was the biggest God damned bar I'd ever seen!! . . . The inside of it must have occupied several acres . . . . They even had an indoor rodeo arena where there was calf-roping and steer wrestling going on at all hours . . . . This was one crazy loud place! Dick had hooked up with an old friend from New Mexico who was the chief pilot for a bank as I remember . . . I got stuck with the banker's co-pilot who was just along for the ride like me. It was still fun and I enjoyed the rodeo events . . . Last time I saw Dick for several hours he was line dancing or square dancing in a conga line or something weird like that . . . Next day in the Sim, Dick showed me how a real professional pilot handles himself . . . Man he was smooth, never in a hurry, no wasted effort doing anything, all about finesse and a velvety smooth touch . . . . He was the best pilot I ever flew with! He went through his required syllabus so quickly that the Sim instructor said we had plenty of time left and asked him if there was anything else he'd like to do . . . As I recall, Dick responded by saying yes, "I'd like to do a single engine, partial panel, raw data NDB with a hold, in severe icing . . . . I'd also like a 30 knot crosswind in the holding pattern and a wind shear event on final" . . . . Holy shit, Chuck Yeager and Bob Hoover together couldn't pull this one off!! Well, I sat back and watched a "master" at work (play for him) . . . . He nailed every aspect, laid in perfect wind correction angles in the holds, flew final like it was an ILS on autopilot, popped the boots to shed the ice whenever the airspeed started to drop a little, and his timing worked out perfectly . . . . What a show . . . . I only got to fly with Dick a dozen times or so before he retired but I have tried to emulate his flying style on every flight I've had since . . . . (not too successfully I must admit)

Once back in Olympia I was scheduled for either King Air 90 or 200 flights every other day and started to get pretty comfortable in both planes fairly quickly. It was always such a pleasure to climb right on through the icing zone in the 200 and pop out on top in the sunshine around FL230 or so. In the 90, since we were limited to 18,000, we were always right in the crap and forced to inflate the de-icing boots quite often. On just one occasion our de-icing best efforts couldn't keep up with the ice accrual rate and we had to turn around before we even got to Whyte intersection on our way to Yakima . . . . When you have to turn around in a King Air, that is the definition of severe icing!

Working traffic in a Cessna was a whole different ball game on the west side of the state. After being used to the slow pace and light traffic on many of the traffic courses on the east side, being thrown into the meat grinder at 320th and I-5, which was very close to the pattern at SeaTac Airport or at Mounts Rd and I-5, right in the pattern at Gray Army Air Field, woke me up in a hurry to the 'real world' of being a traffic pilot! As I said before the weather was the most unpredictable factor and if we wanted to get the job done we were often forced to work in real marginal VFR conditions pretty much right in the tree tops. To keep track of cars flying that low required a lot of really hard banking and crazy rudder work to get parts of the plane out of the way so we could keep the cars and Hwy marks in sight while pulling a lot of G's for hours on end . . . . Man, I have never been so tired in my life as I was after a day of low flying yanking and banking! On days like that if someone asked to go along for a ride we pretty much all just said no immediately . . . . It would have been an automatic puke festival if we had a rider! The close calls with other planes really was amplified on the west side . . . . I just couldn't believe how many private pilots just flew along the I-5 corridor on their cross country trips . . . . Why they had to fly so God Damned low on a clear day just blew me away! It was a daily if not hourly occurrence to come out of a turn and be nose to nose with some dipshit flying right down the middle of the freeway right at our altitude. Eventually the boss installed some early model TCAD units in all of our Cessnas . . . . They picked up another planes transponder but didn't give you any distance information or altitude information . . . They could be set to go off at 1 or 5 miles (I think) which was a great help and we at least had a little warning that there was traffic in our vicinity, if they had their transponder on. Later on, when we replaced all of our older Skylanes with the newer Lycoming IO-540 three bladed prop models, they came factory equipped with state of the art TCAS units which were a tremendous help and virtually eliminated any more close calls. The next big issue to arise was noise complaints while we were turning circles working traffic. We had several 'serial complainers' who would call WSP Headquarters or even the Governor's office every time we worked near their homes. The complaints were always exaggerated beyond reason especially regarding how long we were there and how low we were flying. We had three major complainers; one near I-5 and Marvin Road in Olympia, another in Issaquah near Lake Sammamish on I-90, and a retired airline pilot near Port Angeles along SR101 . . . . Man, if any of these morons even saw a large bird fly by they called in a complaint about us immediately . . . Eventually each one was contacted and interviewed to find out what their major problems were with our operation . . . . As I recall, they 'said' they all supported the traffic safety aspect of our mission but it just boiled down to the fact that they didn't like the specter of 'Big Brother' hovering over them and peering into their backyards (like any of us gave a shit if they were smoking dope back there). For awhile we were limited to only an hour in certain places until we finally got a Chief with some balls. When these same pricks called in complaints during his regime, his reply, forwarded through the chain of command was; "That noise is the price of highway safety and we'll supply you with earplugs if you want them!" I loved that guy but unfortunately he moved on way too soon. My wife faced these same type of assholes in her work . . . . All the biologists called them NIMBYS (not in my backyard types) When some environmental issue or new housing development arose elsewhere that required a few changes, these type folks were all for it, 100% But when it happen to impact their own lakefront property, dock, bulkhead, view, etc . . . or when they had to fix or adjust some man made feature they had constructed (probably without a permit), or wanted to develop their property, all hell would break loose about too much governmental interference, incompetent state employees, and a bureaucracy out of control . . . . Like I said before, a simple painless sterilization laser should be standard equipment for all folks in the law enforcement business and the extent of its usage should be monitored relatively infrequently. (if at all)

Gail Otto helping me hold up a "bed sheet sign" he noticed hanging
from the overpass near Trigger on SR 3. A nearby resident was
trying to warn motorists about the traffic plane overhead.

I was on a King Air 90 flight one morning with Jeff Harshman 311
and just at Vr we encountered a crazy sort of wind shear event where
our 20 knot headwind suddenly turned into a 20 knot tailwind with
no warning whatsoever . . . . We had already broken ground when the
God damned stall horn came on . . . . Jesus, that scared the shit out
of me and my first instinct was to firewall the throttles . . . Well, the
stall horn quit making its racket but I of course had over-torqued the
living shit out of those poor Pratt and Whitney PT6s . . . . Thankfully,
Jeff was quick enough to retard the throttles back to normal takeoff
settings almost immediately but we both recognized they had been way
too high for several seconds. Jeff thought we'd better go back and have
the mechanics take a look at things. They all thought it was hilarious
and after looking up all the over torque time limits for that model of
PT6 in their tech. manuals determined that we hadn't exceeded the
maximum torque for a long enough duration to warrant an inspection
or to have caused any damage . . . . Regardless, from that day forward
my new nickname was 'Red Line Rick', and I had to endure many

snide reminders of all the technical differences between operating reciprocating engines and turbine engines for years to come from the mechanics. During one re-current down at Flight Safety in Wichita my Sim partner, who was a test pilot across the street at Beechcraft, told me that they routinely ran the PT6's in new 200's at red line in an over-torque condition sometimes for a minute or so after takeoff . . . So I don't really know who or what to believe on that issue to this day . . . .

By the summer of 1991 Deb and I finally found a nice ten acre piece of land, not too far from the airport, and decided to buy it. It was a gorgeous spot with a stream and lots of wildlife but had no power or road so we were able to get it pretty cheap. Luckily the folks that owned the adjacent ten acres wanted to build about the same time so we split the costs on the power and road and started building our new homes. The big mistake we made was leaving way too many trees too close to the house. Years later those small cedar and fir trees grew into huge monsters that constantly filled our gutters with needles and crap. Our roof turned green with moss and I spent an inordinate amount of time cleaning out those gutters and spraying vinegar on the roof to kill the moss.

On one of my first flights as PIC in the King Air 200 we had just landed at Prosser and were taxiing over to a very small parking area in front of a big hangar . . . Since there wasn't any good parking places that I could just easily turn into I decided to try out the reversing function of the King Air props for parking purposes. There was a grassy area about a hundred feet in front of that big hangar that looked suitable so I pulled up in front of that spot, turned towards the hangar and stopped. I then put the props into reverse to start backing the plane up. One of the major problems with this type of maneuver is that you can't see where you're going so its usage should be limited to short distances only. Well, things started out OK and I was keeping the plane perpendicular to the hangar while backing up when my co-pilot suddenly yelled out some kind of expletive and said to stop immediately! Shit, I thought I'd backed over somebody or hit another plane but just then I too saw what the problem was . . . . A guy had just come out from between the almost closed hangar doors and was waving at us like crazy to stop! Simultaneously, I noticed the huge dust storm I had been creating as all the propeller thrust was now being thrown forward in a tornado of dirt and debris . . . . What a dumb shit I was to not have anticipated what was going to happen but more importantly, why didn't I notice the mess I was creating sooner!! To make matters worse, when I took the props out of full reverse the damn airplane lurched forward the same distance I had just backed up before I could get on the brakes! Man, that was an embarrassing lesson to learn on the perils of backing up a King Air! Anyway, I just shut that mother down right in front of that guys hangar before I caused any further problems . . . . Sadly, the results and the extent of my stupidity was yet to be seen . . . . After unloading our passengers we located the gentleman that had been frantically waving us off inside his hangar. Before speaking with him I immediately saw why he was so upset . . . . He had been re-skinning an old vintage tail dragger with new fabric and was in the process of applying the dope (glue) to it just when I decided to introduce a swirling tornado of dirt onto his work through that two foot opening between his hangar doors . . . . Oh My God . . . . I was absolutely devastated at the damage I had wreaked and could see by the look on his face that had I not been wearing a gun and badge he would have beat the living shit out of me on the spot! There was dirt stuck to all the fabric that had wet dope on it and one big filthy mess all through his hangar . . . . I have never apologized to someone for so long or too such a degree ever in my life . . . . I told him to please bill me for all the damage, got his name and address, and gave him all my contact information. Thankfully, my veteran co-pilot didn't make me feel any worse by belittling me afterwards which was somewhat consoling. That was a hard lesson to learn and to this day I am always acutely aware of my prop or jet blast and always consider and anticipate where I might be sending it! That gentleman never sent me a bill but I eventually sent him a hundred bucks hoping that small peace offering would at least assuage his anger towards me somewhat . . . .

The big news that summer was when the Beechjet arrived. We had a fairly quiet (Capt Swier didn't want to flaunt the acquisition too much) ceremony down at the hangar and Governor Gardner's wife christened

it by breaking a bottle of champagne on the nose wheel strut. We all
took pictures standing next to it since it was decorated with a huge red
bow wrapped around its fuselage. Capt. Swier and three other of the
most senior pilots were typed in it that year and they had a lot of good
flights back to Washington DC since Governor Gardner was then the
president of the national governors conference. Before the Beechjet
was delivered a couple of the guys arranged for a special registration
number for her . . . In honor of Captain Dick Swier's almost 30 year
career as the commander of the Aviation Section and all the hard work
and dedication he displayed making it grow, it's new N number was
N440DS . . . Dick's personnel/badge number was 44 and of course
his initials followed . . . . The only sad part of this episode was when
they had to park good old King Air N88SP outside for a few months
to make room for the Beechjet in the hangar. She looked so forlorn
and cast aside tied down out in the weeds after serving the state of
Washington so well for so long. I was glad when the new owners took
her away so we didn't have to taxi by her anymore. I started flying
the 200 quite a bit then and was really feeling comfortable in her. Its
only drawback at that time was its antiquated Foster Loran navigation
system. That unit had to have been the most convoluted and non-user
friendly nav. box ever designed by man. Thankfully Captain Swier felt
the same way about it and shortly thereafter had a King KNS 660
Nav Box with a moving map display installed. The KNS 660 wasn't
new but Dick got it for a song from Flight Craft down in Portland
and it was a vast improvement over that Foster Loran. It was very easy
to use and 15 years later was still navigating us accurately around the
country when I retired. Listening to the Beechjet drivers talking about
their flights really made me envious . . . I couldn't wait until some
of those bastards retired or something so I could get into that bird.
They all referred to it as 'the rocket' and were continually bragging
about its fighter like climb rate and seeing ground speeds well over 600
mph (tailwind assisted of course). At first there was no public or media
outrage about the plane since the economy was booming and gas was
cheap. Years later operating that plane became a nightmare and we all
just started calling it the "Bitchjet" . . . . Every time we flew it someone
complained and pitched a bitch, usually to the governor's office. We
even had a guy **within** our own aviation section complaining to the
media and just about anyone else that would listen about its usage . . . .

Talk about biting the hand that feeds you! But for a few years early on, life was good, there were more twin flights than Cessna traffic flights and I couldn't wait to go to work each day.

Delivery day of the brand new Beechjet, June 1991.

One of our primary coffee and lunch destinations in those years was JeffCo (Jefferson County Airport) at Port Townsend. It was a "Who's Who" type pilot destination and one of the waitresses there just happened to be a 'ten'. We just called her Bo, since she was a clone of Bo Derek of the movie *Ten* fame. I think she secretly had a 'thing' for guys in uniform, or possibly thought she might need a ticket fixed at some point in her life, but anyway she was always 'very' friendly to all the WSP pilots. One afternoon on my way back from working traffic up at Birch Bay Lynden, I stopped in for my afternoon cup of panther piss. They weren't too busy so Bo sat down and we were shooting the shit about kitties; her cat had just had a litter under the restaurant's porch and I was telling her tales about our two Burmese kitties Nikki and Teenie. About then I got paged to go look for some idiot running from Bremerton PD on a motorcycle and had to scoot. The next afternoon I was back with one of the other WSP pilots for our afternoon coffee. Bo came over and after pouring she leans over, looks around the room, then very demurely whispers to us if we would like to go out back under the porch and see her 'pussy' . . . . Of course I knew she was talking about her momma kitty and litter but my partner about spewed his coffee all over the table!! I just looked at him and said 'c'mon, this might be fun . . . . I was a little surprised that he came along so eagerly with no questions asked being that he was a happily married man and all . . . . ? When he viewed the "big pussy" and her litter of kittens under the rear deck of the restaurant he seemed somewhat disappointed . . . . As with so many of the guys I worked with over the years, it wasn't long before he too became 'suddenly single' after he succumbed to the wiles of a local "hottie" down in Olympia . . . . Years later, after all the proceedings were over, I was to hear the same refrain from him as I did from all the others troopers I had known who had gone through that process . . . ."Instead of getting married just find some woman you really hate and buy her a house"
. . . .

One weekday while I was stuck doing paperwork at the hangar after being left as Trooper in Charge I got a call from former WSP pilot Ray Riepe. He was now the District Commander (Captain) of the Bremerton area and like my film hero Don Corleone, had an offer for me that I just couldn't refuse. One of his duties was to maintain a close relationship with the U.S. Navy Trident submarine base commander at Bangor. There would often be demonstrations on the Hood Canal Bridge, whenever one of those huge nuclear subs went through, and the Navy and the WSP had to maintain close ties to ward off possible problems and demonstrations there. Anyway, on this particular day he asked if three of us would like to go on an all day VIP cruise on the Ohio Class Trident Submarine USS Georgia, SSBN 729 . . . . Jesus Christ, I couldn't believe this was happening; I immediately told him me for sure and that I would call him back with two other names ASAP since the Navy would have to do a background check on each of us before we could go. At that time there was around fourteen guys in the aviation section and unbelievably just about every person I called said they weren't interested . . . . I thought they were nuts and borderline unpatriotic to pass up an opportunity like this. Finally, two of the guys, Bob Cory and Gary Bade, acted excited and I called Captain Riepe back with all our SS numbers. Apparently we all passed the background check in Washington DC and on the appointed morning we arrived at Bangor around 0430 to board the sub. It was dark and foggy and everything about that morning seemed so eerie that I felt like I was in some crazy Cold War spy movie . . . . The first compartment we descended into upon entering the Georgia was the 'Forest' . . . . It was filled with huge green cylinders, from floor to ceiling, which were the launch tubes for all the Trident nuclear missiles on board . . . I believe there were 24 missiles and man that was a crazy scene knowing that each of those missiles contained multiple warheads and just one sub like the Georgia could annihilate most of the world's largest cities. What struck me as funny were the hammocks strung between the launch tubes where some of the sailors had to sleep . . . . We got a nice tour of the boat then settled down to a nice breakfast. I was amazed at how tight the quarters were and thought there would be a lot more room on such a huge vessel . . . . I had toured several WWII subs and the Trident didn't have a lot more room inside than them, just a lot bigger overall. We left the pier shortly thereafter and headed out into Dabob Bay where the Tridents performed most of their training missions. It wasn't long before Captain Raaz notified everybody we were diving and I soon noticed the deck angle change and found myself leaning backwards. There were also a lot of pressure changes that I noticed in my ears as we submerged. There were some strange noises and sensations as the captain fired some sonic torpedoes. We also toured the torpedo room where there were quite a few conventional torpedoes that looked just like the ones in all the old WWII movies except they seemed a lot longer. At some point the captain performed an 'emergency surface' maneuver which really got our attention . . . . Our ears were popping and we all found ourselves leaning forward like crazy as we zoomed up . . . . Man, this was almost as much fun as flying a P51 . . . almost . . . . The captain gave each of us an opportunity to look through the periscope and I was flabbergasted at how clear the optics were . . . . We were looking at some guys house in Brinnon and you could almost read the numbers on his mailbox from five miles out! Some of the other equipment onboard was quite unique as well . . . They had a desalinization plant that provided continuous fresh water for the crew and another plant that broke up water molecules and separated the oxygen out for breathing purposes . . . . The boat could basically stay submerged until the food ran out . . . . They had a really neat garbage and human waste compacter that compressed and wrapped all the boat's waste into neat stainless steel 'pellets' that were ejected overboard and sunk so the enemy could never follow your garbage trail. After talking with a few of the sailors they all said the food was excellent but after a three month tour, mostly submerged, they longed for fresh fruit and vegetables which were all eaten up in the first couple weeks. The most interesting and scariest part of the trip was watching the men at work in the fire control room (I think it was called). While we watched, the crew simulated a war situation and had to fire their missiles at multiple targets. They went through the whole routine of verifying and double and triple checking everything before two guys at separate locations had to turn keys simultaneously to finally launch each missile . . . . A really sobering exercise for all of us civilians to observe!! The day was over way too soon and what seemed like just a couple hours had lasted nearly ten. I still can't believe to this day why so many of the guys turned down that opportunity . . . . Although none of us were VIP's, I certainly felt like one after being given such a privilege . . . . Thanks again Ray!!

It didn't take long, once I entered the arena of flying politicians around on a regular basis, for me to discover that many of them were the absolute epitome of narcissistic-hypercritical-back stabbers who (in my opinion) actually felt a personal void if they weren't the constant center of attention and adulation for more than a minute . . . . The sad thing was it made no difference if they were Republicans or Democrats . . . . they all acted the same . . . Why do we keep electing the people who have obvious psychological deficits ?? We were coached by our bosses to never reveal what we heard on the aircraft and to carry on as if we were deaf and dumb high paid taxi drivers with no opinions of our own . . . . So . . . . when you love flying high performance jets and turbo-props we all knew that our silence was a small price to pay for the privilege to keep on flying those great machines . . . . But later, after almost fifteen years of it, I started to feel slightly dirty about helping to facilitate the political careers of some of the more offensive elected officials we were forced to fly . . . .

However, I have to say that all of the governors I flew starting with Booth Gardner, then Mike Lowry, Gary Locke, and finally Chris Gregoire were all class acts. Deb and I had known Chris Gregoire since her time as an AAG in Spokane and she always had time to chat with me for a minute during or after a flight to catch up on things and ask after Deb. Booth Gardner had the greatest memory (eidetic) of anyone I have ever known. He came to one of our Aviation Section Christmas parties one year and I introduced him to Debbie . . . just a little five second encounter. About a year later we were standing around on the ramp down at Portland waiting for someone when Booth casually asks me how my lovely bride Debbie was doing . . . . ?! How he could pull someone's name like that out of the thousands he had rattling around in his brain was just wild! On most governor trips around the state the local dignitaries almost always presented them with presents representative of the area they were visiting. In Yakima they got a couple boxes of apples, Wenatchee a couple boxes of cherries, Walla Walla a couple bags of sweet onions, etc . . . . Mike Lowry consistently gave his gift baskets to the pilots which we really appreciated, especially after a visit to wine country!! One of the few non governor politicians we flew, that I had a lot of respect for, was

Senator Alex Deccio of Yakima. He was a decent man, a fellow Italian, and had been a childhood friend of my mother growing up in Yakima.

Myself receiving a "Top Gun" plaque from Governor Booth Gardner for calling out a butt load of violators one year. Sergeant Ken Gunderson looking on. When I retired, my total violator count from the plane was just over 60,000. I held the record until last year when Trooper Johnny Montemayor 426 finished up with nearly 70,000 during his career.

After only a few months in Olympia Trooper Dave Gardner decided he'd spent enough years as the aviation section's flight instructor/ training officer and turned the reigns over to me. At first I didn't realize what a huge responsibility this job was . . . I thought that all the new applicants would be professionals, students of their craft, having constantly strived to improve and perfect their skills, especially when it came to instrument flying . . . . This was very true for the guys already within the section . . . . However, in the next few years there were quite a few retirements and consequently a lot of new recruits who wanted to fill one of those coveted vacancies just as I had. To my utter dismay, some of the recruits applying for a pilot job thought that all they had to do was show up sober for the check flight, prove that they could take off and land a Skylane in VFR weather (like any trained monkey could do) and be able to hold altitude and heading under the hood for a couple of minutes . . . . WRONG!!! When I evaluated these troopers, I could really give a shit about their VFR techniques . . . . All I really cared about was how they responded under the hood or in actual IFR conditions while performing a variety of instrument procedures . . . . If they were cool, calm, and collected in that arena, had soft hands, and flew crisp-precise procedures, they usually got accepted into the section. It just blew me away when some prima-donna, who hadn't spent any time preparing for the evaluation ride, was devastated when he was notified he had failed. All of these guys were usually exceptional road troopers and great guys but those qualities quite often have no direct correlation to being a successful instrument pilot . . . . If you look at the accident statistics for any given year nearly all of those involving fatalities occurred when a so-called "experienced" VFR pilot ventured into IFR conditions, lost control, and killed himself and usually several other passengers that he was trying to impress with his fantastic VFR pilot skills . . . Occasionally the boss would be upset when I rejected some popular "high roller" trooper who came to us highly recommended by his home district . . . Usually, the aviation section backed me up but several times my recommendations were over-ridden, and they hired one of those unqualified guys anyway. In every instance that I was over-ridden it wasn't long until my predictions about that individual's instrument flying skills came to pass. Then when that pilot was transferred out of the section and back to the road, he and his family were extremely embarrassed, the aviation section looked like a ship of fools, and the overall confidence our clientele had in our professionalism took a nosedive . . . . If the brass would have just left the system they put in place for evaluating new recruits alone we could have avoided a number of terribly embarrassing incidents and one major accident, and saved the state millions of dollars . . . .

In my spare time or while sitting in some FBO waiting for our passengers to return I was finally able to draw up a new comprehensive training syllabus for new pilots in the section. Designing it was fairly simple, putting it into practice turned out to be a lot more time consuming than I had realized. I initially thought I could 'check off' all the boxes, included in the ground school and flying portions, in a week . . . . The reality was that the ground school and flying took almost two weeks because I included an overnighter with a considerable amount of night flying . . . . My boss told me it was definitely an excellent syllabus but stressed that these guys were already Commercial Instrument pilots and why did I have to take them back to basics and spend so much time doing so?? This was another of those WTF moments and I just looked at him like he was an alien . . . I diplomatically tried to explain that having some paperwork from the FAA means absolutely nothing if you haven't been honing and practicing your skills routinely . . . . Secondly, some of these guys had been processed through one of those bogus assembly line "rating" schools and thirdly, just about none of them had any actual IFR time . . . The boss just stared at me wishing I wasn't such an argumentative prick . . . He finally compromised and gave me a week and a half to spend with each new guy . . .

Fortunately, not all of the recruits were newbies with the ink still wet on their licenses and instrument ratings . . . Guys like Monty Colver, who was a former airline pilot and C141 Command Pilot in the Air Force, made my job so easy . . . . He had 'soft hands' and was a terrific instrument pilot . . . . I learned more from him than he ever picked up from me. When Army Colonel Tris Atkins came along he was still flying Guard helicopters out of Gray Field . . . . He was another superb instrument pilot who only occasionally tried to hover a Skylane on short final. (sorry Tris) Another Guard helicopter pilot, Paul Speckmaier, was very precise and talented as well . . . . I've never known a guy who had made so many forced landings while flying Chinooks for the Army Guard . . . . His stories about all the mechanical issues he endured while flying those monsters put me off on helicopters for the rest of my life. Paul also told me that whenever an Army helicopter pilot flew IFR they were required to declare an emergency and squawk 7700 on their transponder. I thought that was a bit over the top but believed it was true. A few months later I was sitting at Flight Craft in Spokane savoring my morning cup of cocoa while looking outside at the horrible weather through which we had just shot an approach. All of a sudden there was a tremendous racket and a big old Army Guard Chinook taxis on up and parks on the ramp next to our Beechjet; I thought for a minute it might be Paul. A bunch of high ranking types in flight suits got out and started milling around out on the ramp. A while later I was in the can taking a leak when a bird colonel came in and hit the urinal next to me. Remembering what Paul had told me I casually stated; "So, had to declare an emergency to get in huh?" Man he just snapped a glare at me and I could see that I had really insulted this guy. I knew Paul would love this so I made sure to get the name off his flightsuit. When I told Paul who he was the next day he laughed his ass off and said this guy was really a huge prick and I couldn't have chosen a better comment to nail him with. Steve Bartkowski, the last of the Army chopper pilots I trained, was only with the section for a short time but was also gifted with those soft hands that are mandatory to be a good instrument pilot. Debby Jacobsen was a flight instructor and was a gifted instrument pilot even without the benefit of military training. Anyway, guys like this who had military training or were flight instructors were some of the best new pilots I saw during my time as the instructor pilot in the section. However, in my opinion, the former military pilot's most significant contribution to the WSP Aviation Section was a bit more esoteric; those guys had the best jokes, gross out stories, and gag routines than anyone on earth . . . . Sadly, most of them are unfit for print (make that all of them) but it sure made for stimulating cockpit intercom conversations while cruising along on autopilot somewhere over eastern Montana . . . . I don't think our passengers ever figured out why we kept shutting the cockpit doors from time to time . . . . I think their confidence in the crew might have been somewhat diminished had they caught a glimpse of us convulsing, crying, choking, and laughing so hard we sometimes blew snot and other liquids onto our brand new PFD and MFD displays . . . . Yes sir, those military pilots really raised our professionalism bar to new heights . . . . !?

I also added some realistic flight scenarios in the new syllabus for the new applicants to experience which included the ever popular 'flying into a box canyon scenario' . . . While based in Ephrata I flew Fish and Wildlife agents into some of the canyons of the Colockum Wildlife Area to check on various feeders and watering equipment they maintained. The wildest canyon I saw was the Quilomene . . . . After flying down that twisty narrow monster and having the shit scared out of me by a Wildlife Agent that was supposedly 'guiding me', I felt it was my duty to pass on what I had learned to all the new applicants . . . . When you started down the Quilomene at the top of Colockum Ridge, near the Rye Grass Rest Area on I-90, it looked pretty benign . . . But as you got down closer to the Columbia River it really tightened up and necessitated executing nearly 90 degree banks to stay inside it. The last two sharp turns were just before you reached the river but from a couple hundred yards out it looked like a dead end . . . . It was quite revealing to witness how the FNG pilots reacted to this apparent suicide scenario playing out until they saw that a right 90 followed by a left 90 would pop them out over a sand bar on the wide Columbia River . . . . After apparently just averting death's icy grip we often circled around that sand bar a few times since it was a notorious "nude beach" . . . Of course we were only concerned with any criminal activity that might be going on there?! . . . . That sand bar was right across the river from the "Gorge at George" amphitheater which I used to patrol over when the rock concert traffic coming out got all messed up on the dirt road exit.

Flying the twin engine equipment was a blast but the day to day Cessna 182 flying had its intangible rewards as well. During good weather in Western Washington, which is about three days a year, the views and scenery during our commutes to our traffic course locations were just spectacular! I found myself working traffic in Port Angeles quite often since the commute allowed me to venture deep into the heart of the Olympic Mountains . . . The Brothers Wilderness, The Buckhorn Wilderness, Wonder Mountain Wilderness, All of Olympic National Park, . . . the scenery was just non-stop gorgeous! We occasionally had flights from Bellingham to Spokane and that was when I was privileged to view the North Cascades from on high . . .

I've seen the Alps in France and all of the Rocky Mountains and they have nothing on The Olympics or The North Cascades . . . . On those rare clear mornings climbing out of Olympia it was not uncommon at all to see almost all the volcanoes in Washington and Oregon . . . . Mt Baker was furthest North then Glacier Peak, Mt. Rainier, Mt Adams, Mt St. Helens, Mt Hood, Mt Jefferson, The Sisters, and on a really clear day in the Beechjet, Mt Shasta down in Northern California . . . . Man, it doesn't get any better than that if you're flying for a living!!

When we worked traffic in the Kelso-Longview area we were often asked to take an 'observer' along to witness our traffic ops . . . . If they kept their lunch down the reward after the traffic operations were over was a quick hop up to Mt St Helens for a volcano tour. It can get really rough up there when the winds aloft were high but you could always tell what was going on by watching the movement of the ash and steam in the crater. When the steam was just lazily spiraling upwards and the ash wasn't blowing up a dust storm, it was safe for a tour of the crater. When I first started giving those tours I stayed above the crater rim and kept everything safe and sane . . . . But eventually, especially after observing helicopters right down on the deck inside the crater, I felt it was incumbent upon me to offer my observers the option of the 'up close and personal' crater tour if so desired. Since most of my observers were aggressive, macho, Type A, road troopers, I rarely had one decline my offer . . . . Were they to request the crater over-flight option instead, their reputation as a steely eyed trained killer could become besmirched were the pilot to accidentally mention to that subject's workmates at coffee what type of tour he had requested . . . . Anyway, the center of the crater was occupied by a huge pile of smoldering rock, called the lava dome, which was about 500 feet high then. It was growing taller every day as the mountain slowly rebuilt itself. There was just enough room to get down inside the crater and fly around that pile of rock if you selected approach flaps and stayed in a 45 degree bank while doing a 360 around the dome. The smell of sulfur was pretty strong sometimes and you really couldn't see too much because of the bank angle but my observers always 'raved' about the ride afterwards so I was encouraged to keep improving on my technique.

My most satisfying crater tour was taking one of my old academy instructors for a flight right before he retired . . . . It was sort of a farewell tour for him. He was a real funny guy and during our academy class did a great impression of a Nazi drill sergeant from time to time . . . . However, on one occasion he was showing us a movie on childbirth . . . . Man, the close up scene showing the baby's head coming out was so gross I had to look away so I wouldn't puke . . . . Of course he noticed my reaction and immediately made me pay for it on the spot . . . . After doing 20 push-ups for being a pussy in public, I was then berated by him for other acts of cowardice in the face of the enemy . . . . Well, even after 25 years, I never forgot that personal attack on me and when I saw his name on the flight sheet that day I just knew I was going to convince him he needed to take a volcano tour on his last day of work. I picked him up down at Pearson's in Vancouver but initially he just wanted to fly around Clark County reminiscing about his years of service there. I slowly kept climbing until the mountain came into full view and then casually asked if he'd like to go take a closer look . . . Of course he said sure and off we went. I noticed that the wind was up a bit down in the crater but it looked manageable. At first we just flew around the South Rim where the air was pretty smooth . . . . Finally, after gaining his full confidence, I asked him if he would be interested in a somewhat closer inspection of the lava dome . . . He hesitated for a second or two but agreed that sounded like fun . . . . I maneuvered the 182 to a spot over the deepest part of the crater, chopped the power, went to full flaps, and dropped her right on in to that hole in a tight twisting spiral . . . . I immediately realized that my 30 year quest for revenge had super ceded my common sense somewhat when that vicious crater wind got a hold of us and started slamming us all over the place. Well, there is not a lot of room to maneuver down in there and all I could manage was an out of control 270 around the lava dome and then I punched out of the crater to the north towards Johnson's Ridge . . . . I hadn't even looked at my rider since going to full flaps but did recall him grunting several times since we seemed to pull a lot of g's on a couple of occasions while I desperately tried not to collide with the lava dome or the South Rim . . . Unfortunately, my revenge ploy was a bit 'too' successful as the poor bastard looked pretty messed up afterwards . . . I felt bad about subjecting an old man to that kind of abuse as we quietly headed back towards Vancouver . . . . I was just glad he didn't puke on his last day at work or tell my boss I was some sort of sociopath . . . .

My up close and personal crater tour excursions came to an abrupt end however several years later. I got lazy one day, and instead of overflying the crater to check the conditions out before venturing inside, I just entered it from the blown out North side so I didn't have to waste all that time climbing up to altitude. Anyway, I'm on the back side of the lava dome about a 100 feet off the crater floor in a 45 degree bank when all of a sudden a God Damn tour helicopter appears right at my altitude out of nowhere . . . . Shit O Dear, there was no time to think . . . . At that bank angle I couldn't go over him or under him, but it looked like I could just barely squeeze between him and the South wall of the crater if I cranked in a 90 degree bank to keep my wings from scraping against the wall . . . . All this happened in just a split second so I guess I made it since I'm writing about it . . . I honestly don't know how close it was but after a few seconds I did hear some guy yelling on the crater Unicom frequency wanting to know what my N number was . . . . I nonchalantly turned the volume down on the radio so my passenger wouldn't start asking questions . . . . Thankfully, I had forgotten to radio my intentions and N number to local traffic before my tour began but the flight might have been a little more un-eventful had I done so . . . . I never said a word to anyone about that incident and believe it or not my passenger must have been looking out the right side window 'cause he never mentioned seeing the helicopter . . . . It was only there for the blink of an eye anyway but I still see that bastard in my dreams from time to time . . . .

Flying the crater always brought back memories of dealing with the aftermath of the actual eruption back in May of 1980. The ash that made it as far as Spokane was very fine and resembled gray flour. At noon on May 18th the sky became very dark and then the ash started coming down. There was a little panic at first since no one seemed to know if breathing that stuff was going to cause lung damage or if it was going to destroy our patrol car engines. Someone started distributing those white painting type masks to wear and we were told to start shaking out our air cleaner elements a couple times a day. The worst part was the horrible visibility on the freeway since every passing truck would kick up a snowstorm of ash from the shoulders and median; you couldn't see a thing for a few seconds if you were stopped with a violator. It goes without saying that some of the truck drivers didn't move over or slow down a bit when they saw us out there directing traffic or investigating accidents and made our jobs even more miserable. The Highway Department eventually hosed down all the shoulders on most of the heavily travelled routes and after a week or so things more or less settled down to normal after many road closures and many hours of manual traffic control which I have always detested with a passion anyway! WSP maintenance personnel started retro-fitting huge Kenworth type external air cleaners to the push-bars of our patrol cars which really made them look like a monstrosity . . . . None of us thought that was necessary and I just kept stopping to beat my regular air cleaner element out on the front tire every so often. I was pretty busy at work and hadn't had a lot of time for any home maintenance during that first week or so. We got a fairly heavy rain about then and the media started reporting several roof collapses around town. When I finally got up on our roof to shovel the ash off I found it had the consistency of wet concrete. What had started out as three to four inches of powdery ash became about one inch of thick mud. Shoveling that gunk was a lot of work as each shovel full felt like about 50 lbs!! Most of the ash out on the freeways ended up in the median where for the next twenty years or so it would occasionally come back to life on dry windy days. All of our patrol cars were a disaster and many of them had to be turned in early due to various engine problems. Months later I still dreaded turning my air conditioner on to max-cool as I knew I'd be possibly rewarded with a big puff of ash that had been lurking in the recesses of all that duct work. All in all, I'll take a volcanic eruption every 500 years or so any day rather than have to worry about and then deal with the tornados that my in laws Donna and Kenny Robinson are subjected to almost every year down in Oklahoma City!!

Semi kicking up ash on I-90 near Fishtrap, just after Mt. St. Helens blew
in 1980 . . . . It would have been nice if those guys could have slowed
down when passing a trooper with a car stopped during those months!

After my episode in Moses Lake with the dangling cross-over tube,
other than some really bad icing scares, I really didn't have too many
more hairy situations while flying Skylanes. We went through a period
of faulty voltage regulators for awhile until our technicians changed
vendors, then some magneto issues, followed by vacuum pumps, but
overall those Continental powered 182's were fairly bulletproof. I think
this was largely due to the impeccable maintenance our technicians
performed on all the aircraft in the fleet! Later on, when we traded
in all of our old Skylanes for the new Lycoming IO-540 equipped
units we had a rash of stuck valves, bearing failures, and some other
valve and cam related issues. We started changing the oil every 25
hours and that seemed to help somewhat. The main issue, according
to the factory rep., was the way we operated our Cessnas; he said it
was our fault we were having all those problems because we ran them
at reduced power so much while working traffic . . . . He said those

big ole Lycomings liked to be run wide open and not idling away at 12-14 inches of MP all day . . . . Not much we could do about that since working traffic was our bread and butter! Anyway, according to the maintenance guys, when mechanical issues arose, 99% of the time it was caused by the GILS syndrome (guy in the left seat) . . . . Very funny . . . .

One non-essential part that failed regularly was the push to talk switch installed on the front of the left yoke handle. The engineers designed them to probably last for decades of normal radio usage . . . However, while working traffic, we were keying those things probably ten times per violator and an average number of violators per day was often close to a hundred. We flew those planes seven days a week so you do the math. This didn't even include our normal FAA calls to ATC. After years of working traffic all of us had nicely developed calluses on our left index fingers from punching that tiny little button so much. It was a great relief when the new Lycoming Skylanes arrived equipped with a much larger and softer push to talk button . . . . I know and I'm sorry, this is getting really boring now . . . .

Our technicians were forced to spend an inordinate amount of time trying to quiet the Skylanes down due to all the noise complaints we received while working traffic. Early on, we tried fitting a three bladed prop on one of the older Skylans but it was only marginally quieter and vibrated like crazy. Next we tried a homebuilt muffler that was quite a monstrosity . . . It definitely reduced exhaust noise but we still got just as many noise complaints. It was finally determined that the complaints were definitely being caused solely by all the steep turns we had to continually make while working traffic; the offending noise was just normal prop sounds as we changed directions, sometimes very quickly . . . . Those varying prop 'wows and wumps' were really exacerbated by the Western Washington humidity. The ex-airline captain serial complainer in Port Angeles called us throttle jockeys when he wrongly assumed the noise was caused by frequent power adjustments . . . . Apparently, he had never attended an air show in his life and heard all those crazy prop sounds a Pitts or any other aerobatic plane makes during abrupt maneuvers. Really not much could be done but at least we could report to the complainers that we'd attempted to mitigate the problem and articulate what we tried to do to fix it.

I did have an interesting flight one evening while flying some passengers from Olympia to Bayview (Skagit regional). There was a fairly low overcast so I flew IFR since the freezing level was fairly high that night. The forecast for Bayview was fairly decent, above the NDB approach minimums anyway. When I got within 15 miles of Bayview the Whidbey approach controller cleared me for the NDB approach but I couldn't quite understand the weather reporting portion of his transmission. Then, as I headed for the beacon I thought I noticed things getting a little 'dim' in the cockpit. I turned up all the rheostats but it kept getting dimmer . . . . When Whidbey told me to switch frequencies they couldn't hear my reply and I could barely understand them anymore . . . . I finally realized I was having some sort of electrical issue but was a little occupied shooting this God Damn NDB approach right then. I squawked 7600 but I'm sure no one saw it. I assumed I was down to battery power only and turned everything off except the NDB receiver to save juice. Since it was now very dark in the cockpit, I fished my trusty WSP flashlight out of the side pocket and stuck that crusty thing in my mouth . . . . I flashed it back and forth between my vacuum powered attitude indicator and ADF and tried to act calm. I still had a good needle on the ADF and just prayed the power held out long enough. I had a real good idea of where the terrain was in this area since we worked traffic near here almost every day . . . . I tried to keep my 'terrain free' escape route headings in mind in case the ADF gave up and I had to perform some kind of 'let down' out over the tulip fields west of town . . . . My passengers hadn't said a word but I wouldn't have heard them anyway since I had turned off the intercom. The guy in the right seat finally tapped me on the arm and motioned he would hold my flashlight for me. This was a great help but when I took it out of my mouth and handed it to him it was covered in saliva. We took our headsets off and I told him which instruments I needed him to shine the light at. I tried to use my wristwatch for the timing during the procedure turn and had already decided that 'new minimums' now existed for this approach and they were several hundred feet lower than the published ones. When I finally thought I was pretty well established on the final approach course I had already squeezed about 200 feet off the MDA . . . . I thought I was about a minute from the airport when the ADF needle started to swing around . . . . I thought man, I must have a tailwind and decided I'd better squeeze off another couple hundred feet cause I'm right over the beacon and the airport right now! I still couldn't see a thing outside and then noticed that the ADF needle was slowly rotating aimlessly . . . . I knew I was out of electrical power at that point and told my light-keeper to just aim at the heading indicator and attitude indicator . . . . I just held my last good heading and pinched off an extra two hundred feet and gave myself thirty more seconds . . . . That did the trick. I started seeing some lights (and thankfully no buildings or trees looming dead ahead) as my time ran out but there was no airport in sight . . . . When we broke out of the clouds altogether I saw that it was about 500 OVC and I had about 5 miles of visibility. I thought I saw the lights of Mt Vernon off to the southeast and when I turned to look behind us I finally saw the airport and its rotating beacon . . . . Guess my timing was somewhat off, as usual . . . . After I dropped everyone off and apologized for the somewhat non-standard approach I sat down to calm my nerves a bit and ate my usual dinner out of the vending machine in the terminal. A little front must have just passed through during my arrival 'cause the weather was getting better by the minute. I checked all the reporting stations from there to Olympia and they were all VFR. After hand propping that old Skylane to life, I flew on home with no problems other than a very dark cockpit with no radios . . . The tower was closed by then in Olympia anyway so no big deal. We went back to get everybody in the King Air the next afternoon since the boss felt I had mistreated them so badly during the Cessna flight. Many years later, when I was flying a Citation around the country with another retired WSP pilot, he related experiencing an almost identical incident to mine except it was into Arlington or Paine Field, I don't recall . . . . I guess if you fly single engine planes around IFR long enough it's just a matter of time until some version of this same scenario comes your way too.

Rick Carnevali

A couple of the other King Air pilots, Dave Rheaume and Jeff Harshman had a huge scare in the King Air 90 at Yakima one morning. The plane had just come out of maintenance during which the flap motor had been replaced. Prior to the outer marker they had selected approach flaps followed by the gear at Donny. On a couple mile final they selected another notch of flaps when to their surprise a flap actuating cable snapped resulting in a split flap condition . . . . Approach flaps on the left side and full flaps on the right . . . Now this is one hairy situation and not one that I think I could have survived. Jeff Harshman was flying that day and as the plane started to bank hard left he instinctively knew he had to slow down as much as possible to lessen the severity of the rolling moment . . . From what I remember of his description of that morning they ended up making a series of circles unable to get the plane to fly anywhere near level flight even with maximum cross control and flying at MCA. The best they could hope for was for Jeff to maneuver the plane close to the ground during one of those big circles and try to end up near the right side of the runway, even though the plane was still banking left, cut power, and hopefully slam dunk it down hard and go to full reverse as they passed over the concrete for a few moments. I think they had to switch flying a couple times as their arms got so tired from holding that bitch back from rolling on over. I believe they even considered shutting down the full flap side engine but just reduced power on it to idle instead and ran the other one up as much as they could without increasing their airspeed too much . . . . I still get shivers thinking about those two guys fighting that airplane . . . They finally got it near the concrete, jerked the power off and slammed it down hard and went to full reverse on the full flap side engine in an attempt to stop the turn and straighten it out (I **think** that was the way they did it?!) Unbelievably, they pulled it off without wrecking the plane . . . . They calmly taxied out of the weeds and headed over to the FBO at Noland Decotos as if nothing had happened. In my opinion that was one fantastic piece of airmanship! On Jeff's next visit to Flight Safety in Wichita he told the Sim instructors there what had happened. They told him that his was the first documented case where a King Air in that split flap condition 'ever' made a safe landing . . . . They said every other pilot experiencing that condition had immediately allowed the plane to roll on over followed shortly thereafter by a horrendous crash.

When I went to Flight Safety for my next re-current a few months later, my Sim instructor told me that several of them had tried to land the simulator, programmed in the same split flap configuration that Jeff and Dave had experienced, and not a one of them was able to land it . . . Crashed every time!! So, we were all a bit stunned when Jeff and Dave received no official WSP recognition whatsoever for their fantastic feat of airmanship . . . . The bosses felt that it would draw too much negative publicity to the program and a decrease in clientele confidence . . . . ?

A few years before this incident occurred one of the other pilots had a not quite so heroic episode while flying a Skylane. "Captain Bob" Cory was assigned to Ephrata in Eastern Washington at the time and one day the local media wanted to film him working traffic south of Yakima. Later, after viewing Bob's flying prowess from the ground that day, fellow trooper Chuck Hink, was inspired to write a poem entitled 'Thirty Seconds Over Toppenish' to memorialize the incident. Anyway, Bob is putting on the usual dog and pony show for the media flying above SR 97 demonstrating how the WSP nails speeders from an airborne platform. At some point the media photographer says Bob is flying too high and complains they can't seem to get a decent shot of the traffic airplane calling out the speeders. When that info was relayed to Bob he takes those comments as a direct challenge and personal attack on his manhood and immediately brings the Cessna on down so the nearsighted photographer can get the plane in his viewfinder. Bob brought the Skylane on down for a nice low pass alright but apparently his depth perception went slightly askew for a few seconds and he tore right on through some power lines which he had initially snagged with a wing tip. They sucked the plane towards them until they reached the wing support strut whereupon they snapped and released the plane from their 'surly bonds' . . . From the ground this looked like a disaster movie in the making with lots of sparks, telephone poles bending and swaying, wires snapping and coiling up, and a noisy airplane coming within a few feet of colliding with a bunch of troopers and media personnel filming the whole debacle. Somehow, Bob climbed that sucker the hell out of there without killing anyone although the 182 sustained a considerable

amount of damage. There was also an extensive power outage in the
Toppenish area for quite some time afterwards. In the aftermath, Bob
was sent to Purgatory (demoted to road trooper status) and did his
penance working the road in Ephrata. The FAA allowed the WSP
to handle the pilot's punishment in lieu of any official action on his
certificate. (Thanks to Dick Swier's timely intervention) About 15 years
later at Bob's retirement he was presented with a wonderful going away
gift to commemorate his flying exploits from that day . . . One of the
maintenance technicians awarded Bob with a paint scorched Cessna
182 wing strut with a bunch of high tension wire and some green
glass telephone insulators and other wires wrapped around it in a big
tangled mess . . . . A fitting tribute for one very lucky pilot.

A funny coincidence occurred with myself and the author of that
infamous poem *"Thirty Seconds Over Toppenish"* a few years after
the incident. Undeterred by what he witnessed that day Chuck Hink
wanted to learn to fly and after his transfer to Spokane walked on
in to The Hangar Flying Club one afternoon seeking flying lessons.
He was assigned to me for some unknown reason but we had some
issues almost immediately. Chuck was about 6'8" and weighed around
300 lbs . . . . With me being 6'2" and 230 we could not legally fly
together in either the Beech Sport or a Cessna 150 . . . . We ended up
in a Cessna 172 and just barely met the weight and balance criteria
in that. He was a natural pilot and progressed very quickly to solo.
Unfortunately, I got called up for the next WSP pilot slot about then
and had to turn him over to another instructor.

Dave Rheaume and I were scheduled for a King Air 200 flight to
Pasco one snowy morning in Olympia. There was about three or four
inches of slush on the runway and it hadn't been plowed yet when our
departure time arrived. We discussed all the ramifications of taking off
in the slush and decided to go for it. Prior to departure we opened up
the engine inertial bypass doors (ice vanes) and briefed that we would
cycle the gear a couple times after takeoff to blow off any slush that
might have accumulated on the gear and brakes (this was an early
model 200 with no brake de-ice). Dave was flying and I seem to recall

a little hydroplaning and some slight skidding to and fro during the takeoff roll and a somewhat extended takeoff ground roll . . . . Once airborne everything was cool; we cycled the gear a couple times and made sure our only passenger, Trooper Kermit Gagner, was briefed on what we were doing so he didn't freak out with all the gear noise he would hear. We had a huge tailwind and shortly found ourselves in the pattern at Pasco. The ATIS was reporting icy runways with fair braking action. Dave had nailed Vref as usual and set the old girl down as light as a feather on a very icy section of runway 30. The first few seconds of the landing went very nicely until we came across a section of the runway that was bare and dry . . . . Suddenly, we started rotating to the left until we hit another stretch of icy runway . . . . We then found ourselves skidding sideways on the ice at a 90 degree angle to the runway still doing about 90 mph . . . . We then hit another dry patch of pavement and the turning to the left continued until we had completed almost 270 degrees of rotation . . . . By this time I was looking directly at *Bergstrom Aircraft* out of the front windshield which was an FBO I normally viewed out the co-pilot side window when landing on RWY 30. About this time Dave performed a feat which I still can't believe he had the presence of mind to pull off . . . . In the couple seconds it took for all of this to transpire he had already determined that we had frozen brakes, rightly deduced they were on the left side, and lifted and pulled the right engine power lever past beta into full reverse thrust to stop the plane from spinning to the left before the God Damned gear collapsed . . . Man, I was in a complete fog through the whole episode, and couldn't think of a thing to do while Dave handled everything by himself. We finally came to a stop crossways on the runway just as the tower controller asked if we needed any help out there . . . I just told him to give us a minute until we figured out what had just happened. Dave just calmly said the brakes are frozen up and determined it was just on the left side. We spent a minute or so rocking the plane forward with power, hammering the brakes and then rocking it backwards using full reverse then jamming on the brakes trying to unstick them . . . . They finally broke free while we were in reverse mode and we took off backwards but Dave stopped us before we backed into a snowbank. We taxied on in to *Bergstrom Aircraft* with a corresponding ka—thump, ka—thump, each time the flat spotted tires on the left side made a revolution. I glanced back at our passenger finally and noticed that his eyes were still as big as saucers . . . . I just said frozen brakes and he seemed to get it. Karl Bergstrom inspected our landing gear and said they all looked fine then replaced the two flat spotted tires which he said were down to the cord and were about a millimeter away from blowing out. He also replaced the right side tires since they were also flat spotted just not as bad as the locked up side. He had the work done very quickly and we were able to continue on our mission only slightly behind schedule. What fantastic service! Although Dave could have been the poster boy of a pilot who always rises to the occasion when things turn ugly, when things weren't turning ugly he was known to get very relaxed in short order . . . . Now it really didn't matter if he was in the left seat or right seat but after the gear came up and it looked like both fans were going to keep spinning, he was often out like a light . . . If he was in the left seat all any of us might hear was a faint "It's yours" just as his chin hit his chest . . . . When in the right seat we usually became aware of his state of consciousness when Seattle Approach or Center's radio calls went unanswered . . . . When he got into the right seat of a Cessna, it was lights out when the door closed . . . So, at his retirement I gave him a two hour audio tape of nothing but Cessna 182 engine sounds at cruise . . . . I told him if he ever suffered from insomnia, about thirty seconds of that tape should do the trick for him. Anyway, back to the day in question; we debriefed the flight later and came to the conclusion that in the future if there was any doubt whatsoever about ice accumulation on the brakes after takeoff that we would slam dunk the plane onto the runway upon landing to help unlock them just in case they were frozen. When we got back to Olympia our secretary Denise Poe said that when we took off we had kicked up a huge rooster tail of slush and looked like an unlimited hydroplane on Lake Washington . . . .

On another flight with Dave we were flying our WSP SWAT team to some incident in Eastern Washington in the King Air 200 early one morning. We thought it would be fun to lighten the mood a bit to get their mind off the hairy mission they were about to undertake. We briefed what the plan was then set it into motion. We flipped the radio transmit switch from FAA to cabin speaker then faked a couple routine responses to normal ATC calls about altitude and heading changes. To the SWAT team it just sounded like we were allowing them to hear our ATC calls. After a few minutes I casually mentioned to Dave, with the switch still in cabin speaker for all to hear, that it was a good thing we gassed this pig up before we left so early this morning considering this horrible headwind . . . . He then alarmingly replies "I didn't gas it up, I thought you did!!!" I alarmingly respond "Jesus Christ, we're not gonna make it!!!" Then he says, "Shit, the cabin speaker's on, flip the switch back!" We then gave the scenario about a minute or so to soak in for effect while we pretended to furtively check fuel gauges and give the appearance of calculating our flame out time . . . . We finally both turned around to meet the gaze of eight "very concerned" steely eyed warriors . . . . When we both said "Gotcha" at the same time their response made me fear for my life somewhat . . . . The most tame remarks we heard was something about them "getting us on the ground, ripping our heads off, and shitting down our neck holes" followed by another threat about "gouging our eyes out with a screwdriver and pissing on our brains" . . . . I guess in retrospect we should have tried out this material on a less intense crowd . . . .

While on this theme there was another incident a few years later when Paul Speckmaier and I were on a Beechjet flight with another load of troopers. For years there had been a pair of eyeglasses floating around the pilot's squad room that had lenses about an inch thick. They had been passed down from one generation of pilots to another so Paul and I felt it was about time to pay homage to those old timers with yet another airplane skit at the passenger's expense. These glasses hurt your eyes just to look at them let alone wear them . . . They magnified your face so much the wearer looked like some kind of mad Chinese scientist. Additionally, with his secret military contacts, Paul was also able to obtain one of the original pair of "Billy Bob" teeth. These things were a huge set of buck teeth denture inserts, with the ugliest arrangement of black, brown, and broken off teeth you have ever seen. Anyway, while we were cruising along at FL330 in solid IMC conditions, we pulled out a Washington State road map and start pointing at it furtively and arguing loudly (for all to see and hear) about our position . . . . Paul had already inserted his Billy Bob teeth and donned the glasses. He then turns around pointing at the highway map and excitedly asks our passengers if any of them know where the hell we're at and if they do, can they point to it on this here road map?? Most of the troops thought it was hilarious but one of the more serious dipsticks later scolded us for our lack of professionalism . . . . Anyway, I eventually got my own set of Billy Bob teeth. One day, as I sat in the dentist's chair before my six month cleaning, I popped them in unseen. When the hygienist came over and asked "Are you having any trouble with any of your teeth?" I opened my mouth and pointed at this huge brown broken off snag of a tooth and said "Yeah, this one here is giving me a little discomfort . . ." She recoiled a little and just said "Oh Good Lord . . ." I was hoping for more of a response but I figured she had probably seen worse in her career. She left the room and came back with the doctor; he just said "Hey, where'd you get those?" Then all the other hygienists came in to have a look too . . . Man, I was a hit after all!

One more story about flying with Rheaume. We were on a King Air 200 flight to Wenatchee with the weather there right at minimums again but I was flying this time . . . . We shot the VOR DME Arc approach to Rwy 12 and when we arrived over the airport there was still a fog bank below us obscuring about 75% of the airport which unfortunately included all the approach ends to the runways. The center of the airport was clear and we could clearly see the terminal . . . . Sadly, we weren't flying a helicopter that morning so we called the missed approach, powered up, and headed for the published holding pattern fix to wait and see if the fog might blow away. Just as the gear was coming up and we started to climb, I felt someone grab my shoulder so hard he jerked my right hand off the yoke . . . . This cretin, a WSP Captain no less, then loudly announces, "Hey numb nuts, I saw the airport right back there, where the hell are you going?" Before I could smack that dumbshit in the face myself Dave went into action . . . He reached back and shoved that moron back towards his seat, told him to sit the f**k down, and to never touch or interfere with a flight crew member ever again! The captain was a little dazed to say the least, as was I by Dave's lightening like response . . . From that day forward he was known to me as *"Action Jackson"*. Anyway, after we got established in the holding pattern and I had flipped the autopilot on Dave went back and calmly explained to Captain jerkoff why we didn't land . . . . He was a helluva lot more diplomatic than I would have been and even though Dave was just a trooper like me he never apologized to that idiot even though he was a captain. We both expected some sort of reprisal from Captain Jerkoff but to his credit he never said a word to anyone. We often wondered how such obvious dumb shits ever made rank?

One more story about flying with Mr. Jackson. We had flown into Willapa in the King Air 200, the closest airport to the twin cities of South Bend/Raymond with Governor Gardner one afternoon. There was always a NOTAM published for Willapa concerning Elk on the runway so, as was the custom when we went there in a Skylane, we buzzed the runway fairly low to scare off any Elk that might be grazing close by . . . . Of course we had briefed the governor ahead of time and he later told us that was great fun! Anyway, we landed uneventfully and waited several hours for the governor and his party to return. Even though the departure was at night and there were no runway lights we got out of there OK and turned NE for the quick flight back to Olympia. Just as we leveled off in cruise Dave and I both noticed, almost at the same time, a real strong odor of roasted chicken . . . . We sort of glanced at each other with that all too frequent WTF look . . . . I casually turned around to see if anyone had picked up some KFC or something while in Raymond but that wasn't the case . . . . When we pulled the power back a little, for the descent into Olympia, the odor seemed to diminish somewhat and that's when Dave said he thought he knew what this was. After everyone had gone and we had pulled the King Air into the hangar we opened all the engine side doors to inspect the big screens where the intake air goes into the Pratt and Whitney PT6 engines. Sure enough, just as Dave had predicted, there was a large mass squashed out flat on one of the screens . . . . It turned out to be a cooked bird of some sort and had somehow either had gone through the propeller without getting pulverized and into the air intake on takeoff or was already in there during the engine start . . . Anyway, we peeled it off and it resembled a small piece of auto-floor mat with the little spikes on one side protruding out to dig into the floor carpet . . . . Environmental air for cabin heating is taken from this area of the engine so that was why we got the roasted chicken smell inside . . . . I took the "bird pancake" home to have resident biologist Deb try to determine what the hell it was. It took her awhile but she later determined it to be a Sandpiper.

Myself and Governor Gary Locke in front of King Air 200, May 2004

In 1992 or so we all got a little tired of sweating in our full trooper uniforms in the airplanes, campaign hat included, and started crying to Captain Swier that we needed some wash and wear flight suits or jumpsuits. It was a real drag in the summer when we pitted out our uniforms before noon and consequently the dry cleaning bills really started to add up. Road troopers had nice air conditioners in their patrol cars but our old Skylanes had nothing of the sort other than a flimsy side window . . . . Flying with that open wasn't too bad until you kicked some rudder while maneuvering to keep a violator in view whereupon it slammed you in the elbow usually causing the pilot to drop a stopwatch. Anyway, the Captain finally agreed to hear our grievances and listen to our proposals at a troopers meeting. He was very conservative and we could tell he did not want us to break with WSP tradition and "God Forbid" actually start looking like pilots! He patiently listened to our proposals about obtaining some military type Nomex fire retardant flight suits but eventually he couldn't take it any longer and burst out with a comment to the effect "I don't want you guys looking like a bunch of God Damn Coast Guard Helicopter pilots in orange flight suits . . . ." He went on to dogmatically pronounce that **Cessnas never catch on fire** so why the hell do you guys want Nomex anyway?? The timing of his comment is forever burned into my memory . . . . Now our squad room at the Olympia WSP Hangar was upstairs with a great view of the main runway. During the meeting we all had been glancing out from time to time at a student pilot doing not so gentle touch and goes on runway 17 in a Cessna 172 . . . . As fate would have it no sooner had Captain Swier made that infamous comment when the student pilot landed right on the 172's nose wheel, collapsed it, bent the prop over the cowl, whereupon the damn thing burst into flames!! Captain Swier had his back to the runway as we all watched the unfolding tragedy occur right behind him . . . . I believe it was Joe Anderson 252 who, with perfect comedic timing, casually remarked to the captain something like "Uh, excuse me Captain, but what about that Cessna on fire right behind you there!?" I have to admit he took it pretty well as we all ran outside to assist the young female pilot running away from the conflagration. Well, we didn't get Nomex but he did begrudgingly order us some nice gray cotton flight bags and some handy shoulder harnesses to stick our hoglegs in which made it a lot more convenient on a day to day basis. We just tossed those flight suits in the washer each night and they came out of the dryer just fine not needing to be ironed.

After I'd been in Olympia for only about a year and a half a bunch of the old guard retired and the boss was left with no choice but to promote me to command pilot on the King Air since there was no one else left. I felt totally unprepared but really enjoyed making some decisions for a change. Shortly thereafter the boss approached me one afternoon and asks me if I'm a "numbers sort of guy" . . . I had no idea WTF he was talking about. Then he tells me he is going to send me to Wichita to get typed in the Beechjet in a month or so with Brian Holliday who had just returned to the Aviation Section from his road assignment in Tacoma as a sergeant. This was all a bit overwhelming but I dug into the Beechjet books and started studying jet systems . . . All was going well until one morning when another pilot, Jeff Harshman, announces to everyone that he and Brian will be going to Wichita together to get typed. I thought it was a bit odd that they would send all three of us together so I asked the boss about it. He just casually remarked that he had changed his mind and that he just **forgot** to tell me about it . . . . What a class act! This was the same guy who just **forgot** to tell Debby Jacobsen after several weeks that she wasn't selected to be the new Yakima pilot since some headquarters weenie had hand-picked someone else . . . . Anyway, I was really pissed and I was never told why I was de-selected. But, if I ever wanted to fly that bird there was nothing I could do but soldier on and try to act like I was a real team player and not let anyone see how pissed I was.

It wasn't very long before one of the other Beechjet Captains finally retired. I was asked **again** by the boss if I would like to get typed now . . . . I said I'd like to see some official confirmation from *Flight Safety* with my name on it beforehand . . . . He just gave me one of those "Why you insufferable little prick" looks but assured me that this time it was for real. So, I got all excited again and hit the books pretty hard and also started studying flashcards with my *Flight Safety* partner, Trooper Ron McClinton 600, in preparation for our two week meat grinder in Wichita. My boss graciously allowed me one right seat landing in the Beechjet and then sent me off with the admonition that "A trained monkey could fly one" . . . . I felt sooooo special . . .

Ron and I were staying at the *Tallgrass Inn* down in Wichita, a wonderful place I was to become very familiar with every six months for the next 12 years in a row and a couple more years after that with another outfit). The ground school wasn't too bad but once we started flying the Sim things got ugly pretty fast. We had a terrific

Flight Safety Sim instructor, Phil Jeffries, who did his best to lighten the mood during some of those tense moments shooting single engine ADF approaches and multiple thrust reverser deployments right at V1 . . . . While we were dealing with these catastrophes Phil would sit back in his Sim instructors compartment and breath rapidly and heavily with ever increasing volume into the cockpit intercom adding plenty of extra drama while we struggled to save the airplane from disaster. The call sign on our Beechjet was N440DS (Delta Sierra) . . . . Phil thought the FAA phonetics were way too formal for the Sim and just referred to our plane as 44DuckShit. During one memorable emergency descent right after a window supposedly blew out, Ron was putting on his oxygen mask and accidentally dislodged his hearing aid which fell down between the floorboards of the simulator somewhere . . . . While he was retrieving it, I was also struggling with my oxygen mask, hooked my reading glasses and sent them flying up under the dashboard and then couldn't read the emergency descent checklist to Ron which was a moot point anyway since he couldn't hear me without his hearing aid in . . . . Phil thought this whole scene was hilarious, froze the Sim, and just rocked back in his chair laughing so hard he almost puked . . . . All he could say was "Jesus H. fu**ing Christ, I've got one blind guy and one deaf guy trying to fly a jet together . . . ." Ron and I thought it was real hilarious too, about five years later!

On my very next trip to Wichita for a King Air re-current myself and Dave Peretti arrived about two days after a tornado had ripped through town out near McConnell AFB. Of course being from Washington State we had never seen the aftermath of a serious twister before so this was a real eye-opener. I will never forget seeing hundreds of yards of the cyclone fencing and their posts, (with the concrete still attached) that once protected one side of the Air Force Base. It was now lodged in some huge trees, miles away, wrapped tightly around branches way up high . . . . What a sight! It also dawned on us why the storm drains and gutters on all the major streets were so huge; they could easily swallow up a Yugo or a Mini Cooper . . . The guys at *Flight Safety* told us that it wasn't uncommon to have two feet of water running down the streets during one of those huge storms . . . Years later I was flying over Denver in the Beechjet when a tornado was hitting the area. We were getting a smooth ride at FL430 and were in the clear but our radar was painting a huge magenta (bad) maelstrom down below for us to marvel at. With the radar range scale set at about 100 miles, with each sweep you could clearly see this classic low pressure super cell, with that characteristic "number 6" hook echo, slowly rotating counter-clockwise and moving through the area very rapidly . . . I sure pitied those poor bastards down there taking the brunt of that monster!

Anyway, the big day for our Beechjet check-rides finally came along way too soon and as we sat in the briefing room just prior to our scheduled flight there was a huge commotion in the Beechjet Sim that we'd soon be climbing into. The Sim hadn't even come down off its huge hydraulic cylinders yet nor had the cat-walk descended . . . but some guy was yelling and screaming and trying to get out of it in a real big hurry . . . . It was another student from our Beechjet Initial class who was also the owner/operator of a brand new Beechjet . . . He had been a real pain in the ass throughout our two weeks; he was the know-it-all type who had to constantly bore the whole class with the hair-raising exploits he lived through flying his Bonanza and Baron. Unfortunately for him he had just failed his checkride and was screaming at his rookie co-pilot blaming him for his pink slip . . . . The Sim instructor was in hot pursuit trying to assure this "valued" customer that after a little remedial training he could try again very soon . . . I have to say that witnessing that whole episode didn't set too well with Ron and I . . . We looked at our checkride instructor and wondered if he was going to hammer the shit out of us too?? Since we were a Part 91 crew, the oral wasn't too bad and we prayed that the Sim portion would go as easily. During the Sim test, which was called an 85% ride, we each committed a couple minor miscues, but somehow we both passed that portion. Then we had to head out to the airport to fly the real airplane to complete the remaining 15% of the check ride. Bob Cory and Brian Holliday had graciously flown ole 44DuckShit down to Wichita for our use and we found her on the ramp at ICT (Wichita) with the wings full (427 gal) of Jet A, per Phil Jeffrie's orders, with nothing in the trunk (fuselage tank). Phil Jeffries had Ron do his checkride first which consisted of the stall series, steep turns, a no flap landing, two non-precision approaches to touch and goes, followed by an ILS to a full stop. We then switched seats out on the taxiway, with engines running, and then it was my turn in the hot seat. Everything went quite well until just after my last touch and go while we were climbing out to be vectored for a full stop ILS. Suddenly, the Master Warning starts flashing and the annunciator was for low fuel level in both left and right wing tanks (225 lbs remaining in each). I had been trusting Phil too much and wasn't watching the gas as I should have, being a bit pre-occupied trying to pass the damn ride . . . Phil says it's no big deal so he lets Wichita approach vector us all the way out for a full ILS . . . I was a bit nervous since both the left and right low fuel annunciators stayed lit the whole time and were glaring me right in the face while I was trying to salvage this ILS . . . . But shit, Phil was "The" *Flight Safety* Beechjet check airman so who was I to question? On about a two mile final, the Master Warning starts flashing again and this time the annunciator is for Right and Left fuel feed . . . (less than 10 gal. of gas left per side). I don't think Phil expected to see those and I saw him tense up a bit on short final. I'm sure he was expecting a flame out at any second when he tersely said "I got it" on about a mile final . . . . Well, both of those fuel guzzling Pratt and Whitney JT-15D's kept running and we managed to land and taxi to the ramp without a flame out. I think he was a bit embarrassed by it all as there was not much of a post flight critique to speak of . . . . A quick handshake and brief congrats and that's all there was to it. Regardless, we both got to add MU30/BE40 Type Ratings to our ATP Certificates and were a couple of pretty happy campers on the ride home. Later, out of curiosity, I went out on the ramp and watched the line boy fill up the wings tanks. I still have the numbers in my logbook; it took 417 gal . . . . So there was about 5 gallons left per side . . . . **Nothing really** for a fuel guzzling jet . . . . That was way too close!! Later in retirement, when I was back at *Flight Safety* for a Part 135 PIC oral and checkride for another company, it wasn't quite so easy and both my co-pilot and I were reduced to quivering piles of protoplasm when we finally crawled out of the Sim after that 135 ride . . . One last funny memory from my initial class . . . . One night while Ron and I were each in our separate rooms at the Tallgrass (a two bedroom two bath unit with a common living room) my phone rings. When I answer I was greeted by a very sultry and sexy panting voice who just said "Hi, it's me . . . what are you wearing . . . ?" I immediately recognized the voice of Ron's beautiful wife Barb, who obviously got our numbers mixed up . . . So I thought I'd play along for a minute and said "Oh, nothing, how about you?" . . . . There was a long pause and then she screams "Is this Rick???" We had a great laugh over that one!

Soon after returning home Ron and I had a flight to Yakima together in the Beechjet with the governor. While there I called my Mom and Dad and they came down to the airport for a tour of the plane. According to my Dad he thought it was pretty "fancy smancy" . . . and then told me he liked the look of the King Air a lot better. (I have to agree with Dad . . . no airplane except a P51 looks as good as a King Air 200). Later, they watched from the parking lot at Noland Decotos while we taxied out and took off to the West. Sadly, my Dad got very sick shortly thereafter and passed away in just a few weeks. I was glad he got to see me fly a jet even though it was one he didn't like the looks of. Mom still doesn't like the idea of me flying for a living but says she doesn't worry about me as much in a plane as when I'm riding a motorcycle which I admittedly don't do very well. The double whammy occurred within a few weeks when my good friend and mentor, Jim Kieran, also passed away . . . . of exactly the same illness that got my Dad. That was a rough month for me . . . Losing the two most important role models in my life in such a short time span was pretty upsetting. Flying back from Jim's funeral in Spokane, in a friend's borrowed 182, Deb and I ran into some unexpected weather issues abeam Mt. Rainier. I got a pop-up IFR clearance but then the attitude indicator went south so I got to take Deb home partial panel in solid IFR conditions. To make matters worse, the radio frequency changer knob fell off and rolled away so I improvised a little using Deb's nail clippers to grab that short little stem to change frequencies with. Obviously, she was not impressed with my Rube Goldberg flying style, and I seem to remember some minor screaming and a few profanities directed my way . . . . There is no doubt in my mind that Jim was laughing his ass off at my predicament and probably considered this episode the highlight of his funeral proceedings . . . .

One of the long lasting impressions I have retained from my jet flying period was the new appreciation I gained for high altitude weather and especially the peculiarities of the jet stream. I had some experience with it in the King Air but we rarely got over FL240 on our in-state flights. I was always fascinated watching the winds aloft display on the Collins Pro Line 3 MFD in the Beechjet and later Pro Line 21 FMS in the Cessna CJ2 I flew . . . As we crossed from one weather system to another at FL410 and higher the sometimes wild shifts in wind direction and velocity never failed to astonish me! However, when our 120 knot tailwind suddenly was transformed into a 90 knot headwind component I became less astonished and more aggravated especially when the fuel remaining at destination display went from 1,100 lbs to 250 lbs! (1,000 lbs was the minimum safe fuel we had set for landing in a Beechjet). What I also found very interesting was just how finite the lower and upper levels of the jet stream were sometimes. During a climb out the EFIS wind display might be indicating a moderate wind aloft of 28 knots at 240 degrees or so . . . Quite often you could actually feel a little bump when you went through the lower level of the jet stream . . . Almost simultaneously, at least on the Collins Pro Line 21 equipment, you could watch in amazement as the winds started accelerating very quickly on the MFD screen, usually going well over 100 mph, accompanied by a sometimes drastic shift in wind direction as well. I remember one flight where we got into the jet stream just south of Mt Rainier at about FL270 and watched our tailwind component jump from 30 to 115 mph in less than a minute. We just started talking about what a quick trip this was going to be when all of a sudden we felt another little bump and we were suddenly out of it even though we hadn't even got to our cruise altitude yet . . . It had only been about 1500 feet thick that day . . . Just amazing! The best groundspeed readout I ever saw in the Beechjet was just over 700 mph early one morning which worked out to around a 194 mph tailwind!! . . . We were in level flight at FL210 crossing the Colockum Ridge east of Ellensburg on our way to Spokane after having just departed Olympia. ATC had kept us fairly low that morning for traffic or we would have never encountered the jet stream so low or gone so fast. I knew from experience there was always a good easterly push to be expected in that vicinity of the Colockum but Holy Shit, this was unreal!! I thought it was a malfunction until I looked outside and even at that altitude saw the terrain just whistling by at warp speed! Before we even got to the Ephrata VOR the FMS VNAV alerter let us know we needed to start our descent for Spokane!! . . . That was one quick trip and was the lowest altitude I ever saw the jet stream at in my career!!

Myself and Beechjet 400A in front of WSP hangar in Olympia.

I was working traffic one day up near the Puget Sound convergence zone near Everett when the wind from that effect suddenly hit my plane out of nowhere. It went from a perfectly calm afternoon to tornado like turbulence in five minutes. I started back to Olympia immediately but my groundspeed was only about 70 knots due to a horrendous headwind (normal groundspeed was 135 knots). During convergence zone weather events the wind coming off the Pacific hits the Olympic Mountains and is funneled into two very distinct channels; one is down the straights of Juan De Fuca and the other is up the Chehalis River valley starting at Hoquiam/Aberdeen.

Both channels of wind then hit the rising Cascade Mountains . . . The majority of the wind coming down the Juan De Fuca Straights turns right while the wind coming in from Hoquiam is funneled between Olympia and Shelton and turns left . . . . These winds normally collide and "converge" between Seattle and Everett causing horrendous turbulence, wind shear events, and nearly every other weather phenomenon known to man. Anyway, I'm riding this mother out near Bremerton when I get hit by a tremendous downdraft . . . Even though I had my seat as low as it would go and my belts all tight I was still stretched out upwards and hit my head again on the cabin roof. I immediately felt that same old pain go shooting down my right arm as my hand went numb . . . . Great, just f*   *   *ing great . . . . I finally get typed in the jet and now I'm going to be off for another six months and possibly never fly again!! If I do recover, no doubt Labor and Industries will determine I'm too much at risk for permanent disability and not let me fly for the state anymore. So, I was soon off to Virginia Mason in Seattle for more X-rays, MRI's, and another myelogram. It showed my cervical disk at just C3 was bulged out. They thought that physical therapy alone should take care of it this time. So I spent every third day for the next two months having my neck massaged, ultra-sounded, electrically stimulated, and iced to death. I was given a crazy contraption to use at home twice a day that wrapped around my head and chin and was attached to a ten pound weight I threw over a door that applied traction to my cervical spine to "lift and separate" my vertebrae to relieve the pressure on my disks. Not a fun time for Deb & I. Finally, my Virginia Mason neurologist released me for unlimited flying duties but when I came back to work our new non-flying boss said I couldn't fly until my personal flight surgeon said I was good to go . . . . Wow!! Apparently, the findings and recommendations from a world renowned neurologist who was also one of the team doctors for the Seahawks wasn't good enough . . . . I bit my tongue (almost in half) at this guy's ridiculous requirement but obediently scheduled myself with my flight surgeon, Dr. Jim Patterson in Friday Harbor, to get evaluated. When I told Jim what my WSP boss wanted he laughed his ass off . . . . He just read my neurologist's report and didn't even examine me . . . . He then proclaimed me "fit to fly" and wrote up his report accordingly. To add insult to injury, I was flown up to Friday Harbor in a Cessna by the shittiest pilot in the section, and he had been given strict instructions to **not let me touch** the controls . . . . Good Lord!! This was during an era when we had two different Aviation Section managers who weren't pilots . . . They were nice guys and conscientious managers but knew very little about aviation . . . . One of them used to rip pages out of *Private Pilot Magazine* and taped them all over the office; on the mirror in the toilet, the squad room, behind doors, etc . . . . Most of those articles were intended for student pilots and included such riveting subjects as: "Night Flying . . . Is It Safe?" . . . ."Constant Speed Props Explained" . . . ."Retractable Gear . . . Will It Come Down?" . . . ."Cosswind Landings . . . Are You Up to It?" etc., etc . . . We had several ex-military pilots in our unit, everybody was a Multi Engine ATP, and several guys had 10,000+ hours . . . and this was the level of leadership we had to cope with . . . . Shit oh dear!! My neurologist did recommend that I wear a "crash helmet" while flying a Cessna from then on; he felt that it might dissipate and spread out the impact forces were I to crash into the cabin roof again. So I investigated all the military type helmets out there and the WSP finally provided me with a top of the line USAF standard issue helmet. It was great piece of equipment but even with the seat all the way down in the Cessnas, it was touching the ceiling. When I tried to look left while working traffic I kept banging it against the window and scratching the plexiglass. So ultimately, I wore the helmet while taxiing away from the hangar, in case anybody was watching, but once airborne it went back into its black bag in the back seat to be replaced by my old set of Dave Clarks. Later, when we got another new boss, who was a little more reasonable, (and a pilot!) I was finally allowed to use my best judgment about its usage . . . .

During this episode my fellow "caring and concerned" pilot buddies constantly ragged me about my pitiful and painfully obvious ploy of faking an injury in order to make myself eligible for a full disability retirement wherein my medical insurance would be paid for life . . . . I knew most of them were kidding but also knew for sure that at least one of the "junior" birdmen was praying that I would get that disability retirement which would open up a slot for him in the Beechjet program . . . . When that didn't happen this time around my so called "buddy" decided to go with Plan B. One day on a King Air flight he saw me take a couple red pills from an old tiny Bayer Aspirin sliding metal container I kept in my pocket . . . When he noticed the pills weren't round white (aspirin) tablets, without asking me what they were, he runs excitedly to the boss after landing and tells him I'm popping red painkillers on duty! He told him I was keeping them hidden in some sort of improperly marked container, and that I seemed out of it while flying that day . . . WTF! Shortly thereafter I get called into the boss's office out of the blue whereupon he began to grill me about my suspected drug usage and asked me if I am keeping prescription meds in an unmarked container . . . Man, my jaw hit the floor but I handed over my aspirin box which he discovered only contained little red *Advil* tablets . . . At this point my sergeant backed down, reversed course, and then tried to act concerned about all the pain I must be living with . . . . Wow!? However, he did rat out who the reporting party was . . . . To my face that guy was all nicey nice, and I had actually considered him a friend at one time. But behind that "Sunny Jim" façade of his was a conniving little ladder-climber who just wanted his shot in the Beechjet—NOW!! . . . I am still amazed to this day that he was willing to fabricate facts and tried to ruin a friend's career just to create a vacancy for himself which happened in due time anyway . . . . Whenever I think of this incident, an old song comes to mind that pretty much summed up that episode in a nutshell . . . ."*Backstabbers*" by the O'Jays . . . It went something like: "They smile in your face—all the time they want to take your place—The Backstabbers."

In the years after my last "reported" shot to the neck I had several more incidents while flying in turbulence that aggravated that old injury again and again. Recalling the last debacle where I was banned from flying until the God Damn surgeon general himself was almost called in to OK me for flight, I just kept things to myself and never reported any of those incidents. When I was hurting real bad I just called in sick with the flu for a few days rather than having to go through another one of those ordeals. An additional irritant to my sensitive neck was when they started trading in all the older Skylanes for the new and improved Cessna 182's equipped with three bladed props and the IO-540 Lycoming engines. I have to admit those Lycomings sounded real gnarly and looked real Macho but man were they rough running! . . . . After six hours of thrashing around in one the vibration from that engine-prop combo really aggravated the hell out of my neck disks. I always tried to grab one of the older smooth running Continental units, before anyone else could get to them in the morning; but pretty soon they had all been traded in on new planes and I was forced to fly one of the new "Vultee Vibrators" of the 1990s. The only saving grace with the new 182's was the fantastic King GPS and a great auto-pilot which was sure nice on those long headwind prone commutes back from Bellingham or Eastern Washington!

By now, most of the "old timers" had retired out of the unit and by 1995 I was the senior pilot with the most total time in the section. We had a lot of new guys by then and I was fortunate to be assigned to a lot of flights since we were short on command pilots. Around this time the Department of Corrections began to utilize our Beechjet quite often. Even though its hourly rate was high it was so fast that on any trip over three hours in length it was cheaper to fly the Beechjet than the King Air. The Corrections people were blown away by how many stops we could make on a two day trip, and how many smaller remote airports we could fly into that weren't serviced by a scheduled airline. They still flew commercial when they had simple one way trips with cooperative prisoners to major airports. However, when they had high profile escape risk prisoners or needed to make multiple stops in remote areas of Arkansas and Oklahoma, we got the nod. When the Corrections folks flew commercial to the remote prisons they always ended up at a hub several hours away from their destination. They would have to rent a car, and waste a lot of time and put themselves at tremendous risk hauling those prisoners around. There was usually a good reason those maggots were being transferred and it usually wasn't for good behavior. The Corrections upper management folks determined that when we flew their people in the Beechjet we got the same amount of work done on a two day trip that normally took them four days while flying commercially. We also eliminated much of their per diem and overtime costs and ultimately saved their agency a lot of money. A few years later there was a mandate from the governor's office to reduce prison over-crowding. This gave a tremendous boost to our flight schedule since Corrections was 'forced' to farm out several hundred prisoners a year to less crowded facilities all over the nation. The legislature also passed some kind of 'innovative probation hearing rule' wherein a prisoner had the right to a probation hearing at the original institution he was incarcerated at . . . Since we had moved so many of those guys out of state, guess what? We had to go bring them back home for their hearings . . . . Man, this was the perfect storm of legislation benefiting our Beechjet transportation program and we were flying the shit out of that mother! I ultimately ended up landing in every state in the lower 48 except two or three back East and nearly all of those trips occurred while flying prisoners. A couple of the Corrections lieutenants that we flew with got very creative when planning our trips. It was uncanny how many times we would end up in either Reno or Vegas for our overnight stay . . . . There were big prisons at both locations, a lot of entertainment choices, and I certainly wasn't about to complain since DOC was writing the checks for these flights.

While cruising along at FL450 in the Beechjet with a load of prisoners over some remote part of America it was usually very quiet on the radio as we travelled between ATC sectors. Thankfully, to liven things up a bit, God would occasionally grant us the wonderful gift of a stuck or "hot mike" radio transmission, usually at the expense of some major airline crew. As a result, everyone within listening range got to hear what was supposed to be a private cockpit intercom conversation between two crew members being blasted out on the local center frequency. A stuck mike button, switch that wasn't flipped, or improper avionics selector knob positioning was normally all it took to facilitate one of those events. Those conversations weren't the usual police, adrenaline-charged screaming type episodes at all . . . . After the improper switch was thrown we would quietly hear a crewmember making some routine announcement to his passengers about the flight attendants up-coming trip through the cabin with the beverage cart or that everyone should keep their seat belts fastened . . . . There was always a short pause then that poor sap would casually get back to telling his story to the co-pilot about some X-rated escapade with his crazy girlfriend the night before, or the retelling of some horrible divorce episode, bitching about terrible bosses, lousy working conditions, low pay, etc., etc. Man, some of the shit we heard was just priceless! Sometimes, a crew on another company plane would contact the offending crew on a separate plane to plane radio to let them know about the stuck mike. Usually though the last words we'd hear from the guilty crew went something like this: "Man, it's sure quiet on Salt Lake Center this morning" . . . followed shortly thereafter by an "OMG or WTF" comment of some sort and finally, a squelch break!! When these episodes occurred everyone who heard it had a good laugh but no one ever thought less of the perpetrators.! We always sympathized with them during their moment of personal agony and knew in our hearts that "There but by the grace of God go I."

There were a couple of strange coincidences with prisoners I flew who I had known before they were incarcerated. One guy, worked at an FBO in Olympia which had the state fuel contract for a few years. He was a fuel truck driver and for years we'd see him at all hours of night and day out there in the pouring rain on his ladder filling up our Cessnas, King Air and Beechjet. He was likable and always did a good job and none of us had any complaints. He moved on at some point and I didn't see him until one morning at the local FBO down in Price, Utah. After we gassed up, the guards came out to the plane with the new prisoners we were picking up. As usual, they were all chained up and wearing those ubiquitous orange jump suits. I was standing by the door as they were loading when one of them looked up at me and says "Hi Rick, looks like I finally get to go for a ride in your fancy jet . . ." I recognized him from Olympia and immediately thought back on how many times I'd left my gun laying on the backseat of a Cessna while he was out there gassing it up alone . . . .

The next strange passenger episode hit a little closer to home. When I was a road trooper in Spokane I occasionally had coffee with some of the deputies from the Sheriff's office and once in awhile with some of the Spokane PD guys. After I'd transferred to Olympia from Ephrata I was shocked to hear on the news one night that a Spokane County

Deputy that I knew had been arrested for murdering his wife. To cover it up he went so far as to shoot himself in the stomach then proclaimed that the perps had done it while he was coming to her rescue. That defense didn't work out too well for him since he had bullet entry and exit wounds right next to each other in a roll of his fat where he had obviously pinched it together before shooting himself through it . . . . I used to have coffee with this guy at the Felts Field Café occasionally and was just shocked that he could be capable of such an atrocity. Anyway, several years later I was scheduled for a prisoner flight to Providence, Rhode Island, and was surprised to see his name on the passenger roster. The morning of the flight the two Correction lieutenants brought him into the hangar to take a leak; when he saw me he was friendly and immediately started talking about the old days in Spokane as if nothing had happened. He finally asked me where we were going; the lieutenant gave me the hairy eyeball so I just said "don't know, ask him." Apparently, there had been several threats against his life so he was being moved out of state (way out of state in this case) for his own protection . . . Ex-Cops don't do well in prison . . . . When we stopped for gas in Sioux Falls, S.D. he immediately started talking about our time working the road together in the Spokane Valley like we were old buds and then asked me again where we were taking him. I just said, sorry man, top secret. As we lined up for the approach to Providence we ended up high and quite a ways out over the Atlantic and could clearly see Cape Cod out in the distance . . . . He was sitting on the right side of the plane so I think he finally had a pretty good idea of where he was going if he knew his East Coast geography at all.

In the late nineties the Nicholas Cage movie *Con Air* came out and was a big hit. From then on our secretary, Denise Poe, would always label our prisoner flights on the big flight board in her office as Con Air 1, if it was in the Beechjet or Con Air 2, if it was in the King Air. We also had quite a few one day prisoner flights to California which were normally flown in the King Air. Most of those trips were to Lompoc but we serviced nearly every other major city down there as well. One flight that still makes me laugh involved a short hop over to Spokane, just to pick up one guy, followed by another short hop over to Billings for the drop off. This 'one guy' met the FAA equivalent weight of almost four passengers and we had to plan this flight in great detail. We needed his measurements to see if we could get him through the door, and we would have to use a forklift and pallet to load him since the air-stairs on the Beechjet had a fairly low max weight limitation. We also had to take some seats out so he could fit inside the cabin. Luckily, a couple of the rear seats in the Beechjet could be articulated out away from the bulkhead so with the opposite side seat removed we could actually get him in there and secured in his seat using the seat belt doubler. It also got his weight more centrally located towards the middle of the fuselage. Anyway, when we got to Flight Craft at Geiger Field I was standing outside the plane, waiting for the prison van, shooting the breeze with one of their line girls. She was quite young and naïve and pretty excited about the big "to-do" involving this massive prisoner. When the van showed up, and opened its sliding side door, he filled most of it while getting out; I immediately thought that we weren't going to be able to pull this off. Well, first he had to go inside and go potty, which took about 15 minutes. By the time he came back out, flanked by his prison guards, he had worked up a real sweat. I commented to the young line girl, "Don't see why we need any guards, he couldn't waddle more than 10 feet before he had a heart attack anyway." For some reason she thought my joke was extremely funny and let out a really raucous snorting laugh which caught the prisoner's attention. As he waddled towards the plane, huffing and puffing, he looked over at us and when he saw how cute my snorting partner was he winked at her . . . . Of course, he could have been winking at me I guess . . . . Anyway, I whispered to her, "I think he really likes you!" She started to get the dry heaves and just said "Oh Jesus, gag me with a fork!" or something along those lines. I went on over to "supervise" the loading . . . . He could barely step the four inches up onto the pallet and the small fork lift was really working hard to lift him the three feet up to the aisle entry level. There was a considerable amount of pushing, shoving, grunting, and twisting, but we finally squeezed that sweaty pile of shit through the door . . . Man, he was all lathered up now and really starting to smell bad . . . . That poor Beechjet would never be the same after this guy got done torquing the main spar and stinking up the leather upholstery. While the guards were securing him in the seat I went back over to the cute line girl and told her that while we were loading him he had asked me what her name was . . . . I told her that I thought it would be OK and went ahead and gave him her name and phone number . . . . She just turned white and said in a real low gasp, "You didn't?" I tried to act surprised and hurt by her reaction and just said, "Geez, I thought you'd like having a prison pen pal?" Just then I said, "Well, gotta go" and climbed in. While she was marshaling us out of our parking spot to taxi she was really glaring at me and I really felt bad for a few seconds . . . . My co-pilot noticed her look and asked me what's up her butt and I told him all about the dastardly deed . . . . He laughed his ass off while he turned the A/C to max to help kill the stench in the cabin.

Myself in front of Beechjet wing at Flight Craft in
Spokane during a prisoner flight, 1999

Over the years of flying prisoners we really never had any trouble with any of them other than the occasional smart ass remark. Some of the more violent-escape prone types were required to wear some kind of taser jock-belt apparatus around their crotch and were shown a video of what happens if one of the guards was forced to activate it due to any misbehavior on their part. I never saw the video but was told this device caused the wearer to simultaneously urinate, defecate, ejaculate, vomit, and pass out . . . . The Corrections personnel called its effects "Doing the Funky Chicken" . . . . I imagine some of you more kinky folks out there might enjoy that sort of jolt to the crotch but I'm sure glad I never had to clean up the mess after an activation!! On one trip we picked up a female prisoner down in Pine Bluff, Arkansas. She was bi-polar, schizophrenic, and probably suffering from multiple personality disorder . . . . She was constantly talking out loud and everything that went on in her head she vocalized immediately . . . When she got near the plane for loading she really freaked out and the Corrections lieutenants had a helluva time getting her inside . . . She was jabbering the whole flight and the slightest airplane bump or maneuver would set her off for several minutes of bible quoting and how this airplane was a vehicle for Lucifer and was taking her to her eternal damnation . . . . (actually just Purdy Treatment Center for Women in Gig Harbor). Landing in Olympia really set her off again and she began to really struggle. She also started spitting on the lieutenants . . . Now this was quite an escalation of her behavior so before we could open the door they had to put her in a straight jacket and added some sort of "Bee Bonnet" apparatus to her head so she couldn't spit on anyone else. When we opened the hatch, they had to drag her out screaming, spitting, and struggling . . . . She was quite the sight all bound up in lag shackles, straight jacket, bee bonnet, etc . . . . As luck would have it our new secretary, Aloha Watson, came outside the hangar to witness her first ever prisoner unloading event . . . . I caught a glimpse of her reeling back towards the office door as they drug that deranged wildcat kicking and screaming over to the prison van . . . We walked over to her and she anxiously asked us how everything had gone? Of course, we couldn't pass up this opportunity to act cool and just said; "Pretty boring as usual . . ."

On one prisoner flight down to Bartlesville, Oklahoma, we picked up a kindly looking old man at the FBO to transport to the Walla Walla prison for some reason or other. While we were standing around in the lobby, one of the Corrections Lieutenants, Gary Guffey, was chewing away on the last bearclaw the FBO had left out. The old man politely asked Gary if he could have one too; Gary took another bite then handed the old man what was left. Man, he scarfed that piece down like it was filet mignon. He thanked Gary profusely and I became rather curious about this prisoner who looked like he was about 80 years old or so. I made the fatal mistake to ask Gary what this guy had done even though our bosses had warned us never to ask any questions about our "special" passengers . . . . Gary was all too happy to pass on this guy's history . . . . Apparently, back in the late forties, this unlikely looking fellow had been a serial killer in the Midwest somewhere and not just your run of the mill serial killer . . . . His specialty was torturing and killing pregnant women then cutting out the fetus and eating it . . . . Dammit, I was really angry at myself for asking Gary about this guy and for months afterwards I couldn't get the image of his horrendous crimes out of my brain. As they say, looks can be deceiving and this piece of shit sure fit that bill!! Anyway, that was the last time I ever asked any questions about the maggots we flew . . . .

In 1994 fellow WSP pilot Joe Anderson 252 introduced me to his father-in-law, Mark Aarhaus, who just happened to have his own airport and fleet of planes down in Elma. Mark leaned slightly toward the eccentric side but was one of the most generous guys I'd ever met. His airport, which was located right below the cooling towers of the abandoned Satsop Nuclear Power Plant, was named 'My Airport'. It was a little testy getting in and out of there with all the trees so close and the runway had a nice little built in dogleg to deal with at its west end. Mark built a beautiful hangar next to the strip but felt it was incomplete until he finished it off with a somewhat unusual addition. At the Shelton Airport a few miles away there was a company that scrapped old Boeing airliners. Mark made a deal with them and purchased the front section of a B727 and trucked it down to his airport. It included the first class seats, galley, restroom, and cockpit. He attached it to the south side of his hangar with about 20 feet of it sticking outside. The cockpit was pretty complete and he would take his grandkids up there and give them some dual from time to time. He also had a fleet of 'older' planes; as I remember there was a

Luscombe, Taylorcraft, Ercoupe, Skylane, and a very nice Piper PA12 Super Cruiser, among several others. When I casually mentioned to Mark that I had never flown a tail-dragger he was just incredulous and told me flat out that he was going to immediately rectify that problem and make a **real pilot** out of me immediately! He honestly felt that not being taildragger capable was a serious character flaw and you couldn't really call yourself a pilot until you'd soloed in one.

So began my career as a taildragger pilot. For the next few years, whenever I had some spare time, I was off to Elma to fly that PA12. Mark turned me loose for solo after a few hours and Debbie and I made a lot of trips all over Western Washington in that creampuff. Mark had installed a 150 hp engine and it was a real performer. He would not take any money from me so all I had to do was fill it with gas and go. I happened to notice from time to time that not all the parts on the plane were initially intended for airplane usage. The springs on the tailwheel still had the Ernst Hardware sticker on them, the alternator, oil filter, and several other engine parts were off the shelf items from the local Checker Auto Parts store, but everything worked fine and I never had any mechanical issues with the plane. Mark was a millionaire but when you talked to him he would complain he was just a broken down old logger living on his social security; to emphasize his point he would pull his empty pants pockets inside out and proclaim; "I spent most of my money on women and beer . . . the rest I just wasted . . ." The taildragger time I accumulated in that PA12 really came in handy a couple years later when I was given the opportunity of a lifetime at the Olympic Flight Museum . . . . More on that later.

Although that dead stick landing I made in the Skylane at Moses Lake was the most significant mechanical issue I encountered in my flying career, there were several other incidents that definitely got my blood pressure elevated a little. Getting an Engine Fire Light was a fairly common King Air 200 occurrence, especially if we had just washed the plane. The first time I saw one light up I dutifully announced to the Captain in a not too subdued tone of voice that we had an engine fire . . . . He calmly asked me to look out the window to see if there was any smoke and flames coming out of the affected engine . . . . When I said no he asked if there was any engine gauge readings that might support or indicate a fire and I had to say no, there was not. He finally explained to me what happens when you wash and rinse the engine nacelles too vigorously and get water inside the cowling. Apparently the older King Airs had optical mirror type fire sensors which detected the bright light from an engine fire . . . If those mirrors had water on them, then sometimes during a climbing turn, if the sun hit them just right through a gap in the cowling, the light could be refracted just right to activate the circuitry and give you the fire light in the cockpit . . .

While on a King Air flight from Spokane to Olympia one afternoon we got a chip light (metal debris in the engine) annunciator and master warning light flashing in our faces . . . Had I not just returned from Flight Safety the emergency procedures memory item checklist called for an immediate engine shutdown. However, the well trained ground instructors in Wichita had just instructed me a couple days ago to always look for corresponding engine gauge readings, such as fluctuating oil pressure, rising oil temps, fluctuating torque or prop rpm, vibrations, etc., that would support a precautionary engine shutdown when you got a chip light . . . . Since we didn't have any corroborating data indicating that the affected engine really had a bearing coming apart I decided to keep it running especially since we had the governor on board and he really liked to see both of those big four bladed fans turning all the time. My co-pilot, however, hadn't been to Flight Safety yet and really wanted to shut that mother down—immediately! . . . We had a somewhat heated discussion and I finally acquiesced a little and said we'd reduce power on the affected engine, monitor it, but would not shut it down. Nobody in the back noticed a thing and after landing we advised the maintenance crew about the chip light. They drained the oil and detected some microscopic metal pieces they said were normal. There wasn't enough to warrant anything other than an engine pressure flush and a fresh oil change. We never had any further issues with that engine. Blowing current limiters was a fairly common event on the 200 but we always carried spares in the coffee bar drawer and the tools to replace them;

we usually noticed one was blown just after an engine start. It only took a couple minutes to replace a limiter, since the access panel was just under a carpet flap behind the pilot's seat; normally, we were under way in no time.

The Beechjet was a little more problematic than the King Air . . . . The biggest scare that happened to me **twice** was having to deal with frozen throttle cables that were stuck solid and wouldn't allow me to reduce thrust for a descent. The first time we were only at FL240 in mid winter on a flight from Walla Walla to Olympia. When I went to reduce power and start my let down over Yakima, the throttles wouldn't budge a millimeter. There was no checklist or emergency procedures to cover this eventuality so we were really in the dark as to what to do. We finally concluded that we would probably have to climb in order to slow to gear and flap speed and then hope that with the extra drag from those items we could slowly descend without exceeding their V speed limitations. Then, we hoped that once we got into warmer air the throttles would release. In our excitement, the only back up plan we came up with for landing, if the throttles were still stuck at lower elevations, was to hit the fuel firewall shutoff valves close in to the airport and then make a dead stick landing. However, before we tried the climb we both had an "Aha!" moment and just extended the speed brakes (spoilers) which slowed us down enough to start a slow descent even though we were still at cruise power. We were right at red line on the airspeed tape but we **were** descending, albeit quite slowly. At around 16,000 one of the throttles freed up so we brought that engine to idle. Going through 12,000 the other throttle freed up and we finished the trip with no other problems. When we told the mechanics what happened they seemed to think it was no big deal. They told us in the future to just keep moving the throttles back and forth in the climb and at cruise so they wouldn't freeze up. When I said that the governor probably wouldn't like to hear the power being jockeyed up and down, especially during cruise, they finally acquiesced a little and said they would re-lube the cables with fresh grease. About a month later I was on a prisoner flight to Denver. It was a crystal clear day with +5 ISA temps so frozen throttles didn't enter my mind. However, when we tried to start our descent from

FL370 over the Front Range into Denver I discovered the throttles were stuck in cement again. We popped the speed brakes and began a really high speed descent with the whole plane vibrating like crazy due to the spoilers being extended for such a long period. Finally going through 12,000 the throttles both released at the same time and we were able to make it into Jeffco, which had an authorized Beechcraft service center at the FBO. After briefing the service rep. about our frozen throttle issue he told us right away that there was a two year old Beechcraft service bulletin concerning those original cables and that they should have been replaced long ago. When I called our maintenance supervisor he dodged the issue, got a little testy and just said to go ahead and have them replaced in Wichita and he'd make the appointment for us. So, we flew low level to Wichita where the Beechcraft Service Center supervisor was waiting for us and pulled the plane into the hangar immediately to start the work. He told us that the original cables had the wrong kind of internal grease which tended to thicken up a bit when exposed to the frigid temps at high altitude . . . . I told him a bit sarcastically that the grease was doing a little more than just thickening up . . . He said they had the new and improved throttle cables in stock and that they would do the work overnight! The next morning we were good to go and none of our Corrections folks had any complaints about the extra night on the road. Never had another problem with frozen throttle cables. Later at Flight Safety when I discussed this problem with a Beechjet ground instructor he said it would not have been a smart idea to shut off the fuel firewall valves with the engines at cruise power as that would have collapsed the fuel lines immediately . . . Glad we hadn't over-reacted on that Walla Walla leg!

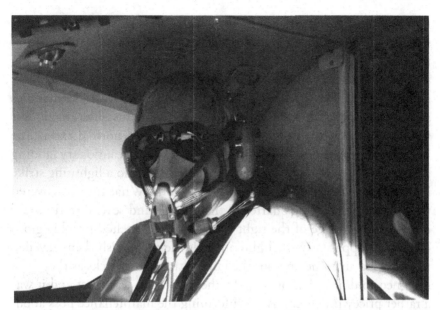

Myself at FL450 (45,000 ft.) in the Beechjet over Eastern Montana. Useful consciousness at that altitude, should the pressurization system fail, is about 5 seconds . . . . One of the pilots usually wore an oxygen mask just in case.

On another prisoner flight we were cruising at FL450 over Indiana and had just made a thirty degree course deviation to the north to avoid a huge thunderstorm build-up probably thirty miles away with tops over fifty thousand feet. It was all magenta on our radar and made the piddily ass thunderstorms of the Pacific Northwest look like a light spring shower in comparison. (The guys at Flight Safety in Wichita called Pacific Northwest thunderstorms **popcorn farts** in comparison to theirs.) Even though we were in the clear we were suddenly blinded by a brilliant white light . . . My vision was totally shot for a few seconds but my hearing was fine because I definitely heard the autopilot disconnect alarm tweedling away. When I could see again I immediately noticed that all our CRT EFIS screens were very black and that we were down to our emergency back-up "peanut gauges" for basic flight information. As usual, there was no emergency procedure checklist for this eventuality. We just couldn't believe that we'd had a lightning strike but everything was sure supporting that conclusion. We checked all the breakers and none of them had popped. While hand flying that mother at FL450, which I have to say is a real dicey situation, we talked our way through the problem. We assumed that the CRT's had overheated, if indeed we had experienced a lightning strike, and had probably shut down to save themselves. So after advising center what we were doing we flipped both master avionics switches off for a minute and then reset them. Just like magic our CRT's sprang back to life and everything seemed normal except the radar wasn't functioning. We decided to make a precautionary landing at Terre Haute and have the FBO personnel there do a lightning strike inspection before we carried on to New York. What they discovered was a hole the size of a quarter in the radome and several static wicks on the trailing edge of the right horizontal stab melted into big globs of plastic. Apparently the lightening hit the radar dish then travelled through the airframe and out the tail melting those wicks as they were designed to do . . . Unfortunately, the radar unit was toast and it was a rather pricey little item. After informing the maintenance boss about the situation he just said to take the bird to Wichita and have a loaner installed. The Terre Haute guys put some 500 mph tape over the hole in the radome and replaced the static wicks with the two spares we always carried with us. And so, we spent another unscheduled night in Wichita with the two Corrections lieutenants again . . . I know they didn't mind a bit when these little diversions occurred and the local jail was always willing to house a couple prisoners for the night. We were forced to eat at the *Outback* again where we were already on a first name basis with the staff; it was only two blocks from the Tallgrass where we always stayed during our Flight Safety recurrents. The next morning we were good to go with our loaner radar installed and continued our trip to Newburgh, New York.

On our next trip to Stewart Field in New York everything went well until our departure. I was flying with Don Tingvall 870 again, the same guy who experienced the lightening hit with me. All was going well during our climb out until we passed through a really weird layer of some kind of hazy material . . . . It wasn't a cloud or dust but it was creating a strange wavy effect that looked to me like a thermo cline Deb and I often experienced when diving in an area where salt water meets fresh water of a different temperature. As we both tried to figure out what it was the stick shaker suddenly activated indicating an impending stall . . . . We both snapped our heads towards the angle of attack and airspeed indicators but saw that we were still in the 250 knot climb mode and nowhere near a stall . . . . What caught our attention was the low and high speed red cue tapes were approaching each other on the sides of the airspeed indicator leaving us about a five knot window to fly in without setting off either the over-speed horn or the stick shaker . . . Another one of those WTF moments! Again, there was no emergency procedures checklist for this condition but the plane was flying perfectly other than the erroneous speed tape indications. We discussed turning around and heading back to Newburgh but felt that the autopilot was handling things fine and knew we could always pull the horn warning circuit breaker to cancel all the noise if this condition didn't go away at cruise . . . Of course we also knew that pulling that breaker cancelled the gear horn . . . But since neither of us had ever landed gear-up we thought we'd chance it. After about five minutes of this craziness the two red speed tapes suddenly parted ways, ascending and descending into their normal positions for a climb . . . . About this time we finally looked outside and realized we could hardly see anything . . . . The windscreen was covered in some kind of material just about obliterating forward vision. Most of the gunk eventually peeled off and when we landed in Sioux Falls for gas we finally discovered what the hell happened. The gunk was actually comprised of several million very small insects. We had apparently passed through their home world on the climb out of Stewart whereupon they proceeded to instantly overwhelm and temporarily clog both our pitot tubes causing those crazy speed tape indications. After we checked with our mechanics in Olympia they advised us that having those pitot heaters on eventually fried them all and turned their little bodies into ash whereupon they blew out the little drain holes in the back of the pitots, resolving the problem . . . . Not quite as exciting or dramatic as running into geese and landing an airliner in the Hudson River but for us it got our blood pressure up for a few minutes!

One winter morning Brian Holliday and I were flying the Chief into Wenatchee in the Beechjet. It was a clear day but the runway was reported to have only fair braking due to ice accumulation. I was flying and wasn't too concerned since the jet had a fantastic ABS braking system and tremendous thrust reversers which in my experience got her slowed down in very short order even on ice. I set her down right on the numbers at Vref and immediately pulled the reversers to max . . . Brian was calling out my speed and as we passed mid point it hadn't decreased much since touch down . . . . Jesus, I was on the brakes as hard as I could and felt the ABS cycling and pounding on the rudder pedals under my feet . . . . I had already exceeded the maximum duration for thrust reverser deployment but wasn't about to bring them in now . . . As we saw the end of the runway coming up quite rapidly, Brian said something like "You'd better get this bitch slowed down Rick . . . !!" Man, I had to laugh . . . like I wasn't already trying my damndest to do just that! Well, we used up every God Damned inch of that 5,700 ft. runway and I barely had room to make the turn-off at the end without getting out into the deep snow . . . . That was the closest I ever came to losing my job . . . . The chief at that time was a very perceptive cat and when he got off the plane he just glared at the two of us and shook his head very disgustedly . . . He never said a word but I for one certainly got his message loud and clear: "You ever do that again and I'll fire your stupid ass!!" . . . . The major issue that day was the ice condition . . . It was compacted from the day before and hadn't been sanded. Additionally, by the time we got there, it had warmed up and there was water on top of the ice which created a perfect storm for super slick conditions . . . I don't know what it was about that place but I sure had a lot of ugly incidents there in my career!

On one sunny morning in Olympia I experienced yet another moment of bad judgment while sitting in the Beechjet chatting with Chief Annette Sandberg waiting for a tardy passenger to show up. Her assistant mentioned to her that I had just come back from a trip to Italy so she asked me if I spoke Italian. I said just a little but I wasn't conversant by any means . . . She then asks me to say something in Italian . . . . Man I freaked out a little with all the pressure and couldn't immediately think of anything appropriate . . . . The only phrase that eventually came to mind was a slang saying that I had picked up recently and thought was very funny . . . So, not wanting to appear to be a dumb shit in front of the Chief and without thinking too much about it I blurted out: "Va' a fare una bella cacata! Ti sentirai meglio." She seemed impressed at my quick response and solid grasp of the language but then asked what it meant . . . . Well, the actual translation is; "Go take a big shit, you'll feel better" . . . . I determined that she wouldn't think that was as funny as I did . . . . So I lied to the Chief of the WSP right to her face and told her that it translated to; "Let's go for a walk, you'll feel better."' I was rather proud of myself that I was able to come up with such a convincing lie on the spur of the moment like that! I think she bought it but no doubt looked up the words later and discovered that I was the one full of 'cacata'!

On another flight with Brian in the Beechjet, with the governor on board this time, we found ourselves about 30 min. out of Richmond, VA when one of the executive protection troopers (who just happened to be Brian's wife Becky) came forward and said the governor was complaining of smoke in the cabin . . . We had noticed a slight odor ourselves and when we turned around and looked backwards the length of the fuselage, you could clearly see a gray oily mist in the air . . . . We both knew that this situation called for us to immediately don our oxygen masks and put our smoke goggles on and begin smoke removal procedures . . . . After talking it over neither of us thought it was quite that bad yet so we decided to ride it out a little longer since we were so close to landing . . . . We tried to isolate which engine the oily smoke was coming from by rotating the cabin pressure source switch from left engine to right engine but before we could determine which one was the problem ATC started us down for Richmond. With the power pulled back and the cabin de-pressurizing during the descent, the odor and oily mist went away almost immediately. We called our maintenance guys upon landing with all the details but they didn't have too much advice for us other than trying to determine which engine it was coming from by selecting one engine pressurization source switch then the other to see which one had the oil leak . . . Well, we had already figured that one out ourselves . . . . So, we tried not to worry about our return flight too much. The next day was spent visiting Brian's son, who was stationed at Norfolk in the Navy, and touring Jamestown Colony near Williamsburg while we both secretly hoped that the cabin didn't fill with smoke again tomorrow! On the climb out at that morning at max continuous thrust we just guessed on which engine to select first . . . . We got lucky selecting the right side engine since there were no further oil smells or smoke for the whole flight home as long as we used it alone as the single cabin pressure source. The next day the mechanics tore into the left engine and soon found a crack in an integral oil line in the engine's compressor section which supplied bleed air to the planes' air conditioning system. It wasn't a big oil leak but bad enough to slowly cause the smoke and oil odor to accumulate in the cabin. After they talked to the engineers at Pratt and Whitney I think they just welded the crack up but can't remember for sure. The whole episode wasn't a real big deal but if we had put on our masks and goggles and then popped the passenger oxygen masks for everyone else, I think we would have really freaked out the governor who wasn't a very good flyer in the first place!

Brian and I had one other interesting incident while flying the chief from Olympia down to The Dalles very early one morning for an officer involved shooting. It was pitch black out with no moon when all of a sudden we witnessed this huge meteor streak across the sky, seemingly right in front of us . . . . Now, we all had seen meteors before and occasionally the aurora on night flights, but this one was bright green and looked like it could have taken out a small city even though it was probably only a few inches in diameter! Neither one of us spoke . . . we just looked at each other with that usual WTF expression on our faces.

It was only a couple weeks later when Monty Colver and I were returning from Spokane in the Beechjet with the governor on board again. We had to shoot an ILS back into Olympia which was always a joy in that plane . . . It had a great auto pilot which would take you right down to minimums and then some . . . . When you finally broke out of the clouds, the plane was never more than a few feet right or left of the centerline. We usually hand-flew all approaches but if we were really tired it was such a relief to let "George" do all the work. Anyway, upon breaking out that night and after the radar altimeter beeped at 50 feet AGL, all I had to do was pull the power levers smoothly to idle thrust, punch the yaw damp off, pitch 10 degrees nose up, and wait for the almost guaranteed greaser . . . . Unfortunately, tonight was a little different! I got the usual greaser (which was always the plane and not the pilot by the way) but a split second later we suddenly experienced a severe torque to the left and began heading for the weeds very fast since our Vref was around 115 knots!! I jumped on the right brake as hard as I could and just then we both heard a tremendous flapping and thrashing noise coming from the left side . . . My first thought was that we'd hit a deer or coyote and it was now somehow jamming the left wheel up! With max reversing and all the pressure I could put on that right brake, where I felt the ABS system pounding my foot very rhythmically, we finally came almost to a stop just on the left edge of the runway but only a few feet from a taxi way turnoff . . . . I didn't want to block the runway for the guy shooting the approach behind us so I gave it some power and thump thumped our way around the corner onto the taxiway and shut it down. The governor's eyes were as big as saucers as we all got out to inspect the damage. There was no deer or coyote to be seen, just a blown out tire torn to shreds. We just couldn't figure out when that tire went flat since the plane had sat on the ramp at Spokane all afternoon and was full of air on departure . . . . For some reason it deflated during that 40 minute leg . . . . Anyway, the governor came up and sort of got in my face and made some sarcastic comment about whether I expected anything else to break on this God Damned plane anytime soon?? I hoped he was kidding, which he was . . . . He slapped me on the back, shook hands, and thanked me for keeping it on the pavement . . . Monty and I stayed with the plane while they all walked back to the hangar through the weeds. Thankfully the gear door wasn't damaged but our jet technicians had to replace the wheel which was pretty beat up. They said that the tire was definitely already flat before touchdown and later contacted Raytheon to see if this was a fleet wide issue with that wheel and tire combo . . . The long angling skid mark to the left, that the flat tire laid down that night on RWY 17, was still there when I retired.

Sometime later I was flying some prisoners to Rockland, Maine. The runway conditions were listed as poor but there was no specific braking action report. As we circled the field evaluating the conditions I heard an FAA mobile at the airport announcing he was going out to the VOR . . . I asked him on Unicom if he could give me a runway braking report . . . He said no problem and proceeded out onto the runway . . . While circling above, we watched as he accelerated then suddenly was sliding sideways and then took a long time to stop . . . Of course he came back and reported that it was very slick. The runway was much shorter than the one I almost slid off at Wenatchee so I started my climb and asked for vectors to our alternate, Portland. My co-pilot was upset with me when I wouldn't try landing at Rockland, even after witnessing the FAA mobile 'test slide'. He was in a hurry to get home for some kind of celebration that night and as I recall had a limo rented and knew this diversion was going to cause some serious delays for him and get him into big trouble with his wife . . . Later on that irresponsible attitude towards adverse weather conditions cost him his flying career.

During my years at the WSP and afterwards I made over thirty trips to Flight Safety, primarily in Wichita, for initials and re-current training in the King Air, Beechjet, and Citation Jet. We got to know most of the ground and sim instructors fairly well and learned to anticipate their little pet peeves, training methods, idiosyncrasies, and various sim tricks which they repeated year after year . . . . When you're dealing with so many clients it must be hard to keep it fresh for everyone but nearly all of them did. If you paid attention during ground school there was nearly always a scenario in the sim the same day that brought home the message about a particular system malfunction discussed during ground school. Some of the instructors just gave you an assembly line of maneuvers, approaches, and emergencies to deal with, one right after another, in order to get you signed off for your 61.58 PIC endorsement as quickly as possible. Others tried to make the sim experience more line oriented and had you fly a normal mission in real time to an airport other than Hutchinson, Wichita, or Salina . . . . (the only three airports we thought the sims had programmed into them). During those line oriented flights you had to deal with normal flight scenarios involving fuel consumption, icing, turbulence, wind shear, headwinds, other lousy weather and a few in flight emergencies to spice things up a bit. A few of the instructors were pretty much sado-masochists; these were the guys who would hit you with multiple unrealistic emergencies on your first takeoff in the sim during the first session. There is no doubt that any or all of those things 'could' happen at some point but having a thrust reverser deployment at V1 followed shortly thereafter by a pitch trim runaway then smoke in the cockpit all in the first ten seconds of a flight is a bit much! During one of my later King Air re-currents we were assigned a part time sim instructor who had just been furloughed by a major airline. He acted quite disgruntled and disinterested but when he found out that my partner and I weren't just civilian pilots working for the State Patrol but were actually troopers, his demeanor went from blasé to semi-vicious in an instant. It was quite apparent that he had a real hard-on for cops and he tried his best to embarrass us to satisfy whatever void or need for revenge he had going on in his life right then. Man, right after gear-up it was just non-stop emergencies piled on worse emergencies . . . He never gave us a chance to get the checklist out for each one before a new one occurred. We finally just tried to do everything from memory and to just keep the plane right side up. Eventually we were down to no generators, a dead battery, a single (surging) engine which we had restarted after initially shutting it down for an engine fire (we shut the other one down for zero oil pressure), a dark cockpit except for our flash lights, severe turbulence in severe icing, all while still in solid IFR conditions at night. With only the vacuum powered instruments and fluctuating engine power we attempted a let-down for an off field landing over an area we knew from personal experience was mostly flat corn fields between Salina and Wichita. When we broke out and it looked like we were going to be able to land on a road he froze the sim a couple hundred feet in the air and told us we had just crashed and killed everyone on board . . . . During the de-brief he said we were incompetent, berated us for bad CRM, not using the emergency checklists, and a host of other things he pulled out of his ass. Eventually, we both just got up and walked out of the briefing room while he was still ranting! He was the first and only sim instructor I had to rip a new asshole on the post Flight Safety session critique form we all had to fill out. My partner did the same and I was quite happy to see this moron's employee photo gone from the waiting room wall in the Flight Safety lobby when we returned six months later for our next re-current. Obviously, one of the full time managerial professionals at FSI had also recognized this cat's personality deficits and canned him. That was the first and only time any of the WSP pilots ever had an issue with any FSI personnel.

For some reason one of my most memorable Flight Safety moments occurred in the King Air sim during a "routine" V1 cut departing San Francisco to the West in night IFR conditions. I cleaned the plane up had Vyse nailed but was told by the instructor that I had to hold my present heading due to conflicting parallel traffic. I knew there was a coastal mountain range coming up and the radar altimeter was winding down very rapidly but he wouldn't let me turn. Suddenly, there was a big shuddering thud as the sim slammed to an abrupt stop near the San Andreas Rift zone. The instructor asked me what I could have done differently, without turning the aircraft, to prevent the crash and clear the ridge . . . . I had no idea and thought it was some kind of trick question. He reset the sim for me and we duplicated the previous flight parameters exactly as before. However, this time right after I cleaned up the failed PT6, he told me to turn the generator off on the operating engine and to just run on battery power during the climb out. I really didn't notice any difference until he told me to look at my rate of climb indicator . . . . Shutting that generator down did give me an extra 100 fpm climb rate and when I got to my previous crash site I sailed over that ridge with room to spare . . . . I had no idea an operating generator created so much drag on an engine! I've long since forgotten all the other lessons learned at Flight Safety but this one has stuck with me . . . .

In 1996 I had my 25 years in with the WSP and could legally retire and maybe go get another flying job out in the real world. But I was still enjoying myself, the patrol still had a decent budget for our Aviation Section, and I didn't have to spend too much time turning circles in the Cessnas. I still enjoyed working traffic and especially nailing the serial tailgaters and other aggressive drivers but the toll it took on my fused cervical vertebrae really caused me a lot of sleepless nights. The problem was that all your neck muscles got really tight when you spent all day with your head cranked to the left, watching traffic down below. When you encountered turbulence in that condition there didn't seem to be any elasticity left in the muscles and tendons. When a big bump was encountered pain and suffering soon followed. As long as I didn't have to work traffic more than two days in a row I was fine but I sure went through a lot of Advil in those years, and my stomach has never been the same since!

A couple years later I was overjoyed to learn that the owner of *Northwest Helicopters*, Brian Reynolds, was going to build a WWII aviation museum at the Olympia airport. Deb and I were still going to the Reno Air Races every year and my love of those old vintage planes had not diminished. As I recall, Brian bought a group of warbirds from Bob Pond from his museum in Minnesota and we soon started seeing them arrive. A P51, F4U Corsair, Douglas Skyraider, TBM Avenger, and a replica Zero flown in the movie *Tora, Tora, Tora.* were just a few of the planes in the collection. Brian named his new enterprise *The Olympic Flight Museum* and it was located just a couple hundred yards south of our hangar. This was an exciting time for me and when I saw Brian taxiing his P51 to the hangar one afternoon I went over and introduced myself. I asked if there were any volunteer opportunities available and he immediately said he needed someone to construct reader boards for each of the planes on exhibit. Thankfully I had hundreds of WWII books containing all the specifications and history of each warbird in Brian's collection so with the help of a gentleman at Kinkos I soon came up with large color reader boards for all the planes. I also built tripods to mount them on and soon the project was done. While I was setting up the last one in front of the museum's AT6 Texan one afternoon Brian and his museum co-founder Richard Potts came over to thank me for all the work. Then, out of the blue Brian asked me if I had any taildragger time. When I said I had a couple hundred hours in a Super Cruiser he just matter of factly asked if I would be interested in flying museum customers in his AT6 . . . . Well, inwardly I was thinking: "Jesus Christ, did the pope shit in the woods?" . . . . But being the consummate professional I responded with a non-chalant "Why yes, I would be interested Brian . . . . Thank you very much." So began the next phase of my aviation career.

CHAPTER 12

THE GLORY YEARS

Brian asked that I get a formal AT6 checkout and a sign off from an experienced Texan operator before he could allow me to begin taking his museum customers up for rides. My cousin, Carl Terrana, had owned and operated a T6 for years so I called him for advice. He recommended his buddy who had his own airstrip down near Winlock and thought he might be able to give me some dual in his T6. I met with him one afternoon but he called me later and said his insurance wouldn't cover him giving instruction. So I made some inquiries and found an outfit down in Kissimmee, Florida that offered a complete AT6 checkout with a 10 hour aerobatic course included. As luck would have it Deb and I already had a trip planned to Disney World the next month so we just added a few days to allow time for the checkout. Thom Richard at *Warbird Adventures* was my instructor pilot and he really put me through the meat grinder in that old bird . . . It was hotter than hell so it was mandatory to keep the canopy open most of the time to stay reasonably cool. The cockpit on this old SNJ4 was a little hard to adjust to after flying a state of the art glass cockpit Beechjet with the latest Collins FMS . . . . All the controls seemed to require a lot of hard pulling, pumping, yanking, twisting, and cranking . . . The gas gauges were hidden down in the floorboards behind the seat and were harder than hell to see. I recall having to manually pump up pressure in the hydraulic system just to put the gear or flaps down . . . . My respect for all those WWII era aviators and the primitive equipment they had to deal with grew with each hour I spent in the old girl. I thoroughly enjoyed the aerobatic course except for the spins . . . . Man those were a real rip-snorter and I remember smelling raw gas venting overboard and hearing a lot of oil-canning sounds coming from the empennage during each one . . . .

My favorite maneuvers were the Cuban eights, eight point hesitation rolls, and the split-ess. I enjoyed doing loops but discovered that it wasn't a good idea to get slow at the top as I regrettably found out a few years later . . . . Several people had mentioned that the T6 had a vicious stall but I found it to be quite predictable even though there was a considerable wing drop when it finally broke. However, the accelerated maneuver stall was a little dramatic, and not a maneuver I wanted to practice too often. Thom had me doing three pointers in no time but I occasionally got confused locking and unlocking the tail wheel while taxiing . . . He had to raise his voice a couple times and yelled into the intercom "Rick, it won't turn with the tail wheel locked" as he shoved the stick forward out of my hands so it would release . . . . Thom's other "Mantra" that has always stuck with me was his emergency egress memory checklist: "Canopy, headset, seatbelt, out!" (roll the canopy all the way back, unplug your helmet, undo your **seatbelt . . . . NOT THE PARACHUTE HARNESS** . . . , then jump out the low side). I continued to use his Mantra for years and briefed all museum riders with it before every flight. That SNJ had a camera out on the wingtip and all my flights were videotaped. I still enjoy watching those tapes with all the Florida country side and lakes upside down and spinning in the background. When I got back to Olympia I had another checkout ride with Ray Chalker then a final one with Brian before I was finally turned loose to give museum rides. I always found it to be such a paradigm shift of technology to jump out of a state of the art, glass cockpit 440 knot jet, and an hour later climb into a 1930's designed round engine crate . . . . But man, I wasn't complaining! Those summers from 1999 to 2004 were some of the most fulfilling of my aviation career. I took many WWII aviators up for their "last ride", some of whom had to be hoisted and assisted into the rear cockpit with much care. When I gave them the stick I was always surprised how smooth they were as if 60 years had no affect whatsoever on their stick and rudder skills. A couple of them had actually been AT6 instructors back in the forties and I was blown away when they flew that plane with such soft hands as if it was just yesterday when they last flew a T6. It was a tremendous privilege and honor to take these guys on those flights . . . something I will never forget. Another memory I'll never forget was when I heard that one of the T6s I had flown in Florida, just a few months before, was destroyed in a crash killing the instructor and student . . . . It wasn't Thom but one of his associates . . . . Raised my pucker factor a bit . . . .

Unusual attitude during my T6 training at Warbird Adventures with instructor Thom Richard waving from backseat . . . Thom also flies the highly modified P51 "Precious Metal" at the Reno Air Races each September.

One afternoon at the museum Teri Thorning, the museum director, arranged a ride for me with some guy named Bruce Mayes. I went out and did my usual thing, a couple aileron rolls, a few touch and goes down at Chehalis, and back to Olympia. He didn't say a word the whole flight. Afterwards, Teri asked me what I thought about Bruce . . . I told her I thought he was awfully quiet for a museum rider. That was when she advised me that he was the aircraft's owner and also a senior B737 captain for *Aloha Airlines* based in Honolulu . . . . Jesus, I wish someone would have advised me in advance! Shortly after flying with Bruce, Brian called me into his office one day and asked if I would be interested in sitting on the board of directors for the Museum . . . It was déjà vou all over again as I thought back on my time as a Port Commissioner in Ephrata . . . I had no idea what someone did sitting on such a board but never being one to show any hesitation, I immediately told Brian "Sure, sounds like fun!" It was fun and I enjoyed learning all about the internal struggles involved with running a flight museum.

I was flying the T6 in a formation flight up to Bremerton one morning when I just about bought the farm over Purdy. Brian was leading the formation in that big old Skyraider, Richard Potts was flying the TBM Avenger, and another guy was in the Tora Zero. After we had all formed up it became apparent that Brian had forgotten to raise the gear on the Skyraider. I glanced over at the Zero pilot who had a huge grin on his face and we both were thinking the same thing . . . who is going to say something first? . . . . Finally, Richard asked Brian on the plane to plane frequency if he was completing some sort of structural integrity test on his gear . . . . The Skyraider gear came up immediately with not a word spoken . . . We were cruising along at only 2500 feet or so and I was still chuckling to myself about Brian's gaff when I noticed I had gotten a few feet low and had drifted slightly behind the Skyraider . . . Suddenly it was payback time for my smug attitude and I found myself nearly inverted before I could wrestle the old girl back up to altitude and into formation. The wake turbulence off that Skyraider was horrendous! I glanced over at the Zero pilot and he was laughing his ass off . . . . again!! He must have thought he really hooked up with a bunch of winners for today's flight . . . .

Had another funny episode, at least I thought it was funny, when I took Deb up for a flight in the T6. I made sure all the turns were gentle and I had to keep the altitude down to around 1,500 ft AGL as she did not like to fly high. When I tried to explain that altitude is your friend in case something happens she got a little excited and wanted to know WHAT was going to happen that I needed altitude for?! . . . . I let it drop and flew low . . . . We had a great lunch up at Bremerton (PWT) where the airport diner has the best halibut and chips in the world. As usual, a small crowd had gathered around the T6 so I made a mental note to try not to ground loop it on departure.

Everything was going quite smoothly until we got to cruise altitude, which obviously didn't take too long. This bird had one little glitch which happened to be a sticky mixture lever. I had trouble with it in the past but today of all days it decided to hang up a little more than usual. When I tried to smoothly pull it back at cruise, to lean out that big ole P&W R-1340 a bit, the lever got stuck. When I applied a bit more pressure to break it free the damn thing suddenly released and momentarily went to a full lean condition and the engine went to idle. I sort of panicked and shoved it all the way forward without thinking . . . . Man, we got the biggest backfire I'd ever seen or heard (louder than a compressor stall during a tailwind start in a Beechjet) accompanied by a huge rolling ball of yellow/orange flame down the right side of the fuselage!! It sort of startled me a bit but its effect on Deb was pretty much catastrophic . . . She commenced a screaming dialogue at me on the intercom that pretty much consisted of an alternating chorus of "Take me down, take me down, take me down and/or put me down, put me down, put me down!!!!" Now you would think that after a few moments most people would calm down somewhat and quit yelling once a person noticed the plane was still flying very nicely but she kept it up until we got back into the pattern at Olympia. I had turned the volume down on the intercom as her screaming was starting to give me a headache . . . When I asked her to be quiet so I could talk to the tower to get permission to land she finally let up. Needless to say, she wasn't speaking to me for several days afterwards and when she did I was accused of viciously doing it all on purpose to exact revenge for some vague infraction she assumed I was paying her back for . . . . She has not flown with me since and unless the aircraft says Boeing on its side, she will not get in it.

In 1999 the WSP Aviation Section celebrated 40 years of accident free flying by hosting an open house at the hangar. It was a huge affair with a lot of 'old timers' in attendance including former Chief Will Bachofner among others. Back in the forties and early fifties there were no 'official' WSP aircraft. Patrolman Bill Gebinini owned an AT6 back in those days and painted the WSP insignia on its side. He patrolled around Western Washington and provided an early form of airborne traffic reporting for the WSP. I asked Bruce if I could attach some temporary WSP stickers to his T6 to resemble Bill's plane from those years and display it at the open house . . . He was fine with it and the plane was a big hit, especially to the old timers who remembered Gebinini. I also wrote an in depth article in the Washington Trooper Magazine about the history of the WSP Aviation Section which seemed to be well received.

Myself in Olympic Flight Museum's North American AT6 with WSP decals attached commemorating Patrolman Bill Gebinini and the T6 he flew for the patrol in the forties.

It was such a shame when shortly after the 40 year anniversary milestone of safe flying a couple of WSP pilots ran our beloved King Air 222KA off the end of the runway in Olympia one morning, collapsed the gear, bent the main spar, and destroyed a prop and engine . . . . Man, we were all really upset after the accident especially since it was 100% pilot error and had ruined our now 42 year perfect safety record . . . . The primary cause for this accident, in my opinion, was when our "commander" at that time scheduled a brand new command pilot with a brand new co-pilot which went against all known Flight Safety doctrine and crewing principles . . . To make matters worse it was the dead of winter during a period of high pressure with lingering morning fog which normally didn't break up until the late afternoon. Besides the crewing error, what we questioned most was the personal integrity of this command pilot who seemed to be in denial about the wreck and tried to evade taking full responsibility for it. Now, to be honest, all of us (including me) knew in our hearts that on a given day any one of us was capable of stacking a plane up . . . I'd come real close myself a couple times. The true test of a man is how he handles the aftermath and this cat was not handling it well! Nobody blamed the rookie co-pilot as he was just along for the ride and trusted the other guy's judgment. But when that command pilot tried to convince a group of very experienced King Air pilots that what happened was just some sort of "unavoidable incident", and then stuck to that story despite overwhelming evidence to the contrary, he clearly exemplified the epitome of irresponsible behavior. As a result of that arrogant attitude, he lost what little credibility he had left with us! . . . . Weeks later he was still sticking to his rendition of events wherein he **supposedly** broke out of the fog (official weather at the time was a 100 ft. ceiling and ¼ mi. visibility) at DH on the ILS, pulled the power off, went to full flaps, and **claimed he was on speed** which **should** have been 99 knots . . . . But, for some "unknown reason" with calm winds, an airplane loaded with 12 people weighing in at 5 & ½ tons that day, just somehow floated almost the entire length of a 5,500 ft runway, **without decelerating**, and touched down 376 feet from its far end . . . . ??? We just couldn't believe that anyone could be so egotistical that he actually believed he could deceive us and the accident investigators with such an implausible rendition of events that defied all the laws of physics and gravity!! Well, the FAA and NTSB didn't believe his story either and eventually suspended his ATP certificate.

At a pilot's meeting after the accident I raised the question of why he didn't perform a balked landing procedure when he saw he wasn't going to get it down in time? To no one's surprise, he got surly and defensive and just blew that option off saying they would have crashed for sure if they had attempted it?? Wow!! A balked landing procedure is in the King Air procedures manual for **exactly** this kind of situation and is a maneuver we all practiced at Flight Safety every six months during our recurrent sessions!! But, that was a long time ago already and I sincerely hope with the passage of time he has finally admitted to himself just how close he came to killing twelve people that day and has come to grips with it.

Anyway, while the King Air was down for repairs myself and Don Tingvall were the only jet pilots left. After a WSP investigation the pilot in question and his "commander" were transferred out of the Aviation Section. The co-pilot on that flight stayed in the Aviation Section but decided to transfer to Eastern Washington as a single engine pilot. As a result, Don and I ended up flying the hell out of the Beechjet to meet our busy schedule. We were on 24 hour/day call for four months straight and it was rough not having a beer for that long!! Finally the King Air was ready for a test flight and I took it up and gave her a thorough workout . . . Everything was perfect and it trimmed up very nicely; our mechanics had done a wonderful job putting her back together and the rebuilt Pratt & Whitney PT6 ran nice and cool! After the investigation was over, Lieutenant Tris Atkins, was appointed as the new commander of the Aviation Section. He was a colonel in the Army National Guard Reserves and brought a wealth of much needed aviation management expertise and maturity into the unit. In some respects the most painful "post accident residue" were the acid remarks we had to endure from our trooper buddies and other professional pilots around the state for the next few years. There was hardly a day gone by when someone didn't ask me if I was the dipstick that ran the King Air off the end of the runway . . . . Man, those kind of comments really got on my nerves and I occasionally reacted with some unkind remarks in response . . . . But, time heals all wounds and with the D.O.C. flights continuing to increase the accident soon became a distant memory.

I used to have a pin map of the United States marking all the airports I'd flown into during my "Con-Air" days . . . . Some of the lesser known airports (at least to me) we flew to were: Bimidgi, MN, International Falls, MN, Bartlesville, OK, Kokomo, IN, McAlester, OK, Toadsuck, AR, Glasgow, MT, Yazoo City, MI, Rockland, MA, Manassas, VA, Pine Bluff, AR and so many others that I've forgotten about. Other than flying the T6 at the museum those were some of the best flights of my career and I sure got to see a lot of rural America and meet some of its wildest and most psychopathic citizens. The flights I had into Los Angeles, Washington DC, Dallas, and other extremely congested areas I did not enjoy in the least . . . technically challenging, but not fun. When taxiing to the GA ramp took longer than the whole approach and often involved several different ground control frequencies and overly complicated airport diagrams I longed for the simple life at Bimidgi or Yazoo City!!

There was one non-WSP flight during that period that I enjoyed even more however! It happened while Deb and I were on a dive trip to Rarotonga in the South Pacific on Air New Zealand. The return trip left about 6pm and after dinner most everyone fell asleep. The plane was only half full so a lot of folks just laid down in the middle row of seats in that 747. After I slept for a couple of hours I was wide awake and bored since I had already read all the books I had brought with me for the trip. For the hell of it I handed my ATP Certificate, Driver's License, Passport, and Trooper's Commission card to a flight attendant and asked him to give it to the Captain to see if I could come up for a cockpit tour . . . . It goes without saying that this was pre-911 . . . . There is no doubt I would be pepper-sprayed, handcuffed, anesthetized, and probably shot if I tried that now. Anyway, the flight attendant was very cordial, took my documents, and disappeared. It was only a couple minutes when he came back and said follow me. Man, I couldn't believe this and even forgot to wake Deb up to tell her where I was going. When I got into the cockpit, the flight engineer went back to take a nap so I sat in his seat. The Captain was a great guy who had his seat way back, shoes off, and a stack of kit airplane magazines on the dash. He said he was driving up to Oregon after we landed at LAX to go over the order for his new RV kit from Vans

Aircraft in Aurora . . . He was so excited about his new RV6 project! The co-pilot was just as friendly and was also a Beechjet pilot who flew the T1A military version. We were just flying over the Equator about this time and the Captain said I was now a Shellback or something along those lines. We chatted for about half an hour when the chief flight attendant suddenly appeared. Man she really gave me a shit stare then gave the same look to the Captain . . . She was not pleased to see a passenger in the cockpit!! After she left, the co-pilot pushed his seat back, got out, said he had to take a leak and told me I was welcome to sit there if I wanted to . . . . Holy Shit . . . this was crazy!! I tried to act calm as I buckled up and slid my seat forward. I was amazed at how antiquated all the flight instruments were . . . this plane was a real throwback to a bygone era! It was a 747-100 Model and the Captain said it was one of the first 747's delivered back in the sixties. Compared to the all glass EFIS equipped 400A Beechjet I was flying, this cockpit with all its steam gauges looked like a Model T in comparison. I was just sitting there taking everything in when all of a sudden the Captain non-chalantly says . . ."You want to fly her?" My heartrate must have jumped to 250 bpm about then but I kept my cool and said sure! He gave me a brief tutorial on what to expect then casually flipped the autopilot switch off . . . . Of course, nothing overt happened . . . it was all trimmed up for cruise and I wasn't about to touch the throttles or try any turns . . . . I just savored those few minutes and kept my heading and altitude spot on with the flight director which was the same exact model and size we had in our 1975 King Air 200. The only thing I asked him was whether or not he was a flight instructor because I certainly planned on logging this time! He was, and to this day I frequently flip back through my old log book to 9/28/96 and look at that entry and the .2 hours of dual in a B741. The co-pilot finally came back after what seemed like quite a long piss and I had to relinquish the right seat to him. Man, what a thrill that was . . . I still think of that night often . . . flying a 747 over the Equator . . . . one of the highlights of my flying career!

When Tris took over as our commander one of his priorities was to deal with the rising fuel costs which was driving much of the criticism of our operation. He had a lot of great ideas including purchasing an old fuel truck then making runs up to Gray Army Air Field to purchase cheap Jet A fuel for our turbine planes. Instead he got us D.O.D. (Dept. of Defense) fuel cards for our planes which allowed us to fly into any National Guard, Army, or Air Force base to buy fuel. This was a tremendous savings for the taxpayers since Jet A was heading towards $7.00/gallon by then. With our D.O.D. cards we were getting it for $.89 cents/gallon . . . . Not too shabby!! So we began stopping in at McChord AFB or the Army base at Gray field when returning from our trips to fill up . . . It was just a ten minute hop from there back to Olympia. On our cross country D.O.C. flights we filled up at military air bases all over the country whenever we could. It was always very interesting to watch the reaction from the military personnel when a civilian jet pulled up to their fuel pits. Other than the two local military bases, I personally was able to enjoy fuel stops and see many interesting aircraft at such bases as: Fairchild AFB in Spokane, Army National Guard at St. Paul, MN, Travis AFB near Sacramento, Davis Monthan in Tucson, and McConnell AFB in Wichita. The other guys stopped at many more and as a result Tris eventually saved the state hundreds of thousands in reduced fuel costs.

Even though the pilots didn't work the road any longer we still attended yearly *In-Service Training* at the WSP Academy in Shelton to get refreshed on driving, shooting, first aid, etc, and were forced to view all the latest police dash mount camera videos of officers getting killed all over the country . . . . Not my favorite class but it sure drove home the message of officer safety and to always watch the bad guys hands! My favorite training exercise was practicing the P.I.T. maneuver out on the huge drive course. To correctly P.I.T a violator you must sneak up on their left or right rear quarter panel, make light contact with your own right or left front fender, then crank your steering wheel to the stop . . . By slamming on your brakes hard you could usually avoid any further contact and the violator spins around and ends up in the ditch backwards. Taking a guy out in a curve was always the easiest since their car was already unloaded and very light contact would start them around quite easily. Man, for some reason I just loved practicing this maneuver and often spent hours out on the drive course even volunteering to ride in the patrol car being pitted just for kicks. My only regret was that I never got to take out a real violator out on I-5 . . . . When I told my sergeant right before I retired that I was going out to P.I.T. the first tail-lighter I saw he became somewhat concerned and sternly advised me that I'd had a great career and to please not go out and screw the pooch as it wound down . . . .

The last time I nearly bought the farm occurred while I was flying Bruce's T6 solo on a proficiency flight over the large metropolis of Rochester, WA. It was the first flight of the season and I was a little rusty to say the least. I climbed to about ten thousand and completed the stall series and some slow flight maneuvers. Now Bruce, I've never told you what happened next so if you ever read this please don't send me any hate mail . . . . I performed a couple aileron rolls and a split ess then thought I'd do a loop. Just as I was going over the top I changed my mind and decided to do a half Cuban eight which necessitated a half roll off the top of the loop . . . . I should have stuck with the loop! Just as I started the half roll all relative motion seemed to stop and I found myself just hanging there by my belts, inverted, rotating slowly but sinking like a greased crow bar!! Man, I could not figure out what to do next especially when moving the stick around and jamming rudder didn't change a thing. About this time that big ole Pratt and Whitney 1340 sputtered to a stop and fuel started pouring out of the gas caps, which apparently weren't sealing very well, and I started choking on the fumes. At least my training kicked in since Thom Richard's mantra of canopy, headset, seatbelt, **out**—was the next thing that crossed my mind . . . In my mind's eye I clearly saw myself floating down in my chute while watching Bruce's T6 auger into some farm house . . . . As I was going through about five thousand I knew I had to make a decision and fast . . . . The only other thing I could remember from my training with Thom was that he once told me that if you ever get into trouble doing aerobatics in a T6 just pull the stick back and hold it there . . . I didn't know what was going to happen but I held it back and waited . . . It took a few seconds but for some aerodynamic reason that is beyond my comprehension that bird eventually snapped into a regular spin and the engine roared back to life all at the same time . . . . At least I was now in a situation I recognized but it took me a few more seconds to determine which way I was spinning . . . . I finally pulled the power to idle which had probably aggravated the situation to begin with . . . . I realize that any aerobatic pilots that might read this are laughing their asses off right now at my stupidity and how long it took me to recover but hey, as I've said before, the WSP only hired me because I was over six feet tall. After closing the throttle I finally determined which way I was spinning and put in the appropriate rudder to stop the rotation. After about a five G pull out I saw that I was down to less than a thousand feet . . . . I hadn't done much praying since leaving the seminary but I said a little thank you prayer at that moment. I thought I better see if the plane was OK and everything checked out fine and I didn't see any popped rivets and the gear and flaps still went up and down OK. I did have to delay my return to Olympia until my hands and knees quit shaking however. Afterwards, when I practiced Cuban eights, I always made sure I was going downhill off the top of the loop and had plenty of airspeed before I did that half roll . . . A lesson I shall never forget! (Thanks for saving my ass Thom!)

I had a less dramatic 'Rochester' area flight around this time that demonstrated just how quickly fatigue can screw up a flight crew. We were scheduled on a two day Dept. of Corrections flight in the Beechjet to Norman, Oklahoma, Kankakee, Illinois, Wilmington, Delaware, Rochester, Minnesota, then home. At the last minute the technicians found a leak in one of the jet's fuel bladders and had to take it out of service. So, we did the flight in the King Air 200 which was almost 200 mph slower than the Beechjet. The problem was trying to meet all the original take-off and departure times at those places without messing up all the pre-arranged schedules of all the various prison departments concerned . . . Instead of a 0600 departure out of Olympia we were wheels up at around 0300 which allowed us may be three hours of sleep that night . . . . By the time we got to the hotel in Wilmington, after delays in both Norman and Kankakee, it was nearly 0300 again!! The Corrections lieutenants said we could sleep in until 0600 since they had another busy day planned for us! Man, after those time zone changes, lack of sleep, and eating meals out of vending machines all day, we were really messed up the next morning . . . . I had filed the flight plan to Rochester (RST) the night before and when

456

we got our clearance the next morning the controller gave us a radar vector to the north with an 'expect further clearance down the road a ways'. So we took off on that heading and almost immediately we both got really drowsy and had to keep talking to stay awake. Even after donning our oxygen masks and cranking them up to 100% for awhile, it still took a 'long time' for us to realize that this radar vector they had us on just didn't seem right . . . . Minnesota is definitely west of Delaware not north . . . . So, I finally asked the controller when we could expect direct to Rochester; his response of "You're already going direct Rochester" kind of threw both of us . . . . I was about to say something sarcastic like "Then how about a 60 degree turn to the left just for the hell of it" when the controller came back apologetically with a turn towards Rochester, Minnesota instead of the vector to Rochester New York (ROC) he had us on . . . . He said once he heard Rochester mentioned on the air he just assumed it was New York and had to look at his strip to see that our destination was actually RST and not ROC . . . . Still, we should have caught the mistake a lot sooner and never after flying 100 miles in the wrong direction . . . I stood my ground in the future when someone tried to cram too much flying and not enough sleep into a trip.

On July 10, 2001 I had the honor to take my Uncle Andy Logozzo up in the T6 for his last ride. He had been a Marine in WWII and saw action at Saipan and Guam during the war. Like so many guys of his generation he rarely talked about the war or the combat he was involved in. When I asked him about his war experiences one time all he would say was that he had been a tail-gunner on a beer truck in Chicago during the war . . . . He also passed on a joke to me which I still tell and laugh about: "What are the three biggest lies that a Montana Cowboy could utter? 1). "My pickup's paid for." 2). "I quit chewin." and 3). "Hey, I was just trying to help that sheep through the fence!" Uncle Andy had passed away the week before and I offered to scatter his ashes out of the T6 over the Bitterroot Mountains near his home in Hamilton, Montana. My cousin Mike Logozzo went up with me after we had secured Uncle Andy's ashes in a biodegradable paper sack . . . . I had heard some stories from other pilots about the problems encountered while scattering ashes from airplanes, where things hadn't gone so well, and thought this method would be a little more efficient . . . Besides, knowing Uncle Andy's crazy sense of humor I knew he'd appreciate going out in style as a party to a high flying "bag job". Mike and I found a nice alpine lake way up high in the Bitterroots; I made a low pass over it, banked hard left, and Mike tossed Uncle Andy out over the side. It was a good drop and we watched as the bag hit some rocks near shore, exploded, and showered his ashes out over the lake . . . . Mike just said "So long Dad" and I said "So long big guy" which is what he had always called me. I did an aileron roll farewell salute over Uncle Andy and headed back to the airport. My other cousins Jack and Micky as well as Andy's long-time companion Dorothy, watched the flight from Hamilton.

Myself and cousin Mike Logozzo in front of T6 at Missoula after having just scattered Uncle Andy's ashes over the Bitterroots west of Hamilton.

One of the greatest birthday gifts I ever received was when Deb presented me with a custom multiple selection fart box machine!! Man, this baby was state of the art; you could play the farts one at a time or sequence all of them together giving listeners an uninterrupted 30 seconds of some of the grossest, wettest, loud & lingering farts imaginable. This made my old laughing box from working the road days immediately obsolete! If Phil was still alive he would have laughed his ass off playing with this thing. Anyway, I tried it out on my patrol car radio a few times, and got no response there . . . . Did get a few positive comments when I used it with the PA while passing local troops who had a violator stopped, but I had the most fun with it right in the hangar. We had a PA function in all of our desk phones for specific parts of the building and could control the volume as well. The most effective use was to turn the volume all the way up and select the hangar speakers. Man, the echo effect was tremendous and the mechanics could hear those long, loud, echoing farts even with their ear protection on while welding something! I tried not to over-use the machine so once a week seemed the appropriate time interval for its usage. I usually would scan who was out in the hangar from upstairs in the break room before cutting loose so as not to scare any unsuspecting civilians. All went well for several months but apparently my hangar scanning had become somewhat lax and I was to pay the ultimate price for my lack of situational awareness . . . Right after I had let loose a sensational ten second blast of the wettest fart in recorded history on the hangar PA, my intercom rang. It was one of the mechanics down in their office who advised me they had a Pratt & Whitney factory rep. in there and that he wasn't amused by the surprise entertainment. Shortly thereafter I got called into the boss's office and he demanded I turn over my fart machine; I said I had already taken it home but he still wanted it. I never did bring it back but I used to scare the deer and raccoons on our property with it using my patrol car PA.

Not long after these events one of our WSP mechanics started acting a little squirrely. He suddenly decided that the state of Washington owning and operating a Beechjet had become a huge issue to all of its citizens . . . . He started preaching to and lobbying anyone who would listen what a huge waste of taxpayer dollars this aircraft was . . . . He cast aside Tris' fuel saving measures as meaningless! He eventually contacted King 5 News out of Seattle and gave them all the "inside" dope. After they completed an exhaustive investigation we all found ourselves on the evening news one night as the feature story. They had determined we were operating the jet as efficiently as possible but that its usage gave the "appearance" of a state agency being too extravagant and recommended we trade it in on another King Air. This outcome didn't satisfy him and it soon became apparent his quest was long from being fulfilled . . . . The next thing he tried was calling the FAA when either the King Air or Beechjet left Olympia in what he determined to be an over gross weight condition. We **never** flew over-gross but the FAA still had to investigate which caused a tremendous amount of internal strife between the pilots and mechanics within our little unit. Then, when the FAA didn't act on any of his complaints, he contacted our own WSP Internal Affairs unit and they were forced to launch an investigation into all our so called illegal over gross weight flying. Needless to say, word soon got out to some of our clients that we were under investigation by several entities . . . . Coming right after the King Air crash, these events did not help our reputation very much or instill confidence in our clientele! Our boss and secretary had to spend almost all of their time just handling the mountains of extra paperwork and public disclosure issues that this guy was creating for them. As a result they were putting in a tremendous amount of overtime which neither of them got paid for . . . . None of us could figure out what was really motivating this guy's since prior to this he had always been a lot of fun, very generous, and a reliable hard working employee. The boss gave him several opportunities to cease and desist without punishment but he just wouldn't leave it alone . . . Why he would self-destruct over an airplane, which was after all his personal job security, was unfathomable to all of us. We just knew that it couldn't go on . . . . When the Internal Affairs investigation found no wrong doing he suddenly turned on one of his fellow mechanics and demanded that this junior man's position, who had a brand new baby at home, was redundant and he should be fired to save the taxpayers money . . . . The situation had now officially become intolerable . . . . It's funny how Karma works sometimes but eventually the tables were turned and he soon found himself under investigation by our Internal Affairs unit for several improprieties separate from his crusade to ruin the WSP Aviation Section. He was eventually given the opportunity to retire in lieu of more serious disciplinary action; he chose to retire. We had all experienced a couple years of hell but things finally got back to normal. I was told after I had retired that he eventually became his old self again, after he had time to reflect on his actions, and he calmed down . . . Apparently, he had just worked for the state too long . . . . A situation I was to experience myself in a couple years . . . .

We got a new WSP Chief around this time, a guy named Ron Serpas. He had been the assistant chief for New Orleans P.D. and prior to that he had worked vice. He didn't realize that he had inherited an air-force with his new assignment so he really took advantage of us throughout his tenure. His first priority after taking office was to travel to every single detachment in the state ASAP for a meet and greet. He kept us pretty busy those first few weeks and he loved to fly. He really let his hair down with the pilots once he got to know us a little and related some pretty 'hairy' stories from his years as an undercover vice cop down in the *Big Easy* . . . He was a natural born entertainer and we always marveled at how he could turn on the professional charm when required to do so; but once that door closed on the Beechjet it was 'Ron Serpas—vice cop' once again . . . We were delighted to say the least! Much to the chagrin of Assistant Chief Porter, who was a spit and polish Marine Corps type, Ron never wore his campaign hat . . . He confessed to us once that he thought it looked pretty goofy and made us all look like characters from *Yogi Bear*. Once again he had scored major points with all of us because in reality that damn hat got in the way just about all the time when you're working the road. Chief Serpas also liked to fly in our Cessnas quite a bit although I'm pretty sure it was only because we almost always let him do the flying. The few times I flew him in a Skylane I have to say that the guy was a natural and kept altitude and heading very well for an FNG pilot. During his brief tenure as chief he instituted some sweeping changes within the department which are still being felt to this day. He was a brilliant man and you did not want to underestimate him just because his language occasionally slipped back into that Louisiana Cajun slang often laced with colorful police metaphors. On King Air or Beechjet flights, when I was the co-pilot, I had an established routine after landing; as I worked my way to the rear of the plane to open the hatch I always commented to whomever might be listening: "Once again science and technology has triumphed over myth and superstition" . . . When Chief Serpas heard that the first time he burst out laughing, got out his pen and wrote it down word for word . . . . Jesus, I didn't think it was that good but was flattered nonetheless! Ron left us to take over as Chief of Police down in Memphis only after a year or so and he's now the Chief of Police in New Orleans where he started out his career. I really miss that guy and wish him all the best!

Olympia WSP Hangar 2002 Standing from left: Chief Ron Serpas 1, Tris Atkins 78, Andy Stoeckle 1088, Don Tingvall 118. Kneeling from left: Paul Speckmaier 1059, myself 305 We had just taken delivery of the new Skylane in background. Paul and I are dressed in the transportation uniforms of 2001.

When the next Chief took over he informed our boss that the pilots weren't writing any tickets and said we needed to start stopping cars while commuting to and from the hangar. He said we were State Troopers first and pilots second . . . . That statement really didn't "fly well" with us since none of us had worked the road in years, the fresh skills needed for us to be safe were non-existent, we weren't issued portable radios or tasers, and were often dressed in our flying gear (sport jacket, tie, and slacks—no body armor). All of us liked the new chief and I personally flew him in one of our Cessnas on many occasions and got to know him pretty well. But we all felt that his new policy was unnecessarily exposing us to a lot of extra risk since we had long ago become "empty holster" corporate pilot types with the reflexes necessary to suddenly deal with a psychopath somewhat diminished! Additionally, on the days we flew a traffic airplane, we usually knocked off 50 to100 violators so we didn't quite understand the urgency for us to get "one more" going to and from work!! However, we certainly realized we were not going to win this one so I just continued stopping to help disabled motorists as I always had . . . . I was not getting paid to be a road trooper at age 55 so this new policy to stop cars or else, finally got me thinking about hanging it up for good. I wasn't about to get shot while driving to the hangar for a governor's flight, just because I felt pressured to pull over some stupid shithead for some meaningless violation. My subsequent lack of activity prompted my sergeant to facetiously categorize my recent enforcement efforts on my next evaluation report as follows: "This employee consistently fails to meet the extremely low standards he sets for himself" . . . . AHHHH, my career summed up in a nutshell!

Deb and I took up diving in the mid-nineties but after completing our initial training in Puget Sound, (alias hypothermia central) we never dove in cold water again . . . For our 25th anniversary we flew to Australia and spent three weeks diving on the Great Barrier Reef outside Port Douglas, Queensland. There had been an incident about a year before in this area where a couple of divers got left behind by the dive boat and eventually drowned. Hollywood made a movie about that incident which scared the shit out of a lot of divers. So, we did our homework and made sure we didn't get mixed up with that outfit! After about a week of diving we asked one of our dive masters during the boat ride back to town one day about that incident . . . . He just looked at us a little strangely and just said, "You do realize this is the same boat and the same captain involved in that incident don't you?" To say we were a little surprised was putting it mildly . . . . The company had simply reorganized, changed its name (as well as the boat's), and was right back in business . . . . Regardless, the diving was spectacular and we saw so many sharks we eventually quit pointing them out or even getting excited about seeing them. We know for a fact that we will never see coral that healthy ever again. The boat ride to and from the reef was two hours each way and we really got pounded each and every time! I thought I had seen a lot of puking while flying traffic planes but man I never saw so much vomit in my whole life as we did during those commutes! There were no refunds if you didn't dive but there were still some folks who just stayed on the boat after we got to the reef . . . . One young Japanese girl just laid down on the slippery barf covered deck, rolled up into the fetal position, and spent a two hour boat ride there rolling around in hers and other people's puke . . . not a pretty sight! However, there were some other more visually appealing sights to behold . . . . A gorgeous young German woman, who was apparently quite confident with her femininity, put on a show for us several times when we got out to the reef. Most of us just put our wetsuits on over a bathing suit . . . . Apparently, that is frowned upon in the German dive community . . . She would strip down naked in front of everyone and then proceed to stuff herself into a very tight wetsuit . . . Sometimes it took her several minutes and I seem to remember getting clobbered by Deb a couple times when I apparently became overly interested as that poor overly-endowed girl struggled to put all her parts into the correct receptacles of that tight little suit . . . . I tried to explain that I thought she might need some assistance and was just being vigilant in case she asked for help . . . . Deb has just never understood my seminarian inspired caring and helpful nature . . . .

We dove in a number of exotic places all over the world in subsequent years but recently have narrowed our dive destinations to just two locations; shore diving in Bonaire, and boat diving off the Kona

Coast. We love hearing the Humpbacks singing under water so we usually hit Kona in February or March. We actually saw a Humpback underwater, up close and personal, while diving in the Turks and Caicos one year and that has been the highlight of our diving careers so far! Shore diving in Bonaire is a snap; we just back our rental pick up close to the water, strap our gear on while sitting on the tailgate, then just fall in and start the dive . . . . Getting out of the water later can be interesting when there is a good surge on and we occasionally end up rolling around like driftwood for awhile after getting knocked down by the breakers . . . .

A very ugly incident occurred in June of 1999 when Deb was to graduate from Evergreen State College with her Master's Degree in Biology. It had been a huge struggle for her to accomplish this, while working full time, having to deal with the death of her father and then handling his estate and legal affairs while working on her thesis. Evergreen President, **Jane Jervis,** allowed a convicted cop killer, Muma Abu Jamal, to give the commencement address, utilizing some sort of video feed from his prison cell, for the graduates to enjoy . . . . !! She approved this monstrous event to occur in spite of a tremendous outcry from most of the graduates beforehand who tried to prevent such a travesty! There were only a couple of **severely deranged graduates** who thought it would be "enlightening" and "very cool" to hear him speak. Unbelievably, **Jervis** acceded to their wishes ignoring the protests of what the majority wanted . . . . !! Deb and I were just beside ourselves with anger that she could be so utterly cold and insensitive to allow such a hideous act to occur . . . . So, Deb didn't go to her own graduation ceremony she had worked so hard towards . . . . She felt it would have been totally dishonorable and disrespectful towards the families and memories of all fallen policemen, especially the troopers I had worked with, for her to attend . . . Deb was devastated, as was I, and to this day I still want to vomit whenever I hear that name . . . .

Eventually, work started to interfere too much with our dive trips so I really started to seriously contemplate retiring and maybe getting a part time flying job somewhere to keep me occupied in between vacations . . . . There were also a couple incidents at work which led me to believe that I had apparently outlived my usefulness there. On one occasion, during a pilot's meeting, one of the FNG's, who wasn't even a King Air co-pilot yet, and wasn't even scheduled to go to King Air Initial at Flight Safety anytime soon, suddenly and angrily got his panties in a real tight wad in front of everyone. He loudly complained that myself and one of the other senior pilots, wasn't nurturing or mentoring him enough about flying King Airs . . . . WTF!!?? Now, a reasonable and prudent person might observe that if a pilot wanted to know something about King Air flying he might go way out on a limb and actually "ask" a King Air driver questions . . . . which he never had . . . . Apparently, reasonable and prudent were not in this cat's lexicon . . . However, being able to lash out at a pilots meeting in front of the boss about the horrible outrage and personal humiliation that he had to silently endure day after day, as we senior guys callously ignored him, was perfectly acceptable and apparently quite a stress reliever for him . . . It was obvious that both of us senior guys had just flat-out failed to recognize this guy's true greatness! . . . . I told my evil co-conspirator that we had really screwed up and should have been giving him a trophy each time he managed to start a Skylane in the morning all by himself without having to call his Mommy for help . . . A few minutes later out in the parking lot he walks by me as if nothing had happened, smiles, casually says see you later and gets in his patrol car . . . . I guess the unloading of all his personal demons, at our expense, had quite the cathartic effect on him as he looked pretty relaxed.

Another time, as I came down the hangar stairs to the reception area, I happened to overhear another young pilot loudly bitching to the boss in the lobby that I was getting too many jet flights. He said he should be taking most of them now since I was an old man way past retirement age who had already enjoyed his share of jet flying and how unfair it was for him now, etc., etc . . . . !! Holy shit . . . . these childish outbursts from supposedly grown men were starting to get a little tiresome . . . . I was reminded of the old Bob Seger song "*Against The Wind*" where the lyrics went something like: "I'm surrounded by strangers I thought were my friends" However, in the aviation world folks get pretty competitive about their rides as I might have been myself when I was their age. So, when the rumors started flying that the jet might be sold pretty soon, due to state budget cuts, the grumbling about crew assignments ramped up considerably . . . Some of the guys were starting to panic that the jet would be sold before they could get typed in it and they wouldn't be able to claim some turbo-jet time on their resumes. I guess I understood how they felt but I thought they could have been a little more professional and respectful while working through their childish frustrations.

When I finally walked into Tris's office and told him that this place was starting to resemble a real "suck shack" and that I was retiring he put on a good show of someone trying to act shocked and surprised. But, I could see the relief on his face and he certainly made no attempt to talk me out of it . . . He knew that I had just given him a solution to at least one of the current morale problems in the section . . . There is no doubt in my mind that some variation of this little drama is played out thousands of times daily all over the world as younger players move up the ladder regardless of what the endeavor or business might be; it's just a fundamental law of nature . . . . I get it! However, it's been quite a few years now and it will soon be their turn to watch their backs as the latest batch of hungry FNG's start putting their moves on them . . . .

On my last flight, as I taxied towards the hangar in old N222KA, I saw a couple of huge Tumwater Fire Trucks parked in front of the hangar. Tris was my co-pilot that day in the King Air and told me to slowly taxi between them enroute to our parking T in front of the hangar. When I got along side of them they each blasted out huge arcs of water over the plane . . . (to wash away all my sins I thought) . . . Tris allowed Deb to go along with us on my last flight and had also arranged for the fire truck hose-down-send off!! . . . . He really made it a special day for both of us! He also arranged a very nice retirement lunch ceremony in the hangar a couple days later where I was given a neat clock made out of the T-Wheel (high compressor turbine wheel) of a Beechjet JT15D-5 Pratt and Whitney Turbofan Engine.

Tris also arranged to have one of the WSP Skylanes re-registered with my initials and old badge number. What used to be N670P became N305RC. At the end of my retirement ceremony, the hangar doors opened and there she was . . . . What a thrill for Deb and I!!! Just then Brian Reynolds roared by in his P51D *American Beauty* . . . . It was just pure co-incidence since that day was the start of the museum's yearly June airshow . . . . But what perfect timing it was to hear that Rolls Royce V12 Merlin growling away at full song just then!! Those were very nice gestures and helped a lot to make up for some of the personnel incidents that occurred at the end of my WSP career. More importantly, I was so thankful that I had survived my road trooper years without getting killed . . . . Curiously though, I was actually more grateful for having never put a scratch on any airplane I ever flew . . . . Some sort of egotistical pride that only an aviator could understand I guess. No WSP retirement ceremony would have been complete without the historical send off gesture proffered to generations of retiring troopers . . . . Before I left the hangar that day one of the active pilots came up to me to ask the traditional retiring trooper going away question; "You know what you are now don't you?" I dutifully responded; "No what?" It was an emotional moment for me that really capped my career . . . ."Just another fu**ing violator!" . . . . Ahhhhh . . . . tears came to my eyes!! Deb and I soon took off for Kauai for three weeks and we finally got to dive the mysterious Island of Niihau. Man, it was spectacular . . . lots of sharks, huge Mantas, and Monk seals . . . some of the best diving we've ever encountered . . . . A fitting end to that chapter of my life!

Tris Atkins (left) and my former Ephrata flying partner Curt Hattell in front of a WSP Skylane that had been re-registered with my badge number and initials for my retirement. Curt is now Deputy Chief of the WSP and Tris is the Director of the Wash State Dept of Transportation's Aviation Division.

Taxiing in on my last official WSP flight and getting hosed down by Tumwater Fire trucks, June16, 2004. Deb got to ride along that day.

My T6 flying at the museum came to an end that summer as well. Bruce Mayes, the owner of the T6, moved to Reno and took the plane with him. I was sure sad to see it go but I'd had six great years flying it and really felt blessed. During the museum's Fall airshow in September Brian surprised me with a ride in his AE1E Skyraider to celebrate my retirement. Bud Granley was the pilot that day and we went out for about half an hour of great flying. Bud let me have the stick right after takeoff and I was just amazed at how light the ailerons were on this old girl. I did a couple of rolls and they were just effortless. Bud helped me a little on the landing as that cockpit sits really high and it was a little tough to judge when to flare. Although flying that big ole bird was a tremendous thrill my favorite warbird is and always will be the Mustang . . . . Before I check out, Deb and I will be making another trip down to Kissimmee to fly *Crazy Horse* one more time!

I thought my WSP flying career was over but a couple months later Tris called me up and asked if I'd be interested in taking a Beechjet flight on a three day DOC prisoner run to Orlando . . . They were down to just two Beechjet pilots by then and one of them was sick so I got the invite. It was a very nice trip with Paul Speckmaier and we also made stops in Wyoming, Arkansas, Kokomo IN, Nebraska, Great Falls MT, and International Falls, Minnesota. There was a guy at the FBO in Minnesota selling locally grown wild rice so I bought a bag. Man, it was the best Deb and I ever had and we still have him ship us five pounds every year or so. About a month later, Tris called me again to share the bad news that the Beechjet had been sold. He asked if I would be comfortable flying it back to Virginia to its new owners . . . . The only wrinkle was, Paul didn't feel comfortable flying with the new owners son, since the kid had just got typed in the plane and had never flown a jet before. I felt OK with it and told Tris I'd be happy to take the flight even though this kid would have to be listed as the PIC since my Beechjet 61.58 currency had just expired. Everything was looking good until I got another call from Tris a week or so later where he broke the news that the kid had just killed himself in the crash of his AT6 Texan back on the family farm . . . . Jesus Christ, what the f**k next? Well, nobody ever said flying a T6 was easy! Now I don't remember if the same family bought the plane after this incident or not but a few weeks later Paul and I were on our way back East on the Beechjet's last WSP flight. We picked up the new owners airplane broker in Olympia, made a gas stop in Lander, Wyoming, and landed in Charleston, S.C. The next day we took the new owners and the broker out on a demo flight in the Hilton Head area. After that flight we took old N440DS on its last leg with a WSP crew, flew over the Master's Course at Augusta, GA then dropped her off at the paint shop in Greenville, S.C. When we shut the engines down at Greenville they were both right at TBO. It was a sad moment and Paul and I shook hands knowing that was the end of the WSP jet era. It had been a good run for me and I had accumulated over 2,000 hours in that bird. I stayed an extra day down in Charleston taking in the Fort Sumpter Civil War Battlefield, the Yorktown Museum, and viewed the Civil War Submarine Hunley, recently retrieved from the bottom of Charleston harbor and being restored at a local shipyard. I finally had to fly home leaving our cherished Beechjet behind. It wasn't long afterwards when I read that the new crew of N440DS had a double engine flameout while descending through an overcast . . . . They were able to get one engine restarted and made a safe landing somewhere. The cause was a simple case of the crew failing to activate the engine anti-ice in visible moisture . . . It was tough pill to swallow knowing that a couple of boneheads were now miss-treating the old girl so badly . . . . But life goes on and so it has for me . . . .

CHAPTER 13

I found a 1967 Triumph Bonneville TT Special at a British motorcycle boneyard in Marne, Iowa while on a prisoner flight several years before I retired. This was the same exact year and model of Triumph that Don Pomeroy was riding up at Rimrock that fateful day almost 40 years earlier. I had it shipped to Olympia and now finally seemed to have the time to begin restoring that old sled. The previous owner had decided to make a chopper out of this classic and had really messed it up. It had been sitting in our garage for quite awhile but I soon had it apart to see what kind of shape it was really in. It was much worse than I thought and it looked like all my early retirement years were going to be spent dealing with this basket case. After getting everything welded and cleaned up, I had the frame and all painted parts bead blasted and powder coated while the engine was being overhauled up in Woodinville. Most of the engine turned out to be junk and needed just about everything replaced including the crankshaft. Almost all TT Specials had been raced hard either at drag strips or flat tracking, and this one was no exception. It actually took several years but I finally found all the original parts, albeit from several different continents, and reassembled the old girl back into her original, just off the assembly line, configuration. Man, she looked and sounded fantastic . . . There was one small wrinkle . . . . I was now afraid to ride her and take a chance of scratching something or, God forbid, lay it down somewhere and "wreck it up" like I had all that farm equipment. So I took the only logical out I had left; I put it up on jacks, and threw a couple sheets over it . . . It became a very nice perch for our garage cats . . . However, just this last year I finally hauled it out of storage, replaced all the easily damaged parts and/or hard to find items with good used ones, and threw some knobbies on it. I've been riding my expensive antique dirt bike around our place out in the sagebrush and apparently scaring the shit out of most of the wildlife here . . . . I occasionally see Deb waving her arms at me and yelling something but I can't hear a thing over those gawd-awful open pipes . . . .

Deb and I in front of our restored '67 Triumph TT Special that occupied much of my time during first few years of retirement.

Anyway, by the next Spring I started to miss flying a little but thankfully got a call from Dave and Mel down at DNR (Dept. of Natural Resources) to be a fill in King Air pilot for them. Brian Reynolds at Northwest Helicopters also wanted me to do some utility flying for his company in their Skylane. I was pretty busy with those guys that Spring, Summer, and Fall. I was surprised when an old Flight Safety instructor friend of mine from Wichita called to tell me about what sounded like an interesting flying job down in Jamaica. It involved flying a Turbo Cessna 206 with a cargo pod and refrigeration unit installed to release insects over the island . . . . Well that definitely sounded like something different, so I called the operator down in Florida to get all the details. Apparently, the citizens of Jamaica were suffering from some sort of flesh eating virus at that time, which was being spread from the horses, pigs, and cattle by an insect called a Screw Worm Fly. Working with the Jamaican government the operator obtained millions of sterile screw worm flies, flown in from Mexico each day in a King Air, which were then loaded into the refrigerated cargo pod of his Stationair. There was an auger assembly connected to the 'chilled' insect hopper which dumped them overboard at a fairly slow rate through a couple of large plastic chutes in the belly of the plane. The sterile flies were supposed to mate with healthy flies and when nothing happened the population would diminish, slowing the virus spread . . . Anyway, the pay was good, meals and housing was included, roundtrip airline tickets were thrown in, it was a brand new airplane, and it was only for six weeks . . . . so I thought what the hell! I took my dive gear with me and blasted off on a new adventure . . . . Apparently, Deb was not as thrilled as I was . . . .

I was put up in a gorgeous resort in Ocho Rios just a few miles from the airport. The plane had a wonderful AgNav GPS unit installed and the moving map display would show which grids I had just released flies on and displayed where I needed to fly on my next pass for maximum coverage . . . The only problem was that the terrain on the East end of Jamaica resembles the Swiss Alps . . . . I had to release the insects at 90 knots and no higher than 400 feet AGL, in the mountains or down in the flats . . . So, it got a little dicey from time to time . . . . They also had huge radio and cell phone towers everywhere with guy wires that extended out for thousands of feet. I immediately saw why the operator chose the Turbo 206 for this job; it had over 300 hp and with the density altitude, I needed every bit of it quite regularly.

Having just spent the last 33 years of my life as a cop it was hard for me to overlook the rampant lawlessness in Jamaica . . . All the resorts had huge fences around them adorned with concertina wire and 24/7 roaming security guards . . . . I felt pretty safe in my unit but man, going to and from the airport was pretty scary at four in the morning! On one of my first flights I looked down and couldn't believe what I was seeing . . . . I was over a huge 'orchard' of marijuana 'trees' . . . . Jesus, these plants were monsters! The technician flying with me thought they were banana trees or something and wanted to know how I knew what they were . . . I explained that I'd spent many years looking for marijuana gardens as a bear in the air up in the National Forests and corn fields of Washington State, but had never seen such a huge orchard type grow like this one. I thought it was an isolated incident but almost every day I saw more and more of those huge grows. The plants were all arranged in tidy rows with state of the art irrigation systems; several of them had guys on little Kubota tractors out there cultivating and cutting the 'weeds' (ha, ha) . . . I casually mentioned this to the boss one day and he told me to just keep quiet about that. I was informed that the Jamaican economy would probably collapse without the marijuana revenue and to just try to ignore what I was seeing . . . . The next thing that struck me was the horrendous poverty on the island . . . . We spent a lot of time releasing flies over the slums of Kingston and over its landfill, just northwest of the airport, which extended right out into a saltwater bay . . . I was horrified to see huge garbage trucks dumping their loads right into the saltwater there . . . . Guess where all the local commercial fishermen were fishing . . . . Just a little ways out from where all this delicious fish food was getting dumped into the water . . . . Needless to say, I did not eat fish once while I was there . . . . When I had a day off I hooked up with a local divemaster who had a friend who had a boat . . . . When I saw the boat and its captain I just had to laugh out loud . . . . The boat resembled the African Queen in that old Bogart movie and the captain looked like a character out of central casting dressed up to resemble a stereotypical guanja smoking Bob Marley Rastafarian . . . Man, I was really hesitant to get on that piece of crap but the divemaster assured me all was well so off we went. The diving was absolutely the lousiest I'd ever seen . . . . No tropical fish, dead coral, engine blocks, old tires, and junk scattered everywhere, water that smelled and tasted like diesel, terrible visibility . . . it was horrendous! Then, when we got back to the surface, no boat! The captain had decided to visit friends while we were down surveying the underwater landfill . . . . After floating around for about half an hour he finally motors on up smoking the biggest joint I'd ever seen . . . . This cat was a living stereotype! That joint made the ones in those Cheech & Chong movies look like toothpicks! I asked my divemaster if there was any better diving on the island and he seemed shocked that I hadn't liked this spot. He said for a few extra bucks he could take me to the best diving on the island but it was a long boat trip. I said fine and we took off. The boat would only do about five knots wide open so it was a long commute. Half way there, the captain veers towards shore and pulled up adjacent to a nice looking resort. It was soon apparent why he had stopped here; this resort was of the clothing optional variety and my two captors were really enjoying the show on shore . . . . Man, I really wanted to get away from these morons ASAP! . . . To make matters worse, most of the folks on shore, who had 'exercised' their clothing option, were in their seventies and eighties and obviously had not missed any meals for decades . . . I finally said I really wanted to get some diving in while it was still daylight . . . . The 'captain' finally motored away. The visibility did look better at the next dive site and I was promised I would definitely see a lot of fish here. When we got to the bottom I didn't see any fish and the coral was all bleached white like the last spot. Man I was pissed! The divemaster kept waving me along and finally got real excited when we got to what looked like a bunch of wadded up cyclone fencing. Sure enough, there were six or seven fish inside this homemade fishtrap, milling around in there looking starved to death. I guess the tender only came by every week or so to harvest his catch . . . When we got back to the boat I told the divemaster flat out that this was the worst diving I'd ever seen. He tried to act shocked again so I asked him if he'd ever been off the island and dove anywhere else in the Caribbean . . . When he said no I sort of understood his predicament but still felt that they should be paying me for this joke of a dive trip. The capper was when we got back to the dock and I started to walk away to call for a taxi; the whacked out boat captain comes over and advises me that it's customary to give him a tip for his services . . . . It was all I could do to not laugh out loud again so I just told him I'd be back with his tip later . . . He seemed pleased and gave me that crazy three tooth grin one last time . . . It took me a long time to get the diesel smell out of my dive gear after that disaster.

Early one morning it was my privilege to experience some pretty hairy instrument flying, minus the instruments . . . . We were getting hit with the remnants of a hurricane that was dissipating several hundred miles away that day . . . . The weather was clear but the turbulence up in the mountains was moderate to severe. After one horrendous smack suddenly the cockpit became filled with thousands of screw worm flies . . . . The turbulence had dislodged a large pipe from the insect hopper to the auger and they were all escaping into the cabin! As I remember, the dry ice normally kept them fairly quiet at a cool 36 degrees in the hopper . . . But once they got out into that warm 95 degree cockpit they perked right up and were soon buzzing all around. Within a minute or so I couldn't see outside as thousands of them were swarming all over me . . . I tried to head back to Kingston but couldn't even see the GPS let alone any of the other instruments. I opened the side windows just to see if my wings were level, and to let some of the flies out . . . We were still up in the mountains so I was honestly concerned about buying the farm up there for a few minutes . . . . I finally made it down to the South coast line and found my way back to Kingston. Meanwhile, the warmed up flies now decided to shit all over the inside of the plane as well. On the approach I was in a full crab up until the last second before touch down 'cause I still had no forward visibility whatsoever as the inside of the windscreen was now covered in fly feces! I was covered in fly shit too, and those fu**ers were in my nose, eyes, ears, and mouth and I think I had swallowed and breathed in quite a few of them! We spent pretty much the rest of the day cleaning the plane up, and ourselves, after that fiasco! Thank God these were the 'clean' flies and not the flesh eating virus carriers!

The six weeks went by fairly quickly and I was putting on a lot of weight eating resort food three times a day. I'd had enough of Jamaica to last me a lifetime so I was thrilled to get back home to the land of no screw worm flies shitting in my face! I started to miss flying jets about this time and began looking on-line to see if there were any Beechjet positions close by. The nearest operator looking for experienced captains was Sunset Air down in Santa Rosa. I applied and was hired immediately. It was supposed to be a two weeks on two weeks off set-up but after they sent me to Flight Safety in Wichita for my Part 135 recurrent training they changed their mind and put me on a regular weekly schedule. That really pissed me off but

---

I assured Deb I would try to get home as much as possible . . . . She was not a happy camper—again . . . . I really enjoyed the flying and most of the Beechjets were the newer Hawker 400XP variants with the extended gross weight kit installed. Unfortunately, the Hawker variants were equipped with the Collins 5000 nav. box which I felt was a real step backwards from the Collins dual 850 nav. boxes I was accustomed to in 440DS. The 5000 was basically a cut and paste type nav. system which I didn't think was very user friendly and reminded me of that old Foster Loran we used to have in the WSP's King Air early on. Most of the other pilots were great, quite a few ex-airline types, but sadly there were a couple redneck bigots in the group that I was forced to fly a couple trips with . . . . Jesus, there just seems to be an unlimited supply of those morons in the world!! I really started to appreciate how professional the WSP Section pilots were (even the backstabbers and bitchers) after flying with those two cretins. The primary mission for Sunset Air was CTDN (California Transplant Donor Network) flights. We were on call to fly anywhere in the country to pick up hearts, livers, kidneys, whatever, and then also pick up and fly the medical transplant teams to wherever they were needed. Sunset was also a fractional ownership company in competition with NetJets, FlexJets, and Citation shares. They had a fairly large fleet of aircraft available for charter including a G5, Hawker 800XP's, several Citations, King Airs and four or five Beechjets. Since most of my flights were into busy airports like Teterboro, White Plains, San Francisco, Dallas, Los Angeles, Houston, etc., I really started to miss those DOC flights into quiet little strips out in the boondocks of Arkansas with no tower . . . I'll never forget the sight one evening taxiing to the East at White Plains, New York. We came up over a little rise where we could see all the departing aircraft heading for the active . . . There was at least twenty planes ahead of us and as we watched the fuel counter tick down we had to re-calculate whether or not we could make it to our gas stop in Scottsbluff. We landed there OK but got below our 1,000 lb. minimum gas landing limit a bit . . . .

My lasting impression from that job was the tremendous wastage displayed by some of the clients. These people would order several thousand dollars of catering for a three hour flight somewhere for just three or four people. The best wine and champagne, dinners served on very nice china and platters, beautiful glasses and silverware, the best linens, everything was top of the line . . . . Guess what happened to all the silverware, china, platters, wine-glasses, and linen at the end of the flight? Right into the old dumpster at the FBO . . . . It just blew me away! Now the untouched food was a different matter . . . . There was always some great stuff left over that hadn't been unwrapped or even taken out of the big coolers . . . . That was pilot booty and man did we score some great stuff . . . . Breakfast burritos to die for, steak sandwiches, huge shrimp platters, smoked salmon, filet mignon, you name it! We took it back to our hotel rooms and dined like kings! . . . . Most of the china and silverware was fished out of the dumpsters at the FBO's by the line personnel for their use and I didn't blame them a bit . . . A couple times when I was in the right seat I was forced to pour wine for some of the clients after closing the hatch and giving the safety briefing. Man, when some of those snobby old dipsticks held out their wine glass for me to fill, as I was trying to get back into the cockpit, it was extremely hard for me not to say something really rude . . . Years before, when I was flying the governor, heads of state, and visiting dignitaries, they always took care of themselves and poured their own drinks while we flew the planes . . . I really started to miss seeing my passengers in orange jump suits, leg shackles and hand cuffs . . . . The main difference between the snobs and the prisoners I used to fly was that the elite crowd smelled slightly better.

The slogan for Sunset Air at the time was "Thrill the Customer" . . . . I agreed with the slogan but my idea of a real thrill for some of our passengers would have been a couple aileron rolls on the climb out and a split ess to a landing . . . . One client had a 15 year old son who was a race car driver. We were supposed to depart San Jose one afternoon right after he got out of school to take him to the Mid Ohio Race Track near Cleveland where he was racing an Indy car the next day. He was very late and we had to re-file the flight plan a couple times. After his Limo finally arrived from school and while Mom was chewing him out, the Limo driver told us the kid had been in detention at school for several hours after creating some sort of disturbance in the classroom . . . , What a "special" young man he was . . . . Later, at a gas stop in Sioux Falls, he talked down to us like we were 'his' personal taxi drivers and it was all I could do to not kick the little shithead in the nuts . . . One of my last flights with Sunset was a five day trip all over the country with a furloughed airline pilot named Scott Giffin. We had a ball and really enjoyed each other's stories from our previous lives. My time at Sunset was cut short after Deb was diagnosed with uterine cancer. After the hysterectomy everything was OK and it's now been seven years of normal checkups. I never went back to work for Sunset.

As luck would have it another former WSP pilot, Don Tingvall, who retired about the same time I did to go fly for NetJets, got a great King Air 200 job right in Olympia flying for Cardinal Glass. He asked me to be his co-pilot from time to time so I was able to keep fairly current in turbine aircraft after leaving Sunset Air. I was still flying for DNR, but very infrequently. Northwest Helicopters had taken on a new client, the Quinault Indian Nation, which afforded me yet another unusual type of flying experience. They installed an array of antennas on their Skylane to locate and track radio collared elk for the Quinault tribe. I spent five years flying their biologists Grover Oakerman and Daniel Ravenel, all over the Quinault Indian Reservation every few months locating their wandering elk. It was a lot of fun and reminded me of my days looking for stolen cars with the Lojack receivers in our WSP Skylanes. The only problem was in order to hear the sometimes faint signals from the elk collar transmitters, that often had weak batteries, you had to turn the squelch and volume up to an ear-splitting level . . . I would often go home with a terrific headache . . . Lately, I've developed tinnitus (ringing in the ears) which my doctor confirmed was no doubt caused by that loud squelch and volume I had to endure for hundreds of hours listening for elk. If you enjoy the sound of a mosquito flying around inside your head 24 hours a day than you might like tinnitus! We also counted eagle hatchlings in the late spring and I have to say that was some of the hairiest flying I've ever done! We had all the eagle nest coordinates saved in the GPS database in the plane but counting the chicks still required a really low pass over the nest, with full flaps right at stall speed in order to make an accurate count . . . Trouble was many of the nests were right on the coastline which was usually obscured with fog even in the summer . . . So, I was forced to occasionally "make up" an IFR approach to the nest ending up at my MAP at about 100 feet AGL, using the GPS and praying that there would be enough visibility (and time) when we hit the fix to see the little eaglets . . .

I also occasionally flew with retired airline pilot Floyd Cummings photographing various highway projects for D.O.T. (Dept. of Transportation) all over the state. He operated a Shrike Commander and a Turbine Commander but I have to say that I was glad my only job was to work the radio, put the gear up and down, and look out for traffic . . . . Watching Floyd set the plane up and fly those photo runs was excruciating . . . . It was like shooting one long ILS approach for several hours at a time . . . perfection was mandatory or the D.O.T. camera guy in the back would ask for another excruciatingly long pass. Floyd was a master at this and made it look very easy but I guarantee you it **was not**!

My next flying job also involved another former WSP pilot. Pat had retired many years back and was fortunate to become the personal pilot for the owner of a small company known as Nighthawk Air based out of Seattle. Nighthawk operated a Cessna Citation CJ2 Jet as well as a brand new Cessna Skylane. The owner kept his planes hangared at Tacoma Narrows Airport about an hour from my house. He made a lot of trips to Long Beach, Las Vegas, and Palm Springs where he had another home. He was typed in the plane but finally realized it would be more relaxing to just sit in the back and watch someone else do all the work . . . . Pat told me he was retiring from Nighthawk in four months so the owner was hiring me to take over the Chief Pilot position from him. When I asked Pat if he was serious about retiring he says "Oh yeah . . . serious as a heart attack!" My reason for asking him (**several times actually**) was because I wanted to make absolutely certain this was going to be a chief pilot position as I most certainly did not want to be somebody's "gear bitch" at this stage of my flying career. So, having known him for over 30 years I trusted that he would keep his word . . . The owner asked me to find myself a new co-pilot ASAP so I excitedly started interviewing several guys and gals (to Deb's consternation) and soon settled on a retired airline pilot who was a great guy who already knew Pat and the owner. In the meantime we cancelled our construction slot date with our home builder in Eastern Wash. (which had taken us a year of waiting to obtain) and postponed building our new home since this great new job had landed in my lap. Then, several weeks later, after things were all settled, out of the blue Pat suddenly announces he doesn't want to retire in **four months,** as agreed upon when I accepted employment, and tells me it would now be **about** 18 months . . . . !? These WTF moments just seemed to pervade my life!! Additionally, my agreed upon (handshake) Chief Pilot salary with the owner, suddenly nose-dived to the FNG co-pilot level and I began to feel very apprehensive about this whole arrangement! When I called the guy who was to be the new co-pilot and gave him the bad news he was pissed as well, as he should have been! However, it was still a great flying situation so I tried to remain upbeat and kept my mouth shut . . . . I got my PIC type rating in the CJ2 at Flight Safety San Antonio, which was quite a cultural shift from the Wichita scene. The CJ2 was equipped with the Collins Pro-Line 21 FMS and it was the finest avionics package I ever had the privilege to sit in front of!

In the winter Pat and I would fly the owner and his lovely wife to Palm Springs, leave the jet there, and fly commercially back home. Usually, about a month later, we would fly back commercially, pick them up in the CJ2 and make a Las Vegas run before heading back to Tacoma. The owner usually stayed at Caesars Palace and put us up there as well. He was very generous to his pilots and almost always bought us dinner at the best restaurants at Caesars. This Palm Springs-Vegas itinerary would be repeated several times each winter with an occasional stop in Long Beach where the boss checked on his real estate holdings. The owner also had family in Boston; during one flight there I stayed in the area while Pat flew back home. I had a week and since I have always been an avid history buff, I rented a car and drove to Gettysburg and Valley Forge. I also toured all the Revolutionary War sites around Boston. I found a couple of Triumph motorcycle restoration shops and picked up some hard to find parts to finish off my TT Special with. When Pat came back we toured Old Ironsides, visited Plymouth Rock, and had a lobster roll in Sandwich, MA. It was a really nice trip and was the highlight of my time with Nighthawk Air. The owner also brought us with him one time on a guided tour of President Reagan's "Western White House" ranch up in the Santa Ynez Mountains northwest of Santa Barbara; that was another great opportunity and a trip I really enjoyed! We also had a couple terrific trips to Alaska; Sitka one summer and Juneau the next. Pat and I were able to go fishing both times and each of us caught some huge halibut and some nice Kings. We had all the fish sent home and Deb and I had to buy another freezer after the Sitka trip to get all the Halibut put away. Shortly after this trip, while hanging out at the Palm Springs airport one afternoon, Pat casually advises me that his retirement plans had changed again and he was now going to stay around as chief pilot for **three** more years . . . . Judas Priest!!

Pat and I were quite surprised one afternoon when we tried to get boarding passes at Palm Springs to fly back commercially to Seattle . . . The counter agent told us we were on some kind of TSA terrorist watch list and wouldn't allow us to board. This was quite a shock for a couple of former state troopers but we found out fairly quickly what brought it on. Apparently, TSA had been monitoring all of our 'one way' airline trips between Seattle and Palm Springs and that's what set off all the bells and whistles. We eventually had to fill out some long questionnaires and write some letters explaining our 'suspicious' behavior before we could get boarding passes without getting called into somebody's back office again. The TSA finally issued us both redress control numbers to attach to our passports in case we had further problems down the road . . . To this day I still get questioned at every check-in and have to present my redress number each time.

I thought the Citation Jet was probably the best handling aircraft I'd ever flown; it had almost exactly the same feel and characteristics of a Cessna 182 . . . . I think a lot of its stability came from that very wide straight wing which also made landings a real piece of cake. The only landing characteristic that gave me a little trouble at first was the CJ's tendency to really float down the runway if you over-flared it just a tiny bit while in ground effect. Even with perfect airspeed control and idle power, that straight winged mother would just not quit flying if you pitched it up even two degrees too high on the flare. The swept-wing Beechjet I flew was just the opposite; once the radar altimeter hit fifty feet and you selected idle power while pulling ten degrees of pitch on the flight director, you would be landing very quickly, no floating!

After about a year and a half with Nighthawk Air, Pat **emails me** early one morning and reveals that he **now doesn't plan on retiring at all** and would remain as chief pilot in perpetuity . . . . Man, that announcement was the final straw for me and I was way beyond pissed this time!! As Homer Simpson once said; "That was the suckiest suck that ever sucked!!" From my point of view I felt I had been hired under false pretenses, continually deceived about my real (read—constantly changing) conditions of employment, and totally disrespected! While having coffee alone with the owner at Caesar's the next morning I unloaded on him about this latest development . . . . He just glared at me like I was some kind of traitor . . . . I could tell this was probably not going to end well for me so I went for broke and said I'd stay with the company if he brought my salary up to what he had originally promised me as a condition of employment 18 months before. With clenched teeth he said he'd let me know very soon . . . . After we got back home he called early the next morning; I immediately sensed the direction the conversation was going, politely interrupted him and informed him that I quit . . . .

Looking back now five years later with 20/20 hindsight, I suppose I should have let myself cool off, stepped back, and thought about the consequences a bit more before giving the boss an ultimatum like that . . . . It really was a good flying job, that most pilots would just kill for, and there were wonderful perks . . . But, at the time, I just could not get past the fact that a colleague I had known and worked with for over 30 years could be so disingenuous and value our friendship so little . . . . I also knew that I could never be civil to him any longer and that we'd likely have zero cockpit crew coordination and CRM on future flights. Just from a flight safety aspect, quitting was really my only option. Regardless of how it ended, I sure enjoyed flying that CJ2.

Deb finally retired from her biologist position with The Dept. of Fish and Wildlife in 2008 after finally reaching her "Dealing With the Public Lifetime Threshold of Frustration" limit. Having to endure the name calling, bitching, harassment, threats, and the constant stream of hyper-critical insensitive individuals at work, had just wore her out as it had me during my road trooper years. The Spotted Owls, Mazama Pocket Gophers, Marbled Murrelets, Oregon Spotted Frogs, and all the other endangered little critters lost a great advocate when she left the department.

As a result of everything that happened that fall, we suddenly had a lot more time to travel and go diving. Bonaire and Kona are our usual destinations now and we never tire of viewing the tremendous undersea life at both spots. Hearing the Humpbacks "singing" underwater at Kona is a huge treat that always thrills us in the winter months!! We both decided to do some volunteer work after retirement; Deb worked at the Thurston County Animal Shelter and to keep busy I became a *Meals on Wheels* driver for three years . . . . What an eye-opener that was; I could write another book just about some of the characters I met during that sojourn!!

After several more years we were finally able to get **another** construction slot with our builder and have since sold the house in Olympia, built our new home in eastern Washington, and moved up into the mountains with our nine cats. We have all kinds of wildlife on our place including elk, deer, turkeys, bears, cougars, hawks, eagles, and nearly every kind of upland game bird. Neither of us are hunters but we thoroughly enjoy keeping track of all the critters and especially their young ones in the spring; we always have our spotting scope and binoculars handy.

I thought I was done flying when a great opportunity opened up at *Bergstrom Aircraft* in Pasco. Malin Bergstrom, who I've known for almost 30 years now, graciously offered me a job as a photo/survey pilot for their company . . . Impossible to pass up working for one of the premier FBOs in the Northwest especially since as an employee I became an automatic member of the *B.A. Flying Club*. The planes available to rent include several C172s, a C182, and best of all a pristine S35 Bonanza!

EPILOGUE

Deb and I are both very proud of our years of public service in spite of the fact that many citizens view retired state employees as common scum that place a heavy drain on an already fragile state economy. That group truly believes that our sole purpose in life was (and is) to bleed "normal" hard working taxpayers dry with our medical benefits and undeserved pensions. I don't know how many times we've heard the snotty little comment from the local yokel crowd about how nice it must be to have **"free"** medical benefits in retirement . . . . Man, if you call paying $1,200.00 a month for our retiree medical insurance "free" then I guess we **are** getting one helluva good deal! Those critical attitudes are not at all surprising to us and we've both developed thick skins over the years dealing with them. We honestly try to consider the source and try not to over-react when some hyper-critical or just plain ignorant person makes a snide or stereotypical comment about public service employees (usually not to your face of course, but just within earshot). However, when the person issuing the negative remark is educated or really should know better, we often become quite exasperated.

Deb and I in our dive gear at Bonaire about to get wet, 2011

In spite of negative attitudes and the abject ignorance of so many folks we dealt with during (and after) our working years Deb and I have both tried very hard to put that all in the past. We are very happy now and really enjoying the peace and quiet of retirement. We both feel extremely lucky to have had such great career opportunities come our way and look upon our dive trips to pristine coral reefs as a gift from God and our quiet reward for those years of service. Mingling with the Moray eels, octopus, turtles, cuttlefish, sharks, Humpbacks, Eagle rays, and so many species of colorful reef fish, really brings us both a tremendous feeling of peace and harmony with the world. Riding my 650 Triumph dirt bike around the place might seem a tad incongruous in comparison and most certainly nullifies the "quiet" aspect of retirement but I find it to be great exercise and **very** relaxing! Sadly, my riding only brings looks of abject disdain from my lovely bride who as a result has lately begun lumping me in with the local yokel redneck crowd.

In those first few months of retirement neither one of us realized just how much daily pressure and stress we had been living under until it slowly started to dissipate . . . . Jesus, what a relief it was to finally unload that burden and begin to relax!! Later, we both began to have lingering doubts whether either of us had actually made a difference during our working years while enforcing traffic or environmental laws . . . . It's really hard to qualify or quantify one's career when so much of what we both did involved preventing future events from occurring that "could" have been harmful to other people or the environment . . . . Of course, when the shallow thinking crowd evaluates your life's work, they assume you were just another lazy government drone, fleshing out some redundant state bureaucracy. They hurry to rash judgments about the validity of your career since there were few tangible results of your life's work that were measurable. I suppose if you spent your career framing houses you could always go drive by them years later and still feel a sense of accomplishment . . . Not so when your job was defined by potentiality and the unknown play out of future events that might or might not have occurred as a result of your actions. Whether it was stopping drunk drivers that **might** have killed a family two minutes further down the road or Deb **having to tell** loggers **not** to drain the oil out of their equipment right into a salmon bearing stream just because it **might** affect the fish, land owners, and fishermen downstream . . . . Yeah, on second thought, I guess the shallow thinkers were right, you just can't measure those types of philosophical non-events.

Rick Carnevali

After many years of retirement we still find it comical when the "golden oldies" of stereotypical remarks about cops or environmentalists resurface. Then as now we just cringe at the ignorance of the people uttering those worn out epitaphs but always enjoy the much needed comic relief at their expense! I just find it totally amazing that so many folks **still** allow the isolated incidents of the bad or outrageous behavior of a few to condemn the other 99% in those groups who consistently do good work, don't have extremist views, personal agendas, or questionable work habits, and just toil along year after year trying their best to serve the public.

Consequently, those of us who had to endure our share of unfair criticism and innuendo, solely because of our job descriptions, with little regard for the **actual** day to day contributions and accomplishments during our working years, tend to withdraw up into the mountains, (or a hundred feet down in crystal clear water), and surround ourselves with peace, tranquility and beauty . . . . Miles away from those who are "vexations to the spirit" . . . . Or, as Thomas Gray more eloquently put it: "Far from the madding crowd of ignoble strife."

A26	Douglas Invader WWII twin engine medium bomber. Used for many Years as a fire bomber all over the Western U.S. and Canada
AAG	Assistant Attorney General
ABS	Anti skid brakes installed on Beechjet Aircraft
ADD	Attention Deficit Disorder
AG	Attorney General
ADF	Automatic Direction Finder . . . Instrument equipped with a needle that Points to the selected nav. beacon giving the pilot a heading to turn to
AFB	Air Force Base
AGL	Above Ground Level
ATC	Air Traffic Control: Ground, Tower, Approach, or Center
AT6	North American Aviation high performance single engine trainer (WWII)
Apache	Twin engine Piper Airplane . . . Used primarily as a trainer
ATIS	Automated Terminal Weather Information System
ATP	Airline Transport Pilot Certificate
Auto Feather	Automatic feature of turbo-prop aircraft that feathers the propeller blades (Aligns the thin edge with the wind for less drag) on a failed engine
Auto Ignition	Automatic system that will energize and provide spark to prevent engine Flameout on a turbine engine. Activates in severe turbulence or icing.
Aztec	Piper twin engine aircraft. WSP's first transport plane, PA23-250 model.
B17	WWII Boeing four engine bomber
B24	WWII Consolidated four engine bomber
BA	Breathalyzer Machine
BB49	Serial number on WSP King Air 200
Beech 18	Beechcraft 1940's era twin engine airplane.

BE 40	Beechjet . . . . Beechcraft twin engine turbo-jet airplane
Bell 47	Korean War vintage helicopter
Bell P63	WWII era single engine fighter plane (Allison engine was behind the pilot).
Bell X-1	Rocket powered airplane Chuck Yeager broke the sound barrier with
BETA	Propeller pitch mode controlled by power lever position that Reduces prop pitch and thrust on turbo-prop aircraft (King Air)
BFD	Big Fu**ing Deal
Bleed Air	Hot air taken from turbo prop/jet engine compressor section Then re-conditioned for pressurization, heating, cooling, anti-ice, etc.
Bonanza	Beechcraft high performance single engine airplane
Bug	WSP Radar units (TR6, MR9, KR11) . . . also known as "The Beam"
C-141	Viet Nam era Lockheed four engine Air Force transport plane
CC & 7	Smooth Canadian Club Whiskey and Seven Up
Cessna 182	Skylane Single engine airplane utilized by WSP for traffic Operations. Early models powered by Continental O-470 engine Later models equipped with Lycoming IO-540 engine
Cessna 310	Twin engine airplane flown by Sky King in TV series (*Songbird*)
Cessna 525	Twin engine turbo-jet airplane
CFII	Certified Instrument Flight Instructor
Collins FMS	Flight Management system installed on WSP Beechjet (Pro-line III)
Compressor Stall	A disruption of airflow into the compressor section of a turbine engine Usually accompanied by a "very" loud bang which scares the bejeezus Out of everyone in the vicinity (mostly the pilot).
Condition Levers	Cockpit control levers that govern the metering of fuel to the fuel control Unit (FCU) of each engine on a turbo-prop aircraft
Chinook	Large Boeing twin engine military transport helicopter

CRM	Cockpit Resource Management . . . Technique wherein crew members use Every item of information (visual, verbal, non-verbal or written) available To maintain flight safety
CRT	Cathode Ray Tubes installed in Beechjets: referred to as a "glass cockpit" Or EFIS . . . electronic flight information system
Current Limiter	A fuse that blows when a source tries to put out too much voltage (Usually blows during an engine start on King Air Aircraft)
DC3	Douglas built 1930's era twin engine airliner. Military designation was C47
DEA	Drug Enforcement Administration
DH	Decision Height . . . . Altitude on precision instrument approach where a pilot Must make decision to either land or go around if ceiling & visibility is low
DIP	Drunk in Public
DME	Distance measuring equipment . . . . Instrument that tells pilot how far he is From a navigation source or fix
DME ARC	Maintaining a fixed distance from a navigation source while Maneuvering in a constant turn during an instrument approach
DMV	Department of motor vehicles
DOA	Dead on arrival
DOC	Department of Corrections
DOL	Department of licensing
DONNY	Final approach fix at Yakima for precision instrument landing approach
Douglas Skyraider	Huge Korean and Viet Nam era single engine propeller driven aircraft Capable of carrying massive loads of ordinance
DWI	Driving while intoxicated . . . Now called DUI
EFIS	Electronic flight information system . . . CRT based panel on a Beechjet Referred to as a "Glass Cockpit"
EMT	Emergency medical technician. WSP troopers trained as EMT's in 1974

F4U	Chance Vought Corsair single engine fighter. Made famous by Pappy Boyington and the Black Sheep during WWII
F7F	Grumman Tigercat WWII era twin engine fighter . . . Later used as Firebomber in Western U.S. and Canada
FAR/AIM	Federal Aviation Regulations and Airman Information Manual
FBO	Fixed Base Operator . . . . Airplane service station whose personnel meet and Greet all flights providing gas, catering, rental cars, lounge, pilot supplies
FISDO	FAA flight standards district office
FL270	27,000 feet above sea level . . . All altitudes above 18,000 feet Are referred to as flight levels (FL)
Flight Director	Pilot instrument that provides precise pitch, roll, altitude, and route information utilizing command bars "bat wings" as an alignment guide
FNG	Fu**ing New Guy
FUBAR	Fu**ed Up Beyond All Recognition
Gear Bitch	Usually a lowly co-pilot position where your only job is to raise and Lower the landing gear and maybe get to talk on the radio
GEORGE	What pilots call an autopilot
GPS	Global positioning system. Satellite based navigation system providing Very exact location and groundspeed data
Hog Leg	What troopers call their duty weapon . . . . Usually refers to the Big and heavy S&W 357 Magnums we carried until 1989
IFR	Instrument flight rules that apply when there are low ceilings and poor visibility requiring strict adherence to prescribed flying protocols
ILS	Precision landing system where the pilot has vertical and lateral Guidance while making an instrument approach in bad weather
IMC	Instrument Meteorological Conditions. Weather conditions with ceiling and Visibility so poor that a pilot cannot fly by visual flight rules

IOC	Inter Office Communique . . . Official WSP office memo usually spelling Trouble if you found one in your mailbox.
ISA	International Standard Atmosphere . . . Temperature on a "standard day" at Sea level is 59 degrees F with a pressure of 29.92 inches of mercury. If the Temperature is colder or hotter than standard then it is reported as either (e.g.) ISA–5 or ISA +5 . . . ISA is extrapolated into the flight levels, According to the standard lapse rate, to help pilots calculate speed, fuel Burn, and eta's and to select the most efficient altitude to fly at.
ISP	Idaho State Police
JAL	Japan Air Lines
King Air	Beechcraft twin engine turbo-prop passenger airplane. WSP operated a 90 Model in the early years and continues to operate a 200 model to this day
KNS 80	
KNS 660	King area navigation units installed in WSP Cessna and King Air aircraft. Older technology that triangulated information from several ground based VOR's (very high frequency omni range) stations to pinpoint aircraft Location or a selected fix. Main problem: you had to be high enough to receive the signals from distant VOR's in a line of sight manner.
KOGA	Self defense tactics taught at WSP Academy 40 years ago Involved a lot of arm twisting and wrist bending.
LERN	Law Enforcement Radio Network . . . Common frequency that all law Enforcement agencies nationwide can access allowing different agencies The ability to communicate anytime especially during an emergency.
MCA	Minimum crossing altitude over terrain as designated on a map
MDA	Lowest altitude a pilot may descend to during a non-precision instrument Approach procedure.
MEA	Minimum Enroute Altitude that can ensure navigation signal reception And obstacle clearance on an instrument flight plan
ME ATP	Multi engine airline transport pilot certificate

Minimums	Lowest published altitude a pilot can descend to during an instrument Approach procedure. If pilots cannot see the runway at minimums they **Must** "Go Around" and execute a prescribed missed approach procedure
MFD	Multi function display: EFIS screen that can display many different functions: checklists, maps, performance info, progress, route list, FMS info
MOA	Military aircraft operating area
MTR	Military training route . . . Depicted on most aeronautical maps
MU30	Mitsubishi Diamond Jet . . . Original Beechjet model before Beechcraft Bought the rights, upgraded and renamed it. Type rating nomenclature On a Beechjet pilot's ATP certificate is: BE40 MU30
N1	Low pressure engine compressor speed; N1 cockpit gauge used to set power Levels on turbine engines in percent of RPM
N2	High pressure engine compressor speed also read in percent of RPM
NDB	Non directional Beacon . . . . Navigation signal station that allows pilots To "home" to the beacon from any direction using an ADF. These stations Have become obsolete with the advent of GPS navigation
NOTAM	Notices to airmen . . . FAA published warnings about flight restrictions, Hazards, closed airspace, runway closures, in/op navigation aids, etc.
OCD	Obsessive compulsive disorder (common among pilots . . . esp. WSP)
OMG	Oh My God
ORV	Off road vehicle park for ATV's and motorcycles
OVC	Overcast
P51	North American Aviation single engine fighter of WWII . . . Best propeller Driven fighter of all time (in my opinion)
PA	Public address system on WSP patrol cars and airplanes . . . Can have embarrassing results when incorrect switch positions selected.
PBY	Catalina . . . Huge WWII era flying boat
PCP	Phencyclidine . . . Powerful powdered drug usually sprinkled on a joint

PFD	Primary flight display: EFIS screen that combines all the standard Flight instruments onto a single integrated presentation display.
Pinch	Trooper slang for writing somebody a ticket
PIT	Police Intervention Technique . . . A maneuver where a car can be spun out By placing your front fender against its rear fender then turning hard into The other car causing it to spin out. WSP policy says this maneuver shall only be used on vehicles travelling below 40 mph . . . Oh Yeah Sure, good one there Boss . . . . Bad guys always travel under 40!!
POH	Pilots operating handbook . . . . Usually found in cockpit of an airplane
Pop Up IFR	Used when a pilot cannot make it to the intended destination flying VFR (under visual flight rules). Usually involves circling under a low cloud Deck with poor visibility while the pilot frantically calls the local ATC Controller to **"air-file"** an abbreviated instrument flight plan. (**if** the pilot Can find the appropriate approach control frequency for that sector!!)
Prop Synchro Phaser	Device on multi-engine airplanes that automatically synchronizes Propeller speeds so the passengers don't have to listen to a constant Wah—Wah—Wah of props rotating at different RPM's or blade pitch
PTO	Power take off . . . . A splined shaft sticking out the rear of most tractors That you can power up various farm implements with: cutters, rotovators, Post hole diggers, etc.
Radar Altimeter	Determines altitude by transmitting a radio pulse from the plane to the ground. It measures true altitude above the ground and is faster than a Sensitive Altimeter which can lag and be in error if it's pressure setting is Incorrect. Radar altimeters are very beneficial and reassuring when flying An instrument approach close to terrain in low visibility.
RCW	Revised Code of Washington . . . Large book all troopers used to carry Defining all the traffic laws of the state by statute and code number.

Reversing
Propellers

System on turbo-prop airplanes that allows prop blade angles to be Be decreased by approximately 10 degrees for quick deceleration. Hot shot pilots often use this function to "back the plane up" on the Ramp to impress the line personnel . . . Usually not very much!

Rotovator

Dangerous piece of farm equipment attached to PTO and 3 point hitch Of a tractor. It is equipped with a circular array of sharp blades to Chop up the top six to ten inches of soil in an eight foot swath.

Rudder
Boost

Airplane System that provides extra force (boost) to a rudder, usually during an engine failure, when that boost is needed to maintain directional control. A Delta P switch senses which engine is producing less power and directs pressure to the applicable rudder pedal to compensate for the asymmetric (unequal) thrust vector created by that failed engine.

Scud
Running

A pilot technique not conducive to long life . . . Involves flying under low Cloud (scud) in marginal visual conditions ratherthan filing an instrument flight plan where you would be saferand flying at higher altitudes usually under ATC radar control. Scud runners often encounter microwave towers, power lines,buildings, big rocks, and trees, often with poor results.

SFF

Airport identifier for Spokane Felts Field (where I learned to fly at "The Hangar Flying Club").

SIM

Flight Simulator . . . . Some are table top; others, like those at Flight Safety International, are massive full motion machines, perched high on huge hydraulic cylinders giving pilots all the sounds, sensations, and visual representations of flight.

Split Ess Maneuver

Box canyon 180 degree escape maneuver where the aircraft is Rolled Inverted, altitude allowing, followed by a 3 or 4 G pull Out to level flight and a chance to reunite with your family.

Stall Speed

The speed where a wing reaches its critical angle of attack Resulting in a turbulent air-flow over the wing and loss of lift.

TBM Avenger	Grumman WWII era Torpedo Bomber many of which Were converted to fire bombers in later years.
TBO	Total time allowed on an engine before it must be overhauled
TCAD	Traffic Collision Avoidance Device that interrogates theTransponders on other aircraft in the vicinity and alerts the Pilot if there is a conflict
TCAS	Traffic Collision Alert System is a more sophisticated version Of a TCAD and actually gives the pilot instructions on what To do to avoid a collision (change altitude or heading)
THC	Active ingredient in marijuana . . . . The higher the content the Better the weed. BC Bud was the hot ticket item during my Years looking for it from the sky . . . . The leaves were discarded And only the huge bud was utilized.
Tomas Torquemada	The "Grand Inquisitor" during the Spanish Inquisition who Tortured and executed thousands for minor infractions
Transponder	Electronic unit that produces a response when it receives an Automated radio frequency interrogation. Pilot's can input a Numerical code for ID purposes, radar control, or collision Avoidance called a sqawk code, e.g. 4563
UHF	Ultra High Frequency radio band utilized by military and Governmental agencies. WSP planes had Wulfsberg variety.
Unicom	Radio frequency utilized at non-tower airports where pilots Self report their position and intentions or call the FBO for gas or a taxi. 122.7, 122.8, & 122.9 are common Unicom freq's.
V1	Pre-Calculated Decision speed during takeoff when (assuming An engine failure on a multi engine aircraft occurs **at that Speed**) the pilot has to make the decision to either abort the takeoff or continue flying. If the engine failure occurs **below** V1 the pilot must abort the takeoff . . . **Above** V1 and the pilot **Must fly** as there may not be sufficient runway left to stop.

V1 Cut	What sadistic simulator instructors like to present to pilots When they are conducting a re-current training session. They Fail an engine at the worst moment (V1) and then sit back and watch the pilot struggle to keep the bird flying on one engine.
VR	Pre-calculated takeoff (rotation) speed for an aircraft Dependent on its weight
VREF	Pre-calculated reference speed for final approach Dependent (primarily) on aircraft weight
VYSE	Best rate of climb speed to maintain after losing an engine, Indicated by a "blue line" on airspeed indicator
VFR	Visual flight rules . . . 1,000 ft ceiling and three miles visibility Required . . . Many General Aviation accidents occur when a Non instrument rated pilot continues VFR into IFR conditions
Vmc	Minimum controllable speed with critical engine inoperative
VNAV	An FMS system that evaluates your altitude and groundspeed Then alerts you when to start your descent so as to arrive at Your destination airport at pattern altitude.
VOR	Very High Frequency Omni Range. These are the big White Bowling Pins you see around airports. They are a line of sight Navigation device with 360 different radials a pilot can dial in And navigate by (if high enough). Being phased out by GPS
Vultee Vibrator	Not what you think . . . . This was a single engine WWII era Advanced trainer that apparently vibrated (especially the Canopy) quite badly.